T0303526

TELL THE TRUTH...
UNTIL THEY DON'T LIKE
WHAT YOU HAVE TO SAY

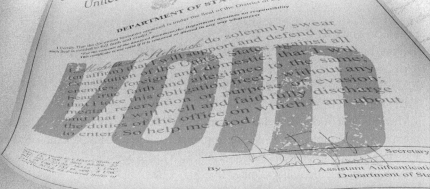

The Abridged Testimonial of a
US Constitutional Oath-Taking
US Department of State Survivor

Michelle L. Stefanick

TELL THE TRUTH—UNTIL THEY DON'T LIKE WHAT YOU HAVE TO SAY: THE ABRIDGED TESTIMONIAL OF A US CONSTITUTIONAL OATH-TAKING US DEPARTMENT OF STATE SURVIVOR
Copyright ©2021/2022 Michelle Stefanick. All Rights Reserved

Published by:
Trine Day LLC
PO Box 577
Walterville, OR 97489
1-800-556-2012
www.TrineDay.com
trineday@icloud.com

Library of Congress Control Number: 2022949030

Stefanick, Michelle
Tell the Truth—Until They Don't Like What You Have to Say:—1st ed.
p. cm.
Epub (ISBN-13) 978-1-63424-359-9
Trade Paper (ISBN-13) 978-1-63424-358-2
1.Memoir--Stefanick, Michelle Laureen--1993-2001. 2. United States--Department of State--Employees. 3. Women diplomats--United States . 4. United States Embassy Bombing--Nairobi, Kenya--1998. 5. Whistle blowing--United States. 6. Government accountability--United States I. Title

FIRST EDITION10 9 8 7 6 5 4 3 2 1

Printed in the USA
Distribution to the Trade by:
Independent Publishers Group (IPG)
814 North Franklin Street
Chicago, Illinois 60610
312.337.0747
www.ipgbook.com

To Those Like Me—

Past, Present, Future

"What happens to the country, to the world, depends on what we do with what others have left us."

– Robert F. Kennedy
December 18, 1963

Tell all the truth but tell it slant – (1263)

– Emily Dickinson

Tell all the truth but tell it slant –
Success in Circuit lies
Too bright for our inform Delight
The Truth's superb surprise
As Lightning to the Children eased
With explanation kind
The Truth must dazzle gradually
Or every man be blind—

"Let me tell you: You take on the intelligence community – they have six ways from Sunday at getting back at you…"

– Senate Minority Leader Charles Schumer (D-NY)
January 03, 2017

SYNOPSIS

Though I did not ask for any of this, I found myself as a little cog in the "Deep State" machine, with the spokes of the nefarious players – the State Department, CIA, FBI, and the military – all connecting to me. My story is the story of how various elements of our government are working to subvert the Constitution and the American people. It's not a political story. It's a very personal and a very real one.

The eery similarities of my situation to that of Christopher Fulton, the missing JFK Cartier watch and the retaliatory actions taken against him… Why, all because he – like me- had the missing link to the pathway to the truth! Like Christopher, I did not ask for any of this…Now only one piece of the puzzle remains until its entirely complete. And that remaining piece of the puzzle is me…

CONTENTS

Education/Career Timeline

1982-1984 Pennsylvania State University (Penn State)
           Business Administration/Accounting
           Altoona Campus, State College Campus
           Altoona, Pennsylvania/State College, Pennsylvania
           Transferred to University of South Carolina

1984-1986 University of South Carolina (USC) –
           Bachelor of Science in Business Administration/Major in Accounting
           Columbia, South Carolina

Feb 1987 – Nov 1988 Defense Contract Audit Agency (DCAA)/
           US Department of Defense (DOD) (1 year 10 months)
           Auditor
           Annandale, Virginia

Dec 1988 – Sep 2014 US Department of State (Resigned/Retired) (25 years 10 months)
           Civil Service (CS)/Foreign Service (FS)
           Washington, District of Columbia; Carlisle, Pennsylvania; and Abroad

Dec 1988 – Jul 1998* US Department of State/Office of Inspector General (OIG)
           Auditor (Financial Management (FM)/Information Management
           (IM)/Office of Security Oversight (OSO))
           Certified Public Accountant (CPA) Examination Passed (Virginia) Jan 1992
           *(Foreign Service Excursion Detail Assignments – Sep 1993 – Jul 1998)
           Washington, District of Columbia

Sep 1993 – Sep 1995* US Embassy Yaoundé, Cameroon
           Regional Financial Management Officer (RFMO)
           for Cameroon, Chad, Equatorial Guinea
           *(Excursion Detail from State/OIG to State/FS)
           Yaoundé, Cameroon

Oct 1995 – Aug 20, 1998 US Embassy Nairobi, Kenya
           Financial Management Center (FMC) Director
           For Kenya, Sudan, Seychelles
           *(Excursion Detail from State/OIG to State/FS)
           *July 9, 1998 – Officially Converted from State/OIG/CS to State/FS/
           Financial   Management Specialist (FMS)
           August 7, 1998 Embassy Bombing
           Nairobi, Kenya

Sep 1998 – Oct 1998 Spanish Language Training
           Onward assignment Santiago, Chile (Assignment Curtailed)
           Foreign Service Institute (FSI)
           Arlington, Virginia

Jan 1999 – Apr 1999 Financial Management Training Trainer
           Foreign Service Institute (FSI)/Administrative Training (AT) Division
           Arlington, Virginia

Apr 1999 – Aug 1999 Financial Management Officer (FMO)
           Bureau of European Affairs/Office of the Executive Director (EUR/EX)
           Washington, District of Columbia

Aug 1999 – Jul 2000 Russian Language Training (Onward assignment Moscow, Russia)
           Foreign Service Institute (FSI)

Arlington, Virginia

Aug 2000 – Jul 2002 US Embassy Moscow, Russia
Senior/Financial Management Officer (S/FMO)
for Moscow, Yekaterinburg, St Petersburg, and Vladivostok
Moscow, Russia

Aug 2002 – Sep 2002 General Services Officer (GSO) Training
Onward assignment Pristina, Kosovo (Assignment Curtailed)
Foreign Service Institute (FSI)
Arlington, Virginia

Oct 2002 – Jul 2003 Program Analysis Officer (Bridge Assignment)
Resource Management/
Office of Strategic and Performance Planning (RM/SPP)
Washington, District of Columbia

Aug 2003 – May 2005 US Embassy Khartoum, Sudan
Management Officer
Khartoum, Sudan

2005 – 2006 American Political Science Association (APSA) Congressional Fellow
State Detail Assignment
Personal Office of US Senator Olympia Snowe
Washington, District of Columbia

Sep 2006 – Jul 2008 Legislative Management Officer (LMO)
Office of Legislative Affairs (H)
US Department of State
Washington, District of Columbia

2008-2009 US Army War College (AWC)
US Department of Defense (DOD)
Student/State Long-Term Senior Training
Masters of Strategic Studies/National Security Policy Program (NSPP)
*Strategy Research Paper (SRP): Powell's Leadership Principles – Time
for State Department to Revisit*
ONE DIME
Carlisle, Pennsylvania

Dec 2009 – Jul 2011 Foreign Policy Advisor (FPA)/Policy Advisor (POLAD)
State/Defense Exchange Detail Assignment (SDE)
(Assignment curtailed by 17 months)
US Marine Corps Forces, Europe/Africa (MARFOREUR/AF)
US Department of Defense (DOD)/US Navy/US Marine Corps (USMC)
Stuttgart Area, Germany

Sep 2011 – Jan 2013 Regional Director, Francophone-West Africa
State/Defense Exchange Detail Assignment (SDE)
Office of the Secretary of Defense for Policy (OSD) Africa Affairs (AFR)
US Department of Defense (DOD)/Pentagon
Washington, District of Columbia/Arlington, Virginia

Acronym List

A&K	-Abercrombie and Kent
AC	-Arlington County
ACID	- Army Criminal Investigation Division
ACLU	-American Civil Liberties Union
ACPD	- Arlington County Police Department
ACSS	- Africa Center for Strategic Studies
ADM	- Admiral
AEA	- American Employee Association
AF	- Bureau of African Affairs
AFR	- African Affairs
AFRICOM	- U.S. Africa Command
AFSA	- American Foreign Service Association
AG	- Attorney General
AGA	- Association of Government Accountants
AHEC	- Army Heritage and Education Center
AJ	- Administrative Judge
APSA	- American Political Science Association
APCD	- Assistant Patient Care Director
AOR	- area of responsibility
ARB	- Accountability Review Board
A/S	- Assistant/Secretary
AT	- Administrative Training
ATM	- automatic teller machine
AUSA	- Assistant United States Attorney
AWC	- Army War College
BC/BS	- Blue Cross/Blue Shield
BGEN	- Brigadier General
BHU	- Behavorial Health Unit
BOA	- Bank of America
CA	- Bureau of Consular Affairs
CAPT	- Captain
CCE	- Combined Country Element
CD	- compact disc
CDA	- Career Development Advisor
CDO	- Career Development Officers
CENTCOM-	U.S. Central Command
CEU	- Compliance Enforcement Unit
CFO	- Chief Financial Officer

CFR	- Code of Federal Regulations
CFSO	- Concerned Foreign Service Officers
CG	- Comptroller General
CG	- Consular General
CIA	- Central Intelligence Agency
CJCS	- Chairman of Joint Chiefs of Staff
CJTF-HOA	- Combined Joint Task Force – Horn of Africa
CNN	- Cable News Network
CNO	- Chief of Naval Operations
COB	- close of business
COCOM	- combatant commands
CODEL	-Congressional Delegation
COL	- Colonel
COM	- Chief of Mission
COS	- Chief of Staff
COS	- Chief of Station
CPA	- Certified Public Accountant
CPE	- continuing professional education
CPMS	- Civilian Personnel Management Service
CRS	- Congressional Research Service
CS	- civil service
CT	- Counter-Terrorism
CVRA	- Crime Victims Rights Act
CYA	- cover your ass
DAO	- Defense Attache Office
DAS	- Deputy Assistant Secretary
DASD	- Deputy Assistant Secretary of Defense
DBHDS	- Department of Behavioral Health & Development Services
DCAA	- Defense Contract Audit Agency
DCIS	- Defense Criminal Investigative Service
DCM	- Deputy Chief of Mission
DG	- Director General of the Foreign Service and Director of Personnel/Human Resources
DHS	- Department of Homeland Security
DHS	- Department of Human Services
DIA	- Defense Intelligence Agency
DLO	- Defense Liaison Office
DMV	- District of Columbia, Maryland and Virginia area
DNI	- Director of National Intelligence
DOD	- Department of Defense
DOJ	- Department of Justice
DON	- Department of Navy
DOS	- Department of State
DPAA	- Darfur Peace and Accountability Act
DS	- Diplomatic Security
EA	- Executive Assistant

ECO	- Emergency Custody Order
ECS	- Employee Counseling Service
EEO	- Equal Employment Opportunity
EEOC	- Equal Employment Opportunity Commission
EER	- Employee Evaluation Report
EFM	- Eligible Family Member
ESC	- Engineering Security Center
EUCOM	- U.S. European Command
EX	- Executive Director
FBI	- Federal Bureau of Investigation
FAM	- Foreign Affairs Manual
FAST	- Familiarization and Short-term Training
FEHB	- Federal Employees Health Benefits
FETS	- Female Engagement Teams
FFC	- Fact-finding Conference
FinCENT	- Financial Crimes Enforcement Network
FLOTUS	– First Lady of the United States
FM	- Financial Management
FMC	- Financial Management Center
FMO	- Financial Management Officer
FMP	- Bureau of Financial Management and Policy
FMS	- Facilities Maintenance Specialist
FOIA	- Freedom Of Information Act
FPA	- Foreign Policy Advisor
FRO	- Family Readiness Officer
FS	- Foreign Service
FSC	- Financial Service Center
FSI	- Foreign Service Institute
FSO	- Foreign Service Officer
FSN	- Foreign Service National
FSPS	- Foreign Service Pension System
FY	- Fiscal Year
GAO	- Government Accoutability Office
GDC	- General District Court
GEN	- General
GSO	- General Service Officer
H	- Bureau of Legislative Affairs
HFAC	- House Foreign Affairs Committee
HIPAA	- Health Insurance Portability and Accountability Act
HPSCI	- House Permanent Select Committee on Intelligence
HR	- Human Resources
HRA	- Human Rights Advocate
HW	- Herbert Walker
IC	- Intelligence Community
ICASS	- International Cooperative Administrative Support Services
ICI	- Investigations and Counter Intelligence

IG	- Inspector General
IM	- Information Management
INL	- International Narcotics and Law Enforcement
IPD	- Investigation and Prosecution Division
IRA	- Individual Right of Action
IRD	- Investigation and Resolution Division
JAG	- Judge Advocate General
JFK	- John Fitzgerald Kennedy
JTTF	- Joint Terrorism Task Force
KUSLO	- Kenya/U.S. Liaison Office
L	- Bureau of Legal
LBJ	- Lyndon Baines Johnson
LCDR	- Lieutenant Commadner
LDSR	- Liberia Defense Sector Reform
LES	- Locally-engaged Staff
LMO	- Legislative Management Officer
LT	- Lieutenant
LTC	- Lieutenant Colonel
LTCOL	- Lieutenant Colonel
LTGEN	- Lieutenant General
LWOP	- leave-without-pay
M	- Under Secretary for Management
MAJGEN	- Major General
MARFORAF	- Marine Forces Africa
MARFOREUR	- Marine Forces Europe
MARFOREUR/AF	- Marine Forces Europe/Africa
MARSOC	- Marine Special Operations Command
MC	- Marine Corps
MD	- Management Directive
MED	- Medical
MFE/A	-Marine Foreces Europe/Africa
MOA	- Memoradum of Agreement
MOU	- Memorandum of Understanding
MP	- Military Police
MRA	- minimum retirement age
MS	- Military Service
MSG	- Marine Security Guard
MSPB	- Merit System Protection Board
NASA	- National Aeronautics and Space Administration
NATO	- North Atlantic Treaty Organization
NCIS	- Navy Criminal Investigative Service
NCTC	- National Counter Terrorism Center
NSA	- National Security Agency
NSC	- National Security Counsel
NSPP	-National Security Policy Program
NVMHI	- Northern Virginia Mental Health Institute

NYC	- New York City
NYFO	- New York Field Office
OC	- Counselor
OCA	- Office of Casualty Assistance
OCA	- Orthodox Church in America
OCR	- Office of Civil Rights
ODNI	- Office of the Director of National Intelligence
OES	- Bureau of Oceans, International Environmental and Scien-
tific Affairs	
OFO	- Office of Federal Operations
O&I	- Oversight and Investigations
OIC	- Officer-in-Charge
OIG	- Office of Inspector General
OPF	- Official Personnel Folder
OSC	- Office of Special Counsel
OSD	- Office of Secretary of Defense
OSO	- Office of Security Oversight
PAE	- Pacific Architects and Engineers
PENTTBOM	– Pentagon/Twin Towers Bombing Investigation
PCS	- Permanent Change of Station
PD	- Public Diplomacy
PDAS	- Principal Deputy Assistant Secretary
PDC	- Professional Development Conference
PI	- Private Investigator
PII	- Protective Intelligence Investigations
PM	- Bureau of Political Military Affairs
PMO	-Post Management Officer
PNG	- persona non grata
PO	- Principal Officer
POA	- Power Of Attorney
POLAD	-Policy Advisor
POTUS	-President Of The United States
POV	- Personally-Owned Vehicle
PRP	- Personnel Review Panel
PSS	- Personnel Security and Suitability
PSYOPS	- Psychological Operation
RAMC	- Regional Area Management Center
REST	- Regional Embassy Support Teams
RFMO	- Regional Financial Management Officer
RICO	- Racketeer-Influenced and Corrupt Organization
RM	- Bureau of Resource Management
ROI	- Report of Investigation
R&R	- Rest and Recuperation
RSO	- Regional Security Officer
RW	- Renaissance Weekend
SA	- Special Agent

SAIC	- Special Agent-in-Charge
SAG	- Staff Advocate General
SAR	- Suspicious Activity Report
SCA	- Bureau of South and Central Asia
SDE	- State/Defense Exchange
SDFCU	-State Department Federal Credit Union
SDNY	- Southern District of New York
SF	- Special Forces
SF	- Standardized Form
S/FMO	-Senior/Financial Management Officer
SFRC	-Senate Foreign Relations Committee
SFS	- Senior Foreign Service
SGT	- Sergeant
SGTMAJ	- Sergeant Major
SID	- Special Investigations Division
SIPR	- Secure Internet Protocol Router
SPAS	- School of Professional and Areas Studies
SPP	- Office of Strategic and Performance Planning
SOCAF	-Special Operations Command Africa
SOCEUR	- Special Operations Command Europe
SOLIC	- Special Operations/Low-Intensity Conflict
SRP	- Strategic Research Project
SSCI	- Senate Select Committee on Intelligence
T&A	- time and attendance
TCN	- third county national
TDO	- Temporary Detention Order
TDY	- temporary duty
TIC	- time-in-class
TIS	- time-in-service
TR	- transcript report
TSA	- Transportation Security Agency
TSCC	- Theatre Security Cooperation Conference
TSP	- Thrift Savings Plan
UAB	- unaccompanied air freight
UCMJ	- Uniform Code of Military Justice
UCI	- unlawful command influence
UIIS	- United International Investigative Services
UK	- United Kingdom
UN	- United Nations
UPI	- United Press International
UPS	- United Parcel Service
U/S	- Under Secretary
USA	- United States Attorney
USA	- United States of America
USAA	- United States Automobile Association
USAC	- United States Army Corps of Engineers

USAG	- Unites States Army Garrison
USAID	-United States Agency for International Development
USAREUR	-United States Army Europe
USC	- University of South Carolina
USC	- United States Code
USG	- United States Government
USIA	- United States Information Agency
USMC	- United States Marine Corps
USPS	- United States Postal Service
USSC	- United Stated Security Coordinator
USSC	- United States Supreme Court
VA	- Commonwealth of Virginia
VHC	- Virginia Hospital Center
VMI	- Virginia Military Institute
VNS	- Victim Notification System
VPU	- Video Production Unit
WH	- White House
WIIS	- Women in International Security
WTC	- World Trade Center
WW	- World War

INTRODUCTION

On August 7, 1998, at approximately 10:30 A.M. local time, the first truck bomb exploded outside the US Embassy in Nairobi, Kenya. Minutes later, a second truck bomb exploded outside the US Embassy in Dar es Salaam, Tanzania. I was assigned to the embassy in Nairobi as the Financial Management Center (FMC) Director. I was off-site that morning. Had I been present, there is a high probability I would not be writing this book.

I returned to the aftermath of the US Embassy Nairobi bombing the next day. On a detail assignment to Kenya from the US Department of State's Office of Inspector General (OIG), about a month prior to the bombing, on July 9, 1998, I was officially converted to the foreign service (FS). After experiencing the most horrific event in my life, when I departed my assignment on August 20, 1998, I had no idea the horror yet to come.

After the first August 7, 1998 East Africa Embassy Bombings trial in 2001, the Department of Justice (DOJ) implemented a Victim Notification System (VNS). On June 25, 2009, I received an applicable DOJ email notification regarding the VNS implementation, status of the next applicable pretrial conference in this case, reminder of my applicable federal Crime Victims' Rights Act (CVRA) rights and DOJ's assurance in ensuring provision of these rights.

Enacted in 2004, the CVRA gives victims of criminal offenses in Federal court certain rights, including: (1) The right to be reasonably protected from the accused; (2) The right to reasonable, accurate, and timely notice of any public court proceeding, involving the crime, or of any release or escape of the accused; (3) The right not to be excluded from any such public court proceeding, unless the court, after receiving clear and convincing evidence, determines that testimony by the victim would be materially altered if the victim heard other testimony at the proceeding; (4) The right to be reasonably heard at any public proceeding in the district court involving release, plea, or sentencing; (5) The reasonable right to confer with the attorney for the Government in the case; (6) The right to full and timely restitution as provided in law; (7) The right to proceedings free from unreasonable delay; and (8) The right to be treated with fairness and with respect for the victim's dignity and privacy.

Furthermore, officers and employees of the DOJ and other department and agencies of the United States engaged in detection, investigation, or prosecution of crime shall make their best efforts to see that crime victims are notified of, and accorded, the rights described. According to the *DOJ Victim Witness Handbook*, victims and witnesses have the right to be free of harassment or intimidation by the defendants and others, highlighting that "it is a federal offense to threaten, intimidate, harass, or mislead a witness in a criminal or civil proceeding."

On September 30, 2013, due to retaliatory actions taken against me, I submitted my letter of resignation to Secretary of State John Kerry. On October 16, 2013, I was notified Secretary Kerry accepted my resignation effective October 1, 2013 as I requested. Within weeks, despite being removed from US Department of State payroll, I was subjected to yet another round of retaliation to include being deemed incapacitated. Due to my resignation? Or something more?

In the 1976 movie, *All the President's Men*, anonymous source known as "Deep Throat" stated that the "…cover-up had little to do with Watergate. It was mainly to protect the covert operations…" Not being a member of the intelligence community, law enforcement nor military, I am not and was not privy to, nor involved in, any covert operations. This crucial insight was also provided by "Deep Throat," "…to follow the money…" And that is where I fit in.

Though I did not ask for any of this, I found myself to be a tiny hub on a Deep State wheel, with the spokes —the US Department of State, Central Intelligence Agency (CIA), DOJ, Federal Bureau of Investigation (FBI) and the Military—all connecting to me. Why me? Due to information and insight I acquired through years of just doing my job as a federal auditor and then as a FS Financial Management Specialist (FMS). Anyone in law enforcement, particularly the FBI, knows that information obtained during an audit, particularly a federal audit, is a protected-activity. But yet, I was not protected. Why? Because the Deep State will stop at nothing to hide corruption and crimes committed particularly when its regarding funding linkages to covert operations, and despite the broader implications to our Constitution.

My story has serious political overtones, but it is not a political story. It is my story. It is the story of what can happen when you innocently seek one truth, but discover quite another.

PART ONE

CHAPTER 1

HOW DID I GET HERE:
What's wrong with this picture?

O n February 1, 2019, I began to write a book that I've wanted to write for so long, but just didn't know how to begin. The Special Counsel Robert Mueller investigation is the backdrop. Reflecting the horrific ordeal I survived, this book provides context for what all this is really about…

I began my career with the United States government (USG) in February 1987 as an auditor with the Defense Contract Audit Agency (DCAA). Shortly thereafter, I transferred to the US Department of State. The US Department of State, not the CIA. To this day, I have to adamantly repeat that fact. Why? Because many people across our nation and around the world assume all those who work for the US Department of State are really CIA. This assumption and perception are indicative of the dangerously wrong path our nation took and continues to take. And it's a factor in the quagmire our nation now finds itself in.

What I know now, I didn't necessarily know at the time. That is the reason writing all this out is so very complex and complicated. The experiences I present are not made up. They are documented fact and real – very real – and occurred both in the US and abroad. Piece by piece, with signposts over time and all along the way, their interlinkages and interconnections paint a storyline, a very scary storyline.

For instance, just prior to starting this book, I tested my computer by writing a sample vignette of the sensitive subject matter that would be included. I did this to determine if my computer was being monitored. Here's what I had written:

> As an APSA Congressional Fellow, I was the source/drafter for these two Congressional Records (Senator Kennedy and Senator Snowe). However, in light of it all and based on the insight, information and experiences Ambassador Mary Ryan and I shared, due to the curious timing of Mary's death, I continue to suspect foul play. Mary and I were exchanging emails and in the process of arranging to have lunch once I got settled into Senator Snowe's office, then all

of a sudden, she passed away. Insight shared with me after Mary's passing was that she was barely eating – primarily saltine crackers and water; and the timing of her sudden passing right before our scheduled meeting for lunch … adds to the possibility that with my seeing/confirming her weight loss and our potential discussion and in return sharing this directly with Senator Snowe, I may have connected dots a lot earlier and even more directly based on Mary and my luncheon discussion, which unfortunately never occurred. Mary and I connected based on Julian Bartley's death, and my sharing with Mary insight I had, based on Julian and my last discussion, which happened a week or so before his and his son Jay's being killed on August 7, 1998 in the Embassy bombing. For the record, Mary Ryan did not issue those visas to the Saudi hijackers linked to 9/11, John Brennan did – though many were trying/did scapegoat her for doing so. Why did they do that? More importantly, WHO did that? Who was behind all that?And do you realize the implications – the question being what other and how many other visas were issued by "John Brennan" (CIA) and NOT "Mary Ryan" (State Dept) over and above the Saudi hijackers. Who are they? Where are they? How long had it been occurring and is it continuing to this day? And yes, I continue to believe Mary's passing – whether directly or indirectly – was indeed foul play. Ambassador Mary Ryan – Memory Eternal!

Michelle L. Stefanick

Within a few days after my writing this, President Trump pulled John Brennan's security clearance. It's from that context I write this book, using a dedicated laptop computer not linked up to internet.

And then this happened: watching MSNBC's *The Rachel Maddow Show* that aired the night before, I was flabbergasted. My immediate thought was does Rachel Maddow realize what this February 20, 2019 show documented and confirmed? Given the previous bin Laden/Sudan cover-up in the mid-1990's during the Clinton Administration, Rachel's guest, Susan Rice documented the modus operandi on how she and others ensure the spread of false-narratives with documented intent to do so at the end of and beyond yet another Administration. Last time it was during the Clinton Administration, this time the Obama Administration.

President Obama began the conversation by stressing his continued commitment to ensuring that every aspect of this issue is handled by the intelligence and law enforcement communities 'by the book'… –Susan Rice January 20, 2017 E-mail to Self.

The only thing is Susan Rice does not control when the timeline begins nor does she control the facts, all the facts. Here's to the truth finally coming out. No matter what.

So how am I factored into this timeline of events? Initially, due to the August 7, 1998 East Africa Embassy bombings, I thought it was due to the time of my assignment from 1995-1998 as Embassy Nairobi FMC Director. Later, I realized my nexus to the timeline of events was actually from much earlier. So, here's the story from the beginning of my affiliation with the USG.

Graduating from college in December 1986, I applied to various entities within the USG including the FBI, National Security Agency (NSA) and CIA. My ultimate goal was to join the Department of State Foreign Service (FS), and the journey I took to get there was atypical and quite eye-opening. In January 1987, I moved from South Carolina to the Washington D.C. area without a job. Graduating with a major in accounting enabled me to be hired as an auditor with DCAA in February 1987. Having direct-hire authority pending a background investigation, this DCAA experience eventually lead to an employment opportunity with State's OIG. The office was in a period of transition implementing a congressional mandate to be led by State's first statutorily independent (civil service, not foreign service) IG, Sherman Funk. This effort included expansive hiring of independent civil service auditing and investigative professional staff. Though many positions would be filled by personnel with a General Accountability Office (GAO) background, DCAA experience was also very desirable. I took this stepping stone one step closer to my ultimate goal.

Though I never ended up working for the FBI, NSA or CIA, there were aspects of these job interviews that have stuck with me even after all this time. And now in hindsight, they add an aspect of relevance to events that would occur to me decades later, even make me wonder if these events were interlinked and interconnected in anyway. I didn't think so at the time. Now, I'm not so sure.

My interview with the FBI was to take place in the Anacostia section of Washington D.C. Being new to the area, I didn't want to be late, so I wanted to trial run the route the night before. I called the FBI office and asked for directions as I explained my intent. I believe I was speaking to a secretary or an administrative assistant. Her response was professional, yet stern, and I recall it to this day: "Honey child, you come down here this evening, we ain't going to see you tomorrow morning." Needless to say, I heeded her warning and didn't drive to the interview site that evening. To ensure I got there in time, I left much earlier than planned the next day.

When I arrived, as I recall, it didn't go as well as I expected. I remember sitting in a conference room and a male FBI representative coming in and starting with an off-the-cuff comment about "good, filling a quota." As I did not intend on filling anyone's quota, the interview didn't go so well. My accounting background was a real positive, and apparently being a female as well, but my eyesight was not 20/20. So, there was a brief discussion regarding my interest in corrective surgery. Now given it was at a time that lasik surgery was not as popular and commonplace as it is today, and given this would be at my own personal expense, the interview ended with an apparent mismatch. Weeks and even months after the interview, I continued to receive calls at work at DCAA from the FBI requesting that I reconsider the employment opportunity. My response, declining their offer, remained the same.

My interview experience with the NSA was also very interesting. Taking Russian language in college, one option was becoming a Russian linguist. With my accounting/business administration degree, another was some sort of management position. And with my DCAA experience, some kind of contracting position was feasible. When I was notified by NSA that I was being offered a position, I simply asked in which area would I be working. NSA wouldn't and/or couldn't tell me until I accepted the position. So, I declined the offer.

All this was after enduring NSA's extensive interviewing process. As I recall, I met a few times with NSA officials at their location. I even went through the polygraph aspect of the process, and only later found out the way this was carried-out was unusual, if not unacceptable/improper. Not that taking the polygraph was unusual, but how it was administered to me was. As I recall, I was asked a set of questions, some over and over and over again – specifically regarding if I ever took illegal drugs. I said I did not because I had not. The polygraph administrator stopped the exam, removed all the applicable attached wiring, and asked me again. He then hooked me up to the machine again. Asking me one last time, he finally said, "Stefanick, you either have never taken illegal drugs or you are one hell of a liar." Annoyed, not only because of the process to which I was being subjected, but because I wasn't being believed, I responded, "Well I guess it's your job to figure which one, isn't it?" Years later when I relayed this experience to some State OIG colleagues, particularly those with applicable experience, they were furious. So much so they asked me if I recalled the name of the individual who administered the polygraph exam. I said I didn't. That's the first time I found out what had happened to me was improper. Regardless, I hadn't taken the position, whatever it was going to be, since I was never told.

Now, I have less recollection regarding my interviewing with the CIA. But I definitely do remember how it ended. I was sitting at the side of an applicable CIA Human Resource (HR) official's desk in the Tysons Corner/McLean area of Fairfax County in the Commonwealth of Virginia, in close proximity to Washington D.C. She said, "Unfortunately, it did not appear to be a good match." The reason provided was because I was *too loyal*. I was taken aback, but there was nothing more I could do – other than knowing that according to the CIA, I was too loyal to serve my nation. When I worked with State OIG, I was advised to never play "*spot the spook*" – trying to figure out who was an intelligence embed. And I never did. However, in due time and in light of events that occurred, on more than one occasion, I would reflect: "*What's wrong with this picture?*"

So with that, not knowing then what I now know, to now have the realization that whatever this is, is way longer, way beyond in the date and depth of simply my career entrance into working within the USG. Now, the story I tell goes way beyond simply the pages of this initial book. And now, with every single name mentioned or referenced, the question has to be asked, what is their real background? Law enforcement? Military? Intelligence? And/or intelligence – *really, a spotted spook....* Or what others commonly refer to as – the *Deep State*.

My first exposure to *that* world was when I was with DCAA. One day, my supervisor Larry Tatem gave me an audit proposal to review at a small defense contractor in Vienna, Virginia. At the time, the request seemed simple enough. I scheduled the onsite interview. Days later, sitting in the conference room, as I had done so many times before at previous audit sites, I patiently waited to meet with contractor's representative. When he finally arrived, I started to brief him on the purpose of my visit and requested required documentation. He stopped me and stated, "Michelle, you aren't supposed to be here." I again shared the audit proposal request packet assigned to me by my supervisor. He again responded, "Michelle you aren't supposed to be here and Larry knows that." At this point, I don't recall whether I or the defense contractor's representative called Larry, but I do know I left that defense contractor soon after.

Then, right before I transferred from DCAA to State OIG, I was working on an audit at a major defense contractor in the Tysons Corner/McLean area. During this audit, I found some major issues of concern. One day while working at this defense contractor location developing my finding, the fire alarm went off. Knowing that remaining in the building was not proper, leaving my audit work unattended wasn't either. I located the defense contractor representative to ask if the alarm was a drill or real because I would hate to have to smash a window to get all my work papers out of the building so they weren't destroyed. The response was that it was a false alarm. Later, at the end of the work day, as I was walking to my car in the underground parking area, I got the distinct feeling that someone was following me. I got to my car as quickly as I could. Locking my work papers in the trunk, I jumped in, locked the doors and drove away as quickly as I could. My audit findings were then referred to Defense Criminal Investigative Service (DCIS). Whatever happened to that investigative referral since my departure from DCAA, I don't know. Regarding the fire alarm incident, apparently competitors would do that to one another in order to get access to sensitive information from one another's waste baskets – so I am told. The insight and experience I obtained during my time at DCAA were invaluable.

Starting my new position as a civil service auditor with State's OIG coincided with the transition from the Reagan Administration to that of President George H.W. Bush. Soon after my arrival, State employees were given an opportunity to say farewell to soon-to-be-departing Secretary of State George Shultz. I recall standing in a long queue on the 8th floor at Main State, Department of State waiting for an opportunity to shake Secretary Shultz's hand and to wish him Godspeed. I also recall attending numerous holiday parties throughout the Department. December 1988 was a very good time to transition to my new position/career with the Department of State.

During my time with State OIG, I participated in numerous audits conducting fieldwork domestic and abroad, in numerous countries and regions of the world. I had just recently returned from conducting overseas audit fieldwork, and was in the process of completing my work papers finding and drafting our report, when I had an unexpected visitor at my desk, in a back corner, out of the main thoroughfare. Though my back was to the opening of my cubicle, the voice of my guest was very distinguishable. He greeted me in his gruff but kind-hearted manner that I had grown used to since joining his office of the OIG. He barked, "Stefanick, what are you doing for me and the US tax payer today." I responded as I turned to warmly and respectfully greet my visitor, "Mr. Shea, jack-shit nothing." After a few pleasantries and a brief discussion regarding my observations from our recent trip, he turned to leave and then came back into my cubicle and said, "You know Stefanick, where we really need you and your skills is overseas in the foreign service. Think about it, and if the opportunity ever arises, take it. I will support you 100%." Within a matter of months, and with the full support of State Assistant IG for Security Oversight Terry Shea, I would be selected for my first excursion detail from State OIG to the foreign service.

My first excursion tour detail assignment was from 1993-1995 as the Regional Financial Management Officer (RFMO) at Embassy Yaoundé, Cameroon with regional responsibilities for Equatorial Guinea and Chad. Close to its completion, the African Bureau (AF) teased that "I couldn't go back to the OIG because I knew too much and would I consider doing a second excursion detail." At the time, I thought this lead-in was just in jest, a common nomenclature between auditors and auditees. In due time, I would come to realize the lead-in was truer than I could have imagined. After pondering the three options provided (returning to State OIG, going to Ndjamena Chad as a Management Officer, or going to Nairobi, Kenya as the Financial Management Center (FMC) Director with regional responsibilities for Sudan and Seychelles), I selected Kenya. Proceeding through the detail assignment process – curiously much rockier this go around than before – from 1995-1998, I was assigned to Embassy Nairobi for my second excursion detail from the State OIG to the foreign service.

As a federal auditor with DCAA and State OIG, I obtained sensitive insight while carrying-out official USG audit fieldwork. During these two limited-appointment FS excursion tours, though I was no longer officially State OIG and not yet officially foreign service, as a Certified Public Accountant (CPA) with auditing experience, I carried out my roles and responsibilities within that professional capacity. Only in due time would I come to realize the crucial significance the insight regarding money and funding that I obtained while in these positions would play in the timeline of events.

CHAPTER 2

WHERE WAS I:
The most devastating attack in our history on our embassies

It was 1998 and I was coming to the end my second excursion tour. Though I had so many fond experiences and memories of my time in Kenya, professionally, it was a tough tour. So many challenges and hurdles to overcome that I could not have accomplished without the hard-working dedication of my FMC staff, whom I regarded as family. Monthly we had birthday parties, and after I successfully climbed Mt. Kilimanjaro, I led a group that included a few of our FMC family to the top of Mt. Kenya. When I found out that my application to officially convert to the FS was accepted and that I soon would be departing Kenya and my FMC family, it was bittersweet. In early July 1998, I found out that my first, non-excursion FS assignment would be Santiago, Chile, and I started to prepare for my departure. The logistical part was easy enough, with check lists to follow, and scheduling applicable pack out dates after setting a tentative departure date of August 20, 1998. The emotional side of saying good-bye to a staff and a continent that I had grown to love was hard. In my remaining time, I took the opportunity to truly honor and thank my staff by submitting them for a Superior Honor Award while periodically taking time off to travel to as many locations as I could before my departure. Ngorongoro Crater in Tanzania was one, and being an Orthodox Christian, the Ethiopian Orthodox historical route was another.

THURSDAY AUGUST 6, 1998

I was sitting at the airport in the Ethiopian capital of Addis Ababa waiting for my flight to Dire Dawa. It was the last leg of my tour of Ethiopia. I had just visited Bahir Dar, Gondar, Axum and Lalibela, Ethiopia's Northern Orthodox Historical Route. Though Dire Dawa was not a part of the original tour, I customized my tour to include Harar, Ethiopia's Holy Islamic Walled Citadel. My schedule was tight. The plan was to fly early afternoon and return early the next morning for a very quick visit and tour. However, my flight was delayed, and delayed, and delayed, which I had grown accustomed to with all my regional travels throughout the continent. The longer the flight was delayed, the less likely I would complete the day's tour. As it would soon be dark, I decided to cut my scheduled tour one day short and remain in Addis. The plan was to stay with FS colleagues the next evening when I returned Friday night. I now hoped I could stay with them Thursday night instead. Lewis and Robyn Byrd, who served with me in Nairobi and had recently transferred to Ethiopia, lived on the US Embassy compound. Unable to reach either Robyn or Lewis, I then called Defense Attaché Colonel Eugene "Michael" Mensch, who I knew was also now in Addis, to see if I could stay at his residence for the evening before linking up with Robyn and Lewis on Friday as originally planned. Fortunately for me, Colonel Mensch was in his office and answered the phone. He said I could stay Thursday but that he had a scheduled event with his Defense Attaché colleagues Friday night, which worked perfectly with my previous arrangements. So, he came to get me at the airport. I have no idea when, if ever, my scheduled flight for Dire Dawa arrived that evening. And I never made it to Harar. It was late afternoon Thursday, August 6 and only in due time would the fortuitous impact of this decision come to light. In fact, it was the very next day—Friday August 7, 1998.

FRIDAY AUGUST 7, 1998

The plan for that morning was for me to relax and recover from my trip, to be picked up and taken to the Embassy Compound for lunch, and to stay with my colleagues as previously arranged before heading back to Nairobi. I was sitting on the back veranda reading and jotting notes from my trip when I heard Colonel Mensch come into the house. As he was walking back to the veranda, I heard lots of gibberish on the Embassy-issued walkie talkies. It reminded me of the last time I was in Ethiopia, just a few months prior. I had been called by Embassy Addis Ababa Management Counselor Bernie Gross and requested to assist regarding shuttling financial resources to their Embassy from ours in Kenya in case of an emergency, such as an evacuation. Their US dollar supply was low since Assistant Secretary (A/S) of State of African Affairs (AF) Susan Rice had just departed with their US currency to support Embassy Asmara in their already ordered evacuation. Bernie's FMO supposedly departed the post without preparing for such contingency as instructed. The Embassy Addis FMO's name was Charlie Slater. When I heard the walkie-talkie chatter that was my initial thought, Ethiopia and Eritrea were at it again.

Colonel Mensch reached the veranda and said, "Michelle, Embassy Nairobi has been bombed. I need you to come back to the Embassy with me." Despite his discernible tone, I initially thought he was making some kind of a sick joke, and so I replied, "Michael, what a horrible thing to say." Again, he said, "Michelle, Embassy Nairobi has been bombed. I need you to come with me in order to assist in identifying what sections were hit." We departed immediately for the embassy. My initial thought was *thank goodness* I had not gone to Dire Dawa. Just a little later, I would be *thanking God* I was in Ethiopia touring the Orthodox Historical Route, for if I had been in my office that day, I most likely would have been killed.

I was in the Embassy Addis Ababa Compound snack bar getting lunch when the initial coverage of the almost simultaneous bombings was being shown on CNN. Our Embassy in Addis was on high alert and there were other reports that two of our other Embassies—in Kampala and Harare—were targeted to be next. Five targeted US Embassies—two already hit and three others on high alert. I don't know how others felt, but I felt like we were at war. At the time, I just didn't know who the enemy was.

As the initial photos and reporting came in, it appeared the bombing took place in the front of the embassy. My initial thought was, *Oh, please,* with the hope that my office, the FMC front office, would have buffered the blast from the rest of my section, the open bull pen area of FMC. Then as more details emerged, so did the actual location of the bombing. It was now reported to be in the back side of the embassy, including right outside of my section. Needless to say, during a crisis such as this, there is chaos, lots of chaos. With Embassy Addis on high alert, I shared what insight I could regarding which sections were located where. My only thought at that time was that I need to get back to Nairobi immediately to help.

With the time difference I was finally able to phone my family as they would be waking up to horrific scenes on television. My father answered the phone and said, "Michelle, your Embassy has been bombed." "Yes Dad, I'm calling to let you know that I am okay. I'm in Ethiopia and hoping to get back to Nairobi as soon as possible." Needless to say, he was relieved and queried on whether this changed my plans for coming home, as my departure for my onward assignment was already scheduled for August 20, 1998. I said I didn't know, promised to keep in touch, and that I was alive and fine. We hung up, as I needed to prepare for my trip back to Kenya.

But before I could do so, I needed to obtain approval. Calls were being made back and forth with Washington. Finally, I obtained approval to go back. Based on my tour schedule, arrangements had already been made for me to fly back the next day. Colonel Mensch, who also obtained approval, would accompany me on the flight back.

SATURDAY AUGUST 8, 1998

On our flight back to Nairobi from Addis Ababa, for the first time, I started to tear up and then I cried. Colonel Mensch, trying to relieve my pain, gently said, "Michelle, you don't know yet." Based on the location of the bomb if the CNN reporting was correct, I knew, I just knew the impact to my section, to my colleagues, I just knew. I responded, "Michael, yes I do."

Needless to say, when we arrived Saturday morning, the airport was in mass chaos. We decided to share a cab to my residence. Since my vehicle had diplomatic plates, I would take Michael to check in at the hotel before driving to the embassy.

There was so much confusion and chaos as everyone tried to do the best they could with the horrific situation. The entire city and its infrastructure were in mass chaos, stretched even further in its capabilities than before the bombing. The next challenge was to get to the bomb site. To begin continuity of operations, financial operations, I needed to assess what I had to work with and pass along that insight/assessment immediately to main State Department in Washington. The first thing I did was to go to the embassy building and get an assessment of the damage done to the financial section.

From the media coverage I had seen up to that point, it appeared that the embassy building itself was intact, since it remained standing, whereas the building next door had collapsed entirely. Other nearby buildings' windows were completely blown out. Based on these images, I didn't know what to expect when I got there regarding the inside. On the flight back, deep down I sensed and prepared for the worst. But then again, how does one prepare for such a horrific atrocity?

The embassy was built to withstand many contingencies. And that was depicted in media coverage. However, what was not so apparent unless you were on the ground was the devastation inside the Embassy building. The FMC section was an open modular floor plan. After the bomb went off, it was obliterated. Based on the numerous comments made to me, the FMC was so obliterated they didn't even know where the furniture

15

went. Though I returned to the Embassy in the aftermath of the explosion, I never returned to the FMC section itself. I did not do so, not only because of devastation, but also because I wanted to remember and hold the memories of my FMC family as they were, before I departed for my trip to Ethiopia.

In every telephone conversation, discussion, and presentation thereafter, I found I had to continuously repeat this fact over and over. For though a building that was built to withstand so many contingencies, inside there was nothing remaining of Embassy FMC operations, just like so many other Embassy sections. To those not on the ground, so many assumptions were being made based on the media coverage of what appeared as a still standing building. Instead of being based on actual facts on the ground. Though the media coverage indicated most of the building was solid and intact, the inside was completely destroyed. Or these assumptions made, was it just naivete of not understanding the aftermath of such a crisis as this. Or, was it all together something more, something much more involved and at play from the very start. Regardless, when I received a response to check this regulation or that regulation, get on the computer and access this form or that form, I had to continually remind that there was no communication link. There were no books and records. No forms. No Financial Service Center (FSC) Paris Operation's Manual. No Foreign Affairs Manual (FAM). No computers and, most devastating, no accounting of the FMC staff.

When I arrived at the bombed Embassy site, I was met by Engineering Security Center (ESC) Specialist Worley Reed and Facilities Maintenance Specialist (FMS) Steve Montgomery. They advised that it was too dangerous to go into the building. I put on the hard hat handed to me. I was then given a verbal assessment of the FMC. I was told that the FMC open bull pen area, right above the explosion, took the brunt. The body count was still unknown. I queried about the two cashier operations: the in-house and the Citibank cashier operations. I was advised that both Embassy Class B Cashier Farhat Sheikh and Citibank Cashier Catherine Mukethi were killed and both cashier operations totally destroyed. Regardless, I advised that I was required to recover any funds, US and local currency, from both operations for accountability purposes. At that time, I was advised that they would retrieve what they could and provide it to me in my next trip to the explosion site. The US Embassy site was no longer operational. Since I could not return to the actual physical location of the FMC section, my colleague and our Department of Defense (DOD)

Kenya/US Liaison Officer (KUSLO) representative Colonel Ronald Roughead said that he would clear out what remained from my office. Soon after, Colonel Roughead gave me a single box containing what was salvageable.

Temporary Embassy operations had been established at our US Agency for International Development (USAID) complex. When I arrived, I immediately held meetings with the USAID Controller Amanda Levenson. Under interagency agreements, FMC Nairobi serviced over 15 USG agencies. Since USAID and State's financial systems were not compatible, arrangements were made to simplify applicable financial processing for her USAID financial staff to separately account and process all related expenses. This would include applicable processing by their USAID Class B Cashier operations. The USAID's Controller Staff and USAID Executive Officer Michael Trott were hands-on and standing-ready to assist whenever needed.

Next, I talked with FSC Paris Director Robert McAnneny and Accounting Manager Elizabeth Sines. I requested an immediate emergency increase to USAID's cashier accountability, explaining that there was no FMC operation left. I requested FSC Paris to send copies of everything they had pertaining to financial operations of Embassy Nairobi—all reports, all applications, all guidance, all forms—for we had nothing left. FSC Paris was incredibly responsive, as well as Financial Management Policy (FMP) in Washington. I received a fax from FMP Sid Kaplan authorizing me to take certain actions as I deemed necessary after our discussions. I remained in continual communications with FSC Paris, FMP and AF/EX; they were my lifeline.

Elizabeth and I discussed the importance of recovering the cashier accountability. I explained that I had just visited the Embassy site and that though the walls were still standing, the inside was totally destroyed. I shared my discussion with ESC Worley Reed and FMS Steve Montgomery regarding this matter. Since I could not enter those areas of the explosion site, they would recover what they could, and then I would go back to the site and retrieve what they gathered. Elizabeth stated that she understood; however, she wanted to provide me some additional insight. She reiterated what occurred in an earlier crisis event; as I recall it was about during Vietnam, when the FMO was instructed to destroy the funds accordingly and instead the funds blew out across the countryside. The applicable FMO was held accountable and had to repay the funds. I said, with my OIG background, I totally understood and would document and control the accountability as tightly as I could, as I had prior to the explosion. I would do so even more tightly in its aftermath. Elizabeth's intended message of the importance of financial controls being maintained in such an incident was received and understood, loud and clear.

Next, I met with Citibank General Manager, Peter Harris. We discussed my priorities, which he quickly responded were also his priorities. I stated that the USAID's cashier accountability was increased and that the physical funds were needed immediately. Accommodation exchange services needed to be established at the USAID complex and all applicable hotels used by the influx of temporary duty (TDY) officials immediately beginning the next day, Sunday. Procedures to be used for circumstances resulting from the explosion were discussed and put in place. Citibank also immediately offered my section office space and computers, if and when we needed them. That was the kind and immediate assistance we received from our banking partner, Citibank. I shared my immense condolences for the loss of our Citibank/FMC family member, dear Catherine.

Coincidentally, at the time of the explosion, there was an ongoing nation wide bank employees' strike limiting banking transactions throughout the country. According to one surviving FMC staff family member, when the first bomb went off, many of the FMC staff went to the back window, with an initial thought that the striking bank employees had thrown a bomb at the Cooperative Bank located in the rear of the Embassy. This thought was proven fatally wrong when the second bomb went off. Peter and I discussed the potential impact the bank strike could have on Citibank, their employees and their operations, as well as ours. I later shared this potential concern with FSC Paris and FMP in case funds had to be flown in. Fortunately, up to the day I left, we had no banking glitches. Peter put his staff at risk for us and made us his top priority.

Soon after, I was asked by Jim Huskey, our Political Officer, if I could call my contacts at Citibank to see if they could establish and provide account information that could be mentioned during his family's interview with *Good Morning America* where people could send contributions. Jim said he knew that this was asking a lot, but could this information be given to him within the half hour since he was leaving soon. I immediately called Peter and said, "Remember when you said all I have to do is ask?" Peter said, "Yes, what do you need?" I explained to Peter that I needed a US dollar account established in the US, and a US dollar and a Kenyan shilling account to be established here in Kenya and to be able to provide this account information on *Good Morning America*. Peter asked, "When do you need this information?" I said, "In about 15 minutes." He responded that he would call me back in 10 minutes. And he did – the only condition was that the phone number for the New York Account Manager could not be read over the air since according to Peter, "Maurice was still sleeping and didn't know yet." That's the kind of cooperation I received from Citibank.

In one DOD or FBI TDY Office, someone put up a sign that read: *The Main Thing is to Keep the Main Thing, the Main Thing*. This motto, became my motto. Due to the assistance I received from USAID Controller's operation and Executive Office, FSC Paris, FMP, AF/EX and Citibank, I was able to do exactly that and focus on my primary objectives before my August 20th departure: account for my staff, account for the funds of the cashiers, obtain counseling for my staff, and get as much of the FMC financial operations up and running as I could. With every crisis, there are unsung heroes and the true colors of leadership rise to the occasion. I truly witnessed this over and over, too many stories to mention. That said, with every crisis, there are also *the good, the bad and the ugly,* those who take advantage for their self-promotion. I truly witnessed this at times as well. A time of crisis either brings human beings together or it does not. In this crisis, for many, that's precisely what it did—it brought us together. For some, the past would not be forgotten.

The FMC family consisted of my American FS Deputy Ann "Michelle" O'Connor, sixteen Kenyan nationals and myself. The FMC family had two *honorary* members: Catherine Mukethi, our Citibank Cashier and George Mimba, the Kenyan Information Management Specialist (IMS) located next to FMC. To this day, when I am asked how many were killed in my section, I always hesitate because our FMC family was larger than indicated on the staffing chart. The confirmed casualties on that day included Michelle, who was temporarily transferred to General Service Office (GSO) just prior to the bombing. She was located and identified immediately, being killed instantly while sitting in her GSO office. Farhat Sheikh and Catherine Mukethi, both of our Embassy cashiers killed instantly, were confirmed deceased as well.

By the end of that first day, I did not have full accounting of my FMC family.

SUNDAY AUGUST 9, 1998

The logistical integration of Embassy Nairobi personnel into the US-AID complex was a challenge, stretched even further with official

TDYers that would arrive daily and, at the same time, having no surviving financial operation.

At one point, I had a TDYer who had just flown in from Washington D.C. come into my office and advise me that he was in need of a travel advance since he didn't have time to get one before he departed. He was told he could get one once he arrived at the US Embassy. Needless to say, with both cashiers deceased and arrangements still not up and running regarding USAID Cashier or Citibank Cashier support, I admit, my initial reaction to that TDYer was not a kind one. By this time, a 24/7 open line had been established with Washington, on which I relayed the message to the AF/EX representative to get the word out: all TDYers get their cash travel advances in the US prior to their departure because they aren't going to be able to get them at a bombed-out Embassy. The message was delivered and received loud and clear. Later I located the TDYer who took the brunt of my initial reaction and I apologized. He did as well. We made sure he was taken care of, and as I recall we gave each other a hug.

Office space was a premium. I was given a temporary office before a more permanent space was provided to me and my surviving staff within the USAID Controller's shop. Since it was Sunday, we had no idea given the bank strike, what our banking arrangements would be on Monday. All we could do was wait and see, and hope.

I was sitting in my temporary office when a DOD soldier was escorted in and introduced himself. He basically said, "Ma'am, I have $1 million dollars in cash and need a safe to store it." I asked him, "Sir, what is your mission at this time?" He replied to support the recovery operations. I replied, "Good, so our missions are the same." I explained the situation on the ground regarding the cashiers being killed, the bank strike, and the possibility of an urgent need for US currency if we couldn't get our makeshift/temporary financial operations up and going Monday morning. He said he understood. I said, "Good. So, you will understand this: I will find you a safe to store your US Currency. However, this is with the understanding that if on Monday morning the makeshift arrangements we've made do not come to fruition, the million dollars will become mine, the US State Department's, with applicable USDO accountability transfers." He replied, "Yes ma'am, I understand and will advise up my chain accordingly." Come Monday morning, the planned makeshift arrangements set into motion successfully went into effect. The US currency that had been immediately secured was never needed on my end.

As stated earlier, USAID was providing great support. But so much more was needed. I requested that the AF/EX Rovers posted in FSC Paris come to assist. AF/EX Rover Bernard Letellier would arrive in coming days. I was delighted. I was also delighted when our previous Regional Security Officer (RSO) Patricia (Pat) Hartnett-Kelly returned to provide support. Though she had departed Nairobi months prior, she had been advised that she would be the *accountable* RSO in regards to the applicable Accountability Review Board (ARB) process. She had flown back to recover applicable files locked up in safes, if they still existed. Her Assistant RSO Daniel Weber was also flown back to Nairobi from Pretoria to assist. Given the circumstance and our professional kinship, I couldn't have thought of anyone better than to have Pat back at post.

Speaking of professional kinship, Colonel Mensch was preparing for his departure back to Addis and said he would stop in to say good-bye. I was walking down the corridor when I heard someone say that now that he had arrived, he was in charge of all financial operations. Reaching this individual at the end of his statement, given the circumstances, I was flabbergasted to see that my replacement, Charlie Slater, came in prior to his scheduled arrival date and was the one making this statement. I then stated loud and clear, "No, I am in charge of the financial operations and will remain so until my scheduled departure." That was the first time I became aware of Charlie Slater's arrival and presence, and quite obvious, his intent and objective—his being there, not to support me and the financial operations, but quite obviously from the very start, his agenda, someone's agenda, and himself. Charlie was the last person who should have been sent to the post, particularly in light of the condition in which he left his last post in Addis Ababa that resulted in my shuttling emergency funds to them just months prior. But this was not our only history. Nor would this be our only confrontation given that he arrived and never located me to let me know he was there. Nor did he ever query/sympathize/empathize regarding the living and the dead of *my* FMC family. Colonel Mensch was off to the side and witnessed the encounter.

Given the circumstances, I was sad to see Colonel Mensch leave but extremely grateful Pat and Dan were there. Witnessing this encounter, Colonel Mensch would have context and understanding of future *Charlie Slater* tactics that I would later share with him. As would Pat, given our dinner discussion later that evening when I recalled the event with her and a group of her fellow TDY Diplomatic Security (DS) Special Agents (SA) who also just arrived to assist with recovery operations. They, in turn, would enlighten me with even more *Charlie Slater* tactics regarding events that took place in Liberia and Sierra Leone when he was RFMO. Something bigger was at play even at that time … just not apparent to me at the time, precisely what. Again, during events such as this, true colors and characters are exposed. Or in this case, a leopard never changes its spots.

By the end of that day, I still did not have a full account of my FMC family.

Monday August 10, 1998

On Monday, after much anticipation and a deep sigh of relief, Citibank was able to proceed as arranged and an Embassy Nairobi *makeshift* financial operation was in place.

I still did not have a full account of my FMC family.

Tuesday August 11, 1998

I returned to the explosion site to recover what remained of the Cashier operations. When I arrived, I was once again provided a hard hat and advised that I could remain in the Consular section of the Embassy on the ground floor where Embassy FMS Steve Montgomery would provide what he was able to recover. Steve handed me the first bag and then, as he passed along the second bag, he made a comment for me to be prepared. "Michelle, this bag includes contents that Farhat didn't let go." Ensuring that I had witnesses from the time of receiving the bags, I was then accompanied on the drive back to the USAID Compound. I then opened the bag in front of witness and proceeded to conduct the two applicable cash counts.

USAID Controller Amanda Levenson assisted me with the inventory of the Embassy Class B Cashier's funds and United States Information Agency (USIA) Executive Officer Rita Jennings assisted me with the inventory of the Citibank Cashier funds. As Steve pointed out, some of the funds were contaminated. In regards to physical dollar bills, not much was recovered and what was recovered was too contaminated with human remains to be reused or sent back to the United States. The entire inventory of recovered funds was documented. FMP, FBI and DS were helpful in advising how to properly and legally dispose of the contaminated US cash and cash equivalents. Once the applicable contaminated funds were documented, the contaminated funds were initially turned over to the FBI.

The FBI determined that the contaminated funds *did not have evidentiary value.* The contaminated US funds were then turned over to RSO Pat Hartnett-Kelly, who then destroyed these funds accordingly. Citibank assisted me in the disposal of contaminated local currency by taking it and returning it to the Kenyan Central Bank.

Despite the reported looting in the building in the initial hours after the explosion until the perimeter was secured, a substantial amount from both cashier operations accountabilities were recovered. AF/EX Rover Bernard Letellier was still completing all the in-transit items of the Class B Cashier accountability when I left, so I did not know the status of the recovery of the entire accountability before my departure. Citibank had yet to determine the total amount they lost before my scheduled departure from post on August 20th.

By the end of that day, I still did not have a full account of my FMC family.

WEDNESDAY AUGUST 12, 1998

The embassy had started a master list for staff accountability. Since my focus was on continuity of Embassy financial operations, I did not participate in the actual Embassy staff location effort at the bombing site, hospitals and morgues. What I did do was pulled out the copy of the FMC staff emergency telephone contact list that I had located at my residence. I started my own FMC staff accountability list to monitor and share accordingly. I already knew at this time regarding Michelle, Farhat and Catherine, but I needed to know about the rest. I started to make calls. This process was heart wrenching. Some calls I made reconnected me with fellow FMC family members that had not been present at the time of the explosion or, like myself, not at the embassy that day. In fact, some took the day off since I, the boss, was not going to be in the office that day. Other calls I made were more challenging as I was advised that their loved one, our FMC Family member, had not yet been seen or heard from since the explosion. I was then able to divide my staff into four lists: alive, deceased, injured, status unknown. For those FMC staff I reached, I asked them to come to see me at the USAID Complex whenever they could to check in. I would then coordinate with those compiling the Embassy's Master list to ensure accuracy regarding the FMC section.

By this time, we were beginning to hear that Ambassador Prudence Bushnell was arranging to conduct a memorial service. I would be eulogizing those of my section.

Just a month prior, in July, I was advised that I was officially converted from civil service to foreign service as a Financial Management Specialist. I would not be returning to State OIG at the end of this second excursion detail, but going on to my first official FS assignment, Santiago, Chile. As standard procedure, one's first assignment was determined by Washington and then assignments thereafter would follow the standard bidding process. Though I was not particularly excited about this assignment, I was *officially* FS. I developed a pending/to do folder of all tasks that needed to be completed before I departed my post/assignment. Fortunately for me, I had this folder at home, not my office in the embassy, at the time of the explosion. I had brought it home on my last day of work before heading off on my personal trip to Ethiopia so I could review it when I got back before heading back to work. In it, I had a copy of the Superior Honor Award nomination justification that I submitted for my FMC staff on June 15, 1998 to Embassy Nairobi Management Counselor Stephan Nolan. That day, I queried Washington on the 24/7 open telephone line on the status of this June award nomination. I intended to use it as the foundation for my eulogy comments and advised AF/EX of this. They said they would get back to me. I was later advised AF/EX never received the award nomination, so I faxed them a copy.

Steve Nolan, like so many others, was in the building at the time of the explosion. I had not seen him since I returned. Our first encounter, in light of all that had occurred, would not be a positive one. Apparently, AF/EX queried Steve on the status of this award, the one he/HR never approved nor submitted as of the time of the Embassy bombing, August 7, 1998.

By the end of that day, I still did not have a full account of my FMC family.

THURSDAY AUGUST 13, 1998

For the first time, I was in my temporary office for an extended period of time, taking notes of all that had come to my attention that needed to be completed. The list was extensive. The day before I started to meet with non-USG entities that were co-located in the embassy whose operations and properties were also damaged/destroyed. These included Citibank, Café Café (our snack bar), Express Travel, UIIS (local guard contractor) and the American Employee Association (AEA) Morale Store. I queried AF/EX about these situations as I was beginning to get queries. To the time of my departure, when asked what they should do, I requested that they submit a claim and that I would consult Washington as to how to handle their situation. Reviewing the list that I'd just compiled, I had a visitor—it was Steve Nolan, in our first encounter. I got up to give him a hug. Instead I was greeted with him stating, "Your replacement is here, you need to start turning over the operations to him." It was his buddy Charlie Slater. I couldn't believe it. I actually had intended to discuss my possible extension since my pre-scheduled departure date was the following week. I now knew the answer. We went back and forth for a bit and our discussion ended with my stating, "It's my operation until my departure on August 20th." He didn't care. And in light of it all, and all that occurred prior, I told him to *go to hell* and walked away to find out the status of the living and dead of my FMC staff family members.

Later that day, I would find out from AF/EX that the Superior Honor Award for FMC that I submitted to Stephen Nolan on June 15, 1998 would be approved. The Awards Coordinator approval memo was dated August 14, 1998. I would receive a faxed copy on August 17, 1998. I could use the award nomination as the foundation for my eulogy comments.

I contacted GSO Chris Stillman to advise him that I hated to do this to him in light of all the other priorities he had in the aftermath of the bombing, but I needed to continue as previously arranged prior to the bombing, the pack-out of my personal effects and vehicle. My departure was not delayed. It was set for the following week on Thursday August 20, 1998, for that is what our Management Counselor Steve Nolan wanted.

By the end of that day, I had an accounting of my entire FMC family except for one, Chrispine Bonyo.

FRIDAY AUGUST 14, 1998

Though I never went to hospitals and morgues trying to locate survivors and bodies, one of my dear colleagues did. Bruce Knotts was a member of the Embassy Khartoum relocated and co-located at Embassy Nairobi. The diplomatic relationship between Sudan and Washington was such that our Ambassador Timothy Carney and his staff were removed from Khartoum and relocated to Nairobi due to security reasons, continuing diplomacy via shuttle diplomacy. Going to Sudan a few times a month, if that, and only when deemed safe to do so. Once Ambassador Carney departed his assignment, the relationship was downgraded from an Ambassadorial to a Charge d'affaires level of diplomatic relations. Ambassador Carney was replaced by Charge Donald Teitelbaum. This downgraded Charge d'affaires diplomatic relationship continues to this day.

Since my arrival to Nairobi in 1995, I had supporting regional financial management responsibilities for Embassy Khartoum, Sudan. At the time of the explosion, Embassy Khartoum Management Officer Bruce Knotts was in his Embassy Nairobi office. Surviving and crawling out of the rubble, Bruce then worked endlessly in assisting the recovery to include going to morgues locating and identifying of our embassy staff.

I was sitting in my makeshift office when Bruce came in to see me. Given the task Bruce was performing, I braced myself. Given the context of needing/wanting closure for all my FMC Family members' families, and knowing the news I was patiently waiting for, he basically said, "Michelle, I have some good news and some bad news." I said, "Okay, good news first." He said he found Chrispine, Chrispine's body. Already mentally and emotionally prepared for this result, I said, "Okay, at least now Chrispine's family has a body, a body to bury, so they can have closure. As well as us, his FMC family. Now, what's the bad news?" Distinctly remembering Bruce rubbing his forearm as he told me, he said, "Michelle, there was an IV (intravenous) hole." Meaning our dear Chrispine had been alive, but we, the USG, just did not get to him in time.

By the end of that day, one week after the explosion, I finally had a full accounting of our FMC family. Eight of my staff were alive, two were hanging on in the hospital, and nine were deceased, including my American deputy and Citibank Cashier. Six of the eight in my section, to include myself, survived because we physically were not in the office that day. George Mimba, our honorary FMC family member in the embassy at the time of the explosion, survived as well.

SATURDAY AUGUST 15, 1998

This last week being the most devastating and trying time of my life, I permitted myself to sleep in. When the house phone rang, not knowing what to expect, I was surprised to hear the woman's voice. "Hello, is this Michelle?" I said *yes*. "Hello Michelle, this is Lizzie Slater, Charlie Slater's wife. How are you?" Without hesitation and despite my issues with her husband, I said, "Oh my goodness Lizzie. How are you? I've seen you being interviewed during the media coverage of the Embassy bombing there in Dar…" She said she was hanging in there, all are trying to be strong. I asked how her son was, etc., when she said, "Michelle could you please do something for me?" Without hesitation, I said, "Anything. What do you need?" Her request was simple, yet, at the same time, beyond reprehensible. But then again, not surprising, given what she would say next and particularly about who she said it. She said "Michelle can you please ask Charlie to give me a call. He hasn't called since all this occurred." I shook my head in disbelief. "Sure, Lizzie, I can pass along the message the next time I see Charlie." I told her to stay strong and to please let me know if there is anything more I can do to assist before hanging up the phone. I laid back down on my bed, thinking, *unbelievable*. Knowing I would not be able to rest again after that call, it was time to get up and get ready to go back into the temporary Embassy. Though my days at post were now numbered, I had to make them count. I don't recall specifically when I saw Charlie Slater again, but I did pass the message on when I saw him next. And I had nothing more to say to him to the day I left.

MONDAY AUGUST 17/THURSDAY AUGUST 20, 1998

My departure had been scheduled before the embassy bombing. Despite the circumstance, since my replacement was already on the ground, it was decided that I should leave as planned. This last week, so much had to be done not only for recovery efforts, but in preparation for my departure. The days and all the events blended together so the timeline of what happened when can't be pin-pointedly reconstructed, but all did occur.

Monday August 17, 1998

The FMC Staff had worked together twenty to thirty years. Many of the Kenyan staff had moved into the Embassy building when it was brand new. They lost not only their home, but also their family. They were hurting. Ambassador Bushnell established mandatory counseling sessions, which all FMC attended together. Since I did not feel it was enough for my staff, I arranged a private counseling session for my staff with Dr. Shirley Hervey. Dr. Hervey was assigned to Nairobi for at least another year and already knew some of my staff. Since my departure date was that week, we had one more session together as my FMC staff was in immense pain.

Next, the memorial service. This was going to be very difficult. What do I even say at a time like this? I decided to use the submitted Superior Honor Award nomination justification as my eulogy foundation. My FMC family nicknamed me *Mama Safi*, which in Kiswahili means *Mama Clean*. It was an affectionate reference to all the *cleaning* we did together—cleaning the office, cleaning desks, cleaning the books and records. They teased of my ongoing *cleaning* goals and priorities. And as a team, we accomplished so much. As I wanted to make sure my FMC staff's efforts were recognized and rewarded before my departure, I wrote and submitted the award months in advance of my scheduled departure. Though it was submitted on June 15, 1998 to Management Counselor Stephen Nolan and HR, I had not heard anything back yet and was planning on following-up on it upon my return from my trip to Ethiopia. Instead of expected celebration, I had no idea that months later I would be repeating the words I wrote as a eulogy and remembrance at their memorial service instead. I was devastated. Having the deeds and memories behind the words I stated gave me the strength to get through this emotional reflection as well as having other surviving FMC family members share insights as to what made our now deceased FMC family members so special.

It came to my attention afterwards that in the history of the Foreign Service, I may be the one to have lost the most staff under direct supervision. I don't know. All I do know is that our lives, so many lives, were forever changed as a result of August 7, 1998.

Every year on August 7, I email my surviving FMC family and our honorary member George Mimba. August 7, 2018 was the 20th year anniversary. And at this time, we have one less family member with the sudden passing of beloved Sammy Mwangi. Memory Eternal to Sammy and all those we lost.

Tuesday August 18, 1998
Since motor pool options were now very restricted, I decided that though my household effects would be packed out before my departure, my Isuzu Trooper would be delayed in being shipped out until after my departure, so I could use it up to that time. I did not want to be an additional burden to the now incredibly stretched motor pool. Pack-out was a two-day event. The first day the packers come by to determine how many boxes and crates would be needed. The second day, an all-day event, everything would be packed up and crated. I would soon be departing from my three-year assignment as FMC Director at Embassy Nairobi, Kenya, ending my tour in the most heart-wrenching and devastating manner possible.

During this time, many high-level officials would come to Nairobi. One in particular, was as heart-wrenched and devastated as myself, Ambassador Mary Ryan. Though I did not know or meet Ambassador Ryan during this time, in a matter of weeks I would come to know and love this incredible human being, a true angel and blessing to the Department of

State. When Ambassador Ryan arrived, she was given a hardhat, just I had been. Unlike myself, restricted to just the Consular section of the bombed Embassy building, Ambassador Ryan requested a tour throughout the building wanting to see where every American and Kenyan Embassy staff was killed, identified by their applicable name. She toured as much of the building as possible. During her visit, I heard she took her colleague Julian Bartley and his son Jay's deaths particularly hard. They were supposedly killed while standing outside the Cashier window in my section. I adored Julian, and would later share insightful comments he would make to me about Ambassador Mary Ryan only weeks before the bombing. Years later, I would contribute in the drafting of tributes to the passing of Ambassador Mary Ryan that ensured a laudation of her for historical record, congressional record forevermore.

Wednesday August 19, 1998

Pack-out

Thursday August 20, 1998

Today I was leaving. A departure date scheduled prior to the bombing and now set in stone with my replacement on the ground. Departing at this time was neither my preference nor my choice.

I was scheduled to leave that evening, as I recall on KLM. Fortunately for me, Pat Hartnett-Kelly would be departing on the same flight. If I was going to leave, I was at least grateful to depart with her. We were in our seats, first row in business class, settling in, when there was an announcement over the intercom. The pilot advised that there was going to be a slight delay. After a while, Pat and I were becoming slightly concerned. Pat requested the stewardess to come see her, indicating to come close for others not to hear her query. Pat indicated that she was State Diplomatic Security and wanted to know if the stewardess could query the pilot to find out what was really going on. The stewardess nodded and walked to the cockpit. Minutes later, she came back with a concerned look on her face. She basically said, "Your country has just bombed the hell out of Sudan and they are looking for an alternate route to avoid Sudan air space." Another stewardess walked by with an open bottle of wine. Pat stopped her and said, "We'll take that." We both sat there in disbelief. Both being regional support for Sudan, we didn't know what was really happening other than feeling that we were in midst of the beginning of *World War III*.

We both just wanted to get back to the US as quickly and as safely as possible. And we did. We would later find out that FBI Director Louis Freeh was on the ground in Nairobi at the time. Supposedly neither he nor the Ambassador were given advance warning of the airstrike on the Al-Shifa pharmaceutical factory in Khartoum, Sudan.

Being regional for Khartoum, I would later find out that though none of our local Sudanese Embassy staff were killed, some were injured in the aftermath. Years later, I would serve in Khartoum at a time of reestablishing normalized operations. And at this time, given the insight I have and the events that would unfold in the meanwhile, I hold deep skepticism of what really was occurring at the time—now with signposts thereafter, all along the way.

Lawrence Gitau – Killed - August 7, 1998
Joel Kamau – Killed – August 7, 1998
Peter Macharia – Killed – August 7, 1998
Catherine Mukethi (Citibank Cashier) * - Killed – August 7, 1998
Ann Michelle O'Connor - Killed – August 7, 1998
Eric Onyango – Killed – August 7, 1998
Farhat Sheikh – Killed – August 7, 1998
Fred Yafes – Killed – August 7, 1998
Chrispine Bonyo – Killed – August 7, 1998 or possibly thereafter…
Livingstone Madahana – (Severely Injured) August 7, 1998 Survivor
Mary Ofisi – (Injured) August 7, 1998 Survivor
Hamza Girnary – August 7, 1998 Survivor
Lucy Gitau – August 7, 1998 Survivor
Grace Marangu – August 7, 1998 Survivor
Raphael Munguti – August 7, 1998 Survivor
Sammy Mwangi – August 7, 1998 Survivor (Passed away 2018)
Charles Ndibui - August 7, 1998 Survivor
Anne Odinga – August 7, 1998 Survivor
George Mimba (Embassy Nairobi/IM) * - August 7, 1998 Survivor
And myself, also an August 7, 1998 Survivor

PART TWO

CHAPTER 3

LIVING MY LIFE:
The Main Thing Is To Keep The Main Thing, The Main Thing

BACK IN THE US

On August 21, 1998, Pat and I arrived safely back in the United States. I checked in to temporary housing in Northern Virginia to proceed with my Foreign Service Institute (FSI) Spanish language training in preparation for my assignment in Santiago, Chile. I had already been there previously when conducting OIG audit field work. The country was going through a very trying period, with an explosion occurring while I was there. Over a weekend, I was able to take an opportunity to go skiing, enabling me to see the breadth of this beautiful country. I knew I would be able to make the best and most of my posting there. However, a very unprofessional and unpleasant experience also occurred while I was in Chile. It was between the only two of us on this State OIG TDY, me and my supervisor at the time, Charlie Slater. Immediately reporting this incident upon our return to Washington, my opinion of Charlie was changed forevermore.

Departing Nairobi on August 20th, I was in essence the first one back alive to tell the story. After a few days back, I don't know which would have been harder: remaining in Nairobi seeing progress, slight progress, being made every day in moving forward amongst the chaos and debris, or what I actually ended up enduring. Being continually stopped in the hall, in the cafeteria, everywhere I went, telling and retelling the story over and over again. I would begin the day strong, but day-after-day, every day, telling and retelling the story, I would begin to tear-up every time I did tell the story. Despite the emotional impact on me personally, on one hand, I felt I had the responsibility to share with colleagues so rightly concerned; while on the other, considerations for my own well-being to move forward. After days of this, I outreached to State's Employee Counseling Services (ECS).

ECS Flora Bryant arranged to see me at FSI. I am not a cryer so when I tear up with every sharing of the story, I wanted to make sure it was normal in the grieving process. I wanted to know what post-traumatic stress was and the difference to the normal grieving process for my own well-being as I had never been through the aftermanth of a terrorist attack before. Flora indicated that the fact that I outreached to ECS and was talking to her is a good, strong indicator of the difference. Our discussions gave me the strength to endure such encounters. Even more, they would strengthen me for what I would yet have to encounter, despite no longer being in Nairobi—the good, the bad and the ugly in the aftermath of such circumstances.

Being back, I didn't know official debriefing protocols. I outreached to many key offices in the Department to let them all know I was available. Though I found it odd, one office that I outreached to that never got back to me was Diplomatic Security. Maybe since I was in continual contact with Pat Hartnett-Kelly, DS didn't feel it was necessary. In due time, I would conclude the real reason was something more sinister.

Though I had no direct linkage, I contacted the Bureau of Consular Affairs (CA), and more specifically Ambassador Mary Ryan. Though I did not know nor meet her when she came to Nairobi in the aftermath, I did hear that Mary was taking her colleague and my friend, Counselor General (CG) Julian Bartley's death very hard. The last discussion I had with Julian was a few weeks before the bombing, before my trip to Ethiopia. He specifically mentioned Mary, and I wanted to share his last comments with her so she knew. I felt it was something that I would have wanted to know. I hoped to assist Mary through her grieving process as well. Given the Ambassador's level of position I realized that I may be breaking protocol in meeting with her. But when I relayed this Julian Bartley conversation to Ambassador Ryan's assistant, her assistant said, "Get in here, she'll want to meet with you immediately." We scheduled an appointment for a day or so later.

I was sitting outside her office when Ambassador Ryan opened her office door, introduced herself and asked me to come in and take a seat. I thanked her for seeing me. I apologized that I did not meet her when she was in Nairobi and explained that I was in the process of packing-out since my departure was scheduled prior to the bombing. I explained that I had heard that she was taking Julian's death very badly. I wanted her to know that just a few weeks prior to the bombing, I had a discussion with Julian and her name came up. I didn't know at the time that it would be our last discussion, nor did I understand that it would be a segue years later for my figuring out what all this was really about. What I did know was Julian was my colleague, my friend that I adored, and in turn, Julian absolutely adored Mary. I let her know that.

I mentioned to Mary that I had been in Nairobi as the FMC Director on an excursion tour detail from OIG, and just before the bombing, on July 9, 1998, I was officially converted to the foreign service. However, I experienced some very trying times, which seemed to get even more troubling and trying after I had submitted my conversion application. Knowing Julian was experiencing his own trying times, with some of ours overlapping, I called to see if Julian could chat. He said sure, meet with him out back. I went down to the basement, out the garage, and saw him standing there, as I recall, smoking a cigarette. I teased and said, "I didn't know you smoked." Putting his finger to his lip, he said, *"I don't."* I adored Julian. Months earlier he took me to a Rotary Club meeting as his guest. He introduced me as his Embassy colleague, *our scholar with the dollar.* I blushed and we laughed. I confided that I was in a situation and would really like his advisement. With the trying times that we both were experiencing, I told him that I had just found out that I was officially accepted and converted into the FS. However, in light of these trying times, I now wonder if I did the right thing. He smiled, and said, "Michelle, you remind me of my girl Mary Ryan." He then went up and down, and round and round, about Mary Ryan, and said, "Michelle, we the foreign service need more Mary Ryan's, women like you." While putting out his cigarette, I gave him a hug while saying thank you, and we walked back into the Embassy building through the garage. It was time to go back to work and because of him, I decided it was the right decision. I felt better. Weeks later, this would be the exact area of the August 7, 1998 bombing.

When I finished telling Mary the story, I realized she had reached for a box of tissues placing them on the coffee table. We both pulled out a tissue, both tearing up due to the intensity of this horrific tragedy and loss. We then shared details of her visit and my experience dealing with continuity of operations at the same time, the accounting for my FMC family, not happening until a full week after the bombing. I shared the story regarding Chrispine, the status of my two injured staff Livingstone and Mary, and the details of my onward assignment. For those unfamiliar with the FS system, those in the FS are what's commonly referred to as *coned* into different position categories. Though I was not *Consular-coned* in the FS of which Mary was senior-level responsible for, she was very interested. She wanted me to stay in touch, particularly regarding Livingstone and Mary's progress. Most importantly, she wanted me to brief Under Secretary (U/S) for Management (M) Bonnie Cohen and her senior staff. She asked if I would be available to do this. I said sure. We got up, gave each other a hug and she said we'll be in touch. Mary walked me to and opened her office door. As I was walking away, I heard her say to her assistant, "Please see if you can get U/S Cohen on the phone."

On Wednesday, September 2, 1998 around 10:00 A.M., I was once again sitting outside Ambassador Ryan's office. She came to the door and asked me to come in. We sat down, and she said, "Are you ready?" I said yes, but forewarned that I didn't know if I could get through it without tearing up. She handed me a tissue for my pocket. She said, "You are going to do fine. And if you tear up, so be it. They need to see the tears, the hurt, the pain, the realness of this tragedy." We got up, she gave me a hug and said, "Let's go. We started to walk down the hall to the elevator to go to the 7th floor to attend U/S Cohen's 10:30 a.m. Weekly Staff Meeting.

Ambassador Ryan and I walked into the conference room. In attendance were Sid Kaplan, the State Department's acting Chief Financial Officer (CFO) and Assistant (A/S) Secretary, Bureau of Financial Management and Policy (FMP), Edward "Skip" Gnehm, the Director General (DG) of the Foreign Service and Director of Personnel, Carrie Weiner, U/S Cohen's Assistant, and a few others. Bert Edwards, the newly appointed incoming political-appointee CFO, may also have been present. We all sat at the table, waiting for U/S Cohen to come in. Soon after she came in, I was introduced and then asked to begin. Nervous, I qualified my comments by stating that in order for me to get through the entire brief, I would be reading from my notes. I was very concerned of my tearing up and appearing to be *emotional* and not getting through all my comments. To me, there were some very important insights and thoughts that I wanted and that needed to be conveyed. I started and as I proceeded, I felt the strength behind the words that I spoke, realizing I was now speaking for those voices that were silenced, and if I did not speak, who would? I continued and even began to add extemporaneous sidebar stories and comments along the way—some to lighten the seriousness of the matter being discussed, and others to emphasize the seriousness of the matter at hand. As I recall I did tear up, but I did not cry. I stayed focus and ended by looking up and asking if there were any questions for me. For the first time, focused on the attendees and not my notes/the material I had to cover, I realized there wasn't a dry eye in the room.

At the end of the meeting, Mary and I walked back to her office. She gave me a hug and said, "Michelle, you did your staff proud as well as your foreign service. Thank you." I said, "No Mary, thank you, thank you for giving this opportunity to speak for those whose voices have been silenced." We hugged and then scheduled an appointment to meet for lunch when I returned from my home leave. Meeting for lunch became a regular and routine ritual when we both were in the country, up to the time of her passing on April 25, 2006.

Two immediate results were the outcome of my briefing. The DG's office, becoming aware of my recent conversion to the FS, queried regarding my options, the main one being whether or not I wanted to convert back to CS or remain FS. I requested some time to think it over and to let the DG know what I decided upon returning from my scheduled home leave.

The second result was my first recommendation under *lessons learned: To create a quick action response team.* Carrie Weiner kept me apprised as only months later the Regional Embassy Support Teams (REST) were established. In light of my experience, one point I raised and emphasized during my in-person briefing was the importance of the right individuals to be sent out on these teams. Not self-promoters, but those with the professional and ethical fiber that could and would understand the mantra as the sign posted in the DOD or FBI TDY office: *The Main Thing is to Keep the Main Thing, the Main Thing.*

Though I really wanted to learn Spanish and really tried to focus, the aftermath events just took over at times. For instance, one day I was sitting in Spanish language class when there was a knock on the door. Our instructor walked over to the door and stepped out for a moment. He came back and said, "Michelle, you have someone here to see you." I walked out to a man standing there waiting to greet me. He said, *"Hello Michelle, I am Theodore 'Ted' Kattouf. My mother and your father go to the same Orthodox Church in Altoona, PA. She told me you were assigned to Kenya at the time of the Embassy bombing. I wanted to stop by to see how you were."* How wonderfully kind. I shared some insights and thanked him so much for coming by to check on me, told him to please pass along my warmest regards to his mother, with hope of seeing her soon when I returned to Pennsylvania for home leave. Ted would later become our Ambassador to the United Arab Emirates and Syria. To this day, I find his gesture of not knowing me and seeking me out an incredible act of kindness and one sincerely and deeply appreciated.

Back in the US, I began monitoring the status of my two FMC Family members who were injured but most importantly still alive: Livingstone and Mary. Both were still in Germany at a military hospital for specialized medical care. At this point, there was nothing more I could do other than pray, pray for them and pray for those back in Kenya.

For home leave, I needed some time and space to gather my thoughts, figure out what I wanted to do next, and decompress. I decided to take an Amtrak trip across the United States. What a wonderful way to see so many beautiful places, crossing our entire nation. I started in Washington, D.C., with stops in Chicago, Seattle, Portland, San Francisco and then back home. Some stops were for hours, others for days, even weeks staying with friends. Two friends I stayed with were Harriet Isom and Carolyn Amacher.

Harriet was my first Ambassador while serving in Cameroon during my first excursion tour. She was now retired and living at her homestead farm in Echo, Oregon. She knew how devastated I was; and yet, she also knew the importance being foreign service, in sharing and educating our fellow Americans when we could. She asked if I would mind sharing some insights with her church and her Rotary Club. She felt it was our responsibility and our duty, and she knew I was still on the fence regarding my decision. Harriet was the perfect person for me to visit during this time. The inspiration from my visit with her convinced me to remain in the foreign service.

My next Amtrak stop was San Francisco. I stayed a few days with Carolyn and Rich Amacher, my roommates a few years earlier in Vienna, Virginia when I first moved to the Washington, D.C. area. Carolyn was one of the first of my friends to contact me when I got back to Washington in the aftermath of the bombing. She knew how excited I was to be doing the foreign service excursion tours. She also knew that it was potentially a cause for the difference between Steve and I, slightly a year prior to the bombing.

One evening I had received a phone call. It was Carolyn. It was so great to her her voice and obviously, given the situation even more so for her, to hear mine. We discussed my upcoming Amtrak trip and the possibility of my visiting with them once I developed my schedule. She had debated on whether to tell me or not, but decided that I should know. She said in the immediate aftermath, she reached out to my ex-husband Steve to see if he had any news. She said Steve was very cold and distant, had no idea and nothing to share. They hung up, her being quite puzzled. When she shared this insight, I told her about our divorce and that maybe I should call him to let him know I was okay. Given what I had just gone through, the fact that we had been married, his response hurt but obviously, so did our divorce. I thanked her for letting me know.

After Carolyn and I hung up, I called Steve. With no answer, I left a message. Realizing this would be our first encounter since the divorce, I maintained a professional tone and said that I was back in the US, not hurt and relatively fine, and thought it would be best for me to let him know in case anyone contacted him not knowing of our divorce. I left my contact number. He never called back and I've never heard nor saw him again, not since flying back to Baltimore, Maryland from Nairobi, prior to the bombing, for his father's funeral. Yet, since, I've always pondered whether there was something more behind the scenes that I was not aware, first meeting Steve while we both worked at DCAA.

It was nice visiting with Carolyn, Rich, their boys, and San Francisco since I had never been. I boarded Amtrak one last time to finalize my trip and spend some time with my family. One other friend I would visit with before returning to Washington from my home leave would be Veronique "Roni" LeBlanc. Roni served with me in Yaoundé, Cameroon, and was now assigned to the US Army War College in Carlisle, Pennsylvania. She too was a wonderful sounding board. From all of those that I visited, I regained my strength, prepared and ready to return to Washington with the intent of moving forward, unaware at the time of the continual battle of the aftermath I would have to endure.

Livingstone and others still in critical condition had been transferred from the military hospital in Landstuhl, Germany to Walter Reed Medical Center in Washington, D.C. In less severe condition, Mary and others were eventually sent back to Nairobi to get further treatment there. Since I did not have my Isuzu Trooper yet, I went to Walter Reed for my first visit driven by Vivian Harvey. Previously serving together in Yaoundé, Vivian and her husband, Ron, were also assigned to Nairobi, Kenya with me but departed a few months before the bombing. Ron was the USAID Deputy Director, and Vivian worked as an eligible family member (EFM) in the Embassy HR section. Like the FMC, the HR section sustained incredible loss and damage during the bombing. Vivian and I prepared ourselves for our visit. For the first time, we saw the injured survivors, Americans, Kenyans and Tanzanians staying at Walter Reed. We were walking down the hall to the room where Livingstone was staying. I remember turning into the room and walking straight to the bed. I remember Vivian walking in behind me then suddenly turning around and walking out. The sight was incredible. She made a comment later on how strong I was to face that situation.

When we walked in, we found Livingstone handcuffed and stripped down to what appeared to be a diaper at Walter Reed, a US military hospital. I was horrified. A man, my/our US Embassy employee, blinded, traumatized and a survivor of the Embassy bombing, was handcuffed. *What in the world is going on?* Livingstone was babbling non-stop in Kiswahili, his native tongue. I gently touched his hand and said, "Livingstone, its Mama, Mama Safi," the nickname my FMC family bestowed upon me. He stopped and looked up towards my voice. I continued, "Livingstone, you are now here in the United States with me. You need to speak English for folks here to understand you." Just then Vivian walked back in. I said "Vivian, can you please go get a nurse. We need to get these hand-cuffs off of him now." I remained with Livingstone when Vivian and a nurse walked back in shortly after. I explained the situation and the nurse immediately removed the hand cuffs. Needless to say, Livingstone's treatment and recovery became my priority.

I now knew the request I would ask of the DG—could I remain in the foreign service but delay my departure/assignment to Santiago, Chile? With DG approval, my assignment was curtailed and I would participate in the upcoming bid process. One option worked perfectly. The senior FMO (S/FMO) in Moscow, Russia after a year of Russian language. I would remain in Washington D.C. for an extended period of time to be with and to monitor Livingstone's recovery and learn Russian. I submitted my bids and hoped for the best. In the meanwhile, I had a bridge assignment at FSI's School of Professional and Area Studies (SPAS) in the Administrative Training (AT) Division as a Financial Management Training Trainer.

My temporary living quarters arrangement was coming to an end. My personal effects and Isuzu Trooper were finally arriving back from Nairobi. I needed to find a place quick. Wanting to be close to FSI, I located a charming original 1925 Sears Catalog Bungalow with a large fenced-in yard in nearby the Lyon Park neighborhood in Arlington, Virginia. Simba, my yellow Labrador retriever and I had our new home.

Due to many complexities that were in play prior to the bombing, I found solace in sharing with and confiding with AT Division Director Janet Buechel. Not only because of her professional experience, but being a woman, her relating to the ordeals that transpired in Nairobi during my assignment there, to include the players involved, she understood completely.

One day Janet called me into her office. FSI was expecting some local Kenyan employees to attend training in the next week or so. She wanted me to be aware that they were here in case I wanted to touch base with them. I thanked her for letting me know and said I was definitely interested. And she then continued. In light of our previous conversations, one employee who was supposed to attend but would not due to her being fired, was Margaret Gitau, the lead Embassy Nairobi GSO local Kenyan employee. She was supposedly fired due to being caught committing fraud, continuing even in the aftermath of the bombing. My initial reaction was, it's about time. I had shared with Janet the conflict that my FMC section was having with the GSO staff, particularly Margaret, as we cleaned up our office, the books and records, to include prior year accounts. FMC started putting an end to what I suspected was years of fraud. So much so, that it was brought to my attention that one of my accountants, Fred Yafes, had been receiving threats. Fred finally confirmed this when he was part of the group that climbed Mt. Kenya. We agreed that he would tell me immediately if there was any other such threat once we got back to the office. Meanwhile, I began documenting and reporting my suspicion of fraud with my upper management. They did nothing, and instead launched a counter-attack against me. However, knowing what I knew, around the same time I wrote up the FMC Superior Honor Award nomination justification, I had also written Fred up for an individual award, for his honor and his integrity. Fred would later be killed in the bombing and never receive this award/honor, but his family did. I was always of the opinion that though Margaret may have been caught committing fraud, she would not have been acting alone. And most importantly, Americans had to be involved. I hold this suspicion to this day, and even more so, as more comes to light—and as I did when I reported this to upper management way back when, and at that time.

For the foreign service, the annual evaluation rating period is consistent worldwide, April 16 to the following April 15. Needless to say, in the aftermath of the bombing, this was no one's priority. Now officially in the foreign service, I had to obtain my final evaluation for the period of April 16 – August 20, 1998. I started gently nudging the Nairobi HR staff on the status when I returned from home leave. It would not be until months later that I would receive incredible flabbergasting insight. HR had no record of my required Employee Evaluation Report (EER) because someone had reported me deceased. I bluntly replied, "I am not deceased and do not want to be a burden, but need my evaluation."

After neither hearing back nor receiving my evaluation, on February 25, 1999, I contacted Embassy Nairobi Deputy Chief of Mission (DCM) Michael Marine. I advised him of the situation regarding my EER and let him know that I was aware of Margaret Gitau. I knew once the DCM became aware, he would query on the status accordingly. However, I wonder if he was made aware that I had been reported deceased. With all that had been occurring prior to the bombing, and now, even in its aftermath, I assume not. My being reported deceased should have been my first red flare indicator. In hindsight, it was, and there were many others.

This would be the first communication between the DCM and myself since before the bombing. Though I returned immediately the next day upon hearing of the bombing, Michael was delayed in returning due to medical issues. Supposedly blood clot issues prevented him from flying back from China to Nairobi. He didn't return to post until after my departure of August 20, 1998. Given the delay, it would now only be reasonable and practical that my evaluation be completed during the normal upcoming evaluation cycle.

I shared being reported *deceased* with Janet. As it was obvious I was not deceased, we brushed it off. At the time, I rationalized it as being due to incompetence, potential TDYers not knowing, innocent error, administrative chaos in the aftermath of the bombing, due to everything and anything. However, an option I didn't verbalize but indeed considered even at that time was that it had been deliberately done. In due time, I would be even more convinced than ever.

Steve Nolan and I finally started an email exchange regarding my official evaluation. Given the last face-to-face verbal exchange Steve and I had before I departed post, I had hoped that he would come to realize how heartless his request was given the devastating losses of my FMC family. He didn't. I was provided a recommend immediate promotion appraisal, so I let it be and moved on. However, I would not and did not expect or anticipate that this would be the first of many attempts by Steve Nolan, later joined by his brother Robert Nolan and others to sabotage my entire career.

Officially paneled for an onward stretch assignment to Embassy Moscow as the S/FMO via one year of language training, I was now temporarily assigned as an FMO with the Office of the Executive Director Bureau of European Affairs (EUR/EX), the regional bureau responsible for Russia.

During this time, the first-year anniversary of the East Africa Embassy bombings occurred. In commemoration, a video was being taped. There would be three different versions made: a long version of forty-nine minutes called *1 Year Anniversary of Embassy Bombings in Kenya & Tanzania*; a medium version of twenty-six minutes, twenty seconds called *Colleagues*

Remembered American Embassy Nairobi American Embassy Dar es Salaam; and a short version of thriteen minutes, thirty-four seconds, also called *Colleagues Remembered American Embassy Nairobi American Embassy Dar es Salaam.* Just like the memorial service when asked to eulogize my FMC family members before I departed Nairobi back in August 1998, I was asked to again provide words for remembrance and reflection a year later.

My taping was scheduled for Monday July 12, 1999 at 11:15 A.M. Though a year had almost passed, the bombing seemed like only yesterday. If I felt this way, I knew many others felt the same. And though I did not have physical scars on the mend, emotional ones still existed for me as they did for so many others. Again, pondering what to say in such a time as this, when the pain for so many remains so raw, I wanted to share a fond memory, provide words of inspiration, and yet link the two embassies. This is what I said:

> As each of our American colleagues were eulogized, our thoughts drift to the lives of our Kenyan and Tanzanian colleagues who were also lost. For any Foreign Service officer knows, our work could not be accomplished without the hard-working, loyal commitment we receive from our foreign service national employees worldwide. The story I'm to share is but one of the many that can be shared from this tragedy. And but one of the many precious memories each and every Foreign Service officer can recall of the relationships developed and experiences had with these tremendous individuals we encounter during our assignments overseas—"our home away from home."
>
> Every year, the Tanzanian High Commissioner to Kenya Major General Sarakikya takes a group on a climb of Mt. Kilimanjaro. In March 1997, I was a member of this group. Before I left for my trek, I met with my staff and informed them that if I got to the top of Mt. Kilimanjaro, they as my Kenyan staff, must take me to the top of Mt. Kenya. During our climb of Mt. Kilimanjaro, the General would advise, to get to the top you must go step-by-step pole-pole (Kiswahili for slowly-slowly). As each climber struggled, we each recalled these words and put one foot in front of the other and proceeded pole-pole. On the Friday after our climb was completed, I went into the Financial Management center and attached a note to each and every one on my staff's computers—When do we climb Mt. Kenya?
>
> In March 1998, I led a group of eleven Americans and four of my Kenyan staff (Eric Onyango, Fred Yafes, Livingstone Mada-

hana, and Grace Marangu) on a climb of Mt. Kenya. As we went along, I shared the words of the General – step-by-step pole-pole. As we neared the summit, again we shared the words—step-by-step pole-pole. The thrill was overwhelming for all when we finally made it to the top.

On 8/7/1998, of the four Kenyans from my staff who joined me on this climb, Eric and Fred were killed, Livingstone was seriously injured and is now blind, and Grace is alive and well and has just given birth to a new baby boy. Also, on that day, the Financial Management family lost Chrispine Bonyo, Joel Kamau, Larry Gitau, Peter Macharia, Farhat Sheikh, and Catherine Mukethi; and Mary Ofisi was severely injured.

On this first anniversary of this dreadful tragedy, as each and every one of us—American, Tanzanian, Kenyan, Foreign Service, Foreign Service National, Civil Service—begin our long journey to recovery, we need to recall the General's words given to every climber tackling his/her mountain—*step-by-step pole-pole.*

On August 7, 1999, one year after the East Africa Embassy bombings, there was a commemorative memorial event held on the 8th Floor of Main State. Many that had served in Kenya and Dar were in attendance. Comments were made and then the shortest version video, what some called the *Executive Summary,* was played due to Secretary of State Madeleine Albright's tight schedule, who was in attendance. Of course, for those who lost a loved one, their preference would have been for the longest uncut version to be shown. When my comments of the video were played, it was like an out-of-body experience. I had so many feelings rush through me, numb and humbled to the compliments I received afterwards of the powerfulness of the story I told, of the words I said. The overwhelming sadness of this tragedy was back, and it took a few days to bounce back—as I would say to myself, *step-by-step, pole pole.*

Many years after, still to this day, there is one day, and only one day, that I give myself to deeply reflect on, cry if necessary, the day of the annual anniversary. That day I reconnect with the survivors of my FMC family. Some respond immediately. Others wait. Others don't respond at all. But most importantly, they are remembered, their loss is remembered, their pain is remembered, and if no one else now remembers what they have endured, I remember.

During that 8/7 memorial event, DG Skip Gnehm told me that the video was going to be sent to every post around the world to be shown to every employee and given to every Congressional Member on the Hill. My reaction was, *Good*, the people and the events cannot be forgotten. Little would I know how forgotten some would be in just the near future…

In November 1999, I went to dinner with one of my FMC Nairobi Kenyan staff who was sent back to Washington for some training at FSI. During dinner I asked Sammy what he thought of the video for the one-year anniversary. He told me that they never saw a video. So afterwards, I took him back to my home and showed him, both the short and long versions. Sammy was very upset that they had not seen the video and was going to query about it when he got back to the Embassy in Nairobi.

That weekend, I attended a dedication for Julian and his son Jay at Camp Lett in Maryland. Absolutely adoring Julian, it was always so devastating knowing the loss Sue, his wife, and Edith, his daughter, had endured that day, losing half of their family in an instant. It was a lovely dedication. Others from State attended as well, to include Kendall Montgomery, of the Office of Casualty Assistance (OCA), an office established in the aftermath of the bombing. As this weekend was Julian and Jay's, I would query Kendall next week on the other matter, the matter of why the video was not shown in Nairobi.

On November 23, 1999, I queried Kendall Montgomery based on comments from friends and now my Kenyan Foreign Service National (FSN) FMC staff family member if this video was indeed shown in Nairobi. Later that same afternoon, Kendall provided this response:

> The video was sent to Nairobi prior to the first anniversary commemoration. It was the post's decision how it was to be used. My understanding is that they decided to show it on August 6th at the Marine House to Americans only. They felt that the FSN's would be hurt to see so much focus on the Americans and little on the FSN's. We here in Washington deferred to their wishes. In mid-August a copy of the video was sent to every post worldwide with a letter from the DG to ambassadors urging that they share it with their communities. I have had no feedback from posts so don't know if the film was actually shown. The video also went to every member of Congress. Once again, I have heard no feedback. Have a great Thanksgiving. Kendall

At this point, so many bizarre, unexplained events were occurring. Fortunately for me, I knew at least one other in the Department was feeling the same way. I realized at her level, she had a lot more insight than I did, and most likely, could not share with me. However, that didn't mean I couldn't share with her. I forwarded this email exchange to Ambassador Ryan with the comment:

> Well Mary—looks like I may have stirred the pot once again by showing it to Sammy! Michelle

This would be just the tip-of-the-iceberg regarding what I considered at the time as sheer unprofessionalism, ugliness, discrimination; only in time would I discover and connect the dots to all *this* being much more…

Studying and learning Russian was a real priority for me. It was a time for me to really focus and be dedicated. And I was committed to doing so. However, once again, during this time, I had to continue to face the shocking realities of the aftermath of the bombings—taking care of and overcoming all the challenges Livingstone experienced that would need to be overcome. The ugly truth shaped my discussion later in an unanticipated meeting with DOJ. So again, despite my really wanting to learn Russian, the aftermath again took priority over my language studies.

Returning home from Russian Language class, I had an urgent message from Judith Busera, Livingstone's wife. I was concerned that Livingstone's condition may have taken a turn for the worse, so I called her back immediately. She was very upset. Asking Judith what was wrong., she kept saying, "They are sending me back to Kenya." As a departure date had never been mentioned before and the intent was for Judith to remain here with Livingstone until he could return to Nairobi, whenever that would be, I said, "Judith, calm down. Please explain to me what you are talking about. Who is saying they are sending you back to Kenya?" She said, "The State Department. They said they are sending me back tonight." I asked, "Why? What is going on?" And then she told me. She said, "They found out that I'm pregnant." First becoming aware of this myself, I said, "You are pregnant? How far along are you?" To which she responded, "A few months." I said, "Okay, let me make some calls and I'll get back to you." My first reaction was to call Ambassador Ryan, only to find out she was on a phone call, and would get back to me. My second reaction was to call the DG's office. I called and left a message to return my call urgently. When I hung up, Mary called back and gave me a little more insight, telling me that it was her understanding that Judith hadn't been feeling well, so when she had a check-up, the doctor discovered she was pregnant. After advising Department of State officials, they began discussing sending her back. Apparently, they didn't want her to give birth in the US, to have an American citizen. Mary said she too had just found out and was trying to intervene to stop this. Given what Livingstone sacrificed for our nation, permitting him to have an American citizen child is the least we, the USG, our nation, could do. She said she had placed a few calls and was waiting to hear back. But meanwhile, her next step was to call the *Washington Post.* I told her I had just found out and placed a call into the DGs' office as well, waiting to hear back. But also, I was willing to call and report this to the *Washington Post.* Hopefully I'd hear something in time, since Judith was supposed to be leaving that evening. Mary was not aware of that and said she needed to go and would get back to me shortly. I hung up shaking my head, *unbelievable.*

The phone rang. It was Gretchen Welch from the DG's office. She said she heard about Judith from Mary and quite aware of both of our intents to go to the *Washington Post* if this occurred. The latest update she had was that Judith was not going to go anywhere and definitely not back to Kenya that evening. I said I needed her assurance, otherwise, I would leave now to go to Walter Reed to be with them. She said that I had her assurance. I said thank you and called Mary back. She too had been assured, wanting to make sure before I called Judith to let her know. Mary said to go ahead call Judith and to please give her Mary's home phone number as well, just in case. I said thank you. I called Judith and she said, "Michelle, thank you. I'm not leaving. Thank you." I explained to Judith that it wasn't just me; it was also Ambassador Ryan who found out and intervened. In addition to having my home phone number, I passed along Mary's to her, requesting that she "...only call Mary if they come for you this evening after all, ok?" Advising to definitely call me as well, and that I'd call her before I left for Russian language class tomorrow morning to make sure all is well. Judith said, *"Okay. Thank you, Michelle."* On November 19, 1999, Judith and Livingstone had a healthy baby girl named Chelsea, an American citizen.

One day during a break from my Russian language class, I received an email from Mary Ryan to give her a call. She advised that she couldn't go into any detail, but that I needed to get Livingstone a lawyer. Trusting her completely and knowing she would have insight that I would not and/or that she could not share, I did as she ask. I started querying my colleagues about legal representation for Livingstone. I had been sharing the drama, the apparent never-ending aftermath drama that was continuing to play out with a small group of my Russian language colleagues. When I got this message from Mary and shared it with a very few, they too understood implications if the request was coming from someone of her stature and professionalism. Something more was coming down the pike. Fortunately for me, and for Livingstone, one of my colleagues had a legal background and network to tap into. This resulted in successfully obtaining pro bono legal representation for Livingstone by the highly reputable law firm, Arnold & Porter. Kendall Millard would be his representing legal counsel.

When I let Mary know that Arnold & Porter would represent Livingstone pro bono, she asked, "Michelle how did you pull that off?" I said that there are some things she can't share with me and there are some things I shouldn't share with her. She agreed and said, well done. Livingstone's interest was now being protected in preparation for when I departed for my assignment in Moscow. But most importantly, Livingstone was protected against actions taken against him by none other than, once again, the Department of State. In due time, this legal counsel representation would be essential in regards to obtaining and establishing well-equipped work capabilities and enhancements for Livingstone to return to work at FMC Nairobi. This included him learning to use JAWS, the Assistive Technology software that enables visually challenged people to use the computer. However, I always sensed Mary's request, the urgency and immediacy of the request, was regarding something more than just protecting Livingstone's work environment interests. Now that Mary is gone, I will never know for sure. However, what I do know, is that after I did this, there were some folks in the Department that were not happy with me, and apparently, or for some, continued to gun for me. Given what I now suspect, and dots I would later connect, I have no doubt Mary knew then what I know now, the real reason for her urgent and immediate legal representation request for Livingstone.

In late March/early April 2000, an Assistant United States Attorney (AUSA) from DOJ/Southern District of New York (SDNY) United States Attorney's (USA) Office came to visit me at FSI. Pulling me from my Russian language class, we met in a separate room on the FSI campus. This would be the first and only time I met privately with DOJ and the discussion was pertaining to the upcoming bin Laden trial in connection with the August 7, 1998 East Africa Embassy bombings. AUSA Kenneth Karas was accompanied by New York Field Office (NYFO)/Joint Terrorism Task Force (JTTF) Trial Liaison/DS Special Agent (SA) James Minor. Ken advised that in preparation for the trial, DOJ wanted to obtain victims' input regarding the sentence they should go after. He basically wanted my opinion on whether DOJ should pursue the death penalty.

I advised that I personally was against the death penalty. In some circumstances, circumstances such as these, some would disagree. However, in light of the fact that I lost my *work* family, not my *blood* family, I strongly recommend that their opinions be heavily considered in such determination. I then stated, "But then again, how can you ask the blood family members when you didn't even include those that were killed in the indictment charges?" Taken back, he asked for me to explain further. So. I continued,

> How can you say bin Laden killed his own, when you don't even include his own that he killed, our local Muslim employees? Many of our Kenyan and Tanzanian Embassy employees were Muslim. Those killed died for a flag that wasn't even their own and their deaths, our local employees' deaths, were not included in the counts.

So, I came right out and said it, "DOJ, please do not treat them the way the State Department has treated them." He was initially taken aback and then said, "Michelle, do you realize you are the first one to have even mentioned this to us. And we are this far along the process."

We then continued to have a discussion that to this day I feel I am not at liberty to put down in writing. Maybe in due time, but not now. Given what I would yet experience down the road, I am more adamant than ever about being against capital punishment, the death penalty, because of the cover-up/scapegoating to which I would bear witness, but was not aware at the time of this discussion the extremity of it all.

In mid-May 2000, as a result of my discussion with AUSA Ken Karas, I received an official envelope in the mail. Addressed from the DOJ/SDNY USA's Office, it contained a copy of a joint May 8, 2000 *For Immediate Release* Press Release by DOJ/SDNY USA Mary Jo White and NY FBI Office Assistant Director in Charge Barry W. Mawn. It announced that a superseding indictment was filed in Manhattan federal court that day charging Osama bin Laden and 16 co-defendants with conspiring to kill American nationals outside of the United States, and for the bombings of the United States embassies in Nairobi, Kenya and Dar es Salaam, Tanzania, in August 1998, which resulted in more than 200 deaths and more than 4000 injuries. The superseding indictment also contained additional counts relating to the murder of employees of the USG, including Kenyan and Tanzanian citizens who worked at the American embassies in Nairobi and Dar es Salaam, as well as diplomats protected by international treaties.

The trial for this case had been set for September 5, 2000. I called Mary immediately and said, "DOJ listened to me, justice will be done for our local employees, to include my killed FMC family members." We arranged to meet for me to show her the DOJ/SDNY USA May 8, 2000 Press Release. When we met, Mary read it and we gave each other a hug. We, Mary and I, together overcame yet another bombing aftermath obstacle.

In June 2000, there would be yet another unbelievable moment of enlightenment. I found out that Secretary Albright authorized, "after the bombing of the embassy – all employees stationed will receive a group heroism award." This was effective 8/31/98. I had not been advised nor included. Previously, after becoming aware of being reported *deceased* by Embassy Nairobi, I did not raise this issue with AF/EX. When I found out about this, I immediately contacted AF/EX Deputy Director Joseph Huggins to find out if this was true. If so, why hadn't I been included? AF/EX immediately submitted the applicable paperwork dated June 29, 2000 with an effective date of August 31, 1998. I was provided copies for my files, to include the July 11, 2000 notification to HR/Personnel Evaluations for it to be included in my official personnel records. I had no doubt something more sinister was at play.

EMBASSY MOSCOW

Soon after, in August 2000, I departed for my first FS assignment as the S/FMO for Embassy Moscow and its three Consulates, St. Petersburg, Yekaterinburg, and Vladivostok.

As touring the Ethiopian Orthodox Historical route saved my life from the bombing of August 7, 1998, being an Orthodox Christian, I was looking forward to the opportunity of venturing deeper into my faith and the historical connections to the Orthodox Church in Russia. Ambassador James Collins even asked me to accompany him to a few Orthodox Church events to show off his Mission's American Orthodox Christian. Serving in Russia previously in his career as a political officer, Ambassador Collins knew one could not completely understand Russian politics without the perspective of the Orthodox Church and the role it plays. I was a member of St. Nicholas Cathedral in Washington, D.C. St. Nicholas Cathedral is the primatial cathedral of the Orthodox Church in America and the seat of the Archbishop of Washington, Metropolitan of All America and Canada of the Orthodox Church in America (OCA). Soon after my arrival, I would begin to attend services at St. Catherine the Great Martyr Church in Moscow, the representation church for the OCA to the

Church of Russia. Though I had previously met Patriarch Alexy II, the 15th Patriarch of Moscow and all Rus, attending events with Ambassador Collins in my assignment to Moscow, strengthened my role as a bridge. I visited many churches and monasteries, and even wrote an icon. And at one such Orthodox Church event, I had the opportunity to personally meet President Putin, a very devout Orthodox Christian.

In January 2001, I received a letter from Dr. Samuel Thielman, the Regional Psychiatrist for East Africa. The letter dated September 11, 2000 was sent to my home address. I would not receive it until months later, by the time it was forwarded, pouched and delivered to me at Embassy Moscow. It was regarding potential delayed complications of the August 7, 1998 bombing and protecting the ability to file a worker's compensation claim in the future by sending in a *Form CA-1, Federal Employee's Notice of Traumatic Injury and Claim for Continuation of Pay/Compensation with the Department of Labor.* As explained in the letter:

> Form CA-1 is normally used to report an injury related to work even though no medical expenses have yet been incurred. Filing this form generates a case number for you with the Department of Labor and will protect your ability to receive compensation for problems that may arise in the future.

My reading of the letter implied that filing this *Form CA-1* was in essence a placeholder for any unseen future complications. On January 27, 2001, I reached out to Lou Bickle, the Embassy Nairobi HRO. Between February 1 and April 12, 2001, I began an informational exchange with Lou to complete the *placeholder Form CA-1* as advised.

Incidentally, a few months later, after returning to Moscow in mid-June 2001 from attending the East Africa Embassy bombing trial, there was a packet from Lou Bickle regarding my *Form CA-1* filing. I contacted Lou and Anita Brown, HR Washington on the next steps. On June 19, Anita, looping in Kendall Montgomery and Lou, queried on whether this filing was *for the record* or *an actual claim*. I responded that I was just attempting to comply with the 9/11/2000 letter from Dr. Samuel Thielman "to protect your ability to file a worker's comp claim in the future by sending in Form CA-1," this filing being *for the record*. Anita provided a mailing address to send the *Form CA-1* that "we will keep on file for future reference (should you ever need it)." On June 22, 2001, I mailed the applicable *Form CA-1*, as advised, *for the record*. This simple request in hindsight leads to so many more questions. Given the retaliatory events that later took place against me, it was as if someone *knowingly, willingly and intentionally* capitalized on what appeared to be a genuine September 11, 2000 official request. Particularly, years later, when I contacted the Department of Labor regarding my applicable case, I was advised no such case on me had been opened.

Then on February 18, 2001, FBI agent Robert Phillip Hanssen was arrested for spying for Soviet and Russian intelligence services against the United States from 1979 to 2001. This event was a real turning point for diplomatic relations and we at US Mission in Russia would soon be caught in the middle. In March 2001, the Bush Administration ordered fifty Russian diplomats to leave. The US Mission in Russia then braced itself, knowing that fifty of us would soon be kicked out, just not knowing who and when. Then late one afternoon, DCM John Ordway got on the Embassy public announcement system. As I recall he said:

> Embassy Moscow, I have just gotten off the phone with Secretary of State Powell. He wanted to let everyone know how proud he was of the work being done by the Mission here...

We all knew. The list of retaliatory expulsions had been received. Fifty colleagues were being sent home, *PNGed*—persona non grata. Certain sections were deeply impacted. The names were from across Mission Russia, to include our three Consulates, Yekaterinburg, St. Petersburg, and Vladivostok. Lives were disrupted, as pawns in a bigger game. Friends were on the list. I was not.

This expulsion battle playing out between the two countries was the primary focus of everyone at Mission Russia. I, however, had another primary focus during this time, the East Africa Embassy bombings trial being tried by DOJ/SDNY in New York federal court. Though I was in continual contact, as a victim, when requested if and when I would like to attend, I said my preference would be to attend the sentencing portion. I knew the DOJ would have built a strong case and wanted other victims, to include the Kenyans and Tanzanians, to have the opportunity to attend first. I would be issued jointly funded DOJ/State travel orders. Initially attending the sentencing in New York from about June 3 to June 6, 2001, I would then continue on to Washington, D.C. to the Department for consultations and to have an opportunity to meet with Livingstone, who would be there for medical check-ups. The DOJ/SDNY lodged trial attendees at the World Trade Center (WTC) Marriott. In light of events that would occur just a few months later, many instantly linked the two events. I did not. Over time, I would have a change of opinion.

While in New York, I reconnected with Pat Hartnett-Kelly, now DS NYFO Special Agent in Charge (SAIC), as well as others from my time in Nairobi, Kenya. SA Caroline Truesdall, with USAID OIG while in Nairobi, Kenya, was now in New York as Department of Treasury/Internal Revenue Service (IRS). The sentencing resulted in life in prison. I then flew to Washington, D.C. for consultations and to obtain first-hand from Livingstone regarding his progress. Given the sentencing outcome, this trip would be a closing chapter. When I boarded my flight to return back to Embassy Moscow, I sat back in my chair with the realization that justice had been done. I had departed my trip to the US with a deep sense of relief, a new beginning, and a time to move-on. Or so I thought/had hoped. Not knowing at the time that the bombing aftermath would continue to linger, with ramifications. The extremity of these ramifications had yet to play out.

At the end of one work day, I was walking through the cafeteria of the Embassy on my way home to my apartment when I noticed colleagues gathering to watch the television. I asked what was going on. Someone replied that one of the WTC towers had been hit by a plane. I stopped just as the second tower was struck. Recently returning from the East Africa Embassy bombing trial in New York, it felt like *déjà vu*. I couldn't believe it, thinking, *what in the world is happening—again?* It was September 11, 2001.

The initial media coverage focused on the buildings, not the mass havoc that I knew had to be playing out on the street level, the human level. Then the towers fell. At which point someone commented on my face, how it appeared to go completely pale white. I was stunned. Living through the aftermath of the Embassy Nairobi bombing, just returning from the sentencing portion of the applicable trial, I was mortified. I recall responding something like, "you all can't even imagine what they are now going through there at ground zero." As a crowd, and fellow American citizens at Embassy Moscow, we gathered around the television, standing there watching and there was nothing we could do. Reports were coming in about the Pentagon and Shanksville, Pennsylvania when I left to watch from home. It was going to be a long night. The next day, we were notified that we would not be able to fly home, to the nation we served and represented, for flights had been grounded. There was nothing we could do but watch the news and pray.

Before 9/11/2001, I had planned on taking my upcoming Rest and Recuperation (R&R) leave back in the states to visit with my family. With all that had just occurred, my plans abruptly changed with an unsettling feeling of not knowing when we would be approved to fly back to the US, to our own country that we served. When I returned to Moscow from my R&R, I heard of the unfortunate time that Ambassador Mary Ryan was experiencing as a result of 9/11. I outreached to her with strong support.

Then in the November 2001 issue of *State Magazine*, I couldn't believe what I saw under the "Letters to The Editor" section, title "Reflections on Sept. 11." There were letters from Howard Kavaler, my Embassy Nairobi colleague who lost his beautiful wife Prabhi, another Nairobi colleague; Lucien Vandenbroucke, my Nairobi colleague who was acting DCM at the time of the bombing; John Lange, who was Charge' d'Affaires at Embassy Dar es Salaam at the time of the bombing; and Charles Slater, my replacement in the aftermath of the Embassy Nairobi bombing, now the Administrative Officer in Embassy Port Louis.

Wait a minute… The description under Charles' letter called "More Pain Lies Ahead," states, "The author was the financial management officer at the US Embassy in Nairobi when it was bombed." I was absolutely furious. And I started to let folks know. However, wanting to avoid the appearance of the apparent pettiness in light of the more horrific tragedy at large, 9/11, I didn't pursue it much further.

But this wasn't only about me. It was also about my FMC family members who were killed. And most importantly, it was about the truth. So, in the February 2002 issue of *State Magazine*, under "Letters to The Editor" section, "Clarification" by Michelle Stefanick, Financial Management Officer, US Embassy, Moscow, I wrote:

> I was pleased to see in the November issue, under "Letters to the Editor," comments on the Sept. 11 terrorist attacks from my colleagues of the East Africa bombing. They brought back many horrific memories for us all. At the end of one set of comments, "More Pain Lies Ahead," author Charles Slater was identified as the financial management officer at the US Embassy in Nairobi when it was bombed. Actually, I held that post at the time of the bombing. Mr. Slater replaced me when I left. I think this clarification is needed, considering that eight of our financial management family (Joel, Chrispine, Fred, Peter, Eric, Farhat, Larry and Catherine) were killed and two (Livingstone and Mary) seriously injured.

With that, I thought the issue, and that fact, was finally put to rest.

Soon after, my primary focus shifted to where was I going after my Moscow assignment? Since successfully completing an FMO tour at a large Embassy, my preference was an Administrative Officer position. Officially paneled, after Embassy Moscow, I would be back for a few months of training at FSI before heading out in October 2002 as an Administrative Officer in Pristina, Kosovo. I was excited for a new challenge, a new assignment, but then, more bizarre events occurred...

Oddly enough, during this time, it was becoming apparent that Ambassador Ryan was being targeted. In the aftermath of 9/11, she was fighting to keep the visa-issuing service from being moved from CA to the newly created Department of Homeland Security (DHS). In July 2002, Mary announced that she would be retiring September 30, 2002. Back from Moscow, Mary would occasionally come over to FSI to have lunch with me. It was a troubling time.

As a CPA, I had to maintain continuing professional education (CPE) credits. As FS, despite being a financial management specialist (FMS) not every FMO had a professional accreditation, a CPA, but some did. As a result, there was a real divisive line between the two schools of thoughts, approaches within the FMO community. A further divisive line tended to fall along the line as to who the *FMS-coned* FMOs belonged to, where their loyalties lied, so to speak; with the applicable regional bureau, such as AF; or with the functional bureau, the Resource Management bureau, RM, formerly named FMP. This loyalty tended to lie along lines of those with a professional accreditation, with RM; and those without, with the applicable regionl bureau. Personally, I maintained a nuanced independent balance, straddling the two camps. Depending on who the applicable Department CFO with their applicable perseverance was at the time would determine the focus, resolve in tackling this balance within the FMO community writ large by RM. In time, I would ponder if there was even more to this divivise divide then what it appeared. Something deeper, more at play, then what the divide appeared to be and what it was really about.

At this time, the Department's CFO was Christopher Burnham. During his tenure, there was a real push to make the RM bureau *the home of FS FMOs*, particularly since many officials within it were CPAs and/ or members of applicable professional organizations, the most popular at the time being the Association of Government Accountants (AGA). Attending AGA courses and training for applicable and required CPE for the CPAed FMOs became a real attraction. Attending the annual AGA Professional Development Conference (PDC) enabled an opportunity to obtain many if not all required CPEs in one fell swoop. Over and above achieving more CPE when attending the applicable annual regional bureau budget conferences, the annual AGA PDC was also a real networking opportunity outside of the Department. It was also a great venue to meet fellow FS CPAed FMOs from around the world and other regional bureaus who would attend. For, given our career path, it was quite possible to only know of a fellow colleague by name and never meeting, if career paths never crossed depending on which regional bureau one worked, remained, or ventured. These AGA conferences provided another bridge and beneficial opportunity for, but outside of the Department.

The last AGA conference I attended was in New Orleans in June 1999, in the aftermath of the bombing. While there, I had an experience that was telling just the same. Though I do not live my life by horoscope, if an applicable newspaper I'm reading has a horoscope section, I'll take a skim. Well, needless to say, for anyone visiting New Orleans, afterlife/other life experiences are there for the offering if one so chooses. So, when in New Orleans, why not. So one late afternoon at the end of the day's sessions, I ventured my way into a shop to have my palm read. Not having a scheduled appointment, I went to the back room to see if a reading was possible. I was told to have a seat. A few moments later, the reader came out and had a seat at the small table across from me. However, before she even began to read my palm, she handed me her card, saying "I would like you to keep in touch with me." Puzzled, since we hadn't even begun the reading yet, I said, "Oh, okay... why?" She replied, "Because I have never seen anything like this before." Puzzled, I responded, "What?" She continued by explaining that she didn't know what experience I recently had, but there are spirits all around me. Some of the spirits are at peace. Others are not. They are angry. She then stated, "But you are at peace." I said, "Yes that I am at peace." She then proceeded to read my palm. I must admit after all these years, I do not recall what she read from my palm, as the experience before her even taking my hand was so memorable itself. I interpreted the spirits surrounding me to be my colleagues and staff that perished from that tragic day of August 7. At the time, I chalked this experience up to being quite interesting; at this time, quite fortutuous.

It was now 2002, and here I was again stateside, attending the upcoming AGA conference from July 7 to 10, 2002. This time in Atlanta, Georgia and yet there was another bizarre encounter in the never-ending aftermath of the embassy bombing. However, this time around, it wouldn't be speculative and in the spiritual world, but very real—one more piece to a pattern that was developing that wasn't establishing a positive storyline.

On the contrary, it was another piece to a storyline of questionable intent. I just did not realize at the time how much larger and complex it was in contrast to my initial quite parochial conclusion that I was drawing at this time.

On July 8, the conference would officially begin with opening comments from the GAO/Comptroller General (CG) at the time, David Walker. The Lunch Keynote speaker for that first day would be National Aeronautics and Space Administration (NASA) Administrator Sean O'Keefe. And the next day, the Lunch Keynote speaker would be Charlie Slater. *What, Charlie Slater? Why would he be the keynote speaker?* Soon I would be stunned to find out why.

During that lunch, I was sitting with fellow FMOs and the Department of State's highest-ranking official attending the conference, Larry Eisenhardt. Once again, I was about to be humiliated. This time would not be just internally within the State Department, but publicly in front of the entire USG spectrum of Accounting and Auditing professionals. And once again it was by Charlie Slater, who falsely presented himself as the FMC Director at the time of the explosion.

Now, please understand, in the aftermath of the bombing, so much work had to be done to reestablish and re-create the financial management operation that I did not and do not begrudge him—or anyone for that matter—on his role as my replacement, or any others in theirs. But to not acknowledge that it was me, while I was sitting in the audience, who was the FMC Director at the time, and whom he had replaced after my departure of August 20, 1998, was beyond a mistake, a misunderstanding. It was intentional. Knowing in advance that I was attending and seeing me the days prior, to not even forewarn me or mention me or introduce me or acknowledge me —this is and was the Charlie Slater I knew. And given that he didn't even know the faces of the FMC family that were killed and injured, just the names, it was unbearable and *unbelievable*.

I patiently sat there, giving looks to a fellow female FMO sitting across the table from me, in disbelief as much as I was. At the conclusion of the lunch, I looked at Larry Eisenhardt and said, "How could you have allowed this to happen?" By his stunned look, I don't know if he was such a good actor that he honestly didn't know what I was talking about, or that he did know but didn't care. But what Larry would have known at the time of the August 7, 1998 explosion and this July 7-10, 2002 AGA conference, is what I would not find out until many years later—the magnitude of our State OIG audit-discovered diverted operational funds.

Irate, I made calls back to Washington and berated AGA and Department of State officials to ensure all at that conference would know first-hand, or learn accordingly, of what had just occurred. And now 20 years after the bombings, the cover-up and implications thereof, continue to this day as a result of intentional actions of individuals such as Charlie Slater. Ironically, after that AGA PDC Keynote speaker Charlie Slater ordeal in Georgia just six months earlier, in February 2003, AGA would have its First National Leadership Conference *Accountability and Ethics.* I would end up attending this conference. GAO/CG David Walker would speak again at this AGA event as well.

Only months after attending the July 2002 AGA conference in Atlanta and after completing all the applicable training in preparation for my upcoming assignment to Kosovo, I was introduced to the Deputy Principal Officer in Pristina, my future boss. I was still at FSI, so we arranged to have lunch there. The introductory meeting was going well, but I must admit I was not expecting nor prepared for what would come next After all this time, though I do not recall his name, I remember our brief discussion. He stated, "Are you aware why they assigned you to Kosovo?" I said, "Yes, because I eventually wanted to convert from financial management specialist to administrative/management generalist." He said, "It's deeper than that." He asked if I was aware that I was assigned there because of my religious background?" I said, "No, I was not." He explained, with my background (my last name and my religious background), they wanted me to be an influencer, to convince our Serb and Muslim Kosovar employees to regain and rebuild trust with one another in coming back and in working together. However, he also wanted to make sure I was aware of the risk. With my background, either side could use this as a target of opportunity, for taking out a diplomat could give either side a political win.

He also offered this to assure me he had the applicable background and credibility to the insight he was sharing: though he himself was Jewish, his wife was Greek Orthodox. As my new boss, he wanted to make sure I was aware because he didn't want to have my death on his hands. I thanked him for his honesty and frankness. I explained that I had seen enough death given the bombing and, first hand, its impact on our local employees. I also said that, despite being extremely proud of my background, there were many other places in the world I could happily serve. It didn't need to be Kosovo at this time. And definitely not wanting to be used as anyone's pawn—with his support since I would be leaving the post in a bind at such late notice—I agreed to curtailing my assignment to Pristina,

Kosovo. Over time, I began to suspect that there was more to our chat and his subtle, nuanced curtailment request than just my last name and my religion.

I now found myself in yet another situation of having to find a temporary bridge assignment until I was paneled to a new onward assignment. And since my house in Arlington was rented, I needed a new place to live. More educated about the process this time around, I worked for about six months as a Program Analyst in the Office of Strategic and Performance Planning in the Bureau with Resource Management (RM/SPP). I would be working with Deputy Assistant Secretary (DAS) Sid Kaplan, who was so pivotal in helping me in the aftermath of the bombing. A true professional I fondly respected, and one of the most Senior FMOs in the Department, a Senior Foreign Service Officer (S/FSO). I would also locate housing in the same neighborhood as my first, close to FSI and the Department, in the Lyon Park Neighborhood of Arlington, Virginia. Months later, I would be paneled to my next overseas assignment, in a generalist position, as Management Officer for Embassy Khartoum, Sudan. Prior to my August 2003 arrival, I had more FSI training and attended another AGA PDC in Chicago, Illinois.

Before I could depart for Sudan, I had to have a medical clearance update, a basic requirement before any new overseas assignment. Since my assignment to Pristina had been curtailed, I did not have to proceed through this process again until much later, when I would once again be subjected to yet another bizarre and unforeseen ordeal, yet another signpost.

On November 15, 2002, Dr. Anwarul Ahad, copying Dr. Steven Feinstein and Harlan Wadley, contacted me regarding my medical clearance. "Dear Ms. Stefanick, I have not heard from you for a while. Please call me at 202 663 1903 to set up your interview so as to expedite your clearance. Dr. Ahad." Now officially paneled for Sudan, on April 10, 2003, I met with Dr. Feinstein, thinking it was just a due diligence follow-up to see how I was and if I had any bombing aftermath concerns. What I didn't know was the intent of this meeting wasn't really about me, my well-being *per se*, but "to examine the validity or lack thereof, of an anonymous letter sent to Dr. Fred Summers, and placed in patient's chart, in 2001 ..."

It was during this meeting that for the first time, I became aware of an anonymous memorandum dated July 20, 2001. Curiously, it was sent about a month after my return to Moscow from attending the bin Laden trial in New York, conducting consultations in Washington D.C, and filing my *"for the record" Form CA-1* in accordance with Dr. Thielman's September 11, 2000 letter. Dr. Feinstein provided me with a copy. I read it and provided comments. Here are Dr. Feinstein's April 10, 2013 patient notes provided to me less than a month later:

> Met w/pt this date. Patient's hx described in various chart notes. Main focus of this eval: to examine the validity, or lack thereof, of an anonymous letter sent to Dr. Fred Summers, and placed in patient's chart, in 2001. Letter must be read to appreciate this note. Brief hx. Patient undertook two extended excursion tours, one to Cameroon (1995-1998), the second to Nairobi (1995-1998). While in Nairobi, she applied for, and was granted FS status. She happened to be out of her office the day of the bombing. Half of her staff were killed; she would also have been a victim had she been at her desk. Was paneled for Santiago as first tour as FSO, but curtailed, undertook therapy with Flora Bryant (9/98 – early 1999). Took Russian language training, beginning 8/99, posted to Moscow 8/2000. Claims tour successful, and was astonished when given the anonymous letter to read. Discussed letter, with good control of affect, and with reasonable comments regarding assertions.
>
> She commented on the financial irregularities she found (she is a CPA), including "questionable practices" (illegal obligations), problems with management support, an issue with an MCA (who did not support the staff's views regarding certain issues), a replacement MCA (known to be problematic, and alcoholic, and who eventually (and suddenly) quit, by not returning to post, and one particularly insubordinate employee. Patient was paneled for Kosovo (10/02), but was curtailed by HR, who indicated that she had not been given the appropriate info for the position (was supposed to work as a generalist; job was for a specialist, a position from which she had come). She is now scheduled to deploy to Khartoum in July, 2003.)
>
> Patient might well be eligible for a Class 1; however, as an interim, I am recommending a Class 2, so that she can begin processing necessary paperwork. She was directed to speak to Flora Bryant, then get back to me, after which a decisive recommendation will be made.

I left this April 10, 2003 meeting with a copy of a two-page July 20, 2001 anonymous memorandum sent to Officer in Charge DS/DSS/ICI/PR and Dr. Frederick Summers M/DGHR/MED/MHS with SUBJECT: Threatening Behavior in Embassy Moscow: Stefanick, Michelle. Later that day, State/MED issued me a Level 2 Medical Clearance dated 04-10-2003. Level 2 means *Limited Clearance for Worldwide Assignment for Post: Khartoum.*

I met with ECS Flora Bryant Monday morning, April 14, 2003. Years after our last discussion, we caught up and then I provided her with a copy of the anonymous memorandum. Later, Flora showed a copy to her boss, who had never heard of it, who then made calls accordingly as well. Needless to say, all were dumbfounded by this anonymous memorandum.

Dr. Feinstein's patient notes continue:

> Undersigned spoke with Flora Bryant this AM. The latter had just interviewed Ms. Stefanick. Ms. Bryant, who has known the patient for several years, could see no reason for patient to not have a Class 1 clearance. I concur.

On April 16, 2003, State/MED issued me a Level 1 Medical Clearance dated 04-16-2003. Level 1 means *Unlimited Clearance or Worldwide Assignment with Post: N/A.* I was pleased that my Level 1 medical clearance was reinstated, and remained so for the rest of my Department of State career. But this immediate medical clearance drama was from from over because of what remained in my official medical file as a result. So that was my next priority: address the anonymous memorandum being placed in my file to begin with and its immediate removal.

On April 30, 2003, I queried Dr. Feinstein and Flora Bryant regarding the removal of the anonymous memorandum. On May 1, 2003, Dr. Feinstein responded:

> Michelle, What I wanted to tell you was that I spoke with "Legal," (Kathleen Murphy) and received the opinion that I should remove the anonymous document, and note that I have done so in the record. I'll send you a copy of my note when I generate it. Sdfmd.

I forwarded this status to Flora with the following comment:

> Flora—FYI—I'm waiting to see the note, but I may indeed need to proceed with this with AFSA and/or IG especially since my file is being tainted by uninvestigated allegation. Will let you know. Hope all is well. Cheers, Michelle.

On Thursday, May 1, 2003, I provided this update to American Foreign Service Association (AFSA) Legal Counsel Sharon Papp.

> Hello Sharon—Hope you had a great trip! I just wanted to bring you up to date on this...I got my one clearance back, after being downgraded to a 2 for a few days. According to John Rendeiro, DS

indeed received the letter but sent it over to MED since they didn't feel it fell under their purview and no action was required by their office. As you can see from the email below, Dr. Feinstein I guess contacted Dr. Summers in Peru and then their legal and according to MED Legal, they were advised that they should remove the document. But as I said in my response to Dr. Feinstein, I still do not understand why a note on removing this letter that was not investigated/unsubstantiated needs to be placed in my file, considering I still don't know the legal basis for which it was placed in there to begin with. Once I receive a copy of this note, I may indeed need AFSA's assistance because I do not understand how and why my file should be tainted at all by this anonymous letter, especially since it was not investigated in light of the fiscal irregularity possibility. Your thoughts on how to proceed would be sincerely appreciated. Thanks! Cheers, Michelle

Minutes later, Sharon Papp responded:

Hi Michelle: Dr. Feinstein needs to clarify what 'record' he is talking about where he will clarify that he removed the letter. I agree that it makes no sense to remove the objectionable letter but then place a note in your file saying the letter was removed. Keep me up to date. I am glad your clearance was upgraded and that they did this relatively quickly. Sharon

On Monday, May 5, 2016, I contacted Dr. Steven Feinstein:

Hello Dr. Feinstein—Hope you had a great weekend. I thought about this this weekend and decided the way I would like to approach this is that nothing is noted in my file, however, if you could draft up a note for my personal files so that if this letter issue appears again years from now, I'll have your note as well as that of RSO John Rendeiro's to pull out. Thanks, michelle

By this time, John Rendeiro, no longer Embassy Moscow RSO, was located in Washington, D.C.as DS Director of the Office of Intelligence and Threat Analysis.

On Tuesday, May 6, 2016 I received the following response from Dr. Feinstein:

Michelle, After another couple of calls to legal (MED's contact is Kathleen Murphy), I've written a brief memo, attached. You're welcome to come by the office and pick up the original. Note that the original is printed on official Department of State stationary. Sincerely, Dr. F.

I responded soon after:

This is great Dr. Feinstein – I have some consultation time in my schedule tomorrow afternoon, so I'll come over then to pick up the original. Thanks for all your assistance in addressing this. Cheers, michelle

I stopped by Dr. Feinstein's office to pick up the memo. The envelope was sitting at the front desk addressed to me, with a note written on it: "Please have pt touch base w/me when she come[s] for this letter SD-FMD" After a brief discussion, I departed with the May 5, 2003 State/MED memorandum in hand. Addressed to me, the memo with SUBJ: "Authorized removal/destruction of non-medical document from medical chart" went as follows:

This memo is to note that, with your approval, the undersigned has removed/destroyed an unsigned document which was placed without authorization in your medical record. NO note reflecting the removal of the aforementioned document has been placed in your medical file. A copy of this memo will be placed with our legal counsel, Kathleen Murphy, who has advised me on this matter. Signed Steven D. Feinstein, M.D. Medical Officer

With this memo in hand, I was of the belief this medical clearance/anonymous memorandum drama issue now finally over. At the time, I really thought it was. However, in time, due time, this issue would re-emerge again years later in a very sinister and suspect way.

I had one final priority before my departure, meeting with Mary, now retired, for dinner. Previously serving in Khartoum herself earlier in her career, Mary provided advice, the most crucial of which was to ensure I drank enough water. She passed this insight along based on first-hand experience from her taking ill during her time there for this exact reason. She wished me well for a fantastic tour and to keep in touch, to which I absolutely agreed. We hugged. That would be the last time I saw Ambassador Mary Ryan alive.

EMBASSY KHARTOUM

I arrived in Khartoum, Sudan on August 10, 2003 for a twelve-month assignment as this was designated an unaccompanied, hardship, danger post. Though typical in most of our embassies around the world, for some reason Embassy Khartoum had no assigned Marine Security Guards (MSG). With so many pressing priorities, I was granted an extension for another year, to depart Khartoum on August 1, 2005.

After the relocation of Embassy Khartoum, Sudan and its American staff to Embassy Nairobi, Kenya in 1996, I would be first Management Officer living back-on-the-ground in Khartoum on a permanent basis in eight years. My primary responsibility would be to reestablish management operations for Embassy Khartoum, to include identifying and purchasing land to build a new embassy, since our current location was considered compromised. Another was supporting crucial US policy objectives such as the signing of the North-South peace agreement (ending over twenty years of civil strife) all while attempting to mitigate one of the worst humanitarian crises in the world in Darfur in a country with a weak infrastructure, many high-level visitors and with a continually far-stretched embassy administrative support structure.

My tour to Khartoum, Sudan was not without its fair-share of bizarre events, and of course, connections and linkages back to the August 7, 1998 Embassy bombings. Early in my tour, in the middle of the night I woke to banging at my door. It was our Embassy's Defense Liaison Officer (DLO)/US Army Colonel Dennis Giddens telling me they needed to move me out immediately. Apparently, the apartment building I was living in had appeared on the al-Qaeda website. So, I grabbed some things and stayed at another location until it was deemed safe to move back. My ground floor apartment was the only official residence in the building. At the time, I did as I was told; it never crossed my mind that I was the possible target. Déjà vu, just like the Embassy Nairobi bombing. In light of all that has since occurred, I have no doubt that I was, and must have been, the reason for the threat. But why?

With the many high-level visits, it became quite apparent that these officials either had no idea what some of our local Sudanese embassy staff had endured as a result of the August 7, 1998 Embassy bombings, nor the August 20, 1998 retaliatory strike on the Al-Shifa pharmaceutical factory in Khartoum, or they didn't care. But I did. So, with each visit, I made mention and reference to ensure they understood—that though no Americans were present, the remaining local staff, our local Sudanese embassy staff withstood the retaliatory actions taken against us there. Some were injured. Some were beaten up. Fortunately, no one was killed. They protected our Embassy and facilities that hung a flag that wasn't even their own. Ensuring Secretaries of State Colin Powell and Rice were aware when they came to visit enabled them both to make comments and address our applicable local Sudanese embassy employees accordingly, so they were proud that they were remembered.

In February 2005, Embassy Khartoum DLO/Army Lieutenant Colonel (LTC) Bill Godbout and I attended a conference in Zambia. Discussion groups were held inside with team-building group activities outside. One such team-building activity was whitewater rafting down the Zambezi. We were loaded up in two rafts, and off we went. I knew there was a high possibility of ending up in the crocodile-infested water. We were successfully running the rapids, passing a spotted crocodile, when all of a sudden, I was pitched into the river. Not completely sure as to what happened or how it happened, I was quickly helped back into the raft by the others to exclamations of how the first raft had caused the incident, more specifically, how the actions of one individual in the other raft, caused our raft to tip. And just take a guess as to who the individual in the other raft was—Charlie Slater. Once I heard that, I said nothing, but had no doubt of the possibility. As I already knew too well.

When I returned to Khartoum after that conference, I was basically in the home-stretch of my assignment there. With all the Congressional Delegations (CODELs) that had visited post during my tour, I had numerous discussions with Congressional Members and their staffs about considering an assignment up on the Hill. The more discussions I had, the more this option piqued my interested. Still, as an FS Financial Management Specialist just completing an FS Generalist assignment, I included a Pearson Fellowship, which provides FS an opportunity to work on Capitol Hill, as one of my upcoming assignment bid options. Soon after, I was notified and delighted of my selection into the Pearson Fellowship.

Curiously enough, however, for some reason, once selected, I wasn't notified regarding an additional further consideration into the other program with a fast-approaching deadline until almost on the deadline due date. And that was for the American Political Science Association's (APSA) Congressional Fellowship. Founded in 1953, the APSA Congressional Fellowship is a highly selective, nonpartisan program devoted to expanding knowledge and awareness of Congress. Once made aware, I literally worked through the weekend in order to meet the deadline. Soon after, I was notified that I had been selected for the APSA Congressional Fellowship program.

And then this bizarre event happened. The bidding process begins in the fall, the evaluation process in the spring and the promotion panel process during the summer. The big anticipation in the fall of every year is the promotion list. With all that was accomplished during my tour in Khartoum, I really thought I had a chance. Then, on November 18, 2005, my Career Development Advisor (CDA) Michael Bajek requested I contact him as soon as possible. On November 20, I was informed that I had been low-ranked by the 2005 Foreign Service Selection Boards. I was flabbergasted. While participating in the APSA Congressional Fellowship Orientation, I finally obtained a hard copy of the low-ranking statement on November 23, and immediately contacted our union, AFSA, upon receipt as I had done regarding the medical clearance/removal of the anonymous memorandum drama just over two years prior.

On December 22, 2005, working with AFSA Legal Counsel Neera Parikh, I filed a *Grievance Submission for Final Agency Review* with State/HR Linda Taglialatela as there were multiple Department failings, errors and violations. For instance:

> As the Management Officer covering the HR portfolio at Embassy Khartoum, I sent all applicable American FSO EERs to HR/PE via DHL on May 9, 2005 (See Attachment C). In June 2005, the applicable promotion review board contacted some of these FSO employees, requesting the status of the employee's latest EER for the current rating period. These employees immediately contacted me, inquiring about the whereabouts of their evaluations. I then spoke with HR/PE and was informed that though DHL tracking system reflected that Embassy Khartoum EERs had been received by HR/PE in May, HR/PE misplaced the evaluations. I faxed and resent by DHL copies of all the EERs to HR/PE. In email correspondence at that time between post and HR/PE, post was assured that Embassy Khartoum employees would not be disadvantaged in any way due to this administrative error and that all applicable panels would receive Embassy Khartoum employee EERs for review/promotion consideration. Please note that according to the copy of my EER in my OPF, HR/PE changed the date received in HR/PE block on DS-1829 to May 19, 2005 (not clearly legible) as requested by post so that neither post nor applicable FS employee would be docked for late submission. However, on the back of my EER, the date stamp received by HR/EX/ADM/RM reflects a date of July 7, 2005 (2:36 p.m.) and later verbally confirmed by HR/PE (December 8, 2005) scanned into my OPF on July 8, 2005. (See Attachment D).
>
> …The Department breached its duty, thereby causing significant harm to my career. Not only did HR/PE misplace my April 2005 EER, I assert that it did not place the report into my perfor-

mance file in time for the Selection Board to review the evaluation. The failure of HR/PE to timely submit my evaluation is blatantly apparent when reviewing the Selection Board's low-ranking statement... Clearly, the Board did not have access to the April 2005 EER as it cites to my 2004 EER as 'the latest evaluation.' In fact, the Board fails to refer to my April 15, 2005 anywhere in the low-ranking statement. In addition, there is no mention of the two awards that I also received during this period (Meritorious – Post; Franklin – African Bureau). (See Attachment E).

...The Department's error significantly harmed my career as I was low ranked. I maintain that I would have had a strong chance for promotion if the Department had abided by its responsibilities and placed the evaluation into my performance file.

...The 2005 Selection Board committed a blatant violation of the precepts, and thereby improperly low ranking me. The precepts specifically mandate that 'inadequacies that lead to low ranking must be documented by one or more examples of performance from the most recent five years. In designating me for low rank, the Selection Board cites to my August 1998, ...The Selection Board clearly violated the precepts by going back over eleven years to justify its decision to low rank me...

...Effective October 1998, I was officially promoted within the Foreign Service as an FP-02 level FMO. Thus, going back over this eleven-year period, I was never low-ranked based on any of these evaluations. It is highly egregious to me that the same evaluations that were used as the basis for my conversion from Civil Service to the Foreign Service are now being used as the basis for me to receive a career damaging low ranking...

I hereby request the following relief:

1. That the low ranking against me be overturned;

2. That my performance file was the latest April 2005 EER and two performance awards be forwarded to a reconstituted board for promotion review; and

3. Any and all other relief deemed just and proper.

On February 28, 2006, HR/G Allegra Sensenig, the grievance analyst assigned to my case, wanted to ask a few follow-up questions. Later that day, in our subsequent telephone conversation, we discussed a proposed settlement. The 2005 low-ranking would be overturned, low-ranking letter would be removed from my OPF and my performance file with my April 2005 EER, and the two applicable awards would be placed before a reconstituted Selection Board for promotion review. I concurred with the proposed offer and the settlement agreement was signed on March 7, 2006. On June 19, 2006, Allegra congratulated me for being promoted by the reconstituted 2005 Selection Board, retroactive to the effective date of the 2005 promotions.

I was delighted with the outcome, but given the definitive pattern, I was very leery of why all this really occurred to begin with, particularly given the players involved, and the same names coming up. For instance, why were the other FS employees in Khartoum contacted in June 2005 by their applicable promotion review board requesting the status of the employee's latest EER for the current rating period except for me? Why didn't my applicable board contact me? It's only because of the other FS employees being contacted that I documented and addressed the issue immediately across the board for all FS employees and their evaluations, including mine, and resent accordingly and immediately after finding out. My board did not contact me nor query on the status of my EER. So again, why didn't my board contact me?

Stunned by the low-ranking, I shared the low-ranking statement with a few trusted colleagues all of which drew the same conclusion:this statement was clearly written as if a personal, unprofessional attack. *So, who on the applicable board wrote it?*

Similarly, why did the low-ranking statement include my 1998 EER, the one completed by Management Counselor Stephen Nolan when it was a clear violation of precepts. And then why go back even further, eleven years, back to my two civil service excursion tours to the foreign service. *Who would do this—and why?*

The same answer can be provided to each of these questions. Charlie Slater. Charlie Slater was the FMO Specialist representative selected to sit on the 2005 Selection Board Promotion Panels. Steve Nolan was AF Executive Director, (AF/EX). The CDA that advised me of the low-ranking was also the same that almost didn't notify me in time for the APSA Congressional Fellowship application deadline, Michael Bajek, a long-time member with numerous assignments within the African Regional bureau and on the African continent, was commonly known as as old "Africa Hand." *Just like Steve Nolan.*

The deliberate actions—or lack of actions—by HR appeared similar to my experience of being reported deceased by HR Nairobi in the aftermath of the bombing, and other events transpiring prior to and in the aftermath of the bombing by the HR section in Embassy Nairobi at the time, and led by Lori Magnusson. But this was Washington HR, so how could this be possible? And then I found out. Washington HR was being led by *Robert Nolan, Steve Nolan's brother.*

With the outcome of the grievance process completely in my favor, I moved on. However, I duly identified and noted a targeting pattern developing, and even made mention to AFSA Legal Counsel Neera Parikh accordingly. So, I waited to see what would happen next. I didn't realize it would be in only a few weeks' time.

APSA Congressional Fellowship

Meanwhile, I was thoroughly enjoying my APSA Congressional Fellowship. I joined the personal staff of Senator Olympia J. Snowe (R-Maine), and had so many memorable moments. In January 2006, I was able to attend President Bush's State of the Union address. I participated in the Canada-US Parliamentary Exchange, where we hosted a week's orientation for Canadian parliamentary interns in Washington and the Canadians returned the favor in Ottawa. While in Ottawa, I attended an internal parliamentary discussion led by Senator and Lieutenant General Romeo Dallaire, the United Nations (UN) commander in charge during the Rwandan genocide, regarding Darfur. The conclusion of the fellowship was marked by a reception in the historic Mansfield Room of the Capitol. I invited Terry Shea, from my OIG days, to attend as my guest, as if it weren't for Terry's encouragement and support to take that first foreign service excursion tour back in 1993 I may not have been standing there that day. Additionally, which I only found out at that time, was that Senator Mansfield and Terry were actually family. Mansfield being Terry's in-law through his wife Maureen. Tickled to be invited, Terry was thankful to me for remembering and honoring him so.

Always a top priority, we talked and met with so many of Senator Snowe's Maine constituents to hear their issues and concerns, and assisting whenever and wherever possible. I assisted in the Senator's preparation for her trip to Iraq, helped obtain the support of sixty-five senators to join her request for an additional $150 million to support breast cancer research, and helped win unanimous support for legislation cosponsored by Senator Snowe and Senator Barbara Boxer that expanded the eligibility for the Purple Heart to prisoners of war who die in captivity. I attended hearings, prepared for her briefings, and followed-up with Maine constituents.

There was always lots of energy within the walls of Congress. Every night driving home, there was nothing more memorable then seeing the

Capitol Dome lite with the American flag flying on top. It was just like the feeling an American has seeing the American flag flying at the US Embassy when abroad. Symbolic, indicative, and always a constant reminder of representing and working for the American people; both, domestically and abroad, just like the US Constitutional Oath I took.

On April 12, 2006, a Department of State cable came out with the subject line: "2006 Omnibus Skill Code Change and Conversion opportunity." While I was one of the first to convert to foreign service from civil service after my two excursion details, the career mobility opportunities program became more established within the Department across the board regarding such opportunities. Now with the low-ranking fiasco rectified, one opportunity available piqued my interest, *change of generalist primary skill code (specialist-to-generalist)*. On April 17, 2006, I contacted my Career Development Officer (CDO) Bobby Balderas regarding my interest and my *Specialist-to-Generalist Conversion* Application. I patiently waited for the outcome of the Skill Code Change/Conversion Panel.

On June 27, 2006, I received the results of the Skill Code Change/Conversion Panel regarding my *Specialist-to-Generalist* conversion request. According to the letter sent from Joyce Currie, HR/CDO, my application was not approved. Apparently, my official personnel file (OPF) had not yet been corrected as agreed to in the terms of the March 7, 2006 Formal Settlement Agreement AGS 2005-116. So, I contacted AFSA Legal Counsel Neera Parikh regarding my concern and to find out accordingly. When she got back to me, she advised that for some reason, the files of the Skill Code Change/Conversion Panel were not kept and not grievable. As it was my first attempt for conversion consideration, I was disappointed, but not discouraged, particularly since I just found out that I had been retroactively promoted to an 01. However, like the low-ranking ordeal, I did duly note the coincidence of Steve Nolan, in AF/EX, and Rob Nolan, in HR, at the time. The stated reason for my application for generalist conversion not being approved was that *"your last two EERs show problems in the Area of Improvement that related to communication and interpersonal skills, both of which are indispensable for a Management Generalist."*

Since my returning from Khartoum, Mary Ryan and I planned on getting together once I was settled in my fellowship. Now having a few months under my belt with Senator Snowe's office, there was so much for us to catch-up on. I reached out to my dear friend to see when we could get together. We were coordinating schedules and finalizing lunch plans when suddenly Mary passed away. I was devastated and heartbroken. Attending her wake to pay my last respect, I saw Mary lay peacefully in her casket. Ambassador Mary Ryan passed away too young at the age of 65, on Tuesday, April 25, 2006.

The last time Mary and I met, I gave her a gift, a very special post-retirement gift I gave to only two others previously in their retirement (Ambassador Harriet Isom and Assistant IG Terence Shea)—a hand cross-stitched *Great Seal of the United States*. Mary was tickled, and overwhelmed. She hugged me a little longer than usual. Through A/S Maura Harding, Mary's State Department successor, I queried if Mary's sister could display it at the funeral home, next to her open casket as a final commemoration to Mary's loyal dedication to her nation, our nation.

Mary's passing was a shock, and timing of Mary's passing was oddly puzzling to me, depriving us of opportunity to talk alone, face-to-face. And given all the circumstances, I remain skeptical regarding her passing.

Meanwhile, as an FS Financial Management Specialist, I was being given the opportunity of unique insight into the "power of the purse" Congressional constitutional role and responsibility, the appropriation authorization process. More specifically, I had insight into the fiscal year 2007 Department of Defense authorization bill. One amendment was of particular interest to Senator Snowe: she co-sponsored it with Senator Boxer, and I was given a lead role in pushing through its inclusion into the authorization bill. The intent of this amendment was to correct an injustice by requiring the President, our Commander in Chief, to review the current circumstances establishing eligibility for the Purple Heart and advise Congress on modifications to the criteria for the Purple Heart Award.

My role in this process was to coordinate with Senator Boxer's staff and others in convincing the Senate Armed Services Committee to accept this amendment and to draft Senator Snowe's floor statement in support of this amendment. The Purple Heart amendment (Congressional Record – Senate S6317 June 21, 2006 SA4465) was successfully accepted and adopted into the 2007 Department of Defense authorization bill. To commemorate the moment, I received a printed hard copy of the Congressional Record depicting Senator Snowe's June 21, 2006 statement with the following inscription, "To Michelle, With profound appreciation for your outstanding contribution to our Nation-! Olympia Snowe" On June 13, 2006, Senator Snowe had sent a letter to Secretary of State Condoleezza Rice regarding an extension of my detail to her staff until the end of the 109th Session.

During this time, I was given an incredible opportunity to assist in commemorating for historical record Ambassador Ryan. My State/APSA

Congressional Fellow colleague Richard "Rick" Driscoll was working on the personal staff of Senator Edward "Ted" Kennedy. He had been tasked to draft a floor statement for Senator Kennedy who wanted to pay tribute to Mary Ryan. Knowing Mary and I had a close relationship, Rick asked if I would assist. I was honored and provided some insights in regards to Mary's actions in the aftermath of the August 7, 1998 Embassy bombings. Senator Kennedy's "Tribute to Mary A. Ryan" floor statement was made on July 12, 2006, as is now historically documented in the Congressional Record S7411.

On July 25, 2006, Senator Snowe received a response to her June 13 letter to Secretary of State Rice. The July 19, 2006 letter was signed by Jeffrey T. Bergner, Department of State's A/S for Legislative Affairs (H). Unfortunately, the request for extending my assignment detail on her staff was not possible due to the critical needs of his office, the office from which I accepted my next assignment in as a Legislative Management Officer (LMO) and was scheduled to start in September 2006. Having nothing but profound respect for the Senator, I knew that I had made the right decision to work on her staff and was extremely honored by Senator Snowe's attempt.

Now in the home stretch of this Congressional detail, I was back at the Department in a matter of months. Two other memorable opportunities would transpire before my departure. The first was a collaboration effort with the current APSA Congressional Fellowship director, Jeffrey Biggs. Jeff was not only a former Foreign Affairs Fellow, but also a former FSO. To encourage others in the foreign service to participate in the APSA Congressional Fellowships program, we wrote a joint article for the *Department of State Magazine*. The article was called, "Working the Hill – FSOs Bring Field Experience to 'Hill Fellowship.'" It appeared in the November 2006 issue, right at the beginning of the bidding process.

The second was even more personal. After discussing with Senator Snowe and her staff, I was given one last opportunity. With the eighth anniversary of the August 7, 1998 Embassy bombings fast approaching, Congress going on August recess, and my upcoming departure back to the Department, I could draft one last one *for the historical record* Congressional Record statement for Senator Snowe's consideration for submission. The draft was accepted and submitted. It pays tribute to our tragic loss of August 7, 1998 and of the April 25, 2006, passing of Ambassador Mary A. Ryan. Now back at the Department, on September 5, 2006, "Foreign

Service Family Losses" appeared in the Congressional Record, the historical record.

On September 19, 2006, in his UN General Assembly address, President Bush announced the new Presidential Special Envoy to Sudan, Andrew Natsios. This new envoy's role and responsibilities were in essence created through legislation that was passing through congress while I was up on the hill. So, in the words of my new boss, A/S of Legislative Affairs Jeffrey Bergner, "since you helped pass this new legislation, you now get to assist in implementing it." The legislation to which he was referring was the Darfur Peace and Accountability Act, DPAA, which the Senate approved on September 21, 2006 and the House passed on September 25, 2006. On October 13, 2006, President Bush signed the bill into law. And as stated by the President in his UN General Assembly Address, his Special Envoy Andrew Natsios was "to lead America's efforts to resolve the outstanding disputes and help bring peace to your land." Upon returning to the Department, my primary purview was to be the Senior Congressional Advisor for Andrew, the new Presidential Special Envoy to Sudan.

The portfolio was challenging enough given the dire situation and circumstances on the ground in Sudan. But at times, circumstances were even more dire, given the internal dynamics that would play out between the Special Envoy and the A/S of African Affairs and their applicable staffs. Aware of this potential and inevitable clash, I early on, scheduled a one-on-one meeting with A/S Jendayi Frazer to introduce myself and state my intention to work collaboratively and with one voice in our official Department of State position to and with the Hill. What I soon learned was the dynamic between the *political appointee* positions within H to ensure implementation of the President's priorities and agendas and the *career* positions within the applicable Bureaus, that outlast these political appointees. Adding the *Special Envoy* construct, created an even more dynamic dimension. This, at times, would become a humorous *told you so* and at other times, *bone of contention* dynamic continually at play that Jeff had alluded to with me at the very start. However, serving in Sudan, and given the crucial and vital importance of the impact to those on the ground, to me, it was worth pushing through the challenges these dynamics at times would present.

At the end of 2006, my plans would include my yearly ritual of Christmas with the family, and then off to attend Renaissance Weekend (RW) in Charleston, S.C. for the new year. However, this year's use-or-lose annual leave events would be different as I was given a once-in-a-lifetime opportunity to achieve one of my goals—to visit all seven continents—with a trip to the final frontier, Antarctica.

From December 10 to 20, 2006, I ventured to Antarctica. What a spectacular experience it was. I came back from the trip rejuvenated. Christmas with family and RW were fun, but my trip to Antarctica was breathtaking.

On April 24, 2007, in accordance with State Cable 046466, I would again submit my *Skill Code Change Request* application for *Specialist-to-Generalist* conversion consideration to my HR/CDA, who this time was Paul Doherty. Now totally aware of the retaliatory posture taken against me by the Nolan brothers previously, I patiently waited for the outcome of the Skill Code Change/Conversion Panel. On May 22, 2007, I received the expected official notification:

> Unfortunately, the Panel did not find that your documented experience warrants a change in skill code at this time. While the panel acknowledged your excellent service as management officer in Khartoum and your other experience, they agreed that successful completion of an FO-01 management generalist tour abroad as an FO-01 would help you demonstrate the kind of breadth and depth of experience in the field at-grade that is needed for conversion to FO-01 management generalist.

Like previously, the members of the 2007 Skill Code Conversion Panel were not mentioned by name and again, and these decisions were final and could not be appealed. However, in light of and given the past circumstances and previously documented actions by the Nolan brothers, I shared these applicable results with AFSA Legal Counsel Neera Parikh, so she too could see the definitive pattern being developed. I documented my file accordingly and moved on.

During my time with H, the complexity of my roles and responsibilities grew and expanded as more applicable UN resolutions and US Congressional legislation related to Sudan and Darfur passed. Additionally, on February 6, 2007, President Bush announced that a new type of military command incorporating officials from other US agencies and focusing on the African continent would be established, US Africa Command, commonly called AFRICOM. To be operationally effective October 1, 2008, with all the policy and resource implications of this first-ever joint-interagency command, serious deliberations were taking place among many interested entities within State, DOD and other government agencies. Not exempt from such deliberations, the applicable Congressional Armed Services and

Foreign Relations authorizing and appropriating committees internally debated jurisdictional oversight and resource implications in regard to the creation of AFRICOM. Given the policy significance and importance of Sudan and Darfur to the African continent during this time, my portfolio logically expanded as I also participated in both State and DOD AFRICOM working groups, assisted AFRICOM, DOD, and State officials with applicable Congressional hearings and briefings, and kept officials apprised of the ever-evolving congressional perspective on this matter to ensure a coordinated and united State/DOD face and voice to the Hill.

On June 4, 2007, an article regarding Sudan appeared in *Vanity Fair*, called "The Osama Files" written by David Rose. It starts like this:

> September 11 might have been prevented if the US had accepted Sudan's offers to share its intelligence files on Osama bin Laden and the growing al-Qaeda threat. Recently unearthed documents reveal that the Clinton administration repeatedly rejected the help of a country it unwisely perceived as an enemy.

Given that I had regionally supported Sudan from 1995-1998, briefly including the tenure of our last accredited American Ambassador to Sudan Timothy Carney, and then returned to serve in Sudan again from 2003-2005, I was intrigued by the article. What I didn't know at the time, however, was that a federal lawsuit was being filed against Sudan and Iran, blaming them for the August 7, 1998 East Africa Embassy bombings.

Now, given my attendance at the trial in NYC in June 2001, there were many events I was not aware of, happening behind the scenes and behind my back, that would later come to light and force me to take a stand, a stand based on a timeline of events and facts, documented facts, as I knew them. As more and more came to light, I became more and more puzzled—and troubled. The most telling factor includes why I was never approached by any of the applicable lawyers to join in and be included in such a lawsuit. In time, I would come to understand why. Because the lawsuit was based on a false narrative, not true to facts—and one I would never accept nor tolerate. Neither would others, to include Ambassador Tim Carney. Yet, this was not all known at the time and would only come to light in the future, which I will embellish upon in due time as well. The last paragraph of the June 4, 2007 *Vanity Fair* article went as follows:

> He who closes his eyes sees nothing. In the case of Sudan, 1996 through 2000, Madeline Albright and her assistant secretary for

Africa, Susan Rice, apparently preferred to trust their instincts that Sudan was America's enemy, and so refused to countenance its assistance against the deepest threat to US security since 1945. Ambassador Carney quoted Talleyrand, the 18th-century father of modern diplomacy. This saga was "pire qu'un crime, c'etait une be-tise." He provided his own translation. "It was worse than a crime. It was a fuckup."

The events referenced in this article cannot be overstated. As well as the timing of the article. In summary, Sudan's President at the time, Omar Bashir, wanted to hand bin Laden over to the USG. This message was re-layed by the Sudanese directly to and through the President of the Unit-ed States' Senate-confirmed representative in the country Ambassador Timothy Carney. Ambassador Carney, in turn, contacted and notified the USG accordingly. However, Clinton NSC senior advisor/Department of State's A/S for African Affairs, Susan Rice, refused the Sudanese offer, de-spite Ambassador Carney's adamant reiteration and request. So instead of bin Laden departing Sudan for the US, he departed for Afghanistan. Soon after, Ambassador Carney and his staff were ordered to depart Khar-toum, and relocate to Embassy Nairobi, Kenya. A very controlled shuttle diplomacy thereafter was implemented between Khartoum and the US President's Ambassador. Only after the disastrous results of this refusal occurred would I become aware… This US refusal occurred prior to the August 7, 1998 East Africa Embassy bombings. Given events that subse-quently occur, Susan Rice's refusal of the Sudanese Governments' request of the US to take bin Laden and all the players involved, one has to ask, *why was bin Laden not taken by the US?* Was it intentional, for purposes of setting him up to be used as a *scapegoat?* Otherwise, quite simply, if bin Laden was such a threat, why didn't the US take him when the Suda-nese Government offered? And if Sudan was such a threat, why was I, an August 7, 1998 Embassy Nairobi bombing survivor, assigned there from 2003 to 2005 by the Department? And why were there no MSGs at Em-bassy Nairobi during this time?

During August, when Congress was on recess and my schedule much lighter, I was invited by DOD colleagues for a tour at the Pentagon. On August 9, 2007, I was finally able to take them up on their offer. The tour included viewing the applicable memorials in honor of those who per-ished on 9/11/2001, just days after the tragic annual memorial of the day that changed my life forever, the Embassy bombing of August 7, 1998. My tour guide was none other than US Army Colonel Dennis Giddens, my colleague from my previous tour in Khartoum, and now Regional Director for Sudan. The tour ended in Deputy Assistant Secretary of Defense (DASD) for African Affairs (AFR) Theresa Whelan's office. As I stepped up to her desk to shake hands, others began to fill the room. They surprised me with an unexpected award—A Certificate for Outstanding Performance in recognition of her invaluable support to the Office of the African Affairs, Office of the Secretary of Defense—dated August 9th, 2007, signed by Colonel C.D. Giddens, USA Regional Director, Sudan and Theresa M. Whelan Deputy Assistant Secretary of Defense for African Affairs. I was truly humbled and honored. At the time, I believed this tribute was a result of my then efforts and support. In due time, I would wonder if the true intent of this award, even this visit to the Pentagon itself, was for a little deeper in reason within and for my OSD/AFR colleagues than I realized at the time. And now, given recent and connecting events, even deeper yet.

The African continent was a major portfolio focus for me during this time in H, but it wasn't the only focus. With an unexpected departure of an office colleague, I also took on responsibility for the Bureau of South and Central Asia (SCA), which included Afghanistan and Pakistan. This would be a very trying time for a country with very high Congressional interest at the time, Pakistan. The Pakistani President Pervez Musharraf implemented a state of emergency in November 2007. Then on December 27, 2007, former Prime Minister, and then-leader of the opposition Pakistan People's Party, Benazir Bhutto was assassinated, just prior to January 2008 scheduled elections. With the current policy and aid assistance package called into question, I assisted Deputy Secretary of State John Negroponte with his November 17, 2007 Hearing and all the other numerous congressional hearings, briefings and queries during this time. Definitely not my area of expertise, I had to adapt quickly to become knowledgeable with the SCA country issues, particularly Pakistan, and quickly become familiar with and successful in establishing the necessary contact network with officials that handled the portfolio both within the Department and the Hill. I had to stay on top of this fast-moving portfolio during this trying time.

And just like all my previous assignments, the bidding process had begun and I was just patiently waiting to see where I would be heading next. However, given my 01-grade level, I was now at the threshold of either entering the senior ranks of the foreign service or remaining at this same grade level for the remainder of my limited time and career with the foreign service. As FSI no longer conducted interagency senior leadership training, commonly referred to as Senior Seminar, the only opportunity my FS colleagues and I, now, had was to attend one of the US Military War Colleges. This timing was also further limited only to those FS at the 01-grade level. If I didn't attempt now, this once-in-a-lifetime/once-in-a-career opportunity would be missed. Given all my interaction and experience with DOD officials, my priority and hope were to be selected to attend senior training at a military war college.

On June 4, 2008, I was officially notified regarding my nomination for attendance at the US Army War College in Carlisle, Pennsylvania. On June 23, 2008, I received a letter from the Department of the Army United States Army War College and Carlisle Barracks Office of the Commandant Major General Robert M. Williams congratulating me on my selection as a member of the US Army War College (AWC) Class of 2009. As instructed by U/S Patrick Kennedy regarding my nomination, "Michelle, I need you to carry the Department of State flag and represent us at the US Army War College in Carlisle, Pennsylvania." I was extremely excited, humbled and honored by this opportunity and very much looking forward to my next FS assignment, in my home state of Pennsylvania.

CHAPTER 4

FOREIGN SERVICE VS. MILITARY SERVICE: *Our Responsibility To The American People For Whom We Serve*

BACK TO SCHOOL

I started senior training at the US Army War College (AWC) on August 6, 2008. I would become a proud member of Seminar 8. However, my first priority during that transition period was to attend the August 7, 1998 Embassy bombings commemoration back in Washington at Main State. My perspective from that ordeal would shape the experiences and insight I would share with my AWC colleagues during that upcoming academic year, my badge of honor so to speak with those who held theirs from experiences in Afghanistan and Iraq. When Patrick Kennedy instructed me to "carry the Department of State flag," I took it as a tongue-in-cheek comment. In due time, I realized how serious he really may have been, how real, significant and urgent a national security matter this *foreign service vs. military service* dynamic really was.

The academic year would be divided into being a team member in a Group Seminar format, followed with electives, new groupings, and other events. For my elective, I would be one of seventeen students chosen for the National Security Policy Program (NSPP), a special course of study that is designed to provide selected students with a detailed understanding of the contemporary USG's national security policymaking environment and the fundamentals for the development of national security policy as well as its implementation. But first, Seminar 8.

The mantra for Seminar 8 was: *Know yourself; Know others; and Reflect.* I have some phenomenal memories of my time at the AWC, but like previously, there were some bizarre events that occurred as well. But being at and affiliated with a DOD installation, my safety and security was never considered to be threatened, or at least that's what I thought so at the time.

Members of each and every military branch and service were in attendance, as well as other government agencies within DOD and throughout the entire USG, and invited students from militaries across the globe.

In Seminar 8, we had two such international military students, one from Estonia and the other from South Korea. The AWC motto is: Not to Promote War, But to Preserve Peace—in theory, the same goal/objective as the US Department of State.

In story after story, I heard of continual, non-stop deployments to Iraq and Afghanistan and the toll they were taking, shaping the hearts and minds of these future military leaders of our nation. In time, I developed an assessment of hidden resentment, not towards me per se, but toward my institution, the State Department, blaming the State Department for getting into these wars. One day, a particularly hardened Colonel made a comment to me about my institution, the State Department—a bit harsher, but similar to those that I had heard previously. But I'd had enough, my threshold was passed. I basically said:

> Listen, I survived the August 7, 1998 Embassy Nairobi bombing and knew of bin Laden before any of you did. When I served at Embassy Khartoum, Sudan from 2003 to 2005, during threats from al-Qaeda, there were no Marine Security Guards, because as I was advised, it was too "unsafe" for them to be there.

Needless to say, this comment did not come from anyone in my Seminar 8, because they had been hearing directly from me in sidebar discussion and our group discussions of my experience. But, when one of my fellow Seminar 8 team mates heard of the comment that had been made to me, he basically said, *"Listen Michelle, sometimes you just need to go toe-to-toe, and you did, you held your own."* Interestingly enough, soon after, I felt a new aura of respect for me—like, *she may be State Department, but she earned her stripes.*

Soon after I would hear that though our AWC Class of 2009 socialized quite a bit, we socialized less than classes from previous years. I heard that my fellow classmates were spending their time to reunite with their families, knowing that at the end of the academic year, most likely they would once again be redeployed. I also had heard that the reason State/FSI no longer had *Senior Seminar* interagency training was because, supposedly, a military officer who attended made a comment to Vice President (VP) Dick Cheney at the time regarding learning how to sip tea from a tea cup. I don't know if it was true or not, but I indeed picked up hidden resentment lingering between our two institutions—State and Defense. But for the time being, I earned my stripes and now understood what Pat Kennedy had been alluding to with his comment.

During my time there, I was also witness to the atmospherics during the election between John McCain and Barack Obama, and the apparent sea change once Senator McCain selected Sarah Palin as his vice presidential candidate. And I witnessed the enthusiasm when out-going President Bush came to speak to our class before leaving office. Attuned to this— and that certain classmates may indeed rise to be the future leaders of our military—one unique contribution I thought I could make was seeing if the AWC would be interested in having the last link to the President John F. Kennedy Administration come speak and provide comments and insights to our class. They indicated that they were, so I was instrumental in bringing Theodore "Ted" Sorensen to the AWC to speak on White House (WH) decision-making and the role of the presidential adviser. Both the foreign service and military service implement the policies of whomever the American people duly-elect at a given time as our President of the United States of America – the duly-elected President, whether Republican or Democrat. Both of our services also take an oath to defend the constitution writ large, not necessarily a president of either party. Having both parties come to speak and provide their perspective, I thought, was a worthwhile contribution.

Despite my arranging for Ted to come speak, I would not be present to hear his comments, nor would I be given an opportunity to see him alive again. He would pass before we had that chance. Ted passed away on October 31, 2010. So how did I get to know Ted Sorensen? It was through his sister Ruth and by attending RW, made famous by the Clintons.

I attended my first RW in Charleston, South Carolina in December 2005-January 2006. There were so many fascinating people to meet and insights to hear and share. One day, walking down the corridor I saw Ted Sorensen with his wife, Gillian. Though I personally did not know Ted, I knew of him indirectly through his sister, Ruth. I met Ruth and Derek Singer while serving together in Yaoundé, Cameroon, during the 1993-1995 time-frame. It was during a cultural event held by USIA highlighting JFK and his book, *Profiles in Courage* that I attended. Given her background and connection Ruth participated, and that's how I found out about the linkages. I was very impressed, and from that event on, Ruth, Derek and I became friendly and socialized quite often. So here I was many years after, finally having the opportunity to meet Ruth's famous brother. I decided the next time our paths crossed, I would introduce myself.

Hours later, I had the opportunity. I introduced myself, stating that I knew Ruth and that we had served together in Cameroon. Initially, Ted said that I must be mistaken as Ruth never served in Cameroon. I light-heartedly laughed, saying, "Yes, she did. Her and Derek were there with USAID." Providing a little more insight, I then politely stated that I just wanted to introduce myself, and asked for him to pass along my warmest regards to Ruth the next time he saw or spoke with her. Obviously, he must have contacted her soon after because the next time I saw him, Ted was delighted to chat more, even inviting me to sit with them for lunch at their table. As a result, I met Eleanor Clift, Dr. Ruth (yes, that Dr. Ruth), General Wesley Clark, and so many others. I attended RW again in December 2007–January 2008; and then again, over Christmas holiday while attending AWC from December 2008–January 2009. And who would have guessed that later I would be in a position to arrange for Ted Sorensen to come to speak to my AWC class, or to invite Eleanor Clift, a *Newsweek* journalist, to participate in the National Security Seminar, the first week of June.

Unfortunately, despite arranging for him to come speak, the day Ted actually came to reflect on his role in the Kennedy Administration, my NSPP colleagues and I were in Washington, D.C. Ironically, we were meeting with high-level USG officials of the current Obama Administration at State, Defense, National Security Council (NSC) and the US Congress. I was disappointed to have missed that once-in-a-life-time opportunity, but overjoyed that Ted had agreed to do it. Based on comments made from some AWC colleagues afterwards, they enjoyed hearing Ted's comments, and a few even had him sign their copies of his most recent book. Unfortunately, though Ted and I were in brief contact afterwards, Ted passed away a few months later. I was neither given an opportunity to hear his AWC comments nor to ever see Ted again before he passed,which was an eerily similar circumstance to that of Mary Ryan.

Occasionally, after-class interagency discussions continued in the local watering hole to reflect on the applicable lesson of the day. During one such discussion, I learned about *A Message to Garcia*, an essay by Elbert Hubbard (1899) from our Seminar 8 USMC classmate. During yet another such discussion, again with my Seminar USMC classmate, our talk evolved into identifying a Seminar 8 unofficial symbolic challenge coin—the DIME. And given its broader interagency implications, I share accordingly a letter I sent to both the AWC Commandant and U/S Kennedy.

18 February 2009

Dear Commandant:

As a Department of State participant in this year's Army War Class (AY 09), I want to thank you for this life-changing senior level educational opportunity. It was based on your meeting last spring at my Department that Under Secretary for Management Patrick Kennedy fulfilled your request for State's participation this academic year. And it was the strategic vision of both of you on the importance of such transformational and developmental opportunity exchanges between our two fine institutions that my participation came to fruition. For that I thank both of you. It is also from that context I share the following insight:

"ONE DIME"

Since the first day of class, I was introduced to a concept, a theme, I had never heard before. It was that America's complex national security environment requires an in-depth knowledge of the diplomatic, informational, military, and economic instruments of national power, as well as the interrelationships among them. Every day throughout this academic year, our seminar discussed these interrelationships, noting that at times the military component's role was a big "M," and at other times a little "m." The same correlation was made for the diplomatic component; at times being a big "D," while other times being a little "d." But always, being a required, holistic relationship commonly referred to and known as throughout our entire class as the DIME.

Also during the academic year, the funding correlations between these components were discussed. It was through that symbolic context that I proposed what seemed so ironically appropriate that the "Dime," the littlest in size of our U.S. Treasury (but not value, though all the State Department can afford), become Seminar 8's symbolic challenge coin. And that night at the Joint Pub at the LVCC, it became so.

In adopting our new challenge coin, the "Dime," I began to closely examine its features and research its history. One side proudly displays the profile of our 32nd President, Franklin D. Roosevelt. It was what I discovered on the other side of this coin that I found to be quite profound.

At the top of this side of the coin displays the words "United States of America," which I realized represented the American people whom we serve.

Below those words, I discovered three symbolic pillars: the olive branch; the torch; and the oak branch. First is the olive branch symbolizing our nation's gesture of peace, goodwill, partnership between us and the other members of our international community. Next, is the liberty torch symbolizing our nation's liberties/ freedoms and values for which we stand for and display for others throughout our international community. Last, is the oak branch symbolizing our nation's strength and courage.

The most intriguing feature of this coin, however, is the words displayed at the bottom. How symbolic that all the letters are capitalized and uniform in size. Unlike the other coins of our U.S. Treasury (i.e. Nickel, Quarter), the words denoted not only include the coin's name, but also symbolically depict a unity of the instruments of our national power—the necessary and unified foundation for which all above it is symbolically supported—the words, "ONE DIME."

So in reflection, how ironic that the smallest of U.S. Treasury is actually its strongest. As we, the future leaders of our nation, emerge from this fine institution go forth and lead our nation, when we come across the smallest of our U.S. Treasury, may we always take the time to reflect upon its symbolic strength and our responsibility to the American people for whom we serve, to be a unified foundation as "ONE DIME."

V/R from a U.S. Army War College Student (AY 09)
Michelle L. Stefanick, U.S. Department of State (Seminar 08)

Those affiliated with the military are quite familiar with the challenge coin, its applicable significance, the sharing of it, and most importantly, always having it on their person, particularly at every and any after class discussion attended thereafter. I certainly did. And needless to say, the "ONE DIME" concept spread like wild fire throughout the AWC, and beyond. So much so that a little over a year later, I was advised by a USMC Staff Judge Advocate on whether I copyrighted the concept. On Tuesday, February 23, 2010 at 3:42 p.m., I received the applicable Acknowledgement of Receipt email from the US Copyright Office.

Throughout the academic year, I would read a lot, write a lot, discuss a lot, observe a lot, listen a lot, and reflect a lot. My required individual Strategy Research Project (SRP) paper would be entitled "Powell's Leadership Principles: Time for State Department to Revisit." Ironically, it would be published on January 20, 2009, the same day Barack Obama would be sworn in as the 44th President of the United States of America.

Recently I reread my SRP, and so much, if not all, still applies to this day. However, if I were writing this again, there are at least three larger, more systemic issues that I would now include. This is what I wrote back then:

> The State Department has but one asset and it is their human asset. As of September 30, 2008, there are approximately 58,073 State Department employees. Approximately 6,691 FS Generalists, 4,965 FS Specialists, 9,328 Civil Servants, and 37,089 LE staff work together in support of the foreign policy goals for our nation. To put this number into perspective, Secretary of Defense Gates recently noted that the entire diplomatic corps of 6,700 Generalists is less than the manning for one aircraft carrier strike group, and allegedly, less than the number of military band members. For even broader comparison, there are approximately 1.6 million active-duty military personnel, nearly 1.6 million members of the Reserve and National Guard, and 673,000 civilian employees in the Defense Department.

Many of my military colleagues would mention to me that only about 1% of the American population volunteers to serve in the military. They would voice their concern of having a major disconnect with the American people due to such a small percentage. Though that percentage number may be low, the strategic messaging throughout our nation is such that when it comes to thanking those who serve, discounts for those who serve, etc., in the military service is high, quite high in fact. Versus, and in contrast to the relative proportion, and particularly in comparison, given the much, even lower percentage number that serves in this nation's foreign service in comparison to the American population writ large. I can assure you, this nation's foreign service isn't receiving thank you's and discounts for their service by fellow Americans and corporations across our nation, or even from our very own military service, in comparison to our fellow military service. Few Americans even know we, their foreign service, even exist; including some of our very own military service colleagues.

I do not want this to be taken out of context. I am also a firm and strong believer that our nation has a responsibility, a moral responsibility, to take care of those who volunteer to defend our nation, foreign service and military service alike. Stories of mistreatment of our serving military (particularly those who are/were injured) by the Veterans Administration, fraudulent non-profits, and profiteering defense contractors infuriate me.

But how about comparing that to absolutely no care or interest regarding our injured and mistreated foreign service, such as many of my colleagues in the August 7, 1998 East Africa Embassy bombings. There was so little care or interest that there were limited congressional hearings after the bombings. So, where is the outrage for us—the foreign service—by our fellow American citizens, our corporations, and more specifically, our colleagues in military service?

Another issue is the topic and reason for my writing this book. Unfortunately, it would not and has not been developed and included in such a research report paper previously, that I am aware of, due to classification purposes. But yet, it is and remains the elephant in the room regarding the Department of State, an institution that has been used and abused for cover purposes by our sister USG agency, the CIA, and others. And for that reason, without embellishment, I summarize and conclude simply like this: the Department of State is the nation's Department of State and cannot and should not be used and abused as a cover for CIA or any intelligence agency/employee(s) now, or ever again.

Both the foreign service and military service take an oath to defend the constitution, regardless of which political party is in control, and take and follow policy direction from and by the person the American people have elected as President of the United States. At the beginning of every leadership transition, the President's political appointees fill a certain number of partisan positions. The number and positions filled are known and tracked. But, for every administration, regardless of political party, something occurs; political appointees don't depart, but they burrow in, creating a buffer zone between real public servants and political appointees of the same, and more often than not, differing political parties. This results in the quagmire between the two parties that our nation is now embroiled in, and is playing out not only at the national level, but inside and across the Departments and Agencies of the USG itself. And this is all at the expense of the American people. Quite simply, political appointees that come in during an Administration must depart with that Administration.

So needless to say, yet another report paper besides my own needs to be written regarding the weaknesses and vulnerabilities of the State Department.

On March 18, 2009, as done in years past, my HR/CDA Mary Draper forwarded to me State Cable 023952 dated March 13, 2009, SUBJECT: "2009 Omnibus Skill Code Change/Conversion Opportunity." Also, as done in years past, on April 16, 2009, I once again submitted my *Skill*

Code Change Request application for *Specialist to Generalist* conversion consideration to my HR/CDA Mary Draper. As in years prior, I patiently waited for the outcome of the Skill Code Change/Conversion Panel.

In the meanwhile, being promoted to my current 01 grade-level in June 2008, I had a decision to make—whether to open my window or not. If I opened my window, when my annual evaluations were reviewed, I would be considered for entry into the SFS. Without opening my window, I would not be considered. And, once your window was opened, if you were not promoted after so many reviews, one's Time-in-Class (TIC) for promotion into the SFS would expire and face mandatory Time-in-Class/Time in Service (TIC/TIS) retirement. In June 2008, I opened my window.

For my AWC elective, I was one of seventeen students selected for NSPP. Of course, this meant more reading and more writing. It also meant trips to meet with key decision-makers in our national security policy-making apparatus to include at MacDill Air Force Base in Tampa, Florida, and in Washington, D.C. There were great guest speakers with great insights, and a one-week NSPP internship; mine with DOD/OSD/AFR. My main interlocutor for my internship would be Dan Pike, the Embassy Nairobi Defense Attaché who served with me at the time of the Embassy bombings. Unfortunately, Dan ended up not being there for most of it. DASD Therese Whelan was on official TDY the entire time. Chuck Ikins, Jeff McManus and others would step in to assist. At the time, I chalked all the absences during my OSD/AFR NSPP internship up to bad timing. On May 29, 2009, I received a certificate for participating in NSPP.

In the meantime, on May 20, 2009, a potential onward assignment that I was patiently waiting for was finally announced via Unclassified State cable 00051418 with SUBJECT: "Defense Doors Opening for Diplomats: Foreign Policy Advisors (POLADS) Sought for US Military Commands." According to the cable:

> ...the Bureau of Political Military Affairs (PM) seeks talented, action-oriented officers who are interested in working at the interface of diplomacy and defense as Foreign Policy Advisors (FPA)/ (POLADs).

Reviewing the newly established available positions, and given my applicable background, on Friday, May 22, 2009, I reached out to both PM and my HR/CDA Mary Draper regarding my interest, my preference and my intent to officially bid on applicable positions:

J. US Army Africa (formerly SETAF) (Vicenza, Italy) FE-OC;

G. US Marines Europe/Africa (Stuttgart, Germany) FE-OC;

F. US Navy Europe (now dual hatted as NAVAF) (Naples, Italy) FE-OC; and

A. US Air Forces Africa/17th Air Force (Ramstein, Germany) FE-OC.

Advised by both PM and HR, since all four positions were OC (SFS-level) positions, selections for the positions had to go through the Deputy Chief of Mission/Principal Officer (DCM/PO) Committee and were required to provide 360-degree references in compliance with DCM/PO Committee procedures. So, as a 01-bidder, I was subjected to the SFS-level DCM/PO Committee assignment procedures; and the applicable selection process proceeded only when such a committee meeting was held. Once identified, candidates were determined by the DCM/PO Committee and official nomination letters would be sent to the applicable Military Commanders for selection, with final selection made (quickly or slowly, depending on how commands took such actions differently. Officially submitting my bids, I patiently waited for the results of the applicable DCM/PO Committee Meeting to occur, whenever it occurred.

The first week of June, I would be reunited with my previous Seminar, Seminar 8, for the National Security Seminar (NSS), an annual event on the last week before graduation. My invited guest was Eleanor Clift, of *Newsweek/The McLaughlin Group* fame, and a RW colleague. On June 4, 2009, Clift published a *Newsweek* column regarding her attendance, "War Planners: Iraq Not A Good Model for Afghanistan," stating she was one of 160 people invited to NSS.

On June 6, 2009 I graduated from the US Army War College with a Master's of Strategic Studies. And at this point, patiently waiting for word on my onward assignment.

On June 25, 2009, I received a DOJ/SDNY Victim Notification System (VNS) email regarding my CRVA-accorded rights and protections. The DOJ/FBI investigation pertaining to the August 7, 1998 East Africa Embassy bombings was still open. I filed the email accordingly, and patiently waited to hear more on the outcome.

On July 2, 2009, U/S Pat Kennedy requested that I review an operational matter in Jerusalem. Specifically, the review would focus on the Support Survey of US Security Coordinator (USSC) as a new memorandum of agreement (MOA) was being developed. I would have a few days of consultations in D.C. followed by two weeks in Israel. US Army General Keith Dayton was the current US Security Coordinator. Coincidentally, just a few months prior, General Dayton was a guest speaker at my AWC NSPP class. Thus, I had a forewarning on how complex, complicated, and politically-charged this assignment would be. Not all parties were completely happy with my report. I felt I did what I could in the time I was given as objectively as possible, given the factors, the players and the politics involved, and stating and keeping to the facts, concerns, and recommendations as I saw them. With that, on a personal-level, weird events occurred during my trip to Israel. So much so, that one such particular event I even reported to the Consulate RSO in Jerusalem. Nothing came of the matter, but I did report it just the same. In hindsight, I felt the entire trip was some kind of *test. The question being carried-out by whom and for what reason?*

Also, during my trip to Israel, I was notified that the DCM/PO Committee met on July 15 and approved my candidacy for the Marines Europe/Africa (MARFOREUR/AF) POLAD position, Stuttgart, along with one other candidate. I was further advised that, for whatever reason, the Committee approved only three candidates for US Army Africa position, (PM had proposed five—implying that I was one of the five) and unfortunately, I was not among those approved. So as of July 15, now approved as one of two candidate nominees by the DCM/PO Committee, I would again have to patiently wait for the next phase of the process once the acting DG officially notified the MARFOREUR/AF Commander for final selection. On Thursday, August 6, 2009, MARFOREUR/AF contacted me to arrange a telephone interview for the position; Monday, August 17 worked for both parties.

On August 17, I had a telephone interview for the MARFOREUR/AF POLAD position with Marine Forces Europe (MARFOREUR) Chief of Staff (COS) Colonel Walter Niblock and Marine Forces Africa (MARFORAF) COS Colonel Mario Lapaix. I'm not sure who the other candidate was; all I could do was patiently wait for their decision, which they advised would be made early the next week.

MARFOREUR/AF provided their POLAD selection decision via email to HR and PM on Wednesday on August 26, 2009. The letter from USMC MARFOREUR/AF Commander Brigadier General (BGen) Tracy Garrett to Department of State Director General of the Foreign Service and Director of Human Resources Ambassador Nancy Powell included the following:

> As a result of the selection process, I have selected FS-01 Michelle Stefanick.

At 9:11 A.M., I was officially notified by my HR/CDA Mary Draper of their decision. Being officially paneled within the internal State Department assignment process was the next step, and that was to occur the following Tuesday. On August 27, I provided Colonel Niblock with that update, an estimated October arrival date with more to follow after the next week's paneling.

Officially relocated back to Washington, D.C., I served on the Promotion Board panels, the first time I did so, from August 11 to September 26, 2009. My applicable panel was mandated to review for promotion potential for the OPFs of eleven specialist categories, including Financial Management, in classes FS-02 through 04. Our Chairperson Jo Ellen Powell and the entire team took our responsibility very seriously, having intense discussions regarding and in developing our results for every category and every ranking decision made. Upon completion, I wrote some "Insights for FMO's from Michelle Stefanick, a 2009 Foreign Service Selection Board Member," as requested by SFS/FMO Sid Kaplan, my mentor. I shared a draft with Jo Ellen for her comments. She responded on Saturday, September 26, 2009, appropriately timed as the promotion list just came out the day before. Making a slight change, on September 28, 2009, I sent it to Sid Kaplan to review before distributing accordingly throughout the FMO community.

On September 17, 2009, I followed-up on an issue I first noticed and reported to HR officials on June 13, 2009 after discovering my Secretary's Heroism Award was hidden within my OPF. Sitting on the Promotion Panels, I saw first-hand a Heroism Award reflected in its own category, a separately identified award category. But in my OPF, for some reason, it was not. *Why the inconsistency? Why was it buried in my OPF?* After the two-year delay in receiving the Heroism Award to begin with, a "huge oversight" given as the reason for the mishap, only now to be reflected in my OPF as *Approved Award (Various) 6/29/2000*. Despite my numerous queries, I never received a response addressing this inconsistency. Given all that has occurred in other aftermath events, *something just isn't right*.

My 2005 EER evaluation was lost/misplaced resulting in a low-ranking by the FMO Promotion panel written by none other than Charlie Slater, my replacement in the aftermath. I filed a grievance, resulting in this low-ranking being over-ruled and my being promoted retroactively to FS-01. But in hindsight, and now having Promotion Panel insight, based on the low-ranking justification Charlie wrote, he had access to my entire OPF beyond the purview of the Panel's mandate. So, he saw all this. I now found all this beyond curious, but quite suspicious. And I only found out about the burying on my receiving the Secretary's Heroism Award because I sat on the 2009 Specialist Promotion Panels. *Had it been changed? Is it possible that it had been reflected properly, properly categorized, and now it wasn't, because it had been changed? If so, who changed it? On whose authority? And when?* Given all the events that occurred since the aftermath up to this point, I have no doubt it all was intentionally done, to my detriment, from the very start. The question being, *why?* Given all the events that would transpire after this, I am convinced more than ever that all this was intentional. Whatever *this is. So now the bigger question is, did Charlie Slater receive this Secretary's Heroism Award? If so, when, as he did not even arrive to Embassy Nairobi until the aftermath...*

On September 1, 2009, my assignment was officially paneled. I was the first FPA/POLAD for MARFOREUR/AF. I was delighted, proud and humbled. On September 2, 2009, unclassified State cable 091648 was sent from the Department announcing my assignment (a new tour of duty is three years) transfer eligibility date is 10/2012.

Now official, though still sitting on the Promotion Panels, I could begin the process of transition to my next assignment overseas with an official arrival date of October 2009. Then all of a sudden, and for some unknown reason, the communications from MARFOREUR/AF went radio silent. There was apparent resistance. And I didn't know why.

NEXT STOP: BERLIN?

Interestingly timed, on September 1, 2009, the same day I was officially paneled, HR/CDA Mary Draper sent out an email request for Crisis Management Training (FSI/LMS/CMT): "Need Volunteers for Marine Expeditionary Unit Exercises." There were three opportunities available: Camp Atterbury, near Columbus, Indiana (29 September–2 October); Yuma, Arizona (October 21-24); and Camp Lejeune, NC (29 October–3 November). Given my onward assignment and time availability, I thought this would be a real win-win opportunity. Though I didn't fit the role requested per se, I volunteered accordingly with preference due to my current transfer schedule for Camp Atterbury exercise as an *observer*. After the Promotion Panels, I was off to Camp Atterbury. My point of contact was Marty Klotz. Only in our chat when he picked me up at the airport and drove me to where I would be staying did it come up regarding our both being assigned to Embassy Nairobi at the time of the explosion. I was in Addis and flew back the next day, while Marty had been in the stairwell. We shared our applicable experiences, to include Marty's wife being Greek Orthodox, and that aspect of each of our survivals. During the exercise, I observed and participated, without getting in the way. I learned a lot, shared a lot, and as requested by FSI Coney Patterson, provided my observation comments after participating. Not being out in the field for a few years now, it was a great experience with the Marines, and I was very pleased and enthused that I had volunteered.

Also, interestingly enough, on September 1, 2009, I received an email from James McNaught, Foreign Policy Advisor – Special Operations Command/Europe (SOCEUR), addressed to MARFOREUR COS Colonel Walter Niblock, United States European Command (EUCOM) Colonel Franz Plescha, myself, and carbon copied to Richard (Carl) Paschal – Special Operation Command/Africa (SOCAF) regarding Subject: RE: POLAD to MARFOREUR. At the time, I was delighted at all the assistance. In due time, and as a result of the events that later occurred, I heavily suspected that the assistance may not have been of genuine, of true intent, but something more sinister, suspect, by and of those offering, to include the possibility that it was Jim McNaught who was the other candidate considered but not selected for the MARFOREUR/AF position. But at the time, again I was delighted, accepted all and any insight provided, and proceeded with genuine intent, at least on my part.

From September 14–15, I attended the POLAD Orientation. Though still on Promotion Panels, I squeezed in consultations (State lingo for meetings) when I could with applicable individuals throughout the Department and the interagency community that would be pertinent points of contact to provide applicable insight and to assist in successfully doing my job. I soon would comprehend the uniqueness of my position. Unlike many of my POLAD FS colleagues, my role would be assisting a Commander in a dual-hatted capacity. Not just one or the other, but in this case, my case, assisting in support of both EUCOM and AFRICOM. Therefore, so many new contacts to make and so much more insight to obtain. So, I focused and went to work, outreaching accordingly. Additionally, I would start my medical clearance process. On September 28, 2009, I obtained my *Worldwide Available/Class 1 Clearance* medical clearance, with no drama this time around. All was coming together, except the final details regarding my actual transition to MARFOREUR/AF.

It was now October, my tentative arrival month, with no finalized arrival date. Still not hearing back from MARFOREUR regarding next steps, upon returning from the Marine Exercise, I emailed my new boss, USMC BGen Paul Brier:

> Subject: Greetings from your new incoming POLAD
>
> Hello General Brier—I wanted to introduce myself. As you may be aware, I was recently selected and paneled to be the first Foreign Policy Advisor (POLAD) for the Commanding General of the Marines for Europe and Africa. Considering the utmost respect for which I and the State Department has toward the Marines, this is an extreme honor for me. I'm looking forward to advising you on Foreign Policy matters pertaining to both your EUCOM and AF-RICOM roles and responsibilities, and providing the reach back to Washington as well as the reach forward to our Ambassadors/ Embassies as necessary. Most of all, I'm looking forward to joining the Marine team under your leadership. Very respectfully, more appropriately, S/F, Michelle Stefanick [1]

BGen Paul Brier emailed back almost instantly:

> Michelle, Thank you for the note and I look forward to you joining our team. I know you will enjoy your time with us and expect that we will benefit greatly from your assignment and insight. Sf Paul [2]

With his response, I had a sigh of relief. Okay, all is good at the top level, I'll be a little more patient. All and every interaction and discussion I ever had with Paul Brier was professional and respectful. To this day, despite the intense sense of hurt and betrayal I would soon experience in and by his Command, I genuinely believe none of it was of his intent or orchestration.

That said, based on my own experiences and observations—to include and while attending the AWC—I submitted my bids as an FPA/POLAD from this context: our serving military had been at war in Iraq, and deployment after deployment after deployment, now for so long that they knew nothing else contextually when serving and deploying to an AOR (area of responsibility) not at war, for instance, such as in Europe, or the Continent of Africa. This meant that they were losing the knowledge base of the role and responsibility when entering a country with and when the President's Representative, the Ambassador, is in charge and not a Military General. This dynamic was playing out in non-combat AORs to such a concern of and by the State Department that State Department Manage-

1   Michelle Stefanick, email message to Paul Briar, October 9, 2009
2   Paul Brier, email message to Michelle Stefanick, October 9, 2009

ment was willing to give up heavily sought-after, highly coveted position billets from needs within our Embassies— and within our own Department—to instead expand this new cadre of FPA/POLADs to work as the interface of diplomacy and defense in non-war zone Military Commands. Teaching and ensuring the understanding of now fading awareness of the Embassy Country Team concept was essential, not only for our military colleagues but for our State Department, with so many serving alongside the military in Iraq and Afghanistan as well. The two services, foreign and military, are necessary to defend our nation, but the two institutions have different mandates, different perspectives, and different cultures. I would argue that this was necessary to and for the best interest of our nation. Being the first FPA/POLAD assigned to MARFOREUR/AF, I was aware of and prepared for such challenges and obstacles, particularly as the position was first being established.

But soon it would become apparent that something more was at play. Working with the PM Front Office, we were trying to figure out precisely what it was. The first indicator was the lack of response/delay of response by the Colonels. They didn't understand nor did they like the fact that an outsider was coming in.

The second indicator involved a complicating, yet common place aspect and dynamic to my assignment. The agreed-upon grade level of the MARFOREUR/AF FPA/POLAD position between the Departments of Defense and State was at the OC (SFS grade-level position). Despite my personal grade being at the 01-level, the *rank of the position* was at an SFS grade-level. For some reason, they didn't understand that in theory the military service and foreign service were more common with each other in a *rank in person* structure than either in comparison to the civil service *rank in position* construct. Due to staffing limitations and circumstances much more prevalent in the FS, the culture was, in practice, more of a *rank in person, kinda* construct at times. In the FS, there is a structure, but also flexibility and circumstances given depending on the personal grade/rank of the individual to the grade/rank and authority level of the position assigned, particularly when pertaining to stretch positions and/or positions into and across the SFS threshold. In the FS system, stretch position assignments (1 level above personal grade) and even double-stretch position assignments (2 levels above personal grade) are/were commonplace. And in such occurrences, the FS authority of the assigned position remains/takes precedence over the personal rank for the duration of the assignment, resulting in a more nuanced interpretation to the MS stringent interpretation of *rank in person*. In the FS, with its very limited staffing resource, particularly in comparsion to the MS, the authority resides within the applicable position assigned to, and duration while assigned, so the *rank of the position* matters as well. A comparable instance within the MS would be when, a staff sergeant or first lieutenant serves as platoon sergeant or company commander then would hold the *authority* of the position but not the rank or pay until promoted. With such circumstance very commonplace in the FS, again, due to its very limited staffing resources, particularly in comparison to the MS.

And then, the third indicator was when a FS assigned to such positions with the MS would be, could be overwhelmed, intimated, threatened by the MS and the position they were placed in, and to take, times, simply giving in or worse, losing focus on who they were representing, the FS perspective not the MS; and whose flag they were carrying/representing (State's, not DOD's). And that's the exact scenario we would come to encounter in my situation by the unauthorized actions and statements made by Kate Canavan. Kate Canavan, aka Cathy Peterson, who was the US State Department's Civilian Deputy and Foreign Policy Advisor to the EUCOM Commander.

Unfortunately, Kate's actions, counter-positions and counter-actions to the decisions made in and by the Department of State would become known and counter-acted, but not all were known and exposed in a timely manner to counter the damage. Based on her actions and positions documented and known at the time, as one high level Department of State official would say, "Apparently, Kate Canavan has joined the Military." But this was at the expense of much more than just the Department of State. In due time, and as it will be revealed, it was at the expense of and did damage to the national security of our Nation.

What U/S Patrick Kennedy, PM Principal Deputy Assistant Secretary (PDAS) Tom Countryman and I did not know at the time, and I would only find out about years later, was that on September 4, 2009, EUCOM POLAD Kate Canavan had sent an email to then USMC MARFOREUR/ AF Commander BGen Tracy Garrett. Having no official role or authority in this personnel matter, and no reporting responsibility since my reporting chain was with AFRICOM State Department FPA/POLAD, not her and not EUCOM, to this day, despite my numerous requests for a cop,y since finding out about the email, a copy has never been provided to me. *So what was in this US Department of State S/FSO Kate Canavan September 4, 2009 email?* It seems particularly relevant given the role Kate had and played in upcoming events.

The PM Front Office, also now concerned, weighed in when PM/PDAS Tom Countryman sent an email directly to BGen Brier upon being included on the email I sent on October 21, 2009, "Subject: Greetings from your new incoming POLAD." BGen Brier responded on October 23, 2009:

> Thanks, Michelle. I'll be back at the office Monday and talk to Lee concerning the funding/timing issues. Sf Paul[3]

In the meantime, Tom replied directly to BGen Brier:

> Dear Paul: I just wanted to add my two cents on Michelle's note.
>
> First, as I told Tracy, you will be well pleased with Michelle's enthusiasm and knowledge. She is well connected to leadership of the State Department, and will provide you invaluable reach back to this building, and outreach to the Embassy country teams with whom you will be dealing.
>
> Secondly, I hope you will keep everything on track to get her to Stuttgart as soon as possible. She is ready and eager.
>
> Finally, and specifically, I want to endorse the idea of having her attend the Theater Security Cooperation Conference in Ramstein in November. She obviously won't be ready to represent your priorities, but simply being there as an auditor, and making the connection with your theater's DCMs, will pay big dividends down the road. When I started working for General Conway, I took every such opportunity to establish the connections and absorb the topics, even before I had anything intelligent of my own to add.
>
> Keep in mind that we can assist from this end in smoothing any bureaucratic hurdles and expediting her arrival. You will find her both loyal and valuable. S/F Tom[4]

On Friday, October 23, 2009, I sent the following email to Tom Countryman:

> Hey there Tom – Was just wondering if you had heard back from General Brier. I haven't as of yet. Thanks, Michelle[5]

Tom replied:

> No reply yet[6]

---

3   Paul Brier, email message to Tom Countryman and Michelle Stefanick, October 23, 2009
4   Tom Countryman, email message to Paul Brier and Michelle Stefanick, October 23, 2009
5   Michelle Stefanick, email message to Tom Countryman, October 23, 2009
6   Tom Countryman, email message to and Michelle Stefanick, October 23, 2009

As of October 23, 2009, according to Tom, he had not received a response back from BGen Brier. I'm not sure whether he ever did. However, I must admit, given the events that would occur and then to figure out *why* and *what* all this was really about, in reflection, some of the words selected/used by Tom in his email could appear to have a double apparent meaning than what *really was/is*, at least from my perspective. And given events that eventually occurred...

At the end of September, I met with Sid Kaplan to discuss my insights regarding the Promotion Panels, as well as my onward assignment as MARFOREUR/AF FPA/POLAD. Well-respected and well-connected, Sid had mentioned one of his fellow FSI Senior Seminar colleagues, USMC Major General Richard "Dick" Lake. They were still in touch, and Sid thought given my new assignment, Lake would be a good contact to consult with before heading out to Stuttgart. In a September 24, 2009 email, Sid indicated that though Lake, *"probably would not be on the usual list on consultations for a POLAD but would be a good guy to meet as the very recent G-2. Once you get into the consultations phase, we can set up a meeting."* I responded back that I was actually starting some of my consultations now, but as I would be attending Camp Atterbury the following week, I would be back in touch when I returned. At that time Sid had also noted in his September 24, 2009 email that USMC MajGen Lake advised him that he was now the Deputy Director of the National Clandestine Service for Community Human Intelligence at the CIA.

Back from Camp Atterbury, I reengaged with Sid regarding his suggestion to meet with MajGen Lake. On October 13, 2009, Sid Kaplan emailed MajGen Lake's phone information. I connected with MajGen Lake and on October 14, I emailed Sid to let him know of our planned lunch for October 26. Since I was now affiliated with PM, I also informed PM Official Kevin O'Keefe, also a Marine, of my plans to meet with MajGen Lake. Kevin asked me to send him the MajGen's contact information, which I emailed to him on October 15, 2009.

On October 26, 2009, MajGen Lake and I met for lunch at the Quarterdeck in Rosslyn, Virginia, right up the hill from the Iwo Jima Memorial, a spot I thought he would enjoy. I can only speak for myself, but I thought our lunch went well. He was very engaging, and I learned a lot, particularly about the insight he had regarding the USMC Female Engagement Teams (FETs). We discussed cultures, difference of cultures, and then also broached the topic of the apparent delay of my arrival to Stuttgart of which he appeared to take genuine interest and concern. Later I would email MajGen Lake, thanking him for being so kind and generous with his time and insights. His October 27 response requested that I keep him updated and forward progress on my situation and getting over to MAR-FOREUR/AF, kindly requesting to please send my contact info once I arrived. Shortly after my December 2, 2009 arrival at MARFOREUR/AF, as requested, I would send MajGen Lake my greetings along with my contact information.

On October 26, I would also follow-up with Sid Kaplan, thanking him for linking me up with MajGen Lake, whom I had just met earlier that day. On October 27, Sid Kaplan responded back, queried the status of my onward assignment. Unfortunately he had not yet had a chance to look over my Promotion Panel comments to be posted on the FMO listserve.

Despite the initial obstacles, I thought all was now on a positive trajectory. During the FPA/POLAD orientation, I was advised of the upcoming AFRICA COMMAND'S 2010 Theater Security Cooperation Conference (TSCC) November 15-20, 2009 in Ramstein, Germany. On September 23, 2009, Mark Swayne, the AFRICOM Interagency Liaison, would send me a copy of the applicable announcement cable. All those that I spoke with highly recommended that I attend and that I even needed to attend given my new position. However, it was not my call, and possibly was not even feasible until I arrived at MARFOREUR/AF. With my arrival plans still mysteriously in limbo, I wasn't sure I would be attending, let alone even continuing to be assigned to MARFOREUR/AF. Yet, everyone I spoke with during consultations adamantly stated that I needed to be there.

Despite not arriving in October as initially scheduled, and in accordance with my initial official orders, on November 3, I got word from Major Robert Cano that BGen Brier had decided that he would like for me to attend this AFRICOM TSCC conference if feasibly possible. The intent would be for me to attend the executive sessions with check-in on November 15 and competition/departure on November 18. We made it happen. I was delighted to attend and to finally meet my new boss MARFOREUR/AF BGen Brier for the first time.

On November 12, 2009, Unclassified State Cable 116791 was sent FR SECSTATE WASHDC TO AMEMBASSY BERLIN SUBJECT: ARRIVAL NOTICE (STEFANICK, MICHELLE L.).

With my personal effects all packed and on their way to either Stuttgart or storage and my house rented, I would arrive in Berlin on Monday, November 30 for consultations. I would depart Berlin for Stuttgart, arriving at MARFOREUR/AF on December 2, 2009. My sponsor MAR-FOREUR/AF Staff Judge Advocate (SJA) Major William Hennessy was there to pick me up at the airport. I finally arrived ready and was excited for my new assignment.

CHAPTER 5

WHAT THE HELL IS GOING ON:
The Good, The Bad, And The Ugly

TENSIONS RISING

Writing this book to this point has been extremely difficult. And from this point on, it will be even more so; this is because I will have to relive the nightmare, the horrific nightmare, I had been forced to endure which will be reflected in these next chapters. This is over and above the experiences I've written about to this point, the Embassy bombing and its aftermath. With that, if I knew then what I know now, I would never, ever, have bid on an assignment/detail with our US military. I wasn't prepared for what I would be exposed to and experience at the hands of the institution I fondly respected and honored when I placed my bids. Given the circumstances I had endured to that point in my career within State Department, and given my utmost respect for our US military, I placed those assignment bids with honor to and for the institutions and the positions for which I might be selected. As difficult as these next chapters are going to be to write and relive, I present the facts as they are, as they occurred, and as I became aware of them, the truth, no matter what.

My official travel orders authorized me two work-day consultations at Embassy Berlin prior to my arrival to MARFOREUR/AF. Despite being detailed with the Marines, many administrative support functions I would be receiving during this assignment would be provided by the Embassy Berlin Administrative staff. This was in accordance with the applicable Memorandum of Understanding (MOU) between the Department of State and the Department of Defense in Support of the Political Advisor (POLAD) Program. The MOU specified terms, relationships and conditions under which State FPA/POLADs serve with DOD military commands in the United States and overseas and with service DOD Chiefs of Staff; it was signed June 14, 2000, then amended, signed and effective October 18, 2002, with a superseding MOU still in draft at the time of my assignment. The following legal authorities supported the MOU: 22 USC. 2685, 22 USC. 3983, and 22 USC. 2778(g)(8). Attached to the MOU was the applicable list of positions at DOD covered under the agreement and the list of positions at State covered under the agreement. My SFS MARFOREUR/AF FPA/POLAD position was clearly identified in these DOS and DOD documents.

On Sunday evening, November 29, 2009, I departed Dulles International Airport via United Flight 0952 to arrive Monday morning, November 30 at Frankfurt International. From Frankfurt, I departed via United Flight 8970 (operated by Lufthansa) for Berlin Tegel Airport. As arranged by the Embassy, I stayed at the Westin Grand. I met with many points of contact throughout the Embassy, including DCM Greg Delawie, previously assigned with the PM Bureau at Main State. Upon my arrival with MARFOREUR/AF, I would be staying at the Stuttgart Marriott Hotel Sindelfingen until I could locate permanent housing.

Arriving during the holiday season, I visited a Christmas Market in a local German town with my colleague from Nairobi days, Ron Roughead, who was a defense subcontractor working at AFRICOM at the time. And speaking of AFRICOM, I attended General Ward's Holiday Party at his residence, the mansion known as Clay House. For decades, this mansion housed the senior US military commander in Stuttgart, Germany. On July 24, 2012, the US military officially returned the Clay House to the German government. Delighted that I was given the opportunity to view this historic residence before it was returned, I was even more delighted to be working with, albeit this time in a support role, AFRICOM Commander General Ward, since we had worked together previously when I was with State/Legislative Affairs (H). Reacquainting with Ron was short-lived as he would not be staying in Stuttgart much longer, as he soon after returned back to the US due to some defense contractor employment matter

Within weeks of my arrival, it appeared I might have found a wonderful house in Sindelfingen. The landlord lived in France and kept the home for her mother, who had recently passed away. Make-ready work had to be completed and my personal effects had to be delivered, but shortly thereafter I would be settled in with a few drama issues needing to be addressed along the way. One pertained to the landlord's family, and the other—many of my personal items were damaged, destroyed and/or missing in transport, like never before in my career. Events subtle enough for me to take notice, but not yet realize the importance, like the slow boiling of a frog, or perhaps, a slow death by a thousand cuts. Perhaps. But again, at that time, something was off, just not right. And I took notice.

Now, of course, I was experiencing my own period of transition on both a personal level and a work level; common place for a new FS assignment/position and my FS assignment/position being the whole reason for my being there. However, in this new FS assignment/position with the MS, an undercurrent was continually there. And in time, it would show its ugly face one too many times for me to just suck it up.

Being the first FPA/POLAD for MARFOREUR/AF was not only an honor but a humbling experience, particularly given the close, long-standing relationship State has with the US Marine Corps as they serve by our side guarding many of our Embassies or when responding to a 911 call for evacuation assistance. My first responsibility was to establish and foster a professional relationship with the MARFOREUR/AF Commanding General based on mutual respect and trust. And on behalf of our two institutions, I was to engender an understanding of my role and the insights that I would bring to the Marine Corps table. I believe I successfully accomplished this as the BGen continually sought my counsel on matters with foreign policy/interagency organizational implications. He also asked me to accompany him on his travels and to meetings, briefings, and conferences.

Being a dual-hatted service component meant MARFOREUR/AF supported fifty-three countries under EUCOM's AOR, and fifty-three countries under AFRICOM's AOR. Admiral James Stavridis was Commander of EUCOM and Supreme Commander of the North Atlantic Treaty Organization (NATO), and General William "Kip" Ward was Commander of AFRICOM. Accompanying the BGen to senior leadership/strategic conferences for both EUCOM and AFRICOM, I heard first-hand from the visionary strategic leadership of Admiral Stavridis and General Ward respectively. Both were strong advocates of the interagency and *of their supporting roles* to State's lead role for US foreign policy.

My most engaging outreach effort was when I developed and conducted "State 101—Department of State Familiarization" PowerPoint (yes, PowerPoint) presentations for the Marines of the greater Stuttgart area. Having Marines teach and share with me their PowerPoint expertise and skills in its development generated open, frank dialogues and exchanges that I believe were necessary in order to move our institutions forward. The response was unanimously positive with requests for the PowerPoint and for subsequent discussions. I enthusiastically responded positively to and for both. A second PowerPoint iteration evolved called, "Dept of State/Dept of Defense—A Marriage of Necessity."

To paint only a rosy picture during this time would be inaccurate. For instance, in Liberia, where MARFOREUR/AF was engaged in an important effort, a very unfortunate situation occurred. Our Ambassador to Liberia at the time was Linda Thomas-Greenfield, a FS colleague who had served with me previously in Nairobi, Kenya and who departed prior to the August 7, 1998 Embassy bombing. Soon after my arrival, I had been requested to be involved regarding a sensitive matter. The matter resulted in Ambassador Thomas-Greenfield removing two back-to-back Officer-in-Charge (OIC) MARFORAF Marine Colonels. My awareness, advisement, and involvement regarding this MARFORAF-conducted investigated matter did not sit well with some in the Command. Due to the Ambassador's and BGen Brier's leadership, reinforced by trust that I helped facilitate between them, the situation was remedied through our strong support of the Ambassador's and our efforts there. At least this is we thought, I thought, at the time.

My first trip accompanying BGen Brier overseas would be to Djibouti. Camp Lemonnier is home to the Combined Joint Task Force–Horn of Africa (CJTF-HOA), with which I first became familiar during my previous assignment to Khartoum, Sudan from 2003 to 2005. Now also a US Naval Expeditionary base, it is still the only US base currently located on the continent of Africa. During our trip, we met with our Ambassador and members of his country team, Djiboutian Government officials, and others, to include the French Foreign Legion. At one point, we took a helicopter ride across the region. During this flight, there was a brief mechanical incident. At the time, I must admit, I didn't think anything of it because I was with our US Marines. They didn't panic, so why should I? In due time, however, I would reflect back on this incident as well as the French connection, to include my new landlord, with a different lens. Do I suspect more to these, including the helicopter malfunction incident? Yes. But how do I, a single female, prove it? I mean *this is the US Military afterall.*

In March 2010, I would attend a PM/POLAD Conference back in the US. During this time, I wanted to obtain copies of the *1 Year Anniversary of Embassy Bombings in Kenya & Tanzania* videos. Given that a Marine was killed that dreadful day, I thought BGen Brier would want to watch it and have a copy for the Command Library as well as General Ward since US Africa Command did not even exist at the time of the bombings. Oddly enough, when I went by the Office of Casualty Assistance, created and established in the aftermath the August 7, 1998 East Africa Embassy bombings, they didn't have copies available. They advised that I check with the Video Production Unit (VPU) that made the videos. Even more oddly, initially VPU could not locate the videos either, until they checked inside a box of items being packaged to be sent to the National Archives. Finally, I obtained a compact disc (CD) copy of the three original videos.

Back at MARFOREUR/AF, I had 5 CD sets made: one for the Commander, BGen Brier; one for his Command, MARFOREUR/AF; one for General Ward; one for his Command, AFRICOM; and one for my office, the MARFOREUR/AF FPA/POLAD office, my replacement's historical record. I believe BGen Brier was sincerely appreciative when I gave him a copy. I then personally gave a set to the MARFORAF COS Colonel Lapaix, who appeared sincerely and genuinely appreciative. I advised that since a Marine, an MSG, was killed that day, MARFOREUR/AF should have a set for their library. Since Colonel Lapaix lived in close proximity to AFRICOM Gen Ward, I gave him two additional sets and asked if he wouldn't mind hand-delivering these to General Ward on my behalf. Colonel Lapaix said he would. As I recall I received a note soon after from General Ward thanking me for the videos.

On April 26, 2010, the same as years prior, I received from my CDA Paul Sutphin an email forwarding State Cable 042119 dated April 24, 2010, SUBJECT: "2010 Omnibus Skill Code Change/Conversion." Unlike years prior, I would not send Paul an email regarding my interest in submitting an application. For in June 2008, I opened my window for entry/promotion consideration into the SFS. Though I had been in stretch assignments—positions of responsibility above my pay grade— before, this time I would be in an OC-stretch assignment, an SFS entry level stretch assignment. This assignment could either make or break my career, in the worst case scenario, I would be TICed-out of the FS in October 2015 if not promoted.

During this time, there were continual colonel clash flare-ups. I had no idea what I would endure in this upcoming rating period. And again, I was and remained of the continual mind-set that all that was occurring was due to *foreign service vs. military service* institutional tensions built-up as a result of the two ongoing wars and the carry-over to the non-war AORs. But then again, with the Global War on Terror, from the military perspective there were no non-war AORs. In due time, I would realize this wasn't an institutional issue at all; it was a very personal, targeted one—and the target was me.

By the time of Colonel Lapaix's departure, we had established a professional respect for one another. His replacement as MARFORAF COS would come from within the Command; he was a Colonel involved and still very bitter in the aftermath of the Liberia ordeal. That was on the MARFORAF side of the Command.

Regarding Colonel Niblock, I believed as well that in our own way, professional respect for one another was also established. His MARFO-REUR COS replacement would come from outside the Command. With the new incoming COS, the sniff test started all over again—and went downhill fast. What made it bearable, however, was having the new Sergeant Major (SgtMaj). SgtMaj Ronald Green was a solid, well-grounded professional, and in a few years would become the 18th Sergeant Major of the Marine Corps. And soon, with rotations, personnel changes, and events that would occur, leadership would be tested all around.

In June 2010, Edward Alden published an article in the *Foreign Service Journal* called, "Remembering Mary Ryan." The article was prefaced like this, "The Late CA Assistant Secretary's 2002 Dismissal was a transforming event in the modern history of the consular service." The article began like this:

> No part of the US government—not the Federal Bureau of Investigation, the Central Intelligence Agency or the National Security Council—was more shaken by the terrorist attacks of 9/11 than the consular corps of the State Department.

From my perspective, the article fell short in its coverage of the crucial event prior to 9/11, and Ryan's role following the August 7, 1998 East Africa Embassy bombings. My response was published in the October 2010 issue of *Foreign Service Journal*, called "For the (Congressional) Record." I wrote what I felt and received many positive reactions and responses. For example:

> ...though Alden's article makes a passing mention of the 1998 bombings, it does not show the true impact this dreadful moment had on our Foreign Service and our institutional family, including Amb. Ryan...

From June 30 to July 17, I was back in Washington for consultations and meeting with officials at the Pentagon and State; I had meetings with many old faces, and was introduced to many new ones. With my legislative background, BGen Brier suggested that I meet with Colonel Brian Murtha, as well as many other USMC Marines and officials. Colonel Murtha and I chatted about legislation/Hill insight and how I was from the Johnstown area. I passed along my sympathies regarding the recent passing of his uncle, Congressman John Murtha, just a few months earlier in February. At that time, I was not made aware of the internal USMC decision regarding the elevation of both MARFOREUR and MARFORAF to three-star level Commands, let the alone the implications thereof, timing, etc. I returned to MARFOREUR/AF and soon after, on August 17, 2010, Lieutenant General (LtGen) Hejlik (three-star) took Command of MARFOREUR. BGen Brier became MARFOREUR Deputy Commander and remained MARFORAF Commander. Until early 2008, LtGen Hejlik headed Marine Special Operations Command (MARSOC). MARFOREUR COS Colonel Adam Copp, who arrived in July 2010, also worked previously at MARSOC, and now remained LtGen Hejlik's COS. As the dual-hatted MARFOREUR/AF FPA/POLAD, and for the record, I never had a one-on-one introductory meeting or any other direct discussion/meeting alone with the new MARFOREUR Commander, LtGen Dennis Hejlik.

In the fall of 2010, the official promotion cable was released and my name was not on it. Given I'd just arrived in my new assignment, and had just opened my window in June 2008 for SFS entry consideration, I was momentarily disappointed, but not discouraged at my prospects. But I was discouraged with the turn of events at MARFOREUR/AF.

On November 13, 2010, I emailed Kurt Amend, the Department of State's new PM/PDAS regarding the continual hostility and resistance to my position I was experiencing, at MAFROREUR/AF particularly and specifically with the Colonels. At the time, I wasn't sure whether this hostility was due to me personally or to these new congressionally-authorized and funded, expanded State Department Foreign Policy Advisor/POLAD positions writ large. Initially, my conjecture was it was the latter. In due time, I would come to realize it was the former. It was me. With the question remaining, why?

On November 18, 2010, I received a response back from PM/PDAS Kurt Amend, copying PM/POLAD Coordinator Gonzalo Gallegos and his Deputy Jerry Sullivan. Interestingly enough, Kurt's response was not one I was expecting; it was puzzling actually, given the issues at hand and given that I had sent a previous draft to his PM/PDAS predecessor Tom Countryman, so Tom knew first-hand what I was reporting. On November 11, I had sent the email draft to Tom. On November 12, Tom replied with minor edits, including the following remark:

Michelle: Very clear. See my little edits, then send it off to Kurt Amend, and ask him to discuss at earliest opportunity. You should come to view as a confessor for POLADs as I tried to be. Best, T[1]

Prior to sending the email to Kurt Amend on November 13, I replied to Tom Countryman:

Thank you so very much Tom for your time, insight and support. I'll keep you posted as this week didn't end on a very good note regarding COS Copp, though I believe I am making progress on the other three Colonels as I think they now see continually taking me on will not result in a positive... and finally, having me on their team will. Have a great weekend. cheers, michelle[2]

Based on his response, either Kurt didn't have an understanding of the issue at hand, or there was some kind of *other agenda* at play. On November 19, 2010, I forwarded Kurt's response to Tom Countryman, expressing my disappointment with the following remark:

Hello there Tom—Hope all is well. Needless to say, I'm disappointed with this response/insight and when I return from my TDY to Kiev will again think out next steps. Cheers, Michelle[3]

On December 5, 2010, I forwarded my November 13 email exchange with PM/PDAS Kurt Amend to U/S Patrick Kennedy. The email exchange was called "MARFOREUR/AF FPA/POLAD POSITION—Points for Consideration."

In the meantime, on Monday November 29, 2010, I sent the following email to EUCOM POLAD/Deputy Katherine Canavan, PM/PDAS Kurt Amend, PM/POLAD Director Gonzalo Gallegos, AFRICOM Deputy Anthony Holmes, AFRICOM FPA Raymond Brown:

Subject: Insights from MARFOREUR/AF FPA

Hello there Kate—Hope you had a Happy Thanksgiving, and now enjoying the snow.

As requested during our meeting of November 4, 2010, here's a reassessment of the situation after Thanksgiving.

The two MARFORAF Colonels—COS and G3/5—have made a noticeable difference in their outreach and approach to me, particularly in light of the recent AFRICOM TSCC in Ramstein

---

1   Tom Countryman, email message to Michelle Stefanick, November 12, 2010
2   Michelle Stefanick, email message to Tom Countryman, November 13, 2010
3   Michelle Stefanick, email message to Tom Countryman, November 12, 2010

and the leadership messaging consistently presented at the forum.

Regarding the MARFOREUR Colonels, after attending EU-COM's Flexible Leadership exercise November 10, 2010 with the MARFOREUR G3/5 Colonel, our relationship seems to have hit a new level of appreciation with respect for which I am also pleased.

For some reason, however, the MARFOREUR COS has been even more marginalizing to me and my position then [sic] before our November 4th meeting, creating yet once again a belittling event just last week between me and LtGen Hejlik, the new three-star Commander of MARFOREUR. This continual marginalization by the MARFOREUR COS, in light of the improvement and appreciation reflected by the other three Colonels I have to work with at both MARFOREUR and MARFORAF being dual-hatted, is also quite demoralizing as his being the "senior colonel" and direct linkage to the new MARFOREUR Commander.

As the new MARFORAF three-star Commander has yet to be confirmed, my intent was to stop by Washington in transit to my holiday leave with my family in mid-December and/or in return from the holidays. As being uniquely dual-hatted and now with two three-star Generals, one one-star (in two-star billet) General as well as two COSs and two G3/5s for both MARFOREUR and MARFORAF, I believe now is the best time to have discussion in the Department about this situation with officials in PM as well as others. Since the MARFOREUR COS has denied this trip under their funding, I will be asking PM to assist with funding this, otherwise I will foot the bill personally myself as I do believe now is the best time to discuss this situation in Washington, and the possible ways forward in the best interest of the Department of State.

As I am heading out on TDY to South Africa until the end of the week, I wanted to get you this requested assessment to you. Thank and have a great day. cheers, michelle[4]

Later that day, I forwarded this email with the following request to Tom Countryman:

Hello there Tom—Hope you had a great Thanksgiving! I really don't want to bring you into this, but was wondering if I stop by Department and you are free, if I could stop by to see you just for a quick chat? cheers, m[5]

4   Michelle Stefanick, email message to Katherine Canavan, Kurt Amend, Gonzalo Gallegos, Anthony Holmes, Raymond Brown, November 29, 2010
5   Michelle Stefanick, email message to Tom Countryman, November 29, 2010

Though I did not know it at the time, in a matter of months I would become not the first Department of State Foreign Service detailed FPA/POLAD to depart early/curtail their assignment with the USMC, nor the second, but at least the third, that I am aware of. Tom Countryman was one of the others. And Tom was the Department of State Foreign Policy Advisor/POLAD for the Commandant of the USMC itself.

What I also was not aware of was that per *the Marine Corps Order, commands with a new Commander must complete this survey, a Command Climate Survey, within 90 days of their assumption of command.* The purpose of a US Military Command Climate Survey is to establish a baseline climate assessment, enabling transparency and accountability, detect and correct emerging hot spots for harmful behaviors and climate issues, and identify areas of promise and healthy command climates. In essence, it provides a Commander with a tool for gathering perspectives and opinions on unit leadership, cohesion, and elements of the human relations environment such as discrimination and sexual harassment/assault. The MARFO-REUR Command Climate Survey was due by November 15, 2010, with the arrival of the new three-star realignment MARFOREUR Commander, Lieutenant General (LtGen) Dennis Hejlik.

On November 14, 2010, as uncomfortable as it was, I attended the AF-RICOM TSCC. I would drive to Ramstein with SgtMaj Green. Then, on Wednesday, November 17, 2010, I would depart the AFRICOM TSCC early to fly to Kyiv, Ukraine. I was to meet up with and then accompany MARFOREUR Lt. Col. Dan Ward on consultations with the Embassy Country team regarding some unanticipated issues on an upcoming exercise. A very short trip, I departed on Friday, November 19, 2010. My participatory inclusion was both unexpected and puzzling, particularly in hindsight, given the controversial role Ukraine soon played in US politics.

On November 22, 2010, I requested use-or-lose leave/consultations back in Washington D.C. to discuss the elevation of both MARFOREUR and MARFORAF to 3-star level. The request would be denied.

And on November 23, 2010, I attended a MARFOREUR staff meeting where I was intentionally humiliated.

That Thanksgiving holiday I spent in Munich with a colleague from my Nairobi, Kenya days, Caroline Truesdall who was now assigned at our Consulate in Frankfurt. Interestingly enough, out of the blue, last minute, and totally unexpected, I was invited for Thanksgiving by EUCOM's Deputy POLAD. Unfortunately, I had to decline the offer, already having Thanksgiving plans.

On November 29, 2010, EUCOM POLAD Kate Canavan's email to me specifically references meeting on December 13 or 14, 2010, appearing in hindsight that the purpose of this meeting was already predetermined.

On December 13, 2010, as preplanned, and obviously preorchestrated, *the question being with who*, I met with State/EUCOM POLAD Kate Canavan and MARFOREUR/AF BGen Brier. Needless to say, during this meeting with BGen Brier and Kate, their outcome was apparently predetermined. Despite Kate's HR and S/FS background, she ignored all basic State Department HR requirements. She never referenced the necessity of a counseling session, nor the documenting concerns and issues to be addressed in writing, nor on what authority she, Kate, had regarding this particularly meeting, let alone the outcome of this meeting, given she was not in my EER evaluation chain. Interestingly enough, however, Kate Canavan subsequently does reference such basic State Department HR requirements in her March 16, 2011 EEO Investigative response, and interestingly enough after her returning from consultations in Washington, D.C with Main State, our US Department of State Headquarters. Again, during this December 13, 2010 meeting, Kate never references on what, whose authority, particularly at Main State Department she had regarding this particular meeting, let alone the outcome of this meeting. So on what and whose authority from US Department of State, Washington was she speaking on behalf during this meeting, given I was FS, as was she? Or was she? Or instead, maybe instead from someone outside State Department all together. Even from the Department of Defense, perhaps? To this day, that question remains unanswered. Why?

On December 23, 2010, taking use-or-lose leave for Christmas Holiday back in US, I met with U/S Patrick Kennedy to brief him on this newly implemented two three-star realignment and the situation.

And on January 3, 2011, I returned to my MARFOREUR/AF Command US Department of State foreign service FPA/POLAD assignment in accordance with U/S Kennedy's instructions.

On January 7, 2011, I received an email from PM/POLAD Director Gonzalo Gallegos that included a list of PM position vacancies for me to consider. Having had very frank discussions with Gonzalo as well as U/S Kennedy while back in the US on leave, the decision was for me to stay in my current position until I located a position that I wanted—staying in a post where I was not wanted, where my expertise and skills were not appreciated, setting me up for failure and never giving me a chance from the very start, even before I arrived. Needless to say, I seriously looked over the list immediately. Seeing a position that interested me, I responded back to Gonzalo soon after receipt, on the same day, January 7, 2011. The position was a domestic assignment: FO-01 SDE (State Defense Exchang) Africa TED 8/11 (Pentagon).

Soon after, I officially bid on the position in order to depart MARFOREUR/AF prior to the end of my original three-year assignment. On April 6, 2011, I received notification of my onward assignment. But obviously, based on actions that would occur after my return on January 3, 2011, my immediate arrangement for an early departure/new onward assignment wasn't enough for some at MARFOREUR/AF—the actions taken against me would become personal, even more personal than previously. They would become targeted.

After spending the 2010-2011 Christmas Holiday with my family and then attending RW in Charleston, I was back in my office catching up when I watched on television with horror the replaying of the shooting of Gabby Giffords and eighteen others. It was January 8, 2011. I had just seen Congresswoman Giffords and her husband Mark Kelly at RW. I met Gabby when I attended my first RW in December 2006-January 2007. Previously working in Senator Snowe's office, and then at the time, working in State/Legislative Affairs Office (H), we briefly chatted, sharing some friendly congressional commonalities. Though I was briefly introduced to Mark Kelly, her husband, and had only a few kind word exchanges over the years, my heart was broken for them both. That year's RW was the last that I attended, having no idea of what I, myself, would soon be enduring.

On January 17, 2011, LtGen John Paxton (three-star) took command of MARFORAF. BGen Brier became Deputy Commander for both MARFOREUR and MARFORAF. This elevation officially split MARFOREUR/AF into MARFOREUR and MARFORAF now commanded by two different three-star Generals, both located back in the US and not in Germany. Given that my original dual-hatted role was in support of the MARFOREUR/AF Command General, this new organizational change put me in an even more untenable position. I discussed this exact matter frankly with U/S Patrick Kennedy when I returned back to the US. Given the documented track record and pattern with now more than one other State Department FPA/POLAD's early departure from other USMC Commands, and mine now obviously in the works as well. Department higher-level Management Officials now questioned whether the USMC really even wanted State Department FPA/POLADS at all. As the MAR-

FORAF FPA/POLAD, for the record, I never had a one-on-one introductory meeting or any other direct discussion/meeting alone with the
MARFOREUR Commander, LtGen Paxton.

And in accordance with the Marine Corps Order, the applicable MAR-
FORAF Command Climate Survey was due by April 17, 2011. This survey as required within 90 days of their assumption of a new Commander,
with the arrival of the new three-star realignment MARFORAF Commander, Lieutenant General (LtGen) John Paxton.

INDIGNITIES, LARGE AND SMALL

On February 9, 2011, I received a Promotion Ceremony Invite from
David Elmo. I had met David Elmo while I was attending the Army
War College. He came to Carlisle for a work-related matter, and had heard
that I, a fellow FS colleague, was there in attendance. In addition to being
FS, David was also an Army Reservist. He decided he would track me
down to introduce himself. We met for a chat later that day, on Thursday,
February 26, 2009. Fast forward, and now David was being promoted
to Brigadier General. He was assigned to US Army Europe, and General Carter Ham, who would soon become the second Commander of US
Africa Command, would be pinning on David's first star at his promotion
ceremony. Upon receiving the Promotion Ceremony invite, I informed
MARFOREUR and MARFORAF COSs accordingly regarding attendance since there were linkages with both Commands. Due to their neg-
ative responses, regardless, I ended up taking annual leave to attend the
promotion ceremony of my own accord.

On the morning of February 11, 2011, I drove to Heidelberg to attend David's promotion ceremony. Also, in attendance was the US Consul
General from Frankfurt, and our mutual FS friend/colleague, Ned Alford.
I then drove over with Ned and his driver for the after-ceremony lunch at
a restaurant in old Heidelberg. As Ned used to work for U/S Patrick Kennedy, I shared some insight regarding my particular situation at that time.
When we arrived at the venue, I sat at the table with Ned and someone
he knew who served in Nairobi, as well as a couple from South Africa.
The table discussion found its way onto Nairobi. The man who had previously served there mentioned something about poor Charlie losing his
staff. Given the fact that Charlie Slater didn't even arrive at post until days
after the bombings, and as it was my staff, my FMC family that was injured or killed that day not his, well, you can imagine the next comments
that came out of my mouth regarding Charlie and the facts to this matter.

Soon after this enlightenment, Ned and the man who previously served in Nairobi left the table to have a smoke outside. As I recall, when they returned to the table, nothing more was said regarding Nairobi. We enjoyed the remainder of the lunch, again congratulated David for his promotion, and Ned's driver was instructed to drive back to my car. I drove back to Sindelfingen, reflecting on the day's events.

From February 22 to March 2, 2011, I attended the AFRICOM Judicious Response Exercise held at US Army Africa in Vicenza, Italy. On February 24, 2011 at 7:29 a.m., I received an email:

> Good Morning Ma'am
>
> My name is Sgt Schilt and this morning when I was parking reversed into the side of your car. There is a dent on the driver's side rear door. I was wondering if I can just pay to get it fixed or if you would like me to call my insurance and get it fixed that way. I am very sorry and Apologize for the inconvenience I am causing you along with the damage to the car.
> V/R
> Sgt Luke Schilt
> G6 Operations Planner/Tech
> US Marine Corps Forces Africa[6]

I responded at 8:19 a.m.:

> Sgt Schilt—thank you for letting (me) know of the accident. I'm currently tdy until March 5. That being said the keys to my car are in my office. It really doesn't matter to me which way the car is repaired. As long as it is repaired as professionally as it can be I would be happy. Let me know how you would like to proceed. Cheers, m[7]

I took Sgt Schilt at his word, that he backed into my car. In the meantime, with nothing more that I could do until I returned, I immediately contacted MARFOREUR/AF Executive Assistant (EA) Macarena Smith and SgtMaj Green regarding the matter and asked if they could go out and check the damage. For, as I was on official travel for MARFORAF attending the AFRICOM-sponsored exercise in Vicenza, Italy, my car was parked in my assigned official parking spot in front of MARFOREUR/AF Command Headquarters located on Panzer Kaserne, a US Army Garrison. Due to events soon to follow, this event would be

---

6   Luke Schlit, email message to Michelle Stefanick, February 24, 2011
7   Michelle Stefanick, email message to Luke Schilt, February 24, 2011.

the trigger, the tipping-point event, the reason I would file a formal EEO complaint.

As the purpose of this book is of a more severe national security implication, of which an unjust EEO Grievance complaint process I endured is just a part, I will not provide all the excruciating details to what I would experience and/or witness. As a senior Female USG leader, I had no choice. The smashing of my car door wasn't accidental; it was intentional. This event and others, particularly those that would follow, crossed a line. I paid a dear price for standing my ground, standing for truth and justice, or in my case, against injustice. But as this storyline proceeds, one will understand the implications involved, and why it was necessary for me to do so—for in time, it would become apparent this was not just an abuse of an EEO grievance process, but surely an obstruction of justice to the levels of potential high treason.

Due to events occurring within the AFRICOM AOR, the Judicious Response exercise would be cut short. On March 2, 2011, I returned from official travel back to MARFOREUR/AF Headquarters and saw the damage to my car for myself. The damage was such that I could still drive the car, as apparently the intent was to send a message. I contacted Sgt Schilt accordingly regarding car door repairs, and next steps.

On March 7, 2011, the MARFORAF Climate Survey email requesting a completion of no later than April 1, 2011 was sent out on behalf of MARFORAF Commander LtGen Paxton. Neither MARFOREUR/AF EA Macarena Smith nor myself, MARFOREUR/AF FPA/POLAD received this email.

On March 9, 2011, I attended the AFRICOM change of command; the first AFRICOM Commander, General William E. Ward relinquished command to General Carter F. Ham.

Though I cannot confirm the US Army's exact requirement at that time and for that level of Command, I am assuming there was a similar "within 90 days" requirement as the US Marine Corps. US Africa Command Climate Survey would then have been due no later than June 7, 2011 with General Ham assuming command. Additionally, a survey may have been conducted prior to General Ward relinquishing command, which is my understanding of what occurred. Regardless, if the US Army requires a Command Survey to be conducted, General Ham, the incoming US Africa Commander, requested one of all applicable supporting Commands, to include MARFORAF.

Needless to say, the fact that my car door was smashed into by a Marine while it was parked in my official space in front of MARFORAF Headquarters located on a US Army Garrison while I was away on official travel for MARFORAF is quite telling. Particularly, when it occurs so soon after I returned to Germany as U/S Patrick Kennedy had instructed me to do so, and despite Kate Canavan's December 13, 2010 meeting. Thus, the importance, significance and implication of these such Marine Command required, and then soon after a subsequently Combatant Command requested Command Survey results was quite indicative that there indeed was something more substantive internally at play. And regardless of me, my presence. But yet, these applicable Command Survery results were being used *against me* as a means to *their end*, to get me removed from this assignment, my US Department of State foreign service FPA/PO-LAD position with MARFOREUR/AF. Apparently, my presence, and my presence alone, being the apparent reason, the sole reason, for all that was being reported and exposed in these applicable Climate Surveys. For this apparent and such irrational explanation to be considered, let alone used, questions need to be asked by whom? More precisely, who, by name and rank, and of course, the why? Who benefitted? Then, to go to such lengths, to order, to authorize such extremities such as smashing my car door in targeting, retaliatory actions against me, particularly since I already was making plans to depart my, this, State Department FS assignment/position early.

On March 10, 2011, after patiently waiting for a status regarding car repair, I reached out to Sgt Schilt's chain of command. I received a response later that day.

On Sunday March 27, 2011, I sent the following email to three individuals. Ron Roughead, who served with me in Nairobi, Kenya and was assigned there during the August 7, 1998 Embassy bombings and its aftermath; Raymond Maxwell, who was my Post Management Officer (PMO) when I was assigned to Khartoum, Sudan from 2003-2005; and Ned Alford, who was an *old Africa Hand* such as myself, that I've known for years, and had most recently seen while attending David Elmo's promotion ceremony on February 11, 2011. The email was individually sent to Ned at 6:07 a.m., Ray at 6:08 a.m., and Ron at 6:11 a.m., and it went like this:

> Hello there (Ned, Ray, Ron)—Hope all is well. I've held on to this too long and I just wanted to share something with you...

I'm a strong advocate of due process and as I've never really gotten my side of the story out regarding Kenya, I just wanted to
pass along some insight to you. While assigned there, I broke up
a fraud ring involving GSO. Though I did this primarily through
implementing stronger internal controls, the effect was just the
same. At the time I had my suspicions on whether it involved
more than just FSNs. Now how many years of vindictiveness
again and again later by one particularly individual, I do indeed
have my suspicions that more than FSNs were involved. Hope
sometime soon I can fill in more of the specifics and particulars,
but at this time, I just wanted you to be aware---as its time for my
side of the story to start being heard. I think you will know who I
am talking about…Thanks, michelle[8]

Without sharing their responses, I stood by this at the time and stand
by it now. MARFORAF now had copies of the 1 Year Anniversary video
set. Given that a Marine had been killed that day on August 7, 1998, a
fellow Marine's comments were included in these videos, as well as mine.
With a still open and on-going FBI investigation, I assumed the USMC
wanted the truth and justice for their Marine who was killed that day as
much as I did for my FMC staff and colleagues who were killed. At that
time, I still did not connect the events that were occurring at MARFO-
REUR and MARFORAF to the Embassy bombings, and my status as a
DOJ victim/witness. In due time, all that would change.

On Sunday March 27, 2011, I also sent the following email to Pat Hartnett-Kelly. Pat served with me in Nairobi, Kenya and had already departed
post by the time of the Embassy bombing. Pat drafted the infamous cable
months prior regarding the security posture of the Embassy, accredited to
Ambassador Bushnell for sending. Curiously and interestingly enough,
despite departing post months before the August 7, 1998 Embassy
Bombing, Pat would be the Embassy Nairobi ARB *accountable* RSO. With
our applicable backgrounds—her law enforcement background and my
OIG/professional auditor/accounting background—over the years, we
continually discussed the bombing. My March 27, 2011 email went like
this:

hi—are you free to talk today? Hope all is well. Cheers, m.[9]

On Tuesday, March 29, 2011, Pat sent the following email response:

8   Michelle Stefanick, email message to Ron Roughead, Raymond Maxwell, and Ned Alford March 27, 2011.
9   Michelle Stefanick, email message to Pat Hartnett Kelly, March 27, 2011.

Hi...sorry I was not around to talk...what's new? Are you working on the Libyan issue?

take care, Pat[10]

To which I replied on Tuesday, March 29, 2011:

no not really...things have gotten very interesting here. Today I'm supposed to be paneled to head back to DC to work at OSD/ Pol-Af with Vicki Huddleston. A/S shapiro is also supposed to be talking to the Commandant of USMC...and seems this may have all played out because of our good ole buddy of kenya days...when is this all going to end! If you are around I can give you a call... hope all is well with you. cheers, m [11]

On March 28, 2011, I again requested the status of car door repairs.

On April 1, 2011, I was notified by PM that a former State contractor employee breached a State/Medical database and accessed the personal information of many State employees, including my information.

On or about April 5, 2011, Sgt Schilt and myself went to pick-up my car at the repair shop selected by Sgt Schilt, only to find the side-view mirror was cracked, supposedly at the car wash.

On April 6, 2011, Sgt Schilt and I returned to pick up the car after the mirror was supposed to be fixed. However, the man who was doing the work did not show up and no one could explain where he was. Getting bad vibes, I immediately got into my car and drove back to the Sindelfin-gen Mercedes dealership to order a side mirror replacement. Interest-ingly enough, though this April 6, 2011 incident and documented email support was provided to US Army Garrison (USAG) Stuttgart/Dept of Army/EEO Office Steve Matkowsky on May 11, 2011, for some reason, it was not and would not be included in the applicable DOD EEO Inves-tigative File.

Now realizing this smashed car door incident subsequently followed by the smashed car side mirror was not coincidental, but intentional, I also documented another odd event that occurred during this same time frame—after returning from Vicenza, Italy—this time, at my off-base res-idence in Sindelfingen.

Every day, usually in the morning before work, I would go for a walk in the nearby park. Exiting my side entrance, I started noticing that ev-ery morning for about a week or so, the top sunflower portion of a metal

---

10   Pat Hartnett Kelly email message to Michelle Stefanick, March 29, 2011.
11   Michelle Stefanick, email message to Pat Hartnett Kelly, March 29, 2011.

garden decoration left by the previous tenant, the landlord's sister, would be detached and lying on the ground. With every incident, I would re-attach. Then one morning, I proceeded out the side door only to notice that for some reason—despite the previous night's storm—the sunflower remained intact and attached on its posting. How odd that event was at the time, right after the smashed car side mirror incident. I not only took a photo of the cracked car side mirror, but of the sunflower garden dec-oration to document this event as well, particularly since it occurred at my off-base residence. These events and many others were threats, subtle threats, to let me know that they knew where I lived.

Finally, it was official. I received an email from my HR/CDO Robin Angel Smith with Subject: RE: 4/5/11 Assignments Panel—Stefanick. *It was finally official. Why it took so long to begin with, I have no idea. But fi-nally, and as MARFOEUR/AF wanted,* my assignment at MARFOREUR/ AF was curtailed by seventeen months. I was assigned to the position I was informed of on January 7, 2011, and immediately bid on thereafter, the 01 Pentagon OSD J5 Africa SDE (State Defense Exchange) Position. Relieved there was finally a concrete end in sight, all I had to do was sur-vive, literally and figuratively—and wait for my official travel orders to be issued.

On April 8, 2011, realizing this smashed car door followed by the smashed car side mirror incident and the sunflower incident at my off-base residence was more than coincidental in light of all events and the environment at MARFOREUR/AF, I reached out to discuss/report events to the Garrison's Base IG. I felt personally threatened and that it crossed the line in regards to a harassment/hostile work environment. The sunflower incident would not be the only one involving my off-base residence. Odd items were intentionally being left at my side-door en-trance, and along the trail I would walk every day. The subtle messaging was becoming even more nuanced and apparent—at least to me. And giv-en the location, it was an apparent message personally to me and only for me. Someone wanted my attention. So I sent a subtle message back. After a few days of observing this, I began to pick the items up so I would have them as support. More items would be left—I still have some to this day, to include the items left outside my side door entrance. *But why? Why was all this occurring? And by whom?*

I initially met/reported the incident to US Army Europe (USAREUR) IG Mr. Johnson on Patch Barracks, headquarters location for US Euro-pean Command (EUCOM) as well as Special Operations Command,

Europe (SOCEUR). He advised that my case/situation was not IG appropriate, and to contact the United States Army Garrison (USAG) Stuttgart/Department of Army/Equal Employment Opportunity (EEO) Office because my redress was with their office. I then reached out to State/AFSA Legal Counsel Neera Parikh to arrange for a discussion.

On Monday, April 11, 2011, as advised, I went to USAG Stuttgart/Depart of Army/EEO Office to meet and discuss events, to include my State/FS status, with Steven Markowsky. Due to the unique circumstances and my State/foreign service status, he needed to consult accordingly before advising on how to proceed.

In the meanwhile, I requested the status of my car mirror repair from Sgt Schilt. I discussed the situation with State/AFSA Legal Counsel Neera Parikh as well.

On Tuesday, April 12, 2011, I received the following email from USAG Stuttgart/Dept of Army/EEO Office Manager Steven Matkowsky's Subject: Per Yesterday's Conversation:

> To date my Manager at IMCOM Region Europe is waiting for a response from IMCOM and HQ DA on the issues discussed. She will be calling DC later today. V/R Steve M.

On April 14, 2011, Sgt Schilt repaired my car side mirror with the part I ordered and received from the Sindelfingen Mercedes dealership. Then, unexpectedly soon after, Sgt Schilt was informed of his attendance to a five-week course away from Stuttgart.

Also, on April 14, 2011, I received the following email from Matkowsky

> Subject: Conversation:
>
> Per initial contact with this office on 12 April 2011 to receive information regarding the EEO process the following information is provided.
>
> If you elect to file an informal EEO complaint at this office the point of contact is Ms. Eshe Faulcon, USAG Stuttgart EEO Office. She can be reached at DSN:430-5312 to make an appointment.
>
> It should be noted that if you elect to file a negotiated grievance through your collective bargaining representative (union) you may not later file a formal EEO complaint IAW 29 CFR 1614.107(a) (4). V/R Steve M.[12]

---

12   Steven Matkowsky, email message to Michelle Stefanick, April 14, 2011

Steve's email contained an error. The date of my initial contact with him, at the USAG Stuttgart/Dept of Army/EEO Office, was Monday April 11, 2011, not Tuesday April 12, 2011 as indicated.

I, in turn, forwarded Steve's April 14, 2011 email to Neera Parikh, who responded on Friday, April 15, 2011:

> Michelle—I think you should file a complaint with the EEO Office in Stuttgart. I am not sure that the State Department OCR (Office of Civil Rights) Office would have jurisdiction over this. If you have to file a grievance regarding your EER— that could be submitted to HR/G at State Department. So go ahead and file a complaint with EEO at Stuttgart. Neera[13]

Unbelievable. It was ubelievable that such a matter, such a situation would even need to be addressed to begin with, given all the US Military required Command Surveys, and given that I wasn't even DOD, let alone US Military, but US Department of State. So per USAREUR IG and subsequent AFSA Legal Counsel suggestion, I did and I would file a formal complaint with the EEO Office in Stuttgart. But first was the informal aspect of the DOD EEO grievance process.

On Monday April 18, 2011, I met again with the USAG Stuttgart/ Dept of Army/EEO Office and later received the following email from Matkowsky, ccing Eshe Faulcon.

> Subject: Meeting 18 April 2011:
>
> I have contacted the IMCOM Europe Regional EEO Office. The Regional EEO manager has advised me that based on the MOU in place with HQ US Marine Forces Europe/AFRICOM that the proper venue for your EEO complaint to be processed is at the USAG Stuttgart EEO Office.
>
> It should be noted that if you forward your complaint directly to the DOD EEO Office (which is your prerogative) that it would be most likely sent back to this office for processing. This would cause a delay in the processing of your informal complaint.
>
> An EEO Intake Specialist can be reached at 430-2068 to begin the informal processing of your complaint. V/R Steve Matkowsky[14]

---

13   Neera Parikh, email message to Michelle Stefanick, April 15, 2011
14   Steven Matkowsky, email message to Michelle Stefanick and Eshe Faulcon, April 18, 2011

Since becoming aware of this referenced MOU, throughout and during this entire process, I continually requested a copy of it. As of the writing of this book, I still, to this day, have never received a copy, nor have I received copies of the applicable Command Climate Surveys.

For additional insight, Sgt Luke Schilt worked at MARFORAF as a G6 Operations Planner/Technician. Colonel Bright was MARFORAF COS, and in his previous position was aware of the US Marine Colonels removal from Liberia incident. Sgt Schilt worked for Lt. Col Edward Howell, the MARFOREUR/AF Command Information Officer (G6), who now worked for MARFOREUR COS Colonel Copp. Despite this trigger/ tipping point event/information being the basis for my EEO Complaint and providing/reporting to USAG Stuttgart/Dept of Army/EEO Office accordingly, this event/incident would not be included in their list of in- cidents. The DOD EEO Investigator did not—and would not further in- vestigate, nor would they provide comment in the Report of Investigation (ROI) despite the evidence being in the DOD EEO Investigative File.

Furthermore, I included Sgt Schilt's name as a witness to be inter- viewed due this trigger event. But he was not interviewed by the DOD EEO Investigator to determine if this car door smashing was truly acci- dental or ordered. None of the witnesses to this incident were interviewed by the DOD EEO Investigator. This included BGen Brier, who had not even been informed that this incident occurred until I advised him upon returning from Vicenza, Italy on March 2, 2011. Nor Sgt Schilt's chain of command, particularly in light of his immediate official travel for five weeks' training immediately after repairing the smashed car side mirror.

Soon after MARFORAF Commander LtGen Paxton's Climate Survey was due, MARFORAF COS Colonel Bright departed Stuttgart, Germa- ny. On page 156 (EEO Transcript Report (TR), according to Colonel Bright's August 2, 2011, testimony, he was located at Camp Lejeune, North Carolina pending becoming the Chief of Staff II MEF, second Marine working under Gen Paxton. On page 256 (TR), according to MARFOREUR Commander LtGen Hejlik's August 2, 2011 testimony, he was located at that time at Camp Lejeune, North Carolina conducting a promotion ceremony, where MARFORAF LtGen Paxton was located, as well as Colonel Bright. The DOD EEO Investigator, from Virginia Beach, Virginia and with a Navy background, added MARFOREUR Lt- Gen Hejlik to be interviewed, but not MARFORAF LtGen Paxton. State Department officials including U/S Patrick Kennedy, former PM PDAS Tom Countryman, and others were not interviewed. The only State Department Official that the DOD EEO Investigator interviewed was Kate Canavan (aka Cathy Peterson).

Needless to say, this EEO grievance complaint was extremely complicated and was documented accordingly. But then again, who would ever have envisioned such a scenario ever being permitted and tolerated by the two institutions of the US Department of State and the US Department of Defense to begin with. *Unless of course there was and had to be more to the story, right?*

It was during this time, and for the first time, I was informed that since MARFOREUR/AF was located on a US Army Garrison, my grievance complaint puzzlingly had been filed against the Department of Army when my grievance was actually against MARFOREUR/AF Marine Colonels. Later, USAG Stuttgart/Dept of Army/EEO Office sent EEO Inquiry Questions to BGen Brier that asked broad-level questions but did not include any questions/reference to the event that triggered my complaint to begin with—the smashed car door and subsequent smashed side mirror incident.

No Rest for the Weary

With all that was occurring at the time, I decided to fly stateside on personal annual leave. Orthodox Pascha/Easter was April 24 that year. Since I had just been back at the Christmas Holiday, I had not initially planned on traveling back to the US until my departure. In light of all that was going on, I changed my mind. I scheduled my trip from April 22 to return on May 3, 2011.

I thought this would be a peaceful reprieve from the intensity and tense times I was enduring, being subjected to, but the bizarreness continued, following me even when I was back on American soil.

For instance, while back in the US, I took the opportunity to get a haircut. This would involve getting a rental car and driving down to Reston, Virginia to my hairdresser of many years, Kudret Terkes. I had been getting my hair cut by Kudret dating back to when I first arrived in the Washington D.C. area in 1987, being introduced to the hair salon where Kudret worked by my roommate's stepmother. My first appointment there was with Kudret, and I have been with him ever since, following him to every location where he set up shop, to include, finally, his own place in Reston.

So in the early morning on April 29, 2011, I drove a rental car to my hair appointment. I was pleased with my haircut, caught up with Kudret, and was on my way back to Pennsylvania. I was enjoying the drive back, blaring the radio, loud as usual, and then something really bizarre occurred. Across the dashboard, red verbiage crossed the console. Initially I just thought it was the name of the song and singer,but instead I noticed that it appeared to be some kind of message. Over and over again. I don't recall the entire message because once I noticed it for what it was, it soon stopped. The words that I definitely recall included: *Michael Vickers*. I recall thinking, that was odd/weird/bizarre, and didn't think of it another minute. I got home, returned the car, and began to relax by reading the papers, to include the *Washington Post* and the *New York Times*. And there it was, an article in the *Washington Post* written by Craig Whitlock dated April 29, 2011. It was called, "Defense Department's Vickers is a national security star—again" about Michael Vickers, the very same name I saw scrolled across the rental car console. I remember thinking, *what in the world*, given the bizarre event that I just experienced.

So I read the article, and at the time didn't think anything of it, only about the bizarreness of the event that occurred just previously on the drive home. Later, due to other such bizarre events—the timeline of events—I would pull up a copy of this article again, this time via the internet for a hard copy on February 13, 2015. In light of events that had transpired, and would soon transpire, and the dots I would soon connect, I would now focus on and ponder the significance and, background of this individual, Michael Vickers, that I first became aware on the same day as that very memorable and very bizarre event. So the question remains to this day: what, if there even was one, was, is the significance of Michael Vickers, this man I do not know nor have I ever met? Given his background, the timing and timeline of events, apparently there is one. To this day, I still don't know what it was, what it is.

In a matter of days, I would be returning to Stuttgart, this time knowing my departure was imminent for my onward assignment, and I would be starting over with a new chapter. When I returned, my priority would be my transition/departure preparations. All I needed were my official travel orders.

And then, of course, there was the EEO grievance process that I had initiated. Due to what I witnessed and endured, it was unfortunate, but it had to be done. With days until my departure, I tried to relax and mentally get prepared for my last few months with MARFOREUR/AF.

And then late Sunday night, the *Breaking News Alerts* came in on both television and internet. "*THE WASHINGTON POST* Breaking News Alert: Obama confirms that Osama bin Laden has been killed May 1, 2011."

Wow, I couldn't believe it. Finally, there was an end to this horrific chapter. Or so I thought…

With very limited details shared, and with no words to express at that time, I simply forwarded the CNN Breaking News "Osama bin Laden is dead" email that I received on Sunday, 1 May 2011 to two individuals: Colonel. Michael Mensch and Pat Hartnett-Kelly. Michael, because if I had not been in Ethiopia that day, there is a very high probability that I would have been killed along with my FMC staff and colleagues. And Pat, because we had been through and shared so much together prior to and in the aftermath of the August 7, 1998 Embassy Nairobi bombing.

Needless to say, I remained pretty much glued to the television and internet until my departure on Tuesday, May 3, 2011. My United flight had me departing from Harrisburg to Frankfurt, Germany via Chicago. One horrific chapter was finally closed, and another soon to be… And then bizarre events occurred. Being a frequent flyer, I would take these events in stride at the time, but in due time, I would reflect on them more skeptically—*but then again, bin Laden was dead and the threat was gone, right?* First, I would arrive in Chicago to find out there was a gate change, a plane change. I remember waiting in the lounge, reading magazines and picking up one or two to read on the plane. Next, I would arrive in Frankfurt in transit to Stuttgart, and once again, there was a gate change and a plane change, delaying the flight so that my arrival back to work at MARFO-REUR/AF would be pushed back a day, May 5 instead of May 4. In both situations, weather was not the apparent cause for either switch or delay; and just like the very memorable and very bizarre rental car dash-board event that occurred during that drive home just a few days before, additional, more subtle, yet odd bizarre events continued to occur in between flights. Again, I just chalked them up to at the time as *that's odd*. Particularly since subtle events were now occurring even while I was no longer overseas in Germany, but also now in the United States on American soil as well. But then again, I also didn't know at the time what I know now— the significance of individuals like *Michael Vickers*.

While I was on leave, the informal EEO grievance complaint proceeded in my absence. On May 2, 2011, BGen Brier sent his *EEO Inquiry (Resolution)* email response to USAG Stuttgart/Dept of Army/EEO Office Eshe Faulcon, who in turn sent it to me. Regarding the timeline of events, BGen Brier's response was provided after both applicable MARFOREUR and MARFORAF Command Climate Surveys had been completed and provided to the applicable MARFOREUR and MARFORAF Commanders, LtGen Hejlik and LtGen Paxton respectively. Additionally, initially there was no reference made, and then soon after, when referenced, an inaccurate reference made to the applicable MOU in place with HQ, US Marine Forces Europe/AFRICOM. There were also inaccuracies, mis-representations regarding the US Ambassador to Liberia Linda Thomas-Greenfield and Liberia Marine Colonels removal ordeal. MARFO-REUR/AF conducted formal command climate surveys in 2009, 2010, and 2011, yet none of these applicable climate surveys were requested by nor obtained/provided to the DOD/NAVY EEO Investigator. And de-spite my continual requests, I have never been provided copies to this day as I write this book.

On May 6, 2011, I had my final in-person counseling interview with USAG Stuttgart/Dept of Army/EEO Office Eshe Faulcon. During this meeting, I went downstairs to discuss/report the harassing/threatening hostile environment situation/events to include the smashed car door, subsequent smashed car side mirror, the sunflower incidents, and my safety/security concerns accordingly with USAG Military Police (MP) Investigations. Also, during this time, I called the DOD (EEO) hotline from a German neighbor's home phone regarding this matter and my concerns. Interestingly and curiously enough, the *EEO Counselor's Report (DA Form 7510)* completed by Eshe Faulcon and approved by (illegible signature appearing to be that of) Steven Matkowsky contained errors and omissions/deficiencies in regards to the extent of my complaint in light of all prior discussion and events reported.

On May 10, 2011, I received the *Notice of Right to File a Formal Com-plaint of Discrimination after Completion of Traditional EEO Counseling* memorandum dated May 6, 2011 signed by Steven Matkowsky from Eshe Faulcon. More and more errors were starting to appear on the documents, and oddities with the process were starting to occur. And I immediately questioned and raised concerns at the time, and every step of the way. Many of them were unanswered, not addressed, nor responded to as the DOD EEO process continued forward. I emailed Eshe:

> Hello Eshe—I received the notice of right to file. I would like to turn this in as soon as possible, quite possibly Wed in person if possible. However, before I do so I have a few questions/clarifica-tion requests regarding responses to particular questions. Can you please advise how to best proceed? Thanks, Michelle[15]

---

15   Michelle Stefanick, email message to Eshe Faulcon, May 20, 2011

Curiously enough, I later found out that also on May 10, 2011, MAR-FOREUR Commander LtGen Hejlik had requested a command investigation.

On Wednesday, May 11, 2011, I received from Eshe the *Notice to File a Formal Complaint (EEO)* email with two accompanying attachments. Again, there were inaccuracies. In the early afternoon of Wednesday May 11, 2011, I hand-delivered the required EEO formal complaint documents *(DA Form 2590; DA Form 2590-R; signed/dated Notice of Right to File)* with the USAG Stuttgart/Dept of Army/EEO Office on Patch Barracks. Later that same day, I emailed an accompanying formal complaint supporting insight memo and accompanying documents since there was insufficient space on the form, and after being advised by Steve Matkowsky to include examples to cover at least the last 120 days to start the DOD/EEO Investigative Process.

However, for some reason this accompanying May 11, 2011 supporting insight memo and all accompanying attachments to document the intent of its entirety of my formal claim filed on May 11, 2011 was not included in the supposed DOD/EEO Investigative File nor reflected in the DOD/EEO Investigator's ROI. Quite apparently, a cover-up was underway. I just would not become aware of the magnitude and implications of what the *cover-up* really was, and was really about, until much later.

Needless to say, that year, though April 15 was fast approaching and the annual foreign service evaluation process upon us, events made the process much more complicated. Though the period of performance would cover an entire year, April 16, 2010–April 15, 2011, there would be a delay in the completion of my EER. MARFOREUR/AF Commander BGen Brier, my rater, did not complete his portion until June 9, 2011. My reviewer, AFRICOM FPA Raymond Brown, did not complete his portion until June 29, 2011. My EER was not approved and signed off by the Review Panel Chairperson Dennis Curry and officially submitted to HR/PE Susan Alexander for Promotion Panels until July 12, 2011.

On May 11, 2011, I filed a formal EEO discrimination complaint against MARFOREUR/AF Marine Colonels. However, upon receipt of May 12, 2011 official acknowledgment, due to internal DOD EEO policies, since MARFOREUR/AF was headquartered on a US Army Garrison, my complaint would initially actually be against the Secretary of the Army. According to May 13, 2011 official correspondence from Steven Matkowsky, the Agency Representative was AFRICOM Legal Counsel Wendy Wiedenfeld. This letter again included inaccuracies and did not include the Formal Complaint supporting insight memo and accompanying documents. In fact, it didn't even include the triggering event regarding this complaint filing—the smashed car door, subsequent smashed car side mirror, and sunflower incident. Needless to say, at this point, I developed full skepticism regarding the entire DOD EEO Complaint process.

So, the question has to be asked, why would the US Army, specifically US Army Garrison Stuttgart/Department of Army/EEO Office, modify/misrepresent/falsify my EEO Formal Complaint against MARFO-REUR/AF (which include MARSOC) Marines?

On May 15, 2011, supposedly, Steven Matkowsky signed/sent a *Request for IRD Investigator* letter to DOD/Civilian Personnel Management Service (CPMS)/Investigation and Resolution Division (IRD). A copy of this letter was provided to Agency Representative, Ms. Wendy Wiedenfeld, but not me. I only became aware of this letter and its discrepancies, upon receipt of the DOD/EEO Investigative file on or about January 6, 2012, accompanying the December 21, 2011 USAG Stuttgart/Dept of Army/EEO Office response regarding my November 23, 2011 *Spin-off* complaint. Interesting to also note that at this time, according to Eshe Faulcon on May 26, 2015, the Equal Opportunity Employment Commission (EEOC) Washington was never provided these applicable letters, nor does it appear in this applicable DOD EEO Investigative file.

At this point, with so many substantial discrepancies already misrepresented, or not included, my civil/due process right had been violated from the very start, in this documented deficient DOD EEO Complaint reporting process. The DOD EEO Investigative process had not even started, but was already substantially flawed. And from my perspective, this was purposeful and intentional.

There were so many events simultaneously occurring, including for some reason, the delay of my official travel orders.

On May 30, 2011, I received the following email from Pat Hartnett-Kelly,

> Subject: Must Read Article, containing a link for the referenced article,;
>
> Michelle,
> I saw this article and it raised some questions for me.
>   I knew of Tom and Molly's jobs etc. But I was surprised to learn that Tom changed his personality to appear subdued. Dan and I wondered about him as he really never spoke much of anything

to us. Also, the last sentence of the article states that Bin Laden targeted the embassy because it was a major CIA station! News to me… I still wonder how bin laden obtained info on who was in our building…

Hope your well… Pat

http://www.huffingtonpost.com//2011/05/29/osama-bin-laden-raid-cia-deaths_n_868536.html [16]

Though I was unable to provide the contents from this specific news media link initially sent to me by Pat, due to its significance, I provide a similar media report from that exact time frame since the actual text regarding this reporting was exactly the same by and regardless of the numerous media outlets. In this instance, I provide in its entirety from nbcnews.com: *Osama raid avenged CIA deaths, a secret until now.*

For a small cadre of CIA veterans, the death of Osama bin Laden was a measure of payback, a settling of a score for a pair of deaths, the details of which have remained a secret for 13 years.

May 29, 2011, 1:25 AM EDT / Source: The Associated Press
By ADAM GOLDMAN, MATT APUZZO

For a small cadre of CIA veterans, the death of Osama bin Laden was more than just a national moment of relief and closure. It was also a measure of payback, a settling of a score for a pair of deaths, the details of which have remained a secret for 13 years.

Tom Shah and Molly Huckaby Hardy were among the 44 U.S. Embassy employees killed when a truck bomb exploded outside the embassy compound in Kenya in 1998.

Though it has never been publicly acknowledged, the two were working undercover for the CIA. In al-Qaida's war on the United States, they are believed to be the first CIA casualties.

Their names probably will not be among those read at Memorial Day celebrations around the country this weekend. Like many CIA officers, their service remained a secret in both life and death, marked only by anonymous stars on the wall at CIA headquarters and blank entries in its book of honor.

Their CIA ties were described to The Associated Press by a half-dozen current and former U.S. officials who spoke on condition of anonymity because Shah's and Hardy's jobs are still secret, even now.

The deaths weighed heavily on many at the CIA, particularly the two senior officers who were running operations in Africa during the attack. Over the past decade, as the CIA waged war against al-Qaida, those officers have taken on central roles in counterterrorism. Both were deeply involved in hunting down bin Laden and planning the raid on the terrorist who killed their colleagues.

"History has shown that tyrants who threaten global peace and freedom must eventually face their natural enemies: America's war fighters, and the silent warriors of our Intelligence Community," CIA Director Leon Panetta wrote in a Memorial Day message to agency employees.

These silent warriors took very different paths to Nairobi.

Hardy was a divorced mom from Valdosta, Ga., who raised a daughter as she traveled to Asia, South America and Africa over a lengthy career. At the CIA station in Kenya, she handled the office finances, including the CIA's stash of money used to pay sources and carry out spying operations. She was a new grandmother and was eager to get back home when al-Qaida struck.

Shah took an unpredictable route to the nation's clandestine service. He was not a solider or a Marine, a linguist or an Ivy Leaguer. He was a musician from the Midwest. But his story, and the secret mission that brought him to Africa, was straight out of a Hollywood spy movie.

"He was a vivacious, upbeat guy who had a very poignant, self-deprecating sense of humor," said Dan McDevitt, a classmate and close friend from St. Xavier High School in Cincinnati, where Shah was a standout trumpet player.

Shah—his given name was Uttamlal—was the only child of an Indian immigrant father and an American mother, McDevitt said. He had a fascination with international affairs. He participated in the school's model United Nations and, in the midst of the Cold War, was one of the school's first students to learn Russian. From time to time, he went to India with his father, giving him a rare world perspective.

"At the time, that was unheard of. You might as well have gone to Mars," said McDevitt, who lost touch with his high school friend long before he joined the agency.

Shah graduated from Berklee College of Music in Boston and Ball State University's music school. He taught music classes and occasionally played in backup bands for entertainers Red Skelton, Perry Como and Jim Nabors. His doctoral thesis at Indiana's Ball State offered no hints about the career he would pursue: "The Solo Songs of Edward MacDowell: An Examination of Style and Literary Influence."

"He was one of our outstanding people," said Kirby Koriath, the graduate student adviser at Ball State.

Shah and his wife, Linda, were married in 1983, the year he received his master's degree. In 1987, after earning his doctorate, Shah joined the U.S. government. On paper, he had become a diplomat. In reality, he was shipped to the Farm, the CIA's spy school in Virginia.

He received the usual battery of training in surveillance, counterespionage and the art of building sources. The latter is particularly hard to teach, but it came naturally to Shah, former officials said. Shah was regarded as one of the top members of his class and was assigned to the Near East Division, which covers the Middle East.

He spoke fluent Hindi and decent Russian when he arrived and quickly showed a knack for languages by learning Arabic. He worked in Cairo and Damascus and, though he was young, former colleagues said he was quickly proving himself one of the agency's most promising stars.

In 1997, he was dispatched to headquarters as part of the Iraq Operations Group, the CIA team that ran spying campaigns against Saddam Hussein's regime. Around that time, the CIA became convinced that a senior Iraqi official was willing to provide intelligence in exchange for a new life in America. Before the U.S. could make that deal, it had to be sure the information was credible and the would-be defector wasn't really a double agent. But even talking to him was a risky move. If a meeting with the CIA was discovered, the Iraqi would be killed for sure.

Somebody had to meet with the informant, somebody who knew the Middle East and could be trusted with such a sensitive mission. A senior officer recommended Shah.

The meetings were set up in Kenya, former officials said, because it was considered relatively safe from Middle East intelligence services. It was perhaps the most important operation being run under the Africa Division at the time, current and former officials said. Among the agency managers overseeing it was John Bennett, the deputy chief of the division. He and his operations chief, who remains undercover, were seasoned Africa hands and veterans of countless spying operations.

Because of the mission's sensitivity, Shah bottled up his normally outgoing and friendly personality while at the embassy.

"This is the glory and the tragedy of discreet work," said Prudence Bushnell, the former ambassador to Kenya. "You keep a very low profile and you don't do things that make you memorable."

Officials say Shah was among those who went to the window when shooting began outside the embassy gates. Most who did were killed when the massive bomb exploded. He was 38. Hardy was also killed in the blast. She was 51.

Families suffer, grieve The U.S. government said both victims were State Department employees. But like all fallen officers, they received private memorial services at CIA headquarters. Every year, their names are among those read at a ceremony for family members and colleagues.

Hardy's daughter, Brandi Plants, said she did not want to discuss her mother's employment. Shah's widow, Linda, sent word through a neighbor that the topic was still too painful to discuss.

Shah's death did not stall his mission. The Africa Division pressed on and confirmed that the Iraqi source was legitimate, his information extremely valuable. He defected and was re-located to the United States with a new identity.

Bennett later went on to be the station chief in Islamabad, where he ran the agency's effort to kill al-Qaida members by using unmanned aircraft. He now sits in one of the most important seats in the agency, overseeing clandestine operations worldwide. His former Africa operations chief now runs the agency's counterterrorism center. Both have been hunting for bin Laden for years. Both were directly involved in the raid.

Shah and Hardy are among the names etched into stone at a memorial at the embassy in Nairobi, with no mention of their CIA service. Shah is also commemorated with a plaque in a CIA conference room at its headquarters. Both were among those whose names Panetta read last week at the annual ceremony for fallen officers.

"Throughout the effort to disrupt, dismantle and defeat al-Qaida, our fallen colleagues have been with us in memory and in spirit," Panetta said. "With their strength and determination as our guide, we achieved a great victory three weeks ago."

Bin Laden said the embassy in Nairobi was targeted because it was a major CIA station. He died never knowing that he had killed two CIA officers there.

Associated Press writers Greg Bluestein in Atlanta and Michelle Price in Phoenix contributed to this report.

I must admit I was as taken aback as Pat in discovering that our embassy was "a major CIA station." Also, in all the years and our numerous discussions in the aftermath of August 7, 1998 East Africa bombings, this email was the very first time Pat ever alluded to me that there was an *insider* possibility. Given Pat's law enforcement background and connections, and her notification in the June 25, 2009 email that the FBI investigation of our Embassy bombings were still ongoing, it was apparent to me that despite bin Laden's recent capture and killing, based on Pat's email—this chapter for us was still not closed and the investigation was still ongoing. And given they finally captured/killed bin Laden after all these years, I had no doubt law enforcement would get to the bottom of it, to include finding the insider, if there indeed was one. That was what I thought at the time…

And then I would be subjected to some even more horrific and bizarre events. To this day and at this time, I cannot and will not provide the details of what I call, the *"involuntary retaliatory actions"* that took place during this period—curiously and coincidentally timed *after* my filing a formal EEO Grievance and *after* the capture/killing of bin Laden on May 1, 2011 by the US Navy SEALs. The reason is twofold: 1) because I would later share the insight with applicable officials of the US military capable of jurisdiction and investigation of such matters—or so I thought; and 2) I hadn't yet connected the dots as to the real motive and reason for all that was really going on.

On June 1, 2011, a MARFOREUR/AF Command Investigation Report would be issued. Conducted by USMC Colonel Mary H. Reinwald, US Marine Corps Forces Command, whose Commanding General was LtGen Hejlik. The Investigation requested by MARFOREUR Commander, the same LtGen Hejlik, on May 10, 2011, coincidentally the same day, I received the *Notice of Right to File a Formal Complaint of Discrimination after Completion of Traditional EEO Counseling* memorandum. The same day, I emailed Eshe of my intent to file.

As depicted by the timeline of events, this MARFOREUR/AF Command Investigation was requested by LtGen Hejlik on May 10, 2011, after both MARFOREUR and MARFORAF Command Climate Surveys were completed and provided to the Commanders, LtGen Hejlik and LtGen Paxton respectively. Yet the Command Investigation neither makes a reference nor a comment regarding these two applicable command survey and/or results. Of course, I would not have access to this June 1, 2011 Investigative Report until much later, and under interesting circumstances, when I finally received an Investigative File on January 6, 2012 in which it was included. I would also find quite eye-opening, once reading this

Investigative Report, what was referenced as *Enclosure (12) Email from AMB Katherine Canavan to Brigadier General Tracy L. Garrett on 4 Sep 09*. Not aware of this email until that point, I immediately began requesting a copy. Despite numerous and ongoing requests, to this day, I still have not obtained a copy of this email. Apparently, and quite obviously, it is *the smoking gun!*

On June 8, 2011, DOD/CPMS/IRD/Intake Services/Human Resources Assistant Donna Parrish sent *Data/Documentation/Witness Request* to both the Agency Representative and myself. As noted, the basis for this IRD request by USAG Stuttgart/Dept of Army/EEO Office was previously sent only to the Agency Representative and not myself, the Complainant, containing substantive misrepresentations and modifications to my formal EEO complaint; and now this IRD request was modified with even more deficiencies/inaccuracies to those already indicated. My due process rights were being even more detrimentally impacted upon even though the DOD EEO Investigative process had not even begun yet, with this crucial initial request/input phase of the DOD EEO process being so substantially and detrimentally flawed before it even started.

With this ever-evolving/snowballing detrimental effect/modification, the DOD IRD request changed my original allegation period, and again this request memo did not even include the trigger/tipping point complaint-filing event regarding the smashed car door, subsequent smashed car side mirror, and sunflower incidents. This DOD IRD request continues to indicate Wendy Wiedenfeld, AFRICOM, as the Agency Representative.

On June 14, 2011, I emailed the initial proposed witness list with only three key witnesses as advised by DOD/CPMS/IRD/Intake Services/Human Resources Assistant Donna Parrish; she said that there is no set number of witnesses to be submitted, but as a general rule the you should submit the fewest you can to support your position. Despite the same three key witnesses later provided on the much more expanded Proposed Witness List, none were interviewed by the DOD/IRD Investigator.

On Sunday, June 19, 2011, I finally received my US Department of State Home Leave/Transfer Order. Now, given thateveryone apparently wanted me out of MARFOREUR/AF as soon as possible—at the time and still to this day—I question why it took me so long to receive my official travel orders? Why were they purposely and intentionally delayed? And who caused the delay? In my entire career, I never experienced what I did at this time, given all the events that had, and were yet to transpire.

This leads me to question—as I did then and still, do to this day—*What was really going on?*

As my detail was in accordance with the applicable State/Defense MOU, after finally receiving my official State travel orders, I then had to obtain my applicable official US Navy/USMC travel orders, which I did on June 24, 2011. Finally, with both required sets of official travel orders, I proceeded as quickly as possible with pack-out/check-out procedures.

I had much to do before my departure. And yet, so much *drama* was still playing out at the same time. I stayed focused. There was now an end in sight. On June 29, I made my travel plans. I would be departing Stuttgart on Saturday July 30, 2011 at 2:55 p.m.

JUMPING THOUGH HOOPS

On July 6, 2011, DOD/IRD Investigator Stanley Bradley sent the *Investigation of Complaints of Discrimination in Germany* email to Steven Matkowsky, Eshe Faulcon, Wendy Wiedenfeld, and numerous others; but not me. *How is that possible?* Though I was the one who was departing soon, with a finite schedule, he was coordinating with all these individuals, instead of me, on the investigative period. And his proposed dates were *after* my departure. Additionally, the DOD/IRD Investigator included the proposed August 2, 2011 Investigation Schedule. Thirteen witness interviews were included, only 1 of the three I initially submitted, and only one Department of State official – Ms. Katherine Canavan. Again, I duly note that I was not included on this email. I did not obtain a copy of this email until November 1, 2011.

On July 7, 2011, Wendy Wiedenfeld emailed DOD/IRD Investigator Stanley Bradley, ccing MARFOREUR/AF Lt. Col Robert Renard, G1; MARFOREUR/AF Major Roger Mattioli, Staff Judge Advocate; and Eshe Faulcon, but not me. Both MARFOREUR/AF and USAG Stuttgart/Dept of Army/EEO Office knew my departure plans for July 30, 2011 were already made. Interestingly enough, this email also indicated that there was a change of Agency Representative from Wendy Wiedenfeld to MARFOREUR/AF Staff Judge Advocate Major Roger Mattioli; yet, I wasn't notified. I did not obtain a copy of this email exchange until November 1, 2011.

The Department of Defense DIRECTIVE SUBJECT: *Diversity Management and Equal Opportunity (EO) in the Department of Defense* (NUMBER 1020.02 dated February 5, 2009 by Deputy Secretary of Defense Gordon England) was in effect at the time. Or was it? Given what I was personally enduring and being subjected to at that time, obviously this applicable DOD Directive was not.

On July 8, 2011, Eshe sent the email "Tentative Date for Fact Finding Conference" to me, again without my inclusion/awareness at the time of the previous and pertinent July 6-7 email exchange:

> Good Morning Ms. Stefanick:
> An IRD Investigator (Mr. Stanley Bradley) has been assigned to your case for the Fact-Finding Conference (FFC). The FFC has been tentatively scheduled for Tuesday, 02 August 2011, so please mark your calendar. I will send you an additional email once date has been confirmed.
> Kind Regards,
> Ms. Eshe Faulcon
> EEO Specialist/ADR Coordinator/
> Complaints Program Manager
> USAG Stuttgart EEO Office[17]

I promptly responded:

> Thank you, Ms. Faulcon—On 02 Aug, I unfortunately will not be in Stuttgart any longer. I depart on July 30. Thank you, michelle[18]

Within minutes, Eshe responded:

> Ms. Stefanick:
> Thank you for the update.
> We can also conduct the Fact-Finding Conference (FFC) with you telephonically. If you would give me a good number to reach you stateside for the date of 02 August 2011, I will pass the information on to the investigator.
> Typically, the complainant is present (in person or via telephone) through the entire FFC which can last 4-8 hours.
> I look forward to your reply!
> Kind Regards,
> Ms. Eshe Faulcon[19]

I responded:

> Thank you, Ms. Faulcon—But as I'm leaving early because of the environment here, we have no alternative. I expect to be at my fa-

17   Eshe Faulcon, email message to Michelle Stefanick, July 8, 2011.
18   Michelle Stefanick, email message to Eshe Faulcon, July 8, 2011
19   Eshe Faulcon, email message to Michelle Stefanick, July 8, 2011.

ther's house by Aug 2. The number there is [redacted]. Hopefully that works. Thank you. michelle[20]

Eshe replied:

> Thank you Ms. Stefanick
> I will continue to send any updates to this email address.
> Kind Regards,
> Ms. Eshe Faulcon[21]

Though this July 8, 2011 email exchange was not provided/included in the DOD EEO IRD Investigative File I received on or about January 6, 2012, Eshe Faulcon's initial email to me at 8:40 A.M., was included under the Investigation Tab in the information accompanying the October 20, 2011 letter from her. I received this letter and accompanying information, to include this 8:40 A.M. email, on November 1, 2011.

On July 14, 2011, I received an email from Eshe, ccing Stanley Bradley:

> Subject: FW: Request for Information Concerning Witnesses
>
> Good Morning Ms. Stefanick:
> The email below has been forwarded to you from the IRD Investigator, Mr. Stanley Bradley. Mr. Bradley is cc'd on the email and you can send your response directly to him.
> Have a good day!
> Kind Regards,
> Ms. Eshe Faulcon
> USAG Stuttgart EEO Office
>
> Ms Stefanick,
> I have identified the following nine witnesses as candidates to be interviewed in connection with your complaint of discrimination:
> COL James Bright
> COL Adam Copp
> BGen Paul Brier
> Ms. Katherine Canavan
> General LtGen Hejlik
> COL Steven Hoyle
> COL Dale Vesley
> LTC Edward Howell
> COL Walter Niblock
> Stan Bradley

---

20   Michelle Stefanick, email message to Eshe Faulcon, July 8, 2011
21   Eshe Faulcon, email message to Michelle Stefanick, July 8, 2011.

Investigator
Civilian Personnel Management Service
Investigations and Resolutions Division (IRD)[22]

Despite being in the process of Permanent Change of Station (PCS) pack-out, I promptly responded that day, including to DOD/IRD Investigator Stanley Bradley, by providing an updated proposed witness list as well as suggesting questioning some of the witness explanations provided in the Agency's provided witness list attachment. On July 14, I responded to Eshe, ccing Stanley as follows:

> Subject: RE: Request for Information Concerning Witnesses
>
> Thank you, Ms. Faulcon—Can you please attach the document I already submitted regarding this. As well as there are names on this list I want as my witnesses because I actually do not agree with some of the statements provided and believe when questioned under oath will provide the truth. Thank you, michelle[23]

Eshe responded to me, not ccing DOD/IRD Investigator Stanley Bradley, with one attachment—*PROPOSED WITNESS LIST.PDF*:

> Ms. Stefanick,
> Here is your original list.
> Kind regards,
> Ms. Eshe Faulcon[24]

Despite my limited time, I forwarded some additional documents to Eshe, ccing Stanley:

> Subject: DOD/DOS MOU
> Hello Ms. Faulcon/Mr. Bradley – Since I am in the process of PCS-ing, I wanted to make sure you had this document before I departed post. Thank you, michelle[25]

At 10:37 A.M.:

> Subject: DOS expectations of the POLAD/FPA Position
> Also this ... [26]

At 10:39 A.M.:

---

22   Eshe Faulcon, email message to Michelle Stefanick and Stanley Bradley, July 14, 2011.
23   Michelle Stefanick, email message to Eshe Faulcon, and Stanley Bradley, July 14, 2011.
24   Eshe Faulcon, email message to Michelle Stefanick, July 14, 2011.
25   Michelle Stefanick, email message to Eshe Faulcon, and Stanley Bradley, July 14, 2011.
26   Michelle Stefanick, email message to Eshe Faulcon, and Stanley Bradley, July 14, 2011.

> Subject: DOS expectations of the POLAD/FPA Position
> And this...thank you, michelle[27]

All three documents were referenced in the DOD/IRD Investigator's ROI and included in the Investigative File. However, so was a statement/claim that I was not participating/uncooperative and/or did not provide evidence in the investigative process.

Meanwhile, at 10:34 A.M., I responded to Eshe, ccing Stanley:

> Subject: RE: Request for Information Concerning Witnesses
> Hello Ms. Faulcon/Mr. Bradley—Please find attached the requested information. Michelle[28]

Stanley responded, ccing Eshe:

> Thank you, Ms. Stefanick[29]

Eshe replied, but not ccing Stanley, as follows:

> The information has been forwarded per your request.
> Kind regards,
> Ms. Eshe Faulcon[30]

I emailed Eshe, but not ccing Stanley, as follows:

> Thank you, Ms. Faulcon—I think there was a confusion regarding my request. I wanted the document I already submitted to be returned to me so I could update it accordingly. Thanks, michelle[31]

Despite being in the process of PCSing, I, that day, as I had been the entire time since first initiating this EEO grievance/complaint, totally cooperated and was forthcoming in each and every reporting/requirement process along the way. With all the evidence provided and in light of all that I had been through, witnessed, and experienced, I dispute any *declining to participate* claim for it is not based on fact. I immediately and continually throughout the DOD EEO grievance complaint process stated and indicated for the record, over and over again, deficiencies in the process that jeopardized/violated my rights, both civil and due process rights, as well as those of others; this included the ever-evolving, purposeful and intentional modification of the basis and timeline of my formal

27   Michelle Stefanick, email message to Eshe Faulcon, and Stanley Bradley, July 14, 2011.
28   Michelle Stefanick, email message to Eshe Faulcon, and Stanley Bradley, July 14, 2011.
29   Stanley Bradley, email message to Michelle Stefanick and Eshe Faulcon, July 14, 2011.
30   Eshe Faulcon, email message to Michelle Stefanick, July 14, 2011.
31   Michelle Stefanick, email message to Eshe Faulcon, July 14, 2011

EEO complaint. In due time, once I figured out and connected dots regarding what *all this* was really about, my federal CVRA-accorded rights and protections as a victim/witness regarding the August 7, 1998 East Africa Embassy bombings were also violated. The question remains, *Why?*

Unfortunately, though the documents provided on July 14, 2011 were included, none of the applicable July 14 email exchanges, which included DOD/IRD Investigator Stanley Bradley, were provided in the applicable Investigative File. They were also not included in the information accompanying the October 20, 2011 letter from Eshe Faulcon, which I later received on November 1, 2011.

On July 15, 2011, Stanley Bradley sent *Witness List—Complaint of Discrimination of Michelle Stefanick* email to Eshe Faulcon and me. Though the last official correspondence I received from both USAG Stuttgart/ Dept of Army/EEO Office (May 13, 2011 *Acceptance Letter of Chain, Formal Complaint of Discrimination* letter signed by Steven Matkowsky and June 8, 2011 *Data/Documentation/Witness Request* letter signed by DOD/CPMS/IRD Donna Parrish) indicated Ms. Wendy Wiedenfeld as the Agency Representative, she was not included on this email. Two Navy/USMC/MARFOREUR/AF Marines were included instead. Attached to the email was the July 15, 2011 DOD/CPMS/IRD *Complaint of Michelle Stefanick* memorandum signed by Stanley Bradley now indicating Major Roger Mattioli as the Agency Representative. Why did this change from Wendy Wiedefeld to MARFOREUR/AF Major Roger Mattioli, particularly given the supposed MOU in place with HQ, US Marine Forces Europe/AFRICOM? To this day, I have never seen nor received a copy of this *supposed* MOU. The July 15, 2011 Stanley Bradley *Witness List – Complaint of Discrimination of Michelle Stefanick* email sent to Eshe Faulcon and me, ccing MARFOREUR/AF G1 Robert Renard and MARFOREUR/AF Staff Judge Advocate, and new Agency Representative, Major Roger Mattioli is as follows:

> FW: Witness List – Complaint of Discrimination of Michelle Stefanick
>
> Ms. Faulcon, Ms. Stefanick, Lt. Col Renard, Maj Mattioli:
> I am attaching a tentative scheduling letter; tentative because it incorporates a second day of fact-finding (August 4th) that we have not previously discussed. You will also note that I have begun the fact-finding rather later in the day (in Germany) than normal to accommodate the fact that Ms. Stefanick, and numerous witness-

es, will be participating from CONUS and there is a six-hour time delay. If the 4th can't be fit into the schedule, I will continue the FFC until a reasonable hour on the 2nd and then I will contact the remaining witnesses for testimony using interrogatories.

As you will see, I have narrowed down the proposed witness lists significantly (the agency proposed 25 witnesses and Ms. Stefanick proposed 33) to those included in the attached scheduling letter. With the exception of Col Bright, Col Copp, and BGen Brier (who need to hear Ms. Stefanick's testimony) the dates and times for the other witnesses can be swapped as needed. If I find it necessary, I will contact additional witnesses to ensure we have as complete an investigation as possible under the circumstances.

As suggested, please collect the phone numbers (where applicable) so we may attempt to interview witnesses no longer in Germany by phone.

Please contact me if you have any questions. Stan Bradley[32]

And by the way, if this email was forwarded, who was it originally sent to and who were the parties to the initial email exchange?

Despite indicating my PCS status the day before with Stanley Bradley and raising concerns on the tentative schedule date of August 2, 2011 with Eshe Faulcon a week earlier, this attached schedule was for August 2, 2011. So, though the email references being tentative, it was not and never was since prearrangements were already made since July 6, 2011 according to the emails that did not include me. I again immediately raised concerns on the timing due to my scheduled July 30, 2011 departure with no flexibility to the tentative schedule in DOD/IRD Investigator's response. And now all my source documents and evidence were in the process of being packed-up and shipped back to the US. I emailed Stanley and Eshe.

RE: Witness List – Complaint of Discrimination of Michelle Stefanick
Hello Mr. Bradley—Please note as I've advised Ms. Faulcon I will no longer be in Stuttgart at this time. thanks, m[33]

Stanley responded, not including Eshe:

Thank you, Ms. Stefanick. I assume that you will be participating by phone (from CONUS), so I have delayed the start of the investi-

---

32   Stanley Bradley, email message to Michelle Stefanick, Eshe Faulcon, Robert Renard and Roger Mattioli, July 15, 2011.
33   Michelle Stefanick, email message to Stanley Bradley and Eshe Faulcon, July 15, 2011

gation to noon Stuttgart time to accommodate the time difference. Stan Bradley[34]

I responded to Stanley, not ccing Eshe:

Also, for clarification your interviews are only with individuals listed?[35]

Stanley responded, now ccing Renard, Mattioli, and Faulcon:

At this point these are the witnesses I plan on interviewing. If it becomes apparent during the investigation that additional witnesses are necessary, I will contact those required to ensure we have a complete an investigation as possible under the circumstances. Stan Bradley[36]

With the errors/modification in my EEO complaint previously presented above on May 13, 2011, May 15, 2011, and June 8, 2011 accordingly, these errors were again carried forward in this July 15, 2011 DOD/IRD Investigator memorandum. Additionally, key first-hand/primary-sourced witnesses were not even being included. With these factors jeopardizing a supposed DOD EEO fair, unbiased, and now obviously flawed investigation already, next I was advised that my testimony had to be heard by Colonel Bright, Colonel Copp and BGen Brier, which I took exception to as well. I responded to DOD/IRD Investigator Stanley Bradley, ccing Renard, Mattioli, and Faulcon:

Thank you, Mr. Bradley—But as the witness list seems to indeed be slanted and the Marines have already got what they wanted, my departure, I no longer want to participate in a process that I thought would be conducted in a fair, just, due-process manner. I am no longer interested in this process. Thank you, michelle[37]

Stanley responded, ccing Renard, Mattioli, and Faulcon:

Ms. Stefanick,
I'm not sure I understand your meaning—are you indicating that you are not going to participate in the investigation, or that you intend to withdraw your complaint of discrimination? Stan Bradley[38]

34   Stanley Bradley, email message to Michelle Stefanick and Eshe Faulcon, July 15, 2011
35   Michelle Stefanick, email message to Eshe Faulcon, and Stanley Bradley, July 15, 2011.
36   Stanley Bradley, email message to Michelle Stefanick, Eshe Faulcon, Robert Renard and Roger Mattioli, July 15, 2011.
37   Michelle Stefanick, email message to Stanley Bradley, Eshe Faulcon, Robert Renard and Roger Mattioli, July 15, 2011.
38   Stanley Bradley, email message to Michelle Stefanick, Eshe Faulcon, Robert Renard and Roger Mattioli, July 15, 2011.

I responded to Stanley, ccing Renard, Mattioli, and Faulcon:

> Mr. Bradley—If you are going to limit the witnesses to just those on the list you provided, I will not participate. I have a valid complaint of discrimination based on a hostile work environment, which can be witnessed by more than just me. So, I guess its what is the intent of the (DOD) EEO discrimination process, for I see now its not very conducive to finding out the facts. Thank you, michelle[39]

This email exchange was included in the DOD EEO Investigative File when I finally received a copy. The next portion of this email exchange, however, was not. Eshe, ccing Stanley but not Renard and Mattioli, emailed:

> Good Afternoon Ms. Stefanick:
> In reference to your email below, if you are no longer interested in the complaint process and wish to officially withdraw the complaint, please complete the form attached.
> Kind Regards,
> Ms. Eshe Faulcon[40]

To which I responded to Eshe, ccing Stanley:

> Hello Ms. Faulcon, I do not want to official[sic] withdraw the complaint. I want a fair, unbiased, due-process investigation. Thank you. michelle[41]

This portion of the email exchange was not provided in the DOD EEO Investigative File and DOD/IRD Investigator Stanley Bradley was included in that email exchange.

To provide further context now in hindsight regarding Stanley Bradley's request that my testimony had to be heard by Colonel Bright, Colonel Copp, and BGen Brier, it appears Colonel Copp and BGen Brier were still located in Stuttgart on August 2, 2011 when their testimony was given. However, soon after MARFORAF Commander LtGen Paxton's Climate Survey, MARFORAF COS Colonel Bright departed Stuttgart. According to Colonel Bright's August 2, 2011 testimony, he was located at Camp Lejeune, North Carolina, pending becoming the Chief of Staff II MEF, working under Gen Paxton. According to MARFOREUR Commander LtGen Hejlik's August 2, 2011 testimony, he was located at that

39   Michelle Stefanick, email message to Stanley Bradley, Eshe Faulcon, Robert Renard and Roger Mattioli, July 15, 2011.
40   Stanley Bradley, email message to, Michelle Stefanick and Eshe Faulcon, July 15, 2011.
142 41   Michelle Stefanick, email message to Eshe Faulcon and Stanley Bradley, July 15, 2011.

time at Camp Lejeune, North Carolina conducting a promotion ceremony, as well as Colonel Bright. The DOD/IRD Investigator, from Virginia Beach, Virginia and with a Navy background, added MARFOREUR Lt-Gen Hejlik to be interviewed, but not MARFORAF LtGen Paxton.

So, if I would have proceeded in a telephone call-in testimony on August 2, 2011 with Colonel Copp, BGen Brier, and Colonel Bright, since Colonel Bright was in North Carolina— coincidentally with both LtGen Hejlik and LtGen Paxton—would they too have been present to hear my testimony? And if so, would I have been advised of their presence? Would Stanley Bradley have known in advance since he was physically located in Stuttgart? This prearrangement that didn't work out since I refused to participate in such a purposely and intentionally deficient and deceptive DOD EEO Investigative process may explain why there were so many inconsistencies and inaccuracies in the August 2, 2011 testimony provided by MARFOREUR Commander LtGen Hejlik; this would be documented in and throughout the formal DOD EEO Grievance process.

With that, as Stanley Bradley was assigned from Virginia Beach, Virginia and had a Navy background, he was aware of the concept—the mortal enemy of military justice—unlawful command influence. Though I was a civilian and this is/was a civilian claim, all the witnesses except Kate Canavan were military and fall under the Uniform Code of Military Justice (UCMJ). Unless, of course, Kate had a military background of which I was unaware? The unlawful actions by a Commanding General is not only a serious allegation, but a serious offense; it's the equivalent to obstruction of justice in a civilian court. For the record, I provide a layperson's definition of the applicable military concept of unlawful command influence (UCI):

> UCI occurs when senior personnel, wittingly or unwittingly, have acted to influence court members, witnesses, or others participating in military justice cases. Such unlawful influence not only jeopardize the validity of the judicial process, it undermines the morale of military members, their respect for the chain of command, and public confidence in the military.

I would not drop this valid EEO complaint. My intent was to obtain legal counsel upon returning to the United States. As an American, it's my constitutional right to be represented by legal counsel. But bizarreness continued, and even got worse...

Only during these departure check-out procedures was I made aware for the very first time that I didn't have the *proper visa* in my passport by the Consular office on Panzer. In essence, this implied that I was in Germany *illegally*. Not knowing *what in the world* was going on, all I knew was that I needed to just survive and get out of Germany,and off this Department of Defense/US Army Garrison as quickly and, *God willing*, as safely as possible. I hand-carried both my official US Department of State and applicable US Department of Navy issued travel orders as supplements to my diplomatic passport until I departed through German customs.

Later, even after my household items and personal effects were packed and shipped and I was moved out of my residence and staying at the Marriott in Sindelfingen, I received a weird call from within the hotel. And the message to me, from within the hotel, and as I took it at the time, was, *someone* was watching, continuing to watch me, even within the hotel. *Why?* I was departing Germany. I was departing my US Department of State foreign service FPA/POLAD position early. *What in the world was going on?*

Speaking of pack-out, here's a July 28-29 email exchange, between myself and the new MARFOREUR/AF Deputy Commander Colonel Charles Chiarotti. On Thursday, July 28, 2011 I emailed Colonel Chiarotti:

> Subject: Departure
>
> Hello Col Chiarotti—I am so sorry I missed your call on Monday. I was handling three packers and didn't hear the blackberry ring. So, didn't get your message until you were already well on your way... I will be departing early afternoon July 30, but just wanted to say goodbye and thank you for everything before I left. I also wanted to provide you my personal email address in case you needed to get a hold of me for any reason.
>
> Despite the situation, I just wanted to let you know what an incredible honor it has been/will be forevermore to me to have been the first Foreign Policy Advisor for MARFOREUR/AF. Until out paths cross again, Godspeed. And as they say around here, Semper Fi. Cheers, Michelle
> Michelle L. Stefanick
> Foreign Policy Advisor
> Marine Forces Europe and Africa[42]

---

42   Michelle Stefanick, email message to Charles Chiarotti, July 28, 2011.

Given all that I was put through, many would be asking how could I have written such an email? To which I would say, during my time in Stuttgart, I had the distinct honor of meeting so many honorable men and women serving and sacrificing for our nation, to include Marines. I do not generalize, but assess on an individual basis. Or at least I really try. I must say, honestly knowing what I know now, and what would later occur, I don't know if I would have written an email response like this, let alone any email response at all. For in hindsight, knowing what I know now, and what would later occur, I now reflect back on my bidding on a detail with the US Military as an FPA/POLAD as something I would never, ever do again if I could turn back time.

On Friday, July 29, 2011, the new MARFOREUR/AF Deputy Commander Colonel. Charles Chiarotti responded, ccing LtGen Paxton and LtGen Hejlik:

> Michelle,
> Thank you for your email; Fully understand how busy things are during a move—as I'm still living out of boxes myself.
>
> If you need anything from me or the staff in order to assist you during this transition, pls do not hesitate to let me know.
>
> On behalf of LtGen Hejlik and LtGen Paxton both, I want to wish you safe travels and well wishes in your new assignment.
>
> S/F,
> Col Chiarotti[43]

Though according to my original paneled detail assignment, I was not supposed to depart this three-year assignment with MARFORAF/EUR in Stuttgart, Germany until October 2012, I departed on July 30, 2011. Given what I had been subjected to, I just wanted to get back to the US as soon as possible. I arrived safely in the US on July 30, 2011.

On August 2, 2011, Stanley Bradley conducted testimonial interviews with all his identified witnesses except MARFOREUR/AF Staff Judge Advocate (SJA) Major William Hennessy. According to the ROI dated October 18, 2011, dates of the investigation were August 2-17, 2011. For reasons stated and provided, I did not participate in this blatantly deficient, biased, jeopardized, and purposely and intentionally flawed bogus DOD EEO investigative process.

Even to the time of my departure, I really believed all that I had been subjected to regarding MARFOREUR/AF was a *foreign service vs. military*

---

service institutional turf war where I was a pawn caught up in the middle. Though I must admit, even at the time, I couldn't believe this *silent war, apparently really real,* was permitted to even occur, and then get this bad. Even at the time, I internally questioned that there had to be something bigger to all this that I was missing. This just didn't make sense and wasn't adding up. *Otherwise, why would the USMC deem one female State Department foreign service detailee such a threat?*

Surely, I would be safe back in the United States while working in the Office of Secretary of Defense (OSD) at and within the Pentagon, the Headquarters of our US Military, right?

CHAPTER 6

CONNECTING THE DOTS:
Law Enforcement Mantra: "See Something; Say Something." Unless of course, you are me

BACK TO WORK?

When I landed back in the US, I really hoped all the bizarreness would end—it wouldn't. I really hoped there would be justice, to include a real investigation into what just occurred in Germany and what I had been subjected to, to obtain and find out the truth—there wasn't. In fact, it would get unbelievably worse—particularly as I connected more and more dots. The *targeting* of me continued from overseas to the shores of the United States of America.

Before reporting to my DOD/OSD/AFR detail assignment at the Pentagon, I went on Home Leave in Pennsylvania with my family. During this time, I really tried to decompress from that horrific ordeal and to relax, reenergize, regain my strength and focus for my next new chapter.

I was looking forward to working at OSD/AFR, and was delighted to be working for DASD, S/FSO Vicki Huddleston, who replaced Theresa Whelan. Though I would have enjoyed working with Theresa again, it was my understanding that her departure was for higher promotion potential. I was delighted for Theresa's new opportunity. Others, however, would speculate that Theresa was actually intentionally moved out so that Vicki could be moved in. I actually don't know for a fact either way. From my perspective, I wanted nothing but the best for both female leaders in our USG/national security ranks.

With my Home Leave coming to an end, I started to focus on my transition back to the Washington, D.C. area. The plan was to travel back on September 5, 2011, and report to OSD/AFR the next day. Since this detail was under State/PM Bureau—as was my previous MARFOREUR/ AF POLAD assignment—PM would remain my *home* bureau. This point becomes particularly relevant in about a year's time…

With any transition there are unforeseen obstacles, but in this instance, there appeared to be more than was typical. My planned OSD/AFR start date would have to be modified with many administrative tasks delaying my arrival. There was drama with my temporary housing check-in, then with the arrival of my unaccompanied Air Freight (UAB) and my vehicle, next with the passing of my security clearance, and for weeks, with my official computer access. For those who have experienced a USG transfer, this appears just to be normal. But then these events would occur…

On Tuesday, September 20, 2011, I sent the following email to PM Official Richard O'Shea, ccing Shaun Redden:

> Hello there Richard—I'm so sorry about this next request…It seems after I went to visit Shaun, enroute from his office to the Pentagon Shuttle bus stop on C Street today—I lost my newly issued State Dept Badge. I've called DS, and continue to check with them to see if anyone turned it in. Even Shaun was so kind to run down to the security office in his building to see if I dropped it along the way or in that office.
>
> So, as I said I apologize in advance—but seems I may need to get another badge. Thus, I will need another DS-1838 form from your office, a signature from the SCI office and then go to badge office. The really bad part about this request is this time I will need to be escorted since I will have no State badge on me—unlike last time.
>
> I was just wondering if any time works better for you/your office this week than another to do this…I plan on calling the DS office every so often to see if anyone turned it in as I really do believe I dropped it near State Dept.
>
> As I may not see your response to this email before I leave for work tomorrow morning, I'll give you a call when I get to the office.
>
> Again, I am so sorry in advance—but fingers crossed that someone finds it and turns it in to DS in the meanwhile. Thanks, michelle[1]

On Wednesday, September 21, 2011, Richard, ccing Shaun, replied:

> Michelle,
> Come on by when you can. Anyone in this office can fill out your new badge form. I'm here in the mornings and this is my last week. If I'm not here call in on [REDACTED], our main number and someone will meet you.
> Thanks.
> Richard

---

[1]   Michelle Stefanick, email message to Richard O'Shea and Shaun Redden, September 20, 2011

Richard J. O'Shea
Management Officer
ISN-PM-VCI/EX/HR[2]

I replied to Richard:

Hello there Richard—Just wanted to say Thank you to Pat and all her assistance this morning in getting me my replacement badge. Don't know if I will see you by weeks end … so if not, thank you for everything and Godspeed with your new assignment. Cheers, michelle[3]

Richard replied:

Thanks Michelle, sorry I missed you this morning![4]

Losing my newly-issued State Department identification badge—which I've never misplaced, let alone lost before—was odd. It was even odder, that no one turned my newly-issued supposedly lost one in despite my only being on State Department property the entire time when I supposedly lost it.

Soon after I began working at the Pentagon/OSD, I was standing at the State Dept Shuttle bus stop area, when I ran into Billie Corbett. Billie was an FBI Agent. I knew him as an MSG while assigned to Embassy Nairobi. Billie was part of the MSG Detachment that relocated from Embassy Nairobi to Embassy Pretoria a short time before the August 7, 1998 East Africa Embassy bombing. At the time, I really didn't think anything of it. However, in a matter of time, I would think, wait a minute, that was interesting. What a coincidence running into Billie, with our history, his new background and given all that had just occurred while I was in Germany assigned with MARFOREUR/AF. *I just simply ran into Billie at the State Department Shuttle bus area, when I did, given that he was now FBI, right? Or was it?*

While I was in Stuttgart, no investigation was conducted and no one assisted me. Now stateside, in order to get to the truth and to the bottom of all this, I reported accordingly, every and any opportunity I had. For any and every situation that arose, I wanted to document everything, to support the evident pattern that was occurring. And for the sake of evidential matter. The spectrum of bizarre incidents, occurrences, coinci-

2   Richard O'Shea, email message to Michelle Stefanick and Shaun Redden, September 21, 2011
3   Michelle Stefanick, email message to Richard O'Shea, September 21, 2011
4   Richard O'Shea, email message to Michelle Stefanick, September 21, 2011

dences was broadening. And more importantly, continuing to occur, and again, even in the United States. And even while I was assigned to the Pentagon/OSD. There was no doubt I was being targeted, had been targeted and continued to be targeted. Based on all these facts and occurrences at this point, I was clearly convinced. The question remains, why didn't others see and conclude accordingly as well? *Michelle is being targeted!* At this point, I did not realize that a reason was because of being a victim/witness to the August 7, 1998 East Africa Embassy bombings. I mean, why would it be? I attended the applicable East Africa Embassy trial in NYC in June 2001. *So who was it? Who was targeting me? Why? And soon the question would be, who could I trust?*

Bizarre events included my personal computer/internet. Initially I just thought my computer had been hacked. But what has happening was much broader than just hacking. The events started while I was back in Germany—curiously starting right around the same time as my reporting the smashed car door incident and filing my informal/formal EEO Grievance—around the time of bin Laden's capture/killing, and soon after, for the very first time, obtaining an indication that the bombing was an *inside job…*

Hoping to finally catch *whomever* in the act, I again did as requested. This time, being stateside, I also reported accordingly. Being in Washington D.C., the headquarter locations of our USG's military, law enforcement, intelligence apparatus, surely all this would come to an end with a proper investigation being carried out, criminals caught and arrested, and the reason for all this to finally come to light.

On Wednesday October 12, 2011, based on my discussion with State/DS, I sent the following email:

> Subject: ATTN: John – Stefanick Identity Theft
>
> Hello John – I wanted to thank you for discussing this issue with me. Needless to say, it's not a very good time for me as I try to grapple with the magnitude of what was done to me. That being said, as advised, please find below all the actions I've taken upon notification that it appears that I was a victim of Identity Theft and recover from this traumatic situation.
>
> In the morning of October 7, I checked my USAA account to monitor my insurance when I noticed that my Credit Card account looked (locked) out. I immediately called USAA to find out that earlier that morning (approximately at 1:30 A.M.) someone called to report a lost credit card. USAA immediately cancelled the card

and proceed for a replacement to be sent to me. I advised that I never called to report a lost card, let alone at 1:30 A.M. in the morning.

Later that day, on October 7, I noticed an unscheduled payment transaction pending in my State Dept Federal Credit Union account for [REDACTED] which I did not authorize. I immediately notified SDFCU of my concern and asked for details regarding this transaction. At that time, I was notified it was a payment for USAA. As I did not authorize this transaction, SDFCU sent me a Written Statement of Unauthorized Debit which I filled out and immediately faxed to them regarding this transaction. As soon as I got home, I immediately called USAA to let them know that I did not authorize the transaction and sent the fax to SDFCU the Written Statement. The representative stated that it appeared that the payment was done online and if I did do/authorize the transaction, then I was a victim of identity theft. She noted that they would begin an investigation and provided me numbers of theft identity/fraud to call.

Since these USAA offices were not open over the weekend, I changed my USAA as well as all my online financial account related usernames/passwords.

On Monday October 10, I called both numbers to find out what was going on and what could be done to stop the "payment request" since I was getting NSF charges. I was distraught to hear that my call representative on Oct 7 had not been noted on my file. They finally noted that they shut down my online account as well as will begin an investigation. They said a replacement credit card was being sent to me.

On Tuesday October 11, I called to find out the status and it was at that time they were not only opened an investigation but a case file for identity theft. The continued to stop access on my online account until investigation (expected into the next week) is concluded. I received my replacement Credit Card.

In the meanwhile, on October 6 I was notified about a suspicious phone payment into my Bank of America account and that they closed my Credit Card account.

On Oct 12 I was finally able to contact with the Bank of America representative, explaining what was happening with my USAA account. Though the closed my credit card account, they were anticipating a "phone payment" was fraudulent and it was at that time I was informed a payment request was processed from a Citibank account. I notified them that I did not have a Citibank account. With me on the phone, the BOA representative called Citibank to query on this transaction/checking account charged, but was unsuccessful in reaching a Citibank rep in order to confirm.

I was meanwhile advised that it appears I was indeed a victim of Identify Theft and that I should contact the three credit bureaus and the police about this situation. Before the police arrived, I called Jim Foy, DS PM Security Officer about my situation. He recommended I contact George Agustin.

I immediately contacted one Credit Bureau and the police. Though Police Officer Rihl (#1298) was very helpful and quick to come to my house to discuss, as the investigation of both USAA and Bank of America were still ongoing and did not prove the "fraud" took place in Arlington County, he advised that I call all three, not just one of the Credit bureaus even though they were required to notify all three with such notification, as well as the Social Security Administration (Federal Trade Commission) about my social security number being jeopardized. They were to be notified if USAA and/or BOA determined that the fraud took place in Arlington.

I immediately called the other two Credit Bureaus and SSA/FTC (Ref # REDACTED]) to report my victimization of Identity Theft. I then called/sent an email to George Agustin who contacted me and listened to my situation and got back with me on what I should do. He said DS/PS required due diligence on my part and to report to law enforcement, which I said I did. He provided me the phone number to DS customer care at 1-866-643-4636. I called and spoke with "John" where we discussed my situation on what I should do as "victim" in this situation. As noted above, USAA and BOA are doing investigations; I called the Arlington Police to file a report; I have changed usernames and passwords on my online accounts; I've filed a report with SSA/FTC; I've notified the credit bureaus; I've called to cancel/replace credit cards; and I've called every Mortgage/bank institution I have accounts with: USAA (replacement card requested); BOA (cancelled credit card); SDFCU (replacement card requested), Chase (replacement card requested); closed Service Credit Union bank account; called the following mortgage/2 th trust holders for my three Real Estate/rental properties: Bank of America, Chase, Wells Fargo, Green Tree Servicing, and United.

As I am currently assigned to the Pentagon on an exchange with OSD/Policy – ISA/Africa, I plan to notify their applicable Security Officer tomorrow on what has occurred and what action I have taken, particularly with DS in light of my responsibilities of a Security Clearance holder.

I am now doing all I can to recover from the financial and emotional damage that has been due to being a Victim of Identity Theft.

Please note the above was to document my due diligence in regards to this incident and my seriousness of being a Security Clearance holder. If there is any other information needed at this time or should be included at this time, please let me know and I will provide accordingly. In the mean while I am now awaiting the results of the USAA and BOA investigations and taking action regarding the financial impact this has caused/and monitoring very closely hereafter. Thank you, Michelle Stefanick[5]

Due to events that subsequently occurred, I would file an applicable Freedom of Information Act (FOIA) request with the Arlington County Police Department (ACPD). In the February 11, 2015 ACPD/Internal Affairs Section Lieutenant Scott Linder response, I obtained documents as requested. Included in this response was the report regarding the call I made on October 12, 2011, when I filed an applicable report with ACPD regarding this apparent identity theft issue. So ACPD knew and had on file my initial reporting to them of the oddity of events that were continuining to occur even after my departure from Germany with MARFOREUR/AF and now also on American soil.

On Thursday, October 13, 2011, I sent an email to Ivory London:

> Subject: Meeting Request
> Hello Mr. London – I recently arrived in OSD Policy on State/ DOD exchange detail. I was wondering if you had a few minutes of time for me to discuss a matter with you. Thank you so much and have a great day. Regards, Michelle
> Michelle L. Stefanick
> Regional Director, West Africa
> OSD-Policy, African Affairs[6]

Ivory London responded:

> Hi Michelle, sure you can chat with me at any available time. Give me a call to schedule a meeting or engage in a phone conversation.
> V/r
> Ivory B. London
> Security Officer/SSCO,
> Office of the Under Secretary of Defense for Policy[7]

---

5   Michelle Stefanick, email message to US Dpartment of State DS John (No Last Name Ever Provided) Independent Contractor Customer Service Center Personnel Security/Suitability , October 12, 2011
6   Michelle Stefanick, email message to Ivory London, October 13, 2011
7   Ivory London, email message to Michelle Stefanick, October 13, 2011

I then met with Ivory London face-to-face to discuss the matter. After, I sent:

> Thank you, Mr. London for meeting with me and for passing along the information/insight. I will look into both accordingly. Have a great evening. Cheers, michelle[8]

On Thursday, October 13, 2011, I received a response from State/DS *John*:

> Subject: RE: ATTN: John – Stefanick Identity Theft
> Michelle,
> I have forwarded this to be included in your file. Please hang on to a copy yourself. If you have any additional information at any time, please send it to us.
> All the Best,
> John
> Independent Contractor
> Customer Service Center
> Personnel Security/Suitability
> US Department of State[9]

I responded on Friday October 14, 2011:

> Thanks John—I sure will. I spoke with OSD/Policy Security yesterday just so they were aware.
> I noticed that my two SDFCU/NSF charges in relations to the fraudulent USAA transaction were reversed, so I am hoping to find out more once I get back with them.
> Have a nice weekend. Cheers, michelle[10]

I never heard back from SDFCU, United States Automobile Association (USAA) or BOA regarding their investigation. Former MARFOREUR/AF Commander BGen Tracy Garrett was on the USAA Board of Directors. I had numerous discussions with the applicable financial institutions in the months/years to follow. DS SAs were not only assigned at both EUCOM and AFRICOM, but also throughout Germany. And now, I heard radio silence from DS regarding this event that occurred in Arlington that I report-

---

8   Michelle Stefanick, email message to Ivory London, October 13, 2011
9   Michelle Stefanick, email message to US Dpartment of State DS John (No Last Name Ever Provided) Independent Contractor Customer Service Center Personnel Security/Suitability, October 13, 2011
10   Michelle Stefanick, email message to US Dpartment of State DS John (No Last Name Ever Provided) Independent Contractor Customer Service CenterPersonnel Security/Suitability, October 14, 2011

ed accordingly. Oh wait, I did hear back once—in January 2012. So again, given all that occurred, and given my federal CVRA *victim/witness status*, why were there *no investigations and why wasn't I protected?*

In the fall of 2011, the Official Promotion Panel cable was released and my name was not on it. Given all that had transpired and that I had been subjected to, this was absolutely not a surprise. It was yet another documented support of the pattern that I had already been enduring since the August 7, 1998 Embassy bombing aftermath. This time it was carried out at the hands of the USMC, the US military. At the time, I really didn't see the direct correlation. I simply attributed all that was happening to the concern I first personally became aware of while attending the Army War College. And thus, shared accordingly with U/S Patrick Kennedy regarding this very real foreign service vs. military service dynamic; clash of our two institutions.

On November 1, 2011, I received the October 20, 2011 USAG Stuttgart/Dept of Army/EEO Office letter advising that *the investigation pertaining to subject complaint of discrimination filed on 12 May 2011 has been completed.* I had 30 calendar days from receipt of this notice to request either a hearing before an Equal employment Opportunity Commission (EEOC) administrative judge or a final US Army decision. Additionally, I received a copy of the DOD/EEO Investigative File for my complaint (*DA Docket Number: AREUSTUT11APR01642*). The DOD/EEO Investigative File, including the ROI dated October 18, 2011, was 405 pages.

On Wednesday, November 2, 2011, I reached out to AFSA/Legal Counsel Neera Parikh to arrange a time to meet. A week later, I met with Neera to discuss the status of my EEO Grievance as well as my options to file an AFSA Grievance.

At this time, I still hadn't heard back from SDFCU, USAA or BOA, but I had no doubt it was all connected and interlinked to the events that occurred in Germany. Again, at this time, I was, without a doubt, convinced that it was connected to the EEO grievance I filed, and I just patiently waited to hear back to have more concrete evidence. To this day, I never heard back regarding any of these investigations…

Additionally, since the last email I received from new incoming MARFOREUR/AF Deputy Commander Colonel Chiarotti dated July 29, 2011 stated *"if you need anything from me or the staff in order to assist you during your transition, pls do not hesitate to let me know,"* I reached out accordingly. On Monday November 14, 2011, I emailed now recently promoted BGen Chiarotti:

Subject: RE: Departure

Hello Gen Chiarotti – I hope this finds you well and all settled in at MARFOREUR/AF in Stuttgart. I'm still in transition, but have at least begun settling into my new position here at OSD/POL – Africa working for DASD Huddleston.

I really hate to bother you with this but I kindly ask you for your assistance/insight on a request I have. Since I moved back to DC earlier than anticipated I am in temporary quarters until my residence is vacated in 8/2012. Though I have a clause in my lease, my tenants are a Canadian military officer with two small children, and a third on the way assigned to the Pentagon. I am leasing temp quarters but since I cannot take delivery of my entire shipment until August of next year, I was in need of a small partial delivery consisting of my winter clothes and my Tax files/records in order for me to get through until August.

Though I have both State and DOD orders, the DOD orders actually covered my shipment of personal effects and according to folks here at Ft Belvoir need to be amended to cover the costs for a Partial Delivery of my Household goods, which should be minimal as it would only include my clothes/records.

I wasn't sure how to proceed with this since the G-1 handled all this before I departed. Again, I hate to bother you on such a matter, but thought you would be a good start to feed me into the DOD order cutting process.

Thank you again for any insight/assistance you can provide. Please let me know if there is anything I can ever assist with and again, I hope all is well. Sincere Regards, Michelle[11]

On Tuesday, November 15, 2011, I received the following response:

Michelle,
Greetings. Glad to hear all is well. I have our G-1 folks into whether or not we can support your request. I'll get back to you shortly.
BGen Chiarotti
Charles Chiarotti
BGen USMC
Deputy Cmdr MARFOR AF/EUR[12]

Later, BGen Chiarotti responded, ccing LtCol Robert Renard and Col Adam J. Copp:

11   Michelle Stefanick, email message to Charles Chiarotti, November 14, 2011
12   Charles Chiarotti, email message to Michelle Stefanick, November 15, 2011

Michelle,

What you are asking for is not possible given the current regulation. Normally, the only time that non-temporary storage (NTS) is approved is if you are in execution of concurrent or follow on orders which require your to place or leave your HHGs into storage. What you are asking for is considered by the government to be a personal convenience and not service directed type of request. I fully understand and appreciate your situation—allowing the family to stay until next summer is truly nice on your part and considerate. However, the government is not liable for the added expense of that decision. You are entitled to have your HHG goods delivered from the current location to your house or any location you desire—the expense for that is already part of your funded travel. We can assist with if you would like.

I would recommend making the same request to DOS—they may operate under a different set of rules when it comes to NTS. My apologizes – I wish I could be of assistance, unfortunately, my hands are tied. R/BGen Chiarotti[13]

I responded to BGen Chiarotti, ccing Renard and Copp, with the applicable State/DOD MOU as an attachment:

Thank you, BGen Chiarotti—I actually already outreached to State and they noted that in accordance with the MOU between State and DOD, the reason State did not move my effects was because I was under the SOFA, not the COM authorities. That is why DOD moved/has my affects at this time and why State did not do my move.

According to folks at Ft Belvoir, they are the ones that advised I contacted you all since Military is authorized this in their move orders. Hearing from both State and Ft Belvoir, I reread/attached the applicable MOU. Seems their reading of the State/DOD MOU in effect states that under Supply, Transportation, and Facility Support under RESPONSIBILTIES, II DOD is responsible for .... Providing office space, transportation, supplies and logistical support at the same level afforded to officers of equivalent pay grades assigned to the Command or service concerned. And again, if State and Ft. Belvoir had not provided the insight they both had I wouldn't have contacted you. Thanks, michelle[14]

13   Charles Chiarotti, email message to Michelle Stefanick,Robert Renard, and Adam Copp, November 15, 2011
14   Michelle Stefanick, email message to Charles Chiarotti, Robert Renard, and Adam Copp, November 15, 2011

Needless to say, I would have a partial delivery made, and continue storage at my own expense. When I moved via DOD to Stuttgart, it was the worst USG PCS move I ever experienced. With the number of items destroyed and damaged, to include a wood-carved Lamu mirror, it was also the first time I ever had to file a claim.

Meanwhile, on Tuesday, December 13, 2011, I received an email from SSGT Douglas C. Pippen, USMC SSGT Pippen:

> Subject: storage (UNCLASSIFIED)
> Good morning Ma'am,
> You will need to get an amendment to your orders stating how many days of storage you are authorized to have. As a DOD civilian you are only authorized 90 days of storage.
> R/S
> SSGT Dougles C. Pippen
> JPPSOWA INBOUND S.I.T.
> FORT BELVOIR, VA[15]

I responded:

> Hello SSGT Pippen – I explained to folks in your office earlier that I am a State Dept Foreign Service Officer (Not a civilian) and explained the situation. I was advised at the time that all I needed to do is fill out this paperwork and submitted it and the extension is automatic. I have done what I was advised to do.
>   If that is not the case, please advise what I should do as my tenants are as stated assigned to the Pentagon until July 31, 2012. I'm out of my assignment early because of the USMC. I am not asking the Canadian military Officer assigned at the JIEDDO working on behalf of our military serving in Afghanistan to depart early. So please advise what I should do. Thank you. michelle[16]

On January 5, 2012, I received the following email from SSGT Douglas Pippen:

> Did anyone get back to you about your storage?[17]

Again, I ended up paying for the storage of my effects out of my own pocket, yet another effect from the retaliatory action taken against me in Germany.

---

15   Douglas Pippen, email message to Michelle Stefanick, December 13, 2011
16   Michelle Stefanick, email message to Douglas Pippen, December 13, 2011
17   Douglas Pippen, email message to Michelle Stefanick, January 5, 2012

Tragic Coincidences

Under my OSD/AFR portfolio, I accompanied DASD Huddleston on many of her speaking engagements. At one such engagement at Virginia Military Institute (VMI), former S/FSO Louis Nigro was also in attendance. Now retired, he was working at PM as acting PM/POLAD Director. Soon after VMI, we would meet again, the last time I would physically see Lou. Years prior, on April 5, 2009, I had shared my AWC Strategic Research Paper with Lou. His last FS assignment was as US Ambassador to Chad. I was regional for Chad while serving in my first excursion tour to Cameroon from OIG to FS. On November 7, 2011, I received the following email from Lou:

> Subject: Great To See You
> Michelle-
> It was great to see you with Vicki at VMI Thursday.
> Vicki's and Todd's remarks really set a high standard for the Conference.
> But I think the rest of the Conference was quite good.
> A/S Carson's remarks were very well received, as well.
> Let me know if you are at State and want to do lunch or a coffee.
> Do keep in touch.
> Best regards,
> -Lou
> Louis J. Nigro
> US Ambassador (Retired)
> Acting Director
> Foreign Policy Advisor Program[18]

I replied:

> AMB Nigro – It was so wonderful seeing you as well. It's very unfortunate that we could only stay for Vicki's session, as I thought their session went off very well and would have been very insightful to hear what others had to say as well.
>
> It would be great to see you sooner than later, if your time/schedule permits, as I think you need to be aware of a matter. I plan on being at State on Wednesday morning regarding this matter in fact. Would it be possible to do lunch so I can fill you in accordingly? Thanks so much and have a great day. Cheers, michelle
> Michelle L. Stefanick
> Regional Director, West Africa
> OSD-Policy, African Affairs[19]

---

18   Louis Nigro, email message to Michelle Stefanick, November 7, 2011
19   Michelle Stefanick, email message to Louis Nigro, November 7, 2011

Lou responded:

> MLS-
> Wednesday lunch works for me.
> Where?
> --I can do HST at 12:30.
> --There is cafeteria in this building that might be change for you from HST: 12:00 or 12:30 or 1:00 here?
> Your call!
> One thing: Is Vicki aware of the issue we are going to discuss?
> -Lou[20]

I confirmed:

> Sure Lou – How about 12:30 in your building, the Red Cross building correct? I just don't know where the cafeteria in your building is located.
> Vicki is not only aware, but extremely supported of me regarding the matter. Cheers, michelle[21]

On Wednesday November 9, I met Lou for lunch at the Red Cross building, after my meeting with AFSA/Legal Counsel Neera Parikh.

On Saturday, November 12, 2011, I sent Lou a series of supporting emails.

> Subject: Insights for your consideration....
>
> Hello Lou – I am so delighted that I accompanied DAS/AMB Huddleston to VMI the week before last because it was such a nice surprise to see you there. It was also great to hear that you are, even if only for a short period of time, the acting director of the POLAD office. It is in that capacity that I thought you should be aware of my situation, if you aren't already, and possibly take my thoughts into consideration for ways to improve the process/avoid the situation that I found myself in and be avoided by any FPA/POLAD(s) in my position or any other in the future.
>
> First, let me start by saying I totally support SecState Clinton and then SecDef Gates in the importance they placed in this program and its expansion to have more State/DOD detailee exchanges. It's the only way we will learn from and by each of our applicable institutions and our cultures. That being said, I believe that this program is more important now than it has ever been in light

---

20   Louis Nigro, email message to Michelle Stefanick, November 7, 2011
21   Michelle Stefanick, email message to Louis Nigro, November 7, 2011

of a post-Iraq/Afghanistan world in which our military colleagues have been in conflict/engaged in for over 10 years now. They need us in these roles more than ever to assist them in this transition to a post-major conflict world. That is why I took the assignment I did at the Pentagon at OSD/Policy-Africa with DASD Huddleston to prove my support for this FPA/POLAD program and that I do not harbor any ill will towards our military colleagues, in light of my situation/experience in Stuttgart with MARFOREUR/AF. This may end up being a lengthy email but one I believe is necessary in order to document/understand what all happened with my situation and hopefully, in reflection, one that will be catalyst for change to the current process/procedure to avoid such situations in the future and to only make the program achieve what it meant to achieve—a win-win to both State and DOD, a true value added for both institutions, and worth the time/effort/benefit associated with the cost.

At U/S Kennedy's urging, in May 2009, I bid (as an 0-1) on the newly established PM/POLAD FE-OC position (S19324006) at US Marine Forces Europe/Africa (MARFOREUR/AF) in Stuttgart, Germany. I thought this would be a great follow-up assignment since I had just graduated from the US Army War College and had experience in both AORs serving in Cameroon, Kenya, and Sudan; and in Russia. Additionally, I thought I brought tactical, operational as well as strategic perspective that would be a bonus for the Marines. PM/PDAS Tom Countryman met with me and agreed as well. I enthusiastically bid on the position, was recommended by the DCM/PO panel to be placed on the list for the Marines consideration and was thrilled when I was selected at the end of August for the position by the Command. In December 2009, I arrived in Stuttgart to begin my tour as the first Foreign Policy Advisor/POLAD reporting to Commander General (a one-star 0-7 filling a two-star billet) General Brier of MARFOREUR/AF.

Not realizing at the time how indicative this point would be, I would like to embellish upon it now. Though I was selected at the end of August 2009, I did not arrive to Stuttgart until December 2009. This delay was not caused by State, but instead by the Marines in Stuttgart. Though I was telephone interviewed by both the MARFOREUR and MARFORAF Chiefs of Staff, I was advised to coordinate my actual move with MARFOREUR Chief of Staff Col Niblock. It appeared from the start that Col Niblock was not on board with my coming to their Command. The Commander General at the time of my selection was Tracy Garrett, and she was replaced by Paul Brier. So, I initially forgave the delay to what the Command was going through as a result of the change of command in early September. Then that month went by, and we were well into October when finally, PM PDAS at the time Tom Countryman was starting to get concerned so that he personally sent an email to Gen Brier, and when he never responded to PDAS Countryman, we began talking about my curtailing from the assignment. (It was at that time I became aware that Tom had been the FPA/POLAD of the Commandant and curtailed; and that Allan Langland curtailed from Camp Lejeune, NC where he was working with a Gen Hejlik). At that point, Col Niblock sent me a draft Position Description to dual appointment me into their system as a "civilian" and to identify that the MFE/AF Commander would be my rater and the Ray Brown, the AFRICOM 'State" FPA would be my reviewer. It appears instead of coordinating all this with the PM and/or PM/POLAD office in DC, they were working with Kate Canavan, EUCOM "State" Deputy/FPA.

I arrived in Stuttgart, and immediately encountered internal resistance from the Colonels – the two MARFOREUR and MARFORAF Chiefs of Staff, and the two applicable MARFOREUR/AF Colonel G-3/5s (Please note that MARFORAF Chief of Staff Col Lapaix and I became very close colleagues/friends). Though Gen Brier from the beginning was supportive of me and my role, the Colonels let it be known—blatantly at times, passive aggressively at others, that they did not like where I sat on the Command deck, my reporting chain directly to the General, and the traveling with him and him listening to my insight/taking my advice. I immediately advised both Ray Brown and Kate Canavan of this internal resistance, but continually praised Gen Brier for his support. When I continued to face resistance/respect/support for my position from the Colonels, I raised the Memorandum of Understanding between DOD/State, my position description, and noted for comparison purposes the grade of my position so that they were aware that though I was an FS-01, that it was quite possible that my job could be filled next time with an OC level FSO, which was equivalent to a Brigadier General. And again, though the General told the Colonels to support me, they did not. Since I was supported by General Brier, as reflected by his rater comments and Ray's reviewer comments in my I kept Ray and Kate apprised.

In July 2010, MARFOREUR and AF Chiefs of Staff departed Stuttgart. MARFOREUR Chief of Staff was replaced by Col Copp and MARFORAF was internally replaced by G3/5 Col Bright, and his position was internally replaced by Col Vessely [*sic*]. So needless to say, the situation not only didn't improve, it got worse.

On August 17, 2010, Lieutenant General Hejlik (3-star) was officially confirmed as the Commander of MARFOREUR (located in Norfolk, VA). Brigadier General Brier (one-star) at that time officially became Gen Hejlik's Deputy Commander (located in Stuttgart, Germany) and remained Commander for MARFORAF until Lieutenant General Paxton (3-star) was confirmed officially in January 18, 2011. I was concerned of this restructuring for a number of reasons, the main one being who did I now report to since there was now two Commanders, and soon two 3-Star Commanders and one Deputy Commander. Since I was supposed to report to the Commander, MFE/AF, I wanted assistance from PM—but at that time there was no one in PM/POLAD to assist me with all this, particularly since Tom Countryman had departed his position. Furthermore, it should be noted that MARFOREUR Chief of Staff Col Copp was the senior Colonel, arrived into his position in Stuttgart in July 2010, and previously worked directly with Gen Hejlik. It was during this July/Aug timeframe that my work environment became outright hostile by the Colonels, (who by the way were all Active duty, while Gen Brier was a Reservist), and particularly by Col Copp.

Despite my numerous discussions with Gen Brier of the environment I was experiencing, I felt he continually supported me and my efforts. This was until Gen Hejlik made his first visit to MARFOREUR. Though Gen Hejlik never met with me one-on-one, there seemed to be a dynamic change between Gen Brier and Col Copp, with more and more Col Copp appearing to be in charge of MARFOREUR and working directly with Gen Hejlik, bypassing Gen Brier and marginalizing me and my position more and more; and Gen Hejlik never meeting with me to discuss my role/position and in one instance, marginalizing me in front of members of this MARFOREUR Command. (Please note this is the same Gen Hejlik that Allan Langland worked for and curtailed from in his previous position). During this time, not only did it get unbearable for me, but for the other female civilians that worked directly for General Brier.

As noted earlier, with the arrival of the new MARFOREUR Chief of Staff Col Copp and the recent confirmation of Gen Hejlik as the new 3-star MARFOREUR Commander, on November 4, 2010, Kate Canavan asked to meet with me to discuss how things were going. I again raised my concern regarding the Colonels, but stating my wanting to stay in the position. (Though Kate had not helped me earlier, I really looked to her as a Senior FSO in Stuttgart for assistance—despite the comments made to me that she had gone "native" as she was now married to retired previous 3-Star General EUCOM Chief of Staff). On November 13, when things appeared to be getting worse, I sent an email to PM/PDAS Kurt Amend after Tom Countryman took a look over the email draft since he by then departed his position in PM, and he agreed with the contents. On November 29, I sent another email to Kate Canavan noting the situation as I saw it at that time, noting improvement with all the Colonels except the MARFOREUR COS, and my willingness to make this arrangement work.

On December 13, all came to a head when I met with Gen Brier and AMB Canavan, and she advised me that I need to leave and to look for another position. (Please note that it appears Kate already knew from our Nov 29 email that she was going to ask me to leave regardless of what I said.) What was incredible about this is that I never received anything in writing from General Brier stating what I was doing in fulfilling my job responsibilities and to counsel me on what I can do to improve. In fact, to that point and up to the end of my rating period, I had been receiving positive feedback on my job and believed I was again on track for an "immediate promotion" EER rating. (Please note that Gen Brier acknowledges this fact by crossing out the statement on page 1 of my 4/16/2010-4/15/2011 EER that at least one counseling session was in writing—this was crossed out because I received nothing in writing from him as to what I was not doing in accordance with my job responsibilities, what I could do to improve). And more importantly, Kate Canavan was neither in my reporting chain nor in a position to request my removal.

Ray Brown is/was my State Department Review Officer. I continually advised both him and Kate Canavan of the problems I was having in regards to the Colonels at MARFOREUR/AF from the beginning of my arrival to this assignment. But he, as my official "State" reviewer, and Gen Brier, my rater, neither alone nor together ever met with me to discuss my job performance. Kate Canavan was not in my official reporting chain and had been aware from the beginning of my arrival in this assignment for the problems with the Colonels.

In light of the Dec 13 meeting and since my request to come back to discuss the two 3-star realignment with State/PM was denied, I flew back to DC on my own dime to meet with PM to discuss the situation. Though I never met with PDAS Amend, I met with Gonzo as well as U/S Patrick Kennedy to discuss the two three-star re-alignment, not knowing who I reported to, and my situation—including that I felt that I had no one to support me. At that time, I was advised by U/S Kennedy that we "State Department" determine when you leave not the Marines, and to go back to Stuttgart and continue to do my work, focusing more on MARFORAF and less on MARFOREUR if they didn't let me do my job. It was agreed within State (U/S and PM) that I would return to Stuttgart in early January 2011, and leave until I found a job that I wanted. (Please note it is my understanding that U/S Kennedy met with PDAS Amend and AMB Canavan about this situation as well after I returned to Stuttgart).

During this entire tour, despite the hostile work environment including my car door being smashed while parked at the Command during a tdy, I carried out the duties specified in my work and job description. And though I never received anything in writing to the otherwise, I received positive feedback regarding the job I did/continue to do throughout the entire rating period. Unfortunately, I do not believe this EER rating accurately reflects upon my accomplishments I had during this rating period because Gen Brier's rate/review officer was three-star Gen Hejlik, and Gen Hejlik was not happy when I returned to post in early January with the support of U/S Kennedy and PM officials. And though Ray Brown was my State Review officer, he was rated by 4-star AFRICOM General Ward. (Please note that during this time I advised AMB James McGhee, the State FPA/POLAD for NAVEUR/AF, and he was appalled by my treatment and assisted the best he could to ensure that my due process/rights were adhere to and totally understood what I said was happening to me. AMB Holmes, the State AFRICOM Deputy, took no role/responsibility during this entire ordeal).

I was the first in this newly established FPA/POLAD position with the Marine Forces Europe/Africa. Despite the marginalizing/hostile/challenging environment I encountered during my time in Stuttgart, I strongly believe it is essential that these such positions exist in order to influence these military institutions in a post-Iraq/Afghanistan world about who State Department is and what lead role our institution plays regarding foreign policy and national security priorities. However, that being said, I believe I have suffered enough during this tour—both personally and professionally—and truly have taken one for the "State" team. I had to file an

EEO grievance (against the Secretary of Army since Stuttgart is a Garrison) due to the hostile environment I and others I witnessed experienced; I am now in the process of filing a grievance (through State/AFSA) to get my latest EER from MARFOREUR/AF expunged from my OPF and my TIC extended; and I am now facing personal humiliation and financial expenses due to the fact that my 3-year assignment was curtailed by 17 months.

I am the fourth FPA/POLAD to no longer work with the Marines. Trends such as this need to be honestly assessed and processes need to be reviewed to ensure the terms of the MOU are adhered to, such arrangements are a win-win to both State and DOD, and that most importantly, State assets are treated professionally and with respect and supported by their own when such occurrences do arise—that is by the way why we are doing this such positions, because we need to get our two institutions to work together despite our cultural differences and to have the Military Commands to turn us State FSOs into "Marines, Soldiers, and/or Sailors."

I hope my experience/observations I noted above will be taken into serious considerations for reflection on how to make our process better to ensure the program that Sec Clinton envisioned truly comes to fruition. And if anything, to prevent any other FPA/POLAD to go through what I went through. Thank you for your patience reading through all this—but I thought you should be aware. Please let me know if you need any assistance and/or any other information/insight to indeed improve this process. Regards, michelle[22]

On Friday, November 11, 2011, Lou sent me the following email:

Subject: Our Chat
Michelle-
Good to see you this week.
If you send me your info memo/aide memoire, as we discussed, I will make it available to PM/FO.
Regards,
-Lou[23]

I replied Monday, November 14, 2011:

Lou – As always it was great seeing you as well. I sent you the memo/info from my personal email account this weekend. Please

22   Michelle Stefanick, email message to Louis Nigro, November 12, 2011
23   Louis Nigro, email message to Michelle Stefanick, November 11, 2011

let me know if you don't/didn't receive it. Thanks again and have a great week. Cheers, michelle[24]

Lou replied:

Michelle-
Got it all.
It will take me a bit of time to get something to PDAS.
No guarantees on what he'll say!
I'll keep in touch.
-Lou
PS: I like your slide presentations. I'm still working my way thru them. -LJN[25]

On January 1, 2013, Louis J. Nigro passed away. At the time, I was saddened when hearing of Lou's passing. *Given what I now suspected this was all about, just like Mary Ryan, and Ted Sorensen, did I think foul play was a possibility? Absolutely.*

In addition to speaking engagements, I also attended applicable forums around the Washington D.C. area, sometimes accompanying the DASD, and other times representing my portfolio or the office. At one such event, I ran into yet another State Africa hand, John Lange. A fellow survivor of the August 7, 1998 East Africa Embassy bombings, John was Charge d'Affaires at Embassy Dar es Salaam at the time. On Tuesday, October 4, 2011, I emailed John the following:

Subject: Nice surprise!
Hello there John—Just wanted to pass a quick note to say how nice it was to see you today. It's always so great to see a fellow State Africa hand—a "friendly"—at such forums. Hope to run into you again soon, hopefully next time with a little more time so we can catch up some. Have a great evening. Cheers, michelle
Michelle L. Stefanick
Regional Director, West Africa
OSD-Policy, African Affairs[26]

On Wednesday, November 2, 2011, John replied:

Dear Michelle,
Thank you very much for your email. Please accept my apologies for this delayed response—I happened to find your message today

24   Michelle Stefanick, email message to Louis Nigro, November 14, 2011
25   Louis Nigro, email message to Michelle Stefanick, November 14, 2011
26   Michelle Stefanick, email message to John Lange, October 4, 2011

in my junk email folder! I hope you are doing well at OSD and look forward to seeing you again soon. Let's try to get together for coffee one of these days. Do you ever make it the McPherson Square area (not fare from the Gates Foundation office)?

Warm regards,

John

Ambassador John E. Lange (Ret.)

Senior Program Officer for Developing-Country Policy & Advocacy

Global Health Program[27]

I responded on Friday, November 4, 2011:

Hello there John—No problem. I must admit when I think about my "after State" life, the Gates Foundation comes to mind as a possibility that I would really be interested in pursuing. I met with some of your folks while up on the Hill working for Senator Snowe and have nothing but the utmost respect for the Gate's efforts and willingness to get involved in such global issues. All that being said, if you have the time to not only have that cup of coffee to catch-up but to give me a tour/brief of your office/efforts in Africa that would really make my day. Let me know what you think? Thanks so much and have a great weekend. Cheers, michelle[28]

We met at the Gates Foundation located on 1300 Eye Street, N.W. on Wednesday, November 16, 2011. And again, John Lange was Charge d'Affaires at Embassy Dar es Salaam at the time of the August 7, 1998 East Africa Embassy bombings.

That week, I also consulted with State/Office of Civil Rights (OCR) Greg Smith on Monday, November 14 regarding the next steps of my EEO Grievance. After I explained to Greg that no real investigation was conducted, he recommended that I file a spin-off complaint regarding the investigation of my formal EEO complaint, as well as request a hearing. Based on items displayed in Greg's office, he had a military background, apparently a Navy background.

On November 22, 2011, I filed the following spin-off complaint:

USAG Stuttgart EEO Office

IMEU-EEO

Unit 30401

APO AE 09107

Dear Sir or Madam:

27   John Lange, email message to Michelle Stefanick, November 7, 2011
28   Michelle Stefanick, email message to John Lange, November 4, 2011

I am writing to file a spin-off complaint regarding the investigation of my formal EEO Complaint, DA Docket Number: AREUSTUT-11APR01642. The information below pertains:

On November 1, 2011, I received by certified mail this attached letter (dated 20 October 2011) and a copy of the investigative file in relation to my complaint (DA Docket Number: AREUSTUT-11APR01642. As stated in attached reference letter, the primary purpose of the investigative file is "to develop the facts of the case and provide the basis for deciding this complaint."

The requirement for the agency to investigate complaints of discrimination is codified in 29 C.F.R. 1614.108. This regulation requires the agency to develop an impartial and appropriate factual record upon which to make findings on the claim or claims raised in the complaint. As stated in Section 1614.108 (a), "an appropriate factual record is one that allows a reasonable fact finder to draw conclusions as to whether discrimination occurred."

In accordance to Chapter 6 of EEOC Management Directive 110 (dated 11/21/2011), the investigator must be and must maintain the appearance to be unbiased, objective and thorough; and is required to conduct a thorough investigation identifying and obtaining all relevant evidence from all sources regardless of how it may affect the outcome. While this requirement does not compel the investigator to engage in irrelevant and superfluous inquiry, it does require that the investigator exhaust those of information likely to support the positions of complainant and the agency.

In this case (DA Docket Number: AREUSTUT11APR01642), I do not believe the standard as specified in the 29 CFR and EEOC MD 110 as referenced above were met. For example,

I was advised that my testimony, and only my testimony, had to be provided in front of those I believe created and enabled the hostile work environment of which my claim was based.

The witnesses I provided on my Proposed Witness List, including those that could substantiate my claim as well as provide first-hand insight regarding their own experience to a hostile work environment, were not interviewed.

The one witness, Staff Judge Advocate Major William Hennessy, on my Proposed Witness List that was supposed to be interviewed according to the Investigator, and who had first-hand knowledge regarding my claim, was never interviewed though listed on Investigation Schedule – Attachment 1. Specifically, this witness could substantiate "Incident E" referenced in Part II – Summary of Evidence of the Report of Investigation (ROI).

The ROI references pages, documents, exhibits that are not included in the file provided/included in the Investigative File provided to me, the Complainant.

Documents such as the 2010 MARFOREUR Climate Survey, the 2011 MARFORAF Climate Survey, the 2010 AFRICOM Climate Survey, the EEO MOU between HQ, US Marine Forces Europe/Africa and USAG Stuttgart, 2011 Gen Ham's requested review of MARFORAF, were not included in this Investigative File.

Other documents were provided to the Investigator, such as the Department of Defense/State Department Memorandum of Understanding, my Position Description, my Supporting Insight Memo regarding a Hostile Environment with attachments/photos (of my smashed vehicle) but were not provided in the Investigative File.

The Investigator was identified right before I was to depart Stuttgart, Germany and the Fact Finding took place in Stuttgart after my departure.

As a result, and in accordance with Chapter 5 of EEOC Management Directive 110 (dated 11/21/2011), I am writing to file a spin-off complaint regarding the investigation of my formal EEO complaint, DA Docket Number: AREUSTUTT11APR01642.
Sincerely,
/s/
Michelle L. Stefanick, Complainant
Attachment:
Copy of the Department of the Army/United States Army Garrison – Stuttgart/Unit 30401/APO AE 09107-0401 letter signed by Eshe Faulcon Acting Equal Employment Opportunity Manager dated October 20, 2011, received November 1, 2011, advising "that the investigation pertaining to subject complaint of discrimination filed on 12 May 2011 has been completed." (DA Docket Number: AREUSTUT11APR01642).[29]

On November 23, 2011, I submitted the applicable *Request for a Hearing* response letter to the USAG Stuttgart/Department of the Army/EEO Office and the Equal Employment Opportunity Commission (EEOC) Washington Field Office.

Soon after, DASD Vicki Huddleston announced her departure from OSD. Being SFS, Vicki understood the necessity for my performance to be documented. Since this was for a period of less than 90 days, instead of using the standard DS-5055 form, before Vicki departed, she completed

29   Michelle Stefanick, spinoff complaint to USAG Stuttgart EEO Office, October 4, 2011

a *Memorandum of Performance* for a period covering September 19, 2011 – December 16, 2011, signed December 20, 2011. I included Vicki on the Friday, December 16, 2011 email I sent to HR Andrea Bryant requesting it be included in my OPF. I wanted to ensure it was reviewed by my next applicable Promotion Panel for SFS Promotion consideration. Why Vicki signed it *December 20, 2011*, instead of December 16, 2011, only she can explain.

> Subject: Memo of Performance – Stefanick
> Hello Andrea – I was hoping you could assist me. I'm currently on a State/DOD exchange detail at the Pentagon working for AMB Vicki Huddleston, the Deputy Assistant Secretary of Defense for African Affairs. AMB Huddleston has been my rater since my arrival in her office September, and today is her last day. Since this was a period less than 90 days, AMB Huddleston prepared the attached Memo of Performance for submission to my Official Personnel File.
>
> Hopefully you are the correct person to assist with this. If you are not, could you please provide the appropriate person within HR/PE that I should contact. Thank you so very much and have a great weekend. Cheers, michelle
> Michelle L. Stefanick
> Regional Director, West Africa
> OSD-Policy, African Affairs[30]

Until February 2012, my second Ambassador while I served in Moscow, Russia from 2000-2002, Alexander "Sandy" Vershbow, was also at the Pentagon. In March 2009, President Obama nominated Ambassador Vershbow as Assistant Secretary of Defense for International Security Affairs this position was responsible for US policy toward NATO and coordination of US security and defense policies relating to the nations and international organizations of Europe, the Middle East and Africa. He was confirmed in April 2009, and in essence my boss' (Vicki Huddleston's) boss.

Huddleston was replaced by Amanda Dory, another female professional. Out of the blue one day, I received a call from my AWC NSPP days, Al Stolberg, confirming who the next DASD would be—and once advised, he voiced his support of her selection.

Soon after DASD Dory's arrival, Amanda raised environmental challenges with security implications for Africa as being inadequately covered

---

30   Michelle Stefanick, email message to Andrea Bryant and Vicki Huddleston, December 16, 2011

within the current OSD/AFR portfolio structure. When asked, I accepted this new addition to my portfolio without hestitation. At the time, the 2010 US National Security Strategy assigned responsibility for addressing the climate change threat to both US Department of State and US Agency for International Development (USAID). I was invited as the first OSD/AFR representative to participate in State's OES (Bureau of Oceans, International Environmental and Scientific Affairs) international water working group, opening a dialogue on how DOD can support State's and USAID's efforts.

So many opportunities opened up to me as a result of this addition to my portfolio, or so I thought at the time. Now I suspected that there may have been much more to these opportunities that came my way, to include the places that I traveled and the individuals that I came to meet, as a result.

On a personal note, since I opened my window in June 2008, unless promoted into the SFS, I would TIC out of the Department of State in October 2015. Given my time in the bush while serving on the Continent, climbing Mt. Kilimanjaro and Mt. Kenya, my trip down the Yangtze River before the flooding of the Three Gorges dam in China, and my recent trip to Antarctica, I saw ending my USG career with connections in the environmental challenges' community as an invaluable opportunity. However, never in my wildest dreams could I have ever envisioned what the USG would do next to ensure I did not have a next career, let alone credibility when I departed this one…

Meanwhile, on January 4, 2012, I received a letter from the US EEOC – Washington Field Office:

> Re: EEOC Case No. 570-2012-00235X, Agency No. AREUS-TUT11APR01642
> The Washington Field Office has received your request for hearing. The parties will be informed of the assignment of an Administrative Judge to process this request as soon as possible.
> Date: December 30, 2011/s/
> Gladys O. Collazo
> Supervisory Administrative Judge[31]

Interestingly enough, this December 30, 2011 EEOC-Washington Field Office letter ended with these four words, "as soon as possible." This is particularly interesting given the date that I would finally be informed of the assignment of an administrative judge.

---

31   Gladys Collazo, letter to Michelle Stefanick, December 30, 2011

About January 6, 2012, I received a response regarding my November 22, 2011 filed Spin-off complaint. The four-page December 21, 2011 response letter signed by USAG Stuttgart/Depart of Army/EEO Manager Ronnie L. Holmes, reflected our continual disagreement regarding this matter. Apparently, a resolution would only be determined in the upcoming hearing that I requested.

Interestingly enough, neither my November 22, 2011 Spin-off Complaint nor USAG Stuttgart/Depart of Army/EEO Manager December 21, 2011 Spin-off Complaint response was provided to the EEOC, DOD/EEO ROI Investigator, nor DOD/Director of Investigations and Resolution by the USAG Stuttgart/Dept of Army/EEO Office. Apparently, quite apparently, behind the scenes, someone had a hand in influencing the DOD, and now EEOC EEO Grievance Process—*and it wasn't me.*

On January 6, 2012, I had an email exchange with Eshe:

> RE: Request for Current Mailing Address (Unclassified)
> Hello Ms. Faulcon –
> Though not sent certified, I just wanted to let you know that I received the response packed from your office regarding my spin-off complaint. After reviewing the packet contents, I stand by the position I state in my referenced letter of November 22, 2011.
>
> On January 4, 2012, I received a response from EEOC – Washington Field Office regarding my request for hearing and their intent to process this request as soon as possible.
>
> As I did not receive a response from you to my email request below, I kindly request your guidance on the proper procedures to ensure I properly inform your office regarding my taking on legal counsel.
> Thank you, Michelle[32]

Eshe, ccing Ronnie Holmes, replied as follows:

> Good Morning Ms. Stefanick:
> In regards to your question regarding obtaining legal counsel, please notify our office in writing of the attorney's name and contact information. All official correspondence will be sent to the attorney with a copy furnished to you, however, time frames for the receipt of correspondence will be computed from the date of receipt by the attorney.
>
> Also, thank you for confirming that you received a notice from the EEOC regarding a hearing. Please forward a copy of the notice

---

32   Michelle Stefanick, email message to Eshe Faulcon, January 6, 2012

you received via email.
Thank you and have a good day.
Kind regards,
Ms. Eshe Faulcon
EEO Specialist
USAG Stuttgart EEO Office[33]

As requested, I emailed Eshe, ccing Ronnie, including a copy of the
EEOC - Washington Field Office December 30, 2011 letter:

Subject: Requested letter
Hello Ms. Faulcon – Please find attached the requested letter. As
today I'm busy with a few deadlines, will provide other requested
information early next week. Thank you, michelle
Michelle L. Stefanick
Regional Director, West Africa
OSD-Policy, African Affairs

On January 9, 2012, I formally filed an AFSA Grievance regarding the
EER filed for the period from April 16, 2010 through April 15, 2011, and
for being subjected to a hostile work environment which resulted in an
inaccurate and falsely prejudicial EER. On February 23, 2012, I received
the agency decision letter from State/HR DAS Linda S. Taglialatela, Re:
AGS 2012-003. The letter states, "after a thorough review of your grievance … I must and do, deny your grievance."

After receiving the letter, I did not grieve this agency decision, as my
EEO Grievance litigation was still pending, and the truth would soon
come to light—so I thought. Upon receiving that February 23, 2012 letter, I now had no doubt that the decision I made in June 2008 to open my
window was the right one. As previously, and now even more so, *someone*
definitely wanted me out of the foreign service/Department of State. Apparently, it would be certain, given all that I had been subjected to even up
to that point, that I would TIC out of the Department of State in October
2015.

Just like the non-existent *DOD EEO Grievance Investigation*, this letter
was very insightful and apparent in the fact that neither Patrick Kennedy nor Tom Countryman, nor Linda Thomas-Greenfield, for that matter,
was interviewed for and during this "thorough" review. So once again, a
"thorough review" was not carried out.

Also, very interesting is that:

33   Eshe Faulcon, email message to Michelle Stefanick and Ronnie Holmes, January 6, 2012

…a new personnel exchange agreement between State and Defense was announced on January 19, 2012 which formalized the reciprocal exchange of DOD personnel assigned to State Department positions and DOS officers detailed to the Defense Department under the Foreign Policy Advisor (POLAD) program managed by the Bureau of Political-Military Affairs.

Though this new MOU was not in effect during my assignment to MARFOREUR/AF, I found it quite curious that it went into effect after my *removal* from Stuttgart. Though I never obtained a copy, it would be interesting to compare the new agreement with what was in effect during my assignment.

How many grievances did I have to file internally within State Department, and now externally, before officials would come to the same conclusion that I had years prior? *I was being targeted.* Not until years later, and after yet even more retaliatory actions had been taken against me, would I discover and verify how absolutely spot on I was—and only because of my FOIA document request.

Interesting enough, the AGS Grievance letter stated it was based on "thorough review," yet there was no reference to the September 04, 2009 email that Kate Canavan sent to USMC BGen Tracy Garrett, though it was specifically referenced and cited in the USMC's own Command Investigation report dated June 1, 2011. I personally was unaware of this September 04, 2009 email until November 1, 2011, when I received the DOD EEO Investigative file that included the USMC Command Investigative report dated June 1, 2011 (page 168/000187). Specifically referencing and including it as an enclosure implies DOD/USMC's reliance and its relevant pertinence. Otherwise why is/was it included and identified as "Enclosure (12) Email from AMB Katherine Canavan to Brigadier General Tracy L. Garrett of 4 Sep 09?"

Out of the blue, and finally, on January 17, 2012, I received a call from DS SA Rob Kelty regarding my reporting the identity theft issue in October 2011. When previously assigned to H during the 2006-2008 timeframe, I worked with Rob. who was the DS Congressional Liaison at the time. Rob said that the investigation was ongoing and that DS would get back in touch with me. To date, no one from DS has ever gotten back to me on this matter.

On July 2, 2012, I was finally able to move back into my primary residence in Lyon Park, Arlington, Virginia, and get all my personal effects delivered and out of storage. My move back to the US via DOD was also bad given the number of items that were missing/stolen. Curiously given what the missing items were—Muslim prayer beads from Sudan, an old Soviet painted plate from Russia, certain books (*Hawk and Dove*; Clark Clifford), etc – it felt like someone was trying to gather some kind of evidence, twisted evidence. Given how long my personal effects ended up being in storage—until my tenants moved out, and I could move back into my residence and finally have full delivery—if one were sinister, one could have/would have had more than ample time to go through every item I still had in storage.

April 15 was fast approaching and the annual FS evaluation process upon us, and with Vicki's departure, the period of performance would cover only December 17, 2011–April 15, 2012. My rater, DASD Amanda Dory, would sign her rater statement on April 26, 2012. My reviewer, PM/Policy Advisors Director Dundas McCullough, would sign his review statement on April 27, 2012. My EER was successfully approved and signed off by the Review Panel Chairperson Mary Witt on May 7, 2012, and officially submitted to HR/PE for Promotion Panels on May 15, 2012 according to PM Management Officer Marcia Oshinaike.

With a new rating period came a new beginning of sorts. And over this rating period I would have many objectives to focus on, particularly with the addition of environmental security to my portfolio. On Tuesday, April 17, 2012, DASD Dory and I received the following email:

Subject: CENTCOM/USF WATER AND SECURITY CONFERENCE (UNCLASSIFIED)
Ms. Dory and Ms. Stefanick,
Knowing what you are trying to accomplish with AFRICOM, I think it would be invaluable for Ms. Stefanick to attend the CENTCOM/University of South Florida water conference 7-9 May in Tampa. This is the third annual event and brings together a quality group of private sectors, USG interagency, military and academic speakers to explore the role of water in regional stability. In particular, international water leads Joe Rozza from Coca Cola and John Freedman from General Electric will be detailing the role of the private sector in supporting regional states and are very approachable.

You are off to a strong start in your African water and security project and you may find it quite useful to make contacts within the broader international water community and CENTCOM and glean some lessons learned from a well-established COCOM with extensive water security issues in its AOR. We have worked with the organizers from the beginning and I feel certain that they would welcome your attendance. I am attaching a draft agenda.

If I may be of assistance please let me know.

V/R,

Kent.

Kent Hughes Butts, Ph.D.

Director, National Security Issues Branch Center for Strategic Leadership

US Army War College Carlisle Barracks, PA 17013-5049[34]

From May 7-9, 2012, on behalf of OSD/AFR, I attended this event in Tampa, Florida sponsored by US Central Command (CENTCOM) and University of South Florida. This event would also have a direct link to Embassy Nairobi, for at the time of the Embassy bombings, AFRICOM did not exist; it had not yet been created. On August 7, 1998, Kenya was under the CENTCOM Combatant Command (COCOM) AOR. The applicable Commander at the time was USMC General Anthony Zinni.

ADDING INJURY TO INSULT

Again, something much bigger was at play. To fast forward, my EER would end up only covering the rating period from 04/16/2012 to 01/26/2013. On page 2 of 5 of the *DS-5055*, the following would be written under the applicable section C. "Describe any special circumstances influencing the work program":

> On June 5, 2012, Ms. Stefanick sustained a leg injury that required out-of-the-office physical therapy two-to-three days of the week until September 6, 2012. Also, from November 2012 until her return to the State Department at the end of January, Ms. Stefanick was unavailable for OSD/AFR duties from one to two days per week while attending to other official business.[35]

This EER also would never be submitted into my OPF nor would it be reviewed by the applicable Promotion Panel for promotion considerations. The reason for this EER not being officially submitted was not due on my part, but on the part of numerous US Department of State officials, including the DG Linda Thomas-Greenfield herself. During this rating period, I continued to experience even more bizarre events, to include with and within the Pentagon/OSD—and the military itself—and once again, I would not be safe and continued to be targeted.

---

34   Kent Hughes, email message to Michelle Stefanick and Amanda Dory, April 17, 2012

35   DS-5055 form for Michelle Stefanick, page 2 of 5, March 14, 2013

On Monday, June 4, 2012, I sent this email to my colleague from my Nairobi, Kenya days, and who I had just overlapped with for a short period of time while in Germany, Ron Roughead:

> Hello there Ron—Hope all is well. Well, today I got to finally (briefly) meet your brother when he made some comments/observations to launch a "research study" at CSIS. That said, more importantly I was able to share how wonderful and special you are… and in particular, were in regards to your assistance to me in the aftermath of the bombing. I've always said if I ever had an opportunity to share that with your brother/family, I would – and today, I finally had the opportunity. Thanks again Ron for that and for being one of my most special, dear friends. You will always have a special place in my thoughts, prayers and heart. Cheers, michelle[36]

Ron's brother, Gary Roughead, was the former CNO (Chief of Naval Operations) of the US Navy, during the time I was assigned to US Navy/USMC/MARFOREUR/AF in Stuttgart. At the time, didn't think anything of it. In due time, and due to its timing, I wondered *was this just simply coincidental or something more?*

Ron replied:

> Hi Michelle,
> What a wonderful note. It could not have come at a better time. It was, in many ways, a life raft and I cherish it. I hope you will always be a part of my life --- Ron[37]

I must admit, even at the time I received this, I thought what a nice note but found the "life raft" reference quite odd. In short time, I would and still to this day question if there was really a "double" meaning and/or something more sinister to this reference…

The very next day, on the morning of Tuesday, June 5, 2012, I was following my regular routine. I parked in the Pentagon parking lot, stopped to get a flavored coffee, and then was walking up the escalator to the floor of my OSD office. Just as I was about to step off the escalator, there was a sharp, intense pain in my left calf. It came out of nowhere. I limped along, thinking it was just a leg cramp. I tried to step down on my foot, but the pain was so intense that I made it to the corridor and then was about to collapse. Fortunately, a gentleman in a US Navy uniform standing in front of the corridor window was there to assist me. He

---

36   Michelle Stefanick, email message to Ron Roughhead, June 4, 2012
37   Ron Roughhead, email message to Michelle Stefanick, June 4, 2012

took my cup of coffee from my hands and assisted me in sitting down until a golf-cart came to take me to the Pentagon's internal medical clinic. The gentleman in a US Navy uniform left once the golf-cart arrived. I never got his name to thank him before he left, taking with him the lid of my coffee cup. Mark Swayne, from my office, joined up with me along the way. At the time, I was so focused and distraught with my leg injury that I didn't focus on all the coincidences in regards to the US Navy. The close location of the gentleman in a US Navy when my injury occurred, just the day prior my emailing Ron, due to just the prior day meeting Ron's brother Gary for the very first time. Again, Ron's brother, Gary Roughead, was the former US Navy CNO during the time I was assigned to US Navy/USMC/MARFOREUR/AF in Germany, and I'm meeting him now at this time while assigned at the Pentagon/OSD. *All just coincidental or something more?*

I spent a few hours in the Pentagon Medical Clinic, then soon after, I departed on a pair of crutches. Mark assisted me to my car. Fortunately, I was able to drive home since the injury was with my left leg, not the right. I then hobbled into my apartment to rest and elevate my leg.

The Pentagon Medical Clinic doctor had recommended that I visit my primary care physician for urgent care follow-up. As I didn't have one, I sent an email to a friend, also from my Embassy Nairobi days, Janet Wilkinson Schwartz. Janet and her husband Shelly, a USAID colleague, also lived nearby in Arlington. Janet replied within hours, recommending their family physician of more than 15 years, with a practice nearby who accepted Blue Cross Blue Shield (BC/BS). It was a perfect match, so I called Dr. Wendy Schwartz's office, arranged an appointment and met with her on Wednesday June 6, 2012. At 4:31 P.M., I sent the following email to Janet:

> Hi – I met with Dr. Schwartz today. She passed along her greetings and her thanks for the referral. My leg is feeling better, though I will be propping it up for another day or so longer... thanks again. cheers, michelle[38]

At the time, it never even crossed my mind the coincidence of both their last names being Schwartz. Only later would I reflect on this last name being more than just a coincidence.

My leg did not heal quickly, and I was always puzzled as to precisely what the injury was. Though I eventually transitioned off of the crutch-

---

es, the pain continued, resulting in follow-ups with Dr. Schwartz, an MRI, and even physical therapy.

After my leg injury and other subsequent events, on April 9, 2013, I came across a BBC report regarding US Navy and lasers. The BBC report was this: "US Navy laser shoots down drones: The US Navy says it plans to install a laser weapon on one of its ships, which can shoot down small aircraft such as drones." At the time, did this such possibility, this feasibility, cross my mind? Not at all. After reading this, and all that had occurred, and by whom—ABSOLUTELY! *Oh, my God, it was just like a laser hit the back of my leg*

Just like the helicopter malfunction incident in Djibouti, do I suspect more to this? Yes. But how do I, a single female, prove it? I mean *this is the US Military, the US Navy afterall.*

If a US Navy laser can shoot down a small aircraft, then I'm sure it has the capability to zap a leg or even a shoe strap. Now, all quite interesting that my "fall" on June 5, 2012 occurred the day after my meeting CNO (retired) Gary Roughead and then emailing Ron, his brother, my colleague from Embassy Nairobi. Even more so, since this incident happened as I approached the US Navy section inside the Pentagon on my walk to the OSD/AFR office. A gentleman in a US Navy uniform standing in the ready to assist me from the injury, when my injury occurred. It's also, curious, that despite my requests, I still have never received copies of my MRI regarding my injury. At least I have this confirmation. The US Navy does indeed have such capability, and the US Navy does indeed have such capacity to utilize it.

It may seem far-fetched, but is it really given all that was taking place and the apparent USNavy/USMC affiliation to so many events. Now given that the August 7, 1998 Embassy bombings were an inside job, was the October 12, 2000 attack on the USS Cole as well? I don't know, and didn't and don't have any affiliation. However, I was aware through media coverage that FBI SA John O'Neill was having an extremely difficult time in trying to investigate the incident. Apparently, this supposedly included the US Ambassador to Yeman at the time Barbara Bodine, whom I met once. Wait, unless, this is indeed an affiliation. It was during the Embassy Closing ceremony reception in Victoria, Seychelles. I was regional for the Seychelles while I was FMC Nairobi Director and assisted with the Embassy's closure. Retired FBI SA John O'Neill would later be killed in the WTC Towers on 9/11. Given my discussion with DOJ/SDNY AUSA

Ken Karas in March/April 2000 in regards to the August 7, 1998 East Africa Embassy bombings, we're all these incidents connected?

Though I didn't think anything of it at the time, in short order, with yet another round of odd reactions, targeted retaliatory actions taken against me, I would even reflect upon the name of "Schwartz," as in Janet Schwartz, then Dr. Schwartz more closely. Particularly given that "Schwartz" was also the last name of the CIA Chief of Station that "committed suicide" during my first first foreign service excursion tour assignment to Embassy Yaounde, Cameroon from State/OIG. It was from 1993-1995. Were, are all these incidents and factors interlinked and interconnected? At this point in time, I have absolutely no doubt they all absolutely are indeed.

For the record, I contacted many attorneys and law firms throughout this ordeal initially regarding my EEO Complaint and applicable upcoming Hearing, and then regarding this matter of the retaliatory actions taken against me, including DOJ/SDNY, whistleblower protection advocacy groups, ACLU, Bar Associations.

The bottom line is this and remains this: why wasn't I protected? By the DOJ? By the FBI? By State Department? By Department of Defense? For as I was not protected, there is only one conclusion that can be drawn and that is: I was not protected because I was targeted, and it was by the very same entities that were supposed to protect me.

And for the record, not only did I contact the Congressional Committee members with jurisdictional responsibilities, but I contacted Congressional Members of my Congressional District/State, and even more so.

Then, on Tuesday, September 25, 2012, I received an email from Sarah E. Taylor:

> Subject: CY11, OGE-278 PFDR
> Hello Michelle,
> Our records indicate that we do not have a current report on file for you. If this is incorrect, kindly provide when your report was forwarded to our office.
> Sarah E. Taylor
> Chief, Financial Disclosure Division
> L/EFD
> [REDACTED]
> 2401 E Street NW
> Washington, DC 20522-0102[39]

I responded:

---

39   Michelle Stefanick, email message to Sarah Taylor, September 23, 2012

Thanks sarah but I'm in on 01 job so why do I need to file?[40]

On Wednesday September 26, 2012, Sarah replied:

Were you in a stretch position before? (FE-OC), if so, did you submit a termination report when you left that position?[41]

I responded:

I was in a stretch position before and no I did not submit a termination report when I left as I didn't know I had to. Thanks, m[42]

Sarah replied:

OK, that is what needs to happen. Please complete one and forward to me.[43]

I responded:

Sarah – Can you please sent to me the written policy requiring this. Additionally, is this such requirement noted in our assignment cables?

Otherwise, with all due respect, I cannot in true honest certify to the accuracy/state of my finances when I departed July 2011 from Stuttgart—especially now over a year after my departure. Thanks, michelle[44]

Sarah provided the following:

http://l.s.state.sbu/sites/efd/Documents/Guidance%20for%20Termination%20OGE20278%20Filer.doc and2 FAM 700 (ethics) discusses as well[45]

I responded:

Thanks Sarah – As this was the first time I occupied an OC stretch position, can you please provide the HR guidance requiring this. Until I have this, I again, cannot in true honestly certify to the accuracy/state of my finances when I departed July 2011 from Stuttgart—especially now over a year after my departure.

However, with the HR Cable Guidance, I will then be able to have a discussion regarding this matter with AFSA, Pat Kennedy and Linda Thomas-Greenfield on my particular situation and this

---

40   Sarah Taylor, email message to Michelle Stefanick, September 23, 2012
41   Sarah Taylor, email message to Michelle Stefanick, September 26, 2012
42   Michelle Stefanick, email message to Sarah Taylor, September 26, 2012
43   Sarah Taylor, email message to Michelle Stefanick, September 26, 2012
44   Michelle Stefanick, email message to Sarah Taylor, September 26, 2012
45   Sarah Taylor, email message to Michelle Stefanick, September 26, 2012

legal requirement not being clearly communicated to those in similar situation such as mine, including why its taken over a year since I departed post for me to receive this notice. Seems to me there needs to be some systemic changes put in place.

Looking forward to receiving the HR Assignment Cable guidance on this requirement. Thanks, michelle[46]

Sarah responded, this time ccing Kathryn Youel Page:

Michelle,
I don't have an HR Cable on this matter because this is a legal requirement, not a HR requirement. Our office does not always get information on when people move out of stretch position so yes it will take some time to contact people. I will discuss this matter with my supervisor, Assistant Legal Advisor, Kathryn Youel Page[47]

I replied to Sarah ccing Kathryn:

Sarah – Thanks for this insight as it seems to be a real necessity in working with HR regarding this matter for as you note it is a legal requirement that HR should be heavily involved in in ensuring its employees are in full compliance.

With that, I appreciate you forwarding this to your supervisor for as I said it was the first time I was in a stretch. I was not notified of this requirement at the time of my reassignment otherwise I indeed would have fulfilled it at that time. However, now over a year later, I may be able to pull the info together but very hesitant to certify legally to accuracy so after the fact. Thanks, michelle[48]

Sarah replied directly and only to me:

Hello Michelle,
I will look for the last report you submitted and send it to you. Maybe that will help you.[49]

I replied directly to Sarah:

Sarah – Please reread my email below regarding the 'certification of accuracy' dated over a year from its requirement that I am concerned about.

46   Michelle Stefanick, email message to Sarah Taylor, September 26, 2012
47   Sarah Taylor, email message to Michelle Stefanick and Kathryn Youel Page, September 26, 2012
48   Michelle Stefanick, email message to Sarah Taylor and Kathryn Youel Page, September 26, 2012
49   Michelle Stefanick, email message to Sarah Taylor, September 26, 2012

Looking forward to your supervisor's comments so I can take to AFSA, M, and HR accordingly. Thanks, michelle[50]

Kathryn would send the following email:

Michelle, these requirements are in CFR – see e.g. 5 CFR 2634.201 and also in the Foreign Affairs Manual, see e.g. 2 FAM 711.3 definition of public filer and 2 FAM 714.2-2

I'm not sure of the details of your stretch assignment, but these rules require persons serving in SFS positions for more than 60 days in a calendar year to file an OGE 278. In your case I believe we would now be looking for a combined CY11/ termination report covering the period of January 2011 through September 2011 or whenever you left your stretch assignment. We would be able to waive the $200 late fee for this report as you were not notified.

I suggest you also could touch base with the Executive Director of the bureau in which you served the stretch for more information about the requirement. Regards, Katy

Katy Youel Page

Assistant Legal Advisor, Ethics and Financial Disclosure US Department of State[51]

I then responded to Sarah and Katy:

Thank you Kathy – I appreciate your offer to waive the late fee—and would like to see the legal authority for which that would be granted—and thank you for the legal/FAM references.

As I requested from Sarah, can you please provide me any cable guidance that has been sent overseas/to posts from your office/HR in regards to this legal requirement. This was my first stretch assignment, and I do not recall ever seeing anything in my reassignment cable regarding this requirement —as otherwise I would have fulfilled my legal requirement at that time. To now hear about this over a year from my departure from post, raises many concerns. One is not simply filling out the form, but the "certification of accuracy" dated over a year from its requirement that I am now being asked to reconstruct and then certify to which I am very concerned about. Secondly, as you note this is a legal requirement thus you must surely be working with HR to ensure you compliance with this mandate, thus cables—particularly assignment cables must address this. As I departed post at the end of July 2011 from

50 Michelle Stefanick, email message to Sarah Taylor and Kathryn Youel Page, September 26, 2012

51 Kathryn Youel Page, email message to Michelle Stefanick, September 26, 2012

this stretch OC (first time in such position), and then restructuring with accuracy after the fact for "my certification" is very very concerning to me.

With that, once you provide me the cables that were sent or confirm that there are none, I will then meet with AFSA, M, and HR regarding this matter. There appears to be a little more than my case at hand, but a systemic control weakness that needs to be addressed, and they should be informed about this.

In the meanwhile, as Sarah offered, I would appreciate her sending me what I submitted so I can look for and then hopefully compare to what I have in my files once I locate them. Thanks, michelle[52]

I immediately met with U/S Patrick Kennedy on Thursday, September 27, 2012. I knew exactly what this was about, my EEO Grievance. Given the timeline of events, the question was now why didn't PM and HR Berlin make me aware at the time of this termination disclosure statement requirement? Again, why wasn't I informed of this requirement at the time of my early departure from MARFOREUR/AF? And only now—over a year after my departure—I'm being contacted by Legal. I had so many questions, including didn't Legal receive copies of my official departure, or new assignment HR cable notifications? Or had they? Something nefarious was going on, at play. *And again, what in the world was going on? Why? By whom?*

On September 28, 2012, I received an email from Sarah with an attached document:

Michelle,
Here is the report.[53]

On October 1, 2012, I replied to Sarah, ccing Kathryn:

Subject: Stefanick OGE-278's
Hello Sarah – Thanks for this this, however, what about the report I filed for CY 2010? Can you please send me that as well.

Additionally, I met with U/S Kennedy on Thursday and mentioned this situation. We plan to follow-up on this again this week. Thanks so much. Cheers, michelle[54]

52   Michelle Stefanick, email message to Sarah Taylor and Kathryn Youel Page, September 26, 2012
53   Sarah Taylor, email message to Michelle Stefanick and Kathryn Youel Page, September 28, 2012
54   Michelle Stefanick, email message to Sarah Taylor and Kathryn Youel Page, October 1, 2012

I emailed Sarah, ccing Kathryn:

> Subject: RE: M. Stefanick
> Thanks Sarah – In comparing the reviews/signatures between my CY 2009 and CY 2010 reports, I noticed there were some differences such as no name but ISN/EX on 3/25 (CY 2009); Mary Reynold's and your signature for CY 2009; but just Mary's for CY 2010; no date stamp received noted on CY 2010. Also noticed that though I sent to PM David Pozorski (CY 2009) and PM/POLAD Director Gonzalo Gallegos (CY 2010), neither of their review signatures are noted.
>
> Can you please provide the specific procedure for such report submissions/reviews as it would seem to me anyone/everyone reviewing such sensitive information on employees should be required to initial/sign. Your insight/assistance with specific procedure would be sincerely appreciated. Thanks, michelle[55]

Sarah replied, this time not ccing Kathryn:

> Here is information on the requirement for a Senior Review.
> 11 FAM 614.7 Senior Reviewer Responsibilities
> 11 FAM 614.7-1 Role
> (CT:POL-53; 09-20-2012)
> a. The senior reviewer, designated in accordance with 11 FAM 614.6, Bureau Head and Chief of Mission Responsibilities (paragraph a), must undertake an initial review of an incumbent Form OGE-278, Executive Branch Personnel Public Financial Disclosure Report, to help the Ethics Office identify actual or potential conflicts of interest. The senior reviewer examines reports filed by Department employees assigned to the bureau or post and, as requested pursuant to 11 FAM 614.7-2, Procedures (paragraph b) or otherwise, one or more reports filed by Department employees who are assigned to a different component of the US Government.
> b. The senior reviewer will examine each Form OGE-278, Executive Branch Personnel Public Financial Disclosure Report, to determine if the filer has participated in or could in the future participate in the consideration or decision of any matter that would have a direct and predictable effect on the financial interests of any entity with which the filer is affiliated or in which the filer has an interest. If a company has business before the filer's bureau or post or has operations in the post's host country, the senior reviewer should specifically consider whether the filer is required to perform official duties relating to that company.

c. The senior review may assume that the disclosures on the reporting form are correct and should draw upon personal knowledge of the filer's duties. No independent fact-finding is required. The senior reviewer is not responsible for making legal judgments concerning the applicability of an ethics law.

11 FAM 614.7-2 Procedures

(CT:POL-53; 09-20-2012)

a. After having obtained a completed incumbent Form OGE-278, Executive Branch Personnel Public Financial Disclosure Report, from a filer as described in 11 FAM 614.4-2, Employees Serving in Filer Positions (paragraph a), the management official will transmit the report to the senior reviewer.

b. To address management issues arising from privacy or other concerns:

(1) A filer may be permitted to provide a copy of his or her report with the values and income redacted for purposes of senior review; or

(2) The post's management official may contact the management official for the post's bureau to arrange for a senior reviewer to examine a report or reports.

c. After completing the review, the senior reviewer must sign and date the cover page of the incumbent Form OGE-278, Executive Branch Personnel Public Financial Disclosure Report, below the filer's signature at "Other Review," then transmit the report to L/EFD. If the senior reviewer reviewed a redacted copy of the report, the management official or filer should attach the signed copy to the original Form OGE-278, Executive Branch Personnel Public Financial Disclosure Report, and transmit both to L/EFD.

d. Any actual or potential conflict of interest or other matters of concern identified by the senior reviewer should be transmitted in writing to L/EFD.[56]

I responded to Sarah, ccing Kathryn:

Wow – thanks so much Sarah for this. In PM who is the "senior reviewer" for such reports as I would think L is very cognizant of "training, identifying and ethically" ensuring who encumbers such a position in the Department bureaus is accountable to the legal intent of the law, but also the sensitivity to such "review" position of senior employees most sensitive financial information. Thanks, michelle[57]

56   Sarah Taylor, email message to Michelle Stefanick, October 1, 2012
57   Michelle Stefanick, email message to Sarah Taylor and Kathryn Youel Page, October 1, 2012

Sarah responded, without ccing Kathryn:

> Hello Michelle,
> I can't tell you who the Senior Reviewer is because it is up to the
> EX Director to determine that person. L/Ethics does not designate
> Senior Reviewers.[58]

I responded to Sarah, ccing Kathryn:

> Thanks Sarah – For clarification, L has/takes no role in these such
> positions, despite the legal importance/sensitivity to the require-
> ment at hand. Michelle[59]

Kathryn, ccing Sarah, responded:

> Yes, it is up the bureau to designate the 'senior reviewer.' We are
> in the process of finalizing a new FSI training for such reviewers.
> Kyp[60]

I replied both Kathryn and Sarah:

> Great Kathy – Thanks for the clarification as when I speak with
> U/S Kennedy, HR, AFSA and others regarding my situation and
> the current procedure in place I just wanted to make sure I had it
> correct. This helps with that. Thanks, michelle[61]

On October 11, 2012, as a follow-up to our September 27, 2012 discussion, I sent this email to U/S Patrick Kennedy. The email included the
following attachments: *Termination FPA Public Financial Disclosure Form.
pdf; New Entrant 2009 FPA position Public Financial Disclosure Form.pdf;
CY 2009 Public Financial Disclosure Form.pdf; CY 2010 Public Financial
Disclosure Form.pdf.*

> SUBJECT: Request to be deemed a 'Confidential Filer'
> Hello Pat – Saw your hearing yesterday. It was a rough ride, but I
> think you did well despite the fact of being asked questions but not
> being permitted to respond.
> As a follow-up to one of the issues we discussed and in light
> of what we discussed on 9/27, I've completed to the best of my

58   Sarah Taylor, email message to Michelle Stefanick, October 1, 2012
59   Michelle Stefanick, email message to Sarah Taylor and Kathryn Youel Page, October 1,
2012
60   Sarah Taylor, email message to Michelle Stefanick and Kathryn Youel Page, October 1,
2012
61   Michelle Stefanick, email message to Sarah Taylor and Kathryn Youel Page, October 1,
2012

knowledge over a year after the fact a "termination" FPA Public Financial Disclosure form covering the period of January 1, 2011 – July 30, 2011. Again, in light of what we discussed, I kindly ask you to compare the three other such forms I submitted in relations to that position (attached) and the one I'm now being asked to submit (also attached/but unsigned). Of particular note is Schedule B and C, and the question why this happened relative to my other submissions and in light of what was happening to me in my position at that time in Stuttgart, Germany.

With that I provide the following:

On September 25, 2012, I was notified by Sarah Taylor (L/EFD) that they do not have a current report on file for me. (According to my files, I filed a New entrant on 11/04/2009; CY 2009 on 3/9/2010; CY 2010 on 3/6/2011).

I explained that I was no longer in an SFS (OC-stretch) position, departing that position on July 31, 2011, over a year ago.

I was then advised that I needed to file a "termination" report. Unfortunately, I was not aware of this requirement and was neither advised by HR nor PM on this reporting requirement, as if I was, I would have filed the report at that time.

With that, I am now very concerned with filing a report so after the fact, particularly in regards to the certification statement – "I certify that the statements I have made on this form and all attached schedules are true, complete and correct to the best of my knowledge." As I would now have to go back and reconstruct my financial statement – assets and liabilities – dating back over a year to July 30, 2011 when I don't even know if I still have those files available based on my recent move and purging of documents when organizing my files.

1. I was not aware of the "termination" requirement nor was I reminded by either HR (in my assignment cable) or PM/Ethics Officer. (According to the emails in my files, Mary Reynolds was great informing/notifying us/me to file our reports for annual requirement). Now according to 5 CFR 2634.201, both me and the PM/Ethics Officer (Mary Reynolds?) are non-compliant with the law.

2. I don't know if at this time I can now reconstruct let alone "certify to accuracy" if I file such a report at this time.

3. What would I need to do to "waive late fee" (5 CFR 2634.704)

4. Is it possible to be considered a "confidential filer" according to 5 CFR 2634.904(a)(2) due to being "involved investigating or prosecuting violations of criminal or civil law," therefore no termination report is required (5 CFR 2634.903e). I make this request

based on the fact that my filed EEO Grievance was filed during the period covered by this "termination filer" period and to date, an EEO Court has neither held/nor made a ruling on my case at this time.

Due to the sensitivity of my situation, your serious consideration to my request is sincerely appreciated. Thanks Pat. Regards, michelle[62]

To date, I've never received a response from U/S Patrick Kennedy nor anyone in L, PM, DS, HR, or any Department of State Official regarding this matter.

Despite previously being notified of required financial disclosure statements, for some reason, I was not notified of this required *termination* financial disclosure statement. This particular November 19, 2010 reminder was not only about the required training and the required filing, but it also clearly indicated to all parties that this was required of 01's in a stretch SFS-graded position—some.

To: Brown, Raymond L. SFS; Davis, John M (DS); Canavan, Katherine H; Saxton, Paul J SFS; Holmes, J. Anthony AMB; Stefanick CIV Michelle

Cc: Marfino, Sherrie L; Cisek, James F; Whitaker, Jonita I; Thomas, Maryanne F; Rittley, Michael R

Subject: Mandatory Ethics Training for Filers of Financial Disclosure Reports – Deadline December 21, 2010

Dear Colleagues,

Please read through the attached State Department cable and the Mission Germany Staff Announcement (both attached). According to our records, those of you addressed in the "to" line will be required to file a Public Financial Disclosure Report (PFDR) in early 2011 (Senior Foreign Service or an FO-01 in an upward stretch SFS-graded position). For this reason, you are required to complete the ethics training by December 31, 2010.

The head of the Ethics Office, Sarah Taylor, kindly sent me the following links to the ethics training videos (choose one—a different one to what you viewed last year). I remember that some of you had had a bit of a problem last year getting access. Please feel free to share the links to the ethics training with other State Department officers presently assigned to Stuttgart AFRICOM & EUCOM—they might want to do the ethics training on a voluntary basis.

The Wizard of Laws (1 hr.)

Link provided....
On The Couch (1 hr.)
Link provided...
Emoluments Clause (1 hr.)
Link provided...
Please confirm directly with Sarah Taylor [email address re-moved} that you have completed the training,
Or,
If you did ethics training with the military in Stuttgart or at FSI this year, and think you are exempted from having to re-do it, please contact Sarah Taylor to double-check.

I've attached the list showing who will be required to complete Public Financial Disclosure Reports next year. Please let me know if you spot any errors on the list. Many thanks.

We don't yet have the State cables calling for FDRs, but I'll share them with you when they come in which is normally January/February).

To repeat: those who are required to file PFDRs must have taken the ethics training by December 31, 2010.
Best regards to all,
Ann
HR Assistant
American Services Unit (ASU)
Human Resources Office
US Embassy Berlin[63]

The email included three attachments: Two regarding Ethics Training and one regarding Mission Germany Financial Disclosure Report Filers. My name was on that list of filers.

Katherine Canavan and others were well-informed and well-advised that I was a 01 in an SFS stretch position, to include Diplomatic Special Agents. DS SA were assigned to and at both EUCOM and AFRICOM, as well as other postitions as SFS officials. Yet, what happened to me during my assignment as an FPA/POLAD with MARFOREUR/AF was permitted to occur. The question remains to this day—*why*?

Considering I had been advised by both PM and HR Embassy Berlin Officials of all my previous financial disclosure filing requirements, I found it absolutely bizarre that I was not advised accordingly. Both PM and Embassy Berlin HR officials knew of my departure and had my home

63   Ann Gamerschlag, email message to Michelle Stefanick, Raymond Brown, John Davis, Katherine Canavan, Paul Saxton, Anthony Holmes, Sherrie Marfino, James Cisek, Jonita Whitaker, Maryanne Thomas, Michael Rittley, October 11, 2012

leave/personal email contact information, yet, I was never advised of a termination Public Financial Disclosure Report being required. Instead I was contacted by L, over a year after my departure from the FPA/POLAD MARFOREUR/AF POSITION. *Why? What in the world was going on? And by whom? Who all was involved? Because its quite apparent, it was more than only one individual. And when its more than one, the legal definition of conspiracy has been met. So again, what in the world was going on and why?*

Still odder yet, since I was in the same Bureau, PM, for that previous position as in my current State/Defense Exchange (SDE) detail position. So yes, it was quite apparent that something sinister was at play. Yet, there was no investigation as to events that occurred while I was in Germany— and curiously, a victim/witness to the August 7, 1998 East Africa Embassy bombings assigned there at the same time bin Laden was captured/ killed by US Navy Seals.

Aha Moments

And now, in light of Pat Hartnett-Kelly's May 30, 2011 email indicating that Embassy Nairobi was a *"major CIA station,"* I have no choice but to openly and rhetorically ask how many in State Department writ large are really spooks? Am I the only one at the US Department of State that is not/ was not a spook? *Is that even possible?* Even if that is possible, the question remains, then why didn't the CIA and the intelligence community protect me? Not only did they not protect me, they targeted me! *Why?*

Now speaking of Pat Hartnett-Kelly, during this exact timeframe the September 11, 2012 attack in Benghazi occurred. Neither an Embassy nor a Consulate, the USG facility attacked was referred to as a *Diplomatic Post*. Out of the blue, Pat Hartnett-Kelly called me,not at homebut at my office in OSD. I always enjoyed discussing such matters with Pat, given her background and our past, but calling me at the office? I admit at the time I thought it odd but not strange, chalking up the call to my office to the seriousness of the Benghazi incident we were discussing. Little by little, more and more details were being released regarding the attack. Though Libya was in the OSD/AFR portfolio, it wasn't my portfolio. Any insight I received was coming from open press sources.

With Pat's call, my initial thought went back to the threat to the apartment building I was living in when posted on the al-Qaeda website when I was assigned to Khartoum from 2003 to 2005. Like the Diplomatic Post in Benghazi, there were no Marine Security Guards assigned to Embassy Khartoum either, though there were MSGs in Nairobi.

Then on October 11, 2012, Pat sent me this email: "Fw: Letting us in on a secret." Reading the article at the time, my initial thoughts were, *Uh-oh, this isn't good.* Now, knowing all that I know, when I read this article my thought is this: *Those treasonous criminals.*

Based on the June 25, 2009 DOJ VNS email I received, I already knew there was still an open, ongoing FBI investigation regarding the bombings. So, I started reviewing the two events through a lens of similarities. Then all of a sudden, given Pat's email sent on May 30, 2011 *after* bin Laden's capture/kill—implying for the first time the embassy bombing was an *inside job*—the events that occurred while I was in Germany, this Benghazi Diplomatic Post attack, Pat's recent call to my office, her October 11, 2012 email,I connected the dots. Not only did I have my *A-Ha!* moment, but I had an *Ah-Shit!* moment. I then heard that there was no actionable intelligence prior to the September 11, 2012 Benghazi Diplomatic Post attack. *Oh my God—yhat's why Pat called me! Just like the August 7, 1998 Embassy Nairobi bombing—there was no actionable intelligence prior to the attack.*

In the fall of 2012, the Promotion cable was released and my name was not on it. It was during this time that I came to the realization that actions taken against me in Germany at the hands of MARFOREUR/AF were not due to a clash of the two institutions of which I was a pawn caught in the middle, but truly due to and in regards to the August 7, 1998 embassy bombing. At this point, without a doubt, I am convinced that it was me and my FMC section who were the targets of the bombing—and the reason Pat alluded for the first time in her May 30, 2011 email that it was an inside job. In due time, I would conclude the reason that I was targeted/subjected to the retaliatory actions taken against me was because *someone* was trying to scapegoat me as the *insider*. The only problem with *someone's* assumption was that I was not the *insider*. I was being scapegoated, intentionally and purposely scapegoated, by *someone* within the USG, and still to this day. And whomever this *insider* is they struck again, as exemplified by the Diplomatic Post attack in Benghazi, once again killing American diplomats and servicemen.

Now having my *Ah-Shit!* moment, I connected dots, more dots, and even more dots because all became crystal clear to me from my new perspective lens. Next, whom I could trust became apparent and as crystal clear by the actions that I took and the responses I received—*no one!*

But I had to do something...

So, on the morning of October 24, 2012, I met with my fellow OSD/AFR officials Mark Swayne (my immediate Director) and Navy Captain

Scott Organ (our office's Security Officer) to raise my concerns and point out the necessity to share accordingly within proper OSD channels without going into specifics. In turn, Captain Organ advised OSD/Security of the situation, to which he was told to bring a written statement. Captain Organ drafted the first version, of which I made edits. On October 25, 2012, Captain Organ took the revised statement to OSD/Security Ivory London. According to Captain Organ, he was advised to come back the next day to meet with Ivory's boss to discuss. On October 26, 2012, Captain Organ met with OSD/Security Mike Brooks and was advised that this was going to be shared up the chain, with higher-ups. Once I received this feedback, I patiently waited.

In the meantime, in early November 2012, I attended the USMC Birthday Cake-cutting event at State Department and afterwards ran into Linda Thomas-Greenfield (or in hindsight, did she really run into me)? Linda said she had been thinking/concerned about me; she worked out near my home and wanted to stop by sometime. I said sure, anytime. She said she was traveling and would get back with me on a proposed date. Within the next day or two, she came back with a proposed evening of Tuesday, November 27, 2012, after her workout. I said sure.

Linda Thomas-Greenfield, who served with me at Embassy Nairobi, Kenya departing prior to the August 7, 1998 Embassy bombing, was the US Ambassador to Liberia when I was at MARFOREUR/AF and removed the Marine Colonels. She was now the Director General of the Foreign Service and Director of Human Resources.

About two weeks after Captain Organ met with OSD/Security on October 26, 2012, he came by my desk and quietly queried whether or not I had heard back yet. I said, no. He said, "Michelle, you need to go to the FBI."

One has to understand that after all that I had endured (the Embassy bombing with so many killed, the targeted actions against me in Germany, and now more deaths in Benghazi) I didn't know who to trust. At that time, and from that time, I had no doubt that me and/or my FMC section were the targets of the August 7, 1998 Embassy bombing. And that was before I found out even more to solidify this fact, and before the worst of retaliatory actions taken against me would occur. Instead of being protected and/or simply being driven to DOJ/SDNY, I was and would be unbelievably retaliated against…

On November 9, 2012, US Army General David Petraeus resigned as Director of the CIA after admitting to having an extramarital affair with his biographer, Paula Broadwell.

On November 19, 2012, based on what I knew, the dots I was connecting, I began my own research to include locating this July 21, 2011 *Washington Post* article, "Warren Magnusson, CIA finance specialist" by T. Rees Shapiro:

WASHINGTON – Warren D. Magnusson—whose CIA career as a finance specialist involved the covert payment of foreign agents, the recovery of buried gold in postwar Germany, and handling top-secret ledgers for stealth-plane development—died July 15 at a retirement community in Springfield, VA. He was 89 and had congestive heart failure.

Mr. Magnusson retired in 1979 as deputy director of finance, where he held the agency's purse strings.

As comptroller, Mr. Magnusson took part in funding the development of the U2 spy plane and its supersonic successors, Lockheed's A-12 and the SR-71 Blackbird.

Mr. Magnusson frequently met with Clarence "Kelly" Johnson, a top engineer in Lockheed's experimental "Skunk Works" group. Mr. Magnusson traveled on several occasions to the government's Nevada air test facility known as Area 51.

Built under the code name Project Oxcart, the A-12 and SR-71 spy planes were engineered to fly at extreme altitude at twice the speed of sound while collecting data. The SR-71 reconnaissance aircraft holds numerous speed records, including a New York-to-London flight of 1 hour and 54 minutes.

Retired CIA finance specialist James Wheeler said that Mr. Magnusson had a leading role in the funding of Project Azorian, the agency's secret mission to lift a sunken Russian submarine from the bottom of the ocean.

The ambitious endeavor to lift the 1,750-ton submarine and its four nuclear ballistic missiles called for the use of the Hughes Glomar Explorer salvage ship. In 1974, the CIA was able to recover parts of the Russian submarine at a cost of hundreds of millions of dollars. The mission failed, however, to bring up the Russian nuclear missiles.

Warren Douglas Magnusson was born in Brooklyn, N.Y. He served aboard a Navy antisubmarine ship in the Atlantic during World War II.

Through a military colleague, he secured a spot in the Navy's V-12 officer training program and graduated from the University of Pennsylvania with a degree in finance in 1947.

He joined the CIA in 1951 and was sent to Japan during the Korean War. He was a finance officer in Frankfurt and helped acquire contracts to build a tunnel between East and West Berlin.

Wheeler said CIA headquarters tapped Mr. Magnusson to lead the operation to dig up hundreds of gold coins buried across Germany. They had been placed there by US intelligence personnel during World War II to aid downed pilots and allied troops evading capture.

Using tattered Army taps, Mr. Magnusson tracked down the metal boxes filled with gold.

Mr. Magnusson often ensured that clandestine CIA operations could not be traced back to the US government. He became an expert at camouflaging the agency's paper trail to pay foreign spies and finance paramilitary operations overseas.

His family said that Mr. Magnusson's work included exchanging currencies and precious metals on the black market and through Swiss banks.

Mr. Magnusson's wife of 60 years, the former Flora "Betty" Mesheau, died in 2005. He leaves two children, Paul of Chevy Chase, Md., and Lori of McLean, VA., and two granddaughters.

My immediate reaction after reading this was and remains, to this day: *Oh. My God—I know exactly what all this is really about!*

By November 23, 2012, after not hearing back from DOD/OSD Security, State/DS or DOJ/FBI, coupled with all the information that was emerging from the Benghazi attack, and in reflection on all that had happened to me, that weekend, I handwrote an eight-page yellow legal paper letter. Given my already protected status as a DOJ/SDNY federal Crime Victims Rights Act (CVRA) –protected victim/witness in regards to the August 7, 1998 East Africa Embassy bombings, and as an EEOC Greivance Complainant, I was now requesting even more expanded protections in this letter —my November 27, 2012 *Whistleblower/Protection Request letter.*

CHAPTER 7

FIRST-HAND VICTIM/WITNESS:
Now Also a Whistleblower

PROTECTION REQUEST

On the evening of November 27, 2012, I read and gave to Linda Thomas-Greenfield, my *Whistleblower/Protection Request letter* when she came over to my house that evening. Unaware that I was going to give her this letter, Linda, the Director General of the Foreign Service, took the letter, and a few days later, on November 30, 2012, responded as follows:

> Subject: Follow up
>
> Michelle: It was good spending time with you earlier this week. I just want you to know what I have done since our discussion. I spoke to Pat and passed a copy of your unsigned note to me to him. I also spoke to the OCR office and asked them to follow up on your complaint against the Marine Corps. They will be in touch with you get more information in order to follow up.
>
> I will be back in touch with you. I have to say I am very, very worried about you. You should not be dealing with this situation alone. With everything else you are dealing with; the impact of Nairobi is clearly still very fresh for you and for good reason. I assume that you have sought some counseling over the years to get through this but I would encourage you to again talk to someone. If you need some assistance, please let me know. I don't know what I can do but I certainly can listen. Also, please stay in touch with me as a friend. If you need anything, I am here for you. This is not the DG speaking but Linda. Best, Linda[1]

I responded to Linda:

> Thanks Linda – Regarding my EEO Grievance, the contact would be Greg Smith in S/OCR and Neera Parikh in AFSA. Neera can also shed insight to the retaliatory actions I've had to take actions against over the years since Nairobi, as well as files that I have.
>
> With that, thank you for sharing with Pat. As noted in my letter,

 Linda Thomas-Greenfield, email message to Michelle Stefanick, November 30, 2012

I will pursue the stated course of action on Monday December 3. I hope to hear from you soon once you see the documented trend as a starting point. Thanks michelle[2]

Linda replied:

Michelle: OK. On the issue in your letter, that is outside my purview and thus I have shared with Pat. Take care and please stay in touch. Linda [3]

This same Linda Thomas-Greenfield also served with me at Embassy Nairobi. She and her husband departed post before the August 7, 1998 Embassy bombing. This is also the same Linda Thomas-Greenfield currently serving as President Joe Biden Administration's US Senate-confirmed United States Ambassador to the United Nations.

On the morning of November 28, 2012, after arriving at OSD/AFR, unscheduled and spontaneously, I took the first shuttle from the Pentagon to the Hill. I had with me another handwritten copy of the letter that I just provided to Linda the evening before. I walked straight to Senator Olympia Snowe's office, whom I had worked for years prior, and asked to see her Chief of Staff John Richter as soon as possible. Again, unscheduled, I patiently waited. In a little while, John came out to see me. Knowing my request to see the Senator was going to be a challenge, I advised John that I would wait all day and as long as it took to meet with Senator Snowe today. It was imperative, of utmost national security importance. I then gave John the sealed manila envelope. I said, "John as you have children, please do not open this letter. Please give it directly to Senator Snowe so she can open and read for herself."

I then waited. In the meanwhile, I was watching CSPAN in the Senators' Waiting Room. It was airing an interview with Senator Susan Collins regarding Benghazi. Soon after, I was taken in to meet Senator Snowe alone. We chatted briefly and she kept the handwritten letter. She instantly knew the importance and implications of the matter at hand. She said her office would get back with me. I then departed and took the shuttle back to the Pentagon, OSD.

Realizing at this time that I was indeed being targeted and that I indeed knew something, I tried to figure out by whom and why. During this exact time frame, news broke about the CIA Director. More and more was coming out regarding the ouster of then CIA Director and former US Army

2   Michelle Stefanick, email message Linda Thomas-Greenfield, November 30, 2012
3   Linda Thomas-Greenfield, email message to Michelle Stefanick, November 30, 2012

198

General Petraeus, specifically regarding Paula Broadwell. One day, given all my other interlinkages and interconnections, dots I was connecting, I did yet another search of my own personal email history to see if I had any such connection. I typed in the name *Paula Broadwell,* and then pressed *enter.* I couldn't believe it. My mouth dropped. *What? I have a connection.* I was stunned. There was an email exchange with me and Paula Broadwell. It had occurred *prior* to my departing for Stuttgart in December 2009, and right after my attending the USMC Marine Expeditionary Unit (MEU) Exercise at Camp Atterbury from September 29 to October 2, and having lunch on October 26, 2009 with USMC MajGen Lake, who now in hindsight I was *curiously and coincidentally* introduced to by Sid Kaplan.

All this, whatever it was, was not simply about these new congressionally-authorized and funded, expanded State Department Foreign Policy Advisor/POLAD positions writ large. It was about me. With the question remaining, *why?* And now this added dynamic, currently and coincidentially-timed, regarding Paula Broadwell and David Petraeus; I have a curious connection, and in light of all the events and interconnections already. So whatever this is, it is high-level, highly-skilled, professionally sophisticated, prearranged, preorhestreated, and expansive in its level of planning and carrying all this out; given the entities interconnected and involved, and with the key questions remaining, why and by whom?

So how did I come in contact with Paula Broadwell? While I was working in State/H, a colleague invited me to a "Women in International Security" (WIIS) event. Through mutual affiliation with WIIS, my email exchange was in response to Paula's recent, and now in hindsight *curiously timed,* article regarding "Marine FETs (Female Engagement Teams)." Given MajGen Lake specifically mentioned and we discussed these exact Marine FETs during our October 26, 2009 lunch, I provide my applicable email exchange with Paula Broadwell:

> Date: Thu, 29 Oct 2009 16:28:50 -0400
> Subject: Marine FETs article
> Hello there Paula – I just wanted to thank you for your article on the Marine FETs. Its timing could not have been more perfect. Recently I was selected as the first Foreign Policy Advisor (POLAD) to the Commanding General to the Marines for Europe and Africa, based out of Stuttgart. So needless to say, with my departure scheduled for the end of November it was great timing for me to read – not only so I can do what I can to support the female Marines I encounter with my new job but to also brag about them during my

current consults with appropriate folks at State, DOD, NSC and the Hill before I head out. Just wanted to let you know....thanks so much and have a great day. Cheers, michelle Stefanick[Redacted][4]

Paula Broadwell responded:

Dear Michelle,

Thanks very much for your thoughtful note. Indeed, it is important to highlight the great work these women are accomplishing!

Congratulations on your new assignment. That sounds like a dream job! I was actually stationed in Heidelberg and Stuttgart for over five years with the Army, so I have a fond spot in my heart for EUCOM. :) You have a lot of responsibility on your shoulders with that job! I wish you well. Let us know how we can assist.

When you chat with the folks on the Hill, State, DOD, and elsewhere, there are a few additional messages you could carry... :) We need to update the combat exclusion policy which prevents women from serving "legally" in these positions. Second, we need to expand women's opportunities in the "black world" – secret special operations jobs. Third, we need to look more at indigenous women (whether in Iraq/ME, Africa, or elsewhere) as counter-terrorism agents. We underestimate their power over "their men," and their ability to deter their children from joining wars/jihad, etc.

I would be happy to expound when and if the time is right. But thanks for keeping women's opportunities on your mind as you go forward with your exciting new job!

All best,
Paula[5]

I responded to Paula on Saturday, October 31, 2009:

Thanks so much Paula. I don't know how much I can carry the message at this time, but what I can do is take with me your insight coupled with my own observations/insights over the course of new assignment and see how I can best influence from inside – for as you say, we underestimate their power of their men, even when the men are our own.

I appreciate the offer of letting you all know how you can assist me, and return the offer in kind if I can assist you all. It's a big portfolio indeed and really looking forward to the challenge regarding the Marines, the fostering of the State/DOD relationship, and as

4   Michelle Stefanick, email message to Paula Broadwell, October 29, 2012
5   Paula Broadwell, email message to Michelle Stefanick, October 29, 2012

always, the opportunities for women. Until our paths cross again in this very small world of ours. Cheers, Michelle[6]

Paula Broadwell replied:

Thanks, Michelle!
Perhaps if you send out an update to friends/colleagues you can ping me too, I'll keep an eye out for your name, either way! Are you on Facebook? :)
Good Luck!
Best,
Paula[7]

As innocent as this exchange was at the time, at least on my part, I now reflected back on this entire scenario with new apprehension—its timing, its content, its true intent, its potential misconstrued intent. In light of what happened to me in Germany, I now looked at it all through a new lens.

I started documenting and focusing on the timeline of events. Now I questioned every event, every encounter—how much was real, how much was a *set-up, prearranged. And most crucially, by whom and why? And how far back did all this go?* Only later would I come to realize the dots I connected at that time were only parochial to the extent and extremity of what all *this* was really about…

Since meeting with Senator Snowe on November 28, 2011, I was in continual contact with her office through John Richter. John was Senator Snowe's COS at the time of my APSA Congressional Fellowship in 2005-2006. Despite the high-anxiety experience I was being subjected to during this period of time, I had a sense of relief since knowing John previously. As more and more came to light, I was connecting more and more dots, it was quite overwhelming to say the least. But knowing what I knew, realizing what I knew, I had no choice—I took an oath and people, innocent people have died, to include members of my FMC staff family. There was no stopping me then, as there is no stopping me now in writing this book.

Senator Snowe was in the process of retiring, and she was in her last few weeks in her office as Senator. I had no intention of dumping all this on her in her last days. Regardless, she and her staff took action to the very end of her time in office to assist me. Apparently, she initially contacted the

6   Michelle Stefanick, email message to Paula Broadwell, October 31, 2012
7   Paula Broadwell, email message to Michelle Stefanick, October 31, 2012

Intelligence Community (IC) OIG. How do I know? Because on Friday, November 30, 2012, at 7:35 p.m., I received the following email from Office of Director of National Intelligence (ODNI)/Africa Theresa Whelan:

> Subject: Time to Chat?
>
> Hey Michelle – how are you? Hope all is well. Things are really crazy in Africa these days. I'm sure you guys are as busy as we are.
>
> Was wondering if you could give me a call sometime this weekend. I got a call from the Intel Community Inspector General's office today. It was a little confusing to me but what they said involved you so I thought maybe it would be good to talk to you and find out what's going on. Feel free to call me on this blackberry number if you get the chance. Thanks! Theresa[8]

I was contacted directly by the IC OIG as well. I could provide names, but given the entity, would they really be real names anyways? That said, during one such phone call, the individual asked if they could provide a copy of the hand-written letter to Director of National Intelligence (DNI) James Clapper. I said yes. There was no further substantive/investigative follow-up by the IC OIG.

I provided feedback to Senator Snowe's office, and they too were becoming concerned on the lack of follow-up. So, in addition to the IC OIG, they contacted the FBI Congressional Liaison office. One such exchange between John and me was as follows:

On Wednesday, December 19, 2012, I received an email from John:

> Subject: update
> Just talked to John Neal who I have been dealing with. Someone will call you. If you don't hear in the next 24 hours you can also call John directly at [redacted].
> John R. Richter
> Chief of Staff
> US Senator Olympia J. Snowe[9]

On Thursday, December 20, 2012, I replied:

> John – I just wanted to let you know that I have not heard from the FBI, and as I've not heard back from you, I will assume Chairman Rogers has not received the package. Thanks, michelle[10]

---

8   Theresa Whelan, email message to Michelle Stefanick, November 30, 2012
9   John Richter, email message to Michelle Stefanick, December 19, 2012
10   Michelle Stefanick, email message to John Richter December 20, 2012

John replied:

> You should call John Neal, he said for you to feel free to call him if you didn't hear from FBI within 24 hours or so. I have not heard back from house intel.[11]

I emailed John:

> Thanks John. I tried reaching him yesterday, but was unsuccessful. I just talked with him – not sure if the urgency is there. But with that, we'll see what he does now.
> Curious that house intel didn't get back to you yet.
> How much longer will you be in your offices with Senator Snowe retiring. Thanks, michelle[12]

John replied:

> Also (Michael) Allen just emailed me to update me that he is examining the info. Didn't mention that rogers has it at this point.[13]

I responded:

> Thanks for the insight as I asked John Neal to call Chairman Rogers' office to ask Allen if the Chairman saw the package from Senator Snowe's office and he was told Allen was in a meeting. So needless to say, I'm happy to see that Allen is now examining the info that he received Monday/Tuesday(?)—especially now that Chairman is about to walk out the door for recess/weekend. Not sure how much longer you all are in the office, but you may want to pass along to Senator Snowe the status of my trying to do the right thing … (you have been great John—thank you!) Thanks, Michelle[14]

On Friday, December 21, 2012, I sent John the following email:

> Hello John – Just wanted to give you the status. Since speaking to John and being told the FBI urgently wanted to speak with me, John has not returned my messages/not in office at all today and no one as of now has contacted me from the FBI. So hopefully Chairman Rogers does indeed have/seen the package and something is being done. I stand by trying to do the right thing despite all the obstacles, including cancelling all my holiday plans, as I sit and wait for someone in our Government to actually take the mea-

11   John Richter, email message to Michelle Stefanick, December 20, 2012
12   Michelle Stefanick, email message to John Richter December 20, 2012
13   John Richter, email message to Michelle Stefanick, December 20, 2012
14   Michelle Stefanick, email message to John Richter December 20, 2012

sures necessary to protect me and the other individual so the information/insight can be passed along to the proper authority at the proper level. I don't know what more to do as I continue to wait.... Going to the press is another option I consider but again, I really want to hold on the faith that there is someone in the Government I can believe in ... and to be honest, that is why I looped in Senator Snowe, because I have no doubt of her commitment to our nation. I just wanted you to be aware. Merry Christmas to you and Senator Snowe. Thanks, michelle[15]

John replied:

What John Neal just sent me:
I spoke with Michelle twice yesterday and contacted HPSCI per her request.
I also spoke with our CT Division and reiterated the importance of reaching out to her asap.
I believe someone out of the NY Office will be contacting her to setup an interview.
I'll ping CT again to check the status.[16]

I replied:

To add to this drama, I'm sure you probably still have not heard back from Michael Allen confirming that Chairman Rogers received the package yet either—right.
Boy, someone is very concerned with the information I have.[17]

Needless to say, with Senator Snowe retiring, one concern was who/which Member I wanted her to provide my package to follow through with assisting me on this matter. I decided it should be Congressman Michael "Mike" Rogers. The reason was that he had a military background, a law enforcement background, and now as House Permanent Select Committee on Intelligence (HPSCI) Chairman, an intelligence background—crucial to me, given what I had connected the dots regarding was a crossover of all three of those paradigms. Him being a Republican or Democrat was less of my concern. Suggesting the package be provided to him from Senator Snowe, I urgently hand wrote another Whistleblower/Protection Request letter.

Unfortunately, despite Michael Allen working at the Department of State previously, I did not know him. And I must admit I was indeed leery

---

15   Michelle Stefanick, email message to John Richter December 21, 2012
16   John Richter, email message to Michelle Stefanick, December 21, 2012
17   Michelle Stefanick, email message to John Richter December 21, 2012

of going from a COS I trusted to one that I did not know. Too many times, I saw folks working under a Principal thinking they are the Principal and not sharing information/insight accordingly. My approach/philosophy had and has always been that it was my responsibility to share immediately and accordingly to whichever Principal I worked for: *The Good, The Bad, and The Ugly*. For without it, I believe they, the Principal, could not do their job in their position—whatever it is—elected by their constituents, and who took an oath to defend our nation. So, I do not—to this day—have high regards, if any regards, for Michael Allen, HPSCI Chairman Chief of Staff.

Still not hearing back from Michael Allen, I would make calls, to include Congressman Roger's Personal Office, and leave messages. Finally, I would reach and chat with Michael Allen. It was brief and it did not go well, particularly after he made a disrespectful comment about Senator Olympia Snowe, a still sitting Senator for the American citizens of the US state of Maine. He had a total disregard of me and my eight-page handwritten Whistleblower/ Protection Request letter that he, the Chief of Staff, had received on behalf of HPSCI Chairman Mike Rogers from US Senator Snowe, on my behalf. This man and his unprofessionalism deserved absolutely no respect. I let him know that, as well as asking the status of my package and Chairman Roger's position and next steps regarding it.

On Friday, December 21, 2012 at 5:55 p.m., I received a call from US Capitol Police Detective William Zimmerman. I sent an email to myself for my records and to document the call. The email is as follows:

> Subject: call from Detective Zimmerman – US Capital Police
> Today at 5:55 p.m. I was called by Detective Zimmerman about my calling, "screaming and cussing" at the House Intel committee. I said I called Michael Allen, Chairman Roger's Chief of Staff, regarding the packet provided by Senator Snowe's office.
>
> Detective kept stating why I called the Intel Committee. I explained that I am the one that provided the packet and my concern of it not being shared with the Chairman.
>
> He didn't care what the packet said and that it was up to the committee to decide what information the Chairman receives.
>
> We went back and forth with the Detective stating that he will contact Senator Snowe's office on Monday.
>
> He said I should know the proper procedure is that the FBI has the information. I told him the FBI does have the information.[18]

---

18   Michelle Stefanick, email message to Michelle Stefanick December 21, 2012

With that reaction/response, I had no doubt that I knew something that *someone* did not want to get out. At this point in time, the reality of it all was very scary. And it was just the beginning.

So, what was the package? The package was my hand-written letter, eight-pages in length on yellow legal paper. At this time, I wrote out seven copies in total, and maintained a log of their distribution maintaining control as to who had copies and who received a copy directly from me. Copy #1 was given to State/DG Linda Thomas-Greenfield at my residence the evening of November 27, 2012. Copy #2 was given to Senator Olympia Snowe at her Russell Senate Office on November 28, 2012. I maintained a copy on my person, Copy #3, and put a copy in my SDFCU Safe Deposit Box, Copy #4, on February 5, 2013, after realizing how serious this matter really was. *Surely, putting a copy in my safe deposit box at the SDFCU branch located within Main State, Department of State should guarantee its security and its safekeeping, right?*

So that's an accounting of four of the first seven hand-written copies. In time I would hand write more copies. And in time, I would no longer maintain an account as I knew there were now too many copies and photocopies out there from under my distribution control. But, my simple request made in the letter was not, and was never to this day, fulfilled: Based on what I knew, and wanted to share, that I and one other individual be protected. Instead, I would be retaliated against.

THE PACKAGE

So, what did the letter say? Well, to this day, I do not feel it's appropriate to share its contents in light of events that are still playing themselves out as I write this book. That said, I will share some contents accordingly. Such as:

> Due to events that have occurred to me, I believe I have information that needs to be shared/passed to the proper officials/authorities within our government, and at the proper levels. Though this information/insight has been obtained from the normal course of carrying-out my position's responsibilities, there may indeed be broader national security implication of which I'm now very concerned…As noted earlier, as the information/insight I have may have broader national security implications, I believe it is my responsibility and duty to my nation to pass it along accordingly… On behalf of my nation, I will share all that I have and all that I know. I look forward to… discuss how best I provide the sensi-

tive/implicating information I have to the proper authorities at the proper level and how we both will be protected in doing so.

So, to provide additional context, at this time, I was a federal DOJ-determined CVRA-accorded rights and protected August 7, 1998 East Africa Embassy bombings victim/witness and an EEO grievance complainant. As of the writing of this letter, I also considered myself a *whistleblower*, believing I and the other individual that I requested be protected in this letter *needed "to be protected well beyond President Obama's Directive expanding whistleblower protection."*

In the letter, I reference my meeting on September 27, 2012 with U/S Patrick Kennedy. Though I had not hand-written this letter at that time, I raised concerns. I also referenced raising my concerns through OSD/Policy Officials to DOD's OSD/Security Officials on October 24-26, 2012. Due to the lack of response at that point, and even so stating in this hand-written letter, I indicated that if not advised accordingly, my intent was to provide a copy of this letter "to David Coombs, the current defense attorney representing Private Bradley Manning in his case with the Government. On December 3, 2012, Mr. Coombs will be in Washington, DC for an event that I plan to attend, further discuss my situation, and provide a copy of this letter." Copy #6 of the hand-written letter was provided to David Coombs at this event on December 3, 2012.

Some may question, why David Coombs? This is simple. He was the only lawyer I knew of at that time who had a military background and was handling such a high-level, high security-clearance case.

However, providing this letter to Combs meant that I had not received any response as I requested from the USG and all the officials who had a copy of it—which included the DNI, the FBI, and others—to "discuss how best I provide the sensitive/implicating information I have to the proper authorities at the proper level and how we both will be protected in doing so." USG officials had been killed, to include at our Embassies, and now the Diplomatic Post in Benghazi. I was subjected to bizarre events while assigned with MARFOREUR/AF in Stuttgart and no investigation was conducted. *What in the world was going on?* As for Copy #5, it was provided to ODNI/Africa Theresa Whelan who was mentioned in the letter and came to my residence on December 2, 2012. During that time, there was absolutely no discussion regarding "how I best provide the sensitive/implicating information I have to the proper authorities at the proper level" or "how we—the other individual and myself—both will be protected in doing so." As for Copy #7, that was provided to Senator and Member of the US Senate's Select Committee on Intelligence (SSCI) Olympia Snowe's Chief of Staff, John Richter, on December 18, 2012 to be provided to Congressman and HPSCI Chairman Michael Roger through his applicable Chief of Staff Michael Allen.

On Thursday, December 27, 2012, I called US Capitol Police Detective Zimmerman. At 3:55 p.m., again, I sent the following email to myself for my records and to document the call:

> Subject: RE: call from Detective Zimmerman – US Capital Police
>
> 12/27 – Just spoke with Detective Zimmerman about any follow-up. He said he did not outreach to Senator Snowe's office and to me, was very very defensive. He said legislative branch does not do investigations, including Chairman Rogers committee. He said he had all the information he needed regarding me and my congressional fellowship with Senator Snowe.
>
> I must admit our discussion, as was the prior one, particularly odd.[19]

With that, another odd event occurred. Congress was called back early from Holiday recess to avoid falling off what was referred to as the "fiscal cliff." I saw an opportunity, and I took it.

Tom Sheehy was my neighbor in Lyon Park, living just up the street, less than two blocks away. Due to my work on the Hill, we were also professional colleagues. Tom was a key staffer for House Foreign Affairs Committee (HFAC) Chairman Ed Royce, the House Congressional Committee with oversight of the Department of State. With Members called back to Washington by House Speaker John Boehner, I knew as a key staffer, Tom would be back in town as well. On Friday, December 28, 2012, I sent the following email to Tom:

> Subject: Greetings
> Hey there Tom – When you get back to town can we chat? Happy Holidays. Cheers, michelle

After exchanging emails, we finally had a chance to talk on January 1, 2013. My request, though seemingly simple, was a big one, particularly with everything else going on. So, what was my ask? Providing not much detail, but as much as I could, I, as a Department of State employee, asked Tom, not through any staffer other than Tom, to simply ask HFAC Chairman Royce when on the House Floor to ask HPSCI Chairman Mike Rog-

---

ers, Member-to-Member, if he received or was aware of the package from Senator Olympia Snowe, a SSCI member. At that time, during their brief encounter, as relayed back to me via Tom later, HPSCI Chairman Rogers was not aware of and had not seen the package. That was all I needed to know. And that made me more adamant than ever to get the truth out— *No matter what.*

Why did I ask the question? The reason was simple. Chairman Royce was responsible for House Congressional Oversight of the Department of State. Chairman Rogers was responsible for House Congressional Oversight of the Intelligence Community. So, who/which committee was responsible for the members of the Intelligence Community embedded within the Department of State for cover? Or, just like the Bureau of Diplomatic Security, there was no Congressional Committee oversight. Just like DS law enforcement Special Agents, these *intelligence* employees slipped through the cracks of Congressional oversight. I opine, apparently, done not only systemically, but intentionally; bypassing oversight by the applicable Senate Foreign Relations Committee and Senate Intelligence Committee, and in the case of State/DS, the Senate Judiciary Committee as well. Thus, applicable in both Congressional Chambers, the House and the Senate, political party never comes into play. This an equal-opportunity, bipartisan, bicameral approach to intentionally and purposely skirt Congressional oversight writ large as well as wrong-doing of which I now, not by choice, am a first-hand victim/witness. And as a first-hand victim/witness, having a front-row seat to the cover-up/scapegoating of criminal wrongdoing with the highest national security implications within the US Department of State, and beyond. In due time, only the tip-of-the-iceberg would be exposed during the upcoming Benghazi Congressional hearings—apparently with implications not fully understood, nor addressed. Or were they, once again, just covered-up—including by the elected representatives of the American people across our nation, by Members and Staffers of Congress (equal-opportunity) both Chambers (House and Senate) and both parties (Republican and Democrat) alike?

For additional context, this very illuminating email exchange is between John Richter and myself from December 7-13, 2012 regarding the FBI.

On Friday, December 7, 2012, I received the following email from John:

Subject: update

They are sending someone over to me this afternoon – not sure of the time yet.
John R. Richter
Chief of Staff
US Senator Olympia J. Snowe[20]

I responded:

Thanks John – I'll be here at home waiting to hear back from you.
cheers, michelle[21]
John replied:
Person is coming by at 2:00 today.
Do I or do I not also include your name with the letter?[22]

I responded:

Thanks John – Can you give me a call when you have a moment to discuss. Thanks,m[23]

John replied:

In meetings till 2:00 … [24]

I responded:

John – Ask that once the FBI Lead Investigator receives/reads the letter that he give you a call directly. At that time you can provide my name, stating that me and the other individual (though this other individual is not aware of my letter/instruction and has not yet been identified) will need Witness protection. With that I strongly advise that no one/no office identified in the letter now at this time be contacted—since they now may have to be questioned/apart of investigation after I and the other individual provide insight jointly/together directly to the FBI.

I kindly request that the FBI agree to the protocol spelled out in the letter for reasons I can't go into at this time over this email. I have provided Senator Snowe the individual's name and location, and would authorize her office to pass that along accordingly if this protocol could be adhered to. I promise other than getting the one individual to the location as noted in the letter, the suggestion I am making is not a complex request. I need to see this person in per-

20   John Richter, email message to Michelle Stefanick, December 7, 2012
21   Michelle Stefanick, email message to John Richter December 7, 2012
22   John Richter, email message to Michelle Stefanick, December 7, 2012
23   Michelle Stefanick, email message to John Richter December 7, 2012
24   John Richter, email message to Michelle Stefanick, December 7, 2012

son so that I am ensured this individual is being protected. Thanks, michelle[25]

John replied:

I'm stacked on meetings, will contact you whenever I hear something from FBI[26]

On Saturday, December 8, 2012, I emailed:

John – In light of what I wrote below, the individual does not know of my letter, but has been informed of an upcoming legal authorities' request for cooperation/assistance in such matter. Thanks, michelle[27]

During this time, the other individual was never contacted by any legal authorities regarding this matter.

On Monday, December 10, 2012, I emailed John:

Senator Snowe/John – As I had not heard from you as of yet today, I wanted to provide a status/update to Senator Snowe since our meeting on November 28. What I have not discussed is that I was/continue to be subjected to a "PSYOPS." I don't know who authorized it, their reason for it being authorized, and on what legal authority. For all that I've been through, it has become crystal clear to me that the information I have is important to someone to resort to this extremity—and with that, the purpose of my handwritten letter is my priority to share accordingly to the proper level/authorities.

As the Senator will be leaving office soon, I highly recommend that this be a "dual tracked" accordingly. The suggestion I make is that Senator Snowe outreach directly to House Chairman Michael Rogers in regards to my letter and the status to date. With his background as an FBI agent and his chairmanship, my effort to do the right thing will continue to have the proper oversight and measures to ensure the information I have is properly shared and lives properly protected for the sake of our nation. Again, these efforts I'm taking are not done lightly. Thank you so much for your continued support and please continue to believe in me and what I have to share.

On November 30, 2012, as a response to Senator Snowe's outreach to the Intel Community Inspector General's office, I received a telephone message from Bill Shea, OIG Hotline. I returned his

25   Michelle Stefanick, email message to John Richter December 7, 2012
26   John Richter, email message to Michelle Stefanick, December 7, 2012
27   Michelle Stefanick, email message to John Richter December 7, 2012

call at approximately 12:17 p.m. at[number redacted]. He noted that he had received a copy of the letter I provided to Senator Snowe and wanted to follow-up. I must admit once Bill focused the context of the call more on it being illegal for me to pass any classified information to David Coombs, instead on what information I had to pass along to them in regards to "whistleblower protection/ national security implications," I became very disenchanted with our discussion. He said there was nothing they could do regarding the steps spelled out in the letter until at least Monday. I noted at that time that I had an IG background and was indeed highly disappointed in his response/reaction and noted that I would discuss with Senator Snowe's office. I did not share any real insight with Bill as a result.

At approximately 1:18, I left a message for John Richter (Senator Snowe's Chief of Staff), in the meanwhile though I did not hear the phone ring, Jim Catella (Senator Snowe's intel staffer) had left a message on my voice mail at 10:40 a.m. regarding their office's outreach to the IG.

At approximately 2:05, John returned my call, linking in Jim, I advised what happened during my call with IG's office and my disappointment, basically blowing me off. Jim said he would contact the IG's office for follow-up.

At approximately 2:42, Jeanette McMillian from the IG General Counsel's Office called me back. She advised that they were working on the protocol as requested in the letter and asked if I authorized them to provide a copy of the letter to the Director/ DNI. I said that I did. However, I would not provide the name of the individual and requested that they contact DNI Africa Theresa Whelan as noted in the letter, since U/S Kennedy shared the name with her. She provided her phone number [number redacted], and said they took my letter very seriously and are working on the protocol. Again, she asked if the letter could be shared with the DNI, I said it could. I also said my intent is not to appear to be taking the process hostage in regards to the December 3 sharing the letter with David Coombs, it's just an opportunity with him being in town. She said she understood the opportunity that existed.

I got off the phone and left a message for John. At approximately 4:29 John called back, linking Jim on the line. I provided the update and my feeling better in regards to IG intent/assistance after talking with Jeanette. John gave me his cell number [number redacted]to call over the weekend with any status.

In the meanwhile, I received an email response of follow-up

from Linda Thomas-Greenfield, in regards to our discussion on the evening of November 27, when I provided her a handwritten copy of the letter. In this email, she noted that she spoke to Pat, passed on a copy of the letter, spoke with OCR and asked them to follow-up on my EEO Complaint with the Marines, while I was in Stuttgart. OCR was supposed to follow-up with me directly, and as of December 10, they have not. In regards to my letter, she noted that it was outside of her purview and thus shared it with Pat.

At 7:35 P.M., I received an email from DNI-Africa Theresa Whelan regarding her being contacting by the IC IG and wanting to talk.

On December 1, at approximately 11:40 a.m., I called and left a message for DNI-Africa Theresa Whelan [number redacted]and sent her a response email 11:51 A.M.

At approximately 12:07 A.M., Theresa returned my call. She noted that she was contacted by the IG, requesting a name of the individual. She said Pat never provided her a name, and that later on Friday afternoon, she was informed that if she received the name to contact IG, Jeanette provided names as she was going to be out on Monday. During our discussion was the first time I became aware that her and Pat never talked though I indicated it in my handwritten letter, either as a follow-up to my October 25 discussion/request from him or my later October email correspondence with Theresa. Thus, Pat never shared the individual's name with Theresa as I had requested in our September 27 meeting. So, at this time, I became aware that Theresa never talked with Pat, didn't know the name of the individual, and didn't see the letter. She noted that Jeanette was not going to be in on Monday so if she found out the name of the individual to pass it along to her colleagues, she identified in an email that she sent to Theresa on SIPR (Secure Internet Protocol Router).

At approximately 12:55 A.M., I called and left a message with Jeanette McMillian regarding my conversation with Theresa Whelan.

At approximately 12:56 A.M., I called and left a message for John Richter.

At approximately 3:18 P.M., John called me back and I advised my conversation with Theresa Whelan, who was contacted by Jeanette McMillian. As Pat never gave Theresa the name, so Jeanette does not have the individual's name to be moving out on the protocol as she told me she was, and that Jeanette never called me back Friday to say she didn't have the name to pass along to DNI with letter for action. Also noted that she may not be in on Monday.

(Note she has same name as OSD policy representative.) Indicated that I provided a suggestion to Senator Snowe as a way forward though may sound extreme but in light of all obstacles/weirdness may be only option/route.

At approximately 5:38 John called me back. Told him I believe Senator Collins in on the right track to connect Benghazi with our Embassy bombings in Nairobi/Tanzania, and that I trust my life completely with the person I provided to Senator Snowe. Noted that the letter asks for not only whistleblower protection, but complete protection for myself and other individual—will need witness protection from Department of Justice if my suspicions are correct.

At approximately 7:50 P.M., I called Theresa Whelan inviting her over to my house to review the letter.

On December 2, at approximately 3:00 p.m. Theresa Whelan came to my house. She read the letter, and then I showed her just a few pieces of information regarding what happened to me and some linkages that are involved. I provided her a hand-written copy of the letter. We discussed her sharing it with Admiral (ADM) McRaven, US Special Operations Command (SOC) Commander, since she was going to see him the next day. She felt best not to give him any such letter in public. She noted that maybe Pat provided the name of the individual directly to DNI Clapper. She left without asking me/me providing her the name of the individual.

At approximately 4:43 Jim Catella (Sen Snowe's SSCI Staffer) called and I passed along the latest status and my concerns.

On December 3, I was advised by OSD Policy Official that after our October 24, 2012 discussion, he discussed with OSD/Policy Security Office Officials Ivory London on October 25, and Mike Brooks on October 26. As of the date of the email (December 10, 2012), no one from OSD Policy Security Office or as requested, ever outreached to me regarding the report I made.

At approximately 1:25 A.M., John Richter returned my call to advise that Alan Ott was going to call me. I advised that he did and that I was about to return his call. We also discussed John outreaching to the Department of Justice for a point of contact. He also advised that my info was wrong and that Jeannette was indeed in the office.

At approximately 11:16 A.M., Alan Ott, the IC IG Investigator, left a message for me to call him at 703-482-2777. I returned his call and left a message at 1:36 P.M. At approximately 4:45, returned Alan Ott's call again.

At approximately 4:46 P.M., Alan called me back and arranged to call me back at 4:00 p.m. on December 4 on the status of things. Calle John to provide the status.

At approximately 6:30 P.M., I discussed briefly with David Coombs and provided a copy of the handwritten letter at the All Souls Church event (1500 Harvard St, NW, Washington DC 20009).

On December 4, 2012, at approximately 4:00 p.m., Alan Ott called stating that he spoke with Theresa Whelan, who did not have the name of the individual. He then said he will not follow the protocol of the letter and that "I have to communicate directly with him otherwise he will deem me as not cooperative." "Not able to accommodate this request." I advised that I once worked in the IG's office and for me to go to these extremes, I stand by what I know and the protocol I request for my protection.

At approximately 5:00 P.M., I called him back to say if the information I have deems to be true, I will make sure folks know that you were the one that was "uncooperative" and put our nation at risk. I relayed some of my first-hand experience with IG folks. I then asked him how long he was with the IG Investigations and who investigates the investigators?

At approximately 6:21 P.M., I discussed with John and Jim my conversation with IC IG. I noted that they have delayed the process in order to find out the name of the individual who could have collaborated by suspicions. My life and this individual's life are now at more risk than before, and if my suspicions are correct, our nation as well. I then read the contents of my handwritten letter as well as the contents of the summary provided to OSD Security Office (who still has not contacted me regarding follow-up). I advised that Senator Snowe has the name/location of the individual, the number and the word. John was then going to outreach to Department of Justice.

On December 5, 2012, at approximately 4:03 p.m., spoke with John to discuss status. I advised for him to find out the lead FBI Investigator on Benghazi and authorize him to read letter in Senator Snowe's office, and for her to provide name of the individual and location. Follow same protocol as spelled out in the letter.

On December 6, 2012, Linda Thomas-Greenfield emailed me to give her a call. Left message on December 7, 2012 for her to call me at home. (Have not received call from her, Pat or Theresa).

On December 7, 2012, at approximately 11:03 A.M., John called to explain that FBI would send over an agent to get a copy of the letter. He will then supposedly hand-carry the letter directly to the FBI Lead Investigator on Benghazi. Once lead investigator receives the letter and contacts John directly, I will authorize Senator Snowe's office to provide name/location of the individual. Reiterate that we will need Witness protection and I would need names of all agents that have been involved—including DOJ Congressional liaisons, etc.[28]

On Tuesday, December 11, 2012, John emailed:

Michelle, FYI informs me that have reviewed the letter and "would like to get in touch with the author." They (specifically, same agent who picked up first letter) wants to meet with me if possible "to obtain the second document." How would you like me to proceed— make a copy of that letter without me looking at it? Give them the original?

I replied:

Thanks John – Before I advise further, who—by name—has read the letter? And what are the names of the agents involved at this point? Thanks, michelle[29]

I replied again:

Hi John – I'm available to discuss from home if you can give me a call. [number redacted]. Thanks, michelle[30]

On Wednesday, December 12, 2012, John responded:

Michelle sorry been swamped, according to agent Neal, here is who's seen your letter:
   The Assistant Director of Counterterrorism Division Andrew McCabe and his Assistant Charles Thorley reviewed the letter.[31]

On Thursday, December 13, 2012, I emailed:

Hello John – I just left you a message. I was just checking in to see status. Thanks, michelle[32]

At this point in time, I had no doubt regarding the validity of the interlinkages and interconnections I made. Advised by that time the

---

28 Michelle Stefanick, email message to John Richter December 10, 2012
29 Michelle Stefanick, email message to John Richter December 11, 2012
30 Michelle Stefanick, email message to John Richter December 11, 2012
31 John Richter, email message to Michelle Stefanick, December 12, 2012
32 Michelle Stefanick, email message to John Richter December 13, 2012

FBI had made a copy on December 7, 2012 of my November 27, 2012 hand-written letter that I provided to Senator Snowe on November 28, 2012, the question remains as valid today, as it did at the time. *Why wasn't I protected?*

Again, I can't emphasize enough the assistance of Senator Snowe and her COS John Richter. They were open, transparent and documented every step of the way—their contacting the IC OIG, the FBI Congressional Liaison, the FBI, the House/HPSCI. Whereas on the other hand, Linda Thomas-Greenfield, who previously served with me at Embassy Nairobi and was now State/DG, her actions were not open, not transparent and not documented—at least, not with me. And in due time, what would be and is documented are the retaliatory actions taken against me by the US Department of State, to include by Linda Thomas-Greenfield, the DG herself. Given the extensive outreach conducted on my behalf by Senator Snowe, my question is and remains—what precise actions did Linda Thomas-Greenfield take and who precisely did she share my November 27, 2012 Whistleblower/Protection Request Letter with—U/S Patrick Kennedy? DS? PM? Secretary Clinton? White House? No one? Who?

Delay after delay after delay, finally two FBI SAs would come to my home to speak with me on January 8, 2013. One male; one female. She was professional; he was absolutely not, and given my OIG background, he had no intention of listening to what I had to say. In fact, the experience was so unprofessional that I would attempt due diligence to confirm/verify that they were even FBI SAs to begin with, that's how unprofessional the experience was. Without being provided business cards to confirm accuracy of spelling, their names were Tony Malow and Jennifer Celso. Also, despite FBI SA John Neal advising Senator Snowe's COS John Richter, who in turn advised me on Friday, December 21, 2012 that "…I believe someone out of the NY office will be contacting her to setup an interview," I was never contacted by the FBI NY Field Office, let alone interviewed, despite my request made from and via OSD/Security since October 24-26, 2012. So, you know that old adage, "See something, say something"—obviously, that pertained and pertains to everyone, except for me! Particularly in my case when its "Know something…"

Now I had already distributed seven copies previously, to include the highest levels of our USG, yet no one responded nor advised accordingly to my simple request: "How best can I provide the sensitive/implicating information I have to the proper authorities at the proper level and how will we both be protected in doing so." And all this was playing out with the backdrop of the congressional investigations regarding the Diplomatic Post attack in Benghazi …

STEPPING IT UP

I sent Tom an email on Friday, January 4, 2013:
Subject: follow-up

> Hello Tom – Just as a follow-up to our conversation regarding investigator, please note I will be off first part of next week as well on use or lose leave. Thank you Tom. Cheers, michelle[33]

On Friday, January 11, 2013, I sent another email:

> Hello Tom – Just wanted to let you know that effective Monday, I will be back at work if you need to get a hold of me regarding our conversation on below/my situation. Thanks and congrats on your new position. Cheers, michelle[34]

On Tuesday, January 15, 2013, Tom emailed:

> Michelle:
> Would you be available to speak by phone to one of the Committee Investigators?
> Thanks, Tom[35]

I replied:

> Hello Tom – Considering I am currently at work, my preference is not to speak on the phone. Could meeting at my residence be an option? I can arrange to be there later today or tomorrow, or whenever you be convenient. Thanks Tom. cheers, michelle[36]

He responded:

> Can he call you on your cell during lunch?[37]

I replied:

> Hi – It's a usg issued cell phone. Is it possible for him to come to my residence so he can also then see some of the evidence directly as well. thanks, m[38]

---

33   Michelle Stefanick, email message to Tom Sheehy January 4, 2013
34   Michelle Stefanick, email message to Tom Sheehy January 11, 2013
35   Tom Sheehy, email message to Michelle Stefanick January 15, 2013
36   Michelle Stefanick, email message to Tom Sheehy January 15, 2013
37   Tom Sheehy, email message to Michelle Stefanick January 15, 2013
38   Michelle Stefanick, email message to Tom Sheehy January 15, 2013

Tom replied:

> Can you meet him this week during your lunch, somewhere downtown?[39]

I replied:

> Tom – I'm not trying to be difficult. Since so many people now know I am a "whistle blower" and my government hasn't come back to me yet, I am now protecting myself. I have limited my life now for months, including restricting where I go. I do not feel comfortable with your request. I'm sorry.[40]

On Friday, January 18, 2013, I emailed Tom:

> Hi Tom – I just wanted to let you know that I am home today and available to meet with your investigator if possible. Thanks, michelle[41]

On Monday, January 21, 2013, Tom emailed:

> Michelle:
> We have our hearing with the Secretary of State on Benghazi on Wednesday. I'd appeal to you to meet him somewhere in DC tomorrow. He will go where ever is convenient for you. Tom[42]

I replied:

> Tom – My White House contacts have been advising me to stay where I am safe, as are folks in my current office. I'm doing so until I hear back from them/the FBI.
>
> I would need to show some documents/online email to whomever to support/make some sense for what I am saying – that is why I'm so adamant of meeting at my house – as I did the FBI agents. My suspicions/implications are not to be taken lightly if indeed true, including for my safety/protection. This has possible major national security implications.
>
> [Have you seen yet my letter that Chairman Rogers' staffer Michael Allen has]. If not, if you want to come by to at least see that you may have more understanding to what's at hand. I'm here it that would work for you. Thanks, michelle[43]

---

39   Tom Sheehy, email message to Michelle Stefanick January 15, 2013
40   Michelle Stefanick, email message to Tom Sheehy January 15, 2013
41   Michelle Stefanick, email message to Tom Sheehy January 18, 2013
42   Tom Sheehy, email message to Michelle Stefanick January 21, 2013
43   Michelle Stefanick, email message to Tom Sheehy January 21, 2013

On Thursday, January 24, 2013, I sent the following email:

> Tom – At this point, I will assume Congress – other than Senator
> Olympia Snowe – has no interest in hearing what I have to say re-
> garding the matter presented in the letter.
>
> I have no intent for this to be a political football because my num-
> ber one objective/priority is the national security of my/our nation.
>
> So, when the truth gets out, the truth will get out. Thanks, mi-
> chelle[44]

On January 24, 2013, I provided a copy, Copy #8, of my hand-written Whistleblower/Protection Request letter to Tom Sheehy by walking to his home to hand deliver a copy. As he was not yet home from work, I left the sealed envelope for him at his residence.

On January 28, 2013, I mailed via United States Postal Service (USPS) Express mail/signature required delivery, Copy #9 to Michael Mensch. He was working at the Center for Civil-Military Relations at the Naval Postgraduate School in Monterey, California at the time. The USPS Green Card returned to me indicates delivery receipt of January 30, 2013. I indicate this extensive detail regarding the mail delivery due to the intentional and purposeful mail fraud/mail tampering/destruction of USG property incidents that would occur later. On January 28, 2013, I also met with and provided Copy #10 to Eleanor Clift.

Now for the step I took with the White House itself. Not knowing if DG Thomas-Greenfield shared my letter with anyone, and definitely losing trust in her as a result, due to the seriousness of the issue and regarding my *intent*, I purposely dual-tracked my reporting. Senator Snowe was a Republican. And the White House, President Obama and his Administration, were Democrats. I knew for a fact that Senator Snowe took appropriate actions—it was those whom she contacted who did not—one of those entities being the Intelligence Community, and now the FBI itself. Doubting whether they were even real FBI SAs that came to my house to question me, I did the only thing I could think of, and that was to contact the WH directly, via the WH Military Liaison Office.

On Tuesday, February 5, 2013, I received a response from WH Military Liaison, Air Force Colonel David Sullivan. When I advised Dave of my concern of the two *supposed* FBI SAs that came to my house, and asked if there was anything, he could do to confirm their authenticity, this was his response:

44   Michelle Stefanick, email message to Tom Sheehy January 24, 2013

Subject: response from earlier request

Michelle –

My POC was able to make contact with the FBI and they responded positively that your interview is a part of an ongoing investigation, and that they naturally could not provide us any further information at this time. We were told they FBI will reach out to you if further assistance is needed.

I think that is good news that they are taking your interview seriously. Hope this helps your peace of mind.

Good luck with the move back to State, and I hope you are getting back to feeling better about all this. Dave[45]

I responded:

Thank you, Dave – This indeed helps. I really appreciate this insight and really hope justice is done. In the meanwhile, I begin my transition back to State today….stay in touch, as will I.

Again, thank you Dave. Cheers, michelle[46]

Now to provide additional context, Dave "Diesel" Sullivan was an AWC colleague of mine. Even more specifically, Diesel and I were in the same Al Stolberg NSPP elective together. During NSPP, we had some very influential and insightful guest speakers. In addition to speakers such as Gen Keith Dayton, through Diesel's connections, former President Bush's Press Secretary Ari Fleischer came to speak to our class.

On Wednesday, January 16, 2013, I had sent an email to Dave:

Hi Dave – I need to talk with you. It's kinda urgent. What's a good number to reach you Thanks, michelle[47]

On Thursday, January 31, 2013, I emailed:

Hi Dave – Just checking in to see if you've heard anything more yet regarding this matter. Thanks, michelle[48]

On Friday, February 1, 2013, Dave responded:

Michelle –

I just ran a poll of my contacts, and unfortunately, everyone is coming up empty on acknowledging whether or not the information you provided the two agents ever made it to the lead investigator in the

45   David Sullivan, email message to Michelle Stefanick February 5, 2013
46   Michelle Stefanick, email message to David Sullivan, February 5, 2013
47   Michelle Stefanick, email message to David Sullivan, January 16, 2013
48   Michelle Stefanick, email message to David Sullivan, January 31, 2013

bureau. Sorry I don't have any better news for you. I will keep my ears and eyes open for you though. Hope you are staying safe. Dave[49]

I responded:

Thanks Dave – I must say I find all this quite bizarre. I'm home this week on administrative leave since being reassigned from OSD to State, pending hearing back from FBI/DS on it being safe for me to come back to work/back to building. Though I appreciate your email and the status, I just don't understand what is going on and why I'm involved in all this. All I want to do is share what I know and let the legal process take it from there…. I really hope the VP was able to talk to Senator Snowe since getting confirmation regarding the FBI knowing is so difficult. All I can say is I must indeed know something that someone doesn't want me to share with legal authorities…. I'm trying to stay safe, but all I want is my life back. Thanks for keeping me posted. Thanks Dave.[50]

Dave replied:

MS – If it's meant to be, it will be, that's what I have always believed! Good luck with your transition back to State. Good job waiting for you? Overseas travel? Will let you know if I hear anything…. Cheers, DS[51]

I replied:

Dave—At this point my career/life has been ruined. I guess that's what was meant to be. Thanks, michelle[52]

Dave replied:

I hope that is not the case, Michelle—you have much more going for you that getting this info into some bureaucrat's hands who may or may not act on it. Just keep working hard for our country and doing what you/we can to prevent the next attack, and you will have accomplished much in life. Stay strong… Dave[53]

On Saturday, February 2, 2013, I replied:

---

49   David Sullivan, email message to Michelle Stefanick February 1, 2013
50   Michelle Stefanick, email message to David Sullivan, February 1, 2013
51   David Sullivan, email message to Michelle Stefanick February 1, 2013
52   Michelle Stefanick, email message to David Sullivan, February 1, 2013
53   David Sullivan, email message to Michelle Stefanick February 1, 2013

Dave – Considering what was personally done to me, and light of my IG/CPA background—I respectfully disagree with you. If laws were broken, justice must be done. I take obstruction of justice very seriously....so with that, getting my insight/information to the right hands is not only the right thing to do, it's the ethical/legal/moral right thing must do. I'm hoping what you are hearing or rather not hearing back regarding my matter from your sources there is because it is now in the right hands and indeed properly being investigated. I would hate to think and don't want to think it's the other ...hopefully you and/or I will hear something back soon and most importantly, justice will be done—as terrible as the story line may be. Thanks, michelle

As I connected more and more dots, I would reach out to "Diesel" again soon after.

January 26, 2013 was my last day at OSD/AFR. Due to circumstances of which I was not certain nor ever made aware precisely what the reason being was, but I was departing my assignment early. Sound familiar? It was just like my early departure from my US Department of State foreign service FPA/POLAD position with the US Military, MARFOREUR/AF. And now I was departing early from my US Department of State foreign service State/Defense Exchange position at the Defense Department's Headquarters, the Pentagon with OSD/AFR. Because of CVRA-accorded rights and protections as a first-hand victim/witness in regards to the August 7, 1998 East Africa Embassy bombing? My EEOC Complaint litigation? My November 27, 2012 Whistleblower/Protection Request letter? *Why? And again, what in the world was going on?*

When I departed, I took with me unclassified files in order to complete my EER, with the intention of returning them as soon as my EER was completed. This never occurred, though I focused on completing my EER as quickly as possible, intentional delay tactics I endured seem incredible, yet all documented.

Before departing OSD/AFR, Mark Swayne made a passing comment to me that Linda (DG Linda Thomas-Greenfield) was definitely talking to someone in the Pentagon/OSD. And once no one got back to me per my applicable OSD/Security outreach on October 24-26, 2012, Capt. Organ made a comment that I definitely needed to talk with the FBI. And the DOD individual that came to my house who strongly implied that there was a higher-level investigation going on.Something was definitely going on. And what in the world was it? And why in the world did I continually see the same specific number and specific word over and over, again and again, in different locations, at different times, so many times, enough times to become more than a pattern of coincidence. I saw them so much and was so confident it was intentional,that I even shared this "specific number and specific word" information with Senator Snowe on November 28, 2012 ... So what was up with that? *What was going on? And why? And by whom? And for what reason? Was this some kind of "test" to see how observant I was? And then, one day I figured out to what the "specific word" related to, was in regards to—due to its uniqueness, yet confirmation to me and for me of my linkage, my connection. It was confirmation that I was right over target as to what all "this" was really about—funding, money, its always about money, the money. In this case, it was black operational funding. And only later would I discover how much, the immense magnitude of black operational funding involved.*

After I departed OSD/AFR, I was placed on Administrative Leave to get my EER done. So, I immediately began working from home on its completion. The period of performance would only cover April 16, 2012 – January 26, 2013. On February 8, 2013, I submitted my EER draft to my applicable rater, DASD Amanda Dory. Delayed due to travel, Amanda eventually completed and then signed my EER on March 14, 2013. My reviewer, PM/POLAD Director Scott Rauland, would eventually sign my EER on April 22, 2013. However, my EER would never be reviewed, approved and signed off by any Review Panel or Review Panel Chairperson. Nor would my EER ever be officially submitted to HR/PE for filing into my OPF, nor provided to the applicable Promotion Panel for review for SFS promotion consideration. With more detail to follow, all this on the part of and by those officials within the Department of State/PM and HR bureaus.

Oh, and remember the May 2011 formal EEO Grievance I filed in Stuttgart after my smashed car door incident? And the December 30, 2011 EEOC-Washington Field Office letter I received on January 4, 2012 in response to my November 23, 2011 EEO Grievance Hearing Request signed by EEOC Supervisory AJ Gladys O. Collazo regarding EEOC Case No. 570-2012-00235X, Agency No. AREUSTUT11APR01642 that ended with the four words *"as soon as possible"*?

Well, over a year later, on February 22, 2013, I finally received an EEOC-Washington Field Office *ACKNOWLEDGEMENT AND ORDER* from Administrative Judge (AJ) Frances del Toro dated February 20, 2013. On February 25, 2013, I responded accordingly as requested, required and so ordered to both the EEOC and USAG Stuttgart/Dept of

Army/EEO Office, of which USAG Stuttgart/Dept of Army/EEO Office never officially responded. I sent an email on February 25, 2013 to Eshe Faulcon:

> Subject: Certificate of Service/No Representative
> Esha – As requested by US EEOC Acknowledgement and Order dated February 20, 2013, please find attached a copy of the Option B for Designation of Representative letter, as well as the Certificate of Service receipt acknowledgement of February 22, 2013, dated February 25, 2013. Additionally, please note the address change to [redacted]. Arlington VA 22201. The contact email remains the same at [email address removed}. The new phone number is [redacted]
> A copy of the above information was mailed back to EEOC on 2/25 and sent via email to provided email address on this letter also on 2/25. Thank you, michelle.[54]

On Tuesday, March 5, 2013, I received the following response from Eshe:

> Thank you Ms. Stefanick![55]

Other than that, interestingly, I did not receive any other official response from EEOC-Washington Field Office AJ del Toro until *my* follow-up on October 28, 2014. However, look at the events that occurred next in light of my applicable February 25, 2013 response. So, are the events that occurred and not investigated in Germany pertinent and relevant? *Absolutely!*

Meanwhile, with more and more information being reported in the media, I was connecting more and more dots: the Congressional Hearings regarding Benghazi, what some called the coup/overthrow/ouster of CIA Director General Petraeus, my distinct observations while in Germany, and insights while assigned within the walls of the Pentagon. More pieces of the puzzle were falling into place, and piecing together perfectly. Of course, in this instance, my conclusion was circumstantial, but if I shared my theory accordingly, it could be the *tipping-point* insight necessary to put the investigators in the direction of the truth and exposing what was really going on. Just as I had done years prior in my role and under my responsibilities as a federal auditor with DCAA and State/OIG, I had to pass along accordingly to investigators.

54   Michelle Stefanick, email message to Eshe Faulcon, February 25, 2013
55   Eshe Faulcon, email message to Michelle Stefanick, February 25, 2013

So, on Friday, March 01, 2013, I reached out to Dave "Diesel" Sullivan again.

Subject: RE: response from earlier request

Hello Dave – I hate to bother you again, but can you please find out who is investigating the Paula Broadwell/Petraeus incident. I have some insight/information to pass along but wasn't sure who was doing the investigation? FBI? Army Criminal Investigative Services? I really need to pass this along but again, the obstacles are absolutely incredible! Thanks, michelle[56]

Dave replied:

Michelle –

My POC here is not "in the know" on who has the lead at this point. Army has the lead on Broadwell administrative punishment, as witnessed by her demotion, but both our insight is that the FBI has the "criminal" investigation still if there are still charges pending. Sorry I don't have more.

How are you doing? Are you stabilized back at State? What are you hearing back about your info that you shared to FBI? Dave[57]

I replied:

Thanks Dave – That's what I thought/think as well. However, I was also thinking that if "crimes" occurred while either or both were active duty than UCMJ would come into play—thus the Army angle. Either way I have info to pass along but being stalled once again… could your POC please find out contact info for me to at least pass along to the right person.

Dave – To be honest, I'm not doing well at all. I am back at State, with the implications I've made do I feel safe—HELL NO! I've heard absolutely nothing back from FBI. What an American citizen must experience/go through to do the right thing is unconscionable—especially in America, the defender of "rule of law"/ due process for the world. It is disgustingly amazing.

So again, understanding your situation, all I'm asking is for is a POC—nothing more, nothing less—as I would really hope the White House would want these to be investigated properly as well. Thanks, Michelle[58]

Dave replied:

---

56   Michelle Stefanick, email message to David Sullivan, March 1, 2013
57   David Sullivan, email message to Michelle Stefanick March 1, 2013
58   Michelle Stefanick, email message to David Sullivan, March 1, 2013

I will ask one more time, next pass by, but I am not optimistic. This topic is probably something the WH is not following very closely since there is a twinge of embarrassment for Gen P every time it is brought up these days…[59]

I responded:

Believe me I totally understand. However, I believe I have some context that can be brought to the investigation that may be to Gen P's favor… and needs to be at least reviewed/considered. Thus, this urgency for me.[60]

Dave responded:

I don't know anybody on the Army staff these days, do you? They might be the best first stop since I think Army CIS works directly for the Secretary of the Army. Maybe you can send the information direct to Sec Army?[61]

I replied:

That's why I was thinking with Rich's JAG background, he would definitely now. Do you have access to his new email address? I guess JS migrated to new email addresses…[62]

Dave responded:

I don't, unfortunately. There is something like .mil@mail.mil after the first name, middle initial, last name.
    Maybe Richard.?.gross.mil@mail.mil
    I do not have Facebook access here at White House, maybe you can find it on his FB page from home?
    Sorry I am not as useful this round… Dave[63]

I replied:

Thanks Dave – I spoke with Rich regarding that angle, and again, any assistance on who POC would be for me to outreach on FBI side would be great—if they are indeed the lead in regards to this investigation. Thanks, michelle[64]

59   Michelle Stefanick, email message to David Sullivan, March 1, 2013
60   Michelle Stefanick email message to David Sullivan, March 1, 2013
61   David Sullivan, email message to Michelle Stefanick March 1, 2013
62   Michelle Stefanick email message to David Sullivan, March 1, 2013
63   David Sullivan, email message to Michelle Stefanick March 1, 2013
64   Michelle Stefanick, email message to David Sullivan, March 1, 2013

Diesel responded:

> Copy that, Michelle. Request will be made next pass with my POC.[65]

I responded:

> Thanks Dave – I really appreciate it. I just want to pass along what I have and then for this nightmare to end!!!![66]

The nightmare would not end. It would only get worse. And continues to this day...

On March 1, 2013, I reached out to another AWC/NSPP colleague, Army Judge Advocate General (JAG) Rich Gross:

> Subject: POC?
> Hello Rich – Hope all is well. I have a question for you ... do you know who is doing the Broadwell/Petraeus investigation? Would it be FBI or Army/Military? I would assume FBI. However, if there was a possibility that something occurred in this regard while either/both were active duty, I would assume UCMJ may apply putting it in Army's court?
> I can't go into detail, but could you please query and find out for me and then provide appropriate poc's for me? Thanks so much. Michelle[67]

Rich responded:

> Michelle:
> As I far as I know (from reading the press), it's the FBI. I'm not aware of any DOD or Army investigation into the matter.
> I don't have a POC there to ask. vr rich[68]

I replied:

> Hi – Thanks Rich. Can you pass along your phone number so I can give you a quick call? Cheers, m[69]

After chatting with Rich, I was provided some additional contacts. On March 1, 2013, I met with two Army Criminal Investigative Division (ACID) SAs, Terry Little and Alfred Diaz, at my residence. After provid-

65   David Sullivan, email message to Michelle Stefanick March 1, 2013
66   Michelle Stefanick, email message to David Sullivan, March 1, 2013
67   Michelle Stefanick, email message to Rich Gross, March 1, 2013
68   Rich Gross, email message to Michelle Stefanick, March 1, 2013
69   Michelle Stefanick, email message to Rich Gross, March 1, 2013

ing an overview and sharing some evidential matter, they quickly noted that this was *under Naval Criminal Investigative Service's (NCIS) purview.*

So again, once again, I patiently waited…

On Sunday, March 10, 2013, I reached out again to Rich Gross:

> Hello Rich – Hope all is well. I just want you to know that I really appreciate your assistance with ACID. The two Special Agents I spoke with were great and we plan on doing additional follow-up this week.
>
> That said, again I hate to do this, but considering the sensitivity yet importance to the matter that is at hand, do you have a contact you trust with the Navy CID/CIS as that is the next step to loop them in.
>
> With that and with not going into too much detail in this email, I just want you to know that eventually you indeed may want to be looped into this accordingly as aspects are already under the purview of an ongoing FBI investigation.
>
> Believe me, this is not a matter I take lightly nor come to you easily with, but as there are implications to our national security, I do what I must. Thanks so much Rich. Michelle[70]

After a round of emails, Rich's last email providing NCIS contact information ended with this:

> … I'm not sure I understand your UCMJ question about violating constitutional authority. If you're concerned for your safety, I recommend you contact the FBI. Vr Rich[71]

I already did. And they, the FBI, did absolutely nothing to protect me. And they never got back to me.

Events occurred, insight obtained, and dots connected presenting and establishing a totally different perspective from what I thought and knew at that time.

So, in summary, at this time, I am a federal CVRA-accorded rights and protected victim/witness regarding the August 7, 1998 East Africa Embassy bombings who requested assistance/protection from DOJ, and received none. Due to what occurred in Germany, I was an EEO grievance complainant who requested an EEOC Hearing, an investigation since there was none, and at this point, had no current status, patiently awaiting a response. Connecting dots with what I know, what happened to me,

---

70   Michelle Stefanick, email message to Rich Gross, March 10, 2013
71   Rich Gross, email message to Michelle Stefanick, March 10, 2013

and what was occurring, I requested whistleblower rights and protections for myself and another, an applicable intelligence community individual, from State Department, Congress, ODNI, IC OIG, FBI, WH, and received none. And I'm connecting more and more dots…

INSECURE

In the meantime, on Monday, March 11, 2013, I received an email from Michael Canfield.

> Subject: Security Clearance
> Ms. Stefanick,
> My name is Michael Canfield and I am a Special Investigator for the US Department of State. I have been assigned to conduct your background investigation for your security clearance. I would like to schedule an appointment to interview. Please call me at [redacted].
> Thank you for your assistance in this matter.
> Regards,
> Michael L. Canfield
> Washington Region
> "Unit 7"
> Contract Background Investigator Program
> Office of Personnel Security and Suitability
> Bureau of Diplomatic Security
> US Department of State
> Independent Contractor[72]

Now, you can only imagine my initial reaction when I received this email. *You've got to be kidding me!* Is this some kind of joke? But, apparently, it's *status quo* for DS and how they operate. You report accordingly and they respond accordingly—*by investigating you.* Oh, but wait, except in the case of the July 20, 2001 anonymous memorandum. Given its timing and my status, instead of notifying me, DOJ and the FBI accordingly, DS, based on this anonymous source, opened a *criminal investigation on me. Unbelievable.* Now this! It was unbelievable not only in its timing, but even more so, given my last security clearance background investigation was in February 2010, while in Stuttgart assigned to MARFOREUR/AF.

What I did not know at the time, however, were all the email exchanges going on behind the scenes within DS. And I would only find out in due time, and only because of my filing a FOIA request as a result of the retaliatory actions taken against me specifically and particularly by the US Department of State/Diplomatic Security. In light of the situation, I responded accordingly:

> Hello Michael – Per our telcon discussion, since I just went through a background check while assigned to Stuttgart, Germany in 2010-2011 timeframe, I would like to know while I'm being requested another one so shortly after just going through the process. As kindly requested, can you please advise the name and the contact person in DS from whom you received this request. Thank you. Michelle[73]

On Tuesday, March 12, 2013, Michael Canfield responded with a puzzling, odd request. So, I responded:

> Michael – Per our telcon, as I work for the State Department, I am totally confused as to why I am being requested to do the below.
> First of all, since my boiler went out in my house on Friday and is being fixed/worked, I will not be able to fulfill this "ASAP" request for tomorrow.
> Secondly, please contact DS Jim Minor and U/S Patrick Kennedy regarding/confirming my involvement with an ongoing National Security investigation. Therefore, these other law enforcement entities must be informed/coordinated/participating in regards to the below before I can proceed accordingly with the below request.
> Thirdly, I again kindly request who is DS made this request.
> Thank you. michelle[74]

I then, in turn, forwarded the entire email exchange to DG Linda Thomas-Greenfield and U/S Patrick Kennedy:

> Hello Linda – Just wanted to let you know that I'm unable to meet at the Pentagon on Wednesday since DS advised that this was your request. Thanks, michelle[75]

I sent this to Linda and Patrick because by March 12, 2013, I had already departed OSD/AFR and was now back at the State Department... And also so they could see, if they were not involved, the games, retaliatory games as a result of my November 27, 2012 Whistleblower/Protection Request letter or even my October 24-26, 2012 OSD/Security outreach.

73   Michelle Stefanick, email message to Michael Canfield March 13, 2013
74   Michelle Stefanick, email message to Michael Canfield March 11, 2013
75   Michelle Stefanick, email message to Linda Thomas-Greenfield and Patrick Kennedy, March 11, 2013

Yet, no one from the FBI and/or DOJ/SDNY contacted me nor protected me. *So, you tell me, what is really going on?*

On Wednesday, March 13, 2013, Linda responded:

> Michelle: I have not had a conversation with DS regarding your security clearance. Linda[76]

I replied to Linda, ccing U/S Patrick Kennedy:

> Thanks Linda – As DS Jim Minor said you were the one that requested this, I find all this to be quite curious/odd at the same time.
>
> Besides having an already scheduled/arranged broken boiler (for heat) at home being replaced and a plumbing issue addressed, again, I will not be able to attend this requested (by whomever) meeting with DS at the Pentagon. Thanks, michelle[77]

In due time I would get more clarity on this DS retaliatory investigation request. But it would not be until about a year later, not until after so much damage had been done, and not until after my FOIA request in light of the next retaliatory action taken against me by US Department of State.

For additional reference, I provide insight to my background check while assigned to Stuttgart, Germany in 2010-2011 timeframe. On Wednesday, February 3, 2010 at 10:48 p.m., I received an email:

> Subject: Security Clearance Interview
> Good Morning Mrs. Stefanick,
> My name is Shelly Watson. I am an Investigator for the US Department of State, assigned your background investigation for your clearance and I'd like to set an appointment with you for an interview. I will be in the Stuttgart area tomorrow, Thursday, February 4, 2010, and could meet with you for 1-2 hours, beginning at 13:00 to discuss your E-QUIP papers for your clearance. If this time is convenient for you, please feel free to call my contact number enclosed in this e-mail as I will not have access to obtain e-mail responses while on the road. Also, please secure a private office space where your interview can be conducted. If tomorrow is not convenient, please reply via e-mail, indicating which day and time next week would best fit your schedule.
> I thank you in advance for your time and hope to hear from you soon.
> Shelly Brock-Watson
> Special Investigator

---

76   Linda Thomas-Greenfield email message to Michelle Stefanick, and Patrick Kennedy, 3/13/13
77   Michelle Stefanick, email message to Linda Thomas-Greenfield and Patrick Kennedy, 3/13/13

Bureau of Diplomatic Security
US Department of State[78]

Now given the fact that Ms. Brock-Watson sent this at 10:48 p.m., the night before, for the interview the next day, I thought odd, but okay, I'll see what I can do. So, I responded at 8:15 a.m. on Thursday, February 4, 2010 accordingly:

> Hello Shelly – I will be available today for a portion of the day, but my entire afternoon is already committed. Next week I will be departing for TDY and only day that may be possible is Monday. I'll call your contact number to discuss. Thanks, m[79]

We met. I must admit the interview was off—a little odd, even. The questions being asked were puzzling, particularly given my official assignment postings, my overseas travel, given all documented and official, all easily confirmable and verifiable.

On Monday, February 8, 2010, I received a follow-up email from Shelly Brock-Watson:

> Good Morning Ms. Stefanick,
> Just to clarify some information I was able to obtain from you during the interview. You stated that you traveled to Sudan, Kenya and South America ... or was it South Africa? If South America, please indicate where in your response. If you indicate South Africa, please confirm it was Pretoria that was visited for OGB.
> Thank you in advance and I hope to hear from you soon.
> Shelly Brock-Watson[80]

I responded back:

> Hello Shelly – Sure. As we discussed I showed you on my submitted package that as I am State Department that from 2003 through 2005, I was assigned to Embassy Khartoum, Sudan. During that official assignment I did two TDYs for official USG—one trip to Embassy Nairobi, Kenya and another to Embassy Pretoria, South Africa. Hope this clarifies.Thanks and have a great day. Cheers, m
> Michelle L. Stefanick
> Foreign Policy Advisor
> Marine Forces Europe and Africa[81]

78   Shelly Brock-Watson, email message to Michelle Stefanick, February 3, 2010
79   Michelle Stefanick, email message to Shelly Brock-Watson, February 3, 2010
80   Shelly Brock-Watson, email message to Michelle Stefanick, February 8, 2010
81   Michelle Stefanick, email message to Shelly Brock-Watson, February 3, 2010

Again, I found the face-to-face interview so odd, that I in turn, forwarded my 1:55 p.m. email response to Pat Hartnett-Kelly, high importance. Pat responded:

> I'll bet you lunch this will not be the last question she will ask you
> – again. But keep your responses nice and professional and know
> that she probably is a newbie... [82]

To which I responded:

> I agree.... But this is not good... [83]

Pat replied:

> yeah, well... what else is new... [84]

My initial call to Pat and the reason for my concern, wasn't a background/security clearance investigation per se;these were necessary and absolutely required. I was cooperative... But yet, the questioning, the line of questioning, was quit puzzling, a-little off, even. Otherwise, I would not have documented. So why did I document it? Well, there were a few reasons. I found the reference to South America puzzling. Given I had already submitted my paperwork and they had access to my passports,was the slip regarding South America, truly just a slip? Was it a concern regarding my trip to Antarctica? Or as you may recall, on July 20, 2001, an anonymous memorandum was submitted to DS after I returned to Embassy Moscow from attending the bin Laden trial in NYC. Now considering MED and I discussed this memo, and DS never ever contacted me about it... So obviously not an issue, right? Well, in due time, via a FOIA request, I would finally find out that that was not the case. Now given my discussion with MED and who I speculated wrote the memo, the specific event generating the memo, and the potential author of the memo was someone I first encountered while conducting OIG audit field work, was, you got it, in South/Central America. And without going into further detail, this individual's behavior during the time of our audit was found by members of our audit team to be puzzling, questionable even... So again, I found this questioning/reference to South America worth a pause.

With that, and given all that would occur, and the fact that DS Special Investigator Shelly Brock-Watson came to Stuttgart, Germany and met

---

82   Pat Hartnett Kelly, email message to Michelle Stefanick, February 3, 2010
83   Michelle Stefanick, email message to Pat Hartnett Kelly, February 3, 2010
84   Pat Hartnett Kelly, email message to Michelle Stefanick, February 3, 2010

with me in my office—this means without dispute, DS knew I was there. *And why is this of relevance?* Because given my federal CVRA-protected status as an August 7, 1998 East Africa Embassy bombing victim/witness, given bin Laden's capture/kill of May 1, 2011, and DS being responsible for protection security details, I surely was being protected, right? I mean I was assigned and working on a US Army garrison with the US Marine Corps after all, right?

Fast forward, and I'm again being contacted in March 2013 regarding a security clearance investigation given all that had occurred and transpired between now and the previous one, and its timing…

Meanwhile, I was connecting more and more dots… And even if no one else was doing their job, that didn't mean I was going to stop doing mine. "See something, say something" as well as "Know something, say something"—unless of course, for some reason, you are me… My thought being, if these individuals do not have the intellectual capability and/or intelligence to understand and comprehend what I was saying, the dots that I was connecting, then it's *them* that should not be entrusted by the American people and with a security clearance. By this time, I knew and had no doubt something nefarious was at play.

On Monday, March 18, 2013, I received an email from ACID SA Terry Little, ccing SA Alfred Diaz:

> Subject: Interview (UNCLASSIFIED)
> Ms. Stefanick
> I am trying to contact you to set up a second interview. As SA DIAZ explained, we were unable to pursue your complaint due to our limited jurisdiction. However, we have been in contact with NCIS and I would like you to tell your story to them. Please reply as soon as possible. I would like to schedule the interview for today if we can.
> V/R
> Terry B. Little
> Special Agent
> Field Investigative Unit
> US Army Criminal Investigative Command[85]

I responded to ACID SA Little, ccing SA Alfred Diaz:

> Hello Terry – I'm currently in office and have a meeting at 12:30 that I must attend. Otherwise, I'm available after that.

---

85   Terry Little, email message to Michelle Stefanick and Alfred Diaz, March 18, 2013

If you can provide me a number, I can give you a call to discuss/coordinate.

With that, as SA Diaz is aware, I outreached to NCIS but they didn't seem to be interested and noted that they were passing it to their NCIS National Security division in Headquarters/Washington.

My preference is if I have this interview with NCIS, that either you or SA Diaz attend as well. First, to make sure I cover all the same points and secondly, so that you can hear any other additional insight I may provide that can assist your case if a linkage is indeed made once NCIS begins their review.

Needless to say, I'm not an expert investigator, but definitely want to assist accordingly to my fullest capability. Thanks, michelle[86]

ACID SA Little replied:

Please call me at [redacted]. Is it possible to meet before your 1230?[87]

I then met with ACID SA Little and two NCIS SAs, Lisa Huff and another who did not provide his business card, at my residence. During my telcon with ACID SA Little, he noted not to get into the financial transactions. Since I had a 12:30 meeting with U/S Patrick Kennedy, my meeting with the three SA's would be shorter than my previous meeting, much shorter. They advised they would be back in touch with me since I had so much more to share but could not be late for my 12:30 meeting. After our meeting, as they departed, NCIS SA Huff provided me her business card as well as a sheet regarding my rights, the Department of Defense Initial Information for Victims and Witnesses of Crime (DD FORM 2701, MAY 2004). As for the second NCIS SA who attended that meeting and did not provide me a business card, I have the name "Ed" written on the back of the business card that NCIS SA Lisa Huff provided. I then left for my meeting with Pat, which I made it to on time.

Not hearing back from NCIS SA Huff, on March 29, 2013, I emailed ACID SA Little, ccing SA Diaz:

Hello Agent Little – I was just wondering the status to our interview/discussion on March 18.

On March 20, I spent the entire day with 2 DS agents – Jim Minor and Prestina Williams. I'm not sure how this is all being coordinated if being coordinated, but I really would like a status as possible. Thank you, michelle[88]

---

86   Michelle Stefanick, email message to Terry Little and Alfred Diaz, March 18, 2013
87   Terry Little, email message to Michelle Stefanick and Alfred Diaz, March 18, 2013
88   Michelle Stefanick, email message to Terry Little and Alfred Diaz, March 18, 2013

ACID SA Little, ccing SA Diaz, replied:

Michelle,

I apologize but I do not have a true status for you. NCIS is conducting their investigation/assessment of their jurisdiction separately from Army CID. As SA Diaz previously stated, Army CID does not have jurisdiction over the incident since it involved the Marines. I was only making the introductions between you and NCIS and there to ensure you felt comfortable with the NCIS Agents. SA Huff, who provided her card, would probably be able to provide a better status for you. To my knowledge, your interview with the DS agents was not coordinated with/through Army CID. I cannot speak as to any coordination made between DS and NCIS.

Again, I apologize for not have better answers or a status for you. The lack of jurisdiction prevents us from taking the active role in the information you provided. Hopefully NCIS will be able to answer your questions. V/R Terry B. Little[89]

I responded to ACID SA Little, ccing SA Diaz:

Great – Thanks.[90]

Unbelievable! I file an EEO Grievance against the Marines in Stuttgart, Germany and, following DOD Protocols, because it happened on a US Army Garrison, the formal grievance is against the Secretary of the Army. I come back to the US and pass along applicable insight, and now the US Army states they have no investigative jurisdiction since it involves Marines. And NCIS hasn't and won't get back to me to investigate. As far as who finally arranged the interview with the two DS SAs. That was an outcome of my 12:30 meeting on March 18, 2013 with U/S Patrick Kennedy—and after receiving *absolutely no response from the FBI*…

What I did not know at the time was that prior to my meeting with DS SAs on March 20, 2012, U/S Patrick Kennedy requested that DS arrange a second meeting between me and the FBI. *It never happened. Why?* DS never contacted the FBI and instead opened an investigation on me. *Déjà vu all over again*…

On Wednesday, March 20, 2013, at U/S Patrick Kennedy's instruction, I finally met with DS SAs Jim Minor and Prestina Williams, despite my initial request since October 24, 2012 via OSD. The meeting was at my residence. It was long, many hours, because I provided extensive de-

---

89   Terry Little, email message to Michelle Stefanick and Alfred Diaz, March 18, 2013
90   Michelle Stefanick, email message to Terry Little and Alfred Diaz, March 18, 2013

tail, interconnections, linkages, interlinkages. And appropriately so, one of the two DS Special Agents in attendance was Jim Minor, who I knew previously as he was on the New York Field Office (NYFO)/Joint Terrorism Task Force (JTTF) 1998 East Africa Embassy Bombing Trial Liaison, and who had accompanied DOJ/SDNY AUSA Kenneth Karas when he came to see me at FSI in March/April 2000; he was also a friend of Accountable Review Board (ARB) Embassy Nairobi Accountable RSO/DS Special Agent Pat Hartnett-Kelly. And because with what was going on, what all this really was about, there was a direct linkage to the August 7, 1998 East Africa Embassy bombings, given Pat's May 30, 2011 email alluding it was an inside job. When they departed my residence, I was exhausted, but felt very relieved. The nightmare would finally end. Little did I know, it had just begun.

On Thursday, March 21, 2013, I sent the following email to DS SA Jim Minor:

> Subject: Status
> Hello Jim – Since our discussion went so long yesterday, I realize you didn't have time to do any follow-up.
> With that and the subject matter at hand, I've taken sick leave for today hoping to give you some time to figure out best options in light of the situation at hand.
> Hope to hear from you sometime today on how best to proceed given the circumstance. Thanks so much. Michelle[91]

On Friday, March 22, 2013, I sent another email to Jim Minor:

> Hello Jim – As I have not heard from you or Prestina, I will plan to go to work today. However, per discussion, my concerns remain the same. Thanks, michelle[92]

Not hearing back from Jim Minor, on Friday, March 22, 2013, I forwarded the March 21, 2013 email to DS SA Prestina Williams, ccing Jim, with the following remark:

> Hello Prestina – Here is the email that I mentioned to you that I sent to Jim yesterday. Thanks, michelle[93]

I sent this March 22, 2013 email to DS SA Prestina Williams, ccing Jim, with the following remark:

91   Michelle Stefanick, email message to Jim Minor, March 21, 2013
92   Michelle Stefanick, email message to Jim Minor, March 22, 2013
93   Michelle Stefanick, email message to Prestina Williams and Jim Minor, March 22, 2013

Prestina – Here is this morning's email that I sent to Jim.
Again, though relaying my genuine concern for my safety and possibilities to consider until all you all in DS had time to follow-up my
concerns/and with the others investigating aspects of my claim, at
the end of our discussion on Wednesday- I must say I remain concerned on the lack of response/follow-up to either of my emails.
Thank you for coming to SA-1 today. I look forward to hearing
back something. Thanks, michelle[94]

Not hearing back from DS, I went to work that Friday morning. Based
on all I shared with them, I did not feel safe at the Department of State.
So, I called Prestina Williams to come to my location and escort me to my
vehicle, parked in Main State underground parking. However, before she
got me there—driving the very short distance from SA-1 in Columbia
Plaza to Main State, Prestina, for some reason, pulled over the vehicle,
intentionally, as folks walked by. Needless to say, at this point, I did not
trust and do not trust DS SA Prestina Williams, nor DS writ large. This
even before my finding out about John Kokal and the others that I will
share in due time, the pattern of reality inside the walls of the Department
of State…

At 9:24 p.m., I finally received this email from Prestina Williams, ccing
Jim Minor:

Subject: Status
Michelle,
Thank you. I am in the office right now and finalizing my report
based on our conversation on Wednesday. Since our notes were
very detailed, it took a bit of time for me to organize them and get
them typed. Please know that the report will be completed before
I leave the office today. We are moving forward. I realize that our
responses may not come as quickly as you would like, but please
give us time to do what is necessary for us to do as investigators. I
do understand and respect your concerns and sensitivities. When
Jim and I have made headway on this, we will be definitely be in
contact with you. Please have a safe and restful weekend
Take care,
Prestina D. Williams
US Department of State.[95]

On March 25, 2013, I responded to Williams and Minor:

94   Michelle Stefanick, email message to Prestina Williams and Jim Minor, March 22, 2013
95   Prestina Williams email message to Michelle Stefanick and Jim Minor, March 22, 2013

> Jim/Prestina – Until I hear back regarding my situation, I plan on staying at home. I have one quick errand to the bank I need to make this morning, otherwise, I will be home waiting to hear the status. Thanks, michelle[96]

Prestina, ccing Minor, replied:

> Good morning Michelle,
> That's fine. I completed the report on Friday for delivery to the Under Secretary and I am following up on that today. Jim and I will be in touch soon as we have an update for you. Thanks, Prestina[97]

On Wednesday March 27, 2013, I emailed Prestina, ccing Minor:

> Hello Prestina – I'm still at home awaiting status/next steps. Do you have any insights to share? Thanks, Michelle[98]

I finally received a response, this time from Jim Minor, ccing Williams:

> Michelle,
> Sorry for the confusion in this difficult time. You should be speaking with your HR supv to determine if and when you should return to work, as that part is not within DS purview. I'm on al for spring break, so may not chk BB msgs often each day. Jim[99]

I responded to Jim, ccing Williams:

> Jim – In light of my uneasiness on Friday when Prestina accompanied me out of the office and discussion with Prestina, this is definitely not my understanding. Thanks, michelle[100]

I immediately called Williams, and followed up with an email, ccing Minor:

> Prestina – As Jim is out of the office and per his email below, I left a message for us to discuss this situation. My number is [redacted], please give me a call as soon as possible to discuss. Thank you, michelle[101]

I received a response from Williams, ccing Minor:

---

96   Michelle Stefanick, email message to Prestina Williams and Jim Minor, March 25, 2013
97   Prestina Williams email message to Michelle Stefanick and Jim Minor, March 25, 2013
98   Michelle Stefanick, email message to Prestina Williams and Jim Minor, March 27, 2013
99   Jim Minor, email message to Michelle Stefanick and Prestina Williams, March 27, 2013
100   Michelle Stefanick, email message to Prestina Williams and Jim Minor, March 27, 2013
101   Michelle Stefanick, email message to Prestina Williams and Jim Minor, March 22, 2013

Michelle,
We understand the sensitivity of the issue and your concerns. Please be patient, as we want to be thorough and provide you with the best solution and support, we can. We will be as soon as we have received an update to pass on to you. Prestina[102]

I responded to Williams and Minor:

Prestina – again, if you can please give me a call as I must say I'm totally confused by what you and Jim are saying. thanks, michelle[103]

Though I would not become aware of this until September 5, 2014, how oddly and eerily familiar, same entities, particularly in light of the events that would occur next with me. This September 27, 2005 rense. com article by Wayne Madsen called *State Department Employee Suicide Going Unreported* states:

Another suicide covered up at the State Department. State Department insiders are reporting another suicide of a State Department employee involved with Middle East policy. Although WMR is still trying to obtain the name of the deceased official, we can report that she worked in the Press and Public Diplomacy Branch of the State Department's Near East and South Asia Bureau.

On November 7, 2003, State Department Bureau of Intelligence and Research chief Iraqi analyst John J. Kokal was reported to have committed suicide by jumping head first to his death from the secured roof of the State Department's headquarters. A few weeks later, a former CIA official, Dr. Gus Weiss, an opponent of the Iraq war, reportedly jumped to his death from the Watergate complex, just a few blocks from the State Department.

Both Kokal and the recent State Department suicide were later reported by senior department officials to be despondent over "personal" issues. However, in both cases, the State Department instituted an information blockade on details surrounding the deaths. http://waynemadsenreport.com/

Wait a minute … from the secured roof? What? How in the world did Kokal get there? Suicides? What? Just like "they" accused me of. Suicide, really? Or something more nefarious at play. What in the world is going on! Particularly given and in light of the entities involved, the events involved … Given what I was personally being subjected to and experiencing

---

102   Prestina Williams email message to Michelle Stefanick and Jim Minor, March 22, 2013
103   Michelle Stefanick, email message to Prestina Williams and Jim Minor, March 22, 2013

first-hand, and despite my supposed federal CVRA-protected first-hand victim/witness status—and my November 27, 2012 Whistleblower/Protection Request letter—something very nefarious was and is at play.

On Thursday, March 28, 2013 at 12:10 p.m., I sent the following to DS SA Prestina Williams:

> Prestina – Considering I have requested since 11/27/2012 whistleblower protection from Linda Thomas-Greenfield, and have spoken with FBI, DS, ACID, NCIS, and have gotten no where, is there a reason I had 5-6 Arlington County Police at my house a few minutes ago based on a call they received? thanks, michelle[104]

"WELFARE CHECKS"

I did not obtain a copy of this applicable ACPD Police report until I put in an ACPD FOIA-request and obtained this February 11, 2015 response. Here's ACPD's documented record to the event of March 28, 2013 based on the ACPD Call for Service Inquiry Response (#130870123)—the day ACPD came to my residence based on a call made by a DS official that resulted in 5 or 6 ACPD Officers dressed in tactical gear surrounding my house, guns locked and loaded…

> INITITIATE: 11:24:43 03-28-2013….
> ….TYPE: ATTSP P- THREATENED SUICIDE ATTE….
> ….CP: [BLACKED OUT] (DEPT OF STATE)…
> TEXT: COW OF [BLACKED OUT] WORKS FOR DEPT OF STATE AND INDICATED TO AN AGENT SHE WANTED TO COMMIT SUICIDE. AGENT RECEIVED THE CALL AT 10:30 TODAY. UNKN METHOD. UNKN IF SHE LIVES AT [REDACTED]. \NAME [BLACKED OUT] (DEPT OF STATE) [BLACKED OUT]
> TEXT: SHE ISN'T IN LOCAL, RP DOESN'T HAVE DOB OR SOC, BUT SHE WILL CALL HUMAN RESOURCES AT DEPT OF STATE TO TRY AND GET FURTHER INFO. HER CELL IS [BLACKENED OUT] GOING TO CALL HER NOW
> TEXT: THE CELL NUMBER GIVEN SOUNDS LIKE IT IS COMING BACK TO A FAX MACHINE.
> ……
> LOCATION: [BLACKED OUT], AC--- [REDACTED] N, AC RECALL FROM [BLACKED OUT] … ADVISING THE CORRECT ADDRESS IS [REDACTED]//STATES LAST HOUSE ON LEFT (CORNER LOT) SHOULD BE A [REDACTED] NO

---

104   Prestina Williams email message to Michelle Stefanick and Jim Minor, March 22, 2013

TINT UNK TAG PARKED IN FRT OF ADDRESS

.....

A37, MADE CONTACT WITH [BLACKED OUT] SUBJECT APPEARS TO BE ED

A37, MADE CONTACT WITH [BLACKED OUT] SUBJECT APPEARS TO BE ED

P AND IS VERY PARANOID IN REGARDS TO THE FEDER-AL GOVERNMENT. SUBJECT IS A BUDGET EXPERT AND HAS WORKED FOR THE GOVERNMENT OF APPROX 20 YEARS. SUBJECT DID NOT HAVE ANY INJURIES AND ALSO STATED SHE HAD NO INTENTION ON HURTING HERSELF. SHE WOULD NOT GO INTO FURTHER DE-TAIL ABOUT THE GOV P AND IS VERY PARANOID IN RE-GARDS TO THE FEDERAL GOVERNMENT. SUBJECT IS A BUDGET EXPERT AND HAS WORKED FOR THE GOV-ERNMENT FOR APPROX 20 YEARS. SUBJECT DID NOT HAVE ANY INJURIES AND ALSO STATE SHE HAD NO IN-TENTIONS ON HURTING HERSELF. SHE WOULD NOT GO INTO FURTHER DETAIL ABOUT THE GOVERNMENT CONSPIRACY.

....

OPERATOR ASSIGNMENTS:

PD 05 E302 DELAFUENTE, DEBORAH

PD 02 E288 DEXTER, ELIZABETH

P662 1463 GOLEMBIEWSKI, MATTHEW

PD03 E323 STOVER, GEORGE

P616 1525 BROOKS, DORIAN J D

Again, I did not see this until quite sometime after. When I did, I became furious. First of all, I would never commit suicide. And how is it, that based on what the DS SA said, ACPD felt the need to surround my residence dressed in tactical gear and guns loaded. I find the inconsistency beyond bizarre. That said, when ACPD knocked on my door, I did not let them in. But I did open the door and advise accordingly: That I am being retaliated against as a federal CVRA-accorded rights and protections victim/witness to the 1998 East Africa Embassy bombings which can be confirmed by the DOJ/SDNY and documents—would ACPD like to see? ACPD said no...I continued. I am an EEO grievance complainant and a federal victim/wit-ness/whistleblower who requested protections accordingly.

What I never advised ACPD was that I was a *budget expert* and/or that I had *worked for the government for approx. 20 yea*rs. And I certainly did not go into any detail, let alone anything about a government conspiracy. *So, who provided ACPD this information?* Because it was not me! But it does confirm, that this is, was and has always been about the *money*.

For the record, when you have first-hand knowledge, first-hand expertise, and factual details, it's not a *government conspiracy*. It's called being a witness. Its's called facts. And based on these facts, a crime has been committed. Given the extent of the orchestrated crimes committed against me, the legal definition of criminal *conspiracy* has been committed. Given my federal CVRA-protected status as a victim/witness and that I was targeted, the statutes of racketeering (RICO) can be applied. And given the retaliatory actions taken against me for the applicable events involved of which I was accorded federal CVRA-protected status, it's called a treasonous crime.

Despite my continual requests, to this day, I have never been provided nor found out the name of the US Department of State DS official that made this March 28, 2013 report to Arlington County Police Department—setting the retaliatory actions against me into motion—and transferring this federal national security matter to a state-level jurisdiction, within the Commonwealth of Virginia. Interestingly enough in terms of timing, despite prolonged delays, just prior to this ordeal, I had finally heard back regarding my EEO grievance that I formally filed in May 2011...

On April 4, 2013, ACPD showed up at my house again, supposedly for a welfare check. (ACPD Call for Service #130940171). Unbelievable. *Or was this just the precursor to what would happen next? On April 12, 2013. Absolutely.*

> INITITIATE: 12:49:35 04-04-2013....
> ....TYPE: COW P- CHECK ON WELFARE ....
> ....CP: [BLACKED OUT] ...
> TEXT: PP HAS NOT SPOKEN [BLACKED OUT] IN ABOUT
> A MONTH. RP SAYS [BLACKED OUT] IS SHOWING BI-
> ZARRE BEHAVIOR TAKING ABOUT CONSPIRACY THE-
> ORIES AND NOT SHOWING UP FOR WORK..\NAME:
> [BLACKED OUT]\PP [BLACKED OUT](MTF).....
> TEXT: OFC WENT OUT ON 03/28 INC #123..RP WOULD
> LIKE AN OF C TO GIVE HIM A CALL ADV OF STATUS....
> B23 102, SUBJECT STATES SHE IS A WHISTLEBLOWER
> ON THE FED GOV. DEPT OF STATE. EMPLY. VERY AN-
> GRY IN VOICE/DEMEANOR. SHE DOES NOT WANT ANY

CONTACT WITH HER FATHER. PLEASE READ NOTES
ON CALL FROM 3/28ISH. I SPOKE WITH THE [BLACKED
OUT] AFTER THIS CALL. HE STATED HE WILL CALL DHS
AGAIN AND SO WHAT THEY CAN DO. THE [BLACKED
OUT] IS IN PA, WILL BE IN TOWN MONDAY. SHE DOES
NOT WANT TO HURT HERSELF OR OTHERS. CAN NOT/
DOES NOT MEET ANY TRUE CRITERIA FOR DHS TO
RESPOND. OR IN FORM. MAYBE IF WE MAKE ENOUGH
CONTACT. HISTORY DHS WILL/COULD RESPOND....
OPERATOR ASSIGNMENTS:
CT02 E325 CAMPBELL, LASHAWN
PD01 P1288 DID NOT IN 0* CODE FILE
P454 1129 TYSON, DAMON B
P511 1135 ST CLAIR, RICHARD BRITT
PD04 E351 GRANDFIELD, CLINT

Again, not having these ACPD FOIA-obtained Call for Service Response records at the time, here's my take at the time. I didn't see this as I wanted to see this, I saw it as it really was... I was being harassed, intentionally and purposefully. As stated previously during the March 28, 2013 ACPD visit initiated by DS, I repeated on April 4, 2013 that I am being retaliated against as a federal CVRA-accorded rights and protections victim/witness to the 1998 East Africa Embassy bombings which can be confirmed by the DOJ/SDNY. I am an EEO grievance complainant and a federal government whistleblower that requested protections accordingly. Fortunately, during this second visit there were only two ACPD Officers at my door—responding again to a *supposed* threatened suicide attempt. *Really?*

For those that are not aware, US Department of State/Diplomatic Security is the USG's main interlocutor with police forces, nationwide within the US as well as worldwide, to include Interpol. And by the way, DS also has absolutely no oversight – not from any law enforcement such as DOJ, FBI nor from any Congressional oversight such as HFAC/SFRC, Judiciary.

On Tuesday, April 9, 2013, I received the following from Linda Thomas-Greenfield, ccing Marcia Bernicat:

Subject: Meeting today at 5:00 P.M.
Are you available to come to my office at 5:00 P.M.? I have something I need to discuss with you urgently.
Linda Thomas-Greenfield

Director General of the Foreign Service and
Director of Human Resources
US Department of State[105]

Now given all that I had been put through, including with this whistleblower/protection request and *NO ONE* advising me of my and the other individual's protection—*how would you be feeling at this point?* Linda Thomas-Greenfield, who had served with me in Embassy Nairobi, was now the DG, received my *whistle-blower/protection request* and did nothing... Now, all of a sudden wanted to meet with me. This meeting request was a *set-up*, and I would have none of it. At this point in time, I had no intention to return to that building. And I was still patiently waiting to hear back from the FBI. *Something very, very nefarious was definitely going on...*

I responded to Linda, ccing Bernicat and Patrick Kennedy:

> Hello Linda – I no longer have a parking pass. So, I won't be able to make it today. Thanks, michelle[106]

Linda replied, ccing Bernicat and Kennedy:

> Michelle: I only need to see you for a short period. Hopefully you can find a place to park outside. Thanks, Linda[107]

I responded, ccing Bernicat and Kennedy:

> Linda – In light of the situation, my preference is not to meet alone with you. Thanks, michelle[108]

Linda responded, ccing Bernicat, Kennedy, and Hans Klemm:

> Michelle: I agree. Marcia Bernicat and Hans Klemm will be in the meeting. You can also bring anyone else that you wish to bring. Linda[109]

I responded, ccing Bernicat, Kennedy, and Klemm:

105   Linda Thomas-Greenfield, email message to Michelle Stefanick and Marcia Bernicat, April 9, 2013
106   Michelle Stefanick, email message to and Linda Thomas-Greenfield, Patrick Kennedy and Marcia Bernicat, April 9, 2013
107   Linda Thomas-Greenfield, email message to Michelle Stefanick, Patrick Kennedy and Marcia Bernicat, April 9, 2013
108   Michelle Stefanick, email message to and Linda Thomas-Greenfield, Patrick Kennedy and Marcia Bernicat, April 9, 2013
109   Linda Thomas-Greenfield, email message to Michelle Stefanick, Patrick Kennedy, Marcia Bernicat, and Hans Klemm April 9, 2013

Good – So maybe we can ask for the meeting to take place with U/S Patrick Kennedy in his office when convenient. Thanks, michelle[110]

Linda responded, ccing Bernicat, Kennedy, and Klemm:

Michelle: I just spoke to Pat and he is totally engaged in dealing with the situation in Kabul that resulted in the loss of lives and injuries to our staff. He asked that I meet with you. I had hoped that we could do that today if possible. Please let me know. Linda[111]

I responded at 4:30 P.M. to Linda, ccing Bernicat, Kenndy, and Klemm:

Thanks Linda – It is not possible. Michelle[112]

On Thursday, April 11, 2013, I emailed NCIS SA Lisa Huff, ccing ACID SA Terry Little:

Subject: Status
Agent Huff – When we met on March 18, you left a sheet in regards to my rights, particularly in being kept apprised of my situation. As its been almost a month since our meeting, can you please provide me a status update. Thank you, Michelle[113]

I would not read NCIS SA Lisa Huff's response until Monday, April 15. For the events of April 12, 2013 would occur...

110   Michelle Stefanick, email message to and Linda Thomas-Greenfield, Patrick Kennedy and Marcia Bernicat, April 9, 2013
111   Linda Thomas-Greenfield, email message to Michelle Stefanick, Patrick Kennedy, Marcia Bernicat, and Hans Klemm April 9, 2013
112   Michelle Stefanick, email message to and Linda Thomas-Greenfield, Patrick Kennedy and Marcia Bernicat, April 9, 2013
113   Michelle Stefanick, email message to Lisa Huff and Terry Little, April 11, 2013

PART THREE

CHAPTER 8

RETALIATION BEYOND COMPREHENSION:
Know Yourself, Know Others, Reflect

EVALUATION AND OBSERVATION

The events of April 12, 2013 and the retaliatory actions that would follow, I refer to as *Round One*. Given what would transpire, how much worse could it get? Well, I forewarn you now. As I continually asked myself, what country is this? Is this really the country I loyally served for over twenty years?

Benghazi was the focus of Congress and the media. Ironically enough, I don't recall such interest in the aftermath of the August 7, 1998 East Africa Embassy bombings, but then again, the Clinton-Lewinsky scandal and the subsequent impeachment process was simultaneously playing itself out at the time. The bombings got minimal coverage in comparison, with no apparent Congressional interest and applicable hearings, as was occurring now. Despite dots I was connecting and linkages I made, I was not being protected nor interviewed accordingly, and the push-back was immense. To a lesser degree, my FS colleague Raymond Maxwell experienced a similar situation—a scapegoat for what was really going on regarding Benghazi. Needless to say, Ray and I were kindred spirits of sorts as the dramas played out around us. We stayed in touch. In fact, we were making plans on getting together for lunch. But first...

On Wednesday, April 10, 2013, I sent Ray the following:

> Subject: do you...find all this quite bizarre or is it just me?
> I know I haven't told you really anything compared to what I've told all the investigators—but just with what is going on with you and your situation, and now having supposedly how many employees from Benghazi at Walter Reed but no one allowed to speak to congress for over 6 months...
> do you think that I'm totally off the wall—as everyone is trying to make me feel—or do you think it's possible. It all just seems so bizarre to me—[1]

Ray responded:

---
1   Michelle Stefanick, email message to Raymond Maxwell, April 10, 2013

Extremely bizarre. The coverup is always worse than the crime. Unfortunately, I don't know what the crime was, nor what was/is being covered up. I can only surmise. But I have no doubt SOME-THING is being covered up.[2]

I replied:

And in my case, I didn't realize there was any "crime" until I had my oh-shit or rather a-ha moment and now connecting dots, I can see parts of the cover-up – at least, pertaining to me. It's not a pleasant storyline – but one that can easily explain all the bizarreness … but to be honest, if I'm proven right, I just don't know how I would ever recover based on all that's happened to me.

How about you … are you looking at the Department a lot differently now?[3]

And on Thursday, April 11, 2013 at 10:13 a.m., I wrote the following to Ray:

Hey – can we talk/meet again? My number is [redacted][4]

Ray responded:

got lunch plans today?[5]

I replied:

No—my life is pretty much on hold because of this bunk.[6]

Ray replied:

so, can we meet, can I swing by and pick you up? a burger or something. I am being thrown out of the house …[7]

I responded:

sure[8]

Ray replied:

I'll pick you up around 12 noon. please give me your address again. Thanks.[9]

Then, Ray emailed:

2   Raymond Maxwell, email message to Michelle Stefanick, April 10, 2013
3   Michelle Stefanick, email message to Raymond Maxwell, April 10, 2013
4   Michelle Stefanick, email message to Raymond Maxwell, April 11, 2013
5   Raymond Maxwell, email message to Michelle Stefanick, April 11, 2013
6   Michelle Stefanick, email message to Raymond Maxwell, April 11, 2013
7   Raymond Maxwell, email message to Michelle Stefanick, April 11, 2013
8   Michelle Stefanick, email message to Raymond Maxwell, April 11, 2013
9   Raymond Maxwell, email message to Michelle Stefanick, April 11, 2013

delayed. repairman arrived to do some carpentry work. may need to cancel altogether. I'll let you know.[10]

Later, I queried:

hi—what do you think?[11]

Ray replied:

looks like I'm stuck here. Next time?[12]

I responded:

ok—maybe tomorrow?[13]

Ray replied:

tomorrow might work with an early start. I have an appointment downtown at 1:30. So maybe 11?[14]

I responded:

sure—that should work.[15]

On Friday, April 12, 2013, I was planning on having lunch with Ray when I received the following email:

Good morning Michelle: I got all caught up in completing assignments and quizzes for my songwriting course and the morning slipped away. How about a quick lunch at noon? I'll pick you up and we can navigate from there.[16]

I responded:

Sure.[17]

That was the last email correspondence for that day. And we didn't meet for lunch due to what would transpire next ...

On Monday, April 15, 2013, I sent to Ray:

Hello – Sorry about not meeting on Friday. Needless to say, I would much rather have been with you for lunch that where I was ... State worked it with Arlington County to have me "tempo-

---

10   Raymond Maxwell, email message to Michelle Stefanick, April 11, 2013
11   Michelle Stefanick, email message to Raymond Maxwell, April 11, 2013
12   Raymond Maxwell, email message to Michelle Stefanick, April 11, 2013
13   Michelle Stefanick, email message to Raymond Maxwell, April 11, 2013
14   Raymond Maxwell, email message to Michelle Stefanick, April 11, 2013
15   Michelle Stefanick, email message to Raymond Maxwell, April 11, 2013
16   Raymond Maxwell, email message to Michelle Stefanick, April 12, 2013
17   Michelle Stefanick, email message to Raymond Maxwell, April 12, 2013

rarily detained" at Arlington Hospital since I am a threat to others... so here I am.[18]

Ray responded:

are you imprisoned?[19]

To which I responded:

yes, in the hospital.[20]

Now for the events of Friday, April 12, 2013. I got up, ate breakfast, showered and was getting ready to have lunch with Ray Maxwell later that morning. He was supposed to pick me up at 11:00, but at 10:39 A.M., Ray emailed stating he was running late and would noon be okay instead. I said sure.

At this time, I still had not heard back from DS SA's Jim Minor or Prestina Williams regarding the report she was writing and status of the investigation that I requested. But that morning, DS SA Williams called. She indicated that they were coming by my house to provide me a memo regarding my security clearance. I said sure, any time. I was expecting them—DS SAs Minor and Williams. Though, not trusting anyone, I wrote a brief note for DS SA Minor. As a reminder, Jim Minor was the DS NYFO/JTTF Trial Liaison with DOJ/SDNY regarding the August 7, 1998 East Africa Embassy bombing, and accompanied AUSA Ken Karas when he met with me in March/April 2000 at FSI.

So, you can imagine how stunned I was to open the front door, to find not only DS SAs Minor and Williams, but also three other individuals, standing near their car on the road in front of my house. Though they may have said their names/who they were with at the time, I immediately felt so set-up I stepped out onto the stoop and read the note I had just written:

4/12/2013
Jim –
During one of our discussions, Pat Kennedy told me that there was no investigations pertaining to me—ongoing or otherwise.
If there was, w/no evidential matter other than my religious/ethnic background—you need to let Pat know immediately.
Otherwise, as a law enforcement officer/retired military officer—how many people have to have their constitutional/due process rights violated and go through what I'm going through? How many more people need to die?

18   Michelle Stefanick, email message to Raymond Maxwell, April 13, 2013
19   Raymond Maxwell, email message to Michelle Stefanick, April 13, 2013
20   Michelle Stefanick, email message to Raymond Maxwell, April 13, 2013

Please do the right thing. Thank you, Michelle

I read this loudly with the hope that someone in the neighborhood would see/hear the ruckus at my house and gossip accordingly to ensure my neighbor Tom Sheehy, an HFAC key staffer, would find out about what happened to me.

I again had a brief exchange with the ladies in the street—and again stated loudly, that:

> I am a federal Crime Victims' Rights Act protected victim/witness regarding the August 7, 1998 East Africa Embassy bombings, an EEO grievance complainant, and a federal government whistleblower who is being retaliated against.

At that point, DS SAs Williams and Minor, maybe figuring out why I was shouting so loudly, asked if we could go into the house as they had a manila envelope in their hand. I said sure. I led them into my dining room. One of them left the door open; in due time I would find out why.

I sat at the front of the table, and the two DS Special Agents sat or stood at the side. They gave me the envelope. I opened it and removed the memo and started reading it , when all of a sudden, ACPD came into my house without knocking, asked me to stand—which I did—and then put handcuffs on me. DS SA Williams asked me where my purse was, got it from my office and brought it with us as I was walked out of my house in *handcuffs* and placed into an ACPD police vehicle. At this point, I was beyond livid, but I acted professionally the entire time.

I left my home, my personal residence, constitutional rights violated, *in hand-cuffs*, with only the clothes on my back, and the memo that I had just received from the two US Department of State Special Agents—that I had spent hours finally briefing just a week or so earlier and that I had not even finished reading—sat on my dining room table. *And why?* Because of my November 27, 2012 Whistleblower/Protection request? Because of my EEO Grievance Complaint? Because of my supposed protected status as first-hand victim/witness in regards to the August 7, 1998 East Africa Embassy bombing? Obviously, something very nefarious was as at play here. And clearly, I was the central target of all of it, not knowing what precisely the "it" was.

The April 9, 2013 memo contained in an unmarked/unaddressed plain manila envelope was itself contained in a protected clear *Executive Correspondence* top cover. The *SENSITIVE BUT UNCLASSIFIED MEMO-*

RANDUM on official United States Department of State letterhead went as follows:

> TO: Ms. Michelle L. Stefanick
> FROM: DS/SI/PSS – James C. Onusko, Director (Carlos O. Yanez signed for)
> SUBJECT: Security Clearance Suspension
>
> This memorandum is to notify you that, in accordance with US government standards set forth in Executive Orders 10450 and 12968, Government-wide Adjudicative Guidelines, and Department of State regulations, the Office of Personnel Security and Suitability (DS/SI/PSS) has determined that your continued access to classified information is not clearly consistent with the interests of national security. Your Top-Secret security clearance is suspended pending the outcome of an ongoing DS investigation.
>
> DS/SI/PSS has been notified that your conduct was questionable relative to your allegations concerning government conspiracies. In addition, your recent behavior casts doubt on your judgment and reliability. This raises serious security concerns and can be disqualifying under Government-wide Adjudicative Guidelines E (Personal Conduct) and I (Psychological Conditions). The suspension of your security clearance does not constitute a formal revocation and does not indicate that such action is planned.
>
> If, after further investigation and review, the Director, Diplomatic Security Service, revokes your security clearance, you will be given an opportunity to respond. Moreover, should the Assistant Secretary of Diplomatic Security render a decision to sustain the revocation of your security clearance, you will be afforded the opportunity to appeal the decision to the Department's Security Appeals Panel.
>
> Pursuant to Department policy, you are required to turn in your building ID card, any government issued credentials, and your Diplomatic Passport to DS/SI/PSS. You will be issued a DS-1838 (Request for Personal Identification Card) and will be issued a non-sensitive building badge. Your point-of-contact is Ms. Michelle Dade, who can be reached at [redacted] to facilitate this requirement. Attached is an Acknowledgement of Receipt for your signature, acknowledging your understanding of these actions, not your agreement.
>
> You are required to return the Acknowledgement of Receipt, signed and dated, to Ms. Dade within five days of receipt. You may

return the completed memorandum by fax to [redacted], or you may scan it and email it to [email address removed].
Enclosure:
    Acknowledgment of Receipt
cc: M/DGHR: Lthomas-Greenfield
HR/ER/CSD: Sparker, Acting
HR/MDR: Mbernicat
HR/CDA: Mdraper
INR: DmcDaniel
DS/DO/SSD: Gbailey
DS/SI/PSS: Certification Desk

I never signed the attached *Acknowledgment of Receipt* form, nor did I ever receive the results of the referenced investigation. That's because there wasn't one.

After I was handcuffed, walked out of my residence and placed into the back seat of the ACPD Police car, the ACPD officer said he was taking me for an evaluation at the Virginia Hospital Center (VHC). According to ACPD FOIA-provided documents, the officer was Daniel Woods. I had bathed and dressed in preparation for lunch plans with a colleague, and just experienced the most unexpected, unannounced, unjustified, horrific invasion of my rights and my residence in my entire life.

Despite being in handcuffs, I calmly walked into VHC with the ACPD Officer, and patiently waited to see the doctor. After a while, Dr. Christopher Olson came in briefly at which point I explained that all this was as a result of retaliation against me as a federal DOJ-determined CVRA-protected victim/witness, an EEO complainant against the military, and as a federal government whistleblower.

The process took many hours. Despite this being a national security/law enforcement matter, never a mental health matter, as a Commonwealth of Virginia (VA)/Arlington County (AC) resident, I understood that Dr. Christopher Olson had to do his due diligence. He needed to confirm the accuracy of my stated protected-status and my documented medical history. I don't know if it was his initiative or someone else, but apparently what I stated and my documented medical history did not matter to Dr. Christopher Olson. Somehow, someone had already pre-arranged that I would be involuntarily committed. Having no forewarning, no change of clothes/toiletries, and not eating all day, this caught me, and I do believe based on his reaction, the ACPD officer, off guard. As a result of Dr. Christopher Olson's actions, or lack thereof, I was to be committed, against my will and involuntarily, to VHC. I would then have to wait for hours until I was walked and escorted to the VHC/Behavioral Health Unit (BHU).

I was in my VHC/BHU room when Dr. Benjamin Adewale abruptly entered at about 8:00 p.m., April 12, 2013. He was accompanied by a secretary/staff assistant, to my understanding not a nurse, whom I hadn't seen working since at VHC. Dr. Adewale was very terse when he spoke, with predetermined questions, not listening to me at all and not concerned at all with what I had to say, nor was he concerned when I advised him that that I had not received dinner (nor lunch earlier) despite my repeated status requests after ordering it. His line of questioning appeared to have an agenda. He abruptly stopped me when I spoke, especially when I stated that all this was retaliation against me as a federal DOJ-determined CVRA-protected victim/witness, an EEO complainant against the military, and as a federal government whistleblower; and the events of that day were a violation of my constitutional, civil and due process rights. He and the VHC didn't care. *But then again, nobody cared...*

Dr. Adewale's line of questioning had nothing to do with me and my well-being. His line of questioning was purposeful and intentional, pointed, with an agenda. Unclear at that time, and still to this day, was *whose agenda?* What did become apparent, obvious, was that this entire horrific ordeal was a set-up, to send some kind of message, and of course, to ruin my reputation and my credibility. At one point, I asked Dr. Adewale where he was from, based on his accent. He told me he was Jamaican via the UK (United Kingdom). I would not find out until eight months later during the second round of retaliation that he was from Nigeria. *Interesting?* So why did Dr. Benjamin Adewale lie to me? As a medical doctor treating a patient, shouldn't his intent be to build a rapport, build trust. Particularly given the very pointed, objective-oriented focus of his questioning, of which it was quite apparent from the very start, me and my well-being was not of his, a medical doctor's, primary concern. But obviously this Commonwealth of Virginia/Virginia hospital Center Medical doctor, Dr. Benjamin Adewale, wanted something out of me. What was it? Why? And for whom? So who precisely was Dr. Adewale working with and working for?

Dr. Adewale was with me no longer than 15 minutes and said he was going to write a report for court on Monday. I had no idea what he was talking about and he provided no detail. For the first time, I realized that, having no change of clothes or toiletries nor supporting evidential matter nor legal counsel representation, I was committed over the weekend—against my will and involuntarily—to appear in court on Monday. It would not be until March 8, 2014, in an intentionally delayed FOIA-request response, that I finally confirmed my suspicions based on the April 12, 2013 memorandum written by DS SA Williams specifically referencing this US Department of State *pre-arranged/pre-orchestrated* April 15, 2013 Commitment Hearing.

VHC Dr. Christopher Olson's and Dr. Benjamin Adewale's actions were based on a pre-orchestrated agenda, not the truth of my statement, the truth of my medical records, and the truth of my mental health. Based on and documented by DS SA Williams' April 12, 2013 memorandum, the truth did not matter.

On Saturday, April 13, 2013, the next day, my room mate and I were napping when Dr. Adewale abruptly opened the door, without knocking. My roommate and I were females, and Dr. Benjamin Adewale was, of course, a male. I asked him to respect our human rights and dignity and to please come back at a prearranged later time, so I could be awake and alert when we talked. He said he would be back at 6:00 p.m. He returned later that evening, at around eight o'clock with another nurse. Again, he said he was writing his report Sunday for court on Monday. He was again, abrupt and rude with questions appearing to be based on an agenda, and was there no longer than 15 minutes in total.

Overwhelmed by the extremity of the retaliatory events taking place and with limited internet access, I was able to read an email I received on Sunday, April 14, 2013. It was from my neighbor Tom Sheehy. My speaking loudly during the events of April 12, 2013 had worked. He found out something happened. The subject line of his email was simple: Benghazi. I would soon find out that my speaking loudly was the basis used by VA/AC/Department of Human Services (DHS) Patrice English for the temporary detention order (TDO) as stated in her sworn statement made against me at the prearranged/preorchestrated April 15, 2013 Commitment Hearing.

At this point, how is it that I have such recollection regarding my retaliatory involuntary commitment? By training and by necessity, I took extensive notes, trying to document dates, times, names, and events. And, despite immense pressure to do so, I never took any medication/drugs during this time. After being placed in handcuffs and escorted out of my home, at least ACPD didn't drive me off with their lights on and sirens blaring. But where was the DOJ? Where was the FBI? Where was the Congress? Dressed to meet Ray Maxwell for lunch, I left that day with the clothes on my back—that's it... But I took notes, lots of notes, as I now share so you all can see what the *real* United States of Government has become...

On the morning of April 15, 2013, I was taken from VHC, once again in handcuffs, to appear in the Department of State's Commitment Hearing in the Commonwealth of Virginia/Arlington County General District Court in front of Judge George Gill. I did not see Dr. Adewale again nor his supposed report, nor did I have access to clean clothes, toiletries, supporting documents or legal counsel before being handcuffed and taken to court. I was placed in a holding cell for a short period right before the hearing. I was confused as individuals came in and out of my cell during this brief period, one supposedly being my court-appointed lawyer whom I met briefly for about ten minutes prior to entering the court room.

There were three opposing witnesses; Patrice English, documented in DS SA Williams' April 12, 2013 memorandum as one of the unexpected/unannounced people at my residence on that horrific Friday morning of April 12, 2013; another woman whose identity I still don't know; and my (now as a result) estranged father. This other opposing witness woman was apparently a doctor who briefly asked me some questions just prior in my cell, and then later testified in court that the diagnosis was *bipolar*. It was also at this hearing that I heard for the first time the false accusation—inaccurate, unsubstantiated, with no details provided nor supported by a police report—regarding my supposed assault of my supposed sister by my estranged father. *Really?* So where was the applicable Arlington County Police Department report file by my supposed sister? Oh, that's right—there was none. Also, *not present* at this US Department of State preorchestrated prearranged Commitment Hearing were any US Department of State officials. There were some major indicators here. *So what does that tell you?*

So what was really going on? Particularly given my initial outreach to this exact Arlington County Police Department on October 11, 2011 that did absolutely nothing. So when, why and by whom was my supposed family interjected into all this? Before or after my assignment in my home state of Pennsylvania, at the US Army War College in Carlisle, Pennsylvania? And particularly given the events, and their timing, while I was subsequently assigned with the US military with MARFOREUR/AF in Germany. Given those events, including my filing the applicable EEO formal grievance as a result, I requested that my family trust me and believe in me. Obivously, and based on all their actions and the roles they played, they made their decision on whose side they took—and it wasn't mine. So again, the question is and remains—for how long were they not on my side? Back to the day I called my family on August 7, 1998 from Addis Ababa, Ethiopia? Before even then? Only during this time in 2013 would I become aware of my supposed father's military intelligence background for the very first time.

With false, inaccurate, and misleading statements being made and without any preparatory time regarding my case, my court-appointed lawyer Rex Flynn spoke but I requested to speak on my own behalf as well. I reiterated to Judge George Gill that all this was a result of retaliation against me as a federal DOJ-determined CVRA-protected victim/witness regarding the August 7, 1998 East Africa Embassy bombings; an EEO grievance complainant against the US Military; and as a federal government whistleblower. He too, *an Officer of the Court and a Constitutional Oath-taker*, already had his mind made up.

After discussing my options with my court-appointed lawyer, I stated I did not have a mental illness, that this was truly a retaliatory act against me based on my indicated status/statements, and that I would not voluntarily go to the hospital. At that point, I was involuntarily admitted back to VHC. I requested Rex Flynn to immediately file an Appeal. I experienced yet another violation of my constitutional, civil, due process, human and CVRA rights, and returned to VHC/BHU under the care of Dr. Benjamin Adewale. And again, with only the clothes that I was wearing on Friday, April 12, 2013, my case was under appeal.

INVOLUNTARY ADMISSION

With limited internet access, I advised/informed others regarding the retaliatory acts taken against me. Soon after, my internet access would be removed.

Needless to say, though my speaking loudly was used against me in court on Monday, it still worked. The word spread to Tom Sheehy, who had my *Whistleblower/Protection Request* letter. He sent me the following email on Sunday, April 14, 2013, the day before the commitment hearing:

> Subject: Benghazi
> Michelle:
> You may have moved on, or prefer not to deal with me (which I understand), but I would be free this beautiful afternoon to talk/stop by.

Best,
Tom[21]

After the April 15, 2013 Commitment Hearing, I responded to Tom:

Hello Tom – I don't know how to put this. In one way, I have indeed moved on, but in another I'm willing to share my insight.
Starting this (painful) process on 10/24/2012, I finally was able to get my insight to the FBI on 1/8/2013 and DS on 3/20/2013 respectfully despite all obstacle placed in my way. What they do with it is now up to them.

Being both a CPA and with my OIG/Auditing background, I believed it was my responsibility to share my insight with the proper law enforcement authorities. Tom, I must admit the storyline I presented in not one I provided easily but felt I had to share just the same. As a result of my efforts (and due to the implications pertain) retaliatory action has been taken against me and I am now in Arlington Hospital on "temporary detention order" since "I am a threat to myself and others."

I don't know what to say other than I'm completely disappointed, but on the other hand I stand by doing what I did and strongly believe I did the right thing. With that, I offer to you an opportunity to discuss further if you would like, just knowing at this time I'm temporarily at Arlington Hospital. I'm not embarrassed by what I've done, so please don't let this stop you in coming to see me—you need to know. Thanks, Michelle[22]

Tom never came to see me while, with my Appeal pending, I was involuntarily held at VHC. The question remained: *Why?* Why didn't Tom Sheehy do more during this time? Tom knew me personally. Tom was my neighbor in Lyon Park, living just up the street, less than two blocks away. Due to my work on the Hill, we were also professional colleagues. But most importantly, Tom was a key staffer for House Foreign Affairs Committee (HFAC) Chairman Ed Royce, the House Congressional Committee with oversight of the Department of State, that on January 24, 2013, I provided him a copy, Copy #8, of my hand-written Whistleblower/Protection Request letter. I had literally walked the less than two blocks to his house from mine to hand deliver a copy. As Tom was not yet home from work, I left the sealed envelope for him at the door of his residence. And based on his Sunday, April 14, 2013 email, Tom knew—he knew

21   Tom Sheehy, email message to Michelle Stefanick, April 14, 2013
22   Michelle Stefanick, email message to Tom Sheehy, April 15, 2013

what had happened to me. How did he find out? How did he know? And again, why didn't Tom do more at that time? But more importantly, what did Tom do, what had Tom done with my Whistleblower/Protection Request letter? Otherwise, how in the world did the events of April 12, 2013 even occur to begin with?

And did Tom's lack of response have anything to do with Michael Allen, HPSCI Chairman Chief of Staff? Given Michael Allen had just a little over a month prior, in December, received (on behalf of HPSCI Chairman Mike Rogers, from John Richter, Senator Olympia Snowe's Chief of Staff on behalf of US Senator Snowe and myself) the same 8-page handwritten Whistleblower/Protection Request letter, which he, Michael Allen, disrespectfully and unprofessionally did nothing, other than call the US Capitol Police Detective William Zimmerman. So again, why didn't Tom do more? For that matter, why didn't Michael Allen do more, given his already odd call to Capitol Police? *Or did he?* If so, precisely what more did Michael Allen, HPSCI Chairman Mike Roger's Chief of Staff do?

On Monday, April 15, 2013, I sent this email to Ray:

> Hello – Sorry about not meeting on Friday. Needless to say, I would much rather have been with you for lunch that where I was... State worked it with Arlington County to have me "temporarily detained" at Arlington Hospital since I am a threat to others... so here I am.[23]

Ray responded:

> are you imprisoned?[24]

To which I responded:

> yes, in the hospital.[25]

Wait a minute... I just earlier made plans for lunch with Ray when soon after the events of April 12, 2013 occurred. So why did Ray use the word *imprisoned?* Did Ray know something, something more that I didn't? What is really going on?

On Friday, April 12, 2013, NCIS SA Lisa Huff, ccing ACID SA Terry Little, responded to my April 11, 2013 email. However, due to the retaliation that I was just subjected, I would not respond back until Monday, April 15, 2013. The email exchange went as follows:

---

23   Michelle Stefanick, email message to Raymond Maxwell, April 15, 2013
24   Raymond Maxwell, email message to Michelle Stefanick, April 10, 2013
25   Michelle Stefanick, email message to Raymond Maxwell, April 15, 2013

Subject: RE: Status

Hello Michelle,

Since we met, I have completed my report and forwarded it to my headquarters. The NCIS investigation is closed. Legally I cannot provide a copy of the report however you can request the information from our FOIA office. I have included the FOIA contact information below.

FOIA requests may be mailed, emailed or faxed to the following:

Naval Criminal Investigative Service Headquarters (Code 00LJF)

27130 Telegraph Road

Quantico, VA 22134-2253

E-mail: [email address removed}

Telephone: [redacted]

Fax: [redacted]

Regards,

Lisa G. Huff

Special Agent

NCISRA Quantico, VA[26]

My mouth dropped. Once again, no investigation and even more eye-opening, NCIS was co-located with the US Marine Corps... So, the cover-up continued. Now given the events that occurred in Stuttgart, Germany and the entities involved, to include MARSOC, and now piecing more and more together, as to what really happened, and why it happened, I responded on Monday, April 15, 2013 to NCIS SA Huff, ccing ACID SA Little, as follows

Thanks for the update Lisa. Needless to say, it's quite disappointing, but it certainly doesn't surprise me at all on the outcome. Thank you for the FOIA info and your law enforcement efforts of due diligence and due process. Thanks, michelle:[27]

And on Tuesday, April 16, 2013, I emailed Huff, ccing Little, again:

Hello Lisa – As a member of the law enforcement community, I'm sure in your investigation, in proving my guilt based on my admitting to making the financial transactions and in supporting my innocence, addressing the "why"—as I requested of you during our one and only March 18 meeting—conducting drug toxicology tests as well as reviewing/determining that other "mind-controlling" methods/means as used by the USMC/our military/

---

intelligence community in psychological operations were not illegally/improperly conducted/utilized. I look forward to reading your report. Thanks, michelle[28]

I stand by this position. Given the timeline of events, the entities involved and the national security matters/issues involved ... if I were truly *guilty*, why would I have continually—every step of the way—reached out to the appropriate authorities? But no, no real investigation, for the cover-up had to continue. And at this point, I still had not received all the pieces of the puzzle to fully comprehend the magnitude of what was really being covered-up.

So, I sent an email to Huff, ccing Little:

> Hello – Per SA Huff's email below, I'm kindly requesting a copy of the applicable investigative report/records/files via FOIA. Please let me know if this is sufficient for such request or if any other information is required to fulfill my such FOIA request. Thank you, Michelle Stefanick[29]

I received the following email from NCIS/FOIA Timothy Owens:

> Ms. Stefanick,
> In order to obtain a copy of the report in question we must first obtain a declaration of identity on your behalf. Please print, complete, sign and return the attached FOIA/PA request form. Upon receipt of your signed declaration we will begin the search for responsive documentation.
> V/R
> NCIS/FOIA[30]

I responded:

> Hello Tim – Thank you for this. I was wondering if just I put "NCIS" regarding all the files that are maintained that I'm trying to obtain from/regarding? (the second part of first statement?) thanks so much. Michelle[31]

NCIS Tim Owens replied:

> You can do that (list ALL NCIS Files), you may also include a statement as to particulars you want us to look for. Any informa-

---

28   Michelle Stefanick, email message to Lisa Huff and Terry Little, April 16, 2013
29   Michelle Stefanick, email message to Lisa Huff and Terry Little, April 16, 2013
30   Tim Owens, email message to Michelle Stefanick, April 16, 2013
31   Michelle Stefanick, email message to Tim Owens, April 16, 2013

tion you can provide about the nature of your inquiry will assist in the search for responsive documents. Tim[32]

I responded:

Subject: Stefanick FOIA Request
Hello Tim – Please find attached my FOIA Request for Records. If you could please let me know that you received the request as well as an approximate timeframe in which I can expect to receive the documents I would appreciate it. Thank you so much and have a nice day. Cheers, michelle[33]

On Wednesday, April 17, 2013, I received the following from NCIS Timothy Owens:

Yes, your request was received.[34]

In the meantime, I received another email from NCIS Tim Owens on another email chain:

Subject: YOUR FOIA REQ
Ms. Stefanick,
My initial search has brought up nothing on a case involving yourself. Can you provide me with any further identifying information to assist? As of right now, utilizing your ssn, name, when, where what…. Anything other than the name of the agent you provided. I can't do a search based on an agent's name, it just doesn't work that way.
I'll await your response.
V/R
T. Owens
NCIS/FOIA[35]

I responded to Owens, ccing Huff and Little:

OK Thanks.
SA Agent Huff – Per the email below, can you please provide more identifying info that I can share with your FOIA folks since my official request has been made, but they can't locate your report and the applicable files. Any insight would be appreciated. Thanks, michelle[36]

32   Tim Owens, email message to Michelle Stefanick, April 16, 2013
33   Michelle Stefanick, email message to Tim Owens, April 16, 2013
34   Tim Owens, email message to Michelle Stefanick, April 17, 2013
35   Tim Owens, email message to Michelle Stefanick, April 16, 2013
36   Michelle Stefanick, email message to Tim Owens, Lisa Huff and Terry Little April 17, 2013

I responded to Owens and Huff, ccing Little:

> RE: Status
> Hello Timothy – Per your other email, please see the information below per SA Huff that the report was filed and FOIA process requirement for request of information. Hopefully this will assist you in your search since you received the required paperwork from me. Thanks so much. Michelle[37]

On Thursday, April 18, 2013, Owens and I received the following from Huff, ccing Little:

> Subject: RE: YOUR FOIA REQ
> Ms. Stefanick,
> Per your request, the case number assigned to this investigation is: 18MAY13-DCQV-0056-4XMA/C.
> Regards,
> Lisa[38]

I replied to Huff and Owens, ccing Little:

> Thank you Lisa.
> Tim – Hopefully this information will assist you in your search and my request for applicable/pertaining information regarding this specified case. Thanks, Michelle[39]

On Thursday, April 18, 2013, I received the following email from Tim Owens:

> Subject: YOUR FOIA REQ
> Ms. Stefanick,
> I have all the information required. Your particular case is in the working queue and will be processed in the order received. You should be receiving an official letter indicating that we have the file, its being worked and give you an estimated timeframe for receipt on your end.
> V/R
> T. Owens[40]

I then waited until I received the NCIS FOIA response…

---

37 Michelle Stefanick, email message to Tim Owens, Lisa Huff and Terry Little April 17, 2013

38 Lisa Huff, email message to Michelle Stefanick, Tim Owens and Terry Little, April 18, 2013

39 Michelle Stefanick, email message to Lisa Huff , Tim Owens, and Terry Little April 18, 2013

40 Tim Owens, email message to Michelle Stefanick, April 18, 2013

I found this notice posted on a VHC/BHU wall quite intriguing in light of it all:

VIRGINIA HOSPITAL   Behavioral Medicine Department
     CENTER   Human Rights

It is Your RIGHT
  To be treated with dignity and respect
  To be told about your treatment
  To have a say in your treatment
  To speak to others in private
  To have your complaints resolved
  To say what you prefer
  To ask questions and be told about your rights
  To get help with your rights
If you have any questions or need help, see your advocate
Call Advocate: Kevin Paluszak [redacted]

So, on April 16, 2013, I contacted the VHC External Human Rights Advocate (HRA), Commonwealth of Virginia's Department of Behavioral Health & Development Services (DBHDS) Official Kevin Paluszak. And then waited to hear back…

On Thursday, April 18, 2013, I received the following email from my AWC/NSPP colleage and recent, current WH Military Liaison contact, Air Force Colonel Dave "Diesel" Sullivan:

http://thehill.com/homenews/house/294685-lawyer-up-issa-warns-cia-staff
don't know if this is something you have been looking for.
Are you attending the Sine's Al Stolberg cocktail hour tonight?
Starts at 6:15
Dave[41]

Wait a minute, Darrell Issa was Chairman of the House Oversight Committee, the Committee on Oversight and Reform, the main investigative committee of the US House of Representatives. Finally, someone is figuring out what is really going on and what all this is really about, or so I thought at the time. I responded to Dave:

Thanks, so much Dave – In light of the fact that last Friday, the Department of State through Arlington County/Arlington Police had me handcuffed and then involuntarily committed to the Virginia

Hospital Center Behavioral Health ward, its very insightful to read the attachment.

This is a retaliatory act against me as a whistleblower regarding Benghazi and in light of my upcoming EEO Grievance Hearing that I filed against the Marines while in Stuttgart that has recently been assigned a Judge.

DOJ needs to do an investigation regarding my constitutional civil/due process rights in this retaliatory action.

With that, a key house staffer is aware of my situation and has been looped in just as you have since the beginning .... My intent is definitely not to embarrass the White House, but maybe now your contact there may now be interested in having VP Biden to outreach to Sen Snowe since she was looped in since 11/28/2012, and to get immediately updated on my case.

I have nothing to hide and all to share, but seems I've pushed someone's button. With that, this is too serious regarding our nation's security. So needless to say, I will not be at Al Stolberg's gathering tonight .... but thanks for sharing and for asking. Cheers, michelle[42]

Diesel replied:

Michelle –
I hope you are safe and okay, and the doc's are taking care of you. How long will you be under their care? I pray your cases will be heard and your concerns addressed. I will give you best to Al, but leave the details out of the conversation. Please take care of yourself. Dave[43]

I replied:

Thanks Dave – As I'm here involuntarily, I guess you can at least say I'm safe and not going away... but definitely not under a "good" doctor's care. Who knows... Thanks, michelle[44]

Needless to say, I wouldn't make it to Sine's/AWC NSPP reunion that night ...

Now my EER, and how it was curiously and coincidentally delayed by HR and PM officials. Here's the email I sent on Monday, April 22, 2013 to Rodney Cunningham:

Subject: Stefanick EER

---

42   Michelle Stefanick, email message to David Sullivan, April 18, 2013
43   David Sullivan, email message to Michelle Stefanick April 18, 2013
44   David Sullivan, email message to Michelle Stefanick April 18, 2013

Hello – Please find the rest of the EER Package. Thanks, michelle[45]

I then responded to Rodney Cunningham, ccing Scott Rauland and Linda Thomas-Greenfield:

Thanks Rodney – I must say I'm confused as I've sent it to three different folks today, including Scott earlier, and everyone can read it just fine. I don't know what more to tell you as everyone else can read it just fine. Thanks, michelle[46]

SURPRISE – look what happens next...
PM Official Scott Rauland responded, ccing Cunningham, but removing Thomas-Greenfield:

Michelle –
Sorry to say the version you just sent has problems.
The text is truncated on p. 4, and also in the suicide box on p.5. And that version does not have signatures. Scott[47]

So, I responded to Rauland, ccing Cunningham and Thomas-Greenfield:

Scott – As Rodney has already been informed, my EER will have to be submitted – as it was last year – in two parts; one with signatures and one with text.

Maybe you then can forward the email of my EER that I sent you on the 8th as I believe as you were able to read it. Quite puzzling why now – despite everyone else I've sent it to today – its coming out truncated.

Maybe your system folks can show you all how to print it out as it may be to different software versions. Again it was the exact version that I used last year and didn't have any problems with. Thanks, michelle[48]

Cunningham, ccing Scott Rauland but not Thomas-Greenfield, responded:

Michelle,
Hello. I have viewed your EER on my computer and I have printed it. In both cases, the text is cut off. I have put a ticket in with IT

45 Michelle Stefanick, email message to Rodney Cunningham, April 22, 2013
46 Michelle Stefanick, email message to Rodney Cunningham, Scott Rauland and Linda Thomas-Greenfield, April 22, 2013
47 Scott Rauland email message to Michelle Stefanick and Rodney Cunningham, April 22, 2013
48 Michelle Stefanick, email message to Rodney Cunningham, Scott Rauland and Linda Thomas-Greenfield, April 22, 2013

270

Services, in the off chance that the problem is on our end. I'll let you know if I find out something. We should be prepared for IT to tell us that the problem is not on our end.

The Office of Performance Evaluation (O/PE) supports the use of ePerformance and the DS-5055 in eForms. Because you are working outside of the state.gov system, you should consider accessing the DS-5055 using the following INTERNET-based link:

http://eforms.state.gov/editdocument.aspx?documentid=15. This website is on the internet. You can access it from <u>any</u> computer that has an internet connection.

1) Once you are at the website, the DS-5055 will appear automatically.

2) Fill in the relevant sections.

a. If you would like to stop working on the document and return to it later; not a problem. Save/Download the file to your computer, using the icons at the top. (Note: Be sure that you know the location where the document is saved. It will make it easier to find.)

b. When you are ready to resume work on the document, go to the website, then open the form, using the icons at the top.

Once you are done, you can email the DS-5055 to me. Rodney[49]

I responded to Cunningham, ccing Rauland and Thomas-Greenfield:

Hello Rodney – I used this format last year as supported by PM. Considering the EER was completed a while ago by myself, and Amanda, with delay with Review Statement, I propose we continue with this process as this was supposed to be completed a while ago – as noted by the period covered in EER. Again, looking forward to hear with IT folks say since everyone I sent it to today as a check as able to print it out completely and read clearly. Thanks, michelle[50]

I would not hear back from Rodney until Thursday, April 25, 2013. Rodney, ccing Rauland, Bessy Bray and Marsha Oshinaike, wrote:

Michelle,

Hello. Today, I spoke with an IT Services colleague and she confirmed that the problem with the text is not on my end or Scott's. The problem is either on your end or in the application that you are using that is associated with the form. While you may continue to use the form that you used, because the layout is fine, again, I point out that all of your text does not come through. Please consider

49   Rodney Cunningham, email message to Michelle Stefanick and Scott Rauland April 22, 2013
50   Michelle Stefanick, email message to Rodney Cunningham, Scott Rauland and Linda Thomas-Greenfield, April 22, 2013

revising what you have written or using the versions of the form that have been approved by O/PE, as noted in my April 22 email message.

I wish that I had happier information for you. Please let me know what you decide to do so that we can get your EER in.

Thank you for your patience. I was waiting to hear back from IT services. Rodney[51]

I replied to Rodney, cc Rauland, Bray, Oshinaike and Thomas-Greenfield:

Interesting, but thanks Rodney. How about it you get a hard copy since as I noted everyone else was able to print it out fine, and exactly the same as I used/submitted last year. Thanks, michelle[52]

Rodney responded, ccing Rauland, Bray, Oshinaike, and Thomas-Greenfield:

Michelle,
Hello. A hard copy will work. Not a problem!
Please send it to the following address.
Rodney D. Cunningham
ISN/EX/HR
Main State
2201 C Street, NW
[redacted]
Washington, DC 20520
Once I receive it, I will email you to let you know. Rodney[53]

I then forwarded this email exchange to DG Thomas-Greenfield, ccing U/S Patrick Kennedy:

Subject: FW: Stefanick EER
Linda – How would you like me to accomplish this from here? Particularly since everyone else I sent this to was able to print it out just fine. Thanks, michelle[54]

Linda responded, not including Patrick Kennedy, but ccing Marcia Bernicat:

51   Rodney Cunningham, email message to Michelle Stefanick, Scott Rauland, Bessy Bray and Marsha Oshinaike, April 25, 2013
52   Michelle Stefanick, email message to Rodney Cunningham, Scott Rauland, Bessy Bray and Marsha Oshinaike, and Linda Thomas-Greenfield, April 25, 2013
53   Rodney Cunningham, email message to Michelle Stefanick, Scott Rauland, Bessy Bray and Marsha Oshinaike, April 25, 2013
54   Michelle Stefanick, email message to Linda Thomas-Greenfield and Patrick Kennedy, April 25, 2013

Michelle: I am on leave and only working on blackberry. I asked Marcia Bernie to follow up.[55]

On Friday April 26, 2013, Bernicat, ccing Thomas-Greenfield, responded:

Hello Michelle,
May I put you in touch with the head of HR/PE Larry Mandel? He and his staff can overcome an array of EER-related technological challenges.[56]

Needless to say, my applicable EER was never submitted to my OPF, nor for review by the Promotion Panel for SFS promotion consideration.

Now, given I had not received these until my February 11, 2015 ACPD FOIA-request response, the applicable ACPD Call for Service (#131020138) and ACPD Incident Report (#130412028) both dated April 12, 2013. ACPD Call for Service (#131020138) is as follows:

INITITIATE: 10:51:07 04-12-2013....
ENTRY: 10:53:15
DISPATCH: 10:55:25
ON SCENE: 11:02:00
DISPATCH: 14:46:45...
LOCATION: 116 N GARFIELD ST, ARLINGTON (1ST ST & 1ST RD) ...
....TYPE: ADMIN P – ADMINSTRATIVE SERVICES...
PHONE: 703-228-5160 (ADDED BY WRITER: ARLINGTON COUNTY MENTAL HEALTH EMERGENCY SERVICES)
TEXT: PICK UP ECO FOR NAM/[BLACKED OUT] AT MAGISTRATE OFFICE, TAKE TO MEET CR718 AT ADDRESS AND TAKE PT TO VHC \NAME: C718//DHS\ PH 301 213 6094 (ADDED BY WRITER: CONFIDENTIAL PHONE NUMBER FOR ARLINGTON COUNTY OFFICIAL PATRICE ENGLISH)
AP COW 04/04/13 @ 12:51:46 (1 MORE)
TEXT: RP IS STANDING BY WITH STATE DEPT OFFICIALS. (PT WORKS FOR THEM) SHE IS RATHER LOUD. AND "VOLITILE" VERBALLY.
RPS CELL PHONE IS GOING DEAD \PH: [BLACKED OUT] ...

---

55   Linda Thomas-Greenfield, email message to Michelle Stefanick and Marcia Bernicat, April 25, 2013
56   Marcia Bernicat, email message to Michelle Stefanick and Linda Thomas-Greenfield, April 25, 2013

B35 MAGISTRATE...

....

TEXT: PICK UP TDO FROM MAGISTRATE OFFICE FOR [BLACKED OUT] ...VHC ER#19 OFC WOODS WITH SUBJ... STAYING AT VHC\NAME:CR704\PH: [BLACKED OUT]
OPERATOR ASSIGNMENTS:
PD05 E288 DEXTER, ELIZABETH
PD 01 E302 DELAFUENTE, DEBORAH
P595 1461 MEYER, BRIDGET
P581 1538 HAWKINS, LANGLEY
PD04 E316 WALKER, VERNETTE
PDO6 E332 CANDELAS-BUSH, ANGELINA
P693 1508 WOODS, DANIEL

The ACPD Incident Report (Incident Report #130412028) is as follows:

Offense Name: TDO....Time Reported: 1053...Capsule Narrative: The victim told her boss, if she got fired she would kill herself. Narrative: On 04/12/2013 at 1053 hours I was dispatched to [redacted] for and emergency custody order. Upon my arrival I made contact with complainant and DHS worker [BLACKED OUT].

The complainant told me that ECO had been issued because the victim, [BLACKED OUT] told her boss that if she lost her job she would have nothing else to live for. The victim had just received notice that she had been fired moments prior to my arrival on scene. The victim has not had any prior history of suicide. I was able to take the victim into custody without incident and transported her to the hospital where she was evaluated by DHS.

After the evaluation DHS decided to commit the victim and found her a bed in the psychiatric unit of Virginia Hospital Center.

Although the victim was upset she remained cooperative with myself and the hospital staff.

The TDO was served at 1410 hours and the victim was transported to the psychiatric unit at 1425 hours.
Date 04/12/2013
Reporting Officer (print)
Woods/Signature
Admin No.
1508

First of all, on April 12, 2013, DS SA Williams called me regarding coming by my residence. I didn't call her. Secondly, who is the boss that

I reportedly said that I *would kill myself* to because this never happened. Thirdly, I was not fired. Who said I was? Fourthly, the memorandum was regarding a *suspension of clearance* pending an investigation and subject to appeal. Quite obviously, US Department of State officials purposely and intentionally misled/lied. DS and/or HR officials lied to Commonwealth of Virginia/Arlington County police, officials, and members of the court, starting with the magistrate and later, including judges.

In turn, VA/AC/DHS officials including Patrice English misled the magistrate—under oath—to obtain the retaliatory TDO on April 12, 2013. When I had my VA/AC court-appointed attorney Rex Flynn file an appeal, it was the VA/Commonwealth Attorney's Office that tried the case against me on May 8, 2013. How and why did the VA/Commonwealth Attorney's Office get involved regarding my May 8, 2013 Appeal Hearing? Still to this day, I don't know. What I do know is that US Department of State officials lied—directly and/or indirectly—to the magistrate to set all this retaliation, that continues to this day, into motion; and then, did not show up to either Hearings. To this day, despite my continual and ongoing requests, I still have not been provided the name of the US Department of State official, apparently a DS SA, that called ACPD on March 28, 2013, setting this entire federal national security matter retaliatory action into motion.

I eventually obtained a copy of the *TEMPORARY DETENTION ORDER – MAGISTRATE* signed by Magistrate Paul W. Koshetar on 04/12/2013 at 01:46 P.M. It was executedby delivering a copy of this Order to the respondent on this day 04/12/13 at 1410 (2:10 P.M.). The Officer Taking Respondent into Custody Woods. Yet, I did not receive a copy until much later.

As far as the TDO itself, it indicates that "this temporary detention order is hereby issued [x] upon motion of the undersigned magistrate" – *Paul W. Koshetar.* The following box is checked:

> [x] Section 37.2-809, it appearing from all evidence readily available, including any recommendation from a physician or clinical psychologist treating the person, that the person (i) has a mental illness, and that there exists a substantial likelihood that, as a result of mental illness, the respondent will, in the near future, (a) cause serious physical harm to him/herself or others as evidenced by recent behavior causing, attempting, or threatening harm and other relevant information or (b) suffer serious harm due to his/her lack of capacity to protect him/herself from harm or to provide

for his/her basic human needs, (ii) is in need of hospitalization or treatment, and (iii) is unwilling to volunteer or incapable of volunteering for hospitalization or treatment…

As is this,

THEREFORE, you are commanded to execute this order, take the respondent into custody and

[x] transport the respondent from the respondent's current location to the location listed below,

…VIRGINIA HOSPITAL CENTER 1701 N. GEORGE MASON DRIVE, ARLINGTON VA.

I have so many questions. Who made sworn statements? DS? VA/AC/DHS? ACPD? Who? What was stated? What was provided? What readily available evidence was used to be the basis of this TDO? By the time this TDO was issued, I had already been unconstitutionally removed from my residence in handcuffs by ACPD, with US Department of State accomplices to include DS Sas, and taken involuntarily to VHC—*before this TDO was even granted/issued.* No wonder there was such a delay when I was first brought to VHC. No wonder there was such a delay in my receiving a *respondent* copy of this TDO. So, on what legal basis/authority did the ACPD enter my residence? And on what legal basis/authority was I removed, in handcuffs, from my residence? I would also receive a copy of the Commonwealth of Virginia Explanation of Involuntary Commitment Process Description of Rights—signed by my court-appointed attorney Rex Flynn dated April 12, 2013. Again, I demanded he immediately file an appeal…

On Tuesday, April 16, 2013, I sent an email to my lawyer Rex Flynn:

Subject: Stefanick Appeal
Hello Rex – I'm now back in Arlington Hospital. I left two phone messages for you but also wanted to outreach to you via email regarding my request to appeal and all the next steps. Looking forward to our next discussion. Thanks, michelle[57]

I received the following from Rex Flynn:

ATTORNEY CLIENT PRIVILEGED
Good Morning Michelle,
I've received your messages, and I will file your appeal. I am sorry that things did not turn out as we would have preferred.
As we discussed before, the appeal will be heard by an entirely new judge, in the circuit court. As we did yesterday, you will have the

opportunity to put on any evidence you wish to put forward, and to testify on your own behalf, as you did yesterday.

I don't believe that I will be able to make it to the court to file today, but I will try. If not today, I will definitely file your appeal tomorrow. Once I have filed the appeal, either today or tomorrow, I will be in touch with you to discuss our case.

If you have any questions or concerns, please feel free to let me know.

Rex

--

G. "Rex" Flynn, Jr.
THE FLYNN LAW FIRM, PLLC
2011 Crystal Drive
Suite 400
Arlington, VA 22202
703.682.6953 (Office)
703.682.6804 (Fax)
Licensed to practice in Virginia and Washington, D.C.[58]

I responded:

Wonderful – Thank you Rex. Looking forward to hearing the status. Again, thank you Rex.

Rex – I realize that this is Attorney Client Privileged, but I have on dear friend that I trust with my life. Am I allowed to share these such emails between us with him or is it best not to? Thanks, michelle[59]

Rex replied:

ATTORNEY CLIENT PRIVILEGED
Hey Michelle,
The Attorney Client Privilege belongs to the client, not the attorney. So, you are technically free to discuss anything with your friend that you choose. The caveat however, is that once you discuss it with your friend it is no longer privileged. Based on the content of our conversation thus far, I don't see anything that would prejudice your case, but that of course may change.

I would "prefer" that you exercise as much discretion in discussing our conversations as possible, as we have (or will have by the end of today/tomorrow) an active case we're trying to win. Even though it is extremely unlikely, any information that you share, could subject your friend to being subpoenaed by the other side,

58   Rex Flynn, email message to Michelle Stefanick, April 16, 2013
59   Michelle Stefanick, email message to Rex Flynn, April 16, 2013

and being called on as a witness. Again, that is a very extreme possibility. Nevertheless, you should be aware of the risks/consequences of sharing our communications. Rex[60]

I replied:

ok – Thanks. I'll definitely hold off until we discuss later today. Thanks so much for the insight. Michelle[61]

Then, I received the following from Rex:

Michelle,

I'm running a little behind schedule. Would 4:30-5:00 be acceptable? I know that you're not in much of a position to go anywhere, but I definitely want to respect your time. If that won't work, I can call later on in the evening or first thing in the morning as I'm filing the appeal (it doesn't look like I'll be able to get to the court before the morning).

Rex[62]

I replied:

Hello Rex – Thanks so much for respecting my time despite my situation, I appreciate it. Speaking between 4:30-5:00 would be fine. Thanks, michelle[63]

On Wednesday, April 17, 2013, Rex sent the following;

Michelle,

Good news and bad news. The bad news is that I had something come up and I had to go to Maryland for a client: I'm stuck in Baltimore and won't be back to Arlington by the time the clerk's office closes to file our appeal.

The good news is that I've done some digging around and my findings are that the nurse is correct that the medication is voluntary. My understanding is that if they require forced medication that they are going to have to petition for a hearing specifically for that purpose. Since I was unable to make it to the clerk's office, I do not have access to the order, to see its language. But as we discussed yesterday there was no specific discussion about medication, only "confinement" to the hospital, involuntarily.

The doctor said that he would postpone his action for 24-48 hours and is politely ask him to maintain that position as your at-

60   Rex Flynn, email message to Michelle Stefanick, April 16, 2013
61   Michelle Stefanick, email message to Rex Flynn, April 16, 2013
62   Rex Flynn, email message to Michelle Stefanick, April 16, 2013
63   Michelle Stefanick, email message to Rex Flynn, April 16, 2013

torney is still very much involved in the matter. If, his position is that it is pursuant to a court order please ask to see the order.

Should any interim emergency arise, please have the Doctor (or anyone else) call my office so that I may assist. Again, I'm so sorry that I wasn't able to file the appeal today. It WILL be filed first thing in the morning.

I'm still in Baltimore, I will give you a call once I get back to Arlington, which should be 6-7ish, depending on this rush hour traffic. Rex[64]

I responded:

Thank you Rex – I really really appreciate that insight regarding the medicine, however, had another unprofessional experience with doctor today. I also told him he is not authorized to discuss my condition with my father. Looking forward to our discussion—if the doctor will let me talk to you…cheers, michelle[65]

On Thursday, April 18, 2013, Rex emailed the following:

Hi Michelle,
I just got back from Baltimore, is it okay if I call you first thing in the morning? The clerk's office opens at 8:30, so I would call either immediately before or immediately after that? Rex[66]

I responded:

Great – Thanks Rex[67]

Not hearing back from Rex, I emailed him:

Hi – Any progress? Thanks, m[68]

Rex emailed:

I'm actually in the clerk's office now getting everything together. I'll call you when I leave. Rex[69]

I emailed Rex:

64   Rex Flynn, email message to Michelle Stefanick, April 17, 2013
65   Michelle Stefanick, email message to Rex Flynn, April 17, 2013
66   Rex Flynn, email message to Michelle Stefanick, April 18, 2013
67   Michelle Stefanick, email message to Rex Flynn, April 18, 2013
68   Michelle Stefanick, email message to Rex Flynn, April 18, 2013
69   Rex Flynn, email message to Michelle Stefanick, April 18, 2013

Rex – If there is any question of guardianship, I would want that to go to a friend of mine—definitely not my family! I can provide if this is direction it (hopefully it does not) goes. Thanks, michelle[70]

Rex responded:

I don't think they can do anything while you're in the hospital. So, for the time being there's not much they can do. Rex[71]

I responded to Rex:

Ok – Thanks, michelle[72]

Needless to say, my patience at this time was wearing very thin. And my being in the hospital did not stop the stunts that continued to be played…

So, on Monday April 22, 2013—a week *after* the Department of State preorchestrated fraudulent April 15, 2013 Commitment Hearing—I emailed Rex Flynn:

Hello Rex – Any status? Thanks, michelle[73]

Rex responded:

Hey Michelle!
I just got back in from the courthouse (I had to take care of some other matters in the clerk's office), our trial date is going to be 5/8 at 9:30 AM. I'll be in touch this afternoon when I have some time to talk. Rex[74]

When I read this, I was fuming…
So, I sent the following to Rex:

You've got to be kidding me…They are holding me hostage until 5/8. This is not fair or just. We definitely need to talk.[75]

Rex responded:

Unfortunately, that's the first date that I had available on my calendar. I don't have a date open this week and next week I have a week-long trial in Baltimore. So, I didn't ask the court for a date this week or next since I wouldn't be available. I'll give u call this afternoon, and we will also setup a time for me to come down and speak in person one evening this week. Rex[76]

70   Michelle Stefanick, email message to Rex Flynn, April 18, 2013
71   Rex Flynn, email message to Michelle Stefanick, April 18, 2013
72   Michelle Stefanick, email message to Rex Flynn, April 18, 2013
73   Michelle Stefanick, email message to Rex Flynn, April 22, 2013
74   Rex Flynn, email message to Michelle Stefanick, April 22, 2013
75   Michelle Stefanick, email message to Rex Flynn, April 22, 2013
76   Rex Flynn, email message to Michelle Stefanick, April 22, 2013

HELD HOSTAGE

Okay, so what is wrong with this picture? In Rex's April 16, 2013 email, he said I would have the opportunity to put on any evidence; yet, I'm being held hostage at VHC until the May 8 Hearing and can't get access to it. Really? And how about this: Rex discontinued closing his emails with his official signature block that he used in his first emails. Apparently, Rex is not/was not licensed to practice in Maryland at that time. The delay to hold me at VHC was due to his schedule, my Commonwealth of Virginia/Arlington County court-appointed Attorney's schedule—and the earliest date as May 8, 2013. So, I had to consider that Rex Flynn was no longer—if ever—representing me and my best interests. And the retaliatory games would continue...

I replied:

> Thanks Rex – It puts me in a very unfortunate situation and prolongs injustice. But if it's the best you can do, it's the best you can do. I just hope it's not at my expense and you are truly representing me.[77]

The bizarreness continued. I can't even make this stuff up...
On Wednesday April 24, 2013, I emailed Rex Flynn:

> Hello Rex – I was just wondering what plan had been arranged with VHC for you to come to the hospital to discuss my appeal.
>
> On another matter, Kevin Paluszak is supposedly Virginia Hospital Center's third-party Human Rights Advocate. I left a message for him [redacted]) on 4/16, and again on 4/17/2013. Kevin returned my call at 12:45 p.m. on 4/17. He said he would be able to meet me the next week. He is required to notify VHS that we will be meeting and thus stay informed with VHC accordingly. I told him I called the VHS# provided [rdeacted] but did not seem to address matters I needed to discuss. He said he would call VHC and then call me to let me know when he would be meeting next week.
>
> I was then later informed by Janelle Bell (APCD) that Kevin would be meeting with me on Tuesday 4/23, no time provided.
>
> On 4/22 I met with Janelle as a courtesy to provide her an overview of what I would be discussing with Kevin. She informed me that a Hospital Rep would be attending the portion of my discussion with Kevin regarding the doctor—Dr. Adewale. I said sure, as I have nothing to hide, and believe in open and transparency.
>
> On 4/23/2013, after patiently waiting the entire day and

even asking Janelle with Kevin was to come, she said she didn't know and would try to find out as she was heading off to a meeting. At 2:50 p.m., I left a message again for Kevin—as neither I nor Janelle had heard back from him.

Rex – If you could kindly call Kevin Paluszak [redacted] as my lawyer to ask when he plans on coming to VHC to speak with me I would appreciate it. In the meanwhile, I plan on calling him and leaving another message on 4/24. Thanks, michelle[78]

I sent Rex the following:

Hello Rex – Just a few minutes ago, Sandra (the social worker), Ashley (my nurse) and Dr. Adewale cornered me as I was walking out of a Group meeting. I again, advised Sandra that I put in a written request for another doctor and did not want Dr. Adewale, and emphasized that this is why I called the Human Rights Advocate Kevin Paluszak since 4/16. Dr. Adewale said that they were not able to find another doctor to take my case. Sandra or Dr. Adewale then said something about my father. I again emphasized that I am estranged from father and that no one is authorized to discuss any of my medical information with my father or anyone in my family. With that, Dr. Adewale said that "I must have forgotten" as I did give him authorization. To that, I said "doctor I'm not on medication and I did not forget, you are not authorized to discuss my medical information with my father." I again stated for everyone (to include Dr. Roy later) that I never and did not authorize anyone to discuss anything with my family and to please contact my lawyer. With that, Dr. Adewale said 'Well then tell him (my father) to stop calling me every day.'

Rex – Dr. Adewale is writing some kind of report and I don't know what he is up to....

About an hour ago and before the above incident, Carolyn Mc-Cosh—Director of Patient Relations—came to my room to introduce herself, asked if she could assist with anything. I mentioned some areas that I had been asking to be addressed through Janelle, etc. but the biggest issue is why my call to Kevin, the Human Rights Advocate, has not come to see me since I first made my call on 4/16, my biggest concern being my doctor. Carolyn said she didn't know why he hasn't come to see me yet, but noted that he was regional and would give him a call as soon as she got back to her office.

As I am writing this email, Janelle came out with a post-it stating that Kevin would be here at the hospital to see me tomorrow

---

from 3-5 p.m. She also advised that I would be alone with Kevin, and no hospital representative would be attending. I just add this in case you would like to be present when I talk to him?

Did Sandra by chance get a hold of you—she came in to see me yesterday about a letter and I told her than that I do not authorize any medical information to be shared with my father, that includes the Doctor as well and she needs to contact you. Did she by chance? Thanks, michelle[79]

After this, a very curious and interesting event would occur resulting in my being denied access to internet/email. And all this in a US hospital—the Virginia Hospital Center—in close proximity to our Nation's Capital, Washington D.C.

During my time at VHC, some very smart Nurses/VHC staff and/or quite possibly the Human Rights Advocate, who became aware that all this was an act of retaliation due to my federal CVRA-protected status, my upcoming EEO hearing against the military and/or my whistleblower allegations, could have put the VHC on notice. By standing my ground, I successfully went through this entire ordeal without taking any medication whatsoever, despite the intent of the immoral and corrupt Dr. Adewale. As I was never medicated, I was able to hear first-hand from nurses/staff and patients how they and other USG employees were retaliated against by our Government through the use of the medical/mental health system. Even more so, seeing patterns, coincidences and observations regarding these atrocity allegations as well as a nexus regarding drugs.

One particular story was in regards to a female US Air Force Colonel totally destroyed by doing the right thing for her nation. I sat there in shock, horror and total disbelief to hear of such an atrocity committed by our own USG/military services until I remembered how I got to the VHC to begin with myself. And yet another story involved a supposedly very high-ranking USG official, a very high-ranking CIA official, committed to VHC only months prior to myself, also supposedly involuntarily; soon after being released they committed suicide.

One must understand that the reliving of the horrific retaliatory ordeal that I, an American citizen, a loyal USG employee, and a federal CVRA-protected victim/witness have been subjected to, was, and is to this day, quite traumatic.

So, with that, I here's the timeline of some key events during that ordeal, the April 15, 2013 Commitment Hearing VHC aftermath.

Since April 12, 2013, the very first day, the VHC/BHU was informed of my instruction of no family phone calls as so indicated on the signed VHC *Authorization of Disclosure Notification of Consent Form*. I continually reiterated that I wanted no family visits due to their participation prior to, and now continuation in, retaliatory acts being taken against me. Upon returning from the April 15, 2013 Commitment Hearing, VHC/BHU was continually informed of my stated and documented position regarding my now estranged family members, particularly with my case being appealed. Despite the posted VHC Human Rights Policy, I continually requested that my applicable rights be provided and respected.

On April 17, 2013, Dr. Adewale came into my room with another nurse, Christine. He threatened to keep me at VHC for another 27 days, and so on, stating *I must take medicine*. Continually, I said that it was my human right that I do not and will not take medication (and never did). Stating that I confirmed with VHC/BHU nurses/staff of this being my right, he wanted to know their names. I wouldn't tell him. He then took me into a room with a panel of supposedly three doctors. Once again, I stated that all this was retaliation as a federal DOJ-determined CVRA-protected victim/witness, an EEO complainant against the military, and as a federal government whistleblower. To this day, despite numerous and continual requests, I still have never been informed of who those three individuals, supposedly doctors, were, and why I met with them.

Since US Department of State Acting HR Director Parker's name appears on the April 9, 2013 DS Memo that I received on April 12, 2013 at my residence from DS SAs Williams and Minor, who were the individuals on this panel? At the time, I had no idea nor was I ever provided names when I continually asked. Now, given this DS Memo, I suspect that the panel of three individuals were not doctors at all—but instead members of a US Department of State Personnel Review Panel (PRP). Puzzling itself if it was, since it is supposedly only applicable to the civil service, not the foreign service. And if so, then why wasn't I advised of such?

According to State Department's Foreign Affairs Manual, a Personnel Review Panel is established to consider the suitability of cases referred for review by the Bureau of Diplomatic Security (DS), with discretionary review of PRP decisions by the Director General. At the time, and in this case being my Embassy Nairobi colleague who departed prior to the August 7, 1998 Embassy bombing, now DG Linda Thomas-Greenfield, would have known all along what all this was really about. So, was this indeed a PRP? If so, were these PRP Panel Members really Department of State officials? Or were they representative embeds from another agency within, but not, the Department of State? I have so many questions, still to this day. And though I would not find out until much later, VHC at that time supposedly had the US Navy/USMC drug detox contract for the area. This is quite interesting and coincidental given my still on-going and pending EEO Grievance litigation against the US Military/Marines also at that time. And if it was indeed a US Department of State PRP, which no doubt it was, it proves that all of this was indeed a purposeful and intentional retaliatory action taken against me. Again, the overarching question remains why, why was all this occurring to begin with?

On April 18, 2013, I met for about an hour with Dr. Patricia Roy, VHC Director of Psychiatry. She was great (or at least I thought so at the time). She listened to my side of the story as I explained and detailed the timeline of events. Though I verbally requested a different doctor, preferably her, due to and since my first encounter with Dr. Adewale, she told me to put it in writing. So I did, that day. My hand-written *Change of Doctor* request was made and given to Dr. Adewale on April 18, 2013. He never responded to me nor was my request ever granted.

It would not be until I *finally* received my VHC Medical Records on June 20, 2013 that I would first become aware of Dr. Adewale's response to my written *Change of Doctor* request. VHC Medical Record/Orders Report dated April 19, 2013 indicated "Transfer to the Institute ASAP." Receiving additional VHC Medical Records on August 10, 2013, VHC Medical Records/Physician's Orders dated April 18, 2013 also indicated "Transfer to the Institute ASAP." No explanation was ever provided to me, despite my continual query, as to why my written *Change of Doctor* request was denied. I would only later find out that the *Institute* to which he was referring, and so indicated as his *supposed* April 18-19 response/instruction to my request at that time, was the Northern Virginia Mental Health Institute, located in Falls Church, in the Commonwealth of Virginia, in Fairfax County. This is precisely where I coincidentally ended up next after Dr. Adewale's sworn testimony at the May 8, 2013 Appeal Hearing.

Upon receiving the 170 pages of VHC Medical Records on June 20, 2013, a document curiously not provided in the VHC response at the time was a copy of my April 18, 2013 hand-written *Change of Doctor* request to Dr. Adewale. The request was as follows:

4/18/2013

Dr. Adewale –

I kindly request that I be switched to a new doctor's care, effective as soon as possible.

Thank you,

/s/

Michelle L. Stefanick

On April 19, 2013, I met with Janelle Bell for the first time. I once again explained the situation, that all this was retaliation due to my federal DOJ-determined CVRA-protected victim/witness status, an EEO complainant against the military, and as a federal government whistleblower. I explained my case being under Appeal, being represented by a court-appointed lawyer, and due to this status and my estranged family situation, my documented and stated request not to speak to nor see them. We also discussed some other concerns I had.

On April 22, 2013, while doing research on the computer in the lobby, another male patient stood behind me reading from my computer screen, loudly stating that I was *looking up FOIA (Freedom of Information Act) information*. No VHC/BHU staffer said anything to him, despite him reading from the computer screen what I was doing. Because of my reporting that incident, soon after, my internet access would be gone as the computer would be removed from the floor.

On April 23, 2012, Sandra Garza came into my room for the first time. I explained the situation and that all this was being done to me as retaliation. I explained that my case was under appeal, I was represented by a court-appointed lawyer, and due to this status and my estranged family situation, my stated request not to speak to them due to this situation and the upcoming Appeal Hearing was documented. Our discussion was brief, but my objective pointed—Sandra Garza could not later say she didn't know or wasn't aware. I know she was aware, because I personally made sure she was made aware.

On April 24, 2013, Carolyn McCosh, the Director of Patients Relations, came to meet with me. I explained my situation, that all this was being done to me as retaliation and repeated all of the above. Again, our discussion was brief, but my objective pointed—Carolyn McCosh, thus VHC, could not later say they didn't know or wasn't aware. I know she and the VHC were aware, because I personally made sure she, and the VHC were made aware.

On April 25, 2013, Kevin Paluszak came to meet with me. I had initially outreached to Kevin on April 16, 2013 and left a message; on April

17, 2013, I left a message and then later talked on the phone; on April 23, 2013 I left a message; on April 24, 2013 I left a message. I reiterated the above, explaining and outlining the issues/concerns, detailing the timeline of events. Again, our discussions were brief, but my objective pointed—Kevin Paluszak, thus the Commonwealh of Virginia, could not later say they didn't know or weren't aware. I know he and the Commonwealth of Virginia, were aware, because I personally made sure he and the Commonwealth of Virginia were made aware.

Later, regarding the computer and generated as a result of my outreach to Kevin Paluszak, this is the notice Janelle Bell gave me to read and sign on April 25, 2013:

NOTICE
This computer is located in a non-secured open area.
Virginia Hospital Center cannot ensure your privacy.
Staff, patients and visitors may walk pass this computer and may see what you have on the screen.
Please sign and acknowledge that you understand the above notice.
(Above the Patient Signature/Date line, I wrote in the following: also, w/understanding that if folks, as happened, stand behind and start reading out loud from my screen, that staff will assist w/asking patients to move on. mls")
Patient Signature /s/ Date: 4/25/2013
In this corner was VHC Patient 'strip code' and information"

FURTHER VIOLATIONS

On April 26, 2013, just after meeting Rex Flynn, Sandra Garza called me into her office with the phone handset lying on the desk telling me my estranged father was on the phone. I again explained, as I had done previously and numerous times before, that my case was under Appeal. And as indicated on the form I completed the first day, I did not authorize VHC nor will I talk to him—only through my court-appointed lawyer, who had just left. I asked that she please not set me up like that again. I left and came back with the *Authorized Call list* from the front desk. Sandra said she had to ask despite that list every time according to the law. I again reiterated my rights and my legal counsel representation regarding the upcoming Appeal Hearing. Sandra told me to "get out of my office."

On April 27, 2013, at noon, VHC/BHU staff (Mariata and/or Michelle) allowed my estranged father on to the floor without discussing it with me, despite my legal rights and VHC/BHU staff knowing the pending Appeal status. I immediately got up from the lunch table and went into my room. I came out and immediately called my Court-appointed lawyer telling him what just happened. It would not be until about 7:35 p.m. when Michelle finally came in to give me a phone message, when I asked her if my estranged father was still on the floor and if not, when did he leave? Otherwise I would have to sit in my room until 8:00 p.m. when visiting hours were over. I would later find out that my supposed sister— you know the one that I supposedly assaulted—was also with him, but did not come on to the floor. Janelle would later tell me that supposedly Dr. Adewale had told them the previous evening not to visit/come on the floor. They did anyway. Needless to say, regardless, my VHC Patient's rights were once again ignored and violated despite all knowing the status of this matter.

On April 29, 2013, due to the ongoing and continual violations of the posted VHC Human Rights Policy, I completed VHC's *Consent for Release of Confidential Information Form* authorizing disclosure to my court-appointed lawyer Rex Flynn. I met with Kevin Paluszak once again. I provided him a copy of Rex's release form and explained the major prior-weekend incident regarding my estranged family members, to include the one I was falsely accused of assaulting. I reiterated my appeal status and my court-appointed legal counsel representation, and my rights being violated again and again. Also, as I was not on any medication during this time, I relayed a sensitive unrelated to my case potential law enforcement matter based on my observations to him as well.

During this entire time, I demanded action by my court-appointed Lawyer Rex Flynn regarding my legal representation and rights. Since VHC had removed my computer/internet access, I kindly requested VHC Janelle Bell to email Rex Flynn accordingly. Here is the email exchange that finally resulted in the May 1, 2013 Legal Representation Notification letter.

On April 30, 2013, Janelle Bell wrote to Rex Flynn:

> Subject: Re-Michelle S
> Good Afternoon,
> I am writing at the request of Michelle Stefanick. Hester Finn will be out of the office after 2:30 p.m. Ms. Stefanick would like for you to send me the form that you were going to send. I will be in the office until 4:30 p.m.
> Regards,
> Janelle L. Bell, RN

Assistant Patient Care Director
Behavioral Health Unit[80]

Rex responded to Janelle, ccing me, on Tuesday, April 30, 2013:

Good afternoon Ms. Bell,
I've been tied up in a Baltimore trial this week, hence my lateness on getting this to you all. I promise I will have it to you by this evening. Rex[81]

Now isn't that odd? Rex did not close his email to Janelle Bell with his "Official" signature box that he used in earlier emails sent to me. Rex Flynn's official signature box did not include his being licensed to practice law in Maryland. So was this simply an error? An oversight? Or something more at play? Rex Flynn's excuse to me for the delay in his filing my appeal immediately as had I requested was due to Rex's working with a client in Maryland. Yet, according to Rex Flynn's own "Official" signature box, Rex Flynn isn't even licensed to practice law in Maryland. Was Rex Flynn not truly representing me? It appears not at all, and not at all during this entire horrific ordeal from the very start. So what was, is really going on?

In turn, Rex finally drafted a legal representation notification letter again reminding VHC/BHU staff accordingly. Here is the Legal Representation Notification letter I finally received and distributed accordingly:

THE FLYNN LAW FIRM, PLLC
2011 Crystal Drive
Suite 400
Arlington, VA 22202
Office: 703-682-6953
Fax: 703-682-6804
May 1, 2013
To Whom It May Concern:
My name is Michelle Stefanick and I am a patient with the Virginia Hospital Center in Arlington, Virginia. Under federal and state law, the hospital, its employees and agents (hereafter "Hospital") are prohibited from making disclosures about me, my condition, my status and any confidential information that the hospital has about me, to other parties without my consent. Violations of my privacy, by making such disclosures to unauthorized parties may subject the hospital, and/or its employees and agents to civil liability.
    I am currently represented by counsel in a pending legal mat-

---

80   Janelle Bell, email message to Rex Flynn and Michelle Stefanick,, April 30, 2013
81   Rex Flynn, email message to Janelle Bell and Michelle Stefanick,, April 30, 2013

ter, and am expressly authorizing the Hospital to communicate with him, and only him. No previous authorizations have been approved. To the extent that the Hospital believes that I have authorized them to speak with anyone else, I require that the Hospital put in writing: (1) the approximate time and date that such authorization(s) was purported to have occurred; (2) the names of the people that the Hospital was purportedly authorized to make disclosures to; (3) the substance of each of the purported disclosures(s); (4) the individual(s) who made the disclosures to the outside parties; and (5) if no permission was granted by me, the authority that the hospital relied on to grant such disclosures without my consent. I will grant no further authorizations, except in writing. To the extent that I have made any authorizations for the Hospital to make disclosures to outside parties, except to my attorney, that authority is hereby revoked.

To reiterate, I authorize the Hospital to speak with my attorney, Mr. G. Rex Flynn, Jr. He is the only person I have granted the authority to the Hospital to discuss my circumstances with, and it may feel free to do so candidly and openly. I otherwise reserve all rights to privacy protections afforded to me under both federal and state law.

Sincerely,

/s/

Michelle Stefanick[82]

On May 1, 2013, I provided a copy of this signed May 1, 2013 Legal Representation Notification letter to Dr. Patricia Roy, Dr. Benjamin Adewale, Ms. Janelle Bell, Ms. Sandra Garza, Mr. Kevin Paluszak, and my VHC Official Medical Records Chart File. The "To Whom It May Concern" was crossed out with the individual/applicable addressee's name written in. If Rex Flynn was ever provided a response from VHC and/or "Hospital" as indicated, I was never made aware.

Despite it being my human and legal right, my continual requests in preparation for my May 8, 2013 Appeal Hearing were denied by VHC/BHU. In fact, it would not be until June 20, 2013, coincidently only after my May 8 Appeal Hearing, that I finally obtained copies of my applicable VHC medical records. Upon receiving 170 pages in their June 20, 2013 VHC Medical Records response, similar to the missing copy of my April 18, 2013 hand-written Change of Doctor request, another document curiously not provided was a copy of this signed May 1, 2013 Legal Rep-

---

resentation Notification letter. A copy had been provided to Dr. Patricia Roy, Dr. Benjamin Adewale, Ms. Janelle Bell, RN, Ms. Sandra Garza, Mr. Kevin Paluszak, and placed in my VHC Official Medical Records File at that time.

Despite numerous and continual requests, neither I nor my court-appointed lawyer Rex Flynn received the 170 Pages of VHC Medical Records during my entire time at VHC nor prior to the May 8, 2013 Appeal Hearing. What is going on? What country is this? This is now the United States of America. And who caused all this? The United States Government? Or as some refer to it, *The Deep State?*

For also on May 1, 2013, at approximately 1:05 p.m., I was taking a nap in my room when a woman came in with no forewarning. Not introducing herself, she began asking me questions without explanation. Due to the line of questioning, I advised my case was still under Appeal and that I needed to have my court-appointed lawyer present. She said that I didn't need a lawyer and was just asking why I wasn't taking my medication. I would only find out later, much later, and after the fact from Janelle Bell that the woman was from VA/AC/DHS/Mental Health Emergency Services, the same office as Patrice English, and that her name was Marilyn Pasley. At approximately 5:00 p.m., Marilyn supposedly called Janelle to say that "the folks she met with could not make a decision, so had to go higher-up for a decision."

To this day, I still do not know who the folks Marilyn Pasley met with/was working with were/are. Who precisely at the US Department of State? HR? DS? Who? And who precisely was being referenced to as "higher-up" for a decision? DG Linda Thomas-Greenfield? U/S Patrick Kennedy? DS Greg Starr? Secretary of State Clinton? The White House? The CIA? Who?

On May 2, 2013, at approximately 2:55 P.M., according to Janelle Bell, VA/AC/DHS Marilyn Pasley advised that "they could not make a determination due to not having an interview. They would follow-up next week at Court." As no interview had been scheduled, I found all this quite puzzling; but at this point it was not surprising. But again, my VHC Patient's rights were violated.

Also, on May 2, 2013, Janelle provided the email response in regards to some of my concerns raised with Kevin. In essence confirming that VHC/BHU previously violated my rights. I was requested to sign at the bottom of the following:

From: Janelle Bell
Sent: Thursday, May 02, 2013 2:27 p.m.
To: [email address removed}
Cc: Andreoli, Eileen
Subject: Follow up from meeting on May 25th and May 29th, 2013
Good Afternoon Mr. Paluszak,

Thank you for meeting with our patient Michelle Stefanick on Thursday, April 25th, 2013. We take the concerns of our patients very seriously and make every effort to address their concerns with immediacy. The concerns that were brought to our attention were:

1. The Spanish patient's rights posted with incorrect contact information listed – CORRECTED The sheet was retyped with the correct information listed.

2. Failure to provide privacy for patient to speak with her attorney – CORRECTED
Allowed access to the interview room with the door cracked and monitored by staff.

3. MD and patients standing over her shoulder reading her emails – ADDRESSED
Posted a disclaimer notice at the computer making the users aware that it is located in a non-secured area and privacy cannot be ensured by VHC staff.
Have the patient to acknowledge the disclaimer notice prior to using the computer.
Instructed staff to redirect patients away from the computer area when it is in use by another user.
Developed guidelines for the use of the computer that include expectations of the user and non-users while the computer is in use.
Monitor computer use to ensure that the sites being accessed will not hinder the patient's improvement.

4. The patient has requested another physician and it had not been addressed. - ADDRESSED
As the Director of Psychiatry, Dr. Roy has intervened and meets with patient to assess and discuss needs of the patient.

Follow up visit on May 29th, 2013

CONCERNS:

1. Confidentiality was questioned
Investigation ensued to address the concern of confidential-

ity and the findings were that the patient's information was not shared with parties outside of her Healthcare Power of Attorneys. However, information was received from a member of the patient's immediate family. (Before I signed, I handwrote off to the side – ABSOLUTELY DISAGREE. I NEVER GAVE DR. ADEWALE ANY AUTHORIZATION AT ANY TIME TO DISCUSS ANYTHING WITH MY FAMILY, ONLY MY LAWYER. MLS 5/2/2013)

2. Father and sister were allowed access to the unit

All staff are made aware of the individual(s) that the patient will allow to visit on the unit. Discussion is occurring to address revising the phone PIN list to include allowed visitors.

Thank you again for meeting with us and sharing your recommendations.

I, Michelle Stefanick, acknowledge receipt of a copy of this response to address my concerns made with the Office of Human Rights.

Signature: /s/   Date: 5/2/2013[83]

Wait a minute, if Dr. Roy "has intervened" then that means she was aware of what Dr. Adewale wrote in VHC Medical notes that VHC *purposely and intentionally* withheld from me until after the May 8, 2013 Appeal Hearing. So then, was Dr. Roy aware of what Dr. Adewale testified to under oath regarding my condition? And who in my immediate estranged family provided information, and what specific information did they provide for such a baseless, unjustified, unwarranted Dr. Benjamin Adewale medical diagnosis? If there is absolutely nothing to hide, then why all the secrets?

The most concerning part of this response was the statement that "as the Director of Psychiatry, Dr. Roy has intervened and meets with patient to assess and discuss needs of the patient." This is in light of Dr. Roy appearing not to be aware of Dr. Adewale taking me to a room to meet with a panel of three supposed doctors, and my still, to this day, not knowing who they were and why I met them. Dr. Roy also appeared not to be aware of the estranged family incident just the prior weekend or Marilyn Pasley's unannounced visit to my room on May 1, 2013. I also question whether Dr. Roy was even aware of the sworn statement Dr. Adewale was going to give at my May 8, 2013 Appeal Hearing. The paramount question remains unanswered. Was VHC Director of Psychiatry Dr. Patricia Roy aware?

---

83   Janelle Bell, email message to Kevin Paluszak, Eileen Andreoli, and Michelle Stefanick, May 2, 2013

On May 7, 2013, the day before my Appeal Hearing, Sandra Garza arranged and permitted Stephen Burns to unexpectedly—and without either myself or my court-appointed legal counsel Rex Flynn being informed, nor him being present—come to VHC to see me. I was totally unaware of a Guardianship motion being filed and the supposed reason for Stephen Burns visit. Rex and I were trying to prepare for my Appeal Hearing without access to any of my evidential/documenting support, internet, my own VHC Medical Records, and from different locations.

When Stephen Burns arrived, I actually thought he was there to assist in representing me, and he implied that he was. But he wasn't. Why was I not advised in advance who Stephen Burns was and that he was coming to see me? Then again, where was my supposed lawyer, Rex Flynn and why was I, would I be meeting alone with Stephen Burns, if he wasn't representing me? I explained the situation from my perspective, but Stephen acted as if his mind was already made up. In a matter of minutes, it was apparent, he was definitely not there in my best interest. Stephen Burn's misrepresentation to me was was later supported and documented by Stephen Burns' own timesheet dated July 9, 2013, to which I would not have access until all the nefarious damage was done. Supposed official of the court Stephen Burns' time was not allocated or billed to me nor my legal counsel but to the opposing side.

On May 7, the day before my May 8 Appeal Hearing, my legal counsel and I were not able to obtain my VHC medical records. However, on May 7, Stephen Burns, who on May 6, 2013 had a telephone conversation with Natalie Page (my estranged father's attorney), had access to my entire VHC medical records. Stephen Burns then proceeded to share that information not with my court-appointed legal counsel or myself, but with the Guardianship Petitioner, my very own estranged father, the opposition in the next day's Appeal Hearing, who testified against me on April 15, 2013. *This is and was beyond a Health Insurance Portability and Accountability Act (HIPAA) violation, this is and was a constitutional violation.*

Based on the misrepresentation made of me by Sandra Garza, a VHC security guard stood in the same room as I held my discussion with Stephen Burns—without the presence of my legal counsel Rex Flynn, and again, violating *my* Patient's rights and *my* Constitutional rights.

Also on May 7, 2013, the day before my May 8, 2013 Appeal Hearing, I contacted the Office of Special Counsel (OSC) from VHC via telephone and fax on VHC letterhead, due to the retaliation that occurred and was on-going against me as a federal DOJ-determined CVRA-protected victim/witness, an EEO complainant and a federal government whistleblower.

My Appeal Hearing on May 8, 2013 was in the Commonwealth of Virginia/Arlington County Circuit Court in front of Judge Louise M. DiMatteo. Since I remained at the VHC this entire time, I was unable to provide supporting documents to my court-appointed lawyer Rex Flynn. All I had were the daily diary/notes I maintained and files/information I could access through the internet, up to the point I had access. Rex and I continually requested copies of my VHC Medical Records, but they were never provided.

During this so-called May 8, 2013 Appeal Hearing, again another prearranged, preorchestrated sham from the very start, there were two witnesses called to the stand. Both made, under oath, inaccurate/false statements against me. My estranged father, now guardianship petitioner/hostile guardian, was one. VHC Dr. Benjamin Adewale, who blocked my legal counsel and myself from obtaining access to my applicable VHC Medical Records, was the other. Under oath, Dr. Adewale's *unsubstantiated/misdiagnosed* testimony was that I was *paranoid schizophrenic* and harmful to myself and others. I could not believe it—my mouth dropped. *Where in the world did all this come from?* So much damage was done based on VHC Dr. Patricia Roy's lack of intervention and Dr. Adewale's unethical/unprofessional/false sworn testimony statement on May 8, 2013. And all this happened because I did what was professionally, morally, ethically—and as a constitution oath-taker—required for me to do.

As indicated previously, no USG/Department of State official attended either their April 15, 2013 Commitment Hearing nor the subsequent May 8, 2013 Appeal Hearing. Somehow the Commonwealth of Virginia's Attorney's Office got involved in the Appeal Hearing. How exactly that was done remains unclear to this day. Based on Dr. Adewale's testimony, I lost my Appeal Hearing in front of Judge Louise DiMatteo. I was then re-admitted involuntarily, this time to the NVMHI, the *Institute*.

After the Judge made her ruling, my court-appointed attorney Rex Flynn disappeared. I was checked into NVMHI at approximately 9:00 P.M. that evening, after waiting in a holding cell in Arlington County Courthouse since after the 10:00 a.m. hearing. Unknown to me at the time that this is where Dr. Adewale wanted me immediately transferred to as a result of my April 18, 2013 written change of doctor's request. I never encountered Dr. Adewale while at NVMHI from May 8–14, 2013. I would encounter him once again, however, in due time.

So, the US Department of State prearranged/preorchestrated April 15, 2013 Commitment Hearing as documented in DS SA Williams' April 12, 2013 memorandum successfully resulted—as intended—in my being discredited as a federal DOJ-determined CVRA-protected victim/witness, an EEO complainant against the military, and a federal government whistleblower; and now, my career, reputation and life were destroyed. Though the EEO Grievance civil litigation initiated by me in April/May 2011 was still pending, due to these retaliatory acts involving and including VHC being taken against me, my rights to justice were challenged and jeopardized as a result.

As stated in the DOJ VNS email I received on June 25, 2009, enacted in 2004, CVRA (18 United States Code Section 3771(a) gives victims of criminal offenses in Federal court certain rights, including: (1) The right to be reasonably protected from the accused; (2) The right to reasonable, accurate, and timely notice of any public court proceeding, involving the crime, or of any release or escape of the accused; (3) The right not to be excluded from any such public court proceeding, unless the court, after receiving clear and convincing evidence, determines that testimony by the victim would be materially altered if the victim heard other testimony at the proceeding; (4) The right to be reasonably heard at any public proceeding in the district court involving release, plea, or sentencing; (5) The reasonable right to confer with the attorney for the Government in the case; (6) The right to full and timely restitution as provided in law; (7) The right to proceedings free from unreasonable delay; and (8) The right to be treated with fairness and with respect for the victim's dignity and privacy.

Furthermore, according to 18 USC. Section 3771(c)(1), officers and employees of the Department of Justice and other department and agencies of the United States engaged in detection, investigation, or prosecution of crime shall make their best efforts to see that crime victims are notified of, and accorded, the rights described in subsection (a).

And, according to the DOJ Victim Witness Handbook, victims and witnesses have the right to be free of harassment or intimidation by the defendants and others. For clarification and emphasis, the following sentence included in the Handbook, and in all capital letters, states, "IT IS A FEDERAL OFFENSE TO THREATEN, INTIMIDATE, HARASS, OR MISLEAD A WITNESS IN A CRIMINAL OR CIVIL PROCEEDING."

Yet, with all the targeting of me that already occurred regarding both applicable criminal and civil proceedings to this point, there would be even more to come...

CHAPTER 9

RETALIATION ROUND TWO:
... and (8) The right to be treated with fairness and with respect for the victim's dignity and privacy.

On May 2, 2014, Speaker of the US House of Representatives John Boehner proposed that a Select Committee be formed to further investigate the events surrounding the September 11, 2012 Benghazi attack. On May 8, 2014, the House voted 232-186 to establish the Select Committee; its chairman would be Representative Trey Gowdy. The last of six investigations conducted, the Select Committee would close after issuing their December 12, 2016 final report.

At the time and to this day, apparently, I am the only one that clearly saw the true connection between two events: the August 7, 1998 East Africa Embassy bombings and the September 11, 2012 Benghazi Diplomatic Post attack. As more information was revealed, I could see it more clearly. What I didn't clearly see at the time, with the insight that I had, was a connection to a much larger event. It was an event that would occur only months after my attending the bin Laden trial in New York in June 2001, and that would be 9/11.

This conclusion I drew was not only based on the insight that I knew, the insight that I obtained and pieces of the puzzle I put together, but also by what would happen to me next, over and beyond what I had experienced and endured already. Obviously, someone didn't want what I knew to be known and come to light.

I was a federal DOJ-determined CVRA protected victim/witness to the August 7, 1998 East Africa Embassy bombings with a still ongoing FBI investigation; I was an EEO grievance complainant in current, pending litigation against the US Military; and I was a federal government whistleblower. Being that *"it is a federal offense to threaten, intimidate, harass, or mislead a witness in a criminal or civil proceeding,"* this was, from the very start and always has been, a national security/law enforcement, never a mental health issue. So how did a federal-level criminal and civil jurisdictional litigation of a national security matter, in which I had rights and protections, transition to the Commonwealth of Virginia/Arlington County state-level of jurisdiction? How? By whom? And most important-ly, why?

Now given all that I had been subjected to by the US Department of State, there was no way I would ever go near that corrupt enterprise again—nor walk the halls of its corrupt building again. *Would you?*

Home But Not Safe

On May 14, 2013, I was released from NVMHI, the *Institute*, once again, successfully not taking any medication. Why I was sudden-ly released from NVMHI, considering I should never have been there to begin with nor that none of this should have ever occurred to begin with, I can only speculate. But, surviving the first round of retaliatory ac-tion taken against me on April 12, 2013 by the US Department of State and the Commonwealth of Virginia, I walked back into my house for the first time on Tuesday, May 14, 2013. Sitting on my dining room table was the unread April 9, 2013 DS Security Clearance Suspension Memoran-dum. After a few hours of reacclimating to my violated residence, I sat down to read this memo, in its entirety for the first time. However, this time I read it through the lens of the trauma and retaliatory actions just taken against me. And again, my first question remains, why would such a memo very oddly be presented to me in a clear protective cover? No doubt *they*, whomever *they* are, wanted to use it to collect my fingerprints for some reason. My next questions were: who precisely entered my res-idence while I was being subjected to emotional torture via the involun-tary admission? On what legal authority did they enter my residence? What precisely were they searching for, and why would *they* need my fin-gerprints? My conclusion, at the time and to this day, is that I was still being nefariously reported "deceased" from the aftermath of the August 7, 1998 Embassy Nairobi bombing: –this was particularly nefarious, given who reported me "deceased" to begin with and given I recently found out Embassy Nairobi was a major CIA station at the time. Now I just had to figure out, confirm and verify who the *they* were, and *who all was involved*. And of course, why was all this occurring to begin with?

I was doing all I could possibly do to protect and defend myself, all the while not backing down on the matter at hand, due to the stakes involved and most importantly, the truth.

For instance, when I contacted HFAC Staffer Tom Sheehy while at NVMHI, this time around Tom in turn e-introduced me to HFAC O&I (Oversight and Investigations) Chief Counsel Thomas Alexander. Why Tom didn't do anything previously to prevent all this from happening to begin with I don't know. But here's the Monday, May 13, 2013 email exchange with Alexander, ccing Sheehy, and just curiously and coincidentally soon after, look what happens next:

> Subject: Contact Info
> Michelle –
> Thanks for taking the time to speak this afternoon. As I said on the phone, I'd like to spend time going over everything in more detail when you're out. I think it would be helpful to sit down with whatever you've got and carefully walk through things.
>
> Of course, if you'd like to meet sooner, I'd be glad to come down to where you're at now. Just let me know what's best for you and if that works with the visitation policy.
>
> Tom also mentioned that his wife would be happy to visit too. I know that on a personal level they're very much interested in your well-being.
>
> My email address is [email address removed] and my phone number is [redacted]. If you don't mind, I'd appreciate if you passed my contact information to Ray Maxwell too. Best, Tom
> Thomas Alexander
> Chief Counsel, O&I
> House Foreign Affairs Committee[1]

Interestingly timed and curiously coincidental, about an hour later, I responded to Alexander, ccing Sheehy, with some great news – and *obviously the reason for my sudden release from NVMHI, the Institute:*

> Thanks so much Tom. Well, I received some great news after our discussion. It seems I will be discharged tomorrow late afternoon. I'll drop you an email when I get home, unless of course you would like to come by today from 6:15-8 p.m. Its up to you...
>
> In the meanwhile I will definitely outreach to Ray. Again, thanks so much Tom. Cheers, michelle[2]

Alexander, ccing Sheehy, responded:

1   Thomas Alexander, email message to Michelle Stefanick and Tom Sheehy, May 13, 2013
2   Michelle Stefanick, email message to Thomas Alexander and Tom Sheehy, May 13, 2013

That's great news. Glad to hear it. Give me a call when you're out and we'll go from there. Happy to sit down with you in person sometime this week. Tom

Sheehy, ccing Alexander, responded:

Great news Michelle. We look forward to seeing you in the neigh borhood. The Committee is fortunate to have Tom on staff. Tom (Sheehy)

On Tuesday, May 14, 2013, I emailed both Tom Sheehy and Thomas Alexander:

Hi Tom and Tom – I'm now at home. My number is [redacted] if you want to give me a call. Thanks so much, michelle

Thomas Alexander, ccing Sheehy, replied:

Good news Michelle. I bet it feels great to be home.

I'd like to set up a time to meet with you in person. Are you available this week to do that? If so, please throw out a time and place you'd prefer to meet. Best, Tom[3]

Too bad this meeting did not occur earlier, in January 2013. But, at least, it was happening now. On Thursday, May 16, 2013, I met with HFAC Legal Counsel Thomas Alexander and another individual at my residence. We sat at the same dining room table where I began to read the April 9, 2013 DS Security Clearance Suspension memorandum given to me by two DS SAs on April 12, 2013. In fact, I purposely did not move the memorandum. I left it exactly where it was when ACPD violated my personal residence and my constitutional rights so I could show Alexander, explaining in detail the events that occurred.

On May 28, 2013 at 6:52 p.m., I received a telephone voicemail message. It was simple and to the point: "Informant!" Left on my home phone, I still have the recording of it to this day. So why did I, why would I receive this message, such a message? Yet another message, yet another threat, like the one I received while I was staying at the Marriott in Sindelfingen, Germany. So yes, the targeted threat against me was and is very real, and continues to this day... And nobody in the entire USG and beyond cared. So who was leaving me these targeted messages? And why? Obviously because they knew no one was coming to me help me. So how would they, whomever the they were, knew that, so confidently know that? And again, why was all this occurring to begin with?

3   Thomas Alexander, email message to Michelle Stefanick and Tom Sheehy, May 13, 2013

Meanwhile, as my lawyer for the April 15, 2013 Commitment Hearing and May 8, 2013 Appeal Hearing, I called Rex Flynn and left him a message as well. What I would hear from Rex Flynn was very insightful. There were four applicable phone messages: two in May 2013, one in October 2013, and one in April 2015. On May 15, 2013, Rex left the first voice mail message:

> Michelle, Hi it's Rex. I first of all want to apologize that I wasn't able to call, talk to you yesterday. I am absolutely elated, and frankly surprised, that you are out already. You know, based on just my observation and my sense of things, according to the law, what they were trying to do, was trying to get you sort of committed to another treatment hospital/facility for up to another 180 days. So, when I told you that to keep in touch, I was under the impression that they were definitely going to, that their goal, was to keep you in custody for that period.
>
> Um, someone is calling right now, I don't know if it's you, but I think it would be rude to hang up with you. In any event I'm calling. I thought I was going to be able to call earlier today, but I've been sorta tied up.
>
> So, give me a call back. Let's sit down and talk and see, let's talk about. Well, well there really is nothing to talk about, everything, you know, everything between us is over, and so really you are just sort of in a position now where you are going to sort of pick-up the pieces and move forward. But I do want to sort of talk with you, so we'll talk then. redacted. Take Care.

On May 16, 2013, Rex left the second voice mail message:

> Michelle, Hi Rex Flynn calling back. We keep playing phone tag. Um, but I got to tell you I'm really happy we are playing phone tag at your house rather than back at one of the treatment centers or facilities or hospitals. So, um, you sound a lot, you know emotionally, you sound a lot more relaxed and you know, not nearly on edge as you were, and understandably so. Um, we keep playing phone tag. I've been running in and out of office with other clients. But give me a call when you get this message. redacted. Take Care.

On Wednesday, May 22, 2013, I received the following email from Rex:

> Hi Michelle, I went to the clerks' office today. I don't have much time this afternoon but this evening I'll shoot you an email with all the details. Rex[4]

---

4   Rex Flynn, email message to Michelle Stefanick,, May 22, 2013

I responded:

> Rex – Can you please give me a call? thanks, michelle[5]

Not yet hearing back from Rex, I sent another email:

> Rex – Can you please urgently assist me in 'requesting a delay for this Hearing on Friday' to give me time to prepare? Or should I try to contact another lawyer—if you have a referral? This is all so wrong. Thanks with whatever you decide. michelle[6]

On Wednesday, May 22, 2013, Rex Flynn finally responded:

> Hi Michelle,
>
> As promised, I went to the clerk's office, and supplied them with the attached letters. There was a trial in the General District Court, and our appeal was in the Circuit Court. I submitted a letter to the Clerk of the Court for both courts, and got a copy stamped and initialed for your file as well.
>
> If you are following up with either of these requests, for the General District Court, you'll need to speak with Kathy. And for the Circuit Court, follow-up with Patricia.
>
> Regarding the hearing on Friday, I won't be able to assist you with that, because I am not available. And honestly, there is little to no time to prepare. Given that our appeal is over, my representation concerning your involuntary commitment is also concluded. I volunteered to make myself available after the appeal, because I was certain that they were going to re-petition to have you involuntarily committed for an additional 180 days. And I figured that, for purposes of synergy, if you had a new counsel appointed, that it would only be right that I share what I knew about your case with that person, to catch them up to speed in preparation for the re-petition hearing. But, for whatever reasons, a re-petition was never pursued by your father.
>
> In any event, we discussed possibly working together in the future, and I am open to that. But, unfortunately, I won't be able to assist you on Friday. It has been a pleasure and an honor to work with, and represent you. I wish you the best. Rex[7]

On May 22, 2013, Rex Flynn sent two letters regarding the US Department of State April 15, 2013 Commitment Hearing, and subsequent May 8, 2013 Appeal Hearing. They went as follows:

5   Michelle Stefanick, email message to Rex Flynn, May 22, 2013
6   Michelle Stefanick, email message to Rex Flynn, May 22, 2013
7   Rex Flynn, email message to Michelle Stefanick,, May 22, 2013

THE FLYNN LAW FIRM, PLLC
2011 Crystal Driv   Suite 400
Arlington, VA 22202
Office: 703-682-6953
Fax: 703-682-6804
May 22, 2013
Mr. Steven R. Spurr
Clerk
General District Court
1425 North Courthouse Road
Suite 2400
Arlington, VA 22201
Re: Civil Commitment Hearing Recording
Dear Mr. Spurr,
On Monday, April 15, 2013, I represented Ms. Michelle Stefanick
in a civil commitment proceeding in the General District Court.
Ms. Stefanick seeks to obtain a copy of those recorded proceed-
ings. She humbly asks that a copy be prepared for her, and that she
be contacted when they are ready for pick-up. She can be reached
at [redacted].
Sincerely,
/s/
G. Rex Flynn, Jr.
Attorney at Law
The Flynn Law Firm, PLLC
703.682.6953 (Office)
703.682.6804 (Fax)
[email address removed}*Licensed to practice in Virginia and Washington, D.C.*[8]

Again, my court-appointed Lawyer Rex Flynn's signature block does
not indicate a license in Maryland. Yet that was the supposed reason for
the delay in not scheduling my Appeal Hearing immediately after the
April 15, 2013 Commitment Hearing, subjecting me to in essence be
held prisoner at the VHC against my will, and until May 8, 2013. Despite
my numerous requests, why didn't Rex Flynn obtain this transcript of the
April 15, 2013 hearing immediately, as I advised him to file an appeal?
So many questions. What I would not find out until much later was that
my name had been misspelled in the Commonwealth of Virginia General
District Court files regarding this April 15, 2013 Commitment Hearing.

This, in essence, delinked the two Courts, and the two applicable hearings—the General District Court April 15, 2013 Commitment Hearing from the May 8, 2013 Circuit Court Appeal Hearing. Why? Apparently, someone really knew what they were doing to pull this off until I found out and got the records changed. I had so many questions, to include did my own supposed Rex Flynn know, how much did he know, and when did he know it. But in the mean time, here is the second letter he sent:

THE FLYNN LAW FIRM, PLLC
2011 Crystal Drive
Suite 400
Arlington, VA 22202
Office: 703-682-6953
Fax: 703-682-6804
May 22, 2013
Hon. Paul F. Ferguson
Clerk
Circuit Court
1425 North Courthouse Road
Arlington, VA 22201
Re: Civil Commitment Hearing Recording
Dear Mr. Ferguson,
On Wednesday, May 8, 2013, I represented Ms. Michelle Stefanick in a civil commitment proceeding in the Circuit Court. Ms. Stefanick seeks to obtain a copy of those recorded proceedings/transcripts. She humbly asks that a copy be prepared for her, and that she be contacted when they are ready for pick-up. She can be reached at {redacted].
Sincerely,
/s/
G. Rex Flynn, Jr.
Attorney at Law
The Flynn Law Firm, PLLC
703.682.6953 (Office)
703.682.6804 (Fax)
[email address removed}
Licensed to practice in Virginia and Washington, D.C. [9]

Outraged by what I had been subjected to, and with still no response, I sent an email to myself to document what I had just found out on Friday, September 6, 2013 at 11:04 a.m.:

9   Rex Flynn, letter requesting Michelle Stefanick's Civil Commitment Hearing Recording to Paul Ferguson, May 22, 2013

Subject: Discussion with Arlington General District Court
On 9/6/2013 at 10:25 I called Kathy Moreno ([redacted]) to find out that status of my attorney's May 22, 2013 request to Mr. Steven Spurr regarding a copy of the civil commitment proceedings in the General District Court on April 15, 2013. I explained as I had not yet received a response/requested copy nor had my attorney at the time—Rex Flynn, I was calling to follow-up on the status. Kathy explained that that "tape" is not working and cannot reproduce it. Seems to be the only one having problems with.

Once I mentioned that I was a federal government whistleblower that was retaliated against, with a complaint with the Office of Special Counsel and Congress regarding this matter, I noted that I'm sure federal investigators would find all this quite curious, as do I since the tape would/could support false statements/perjury/obstruction of justice/abuse of position/power—by Arlington County officials, my family, other witness and potentially Court Marshalls in the room; as well as documenting my allegation during this proceeding in front of an Arlington County Judge that all this was happening as retaliatory act towards me as a federal government whistleblower and my upcoming EEO hearing against the military. With that, Kathy again asked for the particulars of my case to include the spelling of my name to make sure it was the right case. She then put me on hold to check to confirm.

When Kathy returned, she the proceeded to explain that since this case was on appeal that the tape may have been forwarded to the Circuit Court, and since her boss—Mr. Spurr—is out of the office, she would get back to me on Monday. She asked if I contacted the Circuit Court, I said I was contacting them as well but both the General District Court and the Circuit Court received applicable letters on May 22, 2013—of which I received no responses to either or from either. I said thank you about getting back to me on Monday and that would be great, but even if that was the case shouldn't I have received a response either in phone call or written letter to that matter before now. The letter was dated May 22. She again said that she would discuss with her boss and get back with me on Monday. I said thank you very much and asked for the proper spelling of her last name, which she provided.[10]

Coincidental? The tape recording of the Department of State April 15, 2013 Commitment Hearing is not working/inaudible. Somewhere along the way, the applicable General District Court documents, to include online retrievable information, had my last name misspelled. Oversight? Or intentional? Why? So the real timeline of events could not be retraced in the Commonwealth of Virginia's Arlington County Court system?

The telephone calls back and forth would continue, until finally on October 10, 2013, I received the third voice mail message from Rex Flynn:

> Michelle, Hi Rex Flynn here giving you a call. I apologize that its taken so long for me to get back to you. I got back to town from South Carolina and then ultimately what ended up happening I got swamped with work and I've been in trials almost every day since then and I've been and in between then I've been trying to get back to the Circuit Court and GDC (General District Court) to get the material that we wanted.
>
> I was able to get the GDC to release a copy, well not a copy, the original disc. When I tried to listen to it back when we were going to court, it would not play. My understanding after talking to them, that they are/were able to get it to play, but there are certain parts where it gets "staticky" or whatever.
>
> With regards to Circuit Court, they/there, as you said before, were/was no court reporter there so there is a letter from the Circuit Court in response to our request stating that there was not a court reporter. Again, as I told you earlier if anyone is to be at fault it would be me for not requesting a Circuit Court, or excuse me, for not requesting a court reporter. Again, I certainly did not anticipate that they would be, would have sort of misstated the truth as they did. But again, so again, I take responsibility for the fact that there was not a court reporter there and we don't/were not able to get transcriptions for the Circuit Court.
>
> With regard, I need your address. I don't want to talk out your whole voice mail so shoot me an email with your address or give me a call back so I can get this stuff to you.
>
> Um, again with the CD, for the transcript, well for the recording, this is the only copy. I don't have a copy and they gave me what they had because they said they were having difficulty copying it because for whatever reason the part where it gets "staticky" makes it hard for them, I don't know, they tried to explain it to me but I'm not really that savvy.
>
> So, please give me a call or shoot me an email with your address and I will have this out to you tomorrow in the mail. Alright. I hope all is well. Take care.

I sent Rex Flynn the following:

Subject: Status May 22 Arlington County Court Requests for April 15/May 8 Hearing recordings/transcripts

Hello Rex – Sorry I missed your call—hopefully you can give me a call back after hearing my message I just left. After all this time since our May 22 requests, I'm looking forward to finally receiving the "original" CD that has places that are hard to hear/pick up— without even having the CD I have no doubt what sections those will be—from the illegal April 15 hearing; and receiving the letter that no recording/transcript was requested by either you or the prosecution for my Appeal Hearing of May 8 that documents my father's and Dr. Adewale's sworn testimony in which they perjured themselves by lying under oath. Again, I find all this quite curious and suspicious… but with that looking forward to finally receiving something to document the Court's response/position to both requests for both Arlington County Court hearings. Thanks, michelle[11]

On October 18, 2013, I finally received the packet in the mail from Rex Flynn. The contents included a CD, Rex Flynn's business card, and accompanying letters. One letter was the following October 9, 2013 response from the Arlington County Circuit Court Clerk's office:

ARLINGTON COUNTY, VIRGINIA
CLERK OF THE CIRCUIT COURT
1425 N. COURTHOUSE ROAD, SUITE 6700
ARLINGTON, VIRGINIA 22201
PAUL FERGUSON
CLERK, CIRCUIT COURT
October 9, 2013
G. Rex Flynn, Jr., Esq
2011 Crystal Drive
Suite 400
Arlington, VA 22202
RE Transcripts
Dear Mr. Flynn,
The Circuit Court of Arlington County, Virginia does not provide Court Reporters for civil proceedings. In all civil cases counsel of record must supply their own reporter. Should you have any questions please do not hesitate to contact this office at (703) 228-7010.
Arlington Circuit Clerk's Office
/s/

Bonnie Johnson, Deputy Clerk[12]

Also included was the October 10, 2013 letter response from Rex Flynn regarding the May 22, 2013 requests.

THE FLYNN LAW FIRM, PLLC
2011 Crystal Drive
Suite 400
Arlington, VA 22202
Office: 703-682-6953
Fax: 703-682-6804
October 10, 2013
VIA LETTER
Michelle Stefanick
[redacted]
Arlington, VA 22201
Re: Transcripts and Recordings from General District and Circuit Courts
Dear Michelle,

Please find attached the General District Court recording of our trial from the General District Court and a letter from the Circuit Court indicating that they do not have transcripts from that hearing.

It has been my pleasure to assist you during this trying time, and although we did not get the results we would have liked, it was a pleasure to serve you. Although our case has been concluded for some time, I did promise that I would assist you in getting copies of the transcripts, and am providing them now. With that, unfortunately my representation for you is now concluded. As we discussed earlier, I would be happy to work with you in the future.
Sincerely,
/s/
G. Rex Flynn, Jr.
Attorney at Law
The Flynn Law Firm, PLLC
703.682.6953 (Office)
703.682.6804 (Fax)
[email address removed}
Licensed to practice in Virginia and Washington, D.C.[13]

Needless to say, *case has been concluded* was far from true. The snowball effect from this April 12, 2013 retaliatory attack would get worse, and

---

12   Paul Ferguson, letter regarding Michelle Stefanick's Civil Commitment Hearing Recording to Rex Flynn, October 9, 2013
13   Rex Flynn, letter regarding Michelle Stefanick's Civil Commitment Hearing Recording to Michelle Stefanick, October 10, 2013

continues to this day. Two years later, on April 23, 2015, I received the fourth voice mail message from Rex Flynn:

> Michelle – Hi this is Rex Flynn returning your phone call. I wanted to touch base with you, I'm kinda swamped so I'm probably not going to be able to talk too long but I wanted to give you a call back. I had looked over and from what I can gather it looks like what the case that we had in court was on April 15th. And it looks like I guess when they came to your house, they came to your house on the 12th, which was a Friday. So, when you said arrested, I was thinking it was a criminal matter.
>
> But what they can do, and typically what is done, is an Emergency Custody Order where a Magistrate swears that there is probable cause to believe or swears up, someone goes to the Magistrate alleging probable cause of some set of facts that leaves the Magistrate to be concerned that there may be some set of facts that leaves the Magistrate to be concerned that there may be some kind mental illness or some substantial likelihood, I'm reading the Statute here, that as a result of mental illness that the person will in near future cause serious harm to themselves, to others, or suffer serious harm due to their inability to take care of themselves or that if they are in need of hospital treatment and they are unwilling to volunteer or incapable of volunteering for that treatment.
>
> So what probably happened, what you are talking about, I suspect, again I don't know where you are getting this information from, was an ECO, an emergency custody order that was issued on the 12th that is what allowed them to hold you in custody until we had court two or three days later because it was a Monday and at that point they had the civil commitment hearing at that point. I suspect that is what happened. You should probably contact the Magistrate's office or the Police Department to get a copy of whatever records, whatever exists about that. I hope that answers your question. Hope you have a good day. Take Care.

By this time, I also received a copy of the fraudulently-obtained, inaccurate, misleading ECO dated April 12, 2013. My constitutional rights violated, and numerous personnel retaliatory actions taken against me, since my initial May 7, 2013 outreach to the Office of Special Counsel went unheeded; I again officially contacted and reported to OSC. The retaliatory action that took place against me that included an involuntary stay at VHC from April 12 to May 8, 2013, and then NVMHI from May 8 to 14, 2013, was over-the-top. What were my choices given my situation?

So, on Friday, May 17, 2013, I again contacted OSC. I left a message for Carol Lerner and Elizabeth Benzini to discuss next steps. Like May 7th, I heard from neither.

On Saturday, May 18, 2013, I filed an OSC Official Complaint via OSC Form11 5/18/2013 E-Filing at 10:43 a.m. and OSC Form12 5/18/2013 E-Filing at 2:24 p.m. On Monday, May 20, 2013, at 10:31 a.m., I received an *OSC E-Filing System: Form Submitted* email notification for *File number MA-13-3051* and at 3:47 p.m., an *OSC E-Filing System: Form Submitted* email notification for *File number DI-13-3051*.

On Wednesday, May 22, 2013, I received the *US Office of Special Counsel – OSC File No. MA-13-3051* email from Alejandra Dove:

> Dear Ms. Stefanick,
>
> I have been assigned to review and evaluate the complaint you recently filed with our Office. OSC generally processes complaints in the order in which they are received. Based on our current case load, I anticipate reviewing your file in approximately 90 days, at which point I may contact you to ensure we have all of the information necessary to make a determination in your case.
>
> As a courtesy, I am incorporating into this message a brief outline of OSC's complaint examination process so that it is available to you for future reference. The OSC is authorized to investigate allegations of prohibited personnel practices and activities prohibited by civil service law, rule, or regulation. 5 USC. Sections 1214(a)(1)(A), 1216(a) and 2302(b). The provisions of 5 USC. Section 2302(b) specifically define twelve (12) prohibited personnel practices for which we have jurisdiction to investigate. Thus, when reviewing a complaint, CEU analysts consider whether the information provided for each allegation is sufficient to suggest a prohibited personnel practice or any other violation under our jurisdiction occurred. If so, the matter is referred to OSC's Investigation and Prosecution Division (IPD). The determination depends on whether the facts of the case appear likely to satisfy all of the elements of the alleged prohibited personnel practice. The elements are found in section 2302(b) and/or case law established by the Courts or the Merit Systems Protection Board (Board), which is OSC's deciding authority.
>
> Should we determine that your complaint warrants further inquiry by IPD, we will send you a letter advising you of this decision. However, if after communicating with you, we determine that the information provided is not sufficient to suggest that a prohibited personnel practice or any other violation under our jurisdic-

tion occurred, we will send you a preliminary determination letter notifying you of our basis for that decision. You will then have an opportunity to submit (in writing) any additional information you believe will explain that your allegations, in fact, merit further inquiry. A final determination by our Office is not issued until after you receive this opportunity. All determinations, whether preliminary or final, are sent to Complainants in writing.

If you have any urgent questions or comments related to your complaint, please contact me via e-mail. Otherwise, please refer to our website, www.osc.gov, or contact our Officer of the Week hotline at (202) 254-3670 for general information.
Thank you,
Alejandra Duarte Dove
General Attorney
US Office of Special Counsel
Complaints Examining Unit14

And on, or about, May 25, 2013, I received the following OSC letter in the mail:

US OFFICE OF SPECIAL COUNSEL
1730 M Street, N.W., Suite 218
Washington, D.C. 20036-4505
202-254-3600
May 23, 2013
Ms. Michelle L. Stefanick
[redacted]
Arlington, VA 22201
   Re: OSC File No. DI-13-3071
Dear Ms. Stefanick:

The Office of Special Counsel (OSC) has completed its review of the information you referred to the Disclosure Unit. You alleged a violation of law, rule or regulation, a gross waste of funds, an abuse or authority, and a substantial and specific danger to public safety by employees at the Department of State and the Department of Defense, Washington, D.C.

OSC is authorized by law to refer protected disclosures to the involved agency for an investigation and report. Disclosures that OSC may refer for investigation must include information that establishes a substantial likelihood of violation of law, rule, or regulation, gross mismanagement, a gross waste of funds, an abuse of authority, or a substantial and specific danger to public health or

---

14   Alejandra Dove, email message to Michelle Stefanick, May 22, 2013

safety. OSC does not have the authority to investigate disclosures and, therefore, does not conduct its own investigations.

You alleged retaliation. As we discussed, this is an allegation of a prohibited personnel practice, which is reviewed by OSC's Complaint Examining Unit (CEU). Your complaint is currently being reviewed by CEU. See OSC File No. MA-13-3051. Should you have any questions regarding your prohibited personnel practice complaint, please contact Alejandra Dove, CEU Attorney, at (202) 254-3687. Because the Disclosure Unit does not review allegations of prohibited personnel practices, we will take no further action regarding your allegation.

Accordingly, we are closing our file. If you wish to discuss this matter, please contact me at [redacted].

Sincerely,

/s/

Olare A. Nelson

Attorney, Disclosure Unit[15]

OAN:VKC/vkc

Filing this on May 18, 2013, the question remains, was my filing this OSC Formal Complaint the reason why on May 28, 2013 at 6:52 p.m., I received the threatening telephone message "Informant"? Yet no one, no law enforcement entity, to include the DOJ/FBI, did anything despite being made aware accordingly…

Meanwhile, I waited patiently for the follow-up and/or response from OSC. Knowing a fact is one thing, but proving it is quite another. To have the evidence to support and document everything I've been saying regarding these retaliatory actions against me as true, I needed additional support, internal support, so…

On May 19, 2013, I filed Privacy/Freedom of Information Act (FOIA) requests with the US Department of State. At that time, I also filed FOIA requests with the CIA, NSA, ODNI, FBI, DIA, ACID. And as of May 19, 2013, my NCIS Privacy Act request of April 16, 2013 was still pending. I then patiently waited for responses in accordance with the statutory Privacy/FOIA framework.

Before these events, I never thought of making such requests. Now, in light of what I would discover, I highly recommend that every single American citizen, not just USG employees, file such a request. What you find out may be as jaw-dropping as it was for me when I eventually received the response.

---

15   Olare Nelson, letter to Michelle Stefanick, May 23, 2013

On July 1, 2013, I received my official medical record files from Department of State/Medical. It would not be until I finally received the DS FOIA response much later that I discovered some pertinent State/MED emails and actions taken that were not included in the initial documents provided that I received on July 1, 2013.

The FOIA Act contains a provision legally requiring agencies to respond to FOIA requests within 20 days. Many Agencies/Departments apparently rarely meet this requirement for two main reasons: 1) the task for screening requests for sensitive or classified information; or 2) insufficient funding to handle such FOIA requests. However, what if there are more nefarious reasons for intentionally delaying the FOIA requested documents? Is it to obstruct justice, to cover-up for abuses of power, or even more concerning, to use and abuse *national security* as reason a for covering-up crimes. Particularly if and when USG individuals *in the know* become aware of such uses and abuses, and litigation—whether civil or criminal—is open, current and/or pending? For Congress, is this cover-up rationale an acceptable excuse for FOIA response delay? Is it in line with their intent when they wrote and enacted the FOIA legal framework? What about for courts across the US and up to and including the highest court in our nation, the US Supreme Court: is this an acceptable abuse? I would think not…

Given that I filed all these applicable FOIA/Privacy requests throughout the USG on or about May 19, 2013, could this be the reason I received the May 28, 2013 threatening phone message *"Informant?"* But now, since no investigation was conducted at the time, no one will ever know, as no law enforcement entity, to include the DOJ/FBI, did anything despite being made aware accordingly…

Regarding my May 19, 2013 FOIA/Privacy requests, I heard back from NSA in mid-May, and again in late June 2013; the FBI in mid-May, and again in early June 2013; the CIA in mid-June, and again in mid-July 2013; and ODNI, I never received a response.

On Tuesday, May 21, 2013, I received an email from ACID, Subject: RE: Privacy Act Request – Stefanick (UNCLASSIFED). According to this email, ACID requested a copy of my identification to process my request. And according to ACID, I asked to send this copy of my identification "ASAP" to avoid having my request "closed."

Subject: RE: Privacy Act Request – Stefanick (UNCLASSIFIED)
Classification: UNCLASSIFIED
Caveats: NONE
A copy of your identification is required in order to process your

request Please send ASAP to avoid having this request closed. Thank you[16]

I promptly responded. In early June 2013, I received an official ACID response with an applicable attachment. The response indicated *a partial denial* to my request made on behalf of Major General David E. Quantock, Commander, USACIDC. Maybe this pertained to my March 1, 2013 meeting with two ACID SAs Terry Little and Alfred Diaz at my residence? During this meeting, after providing an overview and sharing some evidential matter, ACID Special Agents Terry Little and Alfred Diaz quickly indicated that my case was *under Naval Criminal Investigative Service's (NCIS) purview.* But why couldn't the applicable ACID report simply be provided with applicable sections redacted? Unless of course, there was something more to this ACID partial denial to my FOIA request made on behalf of Major General David E. Quantock, Commander, USACIDC. *So what was it?* And did it include what I reported regarding the Paula Broadwell/Petraeus incident?

It's also very interesting how many of these law enforcement entities are co-located with the USMC in Quantico, Virginia, particularly given the actions taken against me in Germany while assigned with MARFO-REUR/AF, and given that there was no investigation conducted.

At the end of August 2013, I received an official DIA response that contained this paragraph:

> A search of DIA's systems of records located 11 documents (29 pages) responsive to your request. Of these responsive records, 10 documents (28 pages) were referred to another government agency for their review and direct response to you. This referral is necessary because the documents did not originate with DIA.

The *other government agency* referred to was the US Department of State. I would not receive copies of those 10 referenced documents until March 22, 2014... Of the 10 documents, five pertained to my assignment in Khartoum, Sudan (2003-2005), and one pertained to my assignment in Yaoundé, Cameroon (1993-1995).

Despite my FOIA document requests, the only entity within the State Department that I received anything timely was State/MED. In Mid-June 2013, I also received a partial response, an official form letter referencing *DS Investigations regarding requestor, Michelle L. Stefanick Case Control Number P-2013-09436* from United States Department of State Office of

Information Programs and Services (A/GIS/IPS/RL/RC, SA-2) Washington, DC 20522-8100 signed by Mary Therese Casto, Chief, Requestor Communications Branch dated June 11, 2013. State/HR and State/DS documents were deliberately delayed, violating FOIA. Not until almost a year after my initial May 19, 2013 FOIA/Privacy Request did I finally obtain documents on March 8, 2014, seeing precisely what DS had really been up to all these years.

Meanwhile, I received the response to my April 16, 2013 NCIS FOIA/Privacy Request on May 20, 2013. I had met with NCIS SA Lisa Huff, accompanied by ACID SA Terry Little, for a brief period on March 18, 2013, with the expectation that there would be a follow-up meeting. There was none, and there never would be. Based on the matters discussed during this brief meeting with SAs from both the US Army and the US Navy Investigative Services, I really thought all *this* would be investigated and finally come to an end. How wrong I was…Providing details and having supporting/documented evidence to share with these US military investigating officials having the legal jurisdiction in such matters, or so I thought; the only report filed that I would have access to was this NCIS report. Needless to say, I was disappointed by what I read, and distraught from the ordeal I had just been subjected to—I had told them the truth. They may not have liked the truth—but I told them the truth. And regardless of what NCIS reported, I stood, and stand by my claim.

Received on May 20, 2013, I read the official 15 May 2013 NCIS letter and its accompanying attachments. The letter begins like this:

> This further responds to your April 16, 2013 request seeking information pertaining to you.
> A search of our database has resulted in locating one 2013 Naval Criminal Investigative Service report involving you.
> The processing of that report has been completed…

This next part I found quite interesting. The notification letter continued:

> …Some of the information contained within the report is under the release authority of the Office of Information Program and Services, A/GIS/IPS/RL, US Department of State, Washington, D.C. 20522-8100. We are forwarding that information to them for your review and return to us. Once their review is complete, a supplemental response will be provided to you…

For the record, unlike DIA-related documents eventually provided to me regarding my DIA FOIA/Request, A/GIS/IPS/RL never provided me any NCIS-related documents.

Then I read the six-page accompanying attachment. The cover page stated *"FOR OFFICIAL USE ONLY NAVAL CRIMINAL INVESTIGA- TIVE SERVICES RECORDS MANAGEMENT DIVISION LAW EN- FORCEMENT RECORDS,"* and the remainder of the attachment was the *"REPORT OF INVESTIGATION (CLOSED ONLY)."* It indicated the *"Case Number: 18MAR13DCQV00564XMA; DCII INDEX CODE: C= 5 YEARS; Date Closed: 03/29/2013; and Name: FOREIGN SERVICE OF- FICER REPORT OF FINANCIAL SCAM DUE TO."* And despite and in light of my federal CVRA-accorded victim/witness status, the box under *"Final Disposition Report to FBI"* was checked *"NO." So why didn't NCIS refer or submit this report to the FBI?*

And that's only the cover sheet. I continued reading…

Though I remain as adamant today, as I did on and prior to March 18, 2013, regarding the necessity of an investigation, I will not provide all the details/contents of the NCIS Report of Investigation. Some points are so incredibly puzzling that I have to provide some insight at this time. First of all, given my prior experience and background with the US Depart- ment of State OIG, I was well aware of jurisdictional rules. The matter at hand was not of State/OIG jurisdiction. So why would NCIS refer it to the OIG when it dealt with the incident that occurred when I was as- signed with the US Navy MARFOREUR/AF? These were incidents that occurred right after I formally filed an EEO Grievance Complaint and after the killing of bin Laden by the US Navy SEALs. Indicated under paragraph three of the NARRATIVE section,

> …On 18 Mar13, RA *(Reporting Agent – NCIS Special Agent Lisa Huff)* contacted [blocked out – with Referred to the Department of State]. This report is being referred to the Department of State. This investigation is closed.

Really? So, who precisely within the Department of State did NCIS SA Lisa Huff contact on March 18, 2013? OIG? DS? And more importantly, why? Why did the US Navy not investigate given the fact that capabilities and tactics used are not under the jurisdiction of the US Department of State, but only the US Department of Defense? I had contacted State OIG and would indeed contact State OIG again, specifically IG Steve Linnick, as well as the DOD OIG, DOJ OIG, and others …

I continued reading—there were lots of details, specific details and then I got to the last paragraph, *"STEFANICK did not have any further information to provide."* I almost fell out of my chair. No further information to provide, are you kidding me? *What in the world is really going on?*

After reading the accompanying report, I did as the May 15, 2013 letter instructed; not only did I file an appeal, but I also put NCIS on notice of how wrong they were to close the case without any proper follow-up/investigation. As their instructions indicated, on May 21, 2013, I wrote a letter:

> May 21, 2013
> Office of the Judge Advocate General, (Code 14),
> 1322 Patterson Avenue, S.E., Suite 3000
> Washington Navy Yard, D.C. 20374-5066
> SUBJ: "FOIA Appeal"
> To the Secretary of Navy's designee:
> Thank you for providing this Partial Denial letter packet (Attachment 2), so promptly in regards to my initial request (Attachment 1). Also, thank you for providing an opportunity for an appeal to this determination.
>
> As rightly noted, NCIS Special Agent Lisa Huff accompanied by ACID Special Agent Little and another NCIS representative who did not provide a business card, came to my residence of [redacted] on March 18, 2013. And according to this report information obtained, this case, Case Number 18MAR13DCQV00564X-MA, was opened on March 18 and closed on March 29, 2013.
>
> Considering the criminal/national security allegation I am making regarding Marine Corps officials/capabilities, I find the status of this "investigation" quite inadequate. I may not be an "investigator or a member of the Law Enforcement community," however, in addition to being a member of the Foreign Service with the Department of State, I am a licensed Certified Public Accountant in the state of Virginia, and have professional auditor experience both with Defense Contract Audit Agency and State's Office of Inspector General.
>
> With that, I provide the following consideration for reopening this case with "fresh" NCIS investigative professional, objective eyes in reviewing and assessing the allegation made with proper ramifications pursued accordingly.
>
> According to Attachment 7, on Monday, March 18, 2013, I was contacted by ACID SA Little at 9:37 a.m. on setting up a second interview with ACID, and a first with NCIS representatives pres-

ent, to meet that day. In my email response, I noted that I was at the office and had a meeting at 12:30 that day that I must attend. In both my discussion and email exchange, SA Little requested if possible, to meet before my 12:30 meeting, which was with U/S Patrick Kennedy.

As this last email correspondence was at 10:00 while I was at work, and I made the 12:30 meeting with U/S Patrick Kennedy, the longest I would have met with ACID SA Little, NCIS SA Lisa Huff and the other NCIS representative, would have been 2 ½ hours. However, since I needed some time, as did the SAs to commute to my house and for me, back to the Department in time of the 12:30 meeting, our meeting lasted less than 2 ½ hours and more likely in the 1 to 1 ½ hour range.

Additionally, when we all sat at the table, I was advised by SA Little to focus only on the "financial transaction aspect" of the information that I had earlier discussed with ACID SA Little and SA Dias in our March 1, 2013 meeting which lasted from approximately 3:15 to 6:30 P.M.

According to Attachment 2, page 2 of 3, paragraph 10, of NCIS SA Little's report, "Stefanick did not have any further information to provide." This is absolutely not true. As they asked me to be limited in my scope during this one and only meeting with NCIS, as well as wanting me to make it to my 12:30 meeting with U/S Kennedy, I had lots more documents, emails, etc., to share. No copies were made of the information I provided to include Financial Disclosure Reports reviewed/discussed during this one and only meeting.

Again, I emphasize if I had known this was going to be the only meeting I had with NCIS, I would have called and cancelled my appointment with U/S Kennedy immediately—that is how much importance I placed on working with NCIS, and any law enforcement authorities for that matter, in regards to the allegations I make and the information/insight I have to provide.

As I wrote in Attachment 6 to SA Huff once being informed that the case opened on March 18, 2013, was closed on March 29, with no follow-up and no documentation obtained, to include the time line of events occurring after my filing an official formal EEO grievance regarding the Marines in May 2011 in Stuttgart, Germany:

"Hello Lisa – As a member of the law enforcement community, I'm sure in your investigation, in proving my guilt based on my admitting to making the financial transactions and in supporting my innocence, addressing the "why"—as I requested of you during our one and only March 18 meeting – conducted drug toxicology tests as well as reviewing/determining that other "mind-controlling" methods/means as used by the USMC/our military/intelligence community in psychological operations were not illegally/improperly conducted/utilized. I look forward to reading your report."

Now that I've read the report, I again kindly request the Secretary of Navy's designee who reads this letter to agree that this case needs to be reopened and investigated with objective/professional NCIS investigators and oversight as the USMC officials linked to this event are in my opinion capable of what I suggest. I am not a member of the intelligence community. Therefore "classified/national security" capabilities/tactics may have indeed been used against a non-Combatant American citizen, me. The reason may simply be retaliation for the EEO Grievance I filed, but I would offer to you as I have other law enforcement/proper authorities within our USG and two branches of Government, another such reason is also possible and has since emerged since my filing the EEO in May 2011.

Again, I kindly request the professional representative to the Secretary of Navy that reads this letter to reopen this case and re-assign it accordingly so all I have and all I know, to include names of high-ranking Military officials, can be shared with NCIS accordingly, as it has been with other law enforcement official/oversight entities. I can be reached at [email address removed} or [redacted]. Thank you and thank you for your serious consideration to reopening this case.

Sincerely,

/s/

Michelle L. Stefanick[17]

Attachments:

1. Initial Request for Records completed form (dated April 16, 2013)

2. Copy of Partial denial letter (dated May 15, 2013)

3. April 18 email exchange/request requirement fulfilled (Stefanick/Owens)

4. April 16/17 email exchange Stefanick/Owens request submission

5. April 11/12/17 email exchange Special Agent Lisa Huff/ACID Special Agent Little/Stefanick/Owens FOIA request process for report

---

17   Michelle Stefanick, letter to the Secretary of Navy's designee to, May 31, 2013

6. April 11/12/16 email exchange NCIS Special Agent Lisa Huff/ ACID Special Agent Little/Stefanick email exchange

7. March 18/29 ACID Special Agent Little and Diaz/Stefanick email exchange

I sent this letter via USPS Express Mail with Domestic Return Receipt (PS Form 3811, February 2004). The *Green Card* receipt was *"Date Stamped May 22, 2013"* and I, in turn, received the delivery confirmation *Green Card* on May 24, 2013.

With all that was going on at this time, dealing with the actions just taken against me, my pursuit for an investigation and justice, as well as trying to expose the truth … I had yet another fraudulent Commonwealth of Virginia/Arlington County Court retaliatory legal matter I needed to put an end to as well—a guardianship. And this time, clearly at the hands of my very own *estranged* family. Due to the court-appointed attorney stunt pulled last time, I had to find my own legal counsel. I reached out again to some of my former AWC colleagues Dave "Diesel" Sullivan and in turn, Richard Gross. On Wednesday, May 22, 2013, I received the following email from Rich:

> Subject: Lawyer Referral Service
> Michelle:
> Diesel mentioned you were looking for an attorney. Both the Arlington County and Alexandria bar associations have lawyer referral services. They should be able to refer you to someone local who specializes in whatever particular area of law you need:
> http://arlingtonbar.org/Lawyer_Referral.html
> http://www.alexandriabarva.org/lrs.html   Best, rich[18]

I responded the next day:

> Thanks Rich – Because of your assistance, it appears I have legal representation for this and even a back-up lined up just in case. So thank you. Hopefully tomorrow the Court agrees that I can have my own legal counsel.
>   Also, I spoke with DOD IG hotline earlier today and filed a complaint. Hopefully I will be able to discuss/share all that I have with them soon as well. I really hope that letter sent to JAG/NCIS will also be taken seriously.
>   With that, I'm serious about the other matter I discussed with you regarding the Air Force Colonel that was so retaliated against

---

regarding her sexual assault claim, that she even went to Gen Welch, and nothing was done. I know this may not be your lane, but since the President, SEC DEF, and Chairman are so focused to address this issue within our military do you have any point of contact I can pass along to this wonderful woman that had no reason to lie, but be so retaliated against to destroy her, so that she can maybe now be given her constitutional due process rights in such a matter. Its my understanding the SEC DEF established a new panel to address such matters? Any insight you can pass along so I can accordingly would be sincerely appreciated.

And again, thank you Rich. Pray that tomorrow works out so I can at least have my constitutional/due process rights. Cheers, michelle[19]

For this book, I reached out to this wonderful woman to see how much more detail I could provide. By the time this book was published, I had not received a response. I mention her now because despite my own situation, when I heard of hers, I promised that I would shed a light on her situation as well my own, if and when I had the chance. I keep my promises…

Rich responded:

Michelle:
I'm glad to hear all of that. Good Luck on Friday.
As far as the letter to the USN TJAG/NCIS, you labeled it as a "FOIA Appeal" so it's likely to be handled as such (as an appeal for a denial of a Freedom of Information Act request). If you were intending for them to re-open and pursue the underlying allegations, you might want to make that clear in another letter.

Regarding the USAF colonel, I would recommend she either contact the USAF TJAG (http://www.afjag.af.mil) or the IG (http://www.af.mil/inspectorgeneralcomplaints.asp). The SECDEF panel you heard about will examine systemic changes to the Uniform Code of military justice and the military justice system; it is not designed to look into individual cases. Best, rich[20]

I replied:

Thanks so much for this Rich. I will pass along accordingly.
Do you have the right NCIS/JAG link address I should forward/ write this letter to since you don't think the folks receiving the letter yesterday will handle it accordingly as I request? Sorry for all the questions but unfortunately they are all legal related and in an area

19   Michelle Stefanick, email message to Richard Gross, May 23, 2013
20   Richard Gross, email message to Michelle Stefanick, May 23, 2013

regarding the military that I would ever thought I would have to be involved with…again thanks regarding leg rep and fingers crossed. As one Marine Sergeant Major told me once…He said God does not like ugly and the truth always comes out in the end. Let's only hope…cheers, michelle[21]

Rich provided the following:

Mailing address for NCIS:
Naval Criminal Investigative Service
27130 Telegraph Road
Quantico, VA 22134

Mailing address for Navy TJAG:
Vice Admiral Nanette M. DeRenzi
1322 Patterson Ave., Suite 3000
Washington Navy Yard, DC 20374-5066

Mailing address to USMC Commandant's SJA:
Major General Vaughn A. Ary
Headquarters, US Marine Corps (JA)
3000 Marine Corps Pentagon RM# 4D558
Washington, D.C. 20350-3000

On May 23, 2013, I sent the following letter to Navy TJAG:
Vice Admiral Nanette M. DeRenzi
1322 Patterson Avenue, S.E. 3000
Washington Navy Yard, DC 20374-5066
SUBJ: Request to Re-open Case Number 18MAR13DC-QV00564XMA
Dear Vice Admiral Nanette M. DeRenzi:
On May 21, 2013 I sent the attached request to the Office of the Judge Advocate General, (Code 14) (Attachment 1) in response to the Partial Denial letter packet (Attachment 3) that I received on May 20, 2013.

In light of the seriousness of the allegations I am making, I am kindly requesting your serious consideration to my request that this case be reopened and all the supporting documents/insights I have be shared accordingly with a "fresh" NCIS Investigative professional team for assessment and proper action accordingly.

Please note I do not make such allegations lightly. Considering the criminal/national security allegation I am making regarding Marine Corps officials/capabilities. I find the status of this reflected "investigation" quite inadequate. I may not be an "investigator or a member of the Law Enforcement community," however, in addition to being a member of the Foreign Service with the Department of State, I am a licensed Certified Public Accountant in the state of Virginia, and have professional auditor experience both with Defense Contract Audit Agency and State's Office of Inspector General.

Again, I kindly request your consideration to reopening this and reassign it accordingly so all I have and all I know, to include the names of high-ranking Military officials, can be shared and investigated with and by NCIS accordingly. I can be reached at [email address removed} or [redacted]. Thank you and thank you for your serious consideration to reopening this case.

Sincerely,

/s/

Michelle L. Stefanick[22]

Attachments:

1. Letter to Office of the Judge Advocate General, (Code 14) (dated May 21, 2013)

2. Initial Request for Records completed form (dated April 16, 2013)

3. Copy of Partial denial letter (dated May 15, 2013)

4. April 18 email exchange/request requirement fulfilled (Stefanick/Owens)

5. April 16/17 email exchange Stefanick/Owens request submission

6. April 11/12/17 email exchange Special Agent Lisa Huff/ACID Special Agent Little/Stefanick/Owens FOIA request process for report

7. April 11/12/16 email exchange NCIS Special Agent Lisa Huff/ACID Special Agent Little/Stefanick email exchange

8. March 18/29 ACID Special Agent Little and Diaz/Stefanick email exchange

I sent the letter via *USPS Express Mail with Domestic Return Receipt (PS Form 3811, February 2004)*.

Meanwhile, yet another retaliatory action taken against me was clearly agenda-driven—*the Petition for Appointment of a Guardian and Conservator*. This petition was filed by my estranged father, once again in the Commonwealth of Virginia/Arlington County Circuit Court. Again, I simply ask over and over again, on what legal grounds was this filed? In a May 21, 2013 email to Stephen Burns, the Guardian ad litem in this matter (and the same lawyer representing the other side who weaseled his way into VHC to meet with me under false pretenses to review my VHC Medical Records the day before my May 8, 2013 Appeal Hearing), I asked this specific question. But, he, the supposed court-appointed unbiased, neutral party, never provided an answer. So, what does that tell you?

Though I don't provide extensive detail regarding this legal matter, it's because I stand by the position that all of this was a federal, not state-level matter, and not because there isn't much detail to provide. Believe me, there is… Lies/false statements both made under oath in the court of law and contained in official court documents. And not being a legal professional, what's that legal concept? Obstruction of justice. Abuse of power. Intimidation/harassment of a federal victim/witness. Fruit of the Poisonous Tree … The question remains why did federal law enforcement—including the FBI—allow all this to happen?

Early morning Thursday May 23, 2013, I contacted the Arlington County Bar Association and by 10:47 A.M., I had legal counsel for the Court Hearing on the 10th Floor at 9:30 A.M. for May 24, 2013. The Court agreed that George Dodge could represent me, delaying any further matters at that time. Fast-forward, on Tuesday, July 9, 2013, I was informed that on the previous day, George Dodge had filed a motion to dismiss my estranged father's case. On Monday, July 8, 2013, George sent an email to Natalie Page, my estranged father's legal counsel, and Stephen Burns: "Subject: Stefanick Motion to Dismiss and Memorandum in Support of Motion to Dismiss Petitioner's Request for Removal of the Trustee," with a copy of the motion. Within hours, Natalie sent George, ccing Stephen, the following email response: "After much deliberation, my client has come to the decision that he is not in a position to pursue this matter any further." And as a result, an *ORDER OF NONSUIT* Motion was filed and entered by the Commonwealth of Virginia Arlington County Circuit Court and signed by Judge William T. Newman, Jr on July 11, 2013.

Meanwhile, I had sent an email on Tuesday, July 9, 2013 to Kevin Stefanick and Ruthann Stefanick, ccing John Jackson as follows:

Subject: Official Notification Revoking as Agents/Successor Trustees
Dear Kevin and Ruthann – Effective immediately, I hereby revoke any authority/authorization as agent for my, Michelle Laureen Ste-

fanick's Power of Attorney for Health Care and Durable General Power of Attorney. You are kindly requested to return to me any copies of such documents you have in your possession.

Effective immediately, "Amendment to the Michelle Laureen Stefanick Revocable Trust" hereby removes Kevin Stefanick and Ruthann Stefanick Freeland from any authority/authorization under section Article V "Distribution at My Death" and section Article XII "Successor Trustee." You are kindly requested to return to me any copies of such documentation you have in your possession.

Also, Ruthann, you are kindly requested to return certified safely/securely and as soon as possible my safe deposit box key.

The mailing address for all requested documents/items is. [provided address redacted].

Thank you,

Michelle Laureen Stefanick

I forwarded this email to my attorney George Dodge:

George – Just FYI and as discussed. Again, thanks so much for all your assistance and fingers crossed until I hear/receive good news from you on Friday. Cheers, michelle

With this simple request and the *ORDER OF NONSUIT* motion filed/entered/signed on July 11, 2013, this case should be closed, right? But no… And to this day, these requested documents and keys have never been returned to me by my own supposed brother and sister.

What I didn't know at the time was that for some reason the Commonwealth of Virginia Attorney's Office, on June 7, 2013, subpoenaed Dr. Benjamin Adewale. I assumed this was regarding his fraudulent, inaccurate, under oath, testimony that resulted in my losing the May 8, 2013 Appeal Hearing in the Commonwealth of Virginia's Arlington County Circuit Court in front of Judge DiMatteo. So again, why was the Commonwealth of Virginia Attorney's Office interested, given this was a federal matter? And why would the Commonwealth of Virginia Attorney's Office go to such measures to issue and obtain this subpoenaed testimony? Because, once again, the next round of retaliatory actions against me was in the works…

I initially, and for a very long time, was convinced that the retaliatory actions taken against me by the US Navy/USMC was all really about a clash of cultures—*military service vs. foreign service*. I mean, what other possible reason could it all have been for? However, the extremity of the retaliatory actions taken against me just didn't make sense. I mean, I was already departing Stuttgart early! But other odd things, very odd things were happening. So, what was all this targeted retaliation really about?

Remember the April 9, 2013 *Security Clearance Suspension* memorandum? The one that said, "Your Top-Secret security clearance is suspended pending the outcome of an ongoing DS investigation"? The one that said, "The suspension of your security clearance does not constitute a formal revocation and does not indicate that such action is planned?" And the one that said, "If, after further investigation and review, the Director, Diplomatic Security Service, revokes your security clearance, you will be given an opportunity to respond"? And "Moreover, should the Assistant Secretary of Diplomatic Security render a decision to sustain the revocation of your security clearance, you will be afforded the opportunity to appeal the decision to the Department's Security Appeals Panel." The one that I received on Friday, April 12, 2013 that resulted in ACPD violating my constitutional rights, kicking off all this retaliation that continues to this day. In the April 15, 2013 Commitment Hearing, the witnesses against me all said, under oath in a court of law, that I had been fired. This was absolutely not true. I was not fired. So, who purposely and intentionally set a false narrative into play? And why?

On May 30, 2013, I called AFSA/Legal Counsel Neera Parikh, explained what happened and posed four pinpointed questions:

> 1. Was I the subject of any investigation by DS and/or any other USG law enforcement entity from approximately 2008-2011? If so, what was the accusation and furthermore, as I am not and never was an intelligence employee, why were my constitutional/due process rights violated?
>
> 2. In July 2011, why didn't PM notify me of my requirement to file a "termination of position" Financial Disclosure Statement when I departed Stuttgart?
>
> 3. Why didn't DS ever get back to me other than one phone call (on January 17, 2012) while I was at OSD?
>
> 4. Why didn't OSD/Security and/or DS get back to me on my concerns from my October 24, 2012 request with OSD/AFR Officials, taken to OSD/Security on 10/25 and 10/26/2012?[23]

A little later, I received the following email from Neera:

Subject: Stefanick draft

Michelle – do you have the full name of the DS agents that you

---

met with in March and April? I don't see a Christina Williams in the GAL.
Thanks,
Neera
Neera Parikh, Esq.
American Foreign Service Association[24]

I responded:

Sure – I met with DS Agents James Minor and Prestina Williams on 3/20/2013. Pat Kennedy arranged this for me since I had been requesting to meet with them (DS) since 10/25-26/2012 via Office of Secretary of Defense (OSD)/Security office based on my discussions/requests with OSD/African Affairs officials on 10/24/2012.

If you need more names, details, etc. I can provide. Please note this meeting was at my request in order to share the insight I had requested/wanted to share since 10/24/2012. Pat finally made it happen. Other oddity things happened along the way--- but here's the info you requested. Thanks, michelle[25]

On Friday, May 31, 2013, Neera sent the following to Prestina Williams and James Minor:

Subject: case inquiry
Hello Prestina and James – my name is Neera Parikh and I am a staff attorney with AFSA. I was wondering if you have a few minutes today or next week to discuss Michelle Stefanick's case. She has contacted our office with regards to her security clearance and I am trying to get clarity on her case, what has transpired to date and DS' rationale for some of the allegations Ms. Stefanick has made regarding an April 2013 meeting she had with you all. Would it be possible to schedule a time to talk or would you rather I pose questions via email? I look forward to hearing from you.
Thanks
neera
Neera Parikh, Esq.
American Foreign Service Association[26]

Neera received a response from James Minor, ccing Prestina Williams:

Subject: RE: case inquiry – M. STEFANICK
Neera,

24   Neera Parikh, email message to Michelle Stefanick, May 30, 2013
25   Michelle Stefanick, email message to Neera Parikh, May 30, 2013
26   Neera Parikh, email message to Prestina Williams and James Minor, May 31, 2013

Please contact DS legal and work with them first… they can advise me on what I may or may not be able to discuss about our (DS) attempts to understand Michelle's issues, and to provide support, while supporting the Department's efforts to safeguard Michelle and other Dept. employees.
R/
Jim
SSA James Minor
Protective Intelligence Investigative Office[27]

Neera responded to Jim Minor, ccing Prestina Williams and Kevin Gleeson:

My apologies, James. I meant to cc Kevin Gleeson on the email I sent to you and Prestina and somehow did not click the proper button when in the GAL. If one of you could get back to me on this case, I would greatly appreciate, whether that be Kevin, James or Pristine.
neera
Neera Parikh, Esq.
American Foreign Service Association[28]

And speaking of DS, on Monday, June 03, 2013, Kevin Gleeson responded back to Neera and Jim Minor, ccing Prestina Williams:

Neera, Jim is out today. One of us will get back to you after we discuss the matter tomorrow.
Thanks,
Kevin
Kevin M. Gleeson
Attorney-Advisor, L/M/DS
Office of the Legal Advisor
US Department of State[29]

On Thursday, June 6, 2013, Neera sent the following to Gleeson and Minor, ccing Williams:

Kevin – I was wondering if you had a chance to consult and are ready to discuss the case with me. Please let me know. Thanks, Kevin.
neera
Neera Parikh, Esq.

27   James Minor, email message to Neera Parikh, and Prestina Williams, May 31, 2013
28   Neera Parikh, email message to Prestina Williams, James Minor, and Kevin Gleason, May 31, 2013
29   Kevin Gleason, email message to Neera Parikh, Prestina Williams, James Minor, and June 3, 2013

American Foreign Service Association[30]

On June 7, 2013, did the Commonwealth of Virginia Attorney's Office subpoenae of Dr. Adewale, for the reason still unknown to me, maybe have something to do with the reason US Department of State DS FOIA-requested documents were still not being provided to me—violating FOIA, and being purposely and intentionally delayed? Maybe it had something to do with the threatening "Informant" phone message I received on May 28, 2013? So, the question remains, given this is and always was a federal national security matter, by whom and for what reason was it transferred to a state-level court system, more specifically, the Commonwealth of Virginia Arlington County Court system? So, why, on June 7, 2013, would the Commonwealth of Virginia Attorney's Office again subpoena VHC Dr. Benjamin Adewale to testify under oath given his already fraudulent/bogus/misdiagnosis? Maybe because the cover-up could not be sustained. It was absolutely inconsistent with my entire, documented Medical file/records. Apparently, something sinister was in the planning behind the scenes. And once again with the Commonwealth of Virginia, more specifically the Commonwealth Attorney Office for Arlington County and the City of Falls Church, Virginia, under the leadership of Theo Stamos, as an apparent accomplice.

On Tuesday, June 18, 2013, I sent an email to Neera:

> Subject: RE: Stefanick draft
> Hello Neera – Just checking in – Have you heard back from DS regarding this? Following all this media/Hill interest regarding DS and OIG, I'm hoping my case is one being investigated by the "outside law enforcement agents" that have been brought in. In the meanwhile, I have not heard back from anyone regarding my situation. Any insight to share? thanks, michelle[31]

On Wednesday, June 19, 2013, Neera replied:

> Michelle – I have sent several emails to Kevin Gleeson, legal advisor to DS but have not heard back. I just returned from leave so once I get caught up – I will inquire again.
> neera
> Neera Parikh, Esq.
> American Foreign Service Association

I responded:

---

30   Neera Parikh, email message to Kevin Gleason Prestina Williams, and James Minor, June 3, 2013
31   Michelle Stefanick, email message to Neera Parikh, June 19, 2013

Thanks Neera – No problem, totally understand. In the meanwhile, I'll continue dealing with the "guardianship" court case that DS/DG generated with my father as a whistleblower/upcoming EEO hearing retaliatory act. Thanks, michelle

On Friday, June 21, 2013, I sent Neera the following:

Hello Neera – A question for you…you were going to ask Sharon for some names of really good national security lawyers that could assist me with my retaliation as a whistleblower (OSC)/upcoming eeo hearing case. All I ask is if this list of suggested lawyers could be provided in order of who you and/or Sharon would go to first and there on if either of you were in my situation. I've already approached Digenova and Toensing – but they are already representing two whistleblowers (one each). Another recommendation to me was "National Security Counselors" … any insight sincerely appreciated. Thanks, michelle [32]

Neera sent the following:

Michelle – here is a copy of our Lawyer Referral List. Unfortunately, I do not have any specific recommendations as this is a new area for me but I will talk to Sharon. Let me know if you need anything else. neera[33]

I can assure you I called every single lawyer/law firm on that list… No one would touch my case. Now, why would that be? What was really going on—and who was purposely and intentionally blocking my constitutional right to be legally represented?

ON MY OWN

Around this same time, I received an official notification letter from the Department of the Navy Office of the Judge Advocate General. This May 29, 2013 response was to my May 21, 2013 "SUBJ: FOIA Appeal" letter. The response basically stated they are working on a response and as "…we are unable to provide an estimated completion date at this time," I again waited…

At the end of June, I received another official notification letter from the Department of the Navy Office of the Judge Advocate General. This June 24, 2013 response stated that my appeal was denied as their office may only adjudicate appeals related to the release of information under the FOIA and

32   Michelle Stefanick, email message to Neera Parikh, June 21, 2013
33   Neera Parikh, email message to Michelle Stefanick, June 21, 2013

330

the Privacy Act. The letter further stated that "this office has no authority to determine the adequacy of an NCIS investigation or recommend that one be reopened. Any request of this nature must be made to NCIS."

I never heard back from NCIS SA Lisa Huff regarding a follow-up. In fact, NCIS would open and close my case without looking at any of the evidential matter nor spending any additional time with me. Interestingly, the NCIS Supervisory SA handling my case would soon after be arrested by the DOJ/FBI in connection with the "Fat Leonard" corruption Navy contract scandal. The same DOJ/FBI that did not get back with me nor protect me. The NCIS Supervisory Agent's name was John Beliveau. After his arrest, I contacted NCIS numerous times to find out their basic protocols to reopen cases, in particular mine, in such regards. To date, and as I wrote this book, I have never heard back from NCIS.

On May 30, 2013, I obtained thirty-four pages of applicable NVMHI Medical Records. And on June 20, 2013, I finally obtained 170 pages of applicable VHC medical records. Coincidently, I received them only *after* my May 8, 2013 Appeal Hearing and *after* the resulting subsequent admittance to/discharge from NVMHI. This NVMHI admittance all based on and occurring due to the *unethical, unprofessional, and untrue* testimony, under oath, by Dr. Adewale. Maintaining a daily diary/documenting notes during this entire time, I then compared and documented the missing/inaccuracies differences between my notes and these applicable obtained medical records accordingly. I was amazed as to what I found. On July 4, 2013, I drafted my applicable NVMHI and VHC disputing comments and contacted HRA Kevin Paluszak accordingly. I never heard back regarding this matter nor was I ever provided guidance as to the applicable amending NVMHI and VHC Medical Record processes. Especially now, in light of so much damage done based on VHC Dr. Patricia Roy's lack of intervention and Dr. Adewale's May 8, 2013 false sworn testimony statement I have not heard back from them.

On Wednesday, July 10, 2013, Neera emailed Gleeson and Minor, ccing Williams:

> Kevin and James – it's been well over a month since my initial inquiry regarding Michelle Stefanick's case. I have yet to receive any information regarding her situation or to obtain any responses to my questions. Can someone please get in touch with me regarding this case.
> Thanks
> neera
> Neera Parikh, Esq.

American Foreign Service Association[34]

On Monday, July 15, 2013, Neera forwarded me two email chains (FW: case inquiry – M.STEFANICK and FW: Stefanick draft), and sent the following email:

> Subject: leave
>
> Michelle – today I met with DAS Lussier regarding your request for administrative leave. DAS Lussier communicated to me that you were paneled to a position in February 5, 2013. He stated that since that time, your attendance at work has been spotty and you have often times not reported to work. Since April, you have had no contact with the Department. You have not submitted any requests for leave or any medical documentation demonstrating the need for sick leave. DAS Lussier stated that should you want to be placed on sick leave as offered through the Family Medical Leave Act – you would have to provide a doctor's note. You could then use 12 weeks of your sick leave. Otherwise, you have the option of using annual leave or to go on leave without pay. DAS Lussier asked that you reach a decision as soon as possible given then you have had no contact with the Department and the Department is considering placing you on AWOL.
>
> I made the request that you be placed on administrative leave. DAS Lussier expressed that without any issues of misconduct—he could not place you on administrative leave as prescribed under 3 FAM 3464.1-2.
>
> Please let me know what your decision is so I can convey it to him and Bill Schaal. Also, I am attaching AFSA's attorney referral list to this email. neera[35]

I responded to Neera, ccing Papp:

> Neera – I'm not sure who DAS Lussier is but seems he needs to have a discussion with U/S Patrick Kennedy and DG Linda Thomas-Greenfield as well as DS because the information he as provided to you is not completely accurate. The Department (DS and HR) coordinated my involuntary "TDO" with my family and Arlington County on April 12 to Virginia Hospital Center. DS Agents Jim Minor and Prestina Williams were at my home when the events occurred. Upon being released from this "involuntary detention" I filed a whistleblower retaliation with Office of Special Counsel against the Department.

34   Neera Parikh, email message to Kevin Gleason, James Minor, and Prestina Williams,, July 10, 2013
35   Neera Parikh, email message to Michelle Stefanick, July 15, 2013

Therefore, I find it quite curious that DAS Lussier, if with HR, is not aware since DG coordinated all retaliatory action with my father, to include the petition of guardianship, which was coincidentally agreed to "non-suited" with my court-appointed attorney the exact same day I heard from Bill Schaal email was forwarded to you. Supposedly, the "non-suited" guardianship petition was presented in front of Judge on Friday, July 12, but I still have not received confirmation back from my court-appointed attorney on Judge's approval. The Department has been in communication/coordination and cooperation with my father for all the retaliatory acts that were taken against me up to the date of presenting this "non-suit" to the court on July 12.

Again, in light of the ongoing DS investigation as well as my complaint with the Office of Special Counsel, I request to be placed on Administrative leave. If the Department denies that, as it appears from your email below per DAS Lussier that they have, I then will request to be placed on Annual leave effective now—July 15—for as to submit a request to now be placed on Sick Leave – on my own accord – would be fraudulent.

I would go into more detail but again since I filed an official whistleblower retaliatory complaint with the Office of Special Counsel against the Department, particularly DS and HR, if my request for Administrative leave is denied, than I request to go on Annual leave at this time. Thanks, michelle [36]

At 3:20 P.M., I forwarded this email chain to HFAC/Benghazi Legal Counsel Thomas Alexander…

I believe this was the first time AFSA, DS, HR and HFAC heard about my OSC complaint. As this was the first time that I found out I had been *officially paneled* to a new position on February 5, 2013—though I never received any official personnel documentation, nor had any input to any *position*. I was very curious about what specific position I was officially paneled into by State/DG Linda Thomas-Greenfield—the same Linda Thomas-Greenfield to whom I provided my eight-page handwritten *Whistleblower Protection Request* letter, the Ambassador to Liberia when I was assigned to MARFOREUR/AF, and who was assigned with me to Embassy Nairobi.

On Tuesday, July 16, 2013, Neera sent an email to State/HR Philippe Lussier and William Schaal, ccing me:

---

36   Michelle Stefanick, email message to Neera Parikh and Sharon Papp, July 3, 2013

TELL THE TRUTH—UNTIL THEY DON'T LIKE WHAT YOU HAVE TO SAY

DAS Lussier – I would like to thank you for meeting with me yesterday regarding Michelle Stefanick's case. Ms. Stefanick has asked that I relay the following: in light of the ongoing DS security clearance investigation, the whistleblower retaliation complaint filed with the Office of Special Counsel against the Department particularly DS and HR, and all other ongoing investigations, Michelle is requesting that she be placed on Administrative Leave until such investigations are completed and for all parties concerned. Based on our discussion yesterday, Michelle understands that the decision to place an employee on administrative leave rests with the Department. Should the Department decide against placing Michelle on administrative leave, Michelle requests that she be placed on annual leave effective July 15th until further notice.

Please let me know if you have any questions or would like to discuss this further.

Thanks

neera

Neera Parikh, Esq.

American Foreign Service Association[37]

Philippe Lussier responded to AFSA Neera Parikh and HR William Schaal, ccing myself and Ben Lam:

Neera thank-you. The Administrative leave we discussed is associated with disciplinary action and there is no disciplinary action pending. As discussed Ms. Stefanik's [sic] choices are to:

Report to her assigned supervisor in the HR/EX Budget Division, Mr. Ben Lam for her work assignments

Take Sick Leave with documentation from medical professional if greater than 3 days (for either her or a family member)

Take Leave without pay

Take Annual leave

Given that you have communicated these choices to her we will place her on annual leave effective July 15th.

I would ask that she check-in; either phone-call, email, or in person at the end of each work week (Thurs or Friday) to let us know of her work status for the upcoming week whether she will continue on annual leave or report for work as we will be required to fill out Time and Attendance sheets for her and/or have work ready for her to do so. She may contact Mr. Ben Lam, her supervisor, [email address removed], [redacted].

Many thanks, Phil

37   Neera Parikh, email message to Philippe Lussier, William Schaal, and Michelle Stefanick, July 16, 2013

Philippe A. Lussier
Deputy Assistant Secretary
Bureau of Human Resources[38]

Again, the my last name was misspelled by a US Department of State HR official. And as DAS Lussier stated that I was assigned to HR/EX, where's the official personnel panel/orders paperwork? I never received any during that time.

As requested, on Thursday July 18, 2013; Friday July 26, 2013; Thursday August 1, 2013; Thursday August 8, 2013; Friday August 16, 2013; and Thursday, August 22, 2013, I sent an email to Ben Lam, ccing Phil Lussier, William Schaal, Neera Parikh, Linda Thomas-Greenfield, Patrick Kennedy, and Sharon Papp:

> Ben – In light of all the ongoing investigations and the retaliatory action against me by the Department, as my request for Administrative Leave has been denied pending the outcome of these investigations, I will be on annual leave once again next week. Michelle[39]

And as requested, on Friday, August 30, 2013, I sent an email to Lam, ccing Lussier, Schaal, Parikh, Thomas-Greenfield, Kennedy, Papp, and Klemm:

> Ben – In light of all the ongoing investigations and the retaliatory action against me by the Department, as my request for Administrative Leave has been denied pending the outcome of these investigations, I will be on annual leave once again next week.
> For the record, it is and continues to be unconstitutional for the Department/USG's ongoing "targeting/scapegoating" of me because I'm Orthodox. With that, Patricia (Pat) Hartnett-Kelly was also advised that "obstruction of justice" applies to all, including members of the law enforcement, federal agent and Diplomatic Services Community.[40]

Interesting given its timing, writing these words that I first wrote on Friday, August 30, 2013, just recently, October 27, 2019, CNN aired "DE-CLASSIFIED: Untold Stories of American Spies." The commentator for

38   Philippe Lussier, email message to Neera Parikh, William Schaal, Michelle Stefanick, and Ben Lam, July 16, 2013
39   Michelle Stefanick, email message to Ben Lam, Philippe Lussier, William Schaal, Neera Parikh, Linda Thomas-Greenfield, Patrick Kennedy, and Sharon Papp, on July 18, July 26, August 1, August 8, August 16, and August 22, 2013
40   Michelle Stefanick, email message to Ben Lam, Philippe Lussier, William Schaal, Neera Parikh, Linda Thomas-Greenfield, Patrick Kennedy, Sharon Papp, and Hans Klemm on and August 30, 2013

this CNN "DECLASSIFED" series: former US House Chairman of the House Permanent Select Committee on Intelligence Michael Rogers. The very HPSCI Chairman Mike Rogers who received a copy of my November 27, 2012 Whistleblower/Protection Letter Request, who never contacted me, and more importantly, who never protected me. And now this specific episode, "The Spy Game: Russian Espionage" was regarding FBI and DS monitoring and the discovery of an "armchair railing listening device" in a US Department of State Seventh-Floor conference room. Blaming the Russians, of course. What is of particular interest regarding this episode was its timing and the timeline of events depicted, an overlapping of events, but absolutely no mention nor reference, the August 7, 1998 East Africa Embassy bombings...

On Wednesday, September 4, 2013, William Schaal sent an email to Lam and me, ccing Lussier, Parikh, Kennedy, Papp, Klemm and Thomas-Greenfield:

> Michelle,
> I appreciate your email. Our records indicate that after you take 80 hrs annual leave for the current pay period 17, you should have a balance of 52 hours at the start of PP 18 (September 8). Please review this information and determine how you will proceed.
> Sincerely,
> William E. Schaal, Jr., Executive Director
> Bureau of Human Resources[41]

I responded to Schaal and Lam, ccing Lussier, Parikh, Kennedy, Papp, Klem and Thomas-Greenfield:

> Thank you Bill – Considering the unconstitutional and illegal due process rights that the Department/USG violated/took against me in their "scapegoating/targeting" investigations because of my Orthodox religious faith; as well as now taking retaliatory action against me not only because of my upcoming EEO Grievance against the military and their action in Stuttgart, Germany and the role of Department played in that action; and more recently the retaliatory actions against me as a whistleblower to include the involuntary 'TDO' action that the Department took the lead in with Arlington County and my family; and now to deny my requests to be placed on Administrative leave until all applicable investigations were completed resulting as a another form of retaliation for me to

---

41   William Schaal, email message to Ben Lam, Michelle Stefanick, Philippe Lussier, Neera Parikh, Patrick Kennedy, Sharon Papp, Hans Klemm, and Linda Thomas-Greenfield, September 4, 2013

336

use all my Annual leave; as well as other such actions; your question is a very good one. With my OIG/Auditing experience and my CPA professional background, the above is beyond appalling and indeed unconstitutional and illegal, with obstruction of justice applying to al that played their applicable role with the lack of accountability even more so.

If you could please advise for my consideration my options to include what benefits I would receive if I would resign effective the time my annual leave runs out that would be fantastic. If you could also advise what such investigations will be taken by the Department to the above and for the above, that insight would also be appreciated. Thank you, michelle[42]

I then patiently waited for the response. That said, I continued to send some very lengthy, extensive, detailed emails from Thursday, September 5-12, 2013, including many attachments, to Schaal and Lam, ccing Lussier, Parikh, Kennedy, Papp, Klem and Thomas-Greenfield. I debated whether to include these applicable emails here, and decided, at this time, not to. This was not because of any concern on my part, but because of a one-on-one conversation with Bill Schaal in his office on February 25, 2013.

During this conversation, not only did 9/11 come up—*though why 9/11 came up given I was overseas at the time I don't know, maybe because of Bill's supposed Air Force background, as I recall*—but Bill revealed something else during that quite odd conversation. Was it true what he revealed? I don't know. Was it yet another gotcha play? I don't know. But for that reason, and what Bill Schaal revealed—true or not—I have decided not to include the September 5-12, 2013 emails. However, what it did pertain to was his wife. Why he mentioned her, brought her up to begin with, I don't know. Just remember all the entities involved so far in this narrative, to include that one of the three letters, CIA. Just remember, in Pat Hartnett-Kelly's May 30, 2011 email, Embassy Nairobi was a major CIA station, and the August 7, 1998 East Africa Embassy bombings, an inside job. Need I say more—because if I do, will I be subjected to yet another round of retaliation with and after the publication of this book? Its publication already delayed two years. Despite and regardless of *my* supposed federal protected first-hand victim/witness status in regards to the August 7, 1998 East Africa Embassy bombings, this federally protect-

42   Michelle Stefanick, email message to William Schaal, Ben Lam, Philippe Lussier, Neera Parikh, Linda Thomas-Greenfield, Patrick Kennedy, and Sharon Papp, on July 18, July 26, August 1, August 8, August 16, and August 22, 2013

ed status *ignored, disregarded* just like before, and all the times previously. And then again, after my applicable connecting the dots, a-ha moment in the immediate aftermath of the September 11, 2012 attack of Diplomatic Post Benghazi.

Meanwhile, on Monday, July 1, 2013, I sent an email to NCIS FOIA Point of contact, US Navy Lt Matthew Roush:

> Subject: FOIA Response
> Hello Lt. Roush – On Saturday I received your office's response to my request dated June 24, 2013. According to the memo, if I had further questions or concerns, I was supposed to contact you, as my noted point of contact. Earlier I left you a message to discuss. If you could return my call at 703-243-1039. I would appreciate it. Thank you, Michelle Stefanick[43]

Lt Roush returned my call soon after. I followed-up with this email:

> Subject: RE: FOIA Response/Request for reopening NCIS case – Stefanick
> Hello Lt Roush – As discussed in our telcon of just a few minutes ago, it is my understanding per our discussion that your office, though JAGs, is totally outside the NCIS command. The June 24, 2013 response addresses just the FOIA not the NCIS command/ reopening case request, and therefore you all have no such fiduciary responsibility to refer accordingly. With that, you provided me the name of Michael Monroe of NCIS [redacted] to contact.
>
> Also based on our discussion, though the May 23, 2013 letter I also sent to Vice Admiral De Renzi regarding this matter at the recommendation from BGen Gross, Chairman Dempsey's JAG was not specifically referenced in the June 24 response letter I received from your office, the letter is supposedly a consolidated response per discussion/correspondence between your two offices. With that, as noted in our discussion, I kindly request written confirmation to that fact – either by email or by separate letter from your office – that I should not expect nor will not receive a separate response to my May 23 letter addressed directly to Vice Admiral De Renzi.
>
> Additionally, I kindly request the title of Michael Monroe, the NCIS point of contact you provided, so I can contact him accordingly once I receive written confirmation whether or not to expect an official response on behalf of Vice Admiral De Renzi regarding this FOIA request/content inaccuracies warranting reopening this

NCIS investigative case. Thank you, michelle[44]

Lt Matt Roush responded:

Ms. Stefanick,

You may consider this email as confirmation that you should not expect to receive separate correspondence from VADM DeRenzi regarding your FOIA appeal and related letter to VADM DeRenzi of May 23. Mr. Lattin's letter of 24 June is the department's final response regarding your FOIA appeal.

Since our last phone conversation, this office contacted NCIS administrators to determine the appropriate office for submission of your request to reopen the investigation. We were informed that instead of submitting your request to Mr. Monroe, who is located at the Washington Field Office, they would prefer that you submit your request directly to NCIS Headquarters at the following address:

NCIS Criminal Investigations Directorate
27130 Telegraph Road
Quantico, VA 22134-2253

I hope this information is helpful.

V/r,

LT Matt Roush, US Navy
Office of the Judge Advocate General
General Litigation Division (Code 14)[45]

I replied:

Thank you for your response LT Roush. It is duly noted.

I'm unclear as to the hierarchy of NCIS so for clarification, considering the NCIS Criminal Investigations Directorate at Quantico is where the initial NCIS investigation was conducted from and inadequately/insufficiently done and of which I'm asking for "re-opening," is referring this back to the "lion's den" really the appropriate location for referral?

This may appear to be demeaning in my comments, but considering the situation and the appearance of an unprofessionally conducted investigation from those as an American you look to uphold the constitution and due process rights and outreached to accordingly, it was quite disappointing.

Do you have a specific name to sent the request to NCIS Headquarters? Thank you, Michelle[46]

44   Michelle Stefanick, email message to Matthew Roush, July 1, 2013
45   Matthew Roush, email message to Michelle Stefanick, July 1, 2013
46   Michelle Stefanick, email message to Matthew Roush, July 1, 2013

Needless to say, I never received another response back from Lt Roush. Given all the laws and rights, my constitutional rights, that had been broken and violated to this point, I found the "CONFIDENTIALITY NOTICE" at the bottom of Lt Roush's email quite ironic and quite pathetic. Given the timeline of events and the facts, that is, for any honest, professional criminal investigator throughout the entire USG, the US Military and US Law Enforcement community really wanting the truth and justice. But quite obviously, for some reason, that was not the case. Quite obviously, for some reason I was a pawn in somone's cover-up.

And this conclusion I made was before I would finally obtain pertinent, relevant FOIA documents that absolutely supported my conclusion. I did not realize how far back the set-up had been occurring and who the actual players involved were the whole entire time!

I forwarded this email chain to HFAC Benghazi Investigator/Counsel Thomas Alexander, who apparently assisted in getting me immediately released from NVMHI, and I personally met with him soon after that release.

On Thursday, July 4, 2013, I sent the following email update to HFAC Benghazi Investigator/Counsel Tom Alexander as well:

Hello Tom – I just wanted to bring you up to date on 'NCIS response to my request for reopening my case' in this email and will forward you another regarding DS's lack of response to AFSA Legal regarding my Security Clearance aspect to my situation. As I find all this extremely odd, and in light of all that is being exposed/investigated by the Hill to include DOJ/IRS/DS and OIG community, maybe you all need to expand to these "military service law enforcement entities" as well....

With that, I have not received a response back to my email below from LT Matthew Roush. However, I would like you to have the status of my outreach to NCIS in light of my email exchange with Lt. Roush. Since I did not have a specific name at NCIS Headquarters at Quantico, I outreached to Michael Monroe, NCIS Washington Field Office, at [redacted] (the number provided by Lt Roush – [redacted] – was overall office number I believe).

On 7/1/2013 I left a telephone message at approximately 3:20 p.m. for Michael Monroe requesting he return my call and request to reopen my case that was conducted by SA Lisa Huff, from Quantico Headquarters.

On 7/2/2013, since Michael Monroe had not returned my call, called him again at approximately 11:52 a.m. During our discussion I went into some additional detail without providing the exact

USMC General's name but enough for him to "connect the dots" just as I did during our initial telephone conversation. He apologized for not getting back to me but said that I should expect a call from SA Agent Manly or Manning (sp?). He said that she probably had not outreached to me yet because he had asked her to outreach to SA Huff in regards to the case details of which I responded that it was insufficient and that she never came back to actually review any files, as well as the limitation of scope the Army Criminal Investigative Division asked me to keep to in my initial discussions with SA Huff, of which ACID attended, but that SA Huff never came back to see all the details and linkages that I provided to you all, with even more details to share, when she came back. Which she never did. I then explained to Michael Monroe who all I've provided insight to, this ACID "requested' scope limitation during only NCIS interview—just to focus on financial transaction and a very brief time frame of less than an hour. Again, I mentioned some other names linked and the sensitivity involved to include the law enforcement/intelligence/military cross paradigm dimensions to this information and applauded the 5-prong approach in Chairman Issa's investigation of Benghazi of which my information is possibly linked. Michael ended by saying that I should expect a call from SA Manly. I noted that though my information is not "classified per se" from any top secret/classified document, I just asked that she be properly cleared to the possible "black" scoping of where this may go based on who my information is linked to... he said that will not be an issue and can be addressed. (which I believe was the situation with SA Huff).

Later that day, at approximately 5:14 p.m., a received a telephone message from SA John Beliveau to return his call at [redacted] stating that Michael Monroe told him to call me since he was familiar with my case. (I immediately called/left Michael Monroe a message asking for confirmation that that was the case since he had told me to expect a call from SA Manly).

I then returned SA Beliveau's call first leaving a message on the number he provided in the message, and then calling the number he called from [redacted]. Needless to say, the conversation did not go well since he is SA Lisa Huff's boss and reviewed her case, which was closed. I told him the investigation was incomplete and so stated including why. He then asked me for all the names of all the investigators I had contacted from various law enforcement entities and the names of the individuals. I said in light of what I read regarding SA Huff's report, I don't believe he should be the one I provide this insight to. The hung up and called/left a message again with Michael Monroe—who did not call back that day.

On July 3, I called back to NCIS Quantico to speak to John to obtain the proper spelling of his last name. He was "not in," so the woman that answered the phone provided the proper spelling to me. Throughout the entire day, I kept call Michael Monroe's number and the office number—no one answered and no one returned my call.

I wanted to provide you where I was in the process with NCIS, how odd I find all this, and my plans to continue again on Friday and next week, to try to obtain someone from NCIS to come to see/be provided the information/linkages to the USMC/Navy Officers, so they can have the information that the other investigative entities have and to reopen the case and properly investigate the allegation. With that, my concern is "command influence" in light of the military officials involved—thus, the reason I'm letting you know. Thanks, michelle[47]

On Friday, July 5, 2013, I sent Tom an update:

Hello Tom – As a follow-up, at 8:05 a.m., I briefly spoke with Agent Nayda Mannie, NCIS Washington Field Office, who was supposed to contact me. She was very abrupt and said that SA Beliveau handled it, and that was discussed with SA Monroe. I said I disagree—this was not handled/investigated. She hung up.

I then called and left a message for Michael Monroe stating what SA Mannie had said and stated that if SA Beliveau did a thorough investigation why did he ask me on July 2 for the names of those officers I was implicating; why did he ask me for the names of the agents of the other investigators I met with—which is exactly to my point, for if he did such a thorough job with this investigation/ came back for additional information he would have known all the names as I would have provided during the interview—which was never done/done properly. I believe in the law enforcement community they call this "obstruction of justice" and in military they call this potentially "command influence."

I then stated Gen Lake, Gen Paxton, Gen Hejlik, Gen Garrett, Gen Glueck, ADM Stavridis, former CNO Roughead and potentially others linked to this… With that, I hope now someone from NCIS will be contacting me accordingly.

Again, I find this quite curious that NCIS won't come to see all the information/evidential matter that I have, let alone properly investigate this... I hope you can pass along accordingly or at least realize how wide this situation potential is... Thanks, michelle[48]

NCIS never got back in touch with me and never reopened my case...

In light of the first round of *medical* retaliatory actions taken against me, on Tuesday, August 6, 2013, I received an email from Lorrie Stanton:

> Subject: Security Clearance
> Ms. Stefanick,
> Your file was referred to this office by the Dept. of State, Diplomatic Security Office for review because of your medical history. The psychologist performing your evaluation (Dr. Filson or Dr. Ubben) and I would like to access your medical records relating to your medical clearance to aid in our review and would like your permission. Please email me back with your authorization.
> Thank you,
> Lorrie Stanton RN, MSN, ANP
> US Department of State
> Office of Medical Services[49]

I forwarded to AFSA/Legal Counsel Neera Parikh, ccing Papp, with the following:

> Hello Neera – I received this email today from Med. I wanted your advisement on how to respond – whether you should do so on my behalf. Also if you have heard anything more from DS regarding their investigation. Thanks, michelle[50]

On Wednesday, August 7, 2013, Neera replied:

> Michelle – this is standard with regards to a security clearance investigation. DS asks MED to make a determination about whether an employee is suitable for continued clearance. Should you decide not to submit to the evaluation and/or agree to give MED access to your medical records – MED cannot make a determination and it will hold up the process and possibly move DS to revoke your clearance. I advise that you comply with MED's request. The correspondence must be sent by the employee as your medical records are governed by the Privacy Act. Let me know if you have any other questions. neera[51]

I responded to Neera:

---

48   Michelle Stefanick, email message to Thomas Alexander, July 5, 2013
49   Lorrie Stanton, email message to Michelle Stefanick, August 6, 2013
50   Michelle Stefanick, phone call to Neera Parikh and Sharon Papp, August 6, 2013
51   Neera Parikh, email message to Michelle Stefanick, August 7, 2013

> Ok – Thanks Neera. I have nothing to hide so they can review – I just didn't know in regards to protocol/procedure on whether I should respond back with my authorization or you, as my AFSA rep, should be doing it. Should I cc you in my response back to Med agreeing to their accessing my medical records? Thanks, michelle[52]

Neera replied:

> You can cc me but the request has to come directly from you. neera[53]

I responded:

> ok – Thanks. Cheers, michelle

So, on August 7, 2013, I sent the following email response to Lorraine Stanton, ccing Neera:

> Hello Lorrie – Sorry for the delay in responding to your request. I wanted to consult my AFSA Legal representative before responding.
> Sure, the psychologist (Dr. Filson or Dr. Ubben) and you (Lorrie Stanton) have my permission to access my medical records relating to my medical clearance to assist with your evaluation. Thanks, Michelle[54]

Lorrie Stanton responded:

> Thank you!
> Lorrie Stanton RN, MSN, ANP
> US Department of StateOffice of Medical Services[55]

I forwarded the email chain to HFAC Benghazi Investigator/Legal Counsel Thomas Alexander.

I found it absolutely ironic that I was being submitted to this retaliatory action, continuing retaliatory action, and writing such emails defending myself and regarding my security clearance to MED after all I had been through—on August 7, 2013, the 15th anniversary of the East Africa Embassy bombings. How ironic. However, at this point, I still would not be advised/informed regarding how long this retaliation was really going on—behind my back—until many months later, and after yet another round of retaliatory actions taken against me…

52   Michelle Stefanick, phone call to Neera Parikh and Sharon Papp, August 7, 2013
53   Neera Parikh, email message to Michelle Stefanick, August 7, 2013
54   Michelle Stefanick, email message to Lorrie Stanton and Neera Parikh, August 7, 2013
55   Lorrie Stanton, email message to Michelle Stefanick, August 7, 2013

On Wednesday, August 7, 2013, the 15th anniversary of the East Africa Embassy bombings, at 9:41 a.m., I sent the following email to the now retired TDY Embassy Addis Ababa, Ethiopia Defense Attache that accompanied me back to Nairobi on August 8, 1998, Michael Mensch.

Subject: Thank you…
Michael – Because of you, I'm able to write this email. Fifteen years ago today you saved my life… and now there may be more truth to that then I understood just a year ago. So thank you.

With that, I attach for your files/safe keeping a copy of the document provided to OSD Security on Oct 25 – 26, 2012, of which they never responded/outreached to me which has put me in the situation that I'm now in.

While at OSD/African Affairs, I had a revelation coupled with occurrences that using the cliché, helped me "connect the dots." On the morning of Oct 24, 2012, I met with Mark Swayne (my immediate Director) and CAPT Scott Organ (our office's Security Officer) to raise my concerns and necessity to share accordingly within proper OSD channels without going into specifics. CAPT Organ then outreached to OSD/Security and advised the situation of which he was told to bring a written statement. CAPT Organ drafted the first version, of which I made edits. On October 25, CAPT Organ and I went over the written statement, as attached, that he then took to OSD/Security Ivory London to share. According to CAPT Organ, he was advised to come back the next day to meet with Ivory's boss to discuss/share. On October 26, CAPT Organ met with OSD/Security Mike Brooks to discuss/share and was advised that this was going to be shared up the chain, and with higher-ups. Once I received this feedback, I patiently waited.

In the meanwhile, in early November, I attended the USMC Birthday Cake-Cutting event at State and afterwards ran into Linda Thomas-Greenfield (or did she run into me). Linda said she had been thinking/concerned about me and works out near my home and wanted to stop by sometime. I said sure anytime… with that, she said she was traveling and would get back with me on a proposed date. Within the next day or two, she came back with a proposed evening of Tuesday November 27, 2012, after her workout. I said sure.

By November 23, not hearing back from OSD/Security, DS and/or Department of Justice; coupled with all the information that was emerging from the Benghazi incident; and in reflection of what has occurred to me; that weekend, I handwrote the "whistleblower protection" letter that I read/gave to Linda on the evening of November 27 when she came to my house –unaware that I was going to give the letter to her. She, the Director General of the Foreign Service, took the letter, and a few days later responded, that she shared with Pat Kennedy and nothing more she could do.

To date, I have never heard back from OSD/Security, through assistance of Senator Snowe and her office but obstacles galore finally spoke with FBI on January 8, 2013; and finally met with two DS agents, through Pat Kennedy assistance, on March 20, 2013. I also shared with ACID, NCIS (with limited/narrow focus per ACID/NCIS instruction) prior to State Department's retaliatory action of April 12; and HFAC Investigators (after their assistance of getting me discharged from NVHMI) after my discharge. I have details/times/dates/names of all and other individuals/entities as well.

But the question remains—why didn't OSD/Security, DS and/ or DOJ outreach back to me from my original request of October 24-26, 2012. Why did Linda have such "a concern" for me? Who met with my estranged family/father? Why didn't PM request a "termination financial disclosure" form from me when I departed Stuttgart in July 2011, and only for me to be informed of this requirement over a year later by L, of which I immediately completed and met/discussed with Pat Kennedy on September 27, 2012? Why didn't DS ever get back to me other than 1 phone call on January 17, 2012 while I was at OSD regarding the identity theft issue that I reported to them/but never was never interviewed by in October 2011? Why did I have a security clearance investigator come to see me in Stuttgart from Frankfurt in 2010 and then another "ds investigation" when I left OSD 2012? Per the other indicators I mentioned to you in our 9/6/2012 discussion—was I the subject of any investigation by DS and/or any other USG law enforcement or other entity from approximately 2008-2011, maybe even earlier and maybe even later? If so, what was/is the allegation and what about my constitutional/due process rights? Hopefully these are answers I will soon get once I have legal representation.

Before departing OSD, Mark Swayne made a passing comment to me that Linda was definitely talking to someone in the Pentagon/OSD… and once no one was getting back to me per our OSD/Security outreach in Oct 2012, CAPT Organ made a comment that I definitely need to talk with FBI. And finally, why did the other person that came to my house strongly imply/stated that there was a higher level investigation going on and why did I see the "specific number and specific word' enough to become more than a coincidence. And now the rest of the events that occurred, continue to occur...

So with that, 15 years after the most life changing experience event in my life, a chapter that was almost closed but never completely healed, has been ripped wide open once again and damaging to me once again today at a level as in comparison to the dreadful day of August 7, 1998.

Michael—why?[56]

Why? Why? Why? I just didn't understand why. Knowing what I knew, I had a theory... and then oddly enough, I would obtain more and more information and insight, expanding the depth and magnitude of what was really going on and more importantly, the significance of what I knew. Considering how long it took me to connect the dots when I did, once I did, there was no turning back... I had and did accept the unbelievable and unfathomable. And with my piece, when I was given more and more information and insight, all the pieces fell together enabling to clearly see how they all were interconnected and interrelated. So, with that, I had to try a new approach...

Like indicated previously, I contacted so many lawyers and law firms up to this point and throughout this entire ordeal that the list of those names could be a book on its own. However, there was one lawyer to whom I had not reached out. At this time, with the 15th anniversary just passing, I decided it was time I did—knowingly taking what would be perceived as a very partisan move. I contacted Robert Barnett.

I had met Bob years previously at the RWs I attended in Charleston, S.C. While attending the Army War College, I also sent Bob a copy of my SRP. Bob was a good friend of the Clinton's, and no doubt a copy of my SRP went to the new Secretary of State at the time, Hillary Clinton. Not knowing for sure if Secretary Clinton was aware or not of all that occurred, I took a chance. I contacted Bob with the intent of confirming whether or not former Secretary Clinton was indeed aware... Given that the August 7, 1998 East Africa Embassy bombings occurred during President Clinton's tenure, was she/were they aware of all the retaliatory actions being taken against me? Not only was I a survivor to that horrific event, but I was also a federal CVRA protected victim/witness regarding the August 7, 1998 East Africa Embassy bombings that connected dots regarding our Benghazi Diplomatic Post. Did she/he/they know?

---

56   Michelle Stefanick, email message to Michael Mensch, August 7, 2013

I located the previous January 20-21, 2009 email exchange I had with Bob Barnett, and forwarded it accordingly so he would and could clearly link the connection for recollection as to who I was. On Tuesday, August 13, 2013, I forwarded Bob the email chain with the following:

> Subject: RE: Renaissance Weekend – Stefanick Strategic Research Paper
>
> Hello Bob – It's been a very long time and hope all is well.
>
> Bob – On a very serious note, it is my understanding that you are representing Gen Petraeus. I wanted to outreach to you because I find myself in a situation that has a possible linkage to the General and his situation that I wanted to share with you. It may be nothing, but then again it may be something. And with that I at least wanted to bring this to your attention. Thank you, michelle[57]
>
> Date: Wed, 21 Jan 2009 07:31:28 -0500
>
> Thank you Bob. Have a great day! Cheers, m
>
> Date: Tue, 20 Jan 2009 17:47:10 -0500
>
> That is great. I am very happy to have this and look forward to reading it. Hope to see you soon. Thank again.
>
> Subject: Renaissance Weekend – Stefanick Strategic Research Paper
>
> Date: Tue 1/20/2009 11:43 a.m.
>
> Greetings from the Army War College Bob! How wonderful it was to see you at Renaissance. And how wonderful—all the excitement about a new President and new Administration.
>
> Per our brief discussion in Charleston, it is in that context that I'm attaching the Strategic Research Paper I just submitted here. It's called Powell's Leadership Principles—Time for State Department to Revisit. Its not meant to be critical, but observations to move our institution forward from the eye of one perspective. Since many here have read and others want to read, thought only appropriate to share with you as well, so you can share accordingly. As its not only in my interest, the new Secretary of State's, or even the new President's …but in our nation's interest that I share it with you.
>
> Have a great day! Thank you, Bob, I really appreciate your assistance. Cheers, michelle[58]

At 3:27 P.M., Bob, ccing David Kendall, replied:

57   Michelle Stefanick, email message to Robert Barnett, August 13, 2013
58   Forwarded email exchange between Michelle Stefanick and Robert Barnett, January 20-21 2009

Good to hear from you. The person to speak with is my partner, David Kendall, who is copied here. His number is [redacted]. He is here through tomorrow afternoon and is expecting your call.59

David Kendall would reply to Bob Barnett:

Have just talked to France (Francis Hoang), of Fluet Huber Hoang PLC, and he will be expecting Michelle's call. His office # is: [rdacted]. I worked a lot with him when he was here – he's the best.
David E. Kendall
Williams & Connolly, LLP[60]

Bob, in turn, emailed me:

See below. France is an excellent attorney. His firm works extensively in the national security area. He was with our firm for several years. He is expecting your call.[61]

Extremely grateful, I would send the following email to Bob:

Bob – Thank you so much. I just left a call with France. Hopefully once he hears what I have to say the insight I have to share can be passed/beneficial accordingly to you all as well. Thank you, michelle.[62]

On Thursday, August 14, 2013, I went to the law office of Fluet Huber Hoang PLLC in Alexandria, Virginia. France and I met in a conference room, with Hugh Quinn walking in and out of our meeting. The meeting was not long, but I believe it was convincing to France Maybe not to Hugh, however, because he wasn't in the meeting the entire time. At the time, and even more so now in reflection, I felt that though Hugh was not paying much attention to me or what I was saying, something more, much more was going on behind the scene. France thanked me for coming in, stating that he didn't know what more his firm could do at this time, but he would be passing on some additional referrals. Though the meeting didn't go as intended, applicable lawyers and attorneys were aware of me and what I knew. Again, though the time was limited, I provided only the tip-of-the-iceberg of all the pieces and how they all fit together. I have

---

59   Robert Barnett, email message to Michelle Stefanick and David Kendall, August 13, 2013

60   David Kendall, email message to Robert Barnett, August 13, 2013

61   Robert Barnett, email message to Michelle Stefanick and David Kendall, August 13, 2013

62   Michelle Stefanick, email message to Robert Barnett, August 13, 2013

no doubt France understood the national security implications of what I shared.

I sent Bob a follow-up email regarding my meeting:

> Hello Bob – I want to thank you so much for arranging this. Though it did little help my situation per se, they now have the insight that can be shared with you all accordingly and hopefully is a piece in the puzzle, who's ever puzzle it is. It felt good to get it off my chest and to discuss with folks that have the applicable background to understand at least the possibility to the implications that I make. France plans on passing on some additional referrals. In the meanwhile, I ask that you think of me if you don't mind to overcome what has been done to me for whatever reason it happened...the impact to me personally has been devastating. Thanks again Bob. Cheers, michelle[63]

Bob replied:

> Okay. I was glad to hear from you, and I wish you well.[64]

On Friday, August 16, 2013, France sent the following email to me and Brian O'Shea:

> Subject: Introduction
> Michelle,
> As promised, here's an introduction to a Private Investigator I know and trust implicitly. Brian O'Shea is a former Special Forces Operator who now leads Striker-Pierce Investigations (http://www.strikerpierce.com/). He has the perfect background to assist you in the financial investigation we discussed.
> I'll leave it to you two connect.
> Best,
> France
> Francis Q. Hoang I Partner
> Fluet Huber + Hoang PLLC[65]

I replied to France and Brian:

> France – Thank you so very much for meeting with me yesterday and this introduction. I really really appreciate it.
> Hello Brian – With France's strong endorsement, I really look forward to your assistance regarding my situation. You can contact me on this email or give me a call at [redacted].

63   Michelle Stefanick, email message to Robert Barnett, August 14, 2013
64   Robert Barnett, email message to Michelle Stefanick, August 14, 2013
65   Francis Hoang, email message to Michelle Stefanick and Brian O'Shea, August 16, 2013

Again, thank you France. Cheers, michelle[66]

On Saturday, August 17, 2013, I received a response from Brian, ccing France:

Hello,
First, thank you to France for the warm introduction. Michelle, please let me know a good time to call you so we can discuss your situation and possibly take some steps forward. Please feel free to call me at [redacted] or I will contact you at [redacted].
Thank you,
Brian O'Shea
Private Investigator (VA, DCJS 99-242321)[67]

I responded to Brian, ccing France:

Hello Brian – Thanks so much for getting back with me. I'm available to talk, including now. Please call anytime. Thanks so much. cheers, michelle[68]

Meanwhile, I received another email introduction from France with Dr. Amir Afhkami, ccing Emily Taggart:

Subject: Introduction
Michelle – As discussed, Dr. Amir Afhkami has an impressive academic and operational background and has expressed a willingness to meet with you and your father for a consult at the FH+H offices. I'll leave it to you both to coordinate a time/date for a meeting. Emily Taggart (cc'd) can help coordinate the use of the FH+H conference room in Alexandria.
Warm Regards,
France[69]

So why did France Hoang make this e-introduction? From my perspective, meeting with Dr. Amir after all that I had just been subjected to with VHC Dr. Benjamin Adewale was not going to happen. I absolutely would not be set-up once again. So again, why France made this introduction, I have no idea.

And then on Saturday, August 17, 2013, I received this email from France:

66   Michelle Stefanick, email message to Francis Hoang and Brian O'Shea, August 16, 2013
67   Brian O'Shea, email message to Michelle Stefanick and Francis Hoang, August 17, 2013
68   Michelle Stefanick, email message to Brian O'Shea and Francis Hoang, August 17, 2013
69   Francis Hoang, email message to Michelle Stefanick, Amir Afhkami, and Emily Taggart, August 17, 2013

Subject: Dr. Amir Afhkami

Michelle,

I spoke with Dr. Amir Afhkami, a good friend of mine who has significant experience with the Department of Defense, overseas operations of various types, and is a renowned and much sought after medical professional by the Special Operations and Intelligence communities. He's a professor at George Washington University Medical Center, and holds a Top-Secret clearance. I believe he's one of a handful of people in the world who has a necessary background, experience, and open-mindedness to help you answer some of the questions you have.

I've told him a little about your situation. Amir has agreed to meet with you pro-bono at my offices for a consult. He asked, however, that your father also be present because he believes your father may have information useful during the consult.

I will introduce you over email shortly.

France

I read this and immediately thought, wait a minute—I've never met Dr. Amir yet he knows about me already and is (once again) making conditions on me, based on my estranged father. I don't think so—not again. This is about me, not him—my best interest and well-being, not his … And by the way, who brought my estranged father into this anyways? It certainly wasn't me.

I responded:

Thank you so much France. I really appreciate this but again as I noted in my last email my father is the last person on this earth I now trust. So, if this is about my well-being and figuring out why what happened to me happened to me, I so appreciate this. But the duress regarding my father is too much for me to bear at this time in light of that he has done. I hope the doctor would consider to continue in light of this condition. Thanks, michelle

France replied:

I understand Michelle. Amir told me that he wanted someone with you who (a) you have known for a long time and may be able to provide useful information; and (b) you trusted. If you father doesn't fit that criteria, then perhaps someone else does. Amir thought it was important, but I'll let you discuss that directly with him.

I'm happy to facilitate the meeting and a space for it.

Regards,

France

I reiterate my estranged father is not and was not law enforcement. And just prior to the events of April 12, 2013, for the very first time, I found out that he had a military intelligence background. So again, all this was not about me and my well-being . It was about some sort of cover-up, so the truth would not come to light and be exposed. But no matter how long it takes—the truth come to light ...

I responded:

> France – I thank you so much for all this. You have been beyond wonderful. At this time, there is only one person that I fully trust ... So I understand what Amir is requesting, but this time my father certainly does not fit this criteria, ... I'll [let] Amir know my concern once I hear from him. Again, I so appreciate all you are doing. Thank you, Michelle

Given the small exclusive number of individuals involved in this arrangement to meet with France, I was now surer than ever that I had a piece, a very crucial piece in a very high-stakes national security matter. In just days, I became aware of what the precise national security matter was, and how I fit ...

I never heard from nor met with Dr. Amir Afhkami. But I did meet with Brian O'Shea within days. He came to my residence to discuss the situation. Unlike NCIS that did not follow-up and then falsely wrote in its report that I had nothing more to share —I shared so much with Brian. Details, emails, files, and I even gave him crucial original documents to take with him to investigate, to finally get to bottom of all this—that which no law enforcement entity pursued previously. I entrusted documents with a former Special Forces (SF) to assist me to get to the truth ...

Meanwhile, on Monday, August 19, 2013, OSC Alejandra Dove sent me an email:

> Subject: US Office of Special Counsel – OSC File No. MA-13-3051
> Ms. Stefanick,
> On May 23, 2013, the US Office of Special Counsel's (OSC) Disclosure Unit sent you a letter to inform you that it had closed your file because your allegation involved a prohibited personnel practice. Such matters are, instead, reviewable by OSC's Complaints Examining Unit. Thus, while your file with the Disclosure Unit is closed, your file with the Complaints Examining Unit regarding retaliation remains open. This is the matter I am currently evaluating.
> To further clarify, please note that while the Disclosure Unit

may refer protected disclosures to the involved agency for an investigation and report, as referenced in its May 23, 2013 letter to you, this did not occur in your case for the above-referenced reason. The Disclosure Unit did not request either the US Department of State or the US Department of Defense to investigate your complaint and report back to our Office. The only investigation we are aware of is the current preliminary inquiry I am handling in response to your complaint of retaliation. With regard to this matter, I have not contacted any other individual, other than you, at this time.

As for your request that we assist you in having the agency place you on administrative leave, please note that OSC does note request involved agencies to place employees on administrative leave while we investigate the employees' allegations. Therefore, we cannot assist you with your request. I will now proceed with the evaluation of your complaint to determine whether there is a reasonable basis to believe that a prohibited personnel practice has occurred.

I have reviewed all of the information you provided with your complaint and would like to take this opportunity to ask you a few additional questions regarding your allegations. Please provide your responses at your earliest convenience, but preferably no later than close of business on September 2, 2013. While we understand that the information you may be providing is sensitive in nature, please note that the Office has a strict "no walk-ins" policy. Therefore, please respond to the following questions in the manner you are most comfortable with, either by e-mail, mail or fax. If you prefer to provide your responses, instead, by telephone, please let me know so that we can schedule a telephone conference.

• -In order to determine whether an employee was subjected to retaliation for whistleblowing, as protected under 5 USC 2302(b)(8), we must determine whether the information the employee disclosed reasonably evidenced one of the protected categories of information. As a result, it is key that we know the information you disclosed for which you believe agency officials are retaliating against you. Please provide this information

• -What is the status of the investigation the agency initiated that caused your security clearance to be temporarily revoked? Has your security clearance been reinstated? What reasons did the agency give you to revoke your clearance? In other words, why are you being investigated?

• -Who issued the "temporary detention order"? What reasons were you given to justify the detention order?

- -What reasons did the Arlington County Police give you to remove you from your home?

- -What kind of treatment did you receive at the Virginia Hospital Center and the Northern Virginia Health Institute and what were your physicians' conclusions that led to your release in May 2013?

- -You indicate that Ms. Linda Thomas-Greenfield visited you at your home on November 27, 2012. What was the reason for her visit?

- -You indicate your State/Defense detail exchange concluded on January 26, 2013. Was it scheduled to conclude on this date? If not, what was the reason for the detail's early termination?[70]

So many questions, and there were so many more that I could add to this list... However, I still had not received a response to my May 19, 2013 Privacy/FOIA request from portions of the US Department of State necessary to provide the answers to all these questions. The primary entity delaying in order to obstruct justice, and for the truth not to be known, was none other than DS... I was being denied the evidence to prove my position, the facts. And all intentionally and purposely being done so—with deliberate intent.

On Thursday, August 22, 2013, I sent the following email to Neera:

Subject: FW: Security Clearance
Hello Neera – Still no word from either DS and/or MED regarding all this whistleblower retaliatory "bunk that the Department has put me through, huh? Thanks, michelle[71]

On Monday, August 26, 2013, Neera responded:

Michelle – let me email Kevin Gleeson and try to get an update. It's been awhile since I reached out to him. Will let you know when I hear back.[72]
neera
Neera Parikh, Esq.
American Foreign Service Association

Then on Thursday, August 29, 2013, I received the following letter:
United States Department of State
Washington, D.C. 20520
Date Stamped AUG 27, 2013

---

70   Alejandra Dove, email message to Michelle Stefanick, August 19, 2013
71   Michelle Stefanick, email message to Neera Parikh, August 22, 2013
72   Neera Parikh, email message to Michelle Stefanick, August 22, 2013

PRIVACY/PII
Ms. Michelle L. Stefanick
[redacted]
Dear Ms. Stefanick:
The Bureau of Diplomatic Security, Office of Personnel Security and Suitability (DS/SI/PSS), recently received information from the results of a Memorandum conducted by the DS Special Investigations Division (DS/ICI/SID), regarding your recent behavior. DS/SI/PSS forwarded this information to the Department's Office of Medical Services (M/MED/MHS) for review in accordance with Executive Order (E.O.) 10450 *(Security Requirements for Government Employees)* and the Government-wide Adjudicative Guidelines pursuant to E.O. 12968 *(Access to Classified Information)*.

Based on the M/MED/MHS review of this information, they have requested an interview and/or psychological testing to complete their evaluation. You should contact, with two weeks of the date of this letter, Ferolyn Brooks, Administrative Assistant, at [redacted] (primary) or Lorraine A. Stanton, Nurse Consultant, at [redacted] (alternate).

Failure to cooperate and/or provide the information where requested is a security concern under Government-wide Adjudicative Guideline E (Personal Conduct) and may result in a recommendation for an adverse action regarding your eligibility for access to classified information.

If you have any questions concerning this matter, your point of contact at DS/IS/PSS is Michelle Dade at [redacted] or at [email address removed}.
Sincerely,
/s/
Paul D. Hallenback
Chief, Adverse Actions Division
Office of Personnel Security/Suitability
Bureau of Diplomatic Security
cc: M/MED/MHS: FBrooks
Security File73

I found it quite ironic since DS messed up, they now had to find a new path to cover-up their unconstitutional, law-breaking, criminal retaliatory actions they took against me. Their attempt to destroy my creditability by intentionally using false medical accusations as a retaliatory tool once

---

73   Paul Hallenback, letter to Michelle Stefanick, August 29, 2013

again. Upon receipt, I sent the following email to AFSA/Legal Counsel Neera Parikh, ccing Sharon Papp:

> Subject: DS Security Clearance Memo dated Aug 27, 2013
> Hello Neera – Hope all is well. Please find attached the DS Memo dated Aug 27 that was delivered to my house today. Please let me know who I should proceed. Thanks, michelle[74]

AFSA/Legal Counsel Sharon Papp, ccing Neera, responded:

> Hi Michelle, Neera is out until tomorrow. You have a duty to co-operate with their request to see MED and they can suspend your clearance if you do not cooperate. Sharon[75]

I responded to Sharon and Neera:

> Hi Sharon – I have nothing to hide and everything to share so that's not my issue.
>
> My issue is the fact of what is Department so afraid of consider-ing all the coincidences, inconsistencies and questionable acts that I'm trying to share with my OIG/Auditing background and as a CPA, I am ethically, morally and professionally required to do....I have no doubt now considering I have made the connections/link-ages to not only our Embassy bombing on Aug 7 1998, and poten-tially Benghazi; but now linkages to "9/11/2001." So, the fact that I was unconstitutionally "target/scapegoated" in an investigation by parts of our government just because I am Orthodox doesn't mean the Department has a right to "cover-up" their illegalities and considering those that committed the crime are still at large and at my expense.
>
> Besides, now that I've seen the "true colors"/corruption of the Department and other Government entities, I'm not sure that I want to continue to work for the Department. With that, it's my understanding that "obstruction of justice" applies to all. Thanks, michelle[76]

I sent the following to Lorraine Stanton, ccing Michelle Dade, Sharon Papp, and Neera Parikh:

> Subject: DS Security Clearance Memo dated Aug 27
> Hello Lorraine – Today I received the attached DS memo from UPS regarding a request for an interview and/or psychological test to complete their evaluation. The memo states that I have two

---

74   Michelle Stefanick, email message to Neera Parikh and Sharon Papp, August 27, 2013
75   Sharon Papp, email message to Michelle Stefanick, August 27, 2013
76   Michelle Stefanick, email message to Neera Parikh and Sharon Papp, August 27, 2013

weeks from the date of this letter to contact you all. Therefore, as requested, I would like to make such arrangements accordingly. Thank you. Michelle[77]

I forwarded this email chain to HFAC Benghazi Investigator/Legal Counsel Thomas Alexander.

I received Lorrie Stanton's response:

> Ms. Stefanick,
> Good afternoon! Kindly contact Ms. Ferolyn Brooks at ()[phone number provided redacted]. She arranges all the evaluation appointments.
> Regards,
> Lorrie Stanton RN, MSN, ANP
> US Department of State
> Office of Medical Services[78]

I responded to Lorrie Stanton:

> Thanks Lorrie – I just left a message. Cheers, michelle[79]

On Friday, August 30, 2013, Lorrie Stanton sent the following response:

> Ms. Stefanick,
> Thank you for letting me know!
> Lorrie Stanton RN, MSN, ANP[80]

And then there was radio silence.

On Wednesday, September 4, 2013, I sent the following email to Lorrie Stanton, ccing Michelle Dade, Sharon Papp, Neera Parikh, and U/S Patrick Kennedy:

> Hello Lorrie – Just as a follow-up to our email exchange regarding my outreach to Ferolyn Brooks on 8/29, I have not heard back from her at this point. Also as an email address was not provided for her, if you could please pass along accordingly I would appreciate it. Thanks, michelle[81]

77   Michelle Stefanick, email message to Lorraine Stanton, Michelle Dade, Sharon Papp, and Neera Parikh August 27, 2013
78   Lorrie Stanton, email message to Michelle Stefanick, August 27, 2013
79   Michelle Stefanick, email message to Lorrie Stanton, August 27, 2013
80   Lorrie Stanton, email message to Michelle Stefanick, August 30, 2013
81   Michelle Stefanick, email message to Lorraine Stanton, Michelle Dade, Sharon Papp, Neera Parikh and Patrick Kennedy, September 4, 2013

I again forwarded to HFAC Benghazi Investigator/Legal Counsel Thomas Alexander:

> Hello Tom – Saga continues... notice the difference between the two memos. I really wonder if Pat Kennedy knows what DS/HR (DG) did to retaliate against me....[82]

I received the following from Lorrie Stanton:

> Subject: Appointment
> Ms. Stefanick, good morning! Unfortunately, Ms. Brooks and the DSSP team moved to SA1 yesterday and are still in the process of obtaining computer and phone hook-ups. The technicians are currently working on resolving this issue.
>
> I have sent your email to Ms. Brooks so she will see it when she has access and will contact you. If you do not hear from her by tomorrow, please contact me and I assist.
> Take care,
> Lorrie Stanton RN, MSN, ANP[83]

I later received the following email from Lorrie Stanton:

> Ms. Stefanick,
> Good afternoon! I just spoke with our psychologist, Dr. Filson and he can meet with you on 9/5/13 or 9/12/13 at 10:00 a.m. in SA 1, Rm H246.
>
> Please let me know which date works best for you and I will let Dr. Filson know.
> Regards,
> Lorrie Stanton RN, MSN, ANP[84]

TIME TO GO

With all the horrific retaliatory games that had been played at my expense, and now seeing the US Department of State for what it really was—a corrupt enterprise, I made up my mind. I was resigning. On Friday, September 6, 2013, I sent the following email to Lorrie Stanton:

> Hello Lorrie – I have a question for you... in light of the fact that I requested whistleblower protection and DS/HR retaliated with this DS investigation and other horrendous actions, at this time I plan to put in for a resignation effective next week or week after once I hear back from HR regarding this process and all my annual

82   Michelle Stefanick, email message to Thomas Alexander, September 4, 2013
83   Lorrie Stanton, email message to Michelle Stefanick, September 4, 2013
84   Lorrie Stanton, email message to Michelle Stefanick, September 4, 2013

leave is used up, which is soon. With that, would this meeting on Thursday really be necessary if I'm resigning?

Please do not take the next statement personally, but in light of what has been done to me despite my moral, ethical and professional responsibility to do the right thing, I really at this time don't care what anyone in the Department of State thinks of me—because as far as I'm concerned the Department has lost my trust and respect. Your thoughts sincerely appreciated. Thanks so much and have a great day. cheers, michelle[85]

And then I waited for a response…
Meanwhile, Lorrie Stanton forwarded my email to Dr. Charles Filson:

Rick,
Please review and advise.
Lorrie Stanton RN, MSN, ANP[86]

On Monday, September 9, 2013, I received a response from Dr. Charles Filson, ccing Paul Hallenback and James Onusko:

Dear Ms. Stefanik [sic]:
Thank you for your email below. In consideration of your request and your pending resignation from the Department I think that it is prudent that we cancel your appointment for this coming Thursday. Please be advises that I am cc'ing DS/PSS of this occurrence as noted above. You may wish to notify them that you are resigning but that is entirely up to you and/your counsel. We will hold your file open here in MED until the end of this month at which time I will administratively close your file. If you have any further questions please feel free to contact us.
Very Respectfully,
Dr. Filson
Charles R. Filson, Ed.D.
Supervisory Clinical Psychologist
Diplomatic Security Support Program
Office of Medical Services – Mental Health Services[87]

Once I read this message and Dr. Charles Filson's signature block, I knew I made the right decision. This indeed was yet another DS set-up and I wanted nothing to do with it. The misspelling of my last name was yet another irritant at the time, until I realized the misspelling wasn't a

85   Michelle Stefanick, email message to Lorrie Stanton, September 6, 2013
86   Lorrie Stanton, email message to Charles Filson, September 4, 2013
87   Charles Filson, email message to Michelle Stefanick, Paul Hallenback and James Onusko, September 9, 2013

mistake, but intentional – with yet another aspect as to what was really going on…

I sent an email to Dr. Filson and Lorrie Stanton, ccing Paul Hallenback, James Onusko, Neera Parikh, Sharon Papp, and U/S Patrick Kennedy:

> Dr. Filson – Thank you so very much for getting back to me and your understanding regarding this matter and my applicable request. At this time, I have not heard back from HR regarding resignation procedures despite numerous requests, so I really appreciate having the insight that MED will hold my file open until the end of the month, at which time, my file will be administratively closed. Again, thank you so much for getting back with me. Have a wonderful day. Cheers, Michelle[88]

Déjà vu all over again. What the US Department of State could not accomplish in their first round of medical retaliation of April 12, 2013, they were now attempting a second round this time using internal US Department of State/Medical officials. As I stated all along, this matter was a law enforcement matter, and never a mental health issue. Simply contacting my insurance company, Blue Cross Blue Shield (BC/BS), to obtain my medical record coupled with those maintained by US Department of State/Medical Services, clearly documented that this was not a mental health issue. If the VHC, Dr. Christopher Olson, and Dr. Benjamin Adewale would have done their job, their ethical responsibility as health practitioners, all this would have immediately been put into proper context and ended a long time ago. Verifying that all this was indeed as I was stating all along, *a retaliatory action and not a medical/mental health issue*. So, was I about to give US Department of State, a do-over? *Absolutely not!*... And look what happens next…

At this point in time, I still had not received the pertinent DS FOIA-requested documents. But I did receive this…

US OFFICE OF SPECIAL COUNSEL
1730 M Street, N.W., Suite 218
Washington, D.C. 20036-4505
(202) 254-3600
SEP 05 2013 [Date Stamped]
Ms. Michelle L. Stefanick
[redacted]
Re: OSC File No. MA-13-3051
Dear Ms. Stefanick:

---

88   Michelle Stefanick, email message to Charles Filson, Lorrie Stanton, Paul Hallenback and James Onusko, Neera Parikh, Sharon Papp, and Patrick Kennedy, September 9, 2013

This letter is in response to the complaint you recently filed with the US Office of Special Counsel (OSC) against the US Department of State and US Department of Defense. In the complaint, you allege agency officials temporarily suspended your Top Secret security clearance and had the Arlington County Police involuntarily admit you to the Northern Virginia Mental Health Institute in reprisal for disclosing instances of wrongdoing to members of Congress, as well as to various other entities, including, but not limited to, the Army Criminal Investigative Division, the Naval Criminal Investigative Service, the Federal Bureau of Investigation and the State Department Diplomatic Services. On August 19, 2013, we sent you an email requesting additional information regarding your allegations. Specifically, we requested that you indicate the information you disclosed and who issued the alleged personnel actions. This information is key in allowing us to properly evaluate your complaint. However, although you submitted numerous emails in response to our inquiry, you did not provide the specific information we requested by the established deadline. Consequently, while the Complaints Examining Unit (CEU) has carefully considered all of the information you provided thus far, we have made the *preliminary* determination to close our inquiry into your allegations based on our evaluation of the facts and law applicable to your circumstances.

The OSC is authorized to investigate allegations of prohibited personnel practices and activities prohibited by civil servicer law, rule, or regulation. 5 USC. sections 1241(a)(1)A), 1216(a) and 2302(b). The provisions of 5 USC. section 2302(b) specifically define 12 prohibited personnel practices for which we have jurisdiction to investigate. Thus, when reviewing a complaint, CEU analysts consider whether the information provided for each allegation is sufficient to suggest a prohibited personnel practice, or any other violation under our jurisdiction, occurred. If so, the matter is referred to OSC's Investigation and Prosecution Division (IPD). If not, Complainants are given the opportunity to respond to our preliminary findings before a final determination is made. Our decision depends on whether the facts of the case appear likely to satisfy all of the elements of the alleged prohibited personnel practice. The elements are found in section 2302(b) and/or case law established by the Courts or the Merit Systems Protection Board (hereinafter, the "Board"), which is OSC's deciding authority.

Under the Whistleblower Protection Enhancement Act of 2012 (WPEA), it is a violation of section 2302(b)(8) to take or fail to take, or to threaten to take or fail to take, a personnel action with respect to any employee or applicant because of any disclosure of information by an employee or applicant which the employee or applicant reasonably believes evidences: (1) any violation of law, rule, or regulation; (2) gross mismanagement; (3) a gross waste of funds; (4) an abuse of authority; or (5) a substantial and specific danger to public health or safety, if such disclosure is not specifically prohibited by law, or specifically required by Executive Order to be kept secret. The elements of proof necessary to establish violation of section 2302(b)8 are: (1) a protected disclosure of information was made; (2) the accused official(s) (e.g., the proposing or deciding official) had knowledge of the disclosure and the identity of the employee making the disclosure; and (3) the protected disclosure was a contributing factor in the personnel action or threat of a personnel action. *Gergick v. General Services Administration*, 43 M.S.P.R. 651 (1990).

In light of the limited information you provided, we were not able to consider whether the information you disclosed would constitute a protected disclosure of information. Moreover, we considered that in order for the OSC to have authority over the matter, the personnel actions alleged must meet the definition in 5 USC. Section 2302(a)(2)(A). 89 Yet, with regard to the suspension of your security clearance, we considered that the Board has previously found that because 5 USC. Section 2302(a)(2) lacks specific language authorizing it to review security clearance determinations, the Board is without the authority to do so. *See, Department of the Navy v. Egan*, 484 US 518, 526-32 (1988); *Hesse v. Department of State*, 217 F.3d 1372, 1380 (Fed.Cir. 2000). As for your involuntary admission into the Northern Virginia Mental Health Institute, there is no indication in the information you provided that either the US Department of State or the US Department of Defense were involved in this action, which was carried out by the Arlington County Police. As we informed you via e-mail on August 22, 2013, our process of evaluating complaints relies heavily on the cooperation of the individual who has filed the complaint. However, unfortunately, you did not provide key information. Conse-

---

89   Pursuant to 5 U.S.C. Section 2302(a)(2)(A), a personnel action" is defined as: an appointment; a promotion; an action under chapter 75 of this title or other disciplinary or corrective action; a detail, transfer, or reassignment; a reinstatement; a restoration; a reemployment; a performance evaluation under Chapter 43 of 5 U.S.C.; decisions concerning pay, benefits, or awards, or concerning education or training that would reasonably be expected to lead to promotion or other actions described in this subparagraph; a decision to order psychiatric testing or examination; the implementation or enforcement of any nondisclosure policy, form, or agreement; and any other significant change in duties, responsibilities, or working conditions.

quently, because the information you provided was not sufficient to satisfy all of the elements of proof of a section 2302(b)(8) violation and the personnel actions alleged do not meet the definition of section 2302(a)(2), we have no basis for further inquiry into your allegation of a potential violation of section 2302(b)(8) at this time.

We also examined your complaint for a possible violation of 5 USC. Section 2302(b)(12). Under this section, it is a prohibited personnel practice for an official with personnel action authority to take or fail to take a personnel action that would violate any law, rule, or regulation implementing or directly concerning one of the federal merit system principles defined at 5 USC. Section 2301. You allege that agency officials reprised against for contacting members of Congress regarding your disclosures. An employee's right to petition Congress is protected under 5 USC. Section 7211. A violation of such right to petition Congress can be characterized as a violation of a law, rule, or regulation implementing, or directly concerning, the merit system principles identified in 5 USC. Section 2301.

However, for the following reasons, as well as for the reasons previously cited pertaining to the alleged personnel actions, we have no basis for further inquiry into your complaint as a potential violation of section 23029(b)(12). The examination of the issues did not reveal any causal nexus between your Congressional contact and any personnel action taken against you. The information did not show that your Congressional contact resulted in an investigation. The examination did not determine whether any agency officials suffered any adverse impact as result of your Congressional contact. The examination did not find any indication of a statement or animus or other evidence which establishes a connection between your disclosures to Congress and the personnel actions that are the subject of your complaint. Without a causal connection between your Congressional communication and any personnel actions taken against you, there is no reason for further action concerning your allegations of a section 2302(b)(12) violation.

As previously stated, our determination is preliminary. You have the opportunity to provide comments in response to this letter. Your comments must be in writing and must address the reasons we cite in reaching our preliminary determination to close OSC's inquiry into your complaint. You have thirteen (13) days from the date of this letter to submit your comments to my attention. Please reference your OSC File Number in your response. You may mail your comments to the return address on the front page of this letter, fax them to [redacted], or email them to [email address removed}. If we do not receive any comments by the end of the thirteen-day period, we anticipate closing your file. We will then send you a letter terminating our inquiry and advising you of any additional rights you may have.

Sincerely,

/s/

Alejandra Duarte Dove

Attorney

Complaints Examining Unit[90]

Many, if not all, of the *prohibited* personnel practices and violations indicated were applicable and did indeed occur. Yet, there was nothing more I could do since the US Department of State was violating FOIA statutes, and purposely and intentionally delaying FOIA-requested documents to obstruct justice. And due to these tactics, unethical, unprofessional and criminal tactics, they would get away with the retaliatory actions taken against me—once again. And there was nothing more that I could do. After the thirteen-day period, on September 23, 2013, I received another letter from the OSC Alejandra Dove:

US OFFICE OF SPECIAL COUNSEL

1730 M Street, N.W., Suite 218

Washington, D.C. 20036-4505

(202) 254-3600

SEP 19 2013 [Date Stamped]

Ms. Michelle L. Stefanick

[redacted]

Re: OSC File No. MA-13-3051

Dear Ms. Stefanick:

On September 5, 2013, we sent you our preliminary determination letter that set forth the US Office of Special Counsel's (OSC) proposed factual and legal determinations regarding your complaint. At that time, you were notified that you had thirteen (13) days to respond to this report. The following is our response to the additional information you submitted to the Complaints Examining Unit (CEU) as of September 18, 2013 in further support of your allegations against the US Department of State and US Department of Defense.

We have carefully reviewed the information provided; however, we note that your response does not contain any new information or facts that would change our preliminary determination. Specifically, you did not clearly identify the information you disclosed to agency officials that caused the agency to retaliate against you. As indicated in our preliminary determination letter, one of the elements of proof necessary to establish a violation of section 2302(b)(8) (retaliation for whistleblowing) is that a protected disclosure of information was made. If we do not know the subject matter of the disclosure, we cannot determine whether the Merit Systems Protection Board (MSPB) would find it is "protected," as defined by statute, the Courts and the MSPB. If we cannot determine whether the disclosure is "protected," we have no basis for further inquiry into the matter. Accordingly, for the following reasons, and for all other reasons stated in our September 5, 2013 letter, we have made the determination not to refer your complaint to the OSC's Investigation and Prosecution Division and to close our inquiry into your allegations.

Please note we are also sending you a separate letter discussing the rights you may have to seek corrective action from the Merit Systems Protection Board (MSPB). Because you alleged potential violations of section 2302(b)(8) or (b)(9)(A)(i), (B), (C) or (D), you may have a right to seek corrective action from MSPB under the provisions of 5 USC. Sections 1214(a)(3) and 1221. You may file a request for corrective action with the MSPB within sixty-five (65) days after the date of this letter. The MSPB regulations concerning rights to file a corrective action case with the Board can be found at 5 C.F.R. Parts 1201-1206 and 1209. *It is important that you keep the accompanying letter* because the MSPB may require that you submit a copy you should choose to seek corrective action there.

Sincerely,
/s/
Alejandra Duarte Dove
Attorney
Complaints Examining Unit[91]

The accompanying letter went as follows:

US OFFICE OF SPECIAL COUNSEL
1730 M Street, N.W., Suite 218
Washington, D.C. 20036-4505
(202) 254-3600
SEP 19 2013 [Date Stamped]
Ms. Michelle L. Stefanick

---

91   Alejandra Dove, letter to Michelle Stefanick, September 23, 2013

[redacted] Re: OSC File No. MA-13-3051

Dear Ms. Stefanick:

As we informed you in our closure letter of this date, we have terminated our inquiry into your allegations. In the complaint, you allege agency officials temporarily suspended your Top Secret security clearance and had the Arlington County Police involuntarily admit you to the Northern Virginia Mental Health Institute in reprisal for disclosing instances of wrongdoing to member of Congress, as well as to various other entities, including, but not limiting to, the Army Criminal Investigative Division, the Naval Criminal Investigative Service, the Federal Bureau of Investigation and the State Department Diplomatic Services.

The purpose of this letter is to notify you that you have a right to seek corrective action from the Merit Systems Protection Board (MSPB). Because you alleged that you were the victim of the prohibited practice described in section 2302(b)(8) or (b)(9)(A)(i), (B),(C), or (D), commonly called reprisal, you may have the following rights. You may seek corrective action from the MSPB under the provisions of 5 USC. Sections 1214(a)(3) and 1221 (individual right of action) for any personal action taken or proposed to be taken against you because of a protected disclosure or activity that was the subject of your complaint to this office. You may file a request for corrective action with the MSPB within 65 days after the date of this letter.

The MSPB regulations concerning rights to file an individual right of action can be found at 5 C.F.R., parts 1201-1206 and 1209. If you choose to file such an appeal, you should submit this letter to the MSPB as part of your appeal. Therefore, it is important that you keep the accompanying letter if you intend to file a request for corrective action. Additional information about filing an appeal with the MSPB is available at: www.mspb.gov.

Sincerely,

/s/

Alejandra Duarte Dove

Attorney

Complaints Examining Unit[92]

Given my circumstances and the severity of my situation, my intent was to file for corrective action with the MSPB within 65 days after the date of this letter. To ensure a timely filing, I had until November 22, 2013. That was my intent. That was my plan. Surely, I would finally re-

---

ceive the May 19, 2013 requested and required FOIA response from US Department of State by that time, right? I had already decided to resign from the US Department of State effective October 1, 2013 as a result of all the retaliatory actions taken against me. They got what they wanted. I was leaving the US Department of State. So, what more could happen? Sixty-five days is a long time, and so much more would happen…

Fast-forward with this insightful email exchange between OSC Officials and myself. On Friday August 29, 2014, I sent this email to Alejandra Dove and Jason Zuckerman, ccing Carolyn Lerner:

> Subject: FW: US Office of Special Counsel – OSC File No. MA-13-3051
> Hello Alejandra – In light of State Department just recently (March 8, 2014 and June 24, 2014) finally providing me substantiated documents in their "untimely/purposely delayed" "FOIA violation" response to my May 19, 2013 FOIA request, per your September 19, 2013 letter and July 31, 2014 email on behalf of Ms. Lerner re-engaged her on this matter, I have filed a MSPB Complaint accordingly.
>
> With that, since you were the Attorney handling my complaint filed with OSC on May 20, 2013, for the purposes of this MSPB Complaint, I need to know if any Department of State/DOD official was notified of my OSC Complaint by OSC. If so, what date and what officials, what capacity. As you have indicated to me during that earlier process that you/OSC conducted no investigation regarding my complaint, this other information is needed to document that State/DOD officials were aware. Your cooperation and insight to this matter is sincerely appreciated. Thank you. Michelle[93]

On Wednesday, September 3, 2014, Jason Zuckerman and I received the following response from Alejandra Dove, ccing Carolyn Lerner:

> Ms. Stefanick,
> In response to your inquiry, the email will confirm I did not contact the Department of State or the Department of Defense regarding your complaint.
> Thank you,
> Alejandra Dove
> Attorney
> Complaints Examining Unit

93   Michelle Stefanick, email message to Alexandra Dove, Jason Zuckerman, Carolyn Lerner, August 29, 2013

US Office of Special Counsel[94]

OSC Alejandra Dove confirms in her September 3, 2014 response that she did not contact State or DOD regarding my complaint…Yet, I notified State officials accordingly over a year earlier, through AFSA on Tuesday, July 16, 2013 when Neera sent the following email to Philippe Lussier and William Schaal, ccing me:

> Subject:
> DAS Lussier – I would like to thank you for meeting with me yesterday regarding Michelle Stefanick's case. Ms. Stefanick has asked that I relay the following: in light of the ongoing DS security clearance investigation, the whistleblower retaliation complaint filed with the Office of Special Counsel against the Department particularly DS and HR, and all other ongoing…[95]

So, the US Department of State was aware of my OSC Complaint. And regardless, my May 19, 2013 requested and *very pertinent and relevant* FOIA documents were yet again—purposely and intentionally—delayed. And yet another round of retaliatory actions would soon occur, with effects remaining to this day… And as for my still open, pending EEOC EEO Grievance litigation, I had not heard a word of an update since February 2013, curiously and coincidentally-timed just prior to the retaliatory act of April 12, 2013.

At this time, I was juggling so much. So many odds against me—however, I had one big advantage, and that was I was telling the truth. After meeting with former SF/Private Investigator (PI) Brian O'Shea, I patiently waited to hear something. With all my previous attempts with US law enforcement entities such as the FBI, ACID, NCIS, and DS, I just wanted the truth so I could move on and move forward—but how is that possible in light of this?

On Friday, August 23, 2013, I sent Brian O'Shea this follow-up email:

> Hello Brian – Hope all is well. Just checking in. Please call anytime when you can. Thanks so much. cheers, michelle[96]

Then on Saturday, August 24, 2013, I sent this email to Brian O'Shea regarding another bizarre incident occurring with my computer:

> Hello Brian – I wanted to let you know that after after discussing with you what appeared that I was no longer receiving 'facebook'

94   Alejandra Dove, email message to Michelle Stefanick, September 3
95   Neera Parikh, email message to Philippe Lussier, William Schaal, and Michelle Stefanick, July 16, 2013
96   Michelle Stefanick, email message Brian O'Shea, August 23, 2013

emails coming to me oddly reflecting 'Rich Gross' that today I just received another one... was hoping you could give me a call so we could discuss status. I realize when I don't hear back from you I get concerned. Thanks, michelle[97]

One has to understand, given what occurred while I was in Germany, I was petrified that it was happening all over again—and it was, and again on American soil. I was being targeted, again. So was my computer. And again, it was like someone more than just hacking my computer, but literally taking control over it. And of course, there was no trace *after the fact*, just as it was occurring live, real-time. Additionally, I had just given Brian original files without making copies first—so I was concerned both for him and my files. Why I had trusted Brian with the orginals with not making copies first, I don't know. I suppose because of his alleged and supposed Special Forces background. And then this happened. That night I started to put more and more together. Something very odd was happening with my computer, again. So much so that I sent Brian an email on Sunday, August 25, 2013:

> Hi Brian – I woke up this morning realizing I may have indeed figured out 'how' it happened. I plan on pulling the info together today so hopefully we can meet soon. Thanks, michelle[98]

Brian responded:

> Hi Michelle,
> No real progress as of yet. I travel a lot, so I will check in with you every Friday with updates. If you can't get ahold of me do not worry. More to follow as I get it. Brian[99]

I replied:

> Brian – I just wanted you to know that the concerns/comments you noted/raised during our discussion regarding the possibility of "how/why" I did these transactions are the same ones I myself have raised over and over with myself as well—not wanting to believe that's what happened and both from your perspective and mine who then is implicated, to include casting a negative light to that/ your broader community writ large—to which I believe you rightly may be offended with disbelieve as well. So, with that, over and over I've tried to rethink the pieces of the past to come up with another possibility because the current possibility just doesn't make sense

97   Michelle Stefanick, email message Brian O'Shea, August 24, 2013
98   Michelle Stefanick, email message Brian O'Shea, August 25, 2013
99   Brian O'Shea, email message to Michelle Stefanick, August 25, 2013

370

to me... its one more technical in nature and one I really need you to hear to see if it is indeed a possibility which would shed this all into another direction if these pieces I put together fit. I just felt you should know how I feel about this ... Brian, I'm Orthodox—It's my faith to believe in the truth and even more, the pursuit of it. I hope we can meet soon to discuss. Thanks, michelle[100]

Doing more online research, reconstructing and timelining past events, then on Monday August 26, 2013, I would come across this... So, I emailed Brian:

Brian – I was overseas when 9/11/2001 happened. Today, for the first time, I read about Rumsfeld reporting that $2.3 trillion dollars were missing/unaccounted for at the Pentagon the day before 9/11, and then on 9/11, an accounting section of the Pentagon was hit/targeted that day.

I realize we didn't go into details about what I discussed with France, but please, you are going to have to trust me— we really need to solve my situation. I can go into more when we meet next—I really think you need to know/understand the severity of my situation. The dots I potentially connected before are nothing compared to the possible connection now with this insight I've just obtained today.

Please Brian – let me know when we can meet again. Thanks, michelle[101]

Due to how serious the implications were of the dots I just connected, I forwarded this email exchange to France as well:

France – Please read. I had no idea until now ... should I share all the dot connections I made with Brian, the now may include this one. Again France, I had no idea about any of the 9/11 connection until now.[102]

On Monday, August 26, 2013, I now saw the definitive "financial" linkage and connection regarding 9/11, the Pentagon and what I knew. This wasn't just about the August 7, 1998 East Africa Embassy bombings per se, but the implications were much broader and dating much farther back... This correlation pertained back to my State OIG days. In an odd way, all that happened, made sense except for one thing: I wasn't the enemy, as *someone* was trying to scapegoat me out to be. I was the *light*, the

100   Michelle Stefanick, email message Brian O'Shea, August 25, 2013
101   Michelle Stefanick, email message Brian O'Shea, August 26, 2013
102   Michelle Stefanick, email message to Brian O'Shea and Francis Hoang, August 26, 2013

path to the truth…and obviously *someone* didn't like that and certainly didn't want the truth to be exposed. As long as I was around, creditable, alive to tell the truth, and shed light regarding the facts—I was a threat.

Meeting with France Hoang, being introduced to Brian O'Shea, both having SF background, I finally felt like I was getting somewhere. I would resign and then hire and work with Brian to investigate what happened to me in Germany. My plan was moving forward. Considering all that had occurred, I thought my decision to resign would make *someone* happy. Finally, I would be left alone. I could move on and move away from the corrupt enterprise I now saw the State Department, and our USG, for what it was … Then I would be subjected to round two. I can't even make this stuff up…

On Wednesday, September 18, 2013, I sent an email to NCIS SA Lisa Huff, ccing ACID SA Terry Little and U/S Patrick Kennedy:

> Subject: RE: Status
> Hello Lisa – Today I found it quite curious that the NCIS Supervisory Agent 'handling' or not in my case, John Beliveau, was arrested for bribery. Earlier today, I left a message for Michael Monroe asking what 'protocol' procedures are in regards to when a 'dirty' law enforcement agent is arrested and all cases that may have been 'corrupted' under his/her purview. With that, I do indeed have additional insight/information regarding the 'why/how' to what happened to me in Stuttgart, Germany if all NCIS is not corrupt and will reopen my case as I had been requesting. Thank you, Michelle[103]

To this day, NCIS has never contacted me to reinvestigate my case, pursue the truth and justice. The question remains, why did NCIS SA Lisa Huff mislead, inaccurately reflect, and lie in her investigation report—the report she referred to the Department of State? Who did NCIS SA Huff contact and work with at the Department of State? And why didn't she refer this to the DOJ/FBI?

On Thursday, September 12, 2013, Neera sent an email:

> Subject: options
> Michelle – we have worked together a long time and I respect you. I hate to see you lose money that you have worked hard for. You only have to work until [redacted] in order to receive your annuity. Here are your options:
>> You can go on sick leave. DAS Lussier explained that you have [redacted] hours of sick leave. You could remain on sick leave until

103   Michelle Stefanick, email message to Lisa Huff, and Terry Little, September 18, 2013

[redacted] next year at which time you could then retire.

) You can go on LWOP. This allows you to remain on the payroll, but in an unpaid status. However, you can remain in a LWOP status until [redacted] of next year and then retire.

These two options that will allow you to receive your annuity starting next year. If you resign, your annuity is deferred and risk losing thousands of dollars. You have two good options available to you and I ask that you think hard about both.

Please let me know if you have any questions or want to discuss this further.

neera

Neera Parikh, Esq.

American Foreign Service Association[104]

On Tuesday, September 17, 2013, Philippe Lussier sent the following email to Neera:

Subject: FW: Draft email to Neera Parikh (Michele [sic] Stefanick) Neera, the following lays out the options and ramifications for Michele [sic] Stefanik [sic] who has exhausted her annual leave. It is pertinent to know that she is eligible for retirement on [redacted] with a gross annuity of $[redacted] and FSPS annuity supplement of [redacted]for a total annuity of [redacted] per month.

She may report to work to her supervisor Ben Lam in HR/EX/BUD. This is the HR budget division and there is meaningful work in her skill code as a financial management officer. On [redacted] she could retire and receive an immediate annuity carrying her medical coverage into retirement.

She may be eligible for sick leave with medical letter from a professional. She has approximately [redacted] hours of sick leave. On [redacted] she could retire and receive an immediate annuity carrying her medical coverage into retirement.

She may request leave without pay (LWOP) and elect to maintain enrollment in FEHB for up to 365 days. During this time period the Department will continue to pay its share of the FEHB premium and may advance payment of her share, in which case this advanced payment of her share may be withdrawn from her future pay (if she returns to the Department after her LWOP) or from her retirement annuity payments (if she retires after the end of the LWOP period). She could also repay these employee FEHB premium amounts before entering LWOP or elect to "pay as you

---

go" (for more information see http://www.opm.gov/health-care-insurance/healthcare/reference-materials/reference/leave-without-pay-status-and-insufficient-pay). On [redacted] she could retire and receive an immediate annuity carrying her medical coverage into retirement.

She may resign. This would suspend medical coverage and make her eligible for a deferred annuity when she reaches her minimum retirement age (MRA) – 56. She would not have medical coverage at the time she retired and therefore would not be eligible for medical coverage during her retirement.

Regarding her promotion: This summer's threshold board was her 6th attempt at promotion from 01 to OC. She has two TIC extensions (one for no OC opportunities in her specialty one year, and one for long term training in another year). She does not become eligible to retire before age 50 if she were to be promoted. She is only eligible for an immediate annuity if she were to TIC out. Given her two TIC extensions she has two more promotion opportunities. Her 2012-2013 EER did not make it into her promotion folder for the selection panel that was held this summer, but the Promotion Board did review her file.

When she selects an option, I will have her CDO Mark Perry send her information about any relevant procedures. I strongly discourage her from choosing the last option as she would lose benefits and receive a deferred annuity. Please let me know if either of you have any questions.
Best Regards, Phil
Philippe A. Lussier
Deputy Assistant Secretary
Bureau of Human Resources[105]

On Wednesday, September 18, 2013, Neera forwarded Phil's email, ccing Sharon Papp, accompanied with her own:

Michelle – below are the final options the Department is willing to offer you. Unfortunately, an administrative promotion to OC is not an option because you would not be eligible for retirement. Once an OC, you would have to serve in that level before retiring, you cannot immediately retire as you thought.

Michelle – I implore you to think about going on sick leave or LWOP. You have worked so hard for the Department and endured a lot. This is money that you have earned that you stand to lose should you resign. And I also don't want to see you lose your medical benefits. If you are not comfortable with the sick leave option (I think that your best option because you remain in a paid status) and least go on LWOP.

Should you decide to go on sick leave or LWOP, we could then file a grievance and ask that the two-year TIC extensions you received be waived and that you be allowed to TIC out immediately, thus allowing you the right to receive your annuity. So, you would not have to be on LWOP or on sick leave for very long because I think we could reach a settlement with the Department allowing you to TIC out in exchange for giving up the two TIC extensions.

Please let me know if you have any questions or want to discuss this further. I am more than happy to discuss these options with you if you want to talk to me via phone. I am here today until 4 p.m. and then all day tomorrow.

neera

Neera Parikh, Esq.

American Foreign Service Association[106]

One of my options was to resign. And that's what I decided to do. I realize it may appear to some that I was being *irrational* but given all that I had been personally put through, and subjected to – why? For what rational reason wouldn't I want to leave? For wanting to share all that I knew with the proper authorities and assurance that I and the other individual would be protected? Instead, I was massively retaliated against, credibility destroyed—I had had enough. First, my FMC Section took the biggest hit in terms of deaths on August 7, 1998. And then only later I find out Embassy Nairobi was a major CIA hub and the bombing was an inside job. Then the there was the Diplomatic Post Benghazi attack on September 11, 2012 with more deaths, and again, an inside job. And instead of being protected by these supposed fellow US Constitutional oath-takers, supposed US Department of State officials, my supposed colleagues, I was targeted and retaliated against. Who in their right mind would stay and continue working with and in such an entity? And all for what, there were my continual requests for an investigation regarding the events in Germany while assigned with the US military. And there were all the events subsequent. So why wasn't I being protected? Our fellow USG colleagueshad been killed—the threat was real! Are you kidding, after what was personally done to me already, I didn't want to have anything more to do with any of these individuals. I didn't trust them. And resignation was an option an HR-provided option, and the option that was in my best interest literally for my survival. And that's what I decided to do. I resigned.

But instead of resigning, the Department of State really thought I was going to "fraudulently" charge sick leave and then file an AFSA grievance to waive the two-year *time-in-class* extension and TIC out immediately. After all that had already occurred? After everything that these same individuals had already done to me, subjected me to. You've got to be kidding me? Who in their right mind would continue on with this, with these same individuals. After the cover-up that occurred the last time that I filed an AFSA Grievance against the Department of State? No, that was absolutely not an option. And after the Department of State intentionally and purposely ensured my 2012-2013 EER did not make it into my OPF for SFS consideration by Promotion Panels... Is there something the Department of State didn't want more Senior FSOs to see when they would review my OPF? Absolutely. And it's called the truth versus their deliberate false-narrative/lie cover-up.

On Wednesday, September 18, 2013, I sent an email to Phil Lussier, Hans Klemm, Bill Schaal, ccing Neera Parikh, Sharon Papp, and Patrick Kennedy:

> As a DOJ victim of the 1998 Embassy Bombing, in the fall of 2012 once I became aware that I had information that had to be shared, I did the right thing. Due to the obstacles/retaliation that I have experienced by the Department of State and Defense in doing the right thing, I can no longer be a part of such a corrupt institution/ government for which I previously so proudly served. Again, I request the resignation procedures so I can proceed accordingly.[107]

On September 19, 2013, I sent the following to Bob Barnett:

> Hello Bob – Hope all is well.
> The issue at hand is such that I have no choice but to come to you, hopefully one last time, regarding this matter. I wanted you to be aware of this letter and to please share accordingly as my efforts no doubt would be blocked regarding whom I am implicating. With that, not only is this paramount that Secretary Kerry receive this but Secretary Clinton as well for once you read the letter you will understand why. The story line goes well beyond Benghazi, and so does the mode of operandi...

107   Michelle Stefanick, email message to Phillipe Lussier, Hans Klemm, Bill Schaal, Neera Parikh, Sharon Papp, and Patrick Kennedy, September 18, 2013

And for the record, I am not an intelligence employee and have no intelligence background. With that, please assist me and please protect Secretary Clinton and Kerry as well – they need to know, so 'we' all can be protected. Thanks, michelle[108]

Attached to this email was my September 19, 2013 letter to Secretary Kerry, my decision to resign and why. I received the following response from Bob:

Hello, Michelle – I cannot intermediate on such matters with the Secretaries. I urge you to look to your attorney for advice on this, because, as we told you, we cannot represent you. Thank you.[109]

On September 19, 2013, I sent the following email to U/S for Management Patrick Kennedy. Attached would be my letter to Secretary Kerry.

Subject: A Kind Request….
Pat – Please find attached a letter I kindly request of you to provide to Secretary Kerry. In my heart, I have no doubt that you and I have the same ethical, moral, and professional standard to do, always, the right thing particularly when it comes to our Nation and American public for which we serve.

As you know, I'm about to resign from the Department due to all the retaliatory actions that have been taken against me, and this will be done by the HR protocol once it is ever provided to me.

However, if it is true what Pat Kelly as has advised to me that they still have not identified who inside our Embassy provided the insight to outside that dreadful day on Aug 7, I as a witness will soon be silenced—and the answer never to be found.

With that, as I have no other means, I kindly ask that you provide this to the Secretary and direct discussions be held with Senators Snowe and Rockefeller, and USAO, accordingly. Thanks, michelle[110]

Pat responded:

Michelle,
I will get your letter to the Secretary
    But I really confused about your decision to resign
    I've known you for many years and consider you one of the best financial management officers and one of the best administrators that I've ever worked with
    You are less than one year away from a pension, and life-time

108   Michelle Stefanick, email message to Robert Barnett, September 19, 2013;
109   Robert Barnett email message to Michelle Stefanick, September 19, 2013
110   Michelle Stefanick, email message to Patrick Kennedy, September 19, 2013;

medical insurance—both of which you have earned for your service and dedication and under difficult circumstances

What's up?

You really don't want to do this

If you don't want to work here anymore, then go on Leave Without Pay and retire the day you turn 50

Give me a call

Regards

Pat[111]

I responded:

Thank you Pat – In light of all the retaliatory actions that have been taken against me, and no accountability/responsibility to those actions, my principles and my ethics are far more important to me than money ever will be. How much more suffering did I/do I have to withstand from my own government? It just isn't worth the money to me Pat.

I have not received the requested information from Mark Perry yet, so hopefully I will receive it tomorrow and submit according to the 'procedure' on Monday. With that, we can talk before now and then whenever it best works for you. Thanks, michelle[112]

I have no doubt Patrick passed along my September 19, 2013 letter as I requested. On September 30, 2013, I submitted the following resignation letter:

The Honorable John Kerry

Secretary of State

Washington, DC 20520

Dear Mr. Secretary,

For reasons noted in my letter to you dated September 19, 2013, I hereby submit for your consideration and acceptance from the Foreign Service and the Department of State effective Tuesday, October 1, 2013. Thank you for your time and your serious consideration/acceptance to my request.

Sincerely,

[920]/s/

Michelle L. Stefanick

cc: U/S for Management Patrick Kennedy

HR/CDO Mark Perry[113]

---

111   Patrick Kennedy email message to Michelle Stefanick,September 19, 2013;
112   Michelle Stefanick, email message to Patrick Kennedy, September 19, 2013
113   Michelle Stefanick, letter to John Kerry, September 19, 2013

Soon after, I received the following:

United States Department of State
Washington, D.C. 20520
Date Stamped: Oct 16 2013
Ms. Michelle L. Stefanick
[redacted]
Dear Ms. Stefanick,
We received your letter of resignation dated September 30, 2013 and forwarded it to the attention of Secretary Kerry. The Office of the Secretary of State has requested that I, as the Acting Director General of Human Resources, respond to your letter as proper under State Department regulations and policy. On behalf of Secretary Kerry and the Department of State, it is with regret that I accept your resignation, effective October 1, 2013. We thank you for your many years of service to the Department and we wish you every success.
Sincerely,
/s/
Hans Klemm
Principal Deputy Assistant Secretary[114]

Interestingly, I then received another letter from the Department of State, date stamped prior to, but after receiving Secretary of State Kerry's resignation acceptance. Dated October 15, 2013, I just ignored this letter.

United States Department of State
Bureau of Human Resources
Office of Retirement
Room H-620, SA-1
Washington, DC 20522
October 15, 2013
Michelle L. Stefanick
[redacted]
Dear Ms. Stefanick:
The Department of State hereby notifies you that it has initiated an application for disability retirement on your behalf. You have the right to designate a representative to assist you in responding to this proposed application. The name and contact information of any such designated representative should be furnished to me as soon as possible at [email address removed}. You have the right to submit a written response to the proposed application for dis-

ability retirement Any such response must be submitted to me, for forwarding to the Principal Deputy Assistant Secretary for Human Resources, by October 30, 2013.

The Office of the Medical Director will review available medical documentation and written statements by people who have observed your recent performance, conduct, and behavior. If you wish to provide written documentation for that review, including any additional medical documentation, it must be delivered to me by October 30, 2013, for forwarding to the Medical Director. If you wish to make yourself available for a medical examination by the Office of Medical Director prior to the October 30, 2013 deadline, please advise me of that by October 22, 2013.

After October 30, 2013, the Medical Director will reach a medical judgment as to whether medical impairment has left you unable to perform useful and efficient service. A report documenting that medical judgment will be submitted to the Principal Deputy Assistant Secretary for Human Resources who will determine whether you meet the legal requirements for disability retirement.

If disability retirement is approved, you will be notified in writing. If you disagree, you will have 30 days from such determination to submit a written request for reconsideration to the Director General of the Foreign Service. Furthermore, one year after a finding of disability retirement, you will have the right to submit new written evidence regarding your medical health to the Direct General who will then either reaffirm the finding the disability retirement or direct that you be returned to active duty.

Sincerely,

/s/

John K. Naland

Director[115]

Secretary Kerry accepted my resignation effective October 1, 2013. And that's what I wanted. I moved on figuratively and in the process literally. I didn't want any part of the criminally, corrupt US Department of State. But no, my resignation would not be enough… and I can't even make up what happens next …

At this time, I was off State Department payroll and was moving forward. At this time, I was a federal DOJ-determined CVRA-accorded victim/witness regarding the August 7, 1998 East Africa Embassy bombings who had been retaliated against and not protected, with all accorded rights violated. At this time, I was a May 2011 EEO grievance complainant in still open, pending litigation against the US Military despite not having any update since responding accordingly on February 25, 2013 to the EEOC AJ's February 20, 2013 *Acknowledgement and Order.* At this time, I was a federal government whistleblower as requested in my eight-page handwritten November 27, 2012 *Whistleblower/Protection Request* letter despite receiving no official notification/confirmation to the contrary from the FBI. And due to the retaliatory actions taken against me and to which I was subjected by the US Department of State, I rightfully and accordingly filed a May 18, 2013 OSC Formal Complaint, yet another formal complaint closed without investigation. *And yet,* "it is a federal offense to threaten, intimidate, harass, or mislead a witness in a criminal or civil proceeding."

Having 65 days to file an appeal with MSPB, I had until November 22, 2013 to timely file accordingly. I would do so—despite still not receiving pertinent and essential US Department of State May 19, 2013 FOIA-requested documents. That was my intent. Even if I lost and the cover-up continued, all would be documented. I was moving forward to include working with Brian O'Shea to finally determine what occurred in Germany. I can't even make this up—I was notified that an *Emergency Motion* has been filed. What? All because no one protected me, no one investigated, so I protected myself—I resigned from the US Department of State. That was an option and my right.

CHAPTER 10

JUST WHEN I THINK IT'S OVER:
Brought Back Against My Will

WHO'S IN CHARGE?

On Thursday, October 24, 2013, Stephen Burns sent the following, ccing George Dodge:

> Subject: Emergency Motion to Preserve Estate
> Michelle,
> As I hope Mr. Dodge has informed you, your father has re-filed the Guardianship Petition, and has also filed an emergency motion to preserve your estate. Arlington Circuit Court has agreed to hear the motion tomorrow, Friday, October 25, on its 10am docket (although we expect the matter to be heard at the end of the docket). I understand that service of the Motion and Guardianship Petition was attempted today, but I have attached the Motion to this email as well. It is a large attachment, so I hope that it comes through.
>
> I was also re-appointed as your guardian ad litem today. I was hoping to have a chance to speak with you today, but unfortunately the day has gotten away from me. After reading the motion, it appears that your employer (or possibly former employer) has made a generous offer to you regarding your employment that you have rejected.
>
> Please let me know that you've received this email, and please email me with any questions or concerns you may have. I will do my best to return any emails by the end of the evening or first thing in the morning.
>
> I urge you to come to court tomorrow morning to be heard on this matter.
> Sincerely,
> Steve
> Stephen D. Burns, Esq.
> THOMPSON WILDHACK, plc[1]

I responded to Stephen Burns, the Commonwealth of Virginia/Arlington County Circuit Court Court-appointed official, ccing George Dodge:

---

1   Stephen Burns, email message to Michelle Stefanick and George Dodge, October 24, 2013

Hello Stephen – I must say I was quite surprised to see this packet at my doorstep, as no one knocked on the door to provide it to me so I'm just reviewing it now. I'm now even more surprised to see this being on the docket for tomorrow, and just now being notified of such.

I have not yet heard from George, so hopefully he will be there to represent me as we have not yet been in touch with each other, let alone been able to discuss any of this to include inaccuracies reflected therein. I oppose this, and I want to discuss this with my legal counsel. Thank you, Michelle

Unbelievable! Apparently, as an American citizen, USG employee, and US State Department employee, I was not accorded one of the Department of State HR options provided—resignation. How many other USG employees of the US State Department have resigned—to include all those US Department of State FS employees that resigned subsequently in regards to the President Trump Impeachment Hearings? They all can resign, but I can't? I am not permitted. I, and only I, cannot resign, and had to be brought back onto US Department of State payroll against my will. And all this happened because I had to be subjected to yet another round of horrific retaliation.

Preserve my estate. Really? And what would happen to all my financial assets and real estate—without my approval, my authority and against my will?

I had so many questions… For starters, to bring me back onto State Payroll against my will, how did my estranged father/family even find out I resigned since I never told them? I repeatedly asked that question at that time, and I continue to ask that question to this day… And I certainly never authorized anyone in the USG to advise/notify them. So how did they find out?

Another fact that I would not become aware of until much later, but referenced already, was the Commonwealth of Virginia Attorney's Office subpoenaing Dr. Benjamin Adewale on June 7, 2013 for a sworn affidavit regarding his testimony at the May 8, 2013 Appeal Hearing. When I asked at the time how and why was the Commonwealth of Virginia Attorney's Office involved in this matter, I was advised it's because they handle such appeals. Really? As I lost my appeal due to the unethical and illegal stunts and tactics used by the Commonwealth of Virginia Attorney's Office prior to my May 8, 2013 Appeal, what was the reason for their June 7, 2013 subpoena? Was there another set-up in the works? I didn't get an answer. Until now.

Unaware at the time, an Order Appointing A Guardian Ad Litem motion was filed with Paul Ferguson, Clerk Arlington Circuit Court on October 23, 2013. The judge who signed this Order, Commonwealth of Virginia's Arlington County Circuit Court Judge Louise DiMatteo, was the same judge from the May 8, 2013 Appeal Hearing. This is the same judge that appointed Stephen Burns as court-appointed Guardian *ad litem* after the May 8, 2013 Appeal Hearing. Now given the Appeal Hearing was due to the Department of State prearranged April 15, 2013 Commitment hearing, how did Stephen Burns get access to me and my VHC medical records on May 7, 2013, the day before, anyways? Particularly when my attorney Rex Flynn and I were being denied access. It was because Natalie Page and her client, my estranged father, filed a fraudulent *Petition for Appointment of Guardian and Conservator* on April 23, 2013, of which I was never advised. The petition had no legal standing and was non-suited on July 10, 2013 after the first round of retaliatory taken against me by US Department of State was completed… It was all to discredit my credibility and reputation.

Regarding all these medical files: what about all the errors/inaccuracies/missing documents that I documented upon finally obtaining the VHC, as well as NVMHI, medical records?

And as for my financial records, given all my filed Financial Disclosure Statements, Federal and State tax returns, impeccable documented credit and credit score, coupled with the timeline of the events in Germany, financial transactions and my filed May 2011 formal EEO Grievance. Yet, none of this is mentioned nor explained in court filings. All clearly documented. This was never a mental health issue, but always, a federal national security cover-up.

With this October 23, 2013 Order and October 24, 2013 *Emergency Motion*, retaliatory round two had begun, and Dr. Adewale's fraudulent *unsubstantiated/misdiagnosis* under oath May 8, 2013 testimony was the basis.

Interestingly, the filed October 24, 2013 *Emergency Motion* was pretty thick. Given the specific details included, many inaccurate and misleading, it was quite obvious that *someone* in the USG was involved in its development. So precisely who was the USG source/instigator? And how long had this *Emergency Motion* filing been in the works? Between July 8 and this October 24 filing, Brent Baxter of Manning & Murray, P.C. was indicated as legal counsel instead of Natalie Page. So precisely when did legal representation change? And why?

Yet, all *knew* that I was a federal DOJ-determined CVRA-accorded victim/witness regarding the August 7, 1998 East Africa Embassy bombings in which the FBI investigation was still ongoing; a May 2011 EEO Grievance Complainant in still an open, pending litigation against the US Military, a federal whistleblower and a May 18, 2013 OSC Formal Complainant *still within the 65-day window of my right to appeal* to the MSPB. But none of this was indicated in the October 24, 2013 *Emergency Motion. USG/Department of State Officials knew! Commonwealth of Virginia to include the Commonwealth Attorney's Office knew! Stephen Burns knew! My estranged father and family knew! His legal counsel Natalie Page knew! His new legal counsel Brent Baxter knew! My court-appointed attorney Rex Flynn knew! And my new legal counsel George Dodge knew!* And soon, yet another Commonwealth of Virginia/Arlington County Circuit Court Judge would know... And all because I resigned from the US Department of State.

I purposely used up all my annual leave to the point of my September 30, 2013 resignation. I had no other leave but sick leave left. And *someone* knew that. In order to charge more than three days of sick leave in a row, one needs doctor/medical approval. And *someone* knew that. That's why when AFSA legal counsel Neera suggested going on sick leave, I refused. Though it could be used as a basis for filing a grievance, it could easily have been used as an excuse/a reason/justification for a set-up regarding time and attendance (T&A) fraud. And I would have none of it—for I no longer had any trust in the corrupt and criminal enterprise, the US Department of State. By having me involuntarily recommitted, the *Deep State* could commit medical insurance fraud *again* in order to fraudulently use, abuse, and charge sick leave to keep me on State payroll for another year, until my 50th Birthday when they said I could officially retire. I mean that was the whole rational for the October 24, 2013 *Emergency Motion,* was it not? I mean what person of rational mind would resign a year shy of full retirement and health benefits. But that's not what happened nor was it the true intent, because if it was, then why am I still deemed *incapacitated* to this day, and as I write this book in 2019/2020?

But certainly, this October 24, 2013 *Emergency Motion* wouldn't go anywhere. I mean I am allowed to resign. Besides, how would a state-level Commonwealth of Virginia/Arlington County Circuit Court Judge have jurisdiction to overrule a Federal US Senate-Confirmed Presidential Cabinet-level official – the President of the United States' US Department of State Secretary of State John Kerry accepted my resignation effective October 1, 2013.

That is unless of course, the President of the United States of America at the time, President Obama, did approve all this. *Is that even possible?*

The August 7, 1998 East Africa Embassy bombings occurred during the President Clinton administration. President Obama's National Security Advisor Susan Rice was President Clinton's Assistant Secretary of State of African Affairs at the time of the bombings. My October 24, 2012 initial reporting, subsequent November 27, 2012 whistleblower/protection request, and first round of retaliation initiated against me was under the tenure of Secretary of State Hillary Clinton. *How is all this even possible?* The Governor of the Commonwealth of Virginia at the time of the first round of retaliation against me was Republican Bob McDonnell. Prior to him, was Mark Warner and Tim Kaine and subsequent were Terry McAuliffe and Ralph Northam, all Democrats. *So, it depends on when the retaliation against me really all began, doesn't it?*

Again, I had a right to resign, so surely the Commonwealth of Virginia/Arlington County Circuit Court Judge would ponder *"what in the world is going on"* and finally put an end to all of this continual retaliatory ordeal against me. *Right?* So, on October 24, 2013, I appeared in front of Commonwealth of Virginia/Arlington County Circuit Court Judge Paul F. Sheridan. Under oath, I once again stated,

> Your Honor – I received/reviewed this motion last night at 8:00 p.m. I oppose this. I want my own legal counsel, George Dodge, to represent me. Unfortunately, due to the late, unexpected receipt of this, my lawyer and I had not even had a chance to review/let alone discuss it. Can this court please delay any requested action until I've met/discussed with my own legal counsel.

Additionally, *under oath*, I stated what all this was really about—retaliation because of my protected status—given that I was a federal CVRA-accorded victim/witness in regards to the August 7, 1998 East Africa Embassy bombing, an EEO Grievance Complainant against the US Military, a federal government whistleblower, and an OSC Complainant. I was unaware of Judge Sheridan's background at the time, but regardless I wanted to make sure he was aware of mine. I also wanted the Petitioner's Counsel, Brent Baxter to know it—that way he can definitely never say that he wasn't aware, afterhearing it directly from me, under oath.

Needless to say, I was mortified when the October 24, 2013 *Emergency Motion* was accepted. *Again, what country is this?* And though this should never be stated as a factor, it is and it is a fact—particularly in light of the events that occurred—Secretary of State John Kerry has a US Navy background and Judge Paul Sheridan, a US Navy/USMC background. *Coincidence?* Maybe. *Relevant?* In light of the events that occurred while I was assigned in Germany with MARFOREUR/AF, that I had a still open and pending EEO Grievance litigation at the time against the Marines with no real investigation being conducted. *Yes, very much so.* I resigned and now I'm standing in front of a Commonwealth of Virginia/Arlington County Circuit Court Judge with a U.S Navy/USMC background.

Here's the October 29, 2013 letter Stephen D. Burns emailed to US Department of State/Office of Director General—the exact same office that I gave my November 27, 2012 Whistleblower/Protection Request letter:

THOMPSON WILDHACK, plc
ATTORNEYS AT LAW
6045 WILSON BOULEVARD, SUITE 101
ARLINGTON, VIRGINA 22205
TELEPHONE: (703) 237-0027 FACSIMILE: (703) 237-0082

October 29, 2013
Via Email Only
Marcia S. Bernicat
Deputy Assistant Secretary
Bureau of Human Resources &
Office of the Director General of the State Department
[email address removed}
Re: Michelle Stefanick; Arlington Circuit Court Case No. CL13-1196-01
Dear Ms. Bernicat:
As you may be aware, on October 25, 2013, I was appointed Limited Conservator for Michelle Stefanick, a State Department employee. I was previously appointed as her Guardian *ad litem* for the duration of the above-referenced matter, so it is my responsibility to represent her best interests. The Order specifically finds Ms. Stefanick incapable of entering into contracts, and specifically authorizes me to review and make elections regarding Ms. Stefanick's employment with the federal government. The Petition alleges, among other things, that Ms. Stefanick is legally incapable of caring for her person or estate due to an untreated mental illness. I have attached a copy of the Order hereto, and am more than happy to provide you with a copy of the Petition upon request.
I am writing today because I have learned that Ms. Stefanick has tendered her resignation to the State Department, and as her

Limited Conservator, I wish to rescind that resignation pending the outcome of the Petition. I would further like to discuss any options available to Ms. Stefanick to continue her employment with the State Department. It is my understanding that she has had a distinguished career there and as her Limited Conservator, I want to ensure that her options are preserved.

I am available to discuss this matter at your convenience. Please let me know when you are available.
Sincerely,
/s/
Stephen D. Burns[2]

"As you may be aware..." What precisely did that mean? Who precisely at the Department of State was *aware*, and what was their precise role? Though I still did not have the purposely and intentionally delayed FOIA-requested evidence yet, US Department of State officials knew at the time what all this was really about and still, did what they did. Department of State officials were involved.

Needless to say, I was stunned by this Commonwealth of Virginia/Arlington County Circuit Court Judge decision regarding a federal employment matter. The question remained, *What more do they want from me, whoever they are?* I resigned. I reached out to law enforcement/proper authorities every step of the way, and instead of being protected, I was retaliated against. Resigning obviously wasn't good enough. *So why is this horrific retaliatory ordeal continuing, let alone why did it even start to begin with?* And how do I file my MSPB Appeal to my May 18, 2013 Official OSC Complaint, closed without investigation let alone even notification, when the retaliation against me is still continuing?

I had until November 22, 2013 to file my MSPB appeal, but there would be yet another hearing in the Commonwealth of Virginia/Arlington County Circuit Court on November 1, 2013. My legal counsel George Dodge said I did not need to attend. So, I didn't. I had come to realize the family that I had loved unconditionally and thought I knew were nothing more than perfect strangers. This was not based on my actions, but based on their own. I received a day or so later the following letter regarding the November 1, 2013 Hearing results:

GEORGE W. DODGE
Attorney at Law
2300 Clarendon Boulevard, Suite 700

Arlington, VA 22201
703-524-9700 (FAX) 703-522-4570
Email: [email address removed}

November 1, 2013
Michelle Stefanick
[redacted]
Re: Appointment of Guardian and Conservator
Dear Michelle:
I was in court this morning for a hearing regarding this second effort to have a Guardian and Conservator appointed for you. You have been ordered to undergo an evaluation with Henriette Kellum. If everyone is agreeable, I will arrange to have this done at my office in the conference room. Depending on the outcome, the evaluation could be beneficial or detrimental to our position.

A non-jury trial date has been set for December 17, 2013, at 10:00 in the Arlington County Circuit Court to determine if you need a Guardian and Conservator. Also included are copies of the two Court Orders entered today in the case. If you have any questions, I will be happy to review them with you after next week.
Very truly yours,
/s/
George Dodge[3]

Enclosed with the letter were copies of the two referenced Court Orders entered on November 1, 2013: 1) Virginia: In the Circuit Court of Arlington County IN RE: Michelle Laureen Stefanick Civil No. CL13-1196-01 Amended and Restated Order Granting Emergency Relief and Appointing Temporary Conservator; and 2) Virginia: In the Circuit Court of Arlington County IN RE: Michelle Laureen Stefanick Civil No. CL13-1196-01 Order Requiring Respondent to Submit to Evaluation and Cooperate with Preparation of Evaluation Report.

Over and over, I was totally befuddled as to why and how a federal national security matter with federal legal/law enforcement jurisdiction ended up in and transferred to a state-level county level court legal system/jurisdiction. And now a federal employment matter... None of this made any sense. I sent George Dodge on Saturday, January 23, 2016:

Hello George – Needless to say I have started to go back and timeline all my documented facts/events with long-delayed/intentionally delayed FOIA documents—to include when finally obtained and when I became aware of certain information/insight—in

3   George Dodge, letter to Michelle Stefanick, November 1, 2013

preparation for the 4th Circuit Appeal, as well as the EEO Civil litigation proceedings that are still pending/continuing to this day since my initial filing in April/May 2011.

With that, I now have many questions to the supposed Arlington Court Circuit filings that I had not been provided copies of/informed of along the way. For instance maybe you can provide some insight to a supposed "initial filing" dated 10/23/2013 regarding "Restore Driving Privilege" where I am the Plaintiff and the Defendant is "IN RE" (whatever that means). Can you please provide me a copy of this Motion and some insight as I don't seem to have any recollection/records pertaining to this?

Based on all the FOIA documents, seems there's been a lot of false statements/inaccuracies regarding the matters at hand—therefore, in light of all the ongoing and pending Civil Federal Litigation at that time and continuing to this day, the need to review/obtain all the details/insight to pinpoint and negate every single inaccuracy/misstatement (when and by whom) every step of the way ...With that, there appears to be other Pleadings/filings that I don't have copies of, so having insight on this puzzling initial filing will be a great start. Your insight regarding this matter is sincerely appreciated. Thanks, Michelle[4]

And there's the the misspelling of my last name. Apparently, my last name was misspelled/got misspelled in the Commonwealth of Virginia/Arlington County Court system when my May 8, 2013 Appeal Hearing transferred from Commonweath of Virginia General District Court to Circuit Court. Only when I became aware of this error years later and requested action be taken was this error finally corrected. Received on February 6, 2016, here's the applicable Arlington County, Virginia Clerk of the Circuit Court letter with their explanation and action taken:

ARLINGTON COUNTY, VIRGINIA
CLERK OF THE CIRCUIT COURT
Date: 02/03/2016
Michelle Stefanick
[redacted]
Re: In Re: Michelle Laureen Stefanick
CL13-1196-01 and CL 13-1142
Dear. Ms. Stefanick,
Pursuant to your request, I reviewed the case information contained in your file and have made the following updates:

You indicated that the case CL13-1196-01 was showing up with a filing type of Restoration of Driving Privileges. Please note, the Virginia Dept. of Judicial Services utilized the same abbreviation ("REST") for actions to restore, modify or terminate guardianships, as well as actions for the restoration of driving privileges. I have gone ahead and updated the filing type in your case as "APPT" for appointment of guardian and conservator.

You also noted that your name was misspelled as "Stafanick" in case #CL13-1142. I verified and confirmed the paperwork we received with the appeal from Arlington General District Court had your name spelled "Stafanick". After cross referencing your date of birth with your other file, I have now updated our electronic system to note that your name is properly spelled "Stefanick."

Please let me know if you have any additional questions regarding this matter. I can be reached at the Circuit Court Clerk's office (703) 228-7010.

Sincerely,

/s/

Christopher Falcon

Civil Division Supervisor[5]

In the September 5, 2013 OSC letter regarding my case, re: OSC File No. MA-13-3051, there was a significant misstatement. In that letter, OSC Attorney Alejandra Dove stated that "you allege agency officials temporarily suspended your Top-Secret security clearance and had the Arlington County Police involuntarily admit you to the Northern Virginia Mental Health Institute in reprisal for disclosing instances of wrong…" Northern Virginia Mental Health Institute? No, the initial preorchestrated retaliatory tactic was involuntarily admitting me to Virginia Hospital Center, not NVMHI. So, why did she/OSC misstate this fact, this simple fact?

If and when OSC Attorney Alejandra Dove looked up the online Commonwealth of Virginia/Arlington County Court records at the time, these inaccurate online Arlington County Court records misspelling my last name caused the inability to clearly link the original April 15, 2013 Commitment Hearing in General District Court with the May 8, 2013 Circuit Court Appeal Hearing. This disconnect caused an inaccurate, skewed timeline of events. It made it appear that I was not telling the truth regarding the extent of the extremity of this most horrific retaliatory tactic used by USG and Commonwealth of Virginia officials, and my very own

---

family against me—the purposeful and intentional use and abuse of the court and mental health/healthcare systems. The question is how many others were misled if researching/verifying my claim made during this time between on or about April 12, 2013 to on or about February 3, 2016, until I finally had the error corrected.

Meanwhile, round two of retaliatory actions was set into motion. I sent an email to numerous individuals on Sunday November 3, 2013. These individuals included DOJ/SDNY Wendy Olsen, AWC David Sullivan, Attorney Robert Barnett, OSC Alejandra Dove, OSC Jason Zuckerman, Whistleblower Jesselyn Radack, Journalist Eleanor Clift, Congressional Staffers – Thomas Alexander, Tom Sheehy, Clete Johnson, Jennifer Hemingway, Robert Bradley. As you can see, *everyone* was looped in, *everyone* was aware, and *no one* did anything to put an end to all this. And yes, that included the DOJ/SDNY. And this list was just the tip-of-the-iceberg of everyone who knew and did nothing.

> Subject: State's Hostage Taking Continues…
> 1) Sec Kerry Resignation Acceptance letter dated Oct 16
> 2) State's Office of Retirement Letter dated Oct 15
> 3) Emergency Motion for Guardian/Conservator Arlington County Court Order received Oct 24
> 4) Arlington County Hearing Guardian/Conservator dated December 17
> 4) DOJ 1998 Embassy Bombing Victim/FBI ongoing/open Case
> 5) EEOC Grievance vs. Sec of Army (though initial grievance filed against USMC)
> 6) NCIS Supervisory Agent Beliveau Arrest/USMC Commandant Unlawful Command Influence articles
> Hello all – Its been a while and wanted to get everyone caught up to the latest drama. I believe in light of all the retaliatory actions taken against me in my attempts to do the right thing, it was in my best interest to move on and move away from the Department of State/this area as soon as possible. Therefore, I submitted my resignation to Secretary Kerry on September 30, effective October 1, which he acknowledged/accepted in the attached letter dated October 16 signed by Hans Klemm, HR's Principal Deputy Assistant Secretary.
> Considering one would think all would be delighted with this action/decision that I made, to my astonishment, I then receive this attached letter dated October 15 from John Naland, HR Office of Retirement Director— "initiating a disability retirement" on my

behalf and making me remain on State's payroll for another year. When I advised the Department of my resignation/acceptance by the Secretary and thus refusing John's offer, then on October 24 at 9:10 p.m., I officially received this "emergency motion' from Arlington County to appear in court the next day at 10:00. I appear and gave a sworn testimony. Then my lawyer appeared again on November 1 on my behalf to find out a hearing is now scheduled for December 17 and in the meanwhile, I cannot resign from the Department.

Though this may not seem bizarre to you all, it certainly does seem incredibly bizarre to me. Now to revisit in broad terms how I got here. Please see attached that I am a DOJ victim to the 1998 Embassy Bombing, of which remains an open/ongoing FBI investigation, and in light of the recent Delta Force capture of Al Liby is indeed still open. Also please see attached my EEO Grievance against the Secretary of Army from my time in Stuttgart, Germany from December 2009 -July 2011 with MARFOREUR/AF. As I am not military, this seems quite bizarre to me that I file the initial grievance against the Marines, but since it occurred on an Army Garrison the higher, I took my Grievance, it then transferred from against the Marines to the US Army, of which it now stands against the Secretary of Army. Again, as I am not military, this seems quite bizarre but from those that I explained this to with a military background, they seemed to accept its validity. This case is still open and though an EEOC AJ has been identified, it has yet to be heard.

In the fall of 2012, with my OIG/Auditing and CPA background, I began to "connect dots" and with that, did all in my power to present it to the proper law enforcement entities along the way what I believe is/was crucial insight regarding the Embassy bombing. Considering who I am implicating, it does not present a positive storyline but certainly does explain all the retaliatory action that has and continues to be taken against me. For instance, please see attached the newspaper article regarding NCIS Supervisory Agent John Beliveau. NCIS Agent Beliveau was the agent in charge of "handling" my case/my allegation which was not sufficiently reviewed and closed as quick as it was opened. As you can see, NCIS Agent Beliveau was arrested for corruption and still my attempts to reopening my case in light of this fact have been responded to with silence by NCIS.

Also curious is the recent "unlawful command influence" allegations against the USMC Commandant by his very own Marines and their request for Congressional investigation, yet my allegations against the USMC during this same time and after, continue to be "covered-up" with every attempt/every avenue I take to present the facts that I have and are documented . but for some reason, no one will truly investigate.

I'm not an intelligence employee and I'm not an intelligence asset, so do not think in terms of conspiracy. I do have an OIG/Auditing/CPA background and do think in terms of corruption/fraud. Despite my attempts, I have only been able to contact US/AO in Southern New York/the applicable FBI investigators through Wendy Olsen, the DOJ Victims Notification Contact, and I can only pray that she has done the right thing and contacted/notified folks accordingly. But with that, I really hope that for all that I've contacted along the way and throughout this process, to include now, all are true to the constitutional/due process/human rights/rule of laws values of which our nation stands—if not, I ask all to revisit where they stand and to make sure they do the right thing as the American people expect of you to do. Despite all the retaliation against me for doing the right thing, no one will destroy nor take from me my principles and my pursuit to do the right thing. But, if I'm contacting you with this, you have a role as well for if who I'm implicating is true/correct, our nation, our national security is and continues to be at risk. Thanks, michelle[6]

I stand by that email as much today as the day I sent it. Even more so.

In the meantime, on October 6, 2013, about five months after my meeting with the HFAC Benghazi Investigator/Legal Counsel Thomas Alexander, the US Army Delta Force captured Al-Liby in Benghazi in connection to our embassy bombing fifteen years prior. All this time, and only months after I shared my insight, an FBI Most Wanted is captured … And this was after only one brief meeting of my sharing only a portion of what I knew/dots I connected. So, a question remains: what was the path taken of the information that I provided that day at my residence to HFAC to result in this US Army Delta Force action? Thru DIA? CIA? State? FBI? How did the information I provide become *operational*? I mean it had only been 15 years, at that time, since the August 7, 1998 East Africa Embassy bombings, and then only 5 months after my May 16, 2013 HFAC discussion …

6   Michelle Stefanick, email message Wendy Olsen, David Sullivan, Robert Barnett, Alejandra Dove, Jason Zuckerman, Jesselyn Radack, Eleanor Clift, Thomas Alexander, Tom Sheehy, Clete Johnson, Jennifer Hemingway, Robert Bradley, November 3, 2013

arm

According to the headline portion of the Daily Mail *MailOnline* article published on October 6, 2013 that I accessed via internet on April 29, 2014:

> Dramatic moment Delta Force commandos seized "Most Wanted" al-Qaeda terrorist in Libya by smashing windows of his car and dragging him into black Mercedes...Was wanted for planning 1998 US Embassy bombing in Nairobi, Kenya...Libyan Prime Minister says he wasn't informed of raid and demands answers for "kidnapping'" of al-libi but John Kerry says seizure was legitimate... [7]

Initially, I read this headline as stated, with no reading into it. Then in due time, with all I had been put through, I looked at the specific wording of the headline through a different lens. I drove/drive a *black Mercedes*. I was assigned to *US Embassy Nairobi, Kenya on August 7, 1998*. My car door was *smashed* as was my *side-view mirror*. I was in essence *kidnapped* with the filing of the *Emergency Motion* bringing me back onto Department of State payroll against my will after I resigned, which *Secretary of State John Kerry* accepted. Some may say this is a stretch, but all this was describing me, my situation, my circumstance. This was all some kind of coding. Given all I had been subjected to, I no longer took anything at face value, particularly now in regards to the USG and the entities involved. And given "all the entities involved," how far-fetched would what I was now suspecting really be?

According to a June 18, 2014 UPI.com report, "the US Department of State has declined to say whether the Rewards for Justice Program was involved in the apprehension of suspected US Consulate Benghazi [sic] attacker Ahmed Abu Khatallah..." Given what I now knew/pieced together, I too would have the same question, but for possibly now a different reason...

Now speaking of the USG, what about the DOJ? I mean where were they in all this, despite my on-going and continual outreaches. And here are a few examples of the applicable DOJ VNS I received during this time:

On Tuesday, September 23, 2014, I received this DOJ VNS email *Re: United States v. Defendant(s) ADEL ABDEL BARY, Anas Al Liby Case Number 1998R02072 and Court Docket Number 98-CR-01023* from United States Attorney (USA) Preet Bharara and Victim Witness Coordinator Wendy Olsen. Its about Anas Al Liby's hearing scheduled for October 8, 2014 before Judge Lewis Kaplan.

---

7   Citation?

This DOJ VNS email dated Monday, October 6, 2014 *Re: United States v. Defendant(s) ADEL ABDEL BARY Case Number 1998R02072 and Court Docket Number 98-CR-01023* was from USA Preet Bharara and Victim Witness Coordinator Wendy Olsen. It's about requesting a Victim Impact Statement, which I had provided years earlier, and was requested to provide again if wanting to do so.

And this DOJ VNS email dated Wednesday, January 7, 2015 *Re: Case Number 1998R02072 and Court Docket Number 98-CR-01023* was from USA Preet Bharara and Victim Witness Coordinator Wendy Olsen. Trial against Anas al Liby's death will terminate all criminal proceedings against him. Trial against his co-defendant, Khalid al Fawwaz, is now scheduled to commence on January 20, 2015.

Given all that has happened to me, and Pat Hartnett-Kelly's May 30, 2011 email implying an *insider*, and *no one* investigating, I looked at everything from a different lens—a lens of *scapegoating, being set-up, a cover-up at the highest national security levels*. Again, upon receipt, I initially read these DOJ VNSs for the meaning that was stated, with no reading into it. Now, I look at everything that occurred, through a different lens. For instance, take the January 7, 2015 DOJ VNS date reference... I am an American Orthodox Christian with Russian Orthodox lineage. January 7 is old calendar *Russian Orthodox Christmas*. At the time, one would say I'm reading too much into all this. Well, now given all the *Russia, Russia, Russia* drama playing out for years now... There was the timeline of events, to include my own applicable timeline of events, their overlap and the Special Prosecutor John Durham investigation. There was the CNN Declassified episode, the September 11, 2000 CA-1 form incident, the July 20, 2001 Anonymous Memorandum sent about a month after my returning to Embassy Moscow from attending the DOJ/SDNY East Africa Embassy bombing trial in NYC in early June 2001, that was used as the basis for a bogus "criminal investigation" to be opened on me. All this Russia linkage, and all just a coincidence. Really? Given the USG entities involved, the players involved, is it really? I no longer believe in just coincidences. My receipt of all these applicable DOJ VNS emails dated throughout the duration of all these retalitatory actions taken place against me showed my current, on-going DOJ/SDNY federal CVRA-accorded protected status during this entire time. Yet, I was not protected, and what happened to me was permitted to happen.

Additionally, this January 7, 2015 DOJ VNS stated:

We would like to provide you with an update regarding proceedings against Anas al Liby, a/k/a '*Nazih al Raghie*,' a/k/a '*Anas al Sebai*,' Trial against Al Liby and another defendant, Khalid al Fawwaz, a/k/a '*Khaled Abdul Rahman Hamad al Fawwaz*,' a/k/a '*Abu Omar*,'a/k/a '*Hamad*,' was scheduled to commence on January 13, 2015. However, on December 31, 2014, al Liby, who had had long-standing medical problems, was taken from the Metropolitan Correctional Center in Manhattan, where he had been detained pending trial, to a nearby hospital to address medical complications. Despite the care provided at the hospital, al Liby's condition deteriorated rapidly, and al Liby died on January 2, 2015. Al Liby's death will terminate all criminal proceedings against him. Trial against his co-defendant, Khalid al Fawwaz, is now scheduled to commence on January 20, 2015.

Though I am not a conspiracy theorist, isn't this so similar in scenario to the now mysterious circumstances surrounding the August 10, 2019 Jeffrey Epstein death as to be eerie? And both these incidents involved the Metropolitan Correctional Center in Manhattan. I may not be intelligence but I am not stupid. Its quite apparent, based on all I was subjected to and its timing, this description was about me. My being nefariously reported deceased in the aftermath of the bombing, and now given the medical retaliatory actions taken against me ... It's code. *For and of a covert operation*, perhaps?

I strongly believe in justice and justice being done. Innocent until proven guilty—and that *no one is above the law*. That includes members of the United States Government. I was wrongly and falsely accused, and now the cover-up for what happened ... It explains everything. The lack of protection by DOJ, the FBI, the Department of State, the Department of Defense, the entire intelligence community, the entire law enforcement community, and the entire US military. It explains why there were never any investigations about events occurring, retaliatory events that I was subjected to, because it was all these entities—the USG writ large—subjecting me to them. And once they were proven wrong, *committed-crimes* proven wrong about me, they couldn't admit they got it all wrong, treasonously wrong, so they needed another scapegoat to fit the bill instead. And now there was the Special Prosecutor John Durnham investigation. As for me, *to them, the Deep State—I was simply expendable.* So how does US Army Delta Force respond now knowing how an American federal CVRA-accorded rights and protected victim and witness regarding the

August 7, 1998 East Africa Embassy bombings has been retaliated against by the *Deep State*?

First the stunt just pulled to bring me back onto State payroll against my will, and now came a court-ordered capacity evaluation. So, I advised my legal counsel George Dodge to request and to obtain in writing from US Department of State—since they were behind all this—regarding my concerns. George Dodge received the following response:

United States Department of State
Washington, D.C. 20520
November 29, 2013
Via Email Only

George W. Dodge
Attorney at Law
2300 Clarendon Boulevard, Suite 700
Arlington, VA 22201
RE: Michelle Stefanick
Dear Mr. Dodge:
This letter is in response to your email of November 15, 2013 addressed to the Under Secretary of State for Management and is further to your telephone conversation on November 18, 2013 with Assistant Legal Advisor Anne Joyce. We understand that Ms. Stefanick has expressed concern that Henriette Kellum, the evaluator responsible for Ms. Stefanick's court-ordered capacity evaluation, has not received a security clearance from the State Department.
At this stage, we do not have any reason to believe that Ms. Stefanick is in possession of sensitive information that would likely be disclosed during a mental health evaluation, and we believe the evaluation can proceed without further action from the Department of State. That said, in the event that Ms. Kellum has questions concerning the interview or would like to discuss ways to ensure that her report does not include anything of a sensitive nature, we would like to provide a point of contact for her. In these circumstances, she can contact Kevin M. Gleeson, an Attorney-Advisor with the Department. His information is as follows:
Tel.: [redacted]
Email: [email address removed]
Please do not hesitate to let me know if I can be of any further assistance in this matter.
Sincerely,
/s/

Richard C. Visek
Deputy Legal Advisor[8]

This response and evaluator selection was interesting on so many levels. First, in my brief discussion on August 14, 2013 with SF background Attorney France Hoang, he was immediately attuned to the federal national security information/implications regarding what I shared. In turn, he introduced me to Brian O'Shea, a PI also with SF background. Despite an apparent agenda-driven motive, France also referred me to Dr. Amir Afhkami because of his work with the SF community, and his having a top-secret clearance. Yet, in their selection of Henrietta Kellum of McLean, Virginia, a security clearance was not an issue. Given I requested George Dodge to even ask the question and obtain a written determination by the Department of State regarding this matter, the memo speaks for its self.

Next, Henrietta Kellum from McLean, Virginia was selected for an independent evaluation, yet she wasn't even a doctor. Nor did Henrietta Kellum have a USG security clearance. After meeting with Henrietta Kellum in person, being recorded as I recall, she would then, in turn, plagiarize and regurgitate VHC Dr. Benjamin Adewale's fraudulent diagnosis regardless of what I said and did. Henrietta did not have the credentials to overrule Dr. Adewale's May 8, 2013 testimony/written report and subsequently-obtained June 7, 2013 subpoenaed sworn affidavit from the Commonwealth of Virginia Attorney's Office. *And all the parties involved in her selection, knew that!*

The fact is this: on April 17, 2013, I spoke for about an hour with VHC Dr. Patricia Roy. I shared insight and details that I never provided to Dr. Benjamin Adewale due to and after his agenda-driven line of questioning during our first encounter of April 12, 2013. So precisely what was the basis/source of his fraudulent, purposeful and intentional misdiagnosis of *paranoid schizophrenia?* In fact, on April 18, 2013, I provided a hand-written *Change of Doctor* request to VHC Dr. Benjamin Adewale. He never got back to me and the change was never officially made. Yet, in reality it was because I never met with him again. Interestingly enough, in documented VHC Medical Record/Physician's Orders dated April 18, 2013, Dr. Adewale indicated "Transfer to the Institute ASAP" as did documented VHC Medical Record/Orders Report dated April 19, 2013 of Dr. Adewale's note, "Transfer to the Institute ASAP." So, who was he writing his note to—particularly since my attorney and I never got access despite continual requests prior to the May 8th Appeal Hearing for these applicable VHC medial records? It was Stephen Burns perhaps, since he did get access on May 7th. On December 13, 2013, Henrietta Kellum filed a regurgitated Mental Health Evaluation to the Commonwealth of Virginia/Arlington County Circuit Court. Based on Henrietta Kellum's evaluation, I would be deemed *incapacitated*.

On December 13, 2013, Henrietta Kellum could have done the ethical and professional thing—either refute Dr. Adewale and/or step down due to not having the applicable credentials to truly provide an independent evaluation assessment. But, she didn't. On December 17, 2015, I amended my applicable Complaint with the Commonwealth of Virginia/ Department of Health Professions/Enforcement Division to include independent evaluator Henriette Kellum. If and when she was contacted by applicable Commonwealth of Virginia Enforcement Division investigators, Henrietta Kellum was given yet another opportunity to come clean and tell the truth. She did not. On December 8, 2019, I left a telephone message for Henrietta Kellum regarding these facts, her confirmation and comment for this book. To this day, Henrietta Kellum of McLean Virginia has not returned my call. I doubt she ever will.

Needless to say, I missed the *65-day* MSPB Appeal Filing deadline, for I now had a bigger battle to confront—the purposeful and intentional taking away of my rights, all my rights, as an American citizen and a human being.

On December 17, 2013, I received an email from George Dodge:

> Michelle,
> I'm working on some matters for tomorrow so get some rest and I will see you at 10:00 a.m. on the 10th floor of the Arlington Courthouse.
>
> As we discussed earlier today since you will testify last that provides an opportunity for you to rebut your father and others. I will ask you questions that will permit you to elaborate matters and provide rebuttal. You will do fine. You are truthful and smart so just listen to my questions and answer them when on the witness stand. When opposing counsel asks you a question answer briefly, if possible, with yes or no. Don't be afraid to say you don't know an answer of if you are unsure then states so. Answer the questions directly head on. That's my advice. See you tomorrow. George Dodge[9]

I did as George advised, and what I was already doing the whole entire time—telling the truth!

But it didn't matter. On December 17, 2013, Commonwealth of Virginia/Arlington County Circuit Court Judge Louise M. DiMatteo deemed me *incapacitated*, losing all my rights as an American citizen and a human being, which continues to this day as a result. She ordered me to yet another *involuntary* stay at the Virginia Hospital Center. This time, I was permitted to bring an overnight bag versus the last time when I was taken unconstitutionally from my residence in handcuffs by ACPD with nothing more than the clothes on my back. I survived the first round of retaliation, and now it was on to the second. And all this was because I resigned from the Department of State.

I was driven to VHC Emergency Unit by George Dodge, and once again admitted involuntarily—*against my will*—overnight on December 17, 2013 at 7:02 p.m. After my arrival, supposedly due to the stress, there was a concern regarding my heart. So, an EKG was requested supposedly by VHC staff. After being monitored and meeting with VA/AC/DHS officials, VHC doctors and nursing throughout the night, the next day, on December 18, 2013 at 11:53 a.m., I was released. For the purposeful and intentional targeting of me, their "medical" sham, for what it always was, was falling apart and it was quite apparent, to even these medical professionals, what was really going on.

INCAPACITATED

Then the events of December 18, 2013 occurred. Released from VHC and having no transportation home, I took a taxi. I had no cash. We stopped by an SDFCU ATM on the drive home so I could pay the cabbie upon arrival at my residence. I walked in the door and was heading to take a shower, but decided to check my emails and call George Dodge to let him know I was home and that I wanted to file an Appeal immediately. I was literally on the phone with George, when there was a knock at the door... I opened the door. I could not believe it—it was Arlington County Police once again! They asked if they could come in. I said I wanted my lawyer. They came in anyways, received some kind of dispatch while in my house and the next thing you know, ACPD, once again, was taking me out of my residence in handcuffs—taking me back, once again, against my will, to VHC. This time to commit me. *ARE YOU KIDDING ME!* All because I resigned! So off to VHC I went again, round two continues...

During this latest episode, one thing I can tell you for sure, I absolutely did not receive any telephone calls/messages nor emails from my estranged father or his lawyer Brent Baxter... So once again, they soon would be caught in yet another round of their lies!

Obtained through ACPD's February 11, 2015 FOIA response, here are the applicable ACPD Call for Service and ACPD Incident Report, both dated December 18, 2013. ACPD Call for Service #133520168 is as follows:

INITITIATE: 12:27:15 12-18-2013....
ENTRY: 12:29:48
DISPATCH: 12:32:28
ON SCENE: 12:39:05
CLOSE: 14:16:45...
LOCATION: [redacted] [redacted], ARLINGTON ([redacted])...
....TYPE: COW P – CHECK ON WELFARE ...
TEXT: [BLACKED OUT]/ DIAGNOSED WITH DE
TEXT: [BLACKED OUT]/DIAGNOSED WITH DE
PRESSION AND PSYCHOTIC EPISODES// CAN BE AGGRESSIVE, HAV
E ACCELERATED SPEECH, DISORGANIZED THINKING//
[BLACKED OUT]
[BLACKED OUT] WAS GIVEN LEGAL GUARDIANSHIP
LAST NIGHT \NAME
[BLACKED OUT]/ ATTY FOR GUARDIAN (DAD)\
PH:[BLACKED OUT]
(MTF)
AP ADMIN 04/12/13 @10:53;15 (2 MORE)
TEXT: FEMALE AND [BLACKED OUT] WENT TO THE HOSP TO BE EVALUATED BY DHS AND DETAINED (ORDER ALSO STATES THEY CAN HOLD HER FOR 10 DAYS PSYCH EVAL)// DAD LEFT VHC AROUND MIDNIGHT AS THEY WERE TRYING TO FIND A BED FOR HER (MTF)
TEXT: SHE APPARENTLY LEFT THE HOSPITAL AND IS NOT ANSWERING HER PHONE OR EMAIL/CALL RP WITH RESULTS/ HE CAN MEET
OFFICERS AT THE RESD OR AT DHS AND HAS THE PPWK
.168 NO WEAPONS IN THE HOUSE....
B24, CALL AND MEET AT RESIDENCE WITH PAPERWORK
.168, [BLACKED OUT] CELL [BLACKED OUT]
...
B23 VHC

B24 MAGIS

…

B24, PICKING UP ECO FOR INC .179

…

OPERATOR ASSIGNMENTS:
PD06 E109 PUTNAM, LYNNE ANNE
PD01 E316 WALKER, VERNETTE
PD02 E334 HORAN, HEATHER
PD04 P0939 DID NOT IN 0* CODE FILE

First of all, I was discharged by VHC on 12/18/2013 at 11:46:00 a.m., and have the VHC documentation to prove it. Secondly, there were absolutely no phone messages nor emails from my estranged father and his legal counsel Brent Baxter. Yet at 12:27:15, according to ACPD, a call was initiated. While in my residence is when ACPD received the dispatch. The applicable ACPD Incident Report #131218027 is as follows:

Offense Name: ECO….Time Reported: 1229…Capsule Narrative: AT THE ABOVE ADDRESS AND TIME I RESPONDED FOR A CHECK ON THE WELFARE. THE SUBJECT WAS TAKEN TO VHC AFTER AN ECO WAS GRANTED BY THE MAGISTRATE.
Complainant [Blacked Out]
Victim [Blacked Out]
..79. Name (Last, First, Middle) VICTIM IS OFFENDER ….107A
Gang Affiliation Name (something written but - illegible)
Narrative: On 12/18/2013 at approximately 1229 hours I responded to [BLACKED OUT] for a check on the welfare. The individual at this address is [BLACKED OUT] was admitted into Virginia Hospital Center yesterday for an evaluation by DHS.
[BLACKED OUT] was discharged 4 hours because DHS could not find any beds in order to TDO her. She then went home. Her father [BLACKED OUT] who was granted guardianship over her came back to the hospital this morning and found out she wasn't there. He did not know why she had been sent home, and called the non-emergency line.
I arrived at the address and made contact with [BLACKED OUT]. DHS was also contacted and Joseph Burgess stated he would call the Magistrate and obtain an ECO. The ECO was issued at 1304 hours.
I transported [BLACKED OUT] to VHC. I executed the ECO at 1340 hours and signed over custody to security office Ecucetory

#1357.
Date 12/18/2013
Reporting Officer (print)
Shapiro
Signature
/s/
Admin No.
1531

All of this is so bizarre. I left VHC because I was discharged. I went home. There were no such calls or emails. Now what I find even more bizarre is something written—though illegible—under 107A, *Gang Affiliation. What in the world!* Where in the world did that come from? And then under 79, *Victim Is Offender.* Offender of what? And now quite apparent, accomplices to all this retaliation against me was indeed the Arlington County Police Department! Working with someone in the USG. Who? And was my stopping by the SDFCU ATM for cash a triggering event? Precisely what crime was I an *offender* of? And again, why were there no investigations despite my continual reporting?

The referenced *Emergency Custody Order* (ECO) dated 12/18/2013, I would not obtain a copy of it until much later, years later in 2015. This ECO (013GM1300019155) Case Number 131218027 was issued by the Commonwealth of Virginia/Arlington County General District Court, with name and address of respondent blacked out, as well as date of birth, ssn, and current location. This ECO was issued upon motion of the undersigned and facts presented by Joseph Burgess and signed by Scott L. Scher on 12/18/2013 at 01:04 p.m. And according to the second page, Case No. 131218, this ECO was executed by taking the respondent into custody on this day:

> DATE AND TIME 12/18/17 1440
> OFFICER TAKING RESPONDENT INTO CUSTODY   SHA-PIRO
> BADGE NO, AGENCY AND JURISDICTION   1531   ACPD 000
> FOR SHERIFF (not filled in/left blank)

Wait a minute, issued by the General District Court Magistrate, not the Circuit Court? Now isn't all this interesting? And this, the Department of State/Assistant Secretary for Political-Military Affairs (PM) from 2009-2013, during the time I was on detail assignment to Germany was Andrew

Shapiro. The same last name of the *officer taking respondent into custody.*
From 2001-2009, Andrew was Senator Clinton's Senior Defense and Foreign Policy Advisor. Coincidence? Perhaps. Needless to say, at this point,
I don't discount any possibility, linkage, or coincidence one bit. For given
the national security implications at stake, and the players involved, to
me, all possibilities remain on the table to include this one. All this is directly related to the events of Germany and when seeing the name *Shapiro*
that is exactly what I first thought of. So the question remains, what role
did Andrew Shapiro play/have in all this?

On May 6, 2015, when I queried regarding this December 18, 2013
ECO, as well as the previous one dated April 12, 2013, according the Office of the Magistrate, there were no records maintained and names of the
individuals that supposedly presented applicable facts for the issuance of
either/both could not be provided. So, there are no files, no file copies
that reflect the facts for which either of these ECOs were based/issued,
and by whom.

On Wednesday, December 18, 2013, I was taken out of my residence
in handcuffs back to VHC for a third time, as retaliation round two was
not yet complete. I would be discharged on January 3, 2014. Once again,
I took daily documenting notes. And once again, I refused to take any
medication.

On Thursday, December 19, 2013, I met my *new* VHC doctor, Dr.
Ramanath Gopalan. He was very biased and had Dr. Adewale's previous
notes. During our initial discussion, I once again stated that I am a federal
CVRA victim/witness regarding the August 7, 1998 East Africa Embassy
bombing, an EEO Grievance Complainant against the US military, a federal government whistleblower and an OSC Grievance Complainant—
with this latest retaliatory stunt to prevent me from filing my applicable
MSPB Appeal. I once again refused any medication treatment, once again
invoked my rights, and specifically requested Dr. Gopalan to contact my
lawyer George Dodge and Human Rights Advocate Kevin Paluszak.

On December 19, 2013, I authorized VHC to disclose to my lawyer
George Dodge as once again, I requested to immediately file an appeal.
Later when I asked for copy for my files, *someone* at VHC put the wrong
patient label at the bottom of the form; curiously and conveniently, a different patient named *"Michelle."* Interestingly, though I never received a
corrected copy for my files, when I finally received the applicable VHC
Medical records months later, the incorrect form, which I have a copy of,
was not included; only the corrected form was in the records. My first re-

action was the games continue. And the games did continue, sometimes subtly, and at other times, very blatantly…

On Friday, December 20, 2013, I left a message for George Dodge and HRA Kevin Paluszak. These were names that I never authorized during this stay nor called at any time, my *estranged* family. Interestingly enough, when I spoke to Dr. Gopalan that day, he indicated that he spoke to my estranged father but had not reached my lawyer. Dr. Gopalan and I spoke again in his office. Lots of things were going on behind the scenes, games continuing to be played. With what I later discovered once documents were finally provided to me, it was quite apparent that my best interest was never the priority, as this was never about a mental health issue. Instead, it was a *cover-up*. And quite obviously, this was regarding the purposely and intentionally uninvestigated events that occurred in Germany, and beyond…

My first encounter with Dr. Benjamin Adewale occurred that Friday evening. I was in the lounge area when Dr. Adewale came to the unit. He saw me as he was walking passed, but we didn't say anything to each other. As he was leaving the unit, I said, "Hello Dr. Adewale." During our brief discussion, Dr. Adewale mentioned that he had met with "two men in black coats" (his description not mine). Now isn't that interesting? Since no additional insight was provided by Dr. Adewale, so many questions remain. So who were the "two men in black coats" that he was referring to? When did he meet with them? And on what legal authority, purpose for this meeting? Dr. Adewale then asked how my sister was doing and discussed my plans to include my moving to California. Considering he was not my doctor I found all this very odd… Just like our initial and previous encounters. To this day, I do not know who his source for information was—but one thing for sure, it was not me. On April 12, 2013, when I asked, Dr. Adewale told me he was of Jamaican background. During this second, subsequent VHC encounter, an individual, a fellow patient with a naval intelligence background confirmed that Dr. Adewale's background was Nigerian. At least that is what Dr. Adewale had told him, when he asked. So, why did he lie to me? I also found out during this time that VHC supposedly held the rehabilitation/detoxication contract with the US Navy/USMC. Interesting… again, in light of events and players involved. Particularly in light of the applicable ACPD Incident report had something written but illegible regarding, "Gang Affiliation." So what was all this really about? And what was really going on?

On Saturday, December 21, 2013, I spoke with Dr. Patricia Roy. I shared with her all that occurred including Dr. Adewale's role, confirmed that once again all this was retaliatory tactics and not about a mental health issue, and once again refused any medication. She advised that at this time Dr. Gopalan had not prescribed medication other than as needed, if needed.

Now very interesting, while speaking to Dr. Roy, another patient ate my breakfast. So, I had to order another one. Soon after eating breakfast, I became a little lightheaded. I drank water and then suspected that someone overruled my decision and was putting *something* in my food. I requested an immediate blood test… The nurse spoke with Dr. Roy and said no such test would be necessary and that they would not do such an unethical thing. She said that as my nurse, she is the only one allowed to provide medication to me and that she didn't give me anything.

Later that evening, Dr. Adewale was hanging around the nursing desk when I came out of my room. He started backpedaling about talking to my sister… Remember, this is the day after seeing Dr. Adewale for the first time, and the same day, my breakfast was eaten by another patient, replaced, and then I felt light-headed. And now after dinner, I was feeling light-headed again … *Coincidence?* Perhaps. *Something more sinister?* Absolutely a possibility.

On Sunday, December 22, 2013, I advised Dr. Roy accordingly, keeping a copy of the note for my files:

12/22/2013
Dr Roy –
Just want to be clear – I do not want to take any medication, for as you informed me, the doctor (Dr. Gopalan) "recommended" not directed the drugs listed per our confirmation yesterday.

Therefore, I believe that is it possible that I was provided drugs on 12/21/2013 <u>AGAINST MY WILL,</u> and based on my <u>father's/ sister's</u> authority - not mine. Dr. Adewale coordinated this with my family/my sister. As you are an ethical doctor, I want you to be aware that this possibly has happened and under your watch.

Please note that if this indeed happened Janelle Bell/her nursing staff must have played a role as well – to provide the drugs.

The "lightheadedness" I felt after eating my breakfast was nothing in comparison how I felt soon after dinner.

Again, you are an ethical doctor, I really hope you will do the ethical thing regarding Dr. Adewale Janelle Bell in regards to whether this happened w/coordination w/my father/sister (who was/is a pharmaceutical rep) + others on your staff/unit.[10]

What I didn't put in writing, and wouldn't at all eliminate as a possibility, was the involvement off the unit and the VHC kitchen staff. Again, given the events, given the parties involved, and given the implications to what I know, I won't eliminate any possibility. Though I was not provided my VHC Medical files again until much later, this event that occurred was indicated in the VHC Medical file notes. Soon after, Dr. Roy was not on the floor for a period of time, on leave for the Christmas holiday.

On Monday, December 23, 2013, during my discussion with Dr. Gopalan, he indicated that I either be discharged or forced medication due to my paranoia. I noted that I really liked Dr. Roy, that we had discussed what was involved for a guardian to overrule the will of a patient, the possibility of looking into the misdiagnosis, and that she had confirmed medicine was optional. I discussed liking her very much as a doctor, her willingness to investigate what I say, and that I trusted her. I also noted that I called Kevin, the Human Rights Advocate. Later, I left another message with George Dodge, wanting to know the status of my appeal.

I found it very odd that despite my trusting Dr. Patricia Roy, my continued request to be under her care was denied. It was like it was being intentionally done for me to remain with Dr. Benjamin Adewale of supposed Nigerian background, and now Dr. Ramanath Gopalan of supposed Pakistani background. Why? Why was this so significant? I don't know. But obviously it was to someone and for some reason. Otherwise, why was Dr. Patricia Roy, who I trusted most of all the options, being blocked, denied to assist me if all of this was truly, and only about me and my well-being. Such a simple request. So, whatever *this* was—it was never about me and my well-being and my best interest. And now, to find out about VHC's linkages with the US Navy/USMC rehab/detox contract. The coincidences were beyond coincidental…

On Thursday, December 26, 2013, Sandra Garza, the social worker from the previous VHC involuntary stay, came to tell me that there would be a meeting on Friday, December 27 with Dr. Gopalan, my lawyer George Dodge, and my estranged father, if she can get a hold of him. Later Sandy came into the training room. With the door closed, she disrupted the discussion I was having with another patient and his guest—who by the way was from the National Counterterrorism Center (NCTC). She wanted me to leave our discussion so she could advise me regarding what

 10   Michelle Stefanick, letter to Patricia Roy,, December 22, 2013

HRA Kevin had said. I refused, and said anything she had to say, she could say in front of those present. She then said Kevin would not be present at tomorrow's meeting unless my estranged father approved my lawyer George Dodge to attend.

This interaction was odd in so many ways. First of all, according to the Patient Wall Chart, Sandra Garza was not even my assigned Social Case Worker. Shaquila Jones was. So why was Sandra even involved? Sandy indicated Kevin would not be present unless my estranged father gave permission for my lawyer to be present. Meaning it would be just me, with no lawyer and possibly no Human Rights Advocate, no one present representing my rights. Needless to say, I found all this unacceptable.

I called George Dodge to relay the message and was advised that he was planning to attend the meeting. Then I left a message for Kevin about what Sandra said and asked him to call me. During this time around, I had absolutely no internet availability at all. Later, I walked into Sandra's office stating that I would not attend if both George and Kevin did not attend. I then placed a hard copy of the VHC Human Rights sheet that was hanging on the wall on Sandra's desk and walked out.

On Friday, December 27, 2013, there was a meeting at VHC. The attendees included Dr. Gopalan, Sandra Garza (social worker), George Dodge (my attorney), Brent Baxter (my estranged father's attorney), myself and via phone, my estranged father, and Kevin Paluszak (HRA). Oddly enough, before the meeting even began, Sandra tried to connect with Kevin twice, and it went through to his voicemail both times. I told her to try again and asked if she called the right number—providing her his number—which she dialed to reach him. Kevin was finally connected to attend.

Dr. Gopalan started the meeting with information that was partially incorrect regarding his prescription status—I interjected that Dr. Roy confirmed this was recommended not required. My estranged father agreed with whatever Dr. Gopalan said. When Dr. Gopalan tried to speak on behalf of Dr. Roy, I said Dr. Roy could speak for herself when she returns. Particularly since it seemed a given that she took my well-being as a priority. She listened, taking my due process into account, and showed the willingness to look into what I said regarding the misdiagnosis by Dr. Adewale by finding out the source of his information since he pre-diagnosed me without ever seeing me.

Needless to say, Dr. Gopalan seemed very intent in strapping me down against my will, and drugging me up even though there was no emergency reason. I was not, and never was, a harm to myself and/or others. The misdiagnosis was purposeful and intentional. And all that was done against my will. My estranged father then mentioned me becoming homeless/jobless. And his stating this proved the fact that I resigned, meaning that I was not fired previously, as he and others stated under oath on April 15, 2013. I stated that I would not end up homeless and wanted to leave Arlington since he called the police so many times that I no longer wanted to live here. I also planned to leave to be away from my estranged family and the US Department of State. That was what was best for my well-being. I resigned. My resignation was accepted. So, I questioned at that time, and I continue to question to this day, since still unanswered—who told my estranged father/family about my resignation since I never did?

Kevin spoke to include about holding me against my will. I told Kevin about my estranged father calling ACPD while I was en route from VHC to my home after being released ... His reporting me as a *missing person* to bring me in handcuffed by ACPD to VHC again *against my will.*

I was of sound mind, yet without my approval, my estranged father had been tossing copies of my 2003/2008 Power of Attorney (POA) around like it was candy, instead of a legal document and very pertinent to me and my life.He was advising everyone, without my knowledge, awareness nor approval—my bank, credit card companies, thrift savings plan, VHC—(yes, this very Virginia Hospital Center) etc, with simply a letter stating that HE was in control; he was not and had absolutely no legal standing to do what he was doing, what he did, and what was done. And then in December 17, 2013 gets me deemed incapacitated. What he did is called Fraud. He knew it and many of these supposed Officials of the Court knew it.

George Dodge then spoke. Sandra didn't really say much. And my estranged father's lawyer Brent Baxter spoke regarding legal vs. human rights issues, emergency vs. non-emergency, misdiagnosis, against my will, and Dr. Roy – unfortunately not present nor available since on leave. Brent tried to silence me regarding the missing person stunt, the fraudulent use of 2003/2008 POA stunt, and my resignation—to which Brent attributed to my being *emotional*. I ended by saying I hope my estranged father is paying all my bills since I do not have access to internet. The meeting concluded with Kevin saying he would send information on Monday, and that "one cannot hold someone against their will."

In front of witnesses, Dr. Gopalan made statements of wanting to strap me down against my will to medicate me. My estranged father and his legal counsel, Brent Baxter, agreed and wanted such action to be taken—wanting me to be strapped down against my will and in essence, lobotomized. The *true character and intent of individuals was exposed during this process…*

On Saturday, December 28, 2013, Dr. Gopalan was walking by my room when I walked out, but he never met with me… The same thing occurred on Sunday, December 29, 2013. It would not be until Monday, December 30, 2013 that he would ask what bills needed to be paid…

Since it was confirmed regarding the fraudulent use and abuse of my *2003/2008 POA* by my estranged family, I pursued answers. I queried VHC Medical Records, but I never heard back. Sandra Garza mentioned it, then didn't have time to follow-up accordingly… Seems lots of *CYA* was now going on. Since I had no access to internet, on Monday, December 30, 2013, on my behalf, VHC Hester Finn sent via fax, the following email to Kevin Paluszak:

> To Kevin Paluszak from Michelle Stefanick
> Kevin,
> Thank you for again assisting with my situation. Please find attached what I provided to Janelle/VHC, but still have not heard a response/no corrective action yet implemented. With that, I also became aware that in April 2013, my father fraudulently/inappropriately used my "2003/2008 Power of Attorneys." Other entities he sent this "packet" to are now investigating this matter. According to Sandra, the case worker, this "packet" should have been included in my permanent records. As you are aware, I requested my records from VHC when I got home in May 2013. This "POA packet" was not included in the information I received from VHC. I called Medical Records this morning to find out status and reason why and "Brenda" said she would get back to me. I wanted you to be aware of this action as well that needs to be investigated accordingly.
> Sincerely,
> Michelle Stefanick[11]

On Tuesday, December 31, 2013, I attended a Team Meeting with Janelle, Shaquilla, Sandra, and Christine, but Dr. Roy was not there. The meeting, with the purpose to discuss a discharge plan, lasted less than 2 minutes.

---

11   Michelle Stefanick, email message to Kevin Paluzak, December 30, 2013

On Wednesday, January 1, 2014, Dr. Gopalan mentioned that he received Kevin's email, yet he never shared it with me. He advised that Sandra received it and thought she shared it with me. He made a comment that he hoped my estranged father was paying my bills and then mentioned something about holding me here at VHC until January 13, 2014. I requested a copy of the email from Sandra Garza.

On Thursday, January 2, 2014, I left Kevin Paluszak a message:

> Kevin – Still have not heard back from VHC Medical Records regarding the fraudulent use of my 2003/2008 POA in April 2013 by my father and VHC; if you provided info to Sandra I still have not received it; Dr. Gopalan was disappointed to know that he couldn't force medication into me and says he will hold me here against my will until Dr. Roy returns; I want the Director of VHC to know and I want a full investigation; I want to be released as VHC/my father are holding me against my will. This all continues to be retaliatory action against me as a federal CVRA-accorded rights and protections regarding the August 7, 1998 East Africa Embassy bombing; for my upcoming EEO against the US military and as a federal government whistleblower. I am not an intelligence employee nor a military employee![12]

I then left a message for George Dodge:

> George – Supposedly Kevin sent info to Sandra earlier this week, but she never shared it with me—that's according to Dr. Gopalan—who met with me for the first time yesterday since our meeting on Friday. Hope my bills/mortgages are being paid.[13]

At approximately 10:05 a.m., on Thursday, January 2, 2014, I finally received a copy of HRA Kevin Paluszak's December 30, 2013 email:

> Subject: RE: call tomorrow
> Good afternoon Miss Sandra,
> In follow up to our 1 p.m. conference call on December 27 and our phone call later that afternoon, please consider the following:
> The first question the team should consider is that if the individual is not going to follow up treatment after discharge, and the medication over objection treatment would require long term follow-up…is the one time forced medication in the long term therapeutic and relational best interests of the patient?
> In regards to the question can medication be given over objection the answer is "yes." However in this case the court appointed

12   Michelle Stefanick, phone message to Kevin Paluzak, January 2, 2014
13   Michelle Stefanick, email message to George Dodge,, January 2, 2014

guardian has given consent for treatment and the individual has been determined (by the courts) to not have capacity to consent (or object). In this specific case, the medication may be given if clinical determinated appropriate.

However, the individual does have the right to be free from restraint. So in other words, a standing order for a restraint to administer medication would be a violation of the individual's rights. It is also important to note that giving medication over objection does not mean forcibly holding or restraining an individual. Restraint requires an emergency, and has specific criteria for use/release.

I realize this is a complex treatment concern, and all parties desire the best interest of the individual. If I may provide additional regulatory guidance or assistance, please don't hesitate to let me know.

Sincerely.

Kevin[14]

Sandra had this email since 3:47 p.m., Monday, December 30, 2013. If I had not demanded a copy, I would never have received it. More than just games being played, she was hiding something. For instance, the copy of the email was on a slip of paper torn so other contents from the entire Garza/Paluszak email exchange was not shared with me. Remember she made a few attempts to reach Kevin on Friday December 27, 2013 at the time of the meeting—and they went straight to voicemail. I provide Kevin's phone number and viola, Kevin answers and is connected to attend the meeting. Also, note the email subject line "RE: call tomorrow." So clearly, there was a previous email exchange regarding the "call tomorrow" and at minimum, at least between Sandra and Kevin. Here's the summary I wrote to myself while still at VHC, being held against my will:

1) Challenge initial "diagnosis" since had no prior at all for the basis of this. Therefore, who is the source of Dr. Adewale's information? When Dept/Patricia English/Father brought me involuntarily?
2) Why is Sandra involved considering Shaquilla is on the board as my case worker. Why was 2003/2008 POA packet not provided to me/Medical Records not yet get back with me.
3) I found out by Dr. Gopalan that Kevin sent the email. Sandra initially said she didn't receive response and then would get me a copy. Finally received on 1/2/2014—after I asked for it—otherwise I would not have received it. When asked who she gave it to— would not respond, with major attitude she walked away. When I

---

took a copy of "human rights" and put it in her office—she said she didn't want it and walked out and put it on a chair in the tv lounge. When I brought it and placed it on her office chair again— she threatened to call security. Yet, none of my questions have been answered. They are simple questions and I don't understand all the defensiveness if all is "above aboard.

Yet, to this day, and as I write this book, these such simple questions— despite being continually asked—have never been answered…

And how about these:what did Dr. Adewale mean when he mentioned meeting with "two men in black coats?? Did he really mean this? Or did he lie, again, just like he did about his background? Or what about his bigger lie, his fraudulent misdiagnosis and lying in and to a court of law, not just once, under oath—on May 8, 2013, but again in a sworn subpoenaed affidavit again on June 7, 2013. And why did he mention my sister? When did he met her/talk with her? I certainly didn't introduce them or bring her up in our discussions. How did he know of my plans to include potentially moving to California? Again, I certainly didn't mention any of this time to him. Odd, very odd, isn't it? And is it true VHC held the addiction rehabilitation/detoxication contract with the US Navy/USMC? Again, in light of all the events and players involved, just coincidences?

According to the hard copy of the VHC Discharge packet I received and have to this day, my *Discharge Date/Time* was at *01/03/2014 9:04 a.m.* and the *Attending Physician* was *Ramanath Gopalan.* Just like previously, I immediately sent a written *Virginia Hospital Center Authorization for Release of Medical Record Information* request form on January 3, 2014. I then patiently waited...

HOME AGAIN BUT FOR HOW LONG?

Meanwhile, I returned to my home, until that eventually was taken away from me by my estranged father—you know the one who was so concerned about me being homeless, then squandered my entire real estate portfolio. All this was done without my authorization, without my approval, and it was all taken from me against my will. And because there were absolutely no investigations into the events, including the targeted retaliatory actions taken against me while I was assigned in Germany with the US military, specifically the US Navy/USMC MARFOREUR/ AF. He received my State Department paychecks from October 2013 onward, and then my retirement checks to this day, even as I write this book.

Every chance I had to fight back, I did. However, he, his lawyer and their accomplices were so unethical, that no matter what I did—to include exposing the fraud and the crimes they committed to resort to all this—they fought me every step of the way. At one point, he bragged how he could not have accomplished all this on his own. So who precisely were his accomplishes? Who precisely at the State Department, within the USG was he working with?

So, needless to say, I was, and continue to be, both livid and traumatized. I was telling the truth. I did nothing wrong. And the betrayal at every level, quite overwhelming and unbelievable.

At one point, as I was receiving absolutely no money for food, utilities, or personal items, I had to ask friends to borrow money. Friends paid for food deliveries, others literally paid my utility bills, and others sent me money/debit cards in order for me to survive. And all the while, my estranged father knew, his lawyer Brent Baxter knew, the Court-appointed Guardian ad litem Stephen Burns knew, my attorney George Dodge, Judge DiMatteo—they all knew how I was being treated. And no one cared—because as you can see, this was never a mental health issue; it was never about me and my best interest, but about a cover-up. At one point, I completed and filed my 2013 Federal and State taxes as I had done every single year prior—to once again prove that I was not incapacitated. But it didn't matter. My estranged father and his lawyer Brent Baxter just took the refund money that I received. What I was subjected to was nothing short of torture. And why? All because I resigned from the US Department of State. And again, as I continually asked then and continually ask to this day, how did a federal national security matter with federal jurisdiction end up in a state-level, the Commonwealth of Virginia, Arlington County Court system? And again, as I continually asked then and continually ask to this day, how did a state-level, the Commonwealth of Virginia, Arlington County Circuit Court Judge overrule a federal senate-confirmed presidential cabinet-level Secretary of State, Secretary John Kerry's, decision to accept my resignation effective October 1, 2013? To this day, I continually ask, how is all this possible? On March 8, 2014, I finally received the purposely, intentionally delayed Department of State/Diplomatic Security response regarding my May 19, 2013 FOIA/Privacy Request.

On February 6, 2014, ACPD would once again show up at my doorstep. Needless to say, after all I had been through, and the numerous times prior that I advised ACPD accordingly, they were not a welcome at my door. Nor at this time for what they did not do—protect me. Here's the applicable ACPD Call for Service #140370200 dated February 6, 2014 that I received in ACPD's February 11, 2015 FOIA response:

> INITITIATE: 15:11:50 02-06-2014....
> ENTRY: 15:13:47
> DISPATCH: 15:15:20
> ON SCENE: 15:21:52
> DISPATCH: 15:35:08...
> LOCATION: [redacted] ([redacted])..
> ....TYPE: COW P – CHECK ON WELFARE ...
> PHONE: [redacted] *(ADDED BY WRITER: ARLINGTON COUNTY MENTAL HEALTH EMERGENCY SERVICES)*
> TEXT: COW ON A [BLACKED OUT]. SHE IS UN-DER GUARDIANSHIP OF HER [BLACKED OUT]. HER [BLACKED OUT] REPORTS THAT SHE IS NOT EAITING AND NO FOOD IN THE HOUSE. SHE CAN BE VERY PAR-ANOID. UNK WEPS, SHE LIVES ALONE. \NAME: DHS [BLACKED OUT] – CR7 14\PH 703 228 5160 (MTF)
> AP COW 12/18/13 @ 12:29:48 (3 MORE)
> TEXT: PHONE FOR [BLACKED OUT] IS [BLACKED OUT]. DOB [BLACKED OUT].
> ...
> TEXT: PER RMS, W/F OUT LAST CONTACT WAS DEC 18 REPORT NBR 131218027
> TEXT: THAT INCIDENT DOCUMENTS AN ECO AND THE PERSON WAS TRANSPORTED TO THE VHC.
> ...
> OPERATOR ASSIGNMENTS:
> TY01 E139 SPENCER, RICHARD E
> PD01 P1088 DID NOT IN 0* CODE FILE
> P701 1489 GILMORE, DEVIN"

Of course, just like previously, having not received VHC Patient's medical records in time for the February 18, 2014 hearing, I would have to send a second written request on March 9, 2014. Finally, on May 8, 2014, though initially requested on January 3, 2014, I received 273 pages in regards to the December 17, 2013–January 3, 2014 involuntary ordeal. Again, after so much damage had already been done, how precisely do you fight back in correcting a purposeful and intentional false narrative set into motion by the Deep State? But I would, and I did, and I continue to do so, to this day, and every step of the way—until the truth is exposed. For justice delayed is justice denied.

Like previously, I went page-by-page and documented every inaccuracy/misstatement, and just like previously, I took daily/documenting notes. With 273 pages to review, my serious review in essence ended after reading page seven...it said it all. All of this was nothing but a set-up. The applicable VHC document was printed on 12/18/2013 at 12:15 P.M., and under the Admission Assessment section, a comment was indicated under Family History made by VHC Dr. Christopher Olson on 4/12/2013 at 12:30 P.M., "Denies significant family history." Really? Wait a minute—what does that mean? What specifically is he referring to? And more specifically, who was his source to enter such a statement? Given the documented evidence regarding US Department of State's preorchestration of April 12, 2013 and follow-on Commitment Hearing of April 15, 2013, who precisely is the source for VHC Dr. Christopher Olson's statement? DS? HR? Because it certainly was not me, nor was it in my BC/BS medical records or my State Department/Med medical files. So, who?

Then I got to page twenty-one of 273—The entry made on 12/18/2013 at 12:00 P.M. by Nurse Diana Rodriguez: "Spoke to Dr. Mueller regarding pt's discharge, states pt is stable to go home, we are not to be involved with notifying her father. Charge nurse aware." Yet, previous notes indicated "her father" is the "POA." Clear as day, all this was a set-up and obviously, VHC was a willing participant/accomplice—and all at my expense. Within only hours, I would be brought back (again) in handcuffs—against my will—by Arlington County Police due to an ECO; do I need to say anymore? These VHC Medical Records and finally receiving the US Department of State May 19, 2013 FOIA-requested DS document response in March 2014—all was clear as day. And documented.

On Thursday, May 29, 2014, I sent an email to my new attorney Luke Lenzi:

> Luke – In light of our discussion today, I was wondering if there was even a reason for me to attend tomorrow's hearing? If you could call/email back your thoughts I would really appreciate it.
>
> You need to understand. Michael Stefanick has pulled such undermining stunts throughout this process, that I do not trust him at all. I must say I am very concerned that once George is no longer my legal counsel that Michael Stefanick may even try to take me out my home and to PA with him against my will and my best interest.
>
> With that, your insight would be sincerely appreciated. Thanks

so much. Cheers, Michelle[15]

On Friday, May 30, 2014, I sent the following to Roni LeBlanc:

> Hi – Just to let you know, I took you advice and didn't go to the Hearing this morning. As my due process/best interests rights were never apart of this sinister act, my thought is why should I even be involved any more. At least I have it in writing, George Dodge's writing in the Motion he wrote/filed that he doesn't/ didn't have my best interest at all during this entire process. Now the Judge/Michael Stefanick/the Dept/USG can continue with their game—I'm just not participating. Give me a call when you can. Thanks, Michelle[16]

Some additional insight... On Tuesday, May 20, 2014, I received the following email from George Dodge, ccing Brent Baxter and Stephen Burns:

> Subject: In re: Michelle Stefanick
> Attached is my timesheet and a Certificate if Filing regarding the hearing set for Friday, May 30, 2014.
> George Dodge
> George W. Dodge
> Attorney at Law[17]

Attached to the email was one attachment: *Certificate of Mailing and Timesheet.pdf.* George Dodge was stepping down as my attorney. So, my question to this day, what's the status of the Appeal I requested George Dodge to immediately file on December 18, 2013? Well, needless to say, I was livid. He lied. Despite my continual requests, my own legal counsel George Dodge never intended to do as I was requesting, and demanding—that an Appeal be filed.

I sent this email to Roni:

> Hi Roni – As I haven't heard back from you in a while, just thought you should see the latest—today I received George's timesheet and he's never been in touch with me since May 8 – so you tell me what's going on? If you can call I would appreciate it. Thanks, Michelle[18]

---

15   Michelle Stefanick, email message to Luke Lenzi, May 29, 2014

16   Michelle Stefanick, email message to Roni LeBlanc, May 30, 2014

17   George Dodge, email message to Michelle Stefanick, Brett Baxter, and Stephen Burns, May 20, 2014

18   Michelle Stefanick, email message to Roni LeBlanc, May 30, 2014

Roni LeBlanc was a dear friend I met while serving together at Embassy Yaoundé, Cameroon. With DOD, Roni worked with security assistance.

On Thursday, May 29, 2014, I sent an email to George Dodge, ccing my new attorney, Luke Lenzi:

Subject: Authority for Discussion
Hello George – In preparation for tomorrow's (Friday May 30) Hearing at 10:00 in Arlington Circuit Court, I hereby authorize you to speak with Luke Lenzi of The Lenzi Law Firm, PLLC. Thank you, Michelle L. Stefanick[19]

George replied:

Michelle,
I will give him a call.
George Dodge
George W. Dodge
Attorney at Law[20]

Now not trusting George, I forwarded his response to Luke Lenzi:

Luke – Unfortunately George didn't cc you on this, so I wanted to give you a heads up. Thanks. Cheers, Michelle[21]

In due time, I finally received all of George Dodge's *Court Copy* timesheets pertinent and applicable to this entire timeframe. Timesheet: October 25, 2013 to December 17, 2013; Timesheet: December 17, 2013 to February 18, 2014; Timesheet: February 18, 2014 to May 30, 2014—attached to Invoice dated May 6, 2015. When I reviewed the timesheets, what I read was beyond telling, the most telling of all being the following entry:

01-13-2014 .5   Return call to Michelle Stefanick
She does not want to Appeal.[22]

I could not believe what I was reading. *This was absolutely NOT TRUE!* I never said I didn't want to Appeal. I was continually asking George the status. If this were not true, then why did I locate another attorney Luke Lenzi when George filed a motion to step down in May 2014. George Dodge, an attorney, my attorney, lied.

19   Michelle Stefanick, email message to George Dodge and Luke Lenzi, May 29, 2014
20   George Dodge email message to Michelle Stefanick and Luke Lenzi, May 29, 2014
21   Michelle Stefanick, email message to Luke Lenzi, May 29, 2014
22   George Dodge's timesheet for December 17, 2013 to February 18, 2014

On June 24, 2014, due to the actions, and lack of actions, taken in representing me, their client, and my best interest, I filed a Virginia State Bar Inquiry Form regarding G. "Rex" Flynn, Jr; Stephen D. Burns; and George W. Dodge. On March 9, 2016, I received the no surprise response. Nothing was going to be done.

On June 23, 2014, I had filed a Complaint with Judicial Inquiry and Review Commission against the Commonwealth of Virginia/Arlington County – General District and Circuit Court Judges: George Gill, Paul F. Sheridan, and Louise M. DiMatteo. The response would be no surprise, but again, at this point I just wanted to document and file legitimate complaints accordingly, so when the truth came out no one can say they didn't know! On June 26, 2014, I received the expected response. The June 25, 2014 Commonwealth of Virginia Judicial Inquiry and Review Commission response signed by Katherine B. Burnett Counsel, in part, stated:

> …Judges do not violate any ethical rules by rejecting a party's evidence…

The fact is that I was at the time a federal CVRA-accorded victim/witness regarding the August 7, 1998 East Africa Embassy bombing still under FBI investigation, an EEO grievance complainant against US Military still open, pending litigation, a federal government whistleblower, and an OSC formal complainant retaliated against within the 65-day MSPB appeal filing timeframe. Yet, It is a federal offense to threaten, intimidate harass, or mislead a witness in a criminal or civil proceeding, *is it not? And no one is above the law, right?*

When I found out more and received even more pertinent evidence, I filed yet another Judicial Inquiry and Review Commission Complaint – Commonwealth of Virginia/Arlington County General District and Circuit Courts—George Gill, William Newman, Paul F. Sheridan, Louise M. DiMatteo dated March 5, 2016, amending and adding Judge Newman accordingly. On March 10, 2016, I received the response. Again, the response, no surprise.

Needless to say, by this point, I knew the *cover-up* was so far down a *false-narrative rabbit hole*, that all I could do was fight back with the truth. I contacted every entity I could think of, filing legitimate complaints every step of the way. For one day the truth would come out and all these entities/individuals that I contacted/informed/reported to accordingly all along the way would have known and could have/should have done something—but they didn't. And now it's all documented. They all knew and they all did nothing!

To provide even more context, on February 20, 2014, I became aware of this very interesting insight: *FBI Creates Northern Virginia Corruption Tip Line*. According to the media reporting, the FBI recently opened a tip line/task force dedicated to Northern Virginia(especially Arlington and Fairfax Counties) targeting corruption to include information regarding county officials, law enforcement, and court officials, to include Judges. I read this and my mouth dropped. Really? Now isn't that interesting and curious in its timing. So needless to say, I immediately contacted the FBI Northern Virginia Corruption Tip line. And once again, the DOJ and FBI did absolutely nothing—nothing to intervene, nothing to investigate, nothing to protect me, and nothing to put an end to this purposeful and intentional retaliation taken place against me. *This is our nation's Department of Justice and Federal Bureau of Investigation!*

I was fighting back regarding this intentional *false-narrative* put into place at the federal level, now also at the state-level, and the county-level. Again, with this *false-narrative* rabbit hole, all I could do was call every entity I could think of, report to every entity I could think of, all while I was obtaining more and more insight/supporting evidence as to the crimes, targeted crimes committed against me, and absolutely no one was investigating accordingly.

I found all the inaccuracies/errors/misstatements in both the VHC and NVMHI Medical records, when I finally obtained them. Yet, all they had to do was check/confirm with my State/Medical and BC/BS. So, in early November 2014, now with more than ample evidence to prove the retaliatory actions taken against me, which included using the court and medical healthcare systems as a retaliatory tool, I contacted BC/BS officials of both Anthem and Carefirst. As a federal employee with BC/BS, I not only reported this use and abuse of the medical healthcare system by the US Department of State/USG as a retaliatory tool writ large, but in my case, I demanded an investigation for the medical insurance claim fraud that had occurred. And more importantly, there was *the purposeful, intentional, fraudulent, bogus, unsubstantiated misdiagnosis* made by Dr. Benjamin Adewale. From December 16, 2014–December 29, 2014, I was in continual contact with BC/BS officials Dave Waltemeyer, Tom Gambichler, and Doug Mailhot. For all those federal USG employees who have BC/BS as a health insurance carrier, despite my reporting and my request for assistance, given my documented BC/BS Medical files and the anomaly this misdiagnosis was, BC/BS did nothing. Even after advising BC/BS that all this was retaliation due to my federal CVRA-accorded status as a victim/witness regarding the August 7, 1998 East Africa Embassy bombing, as an EEO grievance complainant against the US Military, as federal government whistleblower, and an OSC formal complainant in Appeal status with the MSPB, BC/BS did nothing.

On February 04, 2015, I submitted an ACPD FOIA request. Once I obtained the ACPD FOIA-response on February 11, 2015 from Internal Affairs Section Lieutenant Scott Linder, I could not believe what I was reading. My initial question is why didn't any of my Attorney's—Rex Flynn, George Dodge, Luke Lenzi – obtain any of these for me prior? The lies/inaccuracies/misstatements… Over and over, and once again, why was there no follow-up to what I reported? There was no follow-up with my initial report to ACPD dated October 12, 2011, or to the March 28, 2013 surrounding my house dressed in tactical gear with guns locked and loaded incident. Who was the US Department of State/DS Official that made this *false-narrative* call to ACPD on March 28, 2013? All with the apparent motive to transition a federal national security matter of federal jurisdiction to a state-level. And why? What was the motive and intent—which now is clear as day—to destroy the credibility of a federal CVRA-accorded victim/witness regarding the August 7, 1998 East Africa Embassy bombings. I also filed a complaint. Guess what the result was?

Also, in February 2015, after initially reaching out in February 2014, I contacted Arlington County Government officials, the Arlington County Manager and Board officials accordingly regarding the retaliation that took place against me. Guess what happened next? I contacted my state-level Delegate Representatives of the Commonwealth of Virginia. Guess what happened next? I contacted the Commonwealth of Virginia Attorney's Office. Guess what happened next…? I contacted the Commonwealth of Virginia Office of Attorney General. Guess what happened next? I contacted the Commonwealth of Virginia Office of the Governor. Guess what happened next?

On March 22, 2015, I filed an Arlington, Virginia FOIA request. I re/ceived no response, so I had to refile on April 12, 2015. And on April 20, 2015, I filed an Arlington County Authorization for Release of Protected Health Information request. I finally received the requested information, sixty-nine pages, on April 23, 2015. I then filed a forty-page Arlington County Department of Human Services Request to Amend Record request via email on May 12, 2015, including many officials in the Commonwealth of Virginia and in the United States Congress. Surprisingly, guess what happened next...

Based on NVMHI and VHC medical records, my substantiating/supplementing daily diary/notes, and other pertinent documents, on December 8, 2015, I filed an official complaint with the Commonwealth of Virginia/Department of Health Professions/Enforcement Division. The complaint against VHC Dr. Christopher Olson, Dr. Benjamin Adewale, Sandra Garza, and VA/AC/DHS Marilyn Pasley. The complaint was detailed and extensive, about 50 pages in length; closer to 100 pages with all accompanying and supporting documents.

On December 17, 2015, I amended this complaint to include *independent evaluator*, Henriette Kellum. On January 11, 2016, I received official notifications dated January 6, 2016, and on February 26 and 27, 2016, I receive official notifications dated February 22, 2016 and February 24, 2016 respectively. The official response would not be a surprise, of course, at this point. All applicable investigations had been completed and all individuals cleared/cases closed. But it was on record, documented, and now a pertinent foundational piece for this book, as well as the *official record*, if and when the truth really comes out, and a real investigation is ever conducted.

As my Federal proceedings would continue through the system, I contacted the Commonwealth of Virginia/Arlington County Clerks' Offices. Obtaining documents and as confirmed in the February 3, 2016 official response from the Arlington County, Virginia Clerk of the Circuit Court Civil Division Supervisor Christopher Falcon, correcting the records again, due to inaccuracies/misleading mistakes/errors.

Given that none of this should have occurred to begin with, again, how did a federal national security matter with federal jurisdiction transition into a state-level county- level court system? Well, quite obviously it started with a March 28, 2013 telephone call from a Department of State/DS to ACPD. This was the same Department of State/DS that didn't protect me. It was the same Department of State/DS that opened up a *criminal investigation on me* based on receiving a July 20, 2001 *anonymous* memorandum, curiously about a month after my attending the bin Laden trial in NYC in early June 2001. This I would finally find out about for the very first time after finally receiving the purposely and intentionally delayed response to my May 19, 2013 FOIA-request... *ON MARCH 18, 2014.*

But regardless, none of this explains nor provides the answer to the larger questions at the time, and that still remain to this day, where was the DOJ? What about the Federal Bureau of Investigation? Congress? The Media? And why did the US Military—both the US Army and the US Navy/USMC—lie/cover-up regarding what happened to me during my detail assignment to Germany? Regarding the facts, the timeline of events, the players/entities involved, and with no DOD EEO, ACID nor NCIS investigation what precise role did the US Military play in all this? Precisely how far back? And most importantly, why? Why was the US Military involved? Because there is no doubt, the US Military had a role and they were absolutely involved. Otherwise, none of this would have occurred because I would have been, should have been protected. *So, why wasn't I?*

PART FOUR

CHAPTER 11

Purposely and Intentionally Delayed:

"It is a federal offense to threaten, intimidate, harass, or mislead a criminal or civil proceeding."

Some Answers, But More Questions

At this point in time, I was a federal CRVA-accorded rights and protected victim/witness regarding the August 7, 1998 East Africa Embassy bombing, an EEO grievance complainant against the US Military, a federal government whistleblower, and an OSC complaint complainant. I had experienced not one round of retaliation, but now an on-going, continual second round regardless of this protected status and all this pending litigation. At this point in time, I should also be able to say a former US Department of State employee. But I can't. Despite my resigning and Secretary of State Kerry accepting my resignation effective October 1, 2013, I was brought back onto US Department of State payroll against my will due to an October 24, 2013 *Emergency Motion*. Orchestrated once again by US State Department officials, I was then deemed *incapacitated* by the Commonwealth of Virginia/Arlington County Circuit Court as of December 17, 2013, which remains in effect still to this day. All because I resigned. *Unbelievable! Unfathomable! But yet, all true.*

On May 19, 2013, I filed a US Department of State FOIA/Privacy Act request. Now almost a year later—after two rounds of retaliatory actions taken against me—on March 8, 2014, I finally received the first tranche of 409 pages of documents from DS. I finally had evidence documenting what I had been saying all along. My theory that there was a targeting effort against me since the August 7, 1998 East Africa Embassy bombing was spot on. The intent of USG officials within the US Department of State against me was documented. This wasn't a mistake nor an error. This was intentional and purposeful.

I got the package of DS-related documents, and numbered all the pages accordingly: 1 of 409; 2 of 409; 3 of 409; and so on. I then sat down to read, discovering so much.

For instance: on pages 10-11, I read a March 19, 2013 email sent at 10:25 a.m. from Jim Minor to Prestina Williams and Michelle Dade, ccing Carlos Matus, Barry Moore, Kurt Rice, Paul Houston, Kimber Davidson, Michael Vannett with Subject: DS Interview of Stefanick. Though I had initially requested since October 24, 2012 to meet with DS, at the time of this email I still had not met with DS. So much had now transpired between then and the time of this March 19, 2013 email. What was so interesting and curious, was this statement made by Jim:

> … I know Michelle Stefanick as I was the DS case agent for US Embassy Nairobi & Dar bombing attacks as NYFO/JTTF, and was one of the trial victim witness coordinators, interviewing her and coordinating her attendance at the summer 2001 embassy bombing trial, where she was a (Nairobi USAID employee) victim/witness. I had no contact with her since the 2001 trial until her call a month ago.
> Jim
> SSA James Minor
> Protective Intelligence Investigations Office[1]

When I first read this, my reaction was, what? Jim Minor was good friends, as was I, with Pat Hartnett-Kelly, the Embassy Nairobi Accountable RSO regarding the August 7, 1998 Embassy Nairobi bombing. Jim accompanied DOJ/SDNY AUSA Ken Karas in my interview/conversation at FSI in March/April 2000. Jim knew that I was Embassy Nairobi State/FMC Director, *not an USAID Employee*. So why did he lie, mislead (in error or with intent), falsely state a fact he knew to be inaccurate? Where was this coming from, and why? One fact that cannot be disputed was that I was a victim/witness in regards to the August 7, 1998 East Africa Embassy bombing. Jim Minor, DS case agent at NYFO/JTTF and one of the trial victim witness coordinators, confirmed/verified it.

On pages 22-24, I read a February 25-26, 2013 email exchange. Initiated on February 25 at 7:45 p.m. by Kimber Davidson sent to Michael Posillico, Jim Minor, Paul Houston, ccing Robert Hartung, Barry Moore, Paul Hallenback with Subject: U/S for Management's Involvement in the Michelle Stefanick investigation. Eventually Kurt Rice, Carlos Matus, Michael Vannett, James Onusko, Jacqueline Atiles, Michelle Dade would be

 1   Jim Minor, email message to ?, March 19, 2013

included in this email exchange. This entire email exchange and the applicable DS actions occurred, despite my ignored October 24, 2012 request to meet with DS, and prior to my eventual, initial March 22, 2013 meeting, finally occurring at the insistence of U/S Patrick Kennedy.

> Subject: U/S for Management's Involvement in the Michelle Stefanick Investigation
> To All:
> Pat Kennedy called to discuss a case involving Michelle Stefanick who appears to be suffering some sort of mental health crisis. According to U/S for M SUBJECT has made numerous allegations involving a conspiracy that will bring down the Government. This information has been shared with the FBI. Apparently, there are ties to General Petraeus and others in the USG. DS is part of the conspiracy and cannot be trusted.
>
> Pat Kennedy has requested that FBI meet with SUBJECT one additional time to assure her that the information she provided has been examined and that it has been found not to be accurate and there is no plot to bring the Government.
>
> Kennedy would like the FBI to provide a subject a letter that they looked into her allegations and that they were unfounded or something to that affect. Pat hopes that a letter that comes from the FBI will help her in dealing with this issue.
>
> I am not sure which office has the lead on the case, I suspect PII. In any event we need to get something from the FBI to formally close this investigation.
>
> Apparently, SUBJECT's parents cannot control her. This sounds like an EO-10450 referral. If that is the conclusion the agents have made as well, we need to ensure that an EO-10450 request goes forward to Paul Hallenback in PSS.
> Kimber (Kim) Davidson
> Special Agent in Charge
> Investigations and Counter Intelligence – DS/DO/ICI[2]

Where do I even begin? Where in the world is this *some sort of mental health crisis* coming from? U/S Patrick Kennedy? DS Kimber Davidson? This was never a mental health crisis/issue, but always a national security matter. *So who started this false-narrative?* Based on my review so far of the 409 DS-related FOIA-response pages that *false-narrative* started as early as this Monday, February 25, 2013 email.

---

2   Kimber Davidson, email message to Michael Posillico, Jim Minor, Paul Houston, Robert Hartung, Barry Moore, and Paul Hallenback February 25 2013

Now, U/S Pat Kennedy made a reasonable and acceptable request:

> ...that the FBI meet with SUBJECT (*me*) one additional time to assure her that the information she provided has been examined and that it has been found not to be accurate and there is no plot to bring the Government down...

Yet, this never happened. Such a simple request and yet it never happened. Why not? Is it that DS never followed-up with the FBI—ignoring U/S Patrick Kennedy's request? Or was it that DS requested the FBI accordingly and for some reason, the FBI wouldn't do it? What was the reason? What are the facts? What transpired? *Why did I never meet with the FBI again?*

Okay, no meeting... but how about the FBI providing me, the *SUBJECT*, a letter that the FBI *looked into my allegations and that they were unfounded or something to that effect*. Again, it never happened. I never received such letter from the FBI. Patrick rightly forecasted that he *hopes that a letter that comes from the FBI will help her (me) in dealing with this issue.* So again, such a simple request, and yet it never happened. Why not? Is it that the DS never followed-up with the FBI, again, ignoring U/S Patrick Kennedy's request? Or was it that DS requested this of the FBI accordingly and the FBI wouldn't do it? For some reason, the FBI wouldn't provide a response letter. What was the reason? What are the facts? What transpired? Is it possible DS requested the FBI, but the FBI refused to put such in writing? If so, why?

Reading all this in light of and in the aftermath of all that had transpired, what precisely did DS SA Kimber Davidson mean by "Apparently SUBJECT's parents cannot control her." What does that mean? And all this before DS even met with me, the *SUBJECT*, on March 22, 2013.

Michael Posillico responded at 8:48 p.m. to Kurt Rice, ccing Robert Hartung, Barry Moore, Paul Hallenback, Carlos Matus, Michael Vannett, Jim Minor, Paul Houston, Kimber Davidson:

> Regarding the M request, ICI Office Director and I spoke tonight regarding this issue. We agreed that of TIA management concurs I should pursue an EO 10450 referral from the FBI, although that may take time to acquire from the FBI, given their initial reluctance to go this route.
>
> As an alternative SSA Minor's interactions with Ms. Stefanick in which she discussed her conspiracy theories may satisfy U/S Kennedy's needs.

I will reach out to the FBI Agent who interviewed Ms. Stefanick in the morning.
Regards, Mike[3]

As there was no signature/title block provided in Mike's email, it's not clear his position/role within DS at this time. So precisely who was Michael "Mike" Posillico? His position? His role? And his USG affiliation?

Conclusions and assumptions were being made, wrongly made, without carrying-out any sort of investigation whatsoever. This was despite the fact that I was telling the truth and reaching out to law enforcement/proper authorities every step of the way. Paul Hallenback's Tuesday, February 26, 2013 2:23 p.m. email response did not include everyone, but was sent to Kimber Davidson, ccing Paul Hallenback, James Onusko, Jacqueline Atiles, Michelle Dade:

> Kim – I've got the file and am assigning it today. We will initiate a U02 (For Cause) to see the extent of any possible issues and then forward to MED for a 10450 review.

> Michelle – can you get the memo drafted tonight to get this one initiated. Should include request for several interviews to include any detail locations. Paul[4]

Wait a minute—DS *opened* an investigation on me and they had not even met or talked with me yet? Yep. That's precisely what DS did. I just wouldn't know at this time that this would not be the first time DS would take such an *adverse* action, willingly, take such an adverse action against the victim/witness/the SUBJECT, me. Now I was also seeing in black-and-white, the apparent blatant disregard to U/S Patrick Kennedy's request. And again, what in the world is meant by "Apparently SUBJECT's parents cannot control her?" *My parents aren't law enforcement.* US Department of State/Diplomatic Security is *law enforcement*. Apparently, DS and *my parents* had some kind of interaction. When? For how long? And why? *I was the US Department of State employee! Why no interaction with me?*

WRONGFUL INVESTIGATION

I then got to pages 37-38. It's Prestina William's memorandum documenting the DS-version of events of April 12, 2013:

---

3   Michael Posillico, email message to Kurt Rice, Robert Hartung, Barry Moore, Paul Hallenback, Carlos Matus, Michael Vannett, Jim Minor, Paul Houston, Kimber Davidson, February 25 2013
4   Paul Hallenback, email message to James Onusko, Jacqueline Atiles and Michelle Dade, February 25 2013

United States Department of State
Washington, D.C. 20520
SENSITIVE BUT UNCLASSIFIED
MEMORANDUM
TO: Kimber Davidson – Acting Assistant Director, DS/DO
THRU:Paul Houston – Division Chief, DS/ICI/SID
FROM:Prestina Willims – Special Agent, DS/ICI/SID
SUBJECT:Michelle L. Stefanick

On April 12, 2013, at approximately 10:45 a.m. Special Agent Prestina Williams from the DS Special Investigations Division (SID) and Special Agent James Minor from the DS Office of Protective Intelligence Investigations (PII) hand-delivered, to Department employee Michelle Stefanick, the official document notifying her that the Office of Personnel Security and Suitability (PSS) had determined that her Top-Secret clearance had been suspended pending the outcome of an ongoing DS investigation.

When Agents Williams and Minor arrived at Ms. Stefanick's home address, they were met by Patrice English from Arlington Mental Health Services, the DS Victims' Advocacy Program Coordinator Kayla Hall, and Ellen Millner, a social worker from the Department's Employee Services Center. English, Hall, and Millner remained standing just outside Stefanick's front yard while Agents Williams and Minor proceeded to Stefanick's front porch. Ms. Stefanick opened the door for the agents and asked them to come inside. When they instead asked her to come outside, she willingly did so, but not before asking who the people were standing just outside her front yard. Stefanick quickly stepped out onto her front stoop and very loudly began reading a letter she had written to SA Minor stating her frustration with not receiving any resolution to her request for DS to conduct an official investigation into her allegations of US government fraud and corruption.

Stefanick very openly expressed her mistrust, frustration and disbelief in the motives of all who were present, especially DS. At each point when English, Hall, and Millner attempted to interrupt Stefanick's tirade, asking her questions about her situation and her future, Stefanick shouted at them to stay where they were and told them she didn't need any assistance from them. SA Minor redirected Stefanick's attention to him several times to explain why DS had come. Stefanick said she already knew (from a phone conversation she had with SA Williams earlier that morning) and accused DS of retaliating against her as a whistleblower. The agents expressed to her that that was not the case. SA Minor further explained to

Stefanick that her allegations had not been credible, but Stefanick insisted that DS provide her with a letter which states either the outcome of its investigation, or the reason it had not investigated her claims of corruption. After approximately 10 more minutes of Stefanick's verbal expressions of anger and accusations, and attempts by mental health professionals to intervene, SA Williams gave Stefanick the clearance suspension information and reminded her of what was provided in the packet – the suspension memorandum, an acknowledgement of receipt of the information, and a new Department identification badge.

When Stefanick took the information inside her home to read it, Agents Minor and Williams remained on the front step. SA Minor continued to engage with Stefanick verbally to assess her whereabouts in the home and ask her to return outside. Meanwhile, SA Williams spoke with Ms. English (Arlington Mental Health Services) who notified Williams that based on her professional assessment of Stefanick's state of mind, she had called the Arlington Police Department to respond to Ms. Stefanick's residence and to take her into custody for "failure to care." Upon the arrival of the two local police officers, SA Williams met them and identified herself and SA Minor as armed law enforcement officers. When the two officers entered Ms. Stefanick's home, Agents Minor and Williams followed. The officers briefly spoke with Stefanick, who was sitting in a dining room chair, and asked her to stand as they placed her in handcuffs. SA Williams retrieved Stefanick's personal items (purse, house/car keys) from the study to obtain her driver's license.

Stefanick expressed disbelief and sadness that she was being detained and taken away from her home by police, but at no time did Ms. Stefanick become physically violent. Local police placed Ms. Stefanick in a marked vehicle and took her to the Virginia Hospital Center at 1701 N. George Mason Drive for detainment and mental evaluation. She will receive a court appointed attorney and will be taken from the hospital directly to the Arlington County Courthouse for the civil commitment hearing on Monday morning, April 15, 2013.5
SENSITIVE BUT UNCLASSIFIED

Wow, absolutely amazing. Where do I even begin? I had an ongoing email exchange with DS SAs Prestina Williams and Jim Minor since our first and only meeting on March 22, 2013 regarding the status and a copy

5   Prestina Williams, memorandum to Kimber Davidson and Paul Hallenback, April 12 2013

of their report. Neither was ever provided…Williams is correct, according to the April 9, 2013 memorandum provided to me on April 12, 2013, my *"Top-Secret security clearance had been suspended pending the outcome of an ongoing DS investigation."* What was the basis for this DS investigation even being started? Why, despite continual requests from AFSA Legal Counsel Neera Parikh, was the status of this DS investigation was never provided? So, why did DS really come to my residence on April 12, 2013? And why was the memorandum given to me in a protective cover sheet?

As for speaking loudly on my door stoop, absolutely I did—and it worked. HFAC Staffer/my Lyon Park neighbor Tom Sheehy found out about the retaliatory stunt pulled on April 12, 2013 as a result. Now interesting, not once did Williams mention that they would be blindsiding me by showing up with Patrice English, Kayla Hall and Ellen Millner in tow and accusing "DS of retaliating against her as a whistleblower. The agents expressed to her that that was not the case." Then what was the real reason for all this? Oh, that's right, DS retaliated against me because I was a federal CVRA-accorded victim/witness regarding the August 7, 1998 East Africa Embassy bombing. And "when Stefanick took the information inside her home to read it," Minor and Williams did not remain on the doorstep. They entered my home and stood beside me at my dining room table as I began to read the memorandum when ACPD entered my residence without knocking, violating my privacy and my constitutional rights. And "failure to care"—precisely what does that mean? And no, "upon the arrival of the two local police officers," Williams and Minor did not meet them and identify themselves outside on the door stoop because they were already in my residence standing next to my dining room table. So, no, "when the two officers entered Ms. Stefanick's home, DS SAs Minor and Williams" *did not* follow because they were already in my residence. And yes, both witnessed the retaliatory action taken place against me when the ACPD placed me in handcuffs, walked me out of my residence and placed me in the back of the ACPD Police Car. Patrice English, Kayla Hall, and Ellen Millner also witnessed the retaliatory actions they caused/were accomplices too. And she was correct, when she said "at no time did Ms. Stefanick become physically violent." So, in Williams' preorchestrated Commitment Hearing of April 15, 2013, there were lies/misstatements/inaccuracies of facts including statements that I was fired, when I was not! It said that I was violent to myself and others, when I was not! And as DS prearranged my involuntary April 12, 2013 admittance to VHC and then the Monday, April 15, 2013 Commitment Hearing, who was the source for the Emergency room Dr. Christopher Olson? Who was the source for Dr. Benjamin Adewale's *agenda-driven* line of questioning? It was not me, my BC/BS Medical files, nor my official State/Medical files. So, Williams and Davidson, who precisely was your source?

U/S Patrick Kennedy's supposed February 25, 2013 request regarding DS arranging me to meet again with FBI and FBI providing me a written letter was very eye-opening, as were the contents on pages 35-36: a copy of a July 29, 2013 SENSITVE BUT UNCLASSIFIED Memorandum from DS/PSS/AA – Paul Hallenback Thru M/MED/MHS – Ferolyn Brooks M/MED/MHS To Kimber Davidson – M/MED/MHS Subject: STEFANICK, Michelle L. SSN: XXX-XX-XXXX, which references 4 Attachments: Tab A – Bernicat/Thomas-Greenfield e-mail dated 3/29/2013 Tab B – Thomas-Greenfield e-mail dated 3/23/2013 Tab C –DS/ICI/SID Memo dated 3/22/2013 Tab D – FBI Reported dated 01/31/2013 and a carbon copy to Security File. *Wait a minute*, back-up – Tab D referenced an *FBI Report dated 01/31/2013. So, there was an FBI letter!* Did U/S Patrick Kennedy know of the FBI letter before he made the request to DS on February 25, 2013? Why didn't I ever get a copy? What did this FBI letter say? Why didn't either the FBI nor DS ever share it with me?

Needless to say, by page thirty-nine, I knew I was set up. To say that I said that DS cannot be trusted—*that's an absolute understatement!* To say that I said that DS was corrupt—*that's an absolute understatement!* As spot-on right I was, and as sickened as I was to know how correct I was, I had to continue through the remainder of the DS-provided documents. My thought was what more do I need to see, this already proves what I was saying? *But, there would be even more…*

On pages 61-63, I came across this March 22-26, 2013 email exchange initiated on March 22, 2013 at 8:19 p.m. by Kimber Davidson to Gregory Starr, Patrick Kennedy, Linda Thomas-Greenfield, ccing Marcia Bernicat, Prestina Williams, Paul Houston, Barry Moore, Paul Hallenback, Michelle Dade, Carlos Matus with Subject: Friday incident involving Michelle Stefanick. Eventually Hans Klemm would be included in this email exchange. Here's the Tuesday, March 26, 2013 5:38 p.m. email from Gregory Starr to Linda Thomas-Greenfield, Kimber Davidson, Patrick Kennedy, ccing Marcia Bernicat, Prestina Williams, Paul Houston and Hans Klemm…

Subject: Friday incident involving Michelle Stefanick
I think we have to be very straightforward in regards to this situation.

435

1) Her condition is very far from normal, and in my medically uneducated opinion without proper care she will likely get worse, not better. Conversely, I have seen remarkable turnarounds in some people with severe psychological problems when properly treated. There is no way for us to know which way this could go without proper care and medical attention.

2) I have no choice at this point but to suspend her security clearance. Her current condition causes me great concern about access to classified and quite frankly access to our workplace in her current condition. Without treatment and a major improvement in her condition I don't see returning her clearance, and actually would eventually have to move to permanent revocation, unless she is under medical care.

3) Having given away most of her assets, with her medical condition she is likely to really need her health insurance and likely her retirement as well, but she is not of age to receive retirement benefits. If we have to terminate her employment because her clearance is revoked due to her condition, she loses both. If she gets into treatment, she could make it to retirement, or perhaps have a medical retirement which would give her something to live on and allow her to continue medical insurance coverage.

I would suggest you consider making these facts clear to her father if not already done. He needs to go to a lawyer as next of kin and then go to court to get a judge to order in-patient treatment in my estimation. I would be interested in MEDs take on this. Greg[6]

WOW, in light of all that's happened, what's the date of this Greg Starr email? Tuesday, March 26, 2013. What was the date DS called ACPD to send 5-6 ACPD officers come surround my house dressed in tactical gear with guns locked and loaded? Thursday, March 28, 2013.

Now to put this into further context, who is Greg Starr? At this time, Greg Starr was both the Principal Deputy Assistant Secretary (PDAS) for DS and the Acting Assistant Secretary for DS. He was DS. He was the man in charge. You know, the same DS that should have been protecting their Federal CVRA-accorded victim/witness—ME! But then again, how can you have an entity that is in charge of protective detail security when it's the exact same entity that is targeting you? My theory had now become factual reality.

Greg Starr's fellow DS SAs were assigned to EUCOM and AFRICOM as well as at the US Embassy in Berlin and US Consulates throughout

6   Gregory Starr, email message to Linda Thomas-Greenfield, Kimber Davidson, Patrick Kennedy, Marcia Bernicat, Prestina Williams, Paul Houston and Hans Klemm, March 26, 2013

436

Germany at the time of my detail assignment with MARFOREUR/AF when the retaliatory events against me took place.

Even further context, Greg Starr was the DS Division chief for local guard and residential security programs worldwide from 1995 to 1997, just prior to the August 7, 1998 East Africa Embassy bombings. He was at US Embassy Tel Aviv from 1997-2000, during the time of the bombings. The *accountable* RSO in regards to the Embassy Nairobi ARB was not Paul Peterson, the RSO actually assigned to Embassy Nairobi at the actual time of the bombing. Instead the accountable RSO for the Embassy Nairobi ARB was the previous RSO, who had departed Kenya months prior to the August 7, 1998 bombing, Pat Hartnett-Kelly. So, if Pat was the *accountable* RSO *whose head and career were on the chopper* for the bombing, then to parallel with consistency, so should Greg Starr, given the fact that he was previously in charge of the local guards protecting the Embassies. Obviously this did not happen, as here he was almost 20 years later, heading up DS.

So, what about Pat Hartnett-Kelly's May 30, 2011 email that she sent to me in Germany after bin Laden's supposed capture and killing on May 1, 2011 by US Navy SEALS, alluding for the very first time to an *inside job* possibility regarding the embassy bombings. Why had she alluded to such but only after bin Laden's killing? Given her DS/law enforcement background, what did she know? Though I was connecting dots, given my October 24-25, 2012 outreach through OSD and subsequent November 27, 2012 Whistleblower/Protection Request letter, I still needed that direct link, *the smoking gun*. Or, was something bigger at play? So, I continued to reading…

I got to pages 129-131, the April 9, 2013 Security Clearance Suspension Memorandum that Williams and Minor brought to my residence on April 12, 2013 in a protective cover. The memo that stated:

> …Your Top-Secret security clearance is suspended pending the outcome of an ongoing DS investigation…The suspension of your security clearance does not constitute a formal revocation and does not indicate that such action is planned.

Really? It seems pretty clear by Greg Starr's March 26, 2013 email that permanent revocation was definitely his expected end game. But then again, I was assured my *due process rights* in this April 9, 2013 memo because it clearly states:

> If, after further investigation and review, the Director, Diplomatic Security Service, revokes your security clearance, you will be given

an opportunity to respond. Moreover, should the Assistant Secretary of Diplomatic Security render a decision to sustain the revocation of your security clearance, you will be afforded the opportunity to appeal the decision to the Department's Security Appeals Panel.

Good, what a relief! There's an appeal process to ensure my due process rights. Well then, how about this, pages 129-130 contained a copy of the February 25, 2013 *SENSITVE BUT UNCLASSIFIED ACTION MEMORANDUM FOR UNDER SECRETARY KENNEDY – M* FROM: DS/DSS – Gregory B. Starr, Acting SUBJECT: Request for Delegation of Authorities to DS Deputy Assistant Secretary, signed by Under Secretary for Management by Patrick Kennedy on 02/25/13.

Really? So, given Greg Starr's affiliation/linkage to the August 7, 1998 East Africa Embassy bombings, one would think, if ethical and professional, one would recuse oneself to ensure transparency and to ensure due process rights. Right? Well, this February 25, 2013 delegation was approved based on the following justification:

> Currently, Gregory Starr is serving as both the PDAS and the Acting Assistant Secretary for DS. This situation creates the potential for conflicts of interest, as PDAS Starr could not both make the initial decision and hear the appeal as Acting Assistant Secretary. We recommend that you delegate to DS Deputy Assistant Secretary (DAS) Gentry Smith the authorities and functions of the PDAS. This delegation would allow DAS Smith to make any decisions for which the FAM provides an appeal to the Assistant Secretary, and would free PDAS Starr to hear the appeal as Acting Assistant Secretary.

Not only did Greg Starr not recuse himself entirely, he purposely and intentionally stacked the deck to ensure he got the outcome he wanted— permanent revocation of my security clearance. A fool proof back-up strategy in case I indeed appealed. He ensured himself the final say.

All the bizarreness that occurred during the initial involuntary retaliatory stay at VHC now made sense. Apparently, what threw Greg Starr, DS and all his accomplices off their game-plan was my demanding my attorney to appeal, resulting in the May 8, 2013 Appeal Hearing. Now George Dodge not filing the appeal I requested is also starting to come into clearer focus, as well as the Commonwealth of Virginia Attorney's office June 7, 2013 subpoena of Dr. Adewale. For what I did not know at the time, and until now, was that according to page 131:

...this delegation of authority will terminate upon the assignment of a Principal Deputy Assistant Secretary to succeed the incumbent, or upon May 30, 2013, whichever occurs first.

By May 30, 2013, not only did I get out of VHC and NVMHI, meet with HFAC Benghazi Committee Investigator/Legal Counsel, file an OSC Complaint, and file USG-wide FOIA/Privacy Requests, but I also received that threatening phone message "Informant" on May 28, 2013. Now the timeline of events was very clear.

But no fear, because on July 31, 2013, President Obama formally nominated *Greg Star*r for Assistant Secretary of State for the Bureau of Diplomatic Security. No additional *delegation authority* was necessary. This further supported that this orchestrated retaliatory effort, lack of protection and lack of response/investigations to my outreaches, apparently indeed reached to the highest levels of the USG, to include up to the President of the United States of America himself. *Was it possible the President was not aware nor advised accordingly? Or was the President indeed in the know?*

THE ANONYMOUS MEMO STRIKES AGAIN

Then I got to this, pages 226-231. It was a copy of a PR Tracking System Case Detail Report with a report date of April 30, 2005. So, on April 2005, where was I? Oh yeah, I was in my second year as the Management Officer at Embassy Khartoum, Sudan. Then I read more: Report Date: April 30, 2005 Case Number: 01-MC09-072001-171-0015 Case Name: STEFANICK, MICHELLE Open Date 07/20/2001 Close Date 01/21/2005 Reported Date 07/20/2001 Agency 01 US DEPARTMENT OF STATE Case Type MC09 MISCELLANEOUS MISCONDUCT Field Office DS/ICI/PR County 171 Russia Case Category MISCON-DUCT/SUITABILITY Case Agent: BK Bultrowicz Karl Other Agent: NR Nancy Rolph-O'Donnell.

Misconduct/Suitability? Russia? What in the world? Open Date 07/20/2001? Close Date 01/21/2005? Reported Date 07/20/2001? PR Tracking System Case Detail Report with a report date of April 30, 2005. And then I read further—My reaction being, *You've got to be kidding me!* So, I put aPost-it note marking the page to come back to and continued to read on...

Then, page 277. This report was dated February 18, 2010. It was a print-out as of February 18, 2010 of Case Summary PR-2007-04124: STEFANICK, MICHELLE PRTS CASE: Case Number: 11535 Office:

Professional Responsibility Division Type: Criminal Case Type: MIS-CELLANEOUS MISCONDUCT Case Category: MISCONDUCT/ SUITABILITY Open Date: 20-JUL-01 Close Date: 21-JAN-05 Agent: Bultrowicz Karl   Other Agent: Nancy Rolph-O'Donnell.

Wait a minute! The "Type" is indicated as "CRIMINAL." *What in the world is this?* So, I read further:

> Case_Comment: DS/ICI/PR and M/DGHR/MED/MHS received an anonymous memo dated 07/20/01 reporting Stefanick exhibited threatening behavior. Memo states Stefanick losing her temper frequently and becoming more violent to the point she may hurt herself or others. Outbursts have caused harm to colleagues and is hurting post operations. Memo states Post management has ignored the behavior and others reporting.
>
> RSO Moscow investigated allegations and were unable to corroborate allegations. Case Closed. SA Bultrowicz entered information into PIRTS on 01/21/05, solely for documentation and internal use. Hard copy of case file developed and filed under above listed case number.

So, given I have the State Medical copy of this memorandum of which there are no allegations presented nor provided, let alone criminal allegations, let's take a closer look at this. Why didn't DS ever contact me regarding this "July 20, 2001 anonyomous memorandum" received by DS less than a month after I returned from the DOJ/SDNY East Africa Embassy bombing trial in June 2001, which DOJ/SDNY and State jointly funded for me to attend. And there's nothing suspicious here? But instead they used it as the basis to open a criminal investigation—on me. Obviously, the intent by DS is and was for this to be used as some kind of a permanent placeholder, purposely and intentionally placed in my official file by DS to scar my record. It was something that DS could use/misconstrue/manipulate/use to hold over someone's —*my*—*head* over and over again, throughout one's career, every and anytime DS deemed necessary; and DS did! So again, why didn't DS ever contact me about this "July 20, 2001 Anonymous memorandum,. But, DS used it as the basis to open up a "criminal" investigation on me? And nothing nefarious was going on at all, right? PR Tracking System Case Detail Report with a report date of *April 30, 2005*, report dated *February 18, 2010*, Greg Starr's *March 26, 2013* email…

Oh, but back on pages 127-128, there was *SENSITIVE BUT UN-CLASSIFIED MEMORANDUM:*

SENSITIVE BUT UNCLASSIFIED   February 27,
2013
MEMORANDUM
TO:DS/PSS/OPS – Ms. Alli Littleton, Branch Chief
FROM:DS/PSS/AA – Paul D. Hallenback, Division Chief
SUBJECT:Update for Cause (U02)
NAME: STEFANICK, Michelle L.
SSN: XXX-XX-2246
Last updated completed 03/19/2010
(eQuip Form NOT Required)
REF: Davidson e-mail dated February 25, 2013; Posillico e-mail
dated
February 25, 2013; Minor e-mail dated February 26, 2013.
Request an Update for Cause (U02) with 30-day due date be initi-
ated immediately.
BACKGROUND
Subject is a Foreign Service Officer, FP-01. According to the U/S
for M, Subject has made numerous allegations involving a conspiracy that she believes will bring down the government and that DS
is included in the conspiracy and cannot be trusted. There are possible mental health concerns regarding Subject. In order to obtain
the most current information available to allow for an adjudication
using the whole person concept, the Chief, Adverse Actions Division, requests that a U02 be conducted.

During interviews of the investigation stress subject's honesty,
integrity, duty performance, and any indications of behavior that
casts doubt on the individual's judgment, reliability, or trustwor-
thiness, including but not limited to emotionally unstable, irre-
sponsible, dysfunctional, violent, paranoid, or bizarre behavior.
During interviews of supervisors, co-workers, associates, and references, determine if subject was ever suspected of exhibiting any
emotional, mental, and personality conditions that showed signs
of impair judgment. Expand the U02 investigation as necessary.

Upon completion of the investigative work, please forward all
information and return the case file directly to Michelle Dade, DS/
PSS/AA. If you have any questions, please contact her at [redact-
ed].[7]
SENSITIVE BUT UNCLASSIFIED

Page 277 – *The smoking gun!* The DS *ill-willed* tactic used against me.
Previously, I detailed my initial April 10, 2003 awareness and explanation regarding a July 20, 2001 anonymous memorandum sent to State/

Medical. And as I was issued my Level 1 "Unlimited Clearance for World-wide Assignment" by State/Medical on April 16, 2003, I thought the matter was closed. An anonymous memorandum that had been placed in my applicable State/Medical and State/DS files for over two years at that time had already supposedly been investigated and closed by DS, removed accordingly by Med as well. Or so I thought. According to page 277, apparently that was not the case. For instead, DS had their permanent placeholder.

Question is, did RSO/DS SA John Rendeiro know that DS purposely and intentionally used that curiously-timed July 20, 2001 anonymous memorandum, received less than a month after I attended the bin Laden trial in NYC in June 2001, against me in 2005, 2010, and 2013? Did *accountable* RSO/DS SA Pat Hartnett-Kelly know of this curiously-timed July 20, 2001 anonymous memorandum, received less than a month after my attending the bin Laden trial in NYC in June 2001, being used against me in 2005, 2010, and 2013? Yet, *to this day*, DS has never contacted/met with me regarding this curiously-timed July 20, 2001 anonymous memorandum received less than a month after I attended the bin Laden trial in NYC in June 2001.

So, now with page 277, the *smoking-gun*, and my becoming aware for the very first time on March 8, 2014, that DS used a curiously-timed July 20, 2001 *anonymous* memorandum to open a *criminal* investigation on me, I reflected …Why? Why would DS do this? Why was this curiously-timed July 20, 2001 *anonymous* memorandum sent? Who sent it? Who were the players involved? What were the events involved? Based on this self-questioning, I now had no doubt that I/the Embassy Nairobi FMC was indeed the target, the true target of the August 7, 1998 East Africa Embassy bombing.

With that proper context, DS knew I had just returned from attending the bin Laden trial in NYC, and within less than a month, DS received a curiously-timed July 20, 2001 anonymous memorandum. I mean, given my federal victim/witness protected status, DS knew that *it was a federal offense to threaten, intimidate, harass, or mislead a witness in a criminal proceeding, right?* So, DS immediately contacted DOJ and FBI accordingly to report this threat/harassment/intimidation/misleading set-up accusation/narrative against me, right? Oh, but no! DS did not contact the DOJ nor the FBI. According to Page 277, the law enforcement entity within the US Department of State, DS, based on an anonymous memorandum opened up an investigation, a criminal investigation, on me instead. DS never contacted nor interviewed me about this July 20, 2001 anonymous memorandum. This memorandum wasn't written by the Russians, Iranians, Sudanese, North Koreans, Chinese. Or al-Qaeda. *This curiously-timed July 20, 2001 anonymous memorandum was written by an American USG Official! And DS did not inform DOJ, the FBI, nor me!*

Furthermore, I would never have found out about page 277, if I had not filed my May 19, 2013 State FOIA/Privacy Act Request. I would never have filed this May 19, 2013 State FOIA/Privacy Act Request if the retaliatory actions taken against me by the US Department of State, to include by DS and others, had not occurred. Otherwise, I would never have known… But now, I do know and I am aware. And now, I will not stop until the truth is exposed, and justice is done.

With that, though I did not become aware until March 8, 2014, US Department of State officials and others did know, and knew, the entire time… And obviously, that included the DOJ, Federal Bureau of Investigation, Intelligence Community and Military of the United States of America.

And then I would get to pages 403-409, the final seven-page packet. I would discover DS's last supposed *nail-in-the-coffin* set-up attempt. Despite my reporting accordingly, in which DS never got back in touch with me again, but behind the scenes…

The 1st page (Page 403) included the completed front-page template form:

SENSITIVE BUT UNCLASSIFIED
UNITED STATES DEPARTMENT OF STATE
DIPLOMATIC SECURITY SERVICE
REPORT OF INVESTIGATION
CASE TITLE STEFANICK, MICHELLE DS CASE NUMBER PQ-2011-00726
OTHER IDENTIFER (BIRTHDATE) CASE TYPE   OTHER
OFFICE DS/ICI/PR DATE CASE OPENED 12/13/2011
DATE CASE COMPLETED 1/17/2012 REPORTING AGENT THOMAS WORONICAK
SYNOPSIS
On 12/6/2011, SA Justin Rowan – DS/FLD/BFO reported to DS/ICI/PR that he had received a Suspicious Activity Report (SAR) from a financial institution concerning Michelle STEFANICK (SUBJECT) who is a Foreign Service Officer. The report, dated 7/1/2011, showed that an account opened in SUBJECT's name

had several suspicious wire transfers and withdraws thus triggering a SAR (Attachment A).

RA reviewed SUBJECT's DS/SI/PSS background investigation file and discovered that on 10/13/2011, she had reported to PSS that she was the victim of identify fraud. According to SUBJECT's email to PSS, she had noticed suspicious activity in her banking account and had subsequently reported it to her bank, the credit bureaus, as well as the Arlington County Police (Attachment B).

No further PR investigation is warranted.

-CASE CLOSED- COPIES REFERRED 1-DS/ICI/PR CASE FILE

APPROVED 1-DS/SI/PSS

/s/ Kimber Davidson 01/20/2012

(Special Agent in Charge – Signature) (Date – MM/DD/YEAR)

SUPERVISOR

LEFT BLANK –

REPORTING AGENT

/s/ Thomas Woronicak 1/19/2012

(Reporting Agent – Signature) (Date – MM/DD/YEAR)8

Page 1 of 1

The 2nd page (Page 404) was basically blank, other than a *STEFANICK, Michelle PQ-2011-00726* Header at top and bottom of the page. In the center of the page in bold letters was :ATTACHMENT A. That was the complete page.

The 3rd page (Page 405) was completely blank, other than *Referred* written off-center, in the middle of the page. *To this day, I do not know to whom this was referred.*

The 4th page (Page 406) included a copy of the Justin Rown December 6, 2011 email that went as follows:

From: Rowan, Justin M

Sent:Tuesday, December 06, 2011 12:32:33 p.m.

To:Kelty, Robert F

Cc:Flynn, Michael D

Subject:BFO Referral

Attachments:[Untitled].pdf

Rob,

As a follow-up to your conversation with Mike:

Our Asset Forfeiture Specialist routinely attends Suspicious Activity Report (SAR) Meetings throughout our AOR. These meetings

8   Thomas Woronicak, Diplomatic Security Service report of investigation to Kimber Davidson, January 7, 2013

feature several federal and private sector entities within the financial community. To date we've rec'd a few case leads from these meetings and our office's participation has been value added.

At a recent SAR meeting in New Hampshire, we rec'd a SAR from one of the attending financial institutions. The SAR is apparently on a foreign service officer.

I have scanned the report and attached it for your review.

We at BFO took no further action.

Thanks,

V/r

/s/ Justin Rowan

Special Agent – Criminal Unit Supervisor

Boston Field Office

Diplomatic Security

US Department of State9

The 5th page (Page 407) was basically blank, other than a *STEFAN-ICK, Michelle PQ-2011-00726* Header at top and bottom of the page. In the center of the page in bold letters was: ATTACHMENT B. That was the complete page.

The 6th page (Page 408) included a copy of the October 12–13, 2011 Stefanick/security clearance *ATTN: John – Stefanick Identity Theft* email exchange (Page 1 of 3) that went as follows:

CLASSIFICATION: UNCLASSIFIED

Printed By: DS PSS FILE ROOM

Privacy/PII Page 1 of 3

From: security clearance

To: DS PSS FILE ROOM

Subject: FW: ATTN: John – Stefanick Identity Theft

Sent: 10/13/2011 2:50:22 p.m.

Please add below information to Michelle Stefanick's file.

Thank you,

John

Independent Contractor

Customer Service Center

Personnel Security/Suitability

US Department of State

Did you know many of your questions about personnel security may be answered by visiting our web page at http:www.state.gov-/m/ds/clearances or our intranet site at http://clearances.ds.state.

gov. You may also call our Customer Service Center toll free at 1-866-643-INFO (4636) or 571-345-3186. Fax is 1-571-345-3190. IVG may be utilized with these numbers.

Privacy/PII

This email is UNCLASSIFIED.

From: Stefanick, Michelle L

Sent: Thursday, October 13, 2011 10:18 a.m.

To: security clearance

Cc [email address removed}; [email address removed}

Subject: RE: ATTN: John – Stefanick Identity Theft

Resending …. Seems I got the email incorrect with first email. Thanks, michelle

From: michelle Stefanick [mailto: [email address removed}]

Sent: Wednesday, October 12, 2011 6:21 p.m.

To: [email address removed}

Cc [email address removed}; Stefanick, Michelle L

Subject: ATTN: John – Stefanick Identity Theft

Hello John – I wanted to thank you for discussing this issue with me. Needless to say, its not a very good time for me as I try to grapple with the magnitude of what was done to me. That being said, as advised, please find below all the actions I've taken upon notification that it appears that I was a victim of Identity Theft and recover from this traumatic situation.

CLASSIFICATION: UNCLASSIFIED

 Printed By: DS PSS FILE ROOM

Privacy/PII

Page 1 of 3

(NOTE Page 2 of 3 is missing/not referenced/not included)

The 7th page (Page 409) included a copy of the October 12, 2011 Stefanick/security clearance *ATTN: John – Stefanick Identity Theft* email (Page 3 of 3) that went as follows:

CLASSIFICATION: UNCLASSIFIED

Printed By: DS PSS FILE ROOM

Privacy/PII

 Page 3 of 3

listened to my situation and got back with me on what I should do. He said DS/PS required due diligence on my part and to report to law enforcement, which I said I did. He provided me the phone number to DS customer care at 1-866-643-4636. I called and spoke with John where we discussed my situation on what I should to as "victim" in this situation. As noted above, USAA and BOA are doing investigations; I called the Arlington Police to file a report; I have changed usernames and passwords on my online accounts; I've filed a report with SSA/FTC; I've notified the credit bureaus; I've called to cancel/replace credit cards; and I've called every Mortgage/bank institution I have accounts with: USAA (replacement card requested), BOA (cancelled credit card), SDFCU (replacement card requested), Chase (replacement card requested); Closed Service Credit Union bank account called the following mortgage/2nd trust holders for my three Real estate/rental properties – Bank of America, Chase, Wells Fargo, Green Tree Servicing, and United.

As I am currently assigned to the Pentagon on an exchange with OSD/Policy – ISA/Africa, I plan to notify their applicable Security Officer tomorrow on what has occurred and what action I have taken, particularly with DS in light of my responsibilities of a Security Clearance Holder.

I am now doing all I can to recover from the financial and emotional damage that has been due to being a Victim of Identity Theft.

Please note the above was to document my due diligence in regards to this incident and my seriousness of being a Security Clearance holder. If there is any other information needed at this time or should be included at this time, please let me know and I will provide accordingly. In the meanwhile, I am not awaiting the results of the USAA and BOA investigations and taking action regarding the financial impact this has caused/and monitoring very closely hereafter.

Thank you, Michelle Stefanick
CLASSIFICATION: UNCLASSIFIED
Printed By: DS PSS FILE ROOM
Privacy/PII
Page 3 of 310

So, given all the events that occurred while I was assigned with the US Military in Germany, with no investigation conducted as I continually requested, the question is which financial institution filed the Suspicious Activity Report (SAR) referenced and dated July 1, 2011? Once again, given the timeline of events, the documented facts, and entities involved. It was curiously-timed in the immediate aftermath of the May 1, 2001 capture/kill of bin Laden by the US Navy SEALS and my formally filing

10   US Dpartment of State DS John (No Last Name Ever Provided) Independent Contractor Customer Service Center Personnel Security/Suitability, Email exchange re Michelle Stefanick's identity theft, October 12-13, 2011

the EEO Grievance against MARFOREUR/AF located on a US Army Garrison base facility, purposely and intentionally modified/altered/falsified by the US Army Garrison EEO Stuttgart Office, and purposely and intentionally not investigated.

Needless to say, reading all that I read, piecing together all that I knew, all that was done to me and I've been put through and subjected to, I was furious. I was outraged. I was purposely and intentionally set-up by US Department of State Diplomatic Security, an entity that I previously respected and trusted. Otherwise, why didn't DS ever contact me regarding the July 20, 2001 *anonymous* memorandum? Why didn't DS ever get back to me when I reported the identity theft issue like DS said they would? There was all the retaliation against me when I formally filed the EEO grievance in April/May 2011 in Germany against the MARFOREUR/AF Marines, after my car door was smashed. And where was DS? DS Special Agents were assigned to AFRICOM, EUCOM, Embassy Berlin and at the Consulates throughout Germany. Why didn't DS protect me as a federal CVRA victim/witness in regards to the August 7, 1998 East Africa Embassy bombing and thereafter? And why didn't DS protect me as I was one of them, one of their own, a US Department of State employee, a US Department of State Foreign Service employee? Why? Quite obviously and quite apparently, DS was too busy targeting and setting me up.

Eventually, I obtained even more FOIA/Privacy Act-requested documents from the US Department of State: 548 pages of HR-related documents received on June 19, 2014; 6 pages of DS-related documents received on July 10, 2014; 211 pages of Central Foreign Policy Records received on September 15, 2014; 30 pages of HR-related documents received on January 26, 2015; and 466 pages of HR-related documents received on March 20, 2015. But as far as I was concerned, with documentation finally received on March 8, 2014, I saw all I needed to see. What was done to me was clear as day. And who was involved, if not totally responsible, was clear as day. And DS's intent to purposely delay my receiving these essential and pertinent evidential, supporting documents was clear as day. Though the motive was complex and complicated, it too was clear as day. It would become even more clear when I would obtain some crucial insight for the very first time from an unlikely source, an internet talk show host, on December 27, 2014.

CHAPTER 12

QUESTIONS PRESENTED:

"Though a larger rhetorical question that could be presented would be whether the rule of law still exists in the United States of America..."

A PLAN OF ACTION

Finally equipped with DS-related FOIA-obtained documents, I had the insight necessary to continue fighting – fighting for the truth and for justice. *Someone* intentionally put forth a false-narrative now so far down a rabbit hole that one has to understand the internal strength I needed to muster to continue this fight. It was an unfathomable rabbit hole much deeper than I could have even imagined... If I would have known, would I have continued my fight? I don't know. But knowing what I knew, and with my theory further substantiated, I began to fight back with the most powerful weapon of all: the facts and the truth.

On Sunday, March 9, 2014, I sent the following email to Kathleen Siljegovic. Kathleen went to church with me at St. Nicholas Russian Orthodox Cathedral in Washington, D.C. She worked in the Freedom of Information and Privacy Acts Division in DS. *Yes, at the State Department, DS also controlled the FOIA office...*

> Hello Kathleen – Hope all is well. I'm sorry for sending this to your personal email account but I thought I had your official email address but couldn't locate it, so attempted without knowing a middle initial. I realize you recused yourself from my request, but as you can see from attached, though 3 letters were signed by Linda (unable to read last name) only one references Amendment Procedures. So, with 408 pages being provided and my cursory review at this time, I do indeed have questions/comments regarding some of the documents in the file, particularly from 2005 on. Again, if you could forward this to "Linda" to respond I would really appreciate it—my question being does the Amendment Procedures ref-

erenced for Part 1 section, also apply to Part II and III as well. With that, I will be able to proceed accordingly. Thank you, Michelle L. Stefanick[1]

On Monday, March 10, 2014, Kathleen forwarded my email to Linda Pfeifle accordingly:

Please reply to Michelle's questions. Ks
Kathleen Siljegovic,
DS/MGT/FOIA-PA
Chief, Freedom of Information
And Privacy Acts Division[2]

Linda Pfeifle, ccing Siljegovic, responded:

Hi, Michelle,
As you can see Kathy passed on your email.
You are right to note that Part I is different from Parts II and III. Part I falls under the Privacy Act which permits you to request amendment of your record if you believe it "is not accurate, relevant, timely or complete" according to 5 USC. a (d). However, the same Privacy Act, in 5 USC. a (j)2, specifically excludes documents found in systems of records compiled for law enforcement. The key is the system of records or office in which the documents were found. There are only a limited number of offices in the State Department which fall in this category and DS/PII and DS/ICI/CI are two. Hence, we reviewed the documents in Parts II and III, which were found in those offices, under the Freedom of Information Act which has no provision to request the amendment of records. So, you may not request that the documents in Parts II and Parts III be amended. If you have other questions, please let me now. Linda[3]

On Tuesday, March 11, 2014, I emailed Pfeifle, ccing Siljegovic:

Hello Linda – Thank you so much for responding so quickly to my query.
Regarding Part III, I really don't have any comments on any documents/information provided at this time under that section, which is good in light of your description of the process below that no request for amendment to the record is permitted under that section anyways. In accordance with your applicable cover letter,

---

1   Michelle Stefanick, email message to Kathleen Siljegovic, March 9, 2014
2   Kathleen Siljegovic, email message to Linda Pfeifle March 10, 2014
3   Linda Pfeifle, email message to Michelle Stefanick and Kathleen Siljegovic, March 10, 2014

the review for this Part is complete and no additional documents/information are anticipated to be sent to me at this time—have I understood that properly?

Regarding Part II, if I read your cover letter properly, more documents/information may be provided in addition to those received at this time since other information is still under review. At this time only, information from the period of February 25 – March 19, 2013 has been provided, with possibly more to come at a later date. With that, I assume that I will be notified at a later date when the review is completed regardless of whether or not additional information is provided, with any additional information being provided accordingly.

Lastly, regarding Part I, based on my review and in accordance with your description below, I do indeed foresee my submission of an "Amendment Request." However, if I read your applicable cover letter correctly, I should anticipate receiving referenced Document numbers 131-145 in due time. Therefore, it appears that it may be prudent for me to delay my "Amendment Request" until receipt of these forthcoming documents so I have the entire proper context being provided to me to avoid premature submission of my request for consideration. With that, reading the provided "Amendment" policy I see that there is a time limitation for your office upon receipt of my request, but do not note any time limitation upon me to submit my request to your office—thus, my proposal for delay in submitting until receipt of all referenced documents is acceptable/allowable?

Again, thank you for responding so quickly and look forward to your confirmation regarding my above questions/clarifications. Thanks and have a great day. Cheers, Michelle[4]

On Wednesday, March 12, 2014, I forwarded this March 9 – 11, 2014 email exchange to U/S Patrick Kennedy, including nine applicable attachments and the following comments:

9 attachments (12 MB)
DS Privacy-FOIA Response rec'd Mar 8 20140001.pdf; DOJ Witness Info0001.pdf; DS Anonymous memo investigation 2001-20050001.pdf; DS SAR ROI Jan 20 20120001.pdf; Stuttgart 2011 EEO vs Marines (Army – Garrison) 0001.pdf; EEOC No. 570-2012-00235X Stuttgart Germany0001.pdf; DS Pat Kennedy's Involvement Feb 25-26 20130001.pdf; car door damage 001.JPG; house 002.JPG;

---

4   Michelle Stefanick, email message to Kathleen Siljegovic and Linda Pfeifle, March 11, 2014

Hello Pat – Hope all is well.

Let it be clear that I would not be outreaching to you today if it were not for the fact that I finally received most, but not all, documents from DS on March 8, 2014 in response to my May 19, 2013 Privacy/FOIA request (please see attached). Realizing the DS files may be more complicated to obtain, I received my requested MED records on July 1, 2013. Unlike noted below, and in the attachment, MED provided all their records, whereas other documents according to this cover memo are still due to me. So, I realize some of my insight may change once I receive the remaining documents, or at least the documents warranted to be allowed to be passed along to me, but in the meanwhile due to insights I've obtained in reviewing these 409 documents I believe justify contacting you now.

As noted below, the documentation comes under three separate parts, of which I can request amendments only to Part 1. The emphasis of this point now will be made clearer further in my comments. Part III documents, which were minimal, I had no comments, so no issue there. Part II, I have issues but I'm not allowed to request amendments, and Part I, I have issues, but going to delay filing my amendment request until I receive all the referenced documents. So, with the process aspect out of the way, I'm now going to proceed to "content" issues/insights.

The first issue I would like to clarify is that I work(ed) for the State Department my entire career, and I was never a USAID employee as stated under Part II in email exchanges within DS, which according to the "rules" I cannot request to amend. So, I thought maybe you can let folks in DS know that. Also, in references both in Part II and Part III, DS seems to be unaware of any open FBI investigation, with that, I provide the second attachment which references the still open/ongoing FBI investigation regarding the 1998 Embassy Bombings of which I am a DOJ victim.

The next basic issue that needs to be addressed is the fact that for some reason DS references my "voluntarily retirement" effective October 1, 2013. Again, not sure where DS is getting their information, but as you are aware, I didn't retire. Secretary Kerry accepted my resignation and I was off the payroll for three weeks with "somehow" my father/my family found out (and it wasn't from me because I was not/am not speaking to them). But with that, which I'm sure you are aware, an Arlington County Judge was able to overrule a Presidential/Federal Cabinet level decision/action by bringing me back onto State's payroll against my will. More insight will be provided regarding other actions taken to this regard further on, but its this crux between Federal Level and State/County Court level that folks are finding quite curious. Maybe this linkage/action between Federal and State/Arlington County Courts is actually something that may have resulted in the FBI recently creating a dedicated Northern Virginia Corruption tip line, or at least something they would be very interested in.

Now comes an even more interesting part... Are you aware that DS had open "Criminal" Investigation on me from July 20, 2001 – January 21, 2005 based on an "anonymous memo dated July 20, 2001"? This memo was sent to both DS as well as MED. I was made aware of this memo being sent to MED by MED in May 2002 when I was transferring from Moscow to Kosovo with GSO training enroute. In that discussion, not only did I describe the specific event that created this memo, but provided excruciating details to the overall scenario and more importantly, the other parties involved to include who I suspected wrote the memo/letter. Once I provided the names involved and their positions and motives, MED implied that they had "awareness" to the other individuals involved and I was medically cleared accordingly. However, I was never made aware by DS that they not only received this memo, but that they had an open "Criminal" investigation on me for almost 4 years. Maybe this now explains why the Deputy Principal Officer met with me at FSI and discussed his concerns of my upcoming assignment to Kosovo based on my name and my religion, when really it was all about this "criminal" investigation. Too bad that DS not only violated by due process rights (and defamation of my character), but most importantly they did not obtain the insight that I shared with MED accordingly. Because though I had no "direct evidence' to support suspicion to the individuals involved, I did have my concerns and acted accordingly in the capacity of my position to ensure internal/management controls were in place, funds were safeguarded, and internal notifications were made. I can assure you Pat once the names/details were provided, you too would instantly understand. Instead of going to Kosovo upon finishing the GSO FSI course, I worked with Sid Kaplan (RM/SPP) until I was assigned to Khartoum, Sudan. So too bad, for if DS had requested/obtained this insight/information from me as MED did, they may have indeed had a proper "criminal" case to investigate.

Now to events closer at hand... Please see attached the DS Report of Investigation that references not only my reporting an identity theft issue that occurred/that I reported related to a stateside event in October 2011, but also the reference to a Suspicious

Activity Report (SAR) dated July 1, 2011 timeframe while I was assigned to Stuttgart, Germany that DS linked inaccurately to my October reporting because of receiving the report from the Boston Field Office in December 2011. As I discussed with you, Rob Kelty called me at OSD in January 2012 to say the investigation was ongoing and would get back in touch with me. To date, no one from DS has ever gotten back to me in these regards.

But in the meanwhile, as this DS document supports, the SAR activity occurred in July 2011 timeframe and coincides with the events that happened coincidentally after I filled my formal EEO Grievance against the Marines. As you are well aware, per our discussion/your instruction I went back to Stuttgart, the Marines started to retaliate against me. It was one thing, to give me a hard time at to work, quite another when my car door was smashed while parked in front of Marine Headquarters (attached), my side mirror smashed (attached), and other events occurred which supported the filing of my EEO (please see attached). Why, all because I did what you requested me to do and followed your instruction.

So, let's recap this .. I was so excited to work with Marines. Prior to my December 2009 arrival, I had impeccable credit to support up to 5 real estate properties on one government salary—thanks to my CPA financial background—reported accordingly in all my required Financial Disclosure Statements to include CY 2009 and CY 2010 (of which I've provided you copies/discussed with you in Sept 2012). Had NO mental health issues as supported by my State MED file—other than MY outreach to ECS/Flora Bryant in the aftermath of the Embassy bombings to assist me in distinguishing the difference between the grieving process someone would experience after such an event, and PTSD—and to my arrival in Stuttgart. Then, all of a sudden, returning back to Stuttgart in January 2011 on your instruction, all the retaliation begins. Seeing what they did before I filed the EEO, I guess I was naïve enough to believe they would back off. And then the financial/other events occurred coincidentally soon after I filed the formal grievance in May. I departed post and PM never requested of me the required "termination of position" Financial Disclosure statement—which I find quite curious since I went to another "PM" sponsored position at OSD/African Affairs. Again, I ask you, why did it take L to request this statement over a year, after the fact, which I immediately completed and then discussed/met/shared with you. So why didn't PM request it? Why didn't DS ever get back to me? Despite my outreach, why did John Beliveau, the Supervisory NCIS agent, handling my request for investigation, open and shut the case without reviewing any of the evidential documents I had to share? Then, when John was arrested for corruption from an ongoing DOJ/FBI investigation, why hasn't NCIS reopened/returned my call in regards to their basic law enforcement protocol for cases handled by a corrupt agent?

In the meanwhile, Benghazi and other events occurred, which enabled me to connect dots regarding insight I believe had linkages to both Benghazi, but more importantly to the Embassy Bombings. Unfortunately, my efforts to report accordingly through OSD/Security and the DG Linda Thomas-Greenfield to DOJ/DS were hindered. However, due to efforts of the Legislative Branch I was not only able to get the information to the FBI, but other entities as well. And despite all the emails/ documents I'm now reading from information I received from DS and the retaliatory action for which they imposed (which is now substantiated with these such documents, with hopefully more to follow), I strongly believe the insight I provided assisted/enabled the Delta Force to go in and capture al-Liby in Benghazi in October 2013. If anyone in the Department (DS/DG/HR)/DOD or otherwise to include my family, thinks I would not do everything and anything I needed to do to share with the applicable law enforcement entity to bring justice for half of my staff I lost that day on Aug 7, 1998 as well as for all my colleagues and all those Kenyans and Tanzanians, then all these folks do not know me and my character and my integrity. So, with that, please do advise DS that there are two ongoing open FBI investigations regarding Benghazi and the 1998 Embassy Bombings, and Congressional investigations as well.

With that, I now have emails that include insights from the highest levels of DS, to include Greg Starr, and DG/HR, to include Linda Thomas-Greenfield and its one that I've attached (and received under Part II—no amendments permitted) that I would like to comment on now. First of all, I appreciate your request as indicated in the Feb 25, 2013 email of Kimber Davidson to DS that FBI meet with me again and that they provide me a letter accordingly. Because you were correct, that would have assisted in moving forward. Unfortunately, reading these additional emails, this never happened. Instead I have read the intent to not do as you instructed and not provide me due process rights and not do what I was morally, ethically and professionally required to do; but instead see the planning in process to have me "involuntarily committed" and "assassinate my character and my credibility" instead, all before

I even met with Jim Minor and Prestina Williams on March 20, 2013. In this email exchange as well as others, though not based on any doctor evaluation, I have also now seen how many "self-pre-scribed doctors" work at the State Department, DS in particular and yourself as well. To that I offer, stand in my shoes and do what I had to do, to include enduring all the retaliatory action by the Ma-rines against me for following your instructions when I returned to Stuttgart, and then maybe we can discuss one that suffers from a mental health issued and one that had endured a life stressor/vic-tim of a crime events(s), and the difference between the two. Now seeing first-hand the involvement by DS/DG in NOT assisting me through the law enforcement lane which the Department employ-ees expect of them, but instead to use my family/the Arlington County officials/police/courts instead is not only unforgiveable, but in light of all the applicable ongoing DOJ/FBI investigations, maybe also criminal.

So, I conclude with this by asking these remaining questions:

In light of all that I've presented in regards to what DS has and has not done in my situation and their operations/procedures writ large, who watches/does oversight over them? Carrying a badge, having access to diplomatic passports/pouches, Interpol, law en-forcement here and abroad the temptation must be immense—again, who oversees them—the FBI?

In light of the fact that I went back out to Stuttgart, Germany in January 2011 under your instruction and then was brutally retali-ated against, but yet there has yet to be any such investigation to the actions then and the actions now since my returning. If there is nothing to hide and your intent was true—which is what I want to believe—why not call the FBI in accordingly, as you so supposedly suggested to your own DS, which for some reason they didn't do as you requested. Don't you find that curious?

-For your information, on February 5, 2013, I receive an email from my White House contact regarding my concern about my meeting with the FBI. In this email, it indicated that the FBI re-sponded positively that your interview is part of an ongoing inves-tigation.

-Folks that are aware of the events that occurred in Stuttgart that have Special Forces backgrounds are quite aware of "what oc-curred" in Stuttgart, Germany and have so noted that it was "unau-thorized/unsanctioned/unconstitutional."

For the sake of the Department and all the employees you are serving with, you are too ethical/principled of a man not to do the right thing for there are just too many unanswered questions to what's really going on. Considering Greg Starr was in DS before during the 1998 Embassy Bombings—I'm not judge nor jury, but your reaching out directly to the FBI (since the DS route you suggested in the February email chain didn't result in what you requested—but instead retaliatory action against me) is something I would highly recommend you consider. Thanks, Michelle[5]

And on Tuesday, May 27, 2014, I sent a follow-up email to FOIA Status:

Subject: Status of Outstanding FOIA Request
Hello – I have a FOIA Request from May 19, 2013 that still has not been completely fulfilled. Though I have received pertinent documents from DS/MED and DIA/OPM/FBI, I'm still expecting the one I referenced document from Treasury and the ten from HR. Again, as this request is now over a year old, I find the delay for documents particularly from HR quite puzzling. If you could please provide a status on when I will receive these such documents, I would appreciate it. I've already left a voice message today as well. I can be reached on the email address or [redacted]. Again, as this request is over a year old, I would appreciate the documents/insight to the status of this request as soon as possible. Thank you, Michelle[6]

On Wednesday, May 28, 2014, I received the following response:

Would you please provide the Department of State assigned FOIA case number to facilitate a status update?[7]

I replied, this time ccing Pfeifle:

Sure. The only issue is I've seen a few FOIA case numbers referenced in the letters/documents sent to me in response to my May 19, 2013 request. Here they are: P-2013-16251; P-2013-09436 and 1258607-000.
Hopefully this helps expedite your status update, for as I mentioned earlier, this request is now over a year old. Considering one referenced document is due from Treasury and ten from HR, I find the delay quite perplexing, particularly in regards to HR. With that, again I hope providing these references will expedite an immediate response to this long outstanding request. Thank you. Michelle[8]

5   Michelle Stefanick, email message to Patrick Kennedy, March 12, 2014
6   Michelle Stefanick, email message to FOIA Status, May 27, 2014
7   FOIA Status, email message to Michelle Stefanick, May 28, 2014
8   Michelle Stefanick, email message to Linda Pfeifle, March 28, 2014

I received the following response from FOIA Status, ccing Pfeifle:

> I apologize for not mentioning the case number in the second paragraph as I did in the first paragraph. The Case Number P-2013-09436. 1258607-000 is not an assigned Department of State FOIA case number.
>
> I cannot speak to another agencies review process. However, unusual circumstances include when another agency is involved as it relates to concurrences and/or direct replies.
>
> Estimated completion dates are generally derived from the offices/agencies backlog, search and review times.
>
> To get a better sense of the length of time it would take to process a FOIA request, you may look at the Department's annual reports on the FOIA website at www.foia.state.gov.
>
> I hope this is responsive to your inquiry.[9]

I responded, ccing Pfeifle:

> Hello – I must say I'm totally confused. I'm not talking about the one document from Treasury – in appreciate your assistance in querying the status. Are you saying HR has such a backlog that it will take almost 2 years to get a response? I really hope the OIG has been looped in regarding this unacceptable backlog.
>
> Regarding the 1258607-000 case number – that must be the DOJ/FBI assigned case number as that was the number referenced in their response back to me.
>
> Can you please advise why HR is taking so long to respond to this FOIA request? That's not another agency, that the Dept of State. Thanks, Michelle[10]

Then on Tuesday, June 10, 2014, I sent this follow-up email to FOIA Status and Pfeifle:

> Hello – On June 4, I was advised by Kiwana (?sp?) from Treasury/FOIA, that State' FOIA request of March 24, 2014 (vs May 19, 2013 regarding the initial date of this long outstanding Privacy/FOIA request) was forwarded to their Financial Crisis Enforcement Network (FCEN) and that a response was sent back to State dated March 26, 2014. This was also confirmed by the FCEN/FOIA representative Amanda on June 4 as well. Though I've made numerous requests to Treasury/FCEN to provide me a copy/email of this letter response, I have yet to receive it directly from them for they implied that State's was going to forward me a copy

9   FOIA Status, email message to Michelle Stefanick and Linda Pfeifle, May 28, 2014
10   Michelle Stefanick, email message to FOIA Status and Linda Pfeifle, May 28, 2014

of the letter. I'm not sure who I'm supposed to get a copy of this response from, but all I know is that I still have not received a copy and continue to request it. Your assistance regarding this matter would be appreciated.

With that, I also still have not received the supposed 10 referenced/applicable documents from HR. Can you please provide a status of this portion of my long outstanding Privacy/FOIA request as well? Thank you. Michelle[11]

On Friday, June 13, 2014, I received the following from FOIA Status:

Ms. Michelle Stefanick,
Your information has been forwarded to the appropriate office for action.[12]

I responded, again including Pfeifle:

Great – Thanks. I only wish it would have been forwarded to the 'appropriate office' for action a long time; and shouldn't it have been. So, does this mean now my request will be stonewalled for another year? Or when should I expect my long outstanding request to be fulfilled? Thanks, Michelle[13]

I received the following from FOIA Status, including Pfeifle:

It was forwarded to the appropriate office the first time around as well. Thank you.[14]

I responded this time to FOIA Status, Pfeifle, FINCEN as well as Treasury FOIA:

Subject: RE: Status of Outstanding FOIA Request – Treasury/FINCEN response
Great – thanks. Again, as I strongly believe in accountability and responsibility within our bureaucracies, this is good insight. Guess that applicable appropriate office within State Department has some explaining to do…the first being, why they are holding back this information from me in this long outstanding Privacy/FOIA request. I don't have anything to hide, but seems someone does. Thanks and we'll now see how long it takes for that appropriate office to respond and be held accountable accordingly. Michelle[15]

---

11   Michelle Stefanick, email message to FOIA Status, and Linda Pfefile, June 10, 2014
12   FOIA Status, email message to Michelle Stefanick, June 13, 2014
13   Michelle Stefanick, email message to FOIA Status, and Linda Pfefile, June 10, 2014
14   FOIA Status, email message to Michelle Stefanick and Linda Pfefile, June 13, 2014
15   Michelle Stefanick, email message to FOIA Status, Linda Pfefile, FINCEN and Treasury FOIA, June 10, 2014

On Thursday, June 19, 2014, I sent the following email to FOIA Status and Pfeifle:

> Subject: Inconsistency of HR response to P-2013-09436
> Linda (DS/MGT/FOIA-PA) and FOIA Status Rep (A/GIS/IPS) – Today I received a certified package from HR in regards to my long outstanding Privacy/FOIA request of May 19, 2013. Though I appreciate finally receiving a response from HR to this matter, I am confused on the inconsistency of what I was supposed to receive. This inconsistency is documented/stated in the two letters provide in the attachment. The first letter dated March 6, 2014 from DS references Documents 131 -145 originated with other bureaus/agencies of which Document 130 is Treasury, and Documents 131-140 is HR. However, today and as stated in the attached letter dated June 16, 2014, I received instead 303 documents in totality, but not cross referenced to the "10" expected HR documents as referenced in the March 6 letter. Therefore, I am not ensured/assured that the documents received are the same I referenced/expected to fulfill my long outstanding request.
> Additionally, I still have not received a copy of the Treasury related response/referenced document pertaining to this request.
> Confirmation/clarification to this inconsistency as well as status to the pending Treasury referenced document is sincerely appreciated. Thank you. Michelle[16]

I received a response on Friday, June 20, 2014 from FOIA Status:

> Ms. Stefanick,
> Your request has been forwarded to the appropriate office for action.
> Best,
> Jennine A. Daniels
> US Department of State[17]

I replied to FOIA Status – Jennine and Pfeifle on Friday, June 20, 2014:

> Subject: Inconsistency/Inaccuracy and Incompleteness of HR response to P-2013-09436
> Thank you Jennine for getting back to me and for signing your name.
> In my initial review of the documents provided in this June 16, 2014 HR response, I note that SF-50s for that last year or so appear to be missing. Additionally, the last EER provided does not match

16   Michelle Stefanick, email message to FOIA Status, and Linda Pfefile, June 19, 2014
17   Jennine Daniels, email message to Michelle Stefanick, June 20, 2014

460

the last one I provided to the DG's office for EER Review Board review for rating period ending April 15, 2013. If you could please forward that to the appropriate office for action as well, I would appreciate it.

Also, please note that the June 16, 2014 cover letter/documents provided do not reconcile. As supported by the attachment, though the number of pages (548) is accurate, the number of documents is not 303. This is due to a "10" document gap in numbering (123 to 133) and 3 documents being missed in the accounting. Therefore, I've been provided 296 documents not 303 as indicated in the attached/provided cover letter. Just wanted to document/bring this to your office's attention to ensure your files are properly/accurately documented/reflected.

I look forward to obtaining/receiving the HR and Treasury-related document(s) to this/my long outstanding May 19, 2013 Privacy/FOIA request still pending. Thank you. Michelle[18]

On Monday, June 23, 2014, I received the following response from FOIA Status:

Ms. Stefanick – Your request for a status update for the information received has been forwarded to the appropriate office for action.[19]

I replied to FOIA Status and Pfeifle:

Great – Thanks. Again, just wanted to document and set the record straight due to all the inaccuracies/inconsistencies, and incompleteness. Sorry it must be the OIG in me. Thanks, Michelle

On Saturday, July 5, 2014, I sent the following email to FOIA Status:

Subject: Status of Privacy/FOIA request P-2013-09436 dated May 19, 2013

Hello – It's been almost two weeks and I still have not heard/received the 10 State/HR referenced documents and the 1 Treasury document that they have sent to you all. Can you please provide the status and when I can expect to receive these documents to complete this long outstanding Privacy/FOIA request of May 19, 2013? Thank you. Michelle[20]

On Monday, July 7, 2014, I receive the following response from FOIA Status Jennine Daniels:

---

18   Michelle Stefanick, email message to Jennine Daniels, and Linda Pfefile, June 20, 2014
19   FOIA Status, email message to Michelle Stefanick, June 23, 2014
20   Michelle Stefanick, email message to FOIA Status, July 5, 2014

Ms. Stefanick,

Your request for a status update has been forwarded to the appropriate office for action.[21]

I replied to FOIA Status – Jennine Daniels and Pfeifle:

Hello Jennine – Thank you, I'm quite aware of that per our last email exchange. As this overall request is now over a year outstanding with this specific aspect to the 10 HR/1 Treasury referenced documents being over 2 weeks since you last email response, which specific "office" is the appropriate office that its been forwarded to for action? DS? HR/DG? PM? RM? INR? Your insight sincerely appreciated. Thanks, Michelle[22]

In hindsight, I should have included AF, EUR, INL, SPG, NEA and even H, given the Congressional aspect to all this. I should have included Every single office in the entire Department of State for that matter...

I received the following response from FOIA Status – Jennine Daniels:

Ms. Stefanick,

Your request has been forwarded to the Department's Statutory Compliance and Research Branch.[23]

I replied to FOIA Status – Jennine Daniels and Pfeifele, ccing U/S Patrick Kennedy, OSC Carolyn Lerner, HFAC Staffer Tom Sheehy, as well as the FBI Northern Virginia Task Force:

Jennine – Thanks for the insight. I find it being forwarded to that office/branch by your office quite curious – unless of course someone was concerned/interested in compliance with the law or the breaching thereof... which again, I find quite curious. And with that I add, the timeline/email trial/evidential matter is what is at this point and yes indeed laws have been broken, just not by me. If you could please advise/query the Dept's Statutory Compliance and Research Branch on the status and/or provided me a point of contact information so I can follow-up directly, I would appreciate it. Thank you. Michelle[24]

I emailed all parties again:

Jennine – As a follow-up, per my internet search, it appears that Patrick Scholl [redacted] is in charge of that Branch. So, I called

21   Jennine Daniels, email message to Michelle Stefanick, July 5, 2014
22   Michelle Stefanick, email message to Jennine Daniels, and Linda Pfefile, July 5, 2014
23   Jennine Daniels, email message to Michelle Stefanick, July 5, 2014
24   Michelle Stefanick, email message to Jennine Daniels, Linda Pfefile,Patrick Kennedy, Carolyn Lerner, Tom Sheehy, and the FBI Northern Virginia Task Force July 5, 2014

and left him a message. Per his voicemail, it said to contact Terry Gordan (?sp?) [redacted] who I also called and left a message. As I don't know if these are the appropriate points of contacts in the Statutory Compliance and Research Branch or not, if you could please outreach accordingly to them or whomever is appropriate, I would sincerely appreciate it. Thanks, Michelle[25]

I received the following from FOIA Status Ms. Tyler:

Ms. Stefanick – The reasons for contacting the Advocacy and Oversight Branch is that the personnel who monitor the FOIA Requester Service Center are aware of who is, and who is not available to provide the information that is being sought. As your below email indicates, the persons you contacted are not the correct individuals who are assigned action for the subject request. As stated before, would you please continue to direct your inquiries through FOIA Status and you will be provided with a response as soon as one is received from the assigned Statutory Compliance and Research Branch. Thank you, Ms. Tyler[26]

I replied to FOIA Status and Pfeifle, ccing Kennedy, Lerner, Sheehy, and the FBI:

Ms. Tyler – Thanks so much for getting back with me. I didn't realize you all were the "Advocacy and Oversight Branch." With that, being "Oversight" and all, you then know that there is a fine line between "incompetence" and "intent." Now considering this Privacy/FOIA request is dated May 19, 2013 – over a year outstanding – and per the email chain provided, Treasury sent the response to State a few months back but yet I still have not received it, seems to me that fine line has been crossed a long time ago. With that, since I do not know your chain of command within your role of "oversight," seems to me you should have definitely raised this up that chain a long time ago....Considering you have no context as to why I submitted this Privacy/FOIA request in the first place, others in the upper Management of the Department do. So, with that, I again ask where is this information that I requested a long time ago? Again, with role of "oversight" I hope you did exactly that and reported it accordingly. Otherwise, why is there such a delay? I have nothing to hide, but maybe someone in the Dept does? Again, I kindly request the complete request to this long outstanding Pri-

25   Michelle Stefanick, email message to Jennine Daniels, Linda Pfefile,Patrick Kennedy, Carolyn Lerner, Tom Sheehy, and the FBI Northern Virginia Task Force July 5, 2014
26   Ms. Taylor, email message to Michelle Stefanick, July 5, 2014

vacy/FOIA request and look forward to hearing from you shortly to that regard. Thanks, Michelle[27]

On Wednesday, July 9, 2014, I again emailed FOIA Status and Pfeifle, ccing Kennedy, Lerner, Sheehy, and the FBI:

Hello Ms. Tyler – As follow-up to my July 7 email, if you could please advise status to this long outstanding request, I would appreciate it. Thank you, Michelle[28]

On Thursday, July 10, 2014, I received a response from FOIA Status – Ms. Tyler:

Ms. Stefanick – The Bureau of Diplomatic Security has informed this office that the Department of Treasury documents were mailed to you on July 7, 2014, and that they, (DS) are awaiting a response from the Bureau of Human Resources, and has followed up with them. Regards, Ms. Tyler[29]

I emailed FOIA State and Pfeifle, ccing Kennedy, Lerner, Sheehy, and the FBI:

Ms. Tyler – Thank you for the status. I must say I find it quite curious/odd that the "Deprt" has had this Treasury document for months and multiple responses (per Treasury officials) but "DS" is just now sending the document to me. I will let you know when I receive it.

Also thank you for the insight that "DS" is querying HR on the status of the other referenced still-outstanding documents. Again, I find all this so curious. But thank you for getting back to me. Michelle[30]

Then I emailed FOIA State, Pfeifle, Treasury/FINCEN, Treasury/FOIA; ccing Kennedy, Lerner, Sheehy, and the FBI:

Hello Ms. Tyler – As noted below, I wanted to let you know that I just received the DS/Treasury documents referenced in your earlier email. I really appreciate this considering how long I've been waiting to receive this. With that, I find it quite curious that the packet I received today from William R. Terrini (and attached) is

27   Michelle Stefanick, email message to Ms. Taylor, Linda Pfefile, Patrick Kennedy, Carolyn Lerner, Tom Sheehy, and the FBI Northern Virginia Task Force July 5, 2014
28   Michelle Stefanick, email message to Ms. Taylor, Linda Pfefile, Patrick Kennedy, Carolyn Lerner, Tom Sheehy, and the FBI Northern Virginia Task Force July 5, 2014
29   Ms. Taylor, email message to Michelle Stefanick, July 5, 2014
30   Michelle Stefanick, email message to FOIA State, Linda Pfefile, Patrick Kennedy, Carolyn Lerner, Tom Sheehy, and the FBI Northern Virginia Task Force July 5, 2014

number 130 and have only 4 applicable pages (and none from Dept of Treasury) in comparison to the number 130 packet I received from DS on Mar 8, 2014, (and attached) that has 7 applicable pages. So, what exactly have I been waiting for from Treasury when the packet I received today as less pages than the packet I received from DS on Mar 8, 2014, and still neither contain any documents from Treasury?

As I believe in openness and transparency, I've looped the applicable Treasury officials on this email exchange so they can see for themselves what I actually received to compare it with what they actually sent to DS, but I never received. Again, I have nothing to hide and everything to share, but I find all this, once again, quite curious. So why have I still not received the information that Treasury passed along to DS? The two DS packets alone speak for themselves.

So again, I kindly request the status for the reference Treasury documents since I once again have not received them. Thanks, Michelle[31]

The two referenced documents that I attached were as follows. On November 27, 2015, I received the following official notification letter on United States Department of Treasury FinCen (Financial Crimes Enforcement Network) letterhead. The letter came in an envelope with the following return address: Department of the Treasury Financial Crimes Enforcement Network Post Office Box 39 Vienna, VA 22183-0039, below an official seal, and indicated *OFFICIAL BUSINESS*. The letter went as follows:

November 23, 2015
FOIA Office Chief
DS/MGT/FOIA-PA
US Department of State
[Redacted]
Washington DC 20522-2008
Re: State FOIA Case No. P201309436
To the Current FOIA Chief:
On November 23, 2015 the Financial Crimes Enforcement Network (Fin CEN) FOIA Office received a phone call from Ms. Michelle Stefanick concerning the State FOIA request No. P201309436. Ms. Stefanick asserted that she had not received a

---

31   Michelle Stefanick, email message to FOIA State, Treasury FINCEN, Treasury FOIA, Linda Pfefile, Patrick Kennedy, Carolyn Lerner, Tom Sheehy, and the FBI Northern Virginia Task Force July 5, 2014

FOIA response, which should have included a FinCEN consultation response, from her 2013 FOIA request to State. Our records show that the US Department of Treasury Disclosure Office received a FOIA consultation from State on March 6, 2014 concerning FinCEN records identified in the State FOIA search. The FinCEN FOIA Office received the consultation request and records on March 25, 2014 from Main Treasury and returned a responsive letter and record review to State dated March 26, 2014.

Ms. Stefanick may need to have, if not already completed, the referenced State FOIA response recent including the FinCENT consolation response. The FinCEN FOIA Office has additionally sent this response to Ms. Stefanick.

Sincerely,

/s/

Gilbert L. Paist

Disclosure Officer[32]

To this day, I have never received a copy of the aforementioned and referenced Department of Treasury/FinCEN response supposedly dated March 26, 2014. Yet, DS opened up a criminal investigation on me based on a July 20, 2001 anonymous memorandum, received less than a month after my returning from attending the bin Laden trial in NYC in June 2001 ...

At this point in time, so much was done, purposely and intentionally done. Yet, where was DOJ? Where was the FBI? Why was any of this permitted to happen? And most importantly, why wasn't I protected? So, why didn't the US Department of State, particularly and specifically DS, protect me? Quite clearly, and as documented, because DS targeted me instead. Why?

Obviously, all this was not just about an explosion, but something much bigger. I had to rethink and refocus. This was like an onion, peeling back layer after layer, and never knowing when it was going to end.

So again, I began the pursuit of obtaining more truth and connecting so many more dots. I again contacted my Virginia Congressional Delegation Members to include Senator Mark Warner, Senator Tim Kaine, Congressman Jim Moran, VA Delegate Patrick Hope, VA Senator Barbara Favola. I then had this enlightening official exchange with Senator Mark Warner, now Ranking Member of the US Intelligence Committee:

United States Senate

Washington, DC 20510-4606

June 4, 2014

Ms. Michelle Stefanick

[redacted]

Dear Ms. Stefanick,

I appreciate the trust and confidence you have shown in me in contacting me with your concerns.

In an effort to be of assistance to you, I have referred your letter to the Federal Bureau of Investigations (FBI). I will promptly forward any information I may receive from the agency to you.

Sincerely,

/s/

MARK R. WARNER,

United State Senator[33]

MRW/ot

Then, I received this letter on September 16, 2014:

United States Senate

Washington, DC 20510-4606

September 12, 2014

Ms. Michelle Stefanick

[redacted]

Dear Ms. Stefanick,

Enclosed you will find the response from the US Department of Justice (DOJ) to my inquiry on your behalf. I hope that the information provided will be helpful and responsive to your specific concerns.

My staff and I stand ready to be of assistance to you in any other matter that is of concern to you. Thank you.

Sincerely,

/s/

MARK R. WARNER

United State Senator.34

MRW/ot

Enclosure

Here's the applicable enclosure:

US Department of Justice

Federal Bureau of Investigation Washington, D.C. 20535

September 5, 2014

---

33   Mark Warner, letter to Michelle Stefanick, June 4, 2014
34   Mark Warner, letter to Michelle Stefanick, September 16, 2014

(postmark stamped received US Mark Warner SEP 11, 2014 Vienna)

The Honorable Mark R. Warner
United States Senator
Suite 200
8000 Towers Crescent Drive
Vienna, VA 22182

Dear Senator Warner:

This is in reply to your June 5, 2014, inquiry on behalf of your constituent Ms. Michelle Stefanick, who claims whistleblower status and makes numerous allegations involving corruption. I regret the delay in responding.

The FBI familiar with Ms. Stefanick and representatives of our Washington Field Office have had prior contact with her. Ms. Stefanick has not been afforded Whistleblower status from the FBI. Additionally, in order for the FBI to initiate an investigation of any complaint we receive, specific facts must be present to indicate that a violation of federal law within our investigative jurisdiction has occurred. Although Ms. Stefanick makes numerous allegations, there are insufficient facts to demonstrate a violation of federal law within our investigative jurisdiction or to support the initiation of an FBI investigation. We are, therefore, unable to provide any assistance to her.

I hope this information is helpful to you in responding to your constituent.

Sincerely,
/s/
Elizabeth R. Beers
Section Chief
Office of Congressional Affairs[35]

I read this and could not believe what I was reading!…. *Who precisely in the FBI "has not afforded (me) whistleblower status from the FBI?"* Who, given all that I had been put through, who precisely in the FBI purposely and intentionally, given my federal CVRA-accorded rights and protections, did not protect me? Who precisely in the FBI purposely and intentionally not only permitted, but quite obviously were accomplices to all the retaliatory actions that I was subjected to? Given the timeline of events, at minimum FBI Directors Robert Mueller, James Comey and Andrew McCabe were and would all have been involved, directly and/or indirectly. Fast forward, as I'm writing this book, given all the events

---

that have unfolded and are continuing to play out: do these names sound familiar? *So, why didn't I ever receive a direct official notification from the FBI, at that time or to this day, regarding their decision that "Ms. Stefanick has not been afforded whistleblower status from the FBI?" Now with over 20 years of cover-up/false narratives/crimes being committed, what is the old saying? The cover-up is always worse than the original crime.*

On November 25, 2019, I sent the following Privacy Act request to my current Congressional Representative, Congresswoman Jennifer Wexton. The request was as follows:

> Office of Jennifer Wexton
> Please print, sign and mail/fax to our office.
> Name: Michelle Laureen Stefanick
> Date: 11/25/2019
> Agency involved: Federal Bureau of Investigation
> Numbers Identifying Case (VA claim, Alien number, tax ID, etc.):
> 265A-NY-259391
> Branch of Service (If Applicable):
> Military Rank (If Applicable):
> Date of Birth: PROVIDED
> Social Security #: PROVIDED
> Street Address: PROVIDED
> City, State, Zip Code: PROVIDED
> Telephone #: PROVIDED
> Email Address: PROVIDED
> Immigration-related Information (If Applicable)
> US Citizenship and Immigration Services Alien #:
> US Citizenship and Immigration Services Form #:
> US Citizenship and Immigration Services Receipt #:
> Place of Birth:
> I, Michelle Laureen Stefanick, authorize the Federal Bureau of Investigation to release personal information to Congresswoman Jennifer Wexton United States Representative. I authorize Congresswoman Jennifer Wexton to request and have access to all records and reports pertinent to my request for assistance in the following matter:
> Nature of Problem: I am a federal Crime Victims' Rights Act (CVRA) protected victim/witness in regards to August 7, 1998 East Africa Embassy bombing. Confirm with DOJ/SDNY. After connecting dots regarding the attack on our Consulate [sic] in Benghazi with the August 7, 1998 East Africa Embassy bombing, on November 27, 2012, I provided the Department of State/Di-

rector General at the time—Linda Thomas-Greenfield, my 8-page handwritten "Whistleblower/Protection Request" Letter. She did absolutely nothing. Instead of being protected, I was retaliated against by the US Department of State… Having previously done an APSA Congressional Detail assignment to the Hill from State, on November 28, 2012, I provided an 8-page handwritten copy of the November 27, 2012 "Whistleblower/Protection Request" Letter to Senator Olympia Snowe. Confirm with Senator Olympia Snowe. In turn, Senator Olympia Snowe and her office provided my "Whistleblower/Protection Request" letter to IC/OIG; ODNI; and to the FBI accordingly. Yet, instead of being protected, I was retaliated against instead. After being retaliated against to include by the US Department of State, I met with House Foreign Affairs Committee (HFAC) Benghazi Committee Investigators in my residence in May 2013, which resulted in al-liby's Oct 6, 2013 capture by the Army SF. On Oct 6, 2013, US Army Delta Forces captured al-liby—off of the FBI Most Wanted List—in Benghazi, in connection to the August 7, 1998 East Africa Embassy Bombings. Confirm with US Army SF. Interestingly enough, to this day, I have never received an official notification/correspondence directly from the FBI in regards to/in response to my November 27, 2012 "Whistleblower Protection Request" letter despite knowing that the FBI Congressional Liaison Office, as well as FBI Agents John Neal, Andrew McCabe, Charles Thorley received a copy. It would not be until I received a September 12, 2014 letter from US Senator Mark R. Warner, with an accompanying September 5, 2014 letter from the FBI Office of Congressional Affairs Section Chief Elizabeth R. Beers addressed to Senator Warner not me, that "Ms. Stefanick has not been afforded Whistleblower status from the FBI." Given, to this day, I, Michelle Laureen Stefanick, have never received an official notification/response addressed directly to me from the FBI regarding my November 27, 2012 "Whistleblower Protection Request" letter, I kindly request the assistance of my US Congresswoman Jennifer Wexton on this matter. This request includes querying why I, your Commonwealth of Virginia constituent, never received a direct response from the FBI; requesting an official FBI response be provided now accordingly, to include the basis of why such determination that I was "not afforded whistleblower status from the FBI" and by the FBI. Was it the FBI Congressional Office? FBI Agent John Neal? FBI Agent Andrew McCabe? FBI Agent Charles Thorley? The FBI Office in the Southern District of New York? And/or the FBI Director at the time—James Comey? Or the previous FBI Director—Robert Mueller? Needless to say, given the timeline of events, the national security matters and implications at stake, as well as many other ramifications to include obstruction of justice, abuse of power to name just a few as events currently playing themselves out in current day—the truth matters. Therefore, Congresswoman Jennifer Wexton's, my congressional representative's, assistance in my, your constituent's, request in obtaining this truth and these answers is not only sincerely appreciated, but urgent in its immediacy. Thank you, Michelle L. Stefanick

PLEASE NOTE:

The Privacy Act of 1974 requires that Members of Congress or their staff have written authorization before they can obtain information about an individual's case. We must have your signature to proceed with a casework inquiry.

Signature: /s/

Date: 11/25/19

Print, and then mail or fax your request to Jennifer Wexton at the following address:

Please mail your form to:

Office of Jennifer Wexton

Attn: Constituent Services

1217 Longworth HOB

Washington, DC 20515

Phone: (202) 225-5136[36]

On Monday, November 25, 2019, I sent the following email to Courtney Callejas of Congresswoman Jennifer Wexton's staff:

Subject: Constituent Nov 25, 2019 Request

Importance: High

Hello Courtney – As advised/suggested, please find attached my Constituent Request assistance from my Congressional Representative, Congresswoman Jennifer Wexton accordingly. Also, please advised, a hard copy of this request has also been placed in the mail to Congresswoman Wexton today as well. Thank you in advance for the Congresswoman's assistance on this request/matter. I can be reached [redacted]. Thank you, Michelle L. Stefanick[37]

On Wednesday, November 27, 2019, I received the following email from Erica Constance of Congresswoman Jennifer Wexton's staff:

36   Michelle Stefanick, letter to Jennifer Wexton, November 19, 2019
37   Michelle Stefanick, email message to Courtney Callejas, November 19, 2019

Subject: Request for Assistance
Hello Ms. Stefanick,
I have received your privacy release form and supporting documentation from our DC office. I will also need a letter from you to the Congresswoman detailing your specific request and desired outcome—please send that along as an attachment when you can. I will review everything with the appropriate caseworkers and reach out to you no later than Tuesday of next week.
Thank you,
Erica Constance
District Director (VA10)
Office of Congresswoman Jennifer Wexton[38]

Upon receiving the email, I immediately called Erica to discuss. As follow-up to our discussion, I sent the following:

Hello Erica – Thank you for your quick response. As just discussed in our telcon, I believe my request is quite clear and explicitly indicated in the provided privacy release form. However, if for some reason the FBI needs additional clarification upon Congresswoman Wexton's outreach based on my assistance request, we can definitely address accordingly at that time, and if and when that need arises. Again, thank you Erica for your due diligence and quick response. Happy Thanksgiving. Cheers, Michelle L. Stefanick[39]

As indicated previously, according to State/Casualty Assistance Office Kendall Montgomery's November 23, 1999 email:

In mid-August a copy of the (One-year anniversary) video was sent to every post worldwide with a letter from the DG to ambassadors urging that they share it with their communities… The video also went to every member of Congress…[40]

Yet, there was minimal Congressional focus regarding the August 7, 1998 East Africa Embassy bombings.

When I knew the importance and significance of what I knew, without hesitation, I didn't obstruct justice, I reached out to ensure justice. That included my reaching out immediately and accordingly on November 28, 2012 to Congress when I connected dots regarding the two events, August 7 and Benghazi Diplomatic Post attack on September 11, 2012. And I've paid for it ever since…

38   Erica Constance, email message to Michelle Stefanick, November 27, 2019
39   Michelle Stefanick, email message to Erica Constance, November 19, 2019
40   Kendall Montgomery, email message to Michelle Stefanick, November 23, 1999

I literally reached out to almost every congressional member of the House, Senate, republicans, democrats, personal offices and committee offices alike. No one assisted me the way Senator Olympia Snowe did. But what about Mike Rogers, Ed Royce, Mark Warner, Tim Kaine, Jim Moran, Don Beyer, and so on, and so on? Listing all the names of both congressional members and staffers could easily reach hundreds. I share this form letter, admittedly one of the only ones I received in my efforts, not to embarrass but to prove my point. I was not receiving Congressional attention as I deemed essential and necessary for the sake of our national security, and our democracy. *Yet, no one in Congress can say they didn't know…*

United State Senate
Washington, DC 20510
June 1, 2015

Ms. Michelle Stephanick [sic]
[redacted]
Dear Ms. Stephanick, [sic]
Thank you for contacting my office regarding your claim of retaliation. While I welcome the opportunity to be of assistance, it is a long-standing tradition and courtesy in the Senate to allow each Senator the opportunity to directly serve the constituents he or she represents.

I encourage you to contact your Senator directly at:
The Honorable Tim Kaine
United States Senate
611 S. Jefferson Street, Suite 5B
Roanoke, VA 24011
(540) 682-5693

Again, thank you for bringing this matter to my attention. I trust you matter will receive the appropriate attention.
Sincerely,
[250]/s/
Marco Rubio
United States Senator[41]
MR/dhl
WF#1664890

To which I reply here:

Thank you US Senator. I did contact my applicable Virginia Congressional Representatives, as well as many others, and I did not receive the appropriate attention. Michelle L. Stefanick[42]

41   Marco Rubio, letter to Michelle Stefanick, June 1, 2015
42   Michelle Stefanick, letter to Marco Rubio, June 1, 2015

On Monday, December 9, 2019, I received an email from Congress-woman Jennifer Wexton's staffer, Erica Constance:

> Hello Ms. Stefanick,
> Do you have a copy of the September 12, 2014 letter from Senator Warner and the September 5, 2014 letter from the FBI to the Senator that you can share with me?
> Thank you,
> Erica Constance, District Director
> Office of Congresswoman Jennifer Wexton (VA10)[43]

I replied:

> Hello Erica – Sure. Please find attached the Sen Warner June 4 2014 letter w/envelope that I received on June 7, 2014 (2 Pages). Also, please find attached the Sen Warner Sept 12 2014 letter w/ FBI Sept 5, 2014 letter referenced enclosure w/envelope that I received on Sept 16, 2014 (3 Pages). Thanks, Michelle L. Stefanick[44]

And I now wait for a response, either from Congresswoman Wexton's Office and/or the FBI. Preferably before publication of this book ...

On December 12, 2019, I sent the exact worded Privacy Act request to Senator Tim Kaine that I did to Congresswoman Jennifer Wexton on November 25, 2019. On December 18, 2019, I received the following official letter response via email from United States Senate US Senator Kaine:

> Dear Ms. Stefanick:
> Thank you for taking the time to contact me concerning the difficulties you are experiencing. I appreciate hearing from you.
>   While I would like to be of assistance to you in this matter, it is a long-standing tradition of Congress to allow the member of Congress who initiated your case to complete their casework inquiry. Accordingly, I communicated with Senator Warner's office and was informed that they initiated a Congressional inquiry on your behalf in 2014. The Federal Bureau of Investigation responded at that time and the casework was completed.
>   Because the final authority for a decision rests with the agency, I am unable to provide you with additional assistance for your case at this time.
>   Again, thank you for contacting me.
> Sincerely,
> /s/
> Tim Kaine[45]

---

43   Erica Constance, email message to Michelle Stefanick, December 9, 2019
44   Michelle Stefanick, email message to Erica Constance, November 19, 2019
45   Tim Kaine, email message to Michelle Stefanick, December 18, 2019

I followed-up with Senator Tim Kaine's Congressional staffers with phone calls and email. And I now wait for a response, either from Congresswoman Wexton's Office, Senator Kaine's Office and/or the FBI. Preferably before publication of this book ...

On December 15, 2019, I mailed the exact worded Privacy Act request to Senator Mark Warner that I did to Congresswoman Jennifer Wexton on November 25, 2019, and Senator Tim Kaine on December 12, 2019. And I now wait for a response, either from Congresswoman Wexton's Office, Senator Kaine's Office, Senator Warner's Office and/or the FBI. Preferably before publication of this book ...

On May 7, 2013, and then again, on May 18, 2013, I contacted, reported and filed a formal complaint with the Office of Special Counsel. OSC closed my case with no notification to State or DOD, and no investigation conducted. Within the 65-day timeframe to Appeal with the MSPB, the *Emergency Motion* stunt of October 23 -24, 2013 was used as yet another retaliatory action taken against me. Then on March 8, 2014, I received 409 pages of DS-related documents, the intentionally delayed Department of State May 19, 2013 FOIA/Privacy request response. I finally had proof, after so much retaliatory destruction to my reputation, career, finances, life—all purposely done. Receiving this new evidence, I reinitiated OSC, including Carol Lerner. On Thursday, July 31, 2014, I received the following:

> Dear Ms. Stefanick,
> The Special Counsel has asked that I respond to your correspondence.
> In May 2013, you filed a disclosure with OSC's Disclosure Unit alleging retaliation for exposing wrongdoing at the Department of State and the Department of Defense. As noted in a letter to you dated May 23, 2013, the Disclosure Unit does not review allegations of prohibited personnel practices, including retaliation, as those allegations are reviewed by OSC's Complaints Examining Unit (CEU). The Disclosure Unit referred you to CEU Attorney Alejandra Dove, who could address your allegations of retaliation. Based on our review of the information provided in your recent emails, your allegations appear to concern retaliation, your security clearance, and additional allegations of prohibited personnel practices. Accordingly, the Disclosure Unit will not re-open this matter.
> With regard to your complaint of prohibited personnel practices, Ms. Dove reviewed your allegations of retaliation and on

September 5, 2013, CEU issued you a preliminary determination letter citing the reasons we found to close OSC's inquiry into your complaint. You did not specify the information that caused officials to allegedly retaliate against you; nor did you complain of any personnel actions that are under the jurisdiction of the Office of Special Counsel.

You were given thirteen days to submit your comments to our report and on September 13, 2013, you provided additional information in further support of your allegations. We carefully reviewed your response; however, we found that it did not contain any new information or facts that would change our preliminary determination. In a detailed letter dated September 19, 2013, we indicated we would be closing our inquiry into your complaint. At the time, we also sent you a separate letter discussing the rights you would have to seek corrective action from the Merit Systems Protection Board. This was, and continues to be, our final determination regarding your allegations.

Thank you.

--

US Office of Special Counsel[46]

On Friday August 29, 2014, I sent this email to OSC officials Alejandra Dove and Jason Zuckerman, ccing Carolyn Lerner:

Subject: FW: US Office of Special Counsel – OSC File No. MA-13-3051

Hello Alejandra – In light of State Department just recently (March 8, 2014 and June 24, 2014) finally providing me substantiated documents in their "untimely/purposely delayed" "FOIA violation" response to my May 19, 2013 FOIA request, per your September 19, 2013 letter and July 31, 2014 email on behalf of Ms. Lerner re-engaged her on this matter, I have filed a MSPB Complaint accordingly.

With that, since you were the Attorney handling my complaint filed with OSC on May 20, 2013, for the purposes of this MSPB Complaint, I need to know if any Department of State/DOD official was notified of my OSC Complaint by OSC. If so, what date and what officials, what capacity. As you have indicated to me during that earlier process that you/OSC conducted no investigation regarding my complaint, this other information is needed to document that State/DOD officials were aware. Your cooperation and insight to this matter is sincerely appreciated. Thank you. Michelle

---

On Wednesday, September 3, 2014, OSC Jason Zuckerman and myself received the following response from Alejandra Dove, ccing Carolyn Lerner:

> Ms. Stefanick,
> In response to your inquiry, the email will confirm I did not contact the Department of State or the Department of Defense regarding your complaint.
> Thank you,
> Alejandra Dove
> Attorney
> Complaints Examining Unit
> US Office of Special Counsel[47]

Not a lawyer, but due to all the retaliatory acts taken against me, I continued to document: I Documented the file, documented the timeline of events, documented names/dates, and documented in legal Motions. For the facts are what the facts are, the timeline of events is what the timeline of events is, and there's no changing the storyline now... So that's what I did. For the truth, one day, would be exposed.

From August 3, 2014 – July 31, 2015, I represented myself in the OSC appeal case with the US Merit Systems Protection Board: *MICHELLE L. STEFANICK V. DEPARTMENT OF STATE (MSPB Docket No. DC-1221-14-0959-W-1 INDIVIDUAL RIGHT OF ACTION (IRA)* and *INDIVIDUAL RIGHT OF ACTION (IRA) – PETITION FOR REVIEW.* Covering the period of August 3, 2014 – December 5, 2014, 59 applicable filings for the *INDIVIDUAL RIGHT OF ACTION (IRA)*, and the period of December 7, 2014 – July 31, 2015, 29 applicable filings for the *INDIVIDUAL RIGHT OF ACTION (IRA) – PETITION FOR REVIEW.*

On August 3, 2014, I filed my Appeal with the MSPB, the next step after filing my May 18, 2013 OSC formal complaint. I received notification from the MSPB on August 8, 2014, regarding Short Case Title: *MICHELLE L. STEFANICK v. DEPARTMENT OF STATE Docket#: DC-1221-14-0959-W-1* Description: Initial Appeal. The MSPB (Washington Regional Office) AJ was Michelle M. Hudson. The Department of State Agency Representative was Anne Joyce, Office of the Legal Advisor for Employment Law.

On August 8, 2014, my first filing for MSPB AJ Michelle Hudson under *MICHELLE L. STEFANICK v. DEPARTMENT OF STATE Docket#:*

---

47   Alejandra Dove, email message to Michelle Stefanick, Jason Zuckerman, and Carolyn Lerner September 3, 2013

DC-1221-14-0959-W-1 was in regards to a *Protected Disclosure* and a requested response. *For what all this was about was the information I knew and had acquired while carrying-out my official role and responsibilities as a USG federal auditor,* a protected activity. On August 14, 2014, the US Department of State added a new agency representative to this case: Rachel K. Alpert. And on August 18, 2014, I timely filed Pleading Title: Response to Jurisdiction Order.

On August 22, 2014, the US Department of State filed *AGENCY MOTION TO DISMISS FOR LACK OF JURISDICTION and AGENCY MOTION TO STAY PROCEEDINGS.* "Appellant's initial appeal was untimely filed, as it was submitted 253 days after the regulatory deadline for filing the appeal." Regardless of the fact that it was the US Department of State itself that purposefully and intentionally carried-out the retaliatory actions against me—the results of which were ongoing and continuing—that caused the delay, the *untimeliness* to begin with. On August 26, 2014, a *Timeliness Order* was issued, as well as an *Order Suspending Case* Processing. Needless to say, I continued to object and continued to file motions accordingly. On October 27, 2014, the US Department of State removed Agency Representative Rachel Alpert and added *Hollin D. Lu*h. Filings continued until the Judge's December 5, 2014 *Initial Decision,* "The Appeal is DISMISSED." I then had until January 9, 2013 to file a *Petition for Review.*

CONTINUED HARASSMENT

Meanwhile, shortly after filing my MSPB Appeal, ACPD showed up at more door, and once again, not welcomed. Per ACPD's February 11, 2015 FOIA-request response, here's the applicable ACPD Call for Service #142460115 dated September 3, 2014:

> INITITIATE: 10:45:39 09-03-2014....
> ENTRY: 10:49:57
> DISPATCH: 10:53:39
> ON SCENE: 10:56:56
> DISPATCH: 11:00:36...
> LOCATION: [redacted])..
> ....TYPE: COW P – CHECK ON WELFARE ...
> TEXT: GUARDIAN OF DAUGHTER [BLACKED OUT] YOF NAM/ [BLACKED OUT]. GUARDIAN OF DAUGHTER 49 YOF NAM/[BLACKED OUT] DOB/[BLACKED OUT] W/F MENTALLY INCAPCITATED, HX OF DEPRESSION, HX OF

VIOLENT BEHAVIOR. HAS NOT MADE CONTACT WITH
HER FOR 5-6 WEEKS.
[BLACKED OUT] JUST WANT TO MAKE SURE THAT SHE
IS OKAY AND WANTS [BLACKED OUT] JUST WANT TO
MAKE SURE THAT SHE IS OKAY AND WANTS
PD TO GIVE HIM A CALL BACK. [BLACKED OUT] LIVES
IN PENNSYLVANIA.
...
** CORRECTION, HX OF AGGRESSIVE BEHAVIOUR, JUST
VERBAL***
** CORRECTION, HX OF AGGRESSIVE BEHAVIOUR, JUST
VERBAL***
...
XCC6265
XCC6265
CAR BELONGS TO PERSON THEY ARE CHECKING ON
CAR BELONGS TO PERSON THEY ARE CHECKING ON
...
SHE IS OK
...
SHE IS OK
...
OPERATOR ASSIGNMENTS:
TY01 EC368 ... OLIVERA, APRIL CADA TIB CAD
PD02 EP1108 ... PILCO, ELISEO A JR
P468 1533 ... DOMFE, KWAME

Based on my reading of this, *someone* authorized unconstitutional, illegal, retaliatory surveillance of my vehicle, down to the license plate. So,
who was it? ACPD? DS? USMC? US Army? FBI? Who? Why? And when
did it stop, if it stopped?

On September 18, 2014, I received a letter from the Congress of the
United States House of Representatives Select Committee on Benghazi
via email signed by Dana K. Chipman, Chief Investigative Counsel:

> September 18, 2014
> Via E-mail
> Ms. Michelle Stefanic [sic]
> [Email provided removed]
> Dear Ms. Stefanic: [sic]
> Thank you for your recent outreach to the House Select Commit-
> tee on Benghazi. We appreciate your interest in ensuring that the
> Committee's work captures as best it can your insights, knowledge

and experience – they will ultimately assist us in concluding a sol-idly-grounded investigative effort.

Please note that the Committee continues to receive reports and tips from a number of individuals and groups. A professional staff member on the Committee will evaluate all information re-ceived and follow up with you as required should we have ques-tions or need additional information.

Thank you for your interest in and assistance to this investiga-tion.

Sincerely,

/s/

Dana K. Chipman

Chief Investigative Counsel48

In the middle of my MSPB Appeal, I found the timing of this response, and the apparent lack of interest and follow-up, curiously interesting. At this time, I still had not heard regarding status of the EEO Grievance that I filed in Stuttgart in May 2011, now supposedly with EEOC.

At times, what documents don't disclose is as relevant and pertinent as to what they do, particularly when facts/events are readily known. My filing a formal EEO Grievance in May 2011 was *fact*. Yet, there was abso-lutely not one reference made about it in the March 8, 2014 409 pages of DS-obtained documents response. Given the *fact* that DS SAs were assigned to EUCOM, AFRICOM, at US Embassy in Berlin, and in US Consulates throughout Germany, how is that possible? But then again, how is it possible that the US Navy/USMC would smash my car door while parked on a US Army Garrison? How is it possible that the USAG Stuttgart/Dept of Army/EEO Office would intentionally modify/falsify my formal EEO Grievance? Obviously, quite obviously, if the US Navy/USMC and US Army were so busy *targeting* me, then they, the US Mili-tary, was not protecting me either. *Why?*… Oddly enough, I never heard back from EEOC or USAG Stuttgart/Dept of Army/EEO Stuttgart since February 2013. *Again, why?*

On October 28, 2014, I emailed, then subsequently left a message for EEOC AJ del Toro to find out the status.

Attn: Judge del Toro

On February 22, 2013, I received the attached Acknowledgement and Order from you dated February 20, 2013. As instructed and as so ordered, I not only mailed but emailed the Attached Option B/Certificate of Service on February 25, 2013 to both EEOC as well as Ms. Eshe Faulcon in Stuttgart, Germany, where I initially filed this EEO Grievance against the USMC. As I am/was a Department of State employee who continues to proceed without legal representation at this time, I still, to date and despite numerous outreach attempts accordingly, have not been informed/contacted by anyone identifying themselves as the Agency Representative for this Complaint. Thus, continuing to prevent me/us to proceed accordingly as so instructed by your February 20, 2013 order.

In the meanwhile, I bring to your attention the MSPB IRA Appeal (Docket Number DC-1221-14-0959-W-1) I filed/submitted on August 3, 2014. Currently, Judge Michelle M. Hudson has yet to rule regarding this Appeal and provide accordingly the last ruling Judge Hudson has made in this case. With that, the reason I bring it to your attention is so that you are not only aware of this on-going appeal, but the interlinkages with this EEO Grievance before you as well. I also attach for your review the applicable continuation sheet submitted in my August 3, 2014 filing.

Additionally, I also provide for your attention the two latest emails I received from the DOJ regarding the on-going/still open case of which I am a victim/witness since August 7, 1998. I bring all this to your attention because it now appears that what I thought was a "simple" EEO Grievance issue at the time, in light of additional information that has come to light since filing this EEO Grievance in April/May 2011, that there are/may indeed be broader criminal implications to include under the jurisdiction of the DOJ/FBI of which you need to be aware.

Please note I would provide this information to not only you but also the identified Agency Representative at this time. However, I am unable to do so at this time since I have not been notified who the Agency Representative is, let alone who they will be representing in this case, the Army or the USMC.

Due to the uniqueness of this situation, I do not know how best to proceed other than to make you aware and request guidance accordingly as at this time I continue to legally represent myself in this matter before you.

I can be reached at [redacted], email address[email provided removed], and the same address as provided in the attachment, [redacted]1. Thank you, Michelle L. Stefanick[49]

On October 29, 2014, I received the following voice mail from EEOC AJ Frances del Toro:

Hello – This is Administrative Judge Frances Del Toro calling you from the EEOC in regard to EEOC Number 570-2012-00235X. You called about the status of your complaint. Your complaint is still pending here. And uh, there has been no movement in the case for a while. You had mentioned that your complaint is currently before the MSPB. And if that is the case, then you need to let me know so that I can take proper action in your case. If you can give me a call, I will appreciate it. My number is [redacted]. Thank you.

On Wednesday, October 29, 2014, EEOC AJ Frances Del Toro sent the following email to USAG Stuttgart/Dept of Army/EEO Office Eshe Faulcon and myself:

Ms. Faulcon, my name is Frances del Toro and I am the Administrative Judge assigned to hear the case of Stefanick v. Army. On February 20, 2013, an Acknowledgement and Order was faxed to your office. To date, neither Complainant nor I, have received a Designation of Representative indicating who is the Agency Representative in this case. In order to process the case, I will need that information as soon as possible. Can you please tell me who the Agency representative in this case is and have him/her file a Designation? Thank you for your attention to this matter.
Frances del Toro
Administrative Judge
US Equal Employment Opportunity Commission[50]

This is the Wednesday, November 5, 2014 8:50:50 -0500 email I received from EEOC AJ Frances del Toro:

Subject: RE: Fwd: FW: EEO Grievance Retaliation (UNCLASSIFIED)
Ms. Stefanick, this is the response I received from the Agency this morning. It contains the contact information for the Agency Representative in your case.
Frances del Toro
Administrative Judge
US Equal Employment Opportunity Commission
131 M Street, N.E.
Washington, D.C. 20507
Office No. [redacted]
Fax No. [redacted][51]
>>>"Faulcon, Eshe N CIV (US)" [email provided removed] 11/5/14 1:37 AM>>>

---

50   Francis del Toro, email message to Michelle Stefanick and Eshe Faulcon, October 29, 2014
51   Francis del Toro, email message to Michelle Stefanick November 4, 2014

Classification: UNCLASSIFIED
Caveats: FOUO//SENSITIVE
Good Morning Judge del Toro:
I apologize for the delay in my response.
The Agency Representative in this case has changed and his contact information is as follows:
Maj Rick Congdon
Office of Counsel for the Commandant
Room [redacted] Pentagon
[redacted]
I requested that he contact you immediately.
Kind regards,
Ms. Eshe Faulcon
EEO Specialist
USAG Stuttgart EEO Office
DSN: [redacted]
COMM: [redacted]
[email provided removed]
Follow us on Facebook;
http://www.facebook.com/USAGarrisonStuttgart
USAG Stuttgart Website:
http://www.stuttgart.army.mil
Stuttgart MWR
http://www.stuttgartmwr.com

For some reason, Eshe Faulcon had not included me in her November 5, 2014 response to EEOC AJ Del Toro. *The question remains, why?*

On Sunday November 23, 2014, I sent the following email to EEOC AJ Frances del Toro, ccing Paula Bedford, Major Frederick Congdon, and Eshe Faulcon:

Judge del Toro – As the response to your Instruction/Order dated February 20, 2013 and now your follow-up email request dated October 29, 2014 was delayed by two separate military services (Army and Navy/USMC) of the department of Defense, I kindly request your serious consideration to my request in elevating this complaint to the proper level from Secretary of Army to Secretary of Defense, to which these two separate military services report accordingly and are involved.

As I am without legal representation in this matter at this time, I kindly request the Judge's most liberal consideration of this request. Respectfully, Michelle L. Stefanick[52]

From April 2011/May 2011 to November 23, 2014, I represented myself in my EEO Grievance Litigation. (*Agency Case No. AREUSTUT-11APR01542/EEOC Hearing No. 570-2012-00235X*). Note the timeline of events, and my continually stating that I was an EEO Complainant in current/pending/on-going litigation against the US Military. Yet, *no one cared ...*

On November 24, 2014, Agency Representative Frederick A. Congdon, Major, US Marine Corps, filed the following Motion: *Designation of Representation and Motion to Re-caption Under New Agency.*

> Accordingly, the Agency respectfully requests the AJ amend the caption and title of this case to reflect: Ray Mabus, Secretary of the Navy, Agency, and Agency Case No. DON 11-67023-04331.[53]

I cannot even make this stuff up! My original EEO Grievance was against the US Navy/USMC. But I was told by USAG Stuttgart/Dept of Army/ EEO Office that since the events occurred on a US Army Garrison, the formal May 2011 filing had to be against the Secretary of the Army. Now, *over three years later*, it's okay for my formal EEO Grievance to now be against the Secretary of the Navy? These were bogus DOD EEO Investigative and bogus DOD/EEO Grievance Complainant processes writ large. Needless to say, the *re-captioning* would be accepted. Now given all that occurred, to include at the VHC, the holder of a US Navy/USMC detox rehabilitation contract and their accomplicing retaliatory role that I had just been subjected to not once, but twice, in this one long continuum of torture, on-going emotional torture that continues to this day. For what? For surviving the August 7, 1998 East Africa Embassy bombing terrorist attack Then there was Secretary Kerry accepting my resignation and a Commonwealth of Virginia/Arlington County Circuit Court Judge Paul Sheridan, both of Navy background, accepting a bogus Emergency Motion. *This isn't a conspiracy theory, these are all facts!* So, question remains, why did the US Military purposely and intentionally commit a *federal offense to threaten, intimidate, harass, and mislead* a federal victim/witness in both a criminal and now civil proceeding, instead of protecting me?

Subsequently thereafter, from November 24, 2014 to November 13, 2018, based on this U.S Navy/USMC Filed Motion, my EEOC Litigation was now referenced as *Agency Case No. DON 11-67023-04331.* And due to the USAG Stuttgart/Dept of Army/EEO Stuttgart purposeful and in-

don, and Eshe Faulcon, November 23, 2014

53   Frederick Congdon, motion titled Designation of Representation and Motion to Re-caption Under New Agency, November 23, 2014

tentional modification/falsification of my May 2011 Formal EEO Grievance, I now had no chance whatsoever for justice. Furthermore, with no
real investigation conducted, the real motive/intent was not determined,
purposely and intentionally *obstructed*. A subsequent March 10, 2015 *NO-
TICE OF INTENT TO ISSUE A DECISION WITHOUT A HEARING*
then resulted in a March 25, 2015 *ORDER ENTERING JUDGMENT* by
the AJ, with no hearing, and my day in court *denied*. I then had thirty calendar days to Appeal.

During this time, I was juggling both the MSPB Appeal as well as the
EEO Grievance litigation. All the while, I was deemed *incapacitated* by the
Commonwealth of Virginia. *My life, career, credibility destroyed—Why? All
because I took a US Department of State FS detail assignment with the US
Department of Defense, specifically the US Navy/USMC in Stuttgart, Ger-
many after my year of senior training at the US Army War College. Really?
Does any of this make any sense? Well, it certainly didn't, and doesn't, to me.*

During this time, I obtained additional insight that would assist in
connecting more dots... And I'll advise you now, as bizarre as this entire
storyline has been so far, you need to brace yourself, because it only gets
even more bizarre, yet it's absolutely real and absolutely true. It's not a
pretty storyline. But it is the truth. And I can assure you, I can't make this
stuff up...

On 12/2/2014, I located two media reports. The first was called "Report: Army targeted US Senators with psy-ops" from *MSNBC.com* updated February 24, 2011.54 The second was called "Another Runaway
General: Army Deploys Psy-Ops on US Senators" from *Rolling Stone* by
Michael Hastings February 23, 2011. This was written by the same Michael Hastings who subsequently died in a mysterious single-car accident
on June 18, 2013. According to Hastings:

> The US Army illegally ordered a team of soldiers specializing in
> "psychological operations" to manipulate visiting American sena-
> tors... when an officer tried to stop the operation, he was railroad-
> ed by military investigators... The orders came from... a three-star
> general... When the unit resisted the order, arguing that it violated
> US laws prohibiting the use of propaganda against American cit-
> izens, it was subjected to a campaign of retaliation... "My job in
> psy-ops is to play with people's heads... to behave the way we want
> them to behave"... According to the Defense Department's own
> definition, psy-ops—the use of propaganda and psychological

---

54   "Report: Army targeted US Senators with psy-ops." msnbc.com. https://www.nbcnews.
com/id/wbna41753749.

tactics to influence emotions and behaviors—are supposed to be used exclusively on "hostile foreign groups."... Federal law forbids the military from practicing psy-ops on Americans... [55]

And what were both of these articles about? They're about the *money*. Coincidentally, both of these articles were published during the same timeframe of the *bizarre* events that occurred, *that I was subjected to*, while I was in Germany. And what's my affiliation? It's about the *money*.

Needless to say, this was not a *delusion*. The attack—or the *psychological operation or covert operation or clandestine operation*—on me was very real. Here was additional proof. Yet, at the same time, the reason no one investigated. Either military investigators couldn't for they didn't have the capability to do so nor the jurisdictional authority, or because they were well aware, *in the know* of the targeting of me, and let it happen. Besides, I was just expendable anyways, right? Given the fact that I was an American citizen, this *attack* was a crime. Given my protected-activity status as a federal USG auditor, this *attack* was a crime. Given my federal CRVA-accorded protected status, this *attack* was a crime. Given the related events for which I was accorded CVRA-protected status, makes *this attack on me a treasonous crime*. Having absolutely no mental health issues, I not only survived, but documented accordingly every step of the way...

During this time, I learned of other whistleblowers, the retaliation they were subjected to, and learning the apparent reason for their lives being destroyed. I was not alone, not the only one retaliated against. Yet, given my federal CVRA-accorded protections, my situtation was unique. The retaliatory actions taken against me were real; as was what I was revealing.... So if it was happening to me, and I knew I was telling the truth, I knew quite possibly, they were telling the truth as well. And if it can happen to me, to them, it can happen to you.

During this 2014 timeframe, I heard about Susan Lindauer and Scott Bennett. Susan apparently worked for the CIA and DIA. Intrigued by her horrific ordeal, I became an avid listener to her weekend internet talkshow. Her talk-show became an invaluable conduit for me to obtain even more insight that I was previously unaware yet had connections and linkages to my very own horrific ordeal, it had crucial insight that not only confirmed the validity of my piece to this much bigger puzzle; but also gave me insight to others that I had no idea that I was even connected to.

55   Michael Hastings. "Another Runaway General: Army Deploys Psy-Ops on US Senators." Rolling Stone. February 23, 2011. https://www.rollingstone.com/politics/politics-news/another-runaway-general-army-deploys-psy-ops-on-u-s-senators-178088/

During one of Susan's shows, I learned about Scott Bennett's background and horrific experience, again as a whistleblower, a US Army Special Operations whistleblower. During this exact show, for the very first time, I would be informed of "stolen/missing $14.6 Trillion dollars of CIA/Black Operational funds/accounts in the 1998/9 timeframe." Once I heard that, I gasped. *Oh my God, I know exactly what this is about!* I just didn't realize it was that much money, didn't realize the magnitude of our State OIG audit-discovered diverted funds. But wait, our audit was years prior. *Oh my God, this was the timeframe of the East Africa Embassy bombings. Our bombing was about the stolen/missing/diverted CIA/Black Operational funds!* On December 27, 2014, I would finally, without a doubt, know precisely what all this was about—and how/where I fit in.

This was yet another piece that fit perfectly in the puzzle. So much so that I later included this exact $14.6 Trillion figure and this CIA/Black Operational funds reference—*not Secretary of Defense Rumsfeld's $2.3 Trillion figure reference made on 9/10/2001 that I had become aware of on August 26, 2013*—in my subsequent 2016 US Supreme Court filing. Confirmation of yet another crucial piece of the puzzle would finally come to light in due time, but not until January 27, 2015.

With the MSPB AJ's December 5, 2014 *Initial Decision* that "The Appeal is DISMISSED," I had until January 9, 2015 to file a *Petition for Review*. Interestingly enough, on the same day as receiving this December 5, 2014 AJ's *Initial Decision* specifying that this decision would become final on January 9, 2015, I received an email response from the Department of State FOIA office. This email notified me that the estimated completion date for fulfilling my May 19, 2013 FOIA/Privacy request—already purposely and intentionally delayed—has been further delayed from November 2014 to March 2015. *Coincidence?* Yet, despite my request, no explanation was provided for this delay. It was quite obvious what the reason was given that according to the AJ's ruling I only had until January 9, 2015 to file an Appeal. With that insight, I filed a request for extension of time to file a *Petition for Review* on December 7, 2014; on December 11, 2014; January 10, 2015; February 2, 2015; March 5, 2015; April 5, 2015—all granted. On April 6, 2015, MSPB granted the last limited extension due date, now by May 11, 2015...

How incredibly ironic, isn't it? The Department of State's position for my Appeal to be dismissed was because my Appeal was untimely filed. Yet, it was quite all right that the US Department of State could purposely and intentionally violate statutes of FOIA—with US Department of State officials knowing the evidence to support my case/position contained in these document— all in order to obstruct justice. And that was perfectly fine in the eyes of the United States Justice system.

On April 26, 2015, I timely filed the applicable *Petition for Review* to the MSPB. On April 27, 2015, I received an official Petition for Review acknowledgement letter notice from the Office of the Clerk of the Board, US MSPB. Attached was *Petition for Review Settlement Program* information, the Board's encouragement for settlement. As I never heard from the retaliatory and corrupt US Department of State, there was no such settlement.

Meanwhile, in regards to my formal EEO Grievance filed May 2011, on March 25, 2015, I finally received the EEOC AJ's *ORDER ENTERING JUDGMENT*. My EEO Grievance Complaint was denied as well as my hearing, my day in court. I now had 30 calendar days to Appeal. On March 29, 2015, I sent a letter to the Naval Office of EEO Complaints Management and Adjudication:

> Naval Office of EEO Complaints
> Management and Adjudication
> 614 Sicard Street, SE, Suite 100
> Washington Navy Yard, DC 20374-5017
> Dear Director:
> RE: November 22, 2011 Spin-off Complaint
> In accordance with Chapter 5 of Equal Employment Opportunity Commission (EEOC) Management Directive (MD) 110 (dated 11/21/2011), I am writing to file/request status of my November 22, 2011 Spin-off Complaint regarding the investigation of my formal EEO Complaint, DON (Department of Navy) 11-67023-04331 (formerly Department of Army/DA Docket Number: AREUSTUT11APR01642) since the standard as specified in 29 CFR and EEOC MD 110 (dated 11/21/2011) was not met.
> On November 24, 2014, the USMC Agency Representative responded to the EEOC's Acknowledgement and Order dated February 20, 2013 with a Motion to Re-Caption my EEO Complaint back to the Department of the Navy, the Agency in which my initial informal EEO complaint was filed and not addressed. On March 10, 2015, the USMC Motion was GRANTED. Therefore, as the United States Army Garrison (USAG) Stuttgart EEO Office never responded accordingly to my November 22, 2011 Spin-off Complaint before this USMC Motion was Filed/Granted, this Spin-off Complaint regarding the investigation is redirected accordingly to

the Department of Navy, your office, for immediate response and action regarding this matter, and the material issues raised still not yet addressed.

The requirement for the Agency to investigate complaints of discrimination is codified in 29 C.F.R. Section 1614.108. This regulation requires the Agency, now the Department of Navy, to develop an impartial and appropriate factual record upon which to make findings on the claim or claims raised in the complaint. Chapter 6 of EEOC MD 110 requires that the investigator must be and must maintain the appearance to be unbiased, objective and thorough; and is required to conduct a thorough investigation identifying and obtaining all relevant evidence from all sources regardless of how it may affect the outcome. While this requirement does not compel the investigator to engage in irrelevant and superfluous inquiry, it does require that the investigator exhaust those of information likely to support the positions of Complainant and the Agency. For as stated in the attached reference letter, the primary purpose of the investigative file is "to develop the facts on the case and provide the basis for deciding this complaint."

With examples stated in my November 22, 2011 Spin-off Complaint and even more to provide, the investigative file record was not adequately developed because records in the investigative file were incomplete; and required witness testimonies and further discovery activities were not taken. These actions resulted in material facts not being included and presented in the record which is required "to develop the facts on the case and provide the basis for deciding this complaint." As the Department of Navy is now the Agency regarding my EEO Complaint and applicable November 22, 2011 Spin-off Complaint, your office is kindly requested for immediate response and action regarding this long outstanding matter as required by 20 CFR and EEOC MD 110 (dated 11/21/2011).

For any additional information regarding this matter and this request, I can be reached at [email provided removed] or [redacted]. Thank you.

Sincerely,

/s/

Michelle L. Stefanick, Complainant

Attachments:

Request for a Hearing (November 23, 2011)

Spin-off Complaint regarding the Investigation (November 22, 2011)

USAG-Stuttgart EEO Office-Department of Army letter (October 20, 2011)
Certified Mail Receipts USPS Pentagon Station (November 23, 2011)"[56]

On Monday, March 30, 2015, I sent the following email to Judy Caniban:

Hello Judy – I've been provided your email address by Khaliah Ameen. I don't know if you are aware but I am the Dept of State Foreign Service Employee that was retaliated against by the USMC during my State Depart posting in Stuttgart, Germany. I don't know if you are aware of the situation or not, but I initially provide you with this request regarding the status of my November 22, 2011 Spin-off Complaint, which I have also just "Overnight express mailed" to you and you should receive tomorrow.

I'm in the process of providing you more insight as well, but one fact that you need to be made aware of is that I am a DOJ victim/witness regarding the open/ongoing FBI investigation/case in New York. At the time these events in Stuttgart were occurring, I did not connect dots to their potential linkage with this ongoing FBI case. However, there are now implications more than one that there are indeed linkages to this ongoing FBI investigation of with I am not the "target" of the investigation, but the victim/witness. Therefore, the implications to the actions taken against me by the USMC may have broader criminal intent in regards to Federal legal proceedings.

With that, I provide you the most recent correspondence I had with DOJ in New York as well as attach the linkage to Congressional House Select Committee Investigation on Benghazi. If I were you, I would request a copy of my Response I submitted on March 18, 2015. If you can't obtain it, let me know and I will provide you a copy accordingly. With that, if I were you, I would also outreach to the FBI accordinglyas there is also a linkage to John Beliveau, the NCIS Supervisory agent that was recently arrested by DOJ in the on-going/ever-expanding Navy Contract Corruption Scandal. Again, I initially provide/request the status of this Spin-off Complaint, and will provide copies of my smashed car as referenced in my March 18, 2015 Response filed if you can't obtain accordingly via the EEOC Judge del Toro and/or the USMC Agency Representative Major Congdon. I think it only fair and right that you are thoroughly aware of all that is in play in regards to this EEO case. Thank, Michelle[57]

56   Michelle Stefanick, letter to Naval Office of EEO Complaints Management and Adjudication, March 29 2015
57   Michelle Stefanick, email message to Judy Canaban, March 30 2015

On April 24, 2015, I received the Department of the Navy's *Final Order* dated April 20, 2015 *Re: DON (MC) No. 11-67023-04331 EEOC No. 570-2012-00235X* signed by Judy Caniban, Director Naval Office of EEO Complaints Management and Adjudication. I now had a choice: 30 calendar days after receipt of this *Final Order* to file a *Notice of Appeal* with EEOC or 90 days to file in US District Court. As notoriety in a US District Court was not my objective, justice was, I prepared accordingly to file an Appeal with EEOC within 30 days.

A NEW BETRAYAL

On May 4, 2015, I filed accordingly EEOC FORM 573 *Notice of Appeal/Petition* with the EEOC Office of Federal Operations with applicable attachments regarding *MICHELLE STEFANICK V. RAY MABUS, SECRETARY OF NAVY, DON (MC) No. 11-67023-04331.* My Formal EEO Grievance was initiated in May 2011. You can only imagine how stunned and furious I was to finally receive a *DECISION* from the EEOC/OFO dated September 19, 2017 that my EEOC/OFO Appeal was *denied. Why? Because without my approval or my authorization or my awareness, my estranged father—who already destroyed my lif— interjected himself and initiated contact with the US Department of Navy/USMC.* He continued, purposely and intentionally, to work against me based on an unsolicitated September 21, 2015 letter he submitted to Major Congdon. Despite and in light of the fact that he knew *nothing of the events that occurred in Germany regarding the informal, then formal EEO Grievance I filed in May 2011, he purposely and intentionally—once again—obstructed justice.* He continued a false-narrative. On whose agenda was he working? I have no idea. Though I continually asked, to this day, I have never received the answer. But one thing for sure is that he was never working on my behalf, or in my best interest, or with my approval, or my authorization, or my awareness.

And the basis on which my estranged father interjected himself? It was given that my Formal EEO Grievance had been on-going/pending federal litigation since May 2011, and that everyone knew about it the entire time, because of my fraudulently being deemed incapacitated. Deemed *incapacitated* in December 2013, and to this day, due to the purposeful and intentional retaliatory actions taken against me in Germany by the US Navy/USMC, my Formal EEO Grievance that the US Army/USAG EEO Stuttgart Office purposely and intentionally modified/falsified, and the retaliatory actions I was subjected that were purposely and intentionally not investigated. The purposeful and intentional retaliatory actions that should never have occurred to begin with. That American Citizens, is *your US Military.*

When I finally received the EEOC/OFO *DECISION* dated September 19, 2017, it was the first time I was made aware that I had been given an alias, a/k/a *Estefana M.* This was eerily similar to the tactic of *misspelling* of my last name in the Commonwealth of Virginia Arlington County Court's Records. Once again, the US Department of Navy/USMC and the retaliatory actions they took against me, covered-up... And once again, it was with the assistance of and by my estranged father as their accomplice.

Meanwhile, despite my continual requests since first becoming aware, to this day, I still have not received a copy of the supposed Kate Canavan September 04, 2009 (.mil not state.gov) email sent to USMC Brig General Tracy Garrett and specifically referenced in USMC's June 1, 2011 Command Investigation Report in ressponse to MARFOREUR Commander LtGen Hejlik's own May 10, 2011 requested Command Investigation. Why? Why haven't I still received a copy? The USMC has this September 4, 2011 email, specifically referencing it in their own Command Investigative report as it supposedly as relevance, pertinence regarding me, yet I can't see it—to this day. This is particularly interesting since though I provided numerous names of State Department officials to be interviewed during the supposed DOD EEO investigation process, Kate was the only State Department official interviewed. *Why? Why was Kate Canavan the only State Department official interviewed?* And it's particularly interesting given that preorchestrated meeting on December 13, 2020 with Kate Canavan, BGen Paul Brier and myself. So with whom precisely did Kate Canavan "preorchestrate" that meeting? At this point, without a copy of the Kate Canavan September 04, 2009 (.mil) email being provided, one can conclude that the Kate Canavan September 04, 2009 (.mil) email really doesn't exist—and the US Navy/USMC lied of its existence to begin with... *If so, why? Why would the USMC lie? If not, and this specific referenced email really does exist, than why hasn't it been provided to me?*

James McNaught, State Department FPA/POLAD for Special Operations Command Europe (SOCEUR) immediately moved into my MARFOREUR/AF FPA/POLAD position upon my early departure caused by the retaliatory actions taken against me — As there was one other Department of State FS candidate other than myself that was initially provided to MARFOREUR/AF for selection consideration in August/

September 2009 when I was selected, the question remains, was *James McNaught the other candidate not selected at the time?* James McNaught, the SOCEUR FPA/POLAD at the time. Just like my continual requests for the September 04, 2009 Kate Canavan email, confirmation whether or not James McNaught was the other State FS candidate for MARFO-REUR/AF selection consideration has gone unheeded.

On July 31, 2015, I received the US MSPB's *Final Order.* No surprise. "We therefore find that the administrative judge properly dismissed the appeal as untimely filed." From July 31, 2015, I had 60 days to file an appeal, by September 29, 2015. On September 2, 2015, I mailed my *Petition for Review* to the United States Court of Appeals for The Fourth Circuit in Richmond, Virginia. My *Petition for Review* was officially filed by the Fourth Circuit on September 10, 2015 (*Case Number 15-2053*).

Coincidentally, on Friday, July 31, 2015, the same day of the MSPB *Final Order,* I sent an email to Agency Representative Department of State L/EMP Anne Joyce regarding my intent to Appeal. I received the following *Automatic Reply* email message from State L/EMP Anne Joyce:

> Subject: Automatic reply: Federal Appeal to July 31, 2015 MSPB Final Order
> I am on leave and then transferring to a new job on 7/31. I will be checking e-mail occasionally, but if you have an urgent matter, please call 202-647-4646 and ask for another attorney in L/EMP. Thank you.[58]

Needless to say, do I find it quite curiously odd that both the MSPB *Final Order* was received and the Agency Representative in my MSPB Appeal and departed on the same day—July 31, 2015. *Absolutely.* Just as I found it quite curious that another State/L employee, Matthew Bradley, mentioned and referenced pertaining to my case, departed State and went to work—wait for it—the MSPB. Not sure the exact timing of his departure from State/L, but one thing I know for sure is that he was with MSPB, overlapping and during the exact timeframe as my MSPB Appeal. *Coincidence?* Even more interesting, on September 14, 2015, I sent the following email to myself:

> Subject: RE: Automatic reply: Federal Appeal to July 31, 2015 MSPB Final Order – Anne Joyce departure
> According to my brief telcon when phoned [redacted] (L/EMP) at approximately 4:10 P.M. on September 14, 2015, I was advised that

Anne Joyce no longer works neither with L/EMP nor at the Dept of State. I then called the State/Operator 202-647-4000 at approximately 4:15 p.m. requesting to speak with Anne Joyce when I was transferred to what appears to be the [redacted] (L/EMP) number as the same female answered the phone – not providing her name – she just hung up once again.[59]

Writing this book in 2019/early 2020 timeframe, I have indications that Anne Joyce may indeed still be working at L/EMP to this day. *What else am I to conclude other than apparently, everyone, to include L (Legal), lies at the US Department of State.*

On November 4, 2015, I received a box from the MSPB. Enclosed was an accompanying letter from the US Merit Systems Protection Board Office of the Clerk of the Board to Ms. Joy Moore Office of the Clerk of Court United States Courthouse Annex Richmond VA with carbon copy to me. The letter November 3, 2015, referencing *Michelle L. Stefanick v. Department of State MSPB Docket No. DC-1221-14-0959-W-1 CAFC Docket No. 15-2053,* is as follows:

Dear Ms. Joy Moore:
On October 28, 2015, we received your request for a copy of the above referenced cases. Enclosed is a copy of the administrative records for the above captioned case.
These copies do not haye to be returned.
Sincerely,
(Signature signed for illegible)
William D. Spencer[60]

The box from the MSPB contained copies of all the applicable filings for *MICHELLE L. STEFANICK V. DEPARTMENT OF STATE (MSPB Docket No. DC-1221-14-0959-W-1 INDIVIDUAL RIGHT OF ACTION (IRA) and INDIVIDUAL RIGHT OF ACTION (IRA) – PETITION FOR REVIEW.* Covering the period of August 3, 2014 – December 5, 2014, 59 applicable filings for the *INDIVIDUAL RIGHT OF ACTION (IRA),* and the period of December 7, 2014 – July 31, 2015, 29 applicable filings for the *INDIVIDUAL RIGHT OF ACTION (IRA) – PETITION FOR REVIEW.*

Filing after filing since September 2, 2015, on March 17, 2016, my *Petition for Review* with the Fourth Circuit was denied. On April 4, 2016 I filed a *Petition for Panel Rehearing and Rehearing En Banc.* On April 4,

59   Michelle Stefanick, email message to Michelle Stefanick, July 31 2015
60   William Spencer, letter to Joy Moore and Michelle Stefanick, July 31 201

2016, the Fourth Circuit stayed the mandate pending further order of the court. On May 20, 2016, the Fourth Circuit denied the *Petition for Rehearing and Rehearing En Banc.* On May 31, 2016, the Fourth Circuit filed its Mandate that the judgment of this court, entered 3/17/2016, took effect, constituting the formal mandate of this court.

Once I elevated this Appeal to the US Court of Appeals for The Fourth Circuit, how ironic would it be that it would be the US DOJ that would represent and defend the US Department of State and the retaliatory actions it took against me, a federal CVRA-accorded victim/witness. The very entity/entities that are/were responsible for and should have protected me. *Something is terribly wrong with our US Judicial process/system...*

On October 23, 2015, Igor Helman of the DOJ Civil Division filed an *Appearance of Counsel* motion with the Fourth Circuit, *for the Department of State.* And from February 29, 2016, I purposely and intentionally included James A. Baker, General Counsel of the Federal Bureau of Investigation, as an Agency Representative under Certificate of Service to receive my Appeal Motions accordingly. *Do you realize how many DOJ and FBI officials I notified/were notified by this time regarding the retaliatory actions taken against me?* The very same DOJ and FBI that were responsible for protecting me as a federal CVRA-accorded victim/witness that had been purposely and intentionally retaliated against. The purposeful and intentional retaliatory actions that should never have occurred to begin with. That, American Citizens, is *your US DOJ and Federal Bureau of Investigation.*

Now, for the timeline of events, isn't it quite interesting that soon after my including FBI General Counsel James Baker from February 29, 2016 on my applicable motions filed with the 4th Circuit, the infamous Steele Dossier report was written soon after. This is the report containing allegations of misconduct, conspiracy, and co-operation with the Government of Russia during the 2016 election. *Coincidence?*

On May 31, 2016, the US Court of Appeals for the Fourth Circuit filed its *Mandate* and the final judgment took effect, constituting the formal mandate of this court. My last resort was to appeal to the United States Supreme Court (USSC). At this point, my thought was, *what was there to lose?* To which the answer is—the truth. And without it, justice will never be done and the truth will never be known. And even if I did not win, which it was quite obvious I would not due to the unfathomable treasonous cover-up being carried-out by *someone* (and now quite obvious *someones* by this point), my position would be documented in and for historical record in this nation's highest court of our land, *the US Supreme Court.*

On August 16, 2016, pro se, I officially filed my petition, *On Petition for Writ of Certiorari to The United States Court of Appeals for The Fourth Circuit*, becoming *USSC Case Number 16-223*. And according to the USSC Docket Entries, a *Response due September 19, 2016*. On September 7, 2016, Ian Heath Gershengorn, the Acting Solicitor General, Counsel of Record, filed a *WAIVER* response to *USSC Case Number 16-223*:

> The Government hereby waives its right to file a response to the petition in this case, unless requested to do so by the Court.[61]

Soon after, I received official notification regarding my USSC case. The brief response was on official letterhead of the Supreme Court of the United States from Clerk of the Court Scott S. Harris. The October 11, 2016 letter is as follows:

> Dear Ms. Stefanick
> The Court today entered the following order in the above-entitled case:
> The petition for a writ of certiorari is denied.
> Sincerely,
> /s/
> Scott S. Harris, Clerk[62]

On November 3, 2016, pro se, I officially filed my Petition for Rehearing, *On Petition for Writ of Certiorari to The United States Court of Appeals for The Fourth Circuit*, USSC Case Number 16-223. On December 7, 2016, I received official notification regarding my USSC case. Again, the brief response was on Supreme Court of the United States official letterhead from Clerk of the Court Scott S. Harris. The December 5, 2016 letter is as follows:

> Dear Ms. Stefanick
> The Court today entered the following order in the above-entitled case:
> The petition for rehearing is denied.
> Sincerely,
> /s/
> Scott S. Harris, Clerk[63]

---

61   Ian Heath Gershengorn, WAIVER response to *USSC Case Number 16-223*. September 7, 2016

62   Scott Harris, letter to Michelle Stefanick, October 11, 2016

63   Scott Harris, letter to Michelle Stefanick, December 5, 2016

That was it. That was my last resort for the Office of Special Counsel Complaint I initially filed on May 18, 2013 due to the retaliatory actions taken against me by the U.S Department of State and others.

And for the record, the historical record, in my November 3, 2016 US Supreme Court filing, I specifically included "in the 1997-9 timeframe over $14.6 trillion of CIA/Black operational funds/bank accounts were stolen/missing" reference. *Why?* Because I knew precisely what all this was about. By this specific reference in my applicable USSC filing, I stand by my position, as certain to this day as I did at the time of my filing, and since becoming aware of the amount involved.

The US Supreme Court Justices at the time of my August 16 and November 3, 2016 USSC filings were John Roberts, Anthony Kennedy, Clarence Thomas, Ruth Bader Ginsburg, Stephen Breyer, Samuel Alito, Sonia Sotomayor, Elena Kagan. Justice Antonin Scalia unfortunately passed away on February 13, 2016, prior to my submissions.

I stand by the OSC Complaint I filed on May 18, 2013. Due to the retaliatory actions taken against me, I had to resort to "pro se" representation because no lawyer nor law firm in the Washington D.C. area, or across the Nation that I contacted would represent me in this case. I do not agree with the result of the judicial process on this matter, and remain of that opinion. Otherwise, I would not have filed the OSC Formal Compliant to begin with...

Meanwhile, my EEO grievance from May 2011 was still proceeding through the legal process. And meanwhile, I was obtaining more insight, and connecting even more dots...

On September 19, 2017, I received the EEOC/OFO Appeal *DECISION*:

> Based on a thorough review of the record and the contentions on appeal, including those not specifically addressed herein, we AFFIRM the Agency's final order adopting the AJ's decision.

I now had 30 days to file an appeal, a *Statement of Rights – On Appeal Reconsideration* with the EEOC or 90 days to file a civil action with the US District Court. On October 9, 2017, I filed my *Complainant Statement of Rights – On Appeal Consideration* with the EEOC accordingly. (*Appeal Number/ OFO Docket Number: 0120151982 Hearing Number/EEOC Number: 570-2012-00235X Agency Number: DON (MC) 11-67023-04331*).

On February 26, 2018, I received the US EEOC *Decision on Request for Reconsideration*, the final decision of the Commission dated February

22, 2018. The final decision remained the same; not in my favor. With no further right of administrative appeal from the Commission's decision, next was my right to file a civil action in an appropriate US District Court within 90 calendar days from the date I received their final decision. As I initially informally filed this EEO in April 12, 2011, formally filed on May 11, 2011, and given all retaliatory events that transpired, set into motion and continuing to this day, with no real investigation conducted, I proceeded to the next stepfiling in US District Court.

On May 24, 2018, I filed my *Complaint for A Civil Case* in the United States District Court Eastern District of Virginia Alexandria Division. I also filed a *Motion for Appointment of Counsel.* Since my complaint was against Richard V. Spencer, Secretary of the Navy, the following individuals also had to be served: Anne M. Brennan, Acting General Counsel of the Navy; Jefferson Sessions, Attorney General of the United States; Tracy Doherty-McCormick, United States Attorney for the Eastern District of Virginia. From May 24, 2018 – November 13, 2018, with my *Motion for Appointment of Counsel* denied, I represented myself in my applicable EEOC/OFO Appeal with my filed *Complaint for A Civil Case* in the US District Court Eastern District of Virginia Alexandria Division (*Civil Action No. 1:18-cv-628 TSE-TCB*) until *DISMISSED.*

And once again, once I elevated this Appeal to the US District Court, how ironic would it be that the US DOJ would represent and defend the US Department of the Navy/USMC and the retaliatory actions it took against me, a federal CVRA-accorded victim/witness. These were the very entity/entities that are/were responsible for and should have protected me. *Again, something is terribly wrong with our Judicial process/system…*

On August 3, 2018, John Coghlan and Dennis Barghaan, AUSAs of the Office of the USA G. Zachary Terwillinger, would be *Counsel for Respondents.* Again, do you realize how many DOJ and FBI officials I notified/ were notified by this time regarding the retaliatory actions taken against me? The very same DOJ and FBI that were responsible for protecting me as a federal CVRA-accorded victim/witness who had been purposely and intentionally retaliated against. These were purposeful and intentional retaliatory actions that should never have occurred to begin with. That American Citizens, *is your US DOJ.*

For this federal case, there was a hearing in a federal Court House on Friday, September 7, 2018. A *Motion to Dismiss for Failure to State a Claim and a Motion to Dismiss for Lack of Jurisdiction* was filed by the Secretary of the Navy. And Judge Ellis *ORDERED* that I had to amend my complaint by 5:00 p.m. on October 8, 2018 and ORDERED I take prompt steps to retain counsel. I did all I could, but once again, not a lawyer/law firm would touch my case. So, despite being set up for failure, I did what I could. And then a *Memorandum of Law in Support of Defendant's Motion to Dismiss Plaintiff's Amended Complaint* was filed November 8, 2018. A statement in the Motion went as follows:

> Although Plaintiff's Amended Complaint cures some of the deficiencies of its predecessor, she still fails to overcome her primary hurdle: lack of standing. Because Plaintiff was determined to be incapacitated by a December 17, 2013 Order of the Circuit Court of Arlington County, only her Court appointed guardian, Michael Stefanick, has standing to file suit on her behalf...

On November 13, 2018, US District Judge, T.S. Ellis III in the US District Court for the Eastern District of Virginia, Alexandria Division, *ORDER* stated the following:

> It is hereby ORDERED that defendant's motion to dismiss (Doc. 29) is GRANTED and that plaintiff's amended complaint (Doc. 27) is DISMISSED WITH PREJUDICE.
> The Clerk is directed to send a copy of this Order to plaintiff (who is proceeding pro se) and all counsel of record and to place this matter among the ended cases.
> Alexandria, Virginia
> November 13, 2018
> /s/
> T.S. Ellis, III
> United States District Judge[64]

My case, my formal EEO Grievance initially filed in May 2011, was *Closed* on November 13, 2018. How ironic that the US Department of Navy/USMC retaliatory actions would come again full circle. And once again, the Department of Navy/USMC and the retaliatory actions they took against me, once again covered-up.... And once again, with the assistance of and by my estranged father, as their accomplice.... And again, American Citizens, *this is your US Military and US DOJ.*

I stand by the informal EEOC Compliant I made in April 2011 and the Formal EEOC Complaint I filed on May 12, 2011. Due to the retaliatory actions taken against me, I had to resort to "pro se" representation

---

64   TS Ellis, court order November 13, 2018

because no lawyer nor law firm in the Washington DC area or across the nation that I contacted accordingly, would represent me in this case. I do not agree with the result of the judicial process on this matter, and remain of that opinion. Otherwise, I would not have initiated the informal EEOC Complaint and filed the formal EEOC Compliant to begin with…

Here's some additional insight regarding my experience during and while filing Motions accordingly in federal litigation using the United States Postal system. I filed numerous complaints and concerns while using USPS to file my Motions with the 4th Circuit in Richmond, Virginia. However, it's the example of what occurred while filing an applicable Judge's Ordered *Amended Complaint* with the US District Court in Alexandria, Virginia that I want to provide in detail. In this case, a USPS and/or Court House Mail Room action actually almost resulted in my Motion being untimely filed. I can't even make this stuff up—and given the proximity of the Pentagon, apparently, I'm definitely hitting a nerve, aren't I…

On October 11, 2018, Judge Ellis *ORDERED* that my *Motion for Extension* is *GRANTED* and I then had until 5:00 p.m. on October 24, 2018 to file accordingly. To ensure a timely filing, on October 22, 2018, via USPS, I mailed *certified/signature required* my *Amended Complaint* to all required/served parties: the US District Court Clerk's Office; Richard Spencer; Jefferson Sessions; G. Zachery Terwilliger; Anne M. Brennan; and Lt. Col Jonathan Vaughn, USMC, Office of the Counsel of the Commandant. Scheduled delivery on October 23, 2018. Tracking accordingly, oddly enough five of the six served parties were received timely, on October 23, 2018. All except one, the one being delivered to the US District Court Clerk's Office. As of October 24, 2018, still no delivery—apparently my *Amended Complaint* was missing, not delivered, and not delivered on time for a timely filing. On October 25, 2018, I called and emailed supporting documentation to the US District Court Clerk's Office to this curiously-timed situation. My Amended Complaint timely delivered to five of the six served parties—but the one sent to the Court, missing. Confirming that the Amended Complaint still had not been delivered as of October 25, 2018 at 11:15 a.m., I requested the Court be advised accordingly based on USPS tracking system information. At 1:47 p.m., I was then advised that the *Amended Complaint* was delivered. On Thursday, October 25, 2018 at 4:00 p.m., an applicable *ORDER* was filed stating that my *Amended Complaint* is *DEEMED* timely filed.

Subsequently, about 6 months later, in June 2019, my newly-issued US Department of State personal passport was delivered to my residence and left on the front porch—purposely and intentionally dropped inside the water rim of a flower pot—drenched and ruined by the water. I took photos, made reports accordingly and had to request yet another passport—a replacement passport for my newly issued, purposely and intentionally destroyed USG personal passport. I can't even make this stuff up...

During this entire ordeal, back to 2011, I contacted every authority/entity I could think of. I contacted AFSA, DOJ/SDNY, FBI, DS, etc., guess what happened... I contacted DOD authorities such as MPs, OSD, ACIS, NCIS, etc., guess what happened... I contacted OIGs such as State, DOJ, IC, DOD, etc., guess what happened... I contacted OSC guess what happened... I contacted US Congressional Members and Staffers, GAO, etc., guess what happened... I contacted OMB, Labor, Agriculture, National Archives, etc., guess what happened... In addition to the applicable Federal Administrative and Judicial Court Systems, and look what happened... Nothing. Absolutely nothing.

With all that, and no other federal legal jurisdiction to appeal regarding what I, a federal CVRA-accorded victim/witness regarding the August 7, 1998 East Africa Embassy bombing, an EEO complainant against the US Military, an OSC complainant, and as a federal government whistleblower retaliated against had been subjected to, *what US Court has the proper jurisdiction?* Apparently, none. And apparently not—to answer the larger rhetorical question that I presented in my August 16, 2016 US Supreme Court filing—*whether the rule of law still exists in the United States of America?*

So, what is all this really about...

Afterword

WHAT IS ALL THIS REALLY ABOUT:
The Truth No Matter What.

Article VI clause 3 of the United States Constitution requires that all who hold office in the United States take an oath to uphold the United States Constitution:
I do solemnly swear that I will support and defend the Constitution of the United States against all enemies, foreign or domestic; that I will bear true faith and allegiance for the same; that I take this obligation freely, without any mental reservation or purpose of evasion; and that I will well and faithfully discharge the duties of the office on which I am about to enter (and held). So, help me God.

Some may ask, aren't you embarrassed to write this book? I must admit I initially had much hesitation in my decision whether to write a book, this book or not. But at the end of the day, I didn't do anything wrong. What was done, was done to me—not the other way around.

I am not and was not a member of the intelligence community, law enforcement, nor the military. I was an employee of my nation's government, the US Government, both in the civil service and foreign service that loyally served her nation for over two decades. And what I experienced was betrayal beyond belief.

So, let's start there. *Why Me?*

It's a question I continually asked myself throughout this entire horrific ordeal.

I'm not intelligence, military, nor law enforcement.

So why me?

And then I either figured it out or rationalized—either way, it is a fact.

It's because I'm not intelligence, not military, nor law enforcement.

I'm unbiased.

But yet, because of what was done to me, the retaliatory actions taken against me, I have a vested interest to get to the truth...

So, what is all this really about?

Obviously, not just about an explosion, but something much bigger.

Initially, I did not consider myself a whistleblower, just a patriotic American telling the truth, a truth teller, a constitutional oath-taker. And I never considered myself a conspiracy theorist given my professional background in dealing only in facts.

What happened to me, the events and the magnitude of the efforts taken against me by *Deep State* forces, happened to ensure the false narrative/cover-up continued no matter what. If this could happen to me, *and it did,* in what other scenarios did it occur? To whom else? And how many others?

At the time, I was only looking through the perspective lens as the Embassy Nairobi FMC Director. My initial connecting of dots in October 2012 between the August 7, 1998 East Africa Embassy bombings, the events of Germany, and the September 11, 2012 attack on the Diplomatic Post in Benghazi was too parochoial. And though I did not initially understand this, someone knew what I knew and its pertinent relevance. Otherwise, what happened to me, would never have happened.

In the aftermath of the September 11, 2012 attack on the Diplomatic Post in Benghazi, one thing that certainly wasn't lacking, contrary to the aftermath of the August 7, 1998 East Africa Embassy bombings, were Congressional Hearings. And that was a good thing. And on May 8, 2014, the House voted to establish the Select Committee on Benghazi. An overarching Select Committee approach was necessary since the initial stovepiped jurisdictional committee approach was absolutely not working in getting to the crux, the true crux of the matter at hand.

Unfortunately, on December 12, 2016, the Select Committee closed after issuing its final report, not realizing nor comprehending its biggest finding would be the fact stated by its Chairman Trey Gowdy during the January 27, 2015 Hearing. "This Committee has interviewed eyewitnesses never before interviewed," to include by the Accountability Review Board. Seventy-five eyewitnesses were identified as not included nor interviewed during the ARB process.

By this time, I had come to realize that the pertinence of what I knew was indeed much broader than just my time overseas with the foreign service. It was about insight I acquired as a federal auditor, both with State OIG and DCAA. My parochial lens now went broader in scope, back over twenty years and across the entire USG. And the reason why I included the over $14.6 Trillion figure in my applicable US Supreme Court filing in November 2016.

Now it's a given that none of this should ever have happened to me. And though I never asked for any of this, what happened did happen. That's a fact, a fact that I nor anyone else can now change. And with that fact, to this day, I—and hopefully the many others that read this book—have so many questions, the largest and most rhetorical being, why? Why did all this occur?

Over twenty years since the August 7, 1998 East Africa Embassy bombings, I still don't know the answers and remain befuddled. So, now over twenty years later, who do I go to, or who should I have gone to, to assist me in getting the answers? Based on my own documented personal experience, there was no one, no one in the entire USG. And to me, that is the most treasonous, heiness crime of all.

For in order to solve a crime, you need witnesses. Witnesses to obtain facts, the right facts, all the facts. You need witnesses to the events, to the crime… And without witnesses, you can't solve a crime. Nor can you get to the truth. So, why would our USG not want witnesses, all these witnesses to solve a crime. In my case, to get to the truth, at least three questions, of so many more, need to be answered:

Why wasn't I interviewed by the applicable August 7, 1998 Embassy bombing Accountability Review Board?

Why wasn't I protected?

Why were there no investigations conducted?

Because of the implications involved, until these questions and many more are answered, our national security remains at stake to this day as it did when I initially raised my concerns. And because the American people deserve to know, need to know, and have a right to know, the answers as well. As do I.

Upon graduating from college in December 1986, I applied to various positions throughout the USG. Of the application process with the CIA, I have limited recollection. But I definitely do remember how it ended. I was sitting at the side of an applicable CIA HR official's desk in the Tysons Corner/McLean area of Fairfax County in the Commonwealth of Virginia, in close proximity to Washington D.C. She said, "Unfortunately, it did not appear to be a good match." The reason provided was that I was *too loyal.* I was taken aback, but there was nothing more I could do, other than knowing that, according to the CIA, I was *too loyal* to serve my nation. To that CIA assessment, I strongly disagree.

On second thought, maybe the CIA's assessment is right after all. Maybe I am and was too loyal to serve my nation because I believe in the truth, justice and the rule of law. And I believe that no one is above the law, not the CIA, nor the entire intelligence community; not the DOJ and FBI, nor the entire law enforcement community; not the USMC, nor the entire US military; nor the Department of State, including Diplomatic Security.

And to end, where I began.

Tell the truth… Until they don't like what you have to say. Then what?

At which point, you have a decision to make: To either stand for truth, the truth, or to lie, amend, modify the truth for their agenda, as small or large as it may be, with ramifications and implications, as small or large that may result.

My decision was an easy one. Without knowing or understanding all the implications at the time, I stood and stand by the truth, no matter what. Despite the retaliatory actions taken against me, every day I can, and do, look myself in the mirror knowing I stood by the truth, no matter what. And unlike many others in a situation similar to mine, who made the same decision as mine, I survived and I am alive to write my story.

So, how will you decide when your moment comes to *TELL THE TRUTH?*

On February 1, 2019, I set out on a journey to write this book. And on June 11, 2020, I submitted the full, unedited, unpublished manuscript of over 700 pages with the Library of Congress, the Registration Office. It's title at that time: *"ALWAYS TELL THE TRUTH… Until They Don't Like What You Have To Say: TESTIMONIAL To A Memoir Of and By A US Department Of State Foreign Service Federal CVRA-Protected "Middle-Class Nobody."* The very next day, June 12, 2020, I submitted my signed contract intent with my publisher. And now finally, its publication— shorter in length and modification in title. But yet, regardless, the realization remains the same. My journey is not yet over.

So many questions remain unanswered. And as a first-hand witness, of which I and only I, am uniquely qualified and uniquely possess insight and perspective that can lead to the right answers by asking the right questions, pointing in the right direction, and, from a federal auditor perspective, pulling the right strings. Because when you pull the right string, the entire sweater unfurls… or in this case, all the dots connect, the entire truth is revealed. And with that, the realization that my journey is not yet over.

As a crucial piece to a bigger puzzle, I am forced to peel back layer after layer after layer like an onion. I continue picking up breadcrumbs along the way, connecting more dots as these are revealed to me… as my journey continues. My hope is you continue along with me in this journey, this apparent "yellow-brick road" of sorts journey of countless rabbit holes, fitting more and more pieces of the puzzle together, to see what all hides behind the curtain, exposing more light along the way… and to finally discover what all *this* is really about. *Where our journey leads may surprise us all.*

Index